PSYCHOLOGY

and your life

PSYCHOLOGY

and your life

Robert S. Feldman
University of Massachusetts, Amherst

McGraw Hill **Higher Education**

Boston   Burr Ridge, IL   Dubuque, IA   New York   San Francisco   St. Louis
Bangkok   Bogotá   Caracas   Kuala Lumpur   Lisbon   London   Madrid   Mexico City
Milan   Montreal   New Delhi   Santiago   Seoul   Singapore   Sydney   Taipei   Toronto

 **Higher Education**

PSYCHOLOGY AND YOUR LIFE

Published by McGraw-Hill, a business unit of The McGraw-Hill Companies, Inc., 1221 Avenue of the Americas, New York, NY, 10020. Copyright © 2010 by The McGraw-Hill Companies, Inc. All rights reserved. No part of this publication may be reproduced or distributed in any form or by any means, or stored in a database or retrieval system, without the prior written consent of The McGraw-Hill Companies, Inc., including, but not limited to, in any network or other electronic storage or transmission, or broadcast for distance learning.

Some ancillaries, including electronic and print components, may not be available to customers outside the United States.

This book is printed on acid-free paper.

6 7 8 9 0 DOW/DOW 10 9 8 7 6 5 4 3 2 1

ISBN 978-0-07-337702-5
MHID 0-07-337702-3

Vice president/Editor in chief: *Elizabeth Haefele*
Vice president/Director of marketing: *John E. Biernat*
Sponsoring editor: *Natalie J. Ruffatto*
Developmental editor: *Kristin Bradley*
Senior marketing manager: *Keari Green*
Lead media producer: *Damian Moshak*
Director, Editing/Design/Production: *Jess Ann Kosic*
Lead project manager: *Susan Trentacosti*
Senior production supervisor: *Janean A. Utley*
Designer: *Marianna Kinigakis*
Senior photo research coordinator: *Lori Kramer*
Photo researcher: *Allison Grimes*
Media developmental editor: *William Mulford*
Media project manager: *Mark A. S. Dierker*
Typeface: *11/13 Minion*
Compositor: *Laserwords Private Limited*
Printer: *R R Donnelley, Willard, Ohio*
Credits: The credits section for this book begins on page 560 and is considered an extension of the copyright page.

Library of Congress Cataloging-in-Publication Data

Feldman, Robert S. (Robert Stephen), 1947-
    Psychology and your life / Robert S. Feldman.
        p. cm.
    Includes index.
    ISBN-13: 978-0-07-337702-5 (alk. paper)
    ISBN-10: 0-07-337702-3 (alk. paper)
    1. Psychology—Textbooks. I. Title.
BF121.F35 2010
150—dc22
                            2008047500

The Internet addresses listed in the text were accurate at the time of publication. The inclusion of a Web site does not indicate an endorsement by the authors or McGraw-Hill, and McGraw-Hill does not guarantee the accuracy of the information presented at these sites.

www.mhhe.com

dedication

To Alex, #1

about the AUTHOR

ROBERT S. FELDMAN is Professor of Psychology and Associate Dean of the College of Social and Behavioral Sciences at the University of Massachusetts, Amherst. Feldman, a winner of the College Distinguished Teacher award, also has taught courses at the Lincoln Educational Services system, Mount Holoyoke College, and Virginia Commonwealth University.

Feldman teaches introductory psychology to classes ranging in size from 20 to nearly 500 students. He has served as a Hewlett Teaching Fellow and Senior Online Teaching Fellow, and he frequently gives talks on the use of technology in teaching. He initiated distance learning courses in psychology at the University of Massachusetts.

Feldman is committed to helping students achieve success. He directs the first-year experience course for entering students at the University of Massachusetts, *Power Up for College Success*. He is also author of *P.O.W.E.R. Learning: Strategies for Success in College and Life* and edited *The First Year of College,* books devoted to increasing student success in college.

A Fellow of the American Psychological Association and the Association for Psychological Science, Feldman received a B.A. with High Honors from Wesleyan University and an M.S. and Ph.D. from the University of Wisconsin–Madison. Feldman is actively involved in promoting the field of psychology. He is on the Board of Directors of the Federation of Behavioral, Psychological, and Cognitive Sciences and also is on the Board of the Foundation for the Advancement of Behavioral and Brain Sciences.

Feldman is a winner of a Fulbright Senior Research Scholar and Lecturer award and has written more than 100 books, book chapters, and scientific articles. His books include *Fundamentals of Nonverbal Behavior, Development of Nonverbal Behavior in Children, Social Psychology,* and *Development Across the Life Span,* and they have been translated into a number of languages, including Spanish, French, Portuguese, Dutch, Chinese, and Japanese. His research interests include honesty and deception and the use of nonverbal behavior in impression management, and he has received grants from the National Institute of Mental Health and the National Institute on Disabilities and Rehabilitation Research.

Feldman's spare time is most often devoted to earnest, if not entirely expert, piano playing, and serious cooking. He also loves to travel, and—despite living in New England—is a devoted New York Yankees fan. He has three children and lives with his wife, who is also a psychologist, overlooking the Holyoke mountain range in Amherst, Massachusetts.

brief
TABLE OF CONTENTS

table of
CONTENTS

module 4   Research Challenges: Exploring the Process   36

CHAPTER

Neuroscience and Behavior   46

module 5   Neurons: The Basic Elements of Behavior   48

module 6   The Nervous System and the Endocrine System: Communicating within the Body   56

module 7   The Brain   64

CHAPTER

Development   280

CHAPTER

Personality and Individual Differences   334

Students first.

If I were to use only a few words to summarize my goal for *Psychology and Your Life,* as well as my teaching philosophy, that's what I would say. I believe that an effective textbook must be oriented to students—informing them, engaging them, exciting them about the field, and helping them to learn.

Luckily, psychology is a science that is naturally interesting to students. It is a discipline that speaks with many voices, offering a personal message to each student. Some students see the discipline as a way to better understand themselves, their family members, their co-workers, and people in general. For others, psychology offers information that can help prepare for a future career. Some students are drawn to the field simply because of their interest in psychological topics and how an understanding of psychology can improve their lives.

No matter what brings students into the introductory course and regardless of their initial motivation, *Psychology and Your Life* is designed to draw students into the field by illustrating how psychology will affect them in their career—whether they are studying to become a medical assistant, a graphic designer, or a police officer, or enter any other program. The text integrates a variety of elements that foster students' understanding of psychology and its impact on their everyday lives.

Psychology and Your Life was written to accomplish the following goals:

- To provide broad coverage of the field of psychology, introducing the basic concepts, theories, and applications that constitute the discipline.

- To build an appreciation of the relevance of psychology to everyday life, including learning to apply psychology to students' chosen areas of study.

- To maximize student learning of the material, helping students to think critically about psychological phenomena, particularly those that have an impact on their everyday lives.

The book and its ancillary materials include coverage of the traditional areas of psychology while also emphasizing applied topics. The flexibility of the book's organizational structure is considerable. Each chapter is divided into three or four manageable, self-contained modules, aiding students' reading and studying of the material and allowing instructors to choose and omit sections in accordance with their syllabus.

In addition, *Psychology and Your Life* provides a complete framework for learning and assessment. Clear in-text learning outcomes, tied to each major section of the book, allow students to know exactly what it is they are supposed to learn. These learning outcomes also permit instructors to create assessments based on those outcomes. All the ancillary materials that accompany the text, including every test item in the Test Bank, are keyed to these learning outcomes and tied together by a comprehensive and easy-to-use Asset Map. The

Asset Map, along with the rest of our comprehensive text package, is a part of McGraw-Hill's commitment to connect content with users in new and innovative ways.

Furthermore, *Psychology and Your Life* specifically takes into account the diverse population of students who are enrolled in college today. The book particularly is designed to address the needs of today's students who may work full- or part-time; who may be juggling their education, their families, and their jobs; who may be returning to school in search of a career change; or who are in a specific career-oriented program. I have taken great care to ensure students have an opportunity to explore why psychology is relevant to everyone—no matter what their background is and no matter what their area of study may be.

Psychology and Your Life Promotes Student Success

Psychology and Your Life includes many features designed to maximize students' success in their introductory course. Every chapter follows the same format, allowing students to feel comfortable with the book and be better able to master its content. The examples within the book are drawn from across the spectrum of life, including the worlds of work, family, and community. The vocabulary of the book has received particular focus in order to ensure clarity and ease of learning. Our glossary includes expanded definitions, where appropriate, to ensure that students of all reading levels can gain their fullest understanding of the key terms and their definitions.

Furthermore, *Psychology and Your Life* is divided into 43 short modules grouped into 12 chapters covering the major areas of psychology. An advantage of the modular structure is it allows students to study material in smaller chunks, which psychological research has long found to be the optimal way to learn. The modular approach, therefore, makes already manageable chapters even easier to absorb. Moreover, instructors can customize assignments for their students by asking them to read only those modules that fit their course outline and in the sequence that matches their syllabus. In addition, the Asset Map helps instructors design lessons and assignments that are modular-specific by organizing ancillary material by learning outcome within each module.

At the beginning of each module, *Learning Outcomes* introduce the key concepts covered in the module. For convenience, the learning outcomes are mapped to Bloom's Taxonomy (levels of learning) in the instructor material to reassure instructors that the outcomes, activities, discussion questions, and assignments help students experience multiple types of learning, from understanding and defining concepts to experiencing and analyzing the overarching themes to each module. These key concepts are also the focus of activities available on the Online Learning Center for the text, **www.mhhe.com/psychlife.** In the text, references and icons direct students to **Psych 2.0** activities that correspond to key concepts.

For example, consider the key concept of communication between neurons. The text presentation of this concept includes a verbal explanation and figures plus a text reference and marginal icon prompting students to complete a *Psych2.0* online activity on the nature of neural communication and a follow-up quiz. Additionally, the Online Learning Center provides review exercises and links to other Web sites that offer further information relevant to the key concepts and content for that section.

psych2.0
WWW.MHHE.COM/PSYCHLIFE

Neurons

To further help students learn the material, the book contains dozens of **Study Alerts,** located in the margins by key concepts. *Study Alerts* offer advice and hints for students, signaling them when critical concepts are presented and offering suggestions for learning those concepts effectively.

STUDY ALERT

Use the three steps of problem solving to organize your studying: preparation, production, and judgment (PPJ)

Another great feature that helps connect concepts with career realities is the **From the Perspective of . . .** feature. *From the Perspective of . . .* highlights how psychology impacts a variety of professions. Created to show the correlation between psychology and different professions, the feature helps students learn to comprehend what psychology means to their chosen program of study and answers the "why does psychology matter to me?" question. Whether students are in an allied health, nursing, criminal justice, technology, business, legal studies track, or any other program of study, they will have the chance to make connections between their area of study and their lives after completing their program.

From the perspective of . . .

A MEDICAL OR DENTAL ASSISTANT   How would you handle a patient who is anxiously awaiting treatment and complaining that her pain is getting worse?

In addition, the book contains features designed to engage and excite students. **Try It!** exercises are experiential self-assessment quizzes that reinforce chapter concepts in a nonthreatening (even fun!) manner and enable students to consider, compare, and contrast their preferences, behaviors, and attitudes. Similar to quizzes in popular magazines, students can readily apply their own answers directly to the concepts they are learning—active learning at its best!

try it!

Psychological Truths?

To test your knowledge of psychology, try answering the following questions:

1. Infants love their mothers primarily because their mothers fulfill their basic biological needs, such as providing food. True or false? _____
2. Geniuses generally have poor social adjustment. True or false? _____
3. The best way to ensure that a desired behavior will continue after training is completed is to reward that behavior every single time it occurs during training rather than rewarding it only periodically. True or false? _____
4. People with schizophrenia have at least two distinct personalities. True or false? _____
5. Parents should do everything they can to ensure children have high self-esteem and a strong sense that they are highly competent. True or false? _____
6. Children's IQ scores have little to do with how well they do in school. True or false? _____
7. _____ lead _____ illness _____ false? _____

In the feature **Becoming an Informed Consumer of Psychology,** psychology concepts are discussed in the context of the student as a consumer. These real-life scenarios enable students to consider and even implement psychological concepts within the world around them and apply critical thinking skills to their personal and professional lives. This feature includes scenarios such as how to evaluate advertising, and how to determine if one should seek counseling.

becoming an *informed consumer* **OF PSYCHOLOGY**
Improving Your Memory

Apart from the advantages of forgetting, say, a bad date, most of us would like to find ways to improve our memories. Among the effective strategies for studying and remembering course material:

- *The keyword technique.* If you are studying a foreign language, try the *keyword technique* of pairing a foreign word with a common English word that has a similar sound. This English word is known as the *keyword.* For example, to learn the Spanish word for duck (*pato*, pronounced *pot-o*), you might choose the keyword *pot*; for the Spanish word for horse (*caballo*, pronounced *cob-eye-yo*), the keyword might be *eye.* Once you have thought of

EXPLORING diversity

Rites of Passage: Coming of Age Around the World

It is not easy for male members of the Awa tribe in New Guinea to make the transition from childhood to adulthood. First come whippings with sticks and prickly branches, both for the boys' own past misdeeds and in honor of those tribesmen who were killed in warfare. In the next phase of the ritual, adults jab

full circle   MOTIVATION AND EMOTION

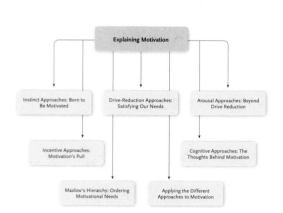

Exploring Diversity features, strategically placed within the modules, address how diversity and perspective relate to the study of psychology. *Exploring Diversity* promotes critical thinking about psychology concepts through the discussion and assessment of cultural and ethnic differences in direct correlation to research, study, and our lives.

The **Full Circle** end-of-chapter concept maps identify the correlation of the overarching chapter key concepts. Visual learners will benefit from the chapter maps that "tie everything together" by revisiting and reinforcing the key concepts for every module within each chapter.

The need to connect the modules with overarching chapter content is addressed in the **Looking Ahead/ Looking Back** feature. *Looking Ahead* introduces the key concepts of every chapter; *Looking Back* summarizes content from the chapter as a whole to reinforce the learning outcomes of each module.

Key terms and their definitions are easily identifiable (bolded and called out in the margins with definitions) within each module and are listed with page references at the end of every module. The glossary includes enhanced definitions— additional explanations of difficult or confusing terms using synonyms or expanded parenthetical definitions—allowing students to expand their knowledge of the terminology associated with psychology. Providing the most clear, accessible definitions helps students recognize, identify, define, and describe the terminology and definitions.

Recap/Evaluate/Rethink end-of-module activities are tied directly to the module's learning outcomes boosting students' opportunities to apply and analyze their knowledge beyond the definitions or simple explanations. These activities allow instructors to move students from memorization to application and analysis in a cohesive, logical manner through a variety of activities and exercises tied to the learning outcomes of the module. Instructors who are familiar with Bloom's Taxonomy or who want to provide activities for students with different learning styles will find a variety of exercises for homework or class discussion.

Found at the end of each chapter, **Case Studies** allow students to apply and analyze the chapter content and discuss what they have learned in the context of a story or situation. Students will analyze a situation through critical thinking, discussion, and interaction with other students whose perspectives may differ from their own.

Psychology on the Web consists of various Web-based activities found at the end of every chapter to promote Internet research of key chapter concepts. This feature is great for active learning and increasing students' abilities to conduct Internet research and critique Internet resources within the context of their psychology class.

The **Online Learning Center** that accompanies the text offers a variety of resources to both instructors and students. This material will help create a dynamic and engaging learning environment.

The **Student Online Learning Center** includes quizzes, activities, and supplementary content to help reinforce key concepts within each chapter.

The **Instructor Online Learning Center** provides an extensive Test Bank, Instructor's Manual, and PowerPoint Presentations. In addition, the OLC includes an Asset Map that breaks instructor material down by Learning Outcome.

McGraw-Hill's *Connect: Psychology* is a Web-based assignment and assessment platform that gives students the means to better connect with their coursework, with their instructors, and with the important concepts that they will need to know for success now and in the future. With *Connect: Psychology,* instructors can deliver assignments, quizzes, and tests easily online. Students can practice important skills at their own pace and on their own schedule. With *Connect: Psychology Plus,* students also get 24/7 online access to an e-book—an online edition of the text—to aid them in successfully completing their work, wherever and whenever they choose.

Students First: The Bottom Line

Based on extensive feedback from reviewers in a variety of schools, I am confident that *Psychology and Your Life* reflects what instructors want: a book that motivates students to understand, learn, and apply psychology in the context of their present and future careers. The book is designed to expose readers to the content—and promise—of psychology, and to do so in a way that will nurture students' excitement about psychology and keep their enthusiasm alive for a lifetime.

Acknowledgments

One of the central features of *Psychology and Your Life* is the hands-on involvement of a wide array of professionals in the review process. The book has benefited substantially from the advice of instructors from a wide range of backgrounds and perspectives. From evaluating the table of contents to commenting on the design and cover, to providing insights on what instructor and student support are most beneficial, the development of this product is the best it can be because of the candid feedback and suggestions from everyone who was part of the development process.

I am extraordinarily grateful to the following reviewers who provided their time and expertise to help ensure that *Psychology and Your Life* reflects the best that psychology has to offer:

Symposium Participants

Mary Alexander, *Ashford University*

Elizabeth Beardmore, *Colorado Technical University Online*

Michael Bowers, *Art Institute of Colorado*

Karen Durand, *Miller-Motte Technical College*

Alfred Ebert, *Brown Mackie College*

Janell Gibson, *Keiser University*

Kerri Holloway, *American Intercontinental University Online*

Barbara Ireland, *Laureate Education, Inc.*

Kristie Kellis, *Globe University/ Minnesota School of Business*

Eric Lance, *ECPI*

Michelle Slattery, *The Bradford School*

Elizabeth Tice, *Ashford University*

Focus Group Participants

Kathleen Hipp, *Brown Mackie College*

Deborah Koysdar, *McCann School of Business & Technology*

Kristie Kellis, *Globe University/ Minnesota School of Business*

Joseph Yasain, *McIntosh College*

Andrea Goldstein, *Keiser University*

Janell Gibson, *Keiser University*

Eric Lance, *ECPI*

Doreen Lewis, *Rasmussen College*

Lois Weber, *Globe University/ Minnesota School of Business*

Text Reviewers

Richard Ackley, *The Chicago School*

Kerri Augusto, *Becker College*

Elizabeth Beardmore, *Colorado Technical Institute Online*

Karen Bedell, *Baker College*

William Bell, *Coyne American Institute*

Michael Bowers, *Art Institute of Colorado*

Allison Brown, *Miller-Motte Technical College*

Alfred Ebert, *Brown Mackie College*

Momika Fileva, *Davenport University*

Dennis Gaynor, *Globe University*

David Gillespie, *Davenport University*

Andrea Goldstein, *Keiser University*

Kathleen Hipp, *Brown Mackie College*

Kristy Huntley, *Briarwood College*

Kristie Kellis, *Globe University/ Minnesota School of Business*

Kevin Kelly, *Andover College*

Doreen Lewis, *Rasmussen College*

Eric Lance, *ECPI*

Bernadette McCallister, *Baker College*

William Neiheisel, *Gwinnett College*

Leslie Rewald, *Trinity College*

Lori Ritter, *The Salter School*

Shelly Shields, *Indiana Business College*

Pamela Simon, *Baker College*

Paula Tripp, *San Joaquin Valley College*

Sharon Vriend-Robinson, *Davenport University*

Donald Webb, *Gibbs College*

Lois Weber, *Globe University/ Minnesota School of Business*

Marc Wilson, *Hesser College*

Brown Mackie Review Panel

Justin Cary, *Cincinnati*

Alfred Ebert, *Northern Kentucky*

Artie Estridge, *South Bend*

Kathy Hipp, *Findlay*

Jeff Laptak-Moreau, *Cincinnati*

Jan Sebestyen, *Merrillville*

Joan Shirley, *Salina*

Julie Smith, *Kansas City*

Marilyn Wells, *Akron*

Many teachers along my educational path have shaped my thinking. I was introduced to psychology at Wesleyan University, where several committed and inspiring teachers—and in particular Karl Scheibe—conveyed their sense of excitement about the field and made its relevance clear to me.

Although the nature of the University of Wisconsin, where I did my graduate work, could not have been more different from the much smaller Wesleyan, the excitement and inspiration were similar. Once again, a cadre of excellent teachers—led, especially, by the late Vernon Allen—molded my thinking and taught me to appreciate the beauty and science of the discipline of psychology.

I'm also grateful to the many students in my classes at the variety of schools at which I've had the privilege of teaching. They include students at career colleges, state colleges, and universities.

My colleagues and students at the University of Massachusetts provide ongoing intellectual stimulation, and I thank them for making the university a fine place to work. Several people also provided extraordinary research and editorial help. In particular, I want to thank John Bickford, who provided superb editorial input on the book. His help was invaluable. I am also grateful to my students, past and present, particularly including Matt Zimbler, Jim Tyler, and Chris Poirier. Finally, I am extremely grateful to Tolley Jones and John Graiff, whose hard work and dedication helped immeasurably on just about everything involving this book.

I also offer great thanks to the wonderful McGraw-Hill team that stands behind the book. My sponsoring editor, Natalie Ruffatto, has been a source of extraordinary support and creativity, with a clear and creative vision for this book. Kristin Bradley has been a terrific developmental editor, with great attention to detail and the ability to see the big picture at the same time. Bill Mulford, media developmental editor, provided great ideas and enthusiasm about the media accompanying the book and made contributions that went well beyond his job description.

As always, it's been a pleasure to work with Susan Trentacosti, project manager for the book, who has done her usual first-rate job. I also want to thank in advance marketing manager Keari Green, on whose skills I'm counting. Finally, I'm grateful to President Jim Kelly and Publisher Liz Haefele, who have provided enthusiastic support. It's a privilege to be part of this world-class publishing team.

Finally, I remain indebted to my family. My parents, Leah Brochstein and the late Saul D. Feldman, provided a lifetime foundation of love and support, and I continue to see their influence in every corner of my life. I am grateful, too, to Harry Brochstein, who has enriched my life and thinking in many ways.

Ultimately, my children, Jonathan, Joshua, and Sarah; my daughters-in-law Leigh and Julie; my grandson, Alex; and my wife, Katherine, remain the focal point of my life. I thank them, with immense love.

Robert S. Feldman
Amherst, Massachusetts

TO THE STUDENTS

Making the Grade: A Practical Guide to Studying Effectively

If you're reading this page, you're probably taking an introductory psychology course. Maybe you're studying psychology because you've always been interested in what makes people tick. Or perhaps you've had a friend or family member who has sought assistance for a psychological disorder. Or maybe you have no idea what psychology is all about, but are taking introductory psychology because it is a required course.

Whatever your reason for taking the course, it's a safe bet you're interested in maximizing your understanding of the material and getting a good grade. And you want to do it as quickly and efficiently as possible.

Good news: You're taking the right course, and you're learning the right material. Several subfields of psychology have identified a variety of guidelines and techniques that will help you learn and remember material not only related to psychology, but also relevant to every other discipline that you will study.

We'll consider a variety of guidelines relating to doing well in your psychology class—and every other class you'll take in your college career. Here's my guarantee to you: If you learn and follow the guidelines in each of these areas, you'll become a better student and get better grades—not only in your introductory psychology classes, but in your other classes as well. Always remember that *good students are made, not born,* and these suggestions will help you become an all-around better student.

Adopt a General Study Strategy

Let's begin with a brief consideration of a general study strategy, applicable to all of your courses, including introductory psychology. Psychologists have created several excellent (and proven) techniques for improving study skills, two of which are described here: "P.O.W.E.R," or *Prepare, Organize, Work, Evaluate,* and *Rethink;* and "SQ3R," or *Survey, Question, Read, Recite,* and *Review.* By employing one of these two procedures, you can increase your ability to learn and retain information and to think critically, not just in psychology classes but also in all academic subjects.

P.O.W.E.R. The *P.O.W.E.R.* learning strategy systematizes the acquisition of new material by providing a learning framework. It stresses the importance of learning outcomes and appropriate preparation before you begin to study, as well as the significance of self-evaluation and the incorporation of critical thinking into the learning process. Specifically, use of the P.O.W.E.R. learning system entails the following steps:

- *Prepare.* Before starting any journey, we need to know where we are headed. Academic journeys are no different; we need to know what our goals are. The *Prepare* stage consists of thinking about what we hope to gain from reading a specific section of the text by identifying specific goals that we seek to accomplish. In *Psychology and Your Life,* these goals are listed as Learning Outcomes at the beginning of every module.

- *Organize.* Once we know what our goals are, we can develop a route to accomplish those goals. The *Organize* stage involves developing a mental road map of where we are headed. *Psychology and Your Life* highlights the organization of each upcoming chapter. Read the outline at the beginning of each chapter to get an idea of what topics are covered and how they are organized.

- *Work.* The key to the P.O.W.E.R. learning system is actually reading and studying the material presented in the book. In some ways *Work* is the easy part, because, if you have carried out the steps in the preparation and organization stage, you'll know where you're headed and how you'll get there. Remember, the main text isn't the only material that you need to read and think about. It's also important to read the boxes and the marginal glossary terms in order to gain a full understanding of the material.

- *Evaluate.* The fourth step, *Evaluate,* provides the opportunity to determine how effectively you have mastered the material. In *Psychology and Your Life,* a series of questions at the end of each module permits a rapid check of your understanding of the material. Quizzes on the text's Web site, or Online Learning Center (www.mhhe.com/psychlife), and within *Psych2.0* provide additional opportunities to test yourself. Evaluating your progress is essential to assessing your degree of mastery of the material.

- *Rethink.* The final step in the *P.O.W.E.R.* learning system requires that you think critically about the content. Critical thinking entails reanalyzing, reviewing, questioning, and challenging assumptions. It affords you the opportunity to consider how the material fits with other information you have already learned. Every major section of *Psychology and Your Life* ends with a *Rethink* section. Answering its thought-provoking questions will help you understand the material more fully and at a deeper level.

SQ3R. Use of the SQ3R learning system entails the following specific steps:

- *Survey.* The first step of the *SQ3R* method is to *survey* the material by reading the outlines that open each module, the headings, figure captions, recaps, and *Looking Ahead* and *Looking Back* sections, providing you with an overview of the major points of the chapter.

- *Question.* The next step—the "Q"—is to *question.* Formulate questions about the material, either aloud or in writing, prior to actually reading a section of text. The questions posed at the beginning of each module and the *Evaluate* and *Rethink* questions that end each part of the chapter are examples.

- *Read.* Read carefully and, even more important, read actively and critically. While you are reading, answer the questions you have asked yourself. Critically evaluate material by considering the implications of what you are reading, thinking about possible exceptions and contradictions, and examining underlying assumptions.

- *Recite.* This step involves describing and explaining to yourself (or to a friend) the material you have just read and answering the questions you have posed earlier.

Recite aloud; the recitation process helps to identify your degree of understanding of the material you have just read.

- *Review.* In this final step, review the material, looking it over, reading the Looking Back summaries, and answering the in-text review questions.

Manage Your Time

Without looking up from the page, answer this question: What time is it?

Most people are pretty accurate in their answer. And if you don't know for sure, it's very likely that you can find out. There may be a cell phone in your pocket; there may be a clock on the wall, desk, or computer screen; or maybe you're riding in a car that has a clock in the dashboard. Even if you don't have a timepiece of some sort nearby, your body keeps its own beat. Humans have an internal clock that regulates the beating of our heart, the pace of our breathing, the discharge of chemicals within our bloodstream, and myriad other bodily functions.

Managing your time as you study is a central aspect of a successful plan. But remember: The goal of time management is not to schedule every moment so we become pawns of a timetable that governs every waking moment of the day. Instead, the goal is to permit us to make informed choices as to how we use our time. Rather than letting the day slip by, largely without our awareness, the time management procedures we'll discuss can make us better able to harness time for our own ends.

We'll consider a number of steps to help you improve your time management skills.

Create a Time Log. A *time log* is simply a record of how you actually have spent your time—including interruptions—and is the most essential tool for improving your use of time. It doesn't have to be a second-by-second record of every waking moment. But it should account for blocks of time in increments as short as 15 minutes.

By looking at how much time you spend doing various activities, you now know where your time goes. How does it match with your perceptions of how you spend your time? Be prepared to be surprised, because most people find that they're spending time on a lot of activities that just don't matter very much.

You should also identify the "vacuums" that suck up your time. We all waste time on unimportant activities that keep us from doing the things we should be doing or want to do. Suppose you're studying and your cell phone rings. Instead of speaking with a friend for a half hour, you might (a) let the phone ring but not answer it; (b) answer it, but tell your friend you are studying and will call her back; or (c) speak with her for only a short while. If you do any of these three things, you will have taken control of your time.

Set Your Priorities. By this point you should have a good idea of what's taking up your time. But you may not know what you *should* be doing.

To figure out the best use of your time, you need to determine your priorities. *Priorities* are the tasks and activities you need and want to do, rank-ordered from most important to least important. There are no right or wrong priorities; maybe spending time on your studies is most important to you, or maybe your top priority is spending time with your family. Only you can decide. Furthermore, what's important to you now may be less of a priority to you next month, next year, or in five years.

The best procedure is to start off by identifying priorities for an entire term. What do you need to accomplish? Don't just choose obvious, general goals, such as "passing all my classes." Instead, think in terms of specific, measurable activities, such as "spend one hour each day reading the textbook to prepare for upcoming psychology classes."

Identify Your Prime Time. Do you enthusiastically bound out of bed in the morning, ready to start the day and take on the world? Or is the alarm clock a hated and unwelcome sound that jars you out of pleasant slumber? Are you zombielike by 10:00 at night, or a person who is just beginning to rev up at midnight? Each of us has our own style based on some inborn body clock. Being aware of the time or times of day when you can do your best work will help you plan and schedule your time most effectively. If you're at your worst in the morning, try to schedule easier, less-involving activities for those earlier hours. On the other hand, if morning is the best time for you, schedule activities that require the greatest concentration at that time.

Master the Moment. You now know where you've lost time in the past, and your priority list is telling you where you need to head in the future. You've reached the point where you can organize yourself to take control of your time. Here's what you'll need:

- A *master calendar* that shows all the weeks of the term on one page. It should include every week of the term and seven days per week. Using your class syllabi, write on the master calendar every assignment and test you will have, noting the date that it is due. Pencil in tentative assignments on the appropriate date. Also include on the master calendar important activities from your personal life, drawn from your list of priorities. And don't forget to schedule some free time for yourself.

- A *weekly timetable,* a master grid with the days of the week across the top and the hours, from 6:00 A.M. to midnight, along the side. Fill in the times of all your fixed, prescheduled activities—the times that your classes meet, when you have to be at work, the times you have to pick up your child at day care, and any other recurring appointments. Add assignment due dates, tests, and any other activities on the appropriate days of the week. Then pencil in blocks of time necessary to prepare for those events.

- A *daily to-do list.* Your daily to-do list can be written on a small, portable calendar that includes a separate page for each day of the week, or you can maintain a calendar electronically, if that is your preference. List all the things that you intend to do during the next day, and their priority. Start with the things you know you *must* do and that have fixed times, such as classes, work schedules, and appointments. Then add in the other things that you *should* accomplish, such as an hour of study for an upcoming test; work on research for an upcoming paper; or finish up a lab report. Finally, list things that are a low priority but enjoyable, like a run or a walk.

Controlling Time. If you've followed the schedules that you've prepared and organized, you've taken the most important steps in time management. However, our lives are filled with surprises: Things always seem to take longer than we've planned. A crisis occurs; buses are late; computers break down; kids get sick.

The difference between effective time management and time management that doesn't work lies in how well you deal with the inevitable surprises. You can take control of your days and permit yourself to follow your intended schedule in several ways:

- **Just say no.** You don't have to agree to every request and every favor that others ask of you.

- **Get away from it all.** Go to the library. Lock yourself into your bedroom. Find an out-of-the-way unused classroom. Adopt a specific spot as your own, such as a corner desk in a secluded nook in the library. If you use it enough, your body and mind will automatically get into study mode as soon as you seat yourself at it.

- **Enjoy the sounds of silence.** Although many students insist they accomplish most while a television, radio, or CD is playing, scientific studies suggest otherwise—we are able to concentrate most when our environment is silent. Even experiment and work in silence for a few days. You may find that you get more done in less time than you would in a more distracting environment

- **Take an e-break.** We may not control when communications arrive, but we can make the message wait until we are ready to receive it. Take an e-break and shut down your communication sources for a some period of time. Phone calls can be stored on voice-mail systems, and text messages, IMs, and e-mail can be saved on a phone or computer. They'll wait.

- **Expect the unexpected.** You'll never be able to escape from unexpected interruptions and surprises that require your attention. But by trying to anticipate them in advance, and thinking about how you'll react to them, you'll be positioning yourself to react more effectively when they do occur.

- **Combat procrastination.** Even when no one else is throwing interruptions at us, we make up our own. *Procrastination,* the habit of putting off and delaying tasks that are to be accomplished, is a problem that many of us face. If you find yourself procrastinating, several steps can help you:
  1. Break large tasks into small ones.
  2. Start with the easiest and simplest part of a task, and then do the harder parts.
  3. Work with others—for example, a study session with several of your classmates.
  4. Keep the costs of procrastination in mind.

Reading Your Textbook Effectively

Reading a textbook is different from reading for pleasure. With textbooks, you have specific goals: understanding, learning, and ultimately recalling the information. You can take several steps to achieve these goals:

- **Read the frontmatter.** If you'll be using a text extensively throughout the term, start by reading the preface and/or introduction and scanning the table of contents—what publishers call the *frontmatter.* It is there that the author has a chance to explain, often more personally than elsewhere in the text, what he or she considers important. Knowing this will give you a sense of what to expect as you read. (Note: You're reading part of the frontmatter at this very moment!)

- **Identify your personal objectives.** Before you begin an assignment, think about what your specific objectives are. Will you be reading a textbook on which you'll be thoroughly tested? Or will your reading provide background information for future learning but it won't itself be tested? Is the material going to be useful to you personally? In your program? Your objectives for reading will help you determine which reading strategy to adopt and how much time you can devote to the reading assignment. You aren't expected to read everything with the same degree of intensity. Some material you may feel comfortable skimming; for other material you'll want to put in the maximum effort.

- **Identify and use the advance organizers.** The next step in reading a textbook is to become familiar with the *advance organizers*—outlines, overviews, section objectives, or other clues to the meaning and organization of new material—provided in the material you are reading. For example, *Psychology and Your Life* includes "Learning Outcomes" in every module. These learning outcomes direct you to the key points of every section in this textbook. If you can work through the concepts presented in the learning outcomes, you have gained an understanding of exactly what each module is designed to do!

- **Stay focused as you read.** There are a million and one possible distractions that can invade your thoughts as you read. Your job is to keep distracting thoughts at bay and focus on the material you are supposed to be reading. Here are some things you can do to help yourself stay focused:

  - **Read in small bites.** If you think it is going to take you four hours to read an entire chapter, break up the four hours into more manageable time periods. Promise yourself that you'll read for one hour in the afternoon, another hour in the evening, and the next two hours spaced out during the following day.

  - **Take a break.** Actually, plan to take several short breaks to reward yourself while you're reading. During your break, do something enjoyable—eat a snack, watch a bit of a ball game on television, play a video game, or the like. Just try not to get drawn into your break activity to the point that it takes over your reading time.

- **Highlight and take notes as you read.** Highlighting and taking notes as you read a textbook are essential activities. Good annotations can help you learn and review the information prior to tests, as well as helping you to stay focused as you read. You can do several things to maximize the effectiveness of your notes:

  - **Rephrase key points.** Make notes to yourself, in your own words, about what the author is trying to get across. Don't just copy what's been said. Think about the material, and rewrite it in words that are your own. The very act of writing engages an additional type of perception—involving the physical sense of moving a pen or pressing a keyboard.

  - **Highlight or underline key points.** Often the first or last sentence in a paragraph, or the first or last paragraph in a section, will present a key point. Before you highlight anything, though, read the whole paragraph through. Then you'll be sure that what you highlight is, in fact, the key information. You should find yourself highlighting only one or two sentences or phrases per page. *In highlighting and underlining, less is more.* One guideline: No more than 10 percent of the material should be highlighted or underlined. You may find it helpful to highlight only the information that helps you work through the concepts presented in the Learning Outcomes.

  - **Use arrows, diagrams, outlines, tables, timelines, charts, and other visuals to help you understand and later recall what you are reading.** If three examples are given for a specific point, number them. If a sequence of steps is presented, number each step. If a paragraph discusses a situation in which an earlier point does not hold, link the original point to the exception by an arrow. Representing the material graphically will get you thinking about it in new and different ways.

The act of creating visual annotations will not only help you to understand the material better but will also ease its later recall.

- **Look up unfamiliar words.** Even though you may be able to figure out the meaning of an unfamiliar word from its context, look up unfamiliar words in a dictionary or online. You'll also find out what the word sounds like, which will be important if your instructor uses the word in class. *Psychology and Your Life* includes a glossary with definitions designed to help you gain a clear understanding of all the key terms in the text. Be sure to check it out if you need further clarification on any of the key terms within the modules.

Taking Good Notes in Class

Perhaps you know students who manage to write down nearly everything their instructors say in class. And perhaps you have thought to yourself: "If only I took such painstaking notes, I'd do much better in my classes." Contrary to what many students think, however, good note taking does not mean writing down every word that an instructor utters. With note taking, less is often more. Let's consider some of the basic principles of note taking:

- **Identify the instructor's—and your—goals for the course.** On the first day of class, most instructors talk about their objectives for the course. Most review the information on the class syllabus, the written document that explains the assignments for the semester. The information you get during that first session and through the syllabus is critical. In addition to the instructor's goals, you should have your own. What is it you want to learn from the course? How will the information from the course help you to enhance your knowledge, improve yourself as a person, achieve your goals?

- **Complete assignments before coming to class.** Your instructor enthusiastically describes the structure of the neuron, recounting excitedly how electrons flow across neurons, changing their electrical charge. One problem: You have only the vaguest idea what a neuron is. And the reason you don't know is that you haven't read the assignment.

  Chances are you have found yourself in this situation at least a few times, so you know firsthand that sinking feeling as you become more and more confused. The moral: Always go to class prepared. Instructors assume that their students have done what they've assigned, and their lectures are based upon that assumption. Don't forget to bring your textbook to class—during those times when you aren't as prepared, you will at least be able to use your text to follow along with your class discussions!

- **Use a notebook that assists in note taking.** Loose-leaf notebooks are especially good for taking notes because they permit you to go back later and change the order of the pages or add additional material. Whatever kind of notebook you use, *use only one side of the page for writing; keep one side free of notes.* There may be times that you'll want to spread out your notes in front of you, and it's much easier if no material is written on the back of the pages.

- **Listen for the key ideas.** Not every sentence in a lecture is equally important. One of the most useful skills you can develop is separating the key ideas from supporting information. Good lecturers strive to make just a few main points. The rest of what they say consists of explanation, examples, and other supportive material that expand upon the key ideas. To distinguish the key ideas from their support, you need to be alert and always searching for the *meta-message* of your instructor's words—that is, the underlying main ideas that a speaker is seeking to convey.

How can you discern the meta-message? One way is to *listen for keywords*. Phrases like "you need to know . . . ," "the most important thing that must be considered . . . ," "there are four problems with this approach . . . ," and—a big one—"this will be on the test . . ." should cause you to sit up and take notice. Also, if an instructor says the same thing in several ways, it's a clear sign that the material being discussed is important.

- **Use short, abbreviated phrases—not full sentences—when taking notes.** Forget everything you've ever heard about always writing in full sentences. In fact, it's often useful to take notes in the form of an outline. An outline summarizes ideas in short phrases and indicates the relationship among concepts through the use of indentations.

- **Pay attention to what is written on the board or projected from overheads and PowerPoint slides.**

  - **Listening is more important than seeing.** The information that your instructor projects on-screen, although important, ultimately is less critical than what he or she is saying. Pay primary attention to the spoken word and secondary attention to the screen.

  - **Don't copy everything that is on every slide.** Instructors can present far more information on their slides than they would if they were writing on a blackboard. Oftentimes there is so much information that it's impossible to copy to it all down. Don't even try. Instead, concentrate on taking down the key points.

  - **Remember that key points on slides are . . . key points.** The key points (often indicated by bullets) often relate to central concepts. Use these points to help organize your studying for tests, and don't be surprised if test questions directly assess the bulleted items on slides.

  - **Check to see if the presentation slides are available online.** Some instructors make their class presentations available on the Web to their students, either before or after class time. If they do this before class, print them out and bring them to class. Then you can make notes on your copy, clarifying important points. If they are not available until after a class is over, you can still make good use of them when it comes time to study the material for tests.

  - **Remember that presentation slides are not the same as good notes for a class.** If you miss a class, don't assume that getting a copy of the slides is sufficient. Studying the notes of a classmate who is a good note taker will be far more beneficial than studying only the slides.

Memorizing Efficiently: Using Proven Strategies to Memorize New Material

Here's a key principle of effective memorization: Memorize what you need to memorize. *Forget about the rest.*

The average textbook chapter has something like 20,000 words. But, within those 20,000 words, there may be only 30 to 40 specific concepts that you need to learn. And perhaps there are only 25 keywords. *Those* are the pieces of information on which you should focus in your efforts to memorize. By extracting what is important from what is less crucial, you'll be able to limit the amount of the material that you need to recall. You'll be able to focus on what you need to remember.

You have your choice of dozens of techniques of memorization. As we discuss the options, keep in mind that no one strategy works by itself. Also, feel free to devise your own strategies or add those that have worked for you in the past.

Rehearsal. Say it aloud: rehearsal. Think of this word in terms of its three syllables: re–hear–sal. If you're scratching your head as to why you should do this, it's to illustrate the point of *rehearsal:* to transfer material that you encounter into long-term memory.

To test if you've succeeded in transferring the word *rehearsal* into your memory, put down this book and go off for a few minutes. Do something entirely unrelated to reading this book. Have a snack, catch up on the latest sports scores on ESPN, or read the front page of a newspaper. If the word *rehearsal* popped into your head when you picked up this book again, you've passed your first memory test—the word *rehearsal* has been transferred into your memory.

Rehearsal is the key strategy in remembering information. If you don't rehearse material, it will never make it into your memory. Repeating the information, summarizing it, associating it with other memories, and above all thinking about it when you first come across it will ensure that rehearsal will be effective in placing the material into your memory.

Mnemonics. This odd word (pronounced with the "m" silent—"neh MON ix") describes formal techniques used to make material more readily remembered. *Mnemonics* are the tricks of the trade that professional memory experts use, and you too can use them to nail down the information you will need to recall for tests.

Among the most common mnemonics are the following:

- **Acronyms.** *Acronyms* are words or phrases formed by the first letters of a series of terms. The word *laser* is an acronym for "light amplification by stimulated emissions of radiation," and *radar* is an acronym for "radio detection and ranging."

  Acronyms can be a big help in remembering things. For example, Roy G. Biv is a favorite of physics students who must remember the colors of the spectrum (red, orange, yellow, green, blue, indigo, and violet). The benefit of acronyms is that they help us to recall a complete list of steps or items.
- **Rhymes and jingles.** "Thirty days hath September, April, June, and November." If you know the rest of the rhyme, you're familiar with one of the most commonly used mnemonic jingles in the English language.

Involve Multiple Senses. The more senses you can involve when you're trying to learn new material, the better you'll be able to remember. Here's why: Every time we encounter new information, all of our senses are potentially at work. Each piece of sensory information is stored in a separate location in the brain, and yet all the pieces are linked together in extraordinarily intricate ways.

What this means is that when we seek to remember the details of a specific event, recalling a memory of one of the sensory experiences can trigger recall of the other types of memories. You can make use of the fact that memories are stored in multiple ways by applying the following techniques:

- **When you learn something, use your body.** Don't sit passively at your desk. Instead, move around. Stand up; sit down. Touch the page. Trace figures with your fingers. Talk to yourself. Think out loud. By involving every part of your body, you've increased the number of potential ways to trigger a relevant memory later, when you need to recall it. And when one memory is triggered, other related memories may come tumbling back.

- **Draw and diagram the material.** It's often useful to structure written material by graphically grouping and connecting key ideas and themes. In contrast to an outline, such drawings help visually show related ideas fit together. (The *Full Circle* features at the end of each chapter in this book are an example of this.) Creating drawings, sketches, and even cartoons can help us remember better.

- **Visualize.** You already know that memory requires three basic steps: the initial recording of information, the storage of that information, and, ultimately, the retrieval of the stored information. *Visualization* is a technique by which images are formed to ensure that material is recalled. Don't stop at visualizing images just in your mind's eye. Actually drawing what you visualize will help you to remember the material even better. Visualization is effective because it serves several purposes. It helps make abstract ideas concrete; it engages multiple senses; it permits us to link different bits of information together; and it provides us with a context for storing information.

Overlearning. Lasting learning doesn't come until you have overlearned the material. *Overlearning* consists of studying and rehearsing material past the point of initial mastery. Through overlearning, recall becomes automatic. Rather than searching for a fact, going through mental contortions until perhaps the information surfaces, overlearning permits us to recall the information without even thinking about it.

Test-Taking Strategies

Preparing for tests is a long-term proposition. It's not a matter of "giving your all" the night before the test. Instead, it's a matter of giving your all to every aspect of the course.

Here are some guidelines that can help you do your best on tests.

Know What You Are Preparing For. Determine as much as you can about the test *before* you begin to study for it. The more you know about a test beforehand, the more efficient your studying will be.

To find out about an upcoming test, first ask this question:

- Is the test called a "test," "exam," "quiz," or something else? The names imply different things:
  - *Essay:* Requires a fairly extended, on-the-spot composition about some topic. Examples include questions that call on you to describe a person, process, or event, or those that ask you to compare or contrast two separate sets of material.
  - *Multiple-choice:* Usually contains a question or statement, followed by a number of possible answers (usually four or five of them). You are supposed to choose the best response from the choices offered.

- *True–false:* Presents statements about a topic that are either accurate or inaccurate. You are to indicate whether each statement is accurate (true) or inaccurate (false).
- *Matching:* Presents two lists of related information, arranged in column form. Typically, you are asked to pair up the items that go together (e.g., a scientific term and its definition, or a writer and the title of a book he wrote).
- *Short-answer:* Requires brief responses (usually a few sentences at most) in a kind of mini-essay.
- *Fill-in:* Requires you to add one or more missing words to a sentence or series of sentences.

Match Test Preparation to Question Types. Each kind of test question requires a somewhat different style of preparation.

- **Essay questions.** Essay tests focus on the big picture—ways in which the various pieces of information being tested fit together. You'll need to know not just a series of facts, but also the connections between them, and you will have to be able to discuss these ideas in an organized and logical way.

    The best approach to studying for an essay test involves four steps:

    1. Carefully reread your class notes and any notes you've made on assigned readings that will be covered on the upcoming exam. Also go through the readings themselves, reviewing underlined or highlighted material and marginal notes.

    2. Think of likely exam questions. For example, use the key words, phrases, concepts, and questions that come up in your class notes or in your text. Some instructors give out lists of possible essay topics; if yours does, focus on this list, but don't ignore other possibilities.

    3. Without looking at your notes or your readings, answer each potential essay question—aloud. Don't feel embarrassed about doing this. Talking aloud is often more useful than answering the question in your head. You can also write down the main points that any answer should cover. (Don't write out *complete* answers to the questions unless your instructor tells you in advance exactly what is going to be on the test. Your time is probably better spent learning the material than rehearsing precisely formulated responses.)

    4. After you've answered the questions, check yourself by looking at the notes and readings once again. If you feel confident that you've answered specific questions adequately, check them off. You can go back later for a quick review. But if there are questions that you had trouble with, review that material immediately. Then repeat the third step above, answering the questions again.

- **Multiple-choice, true–false, and matching questions.** Whereas the focus of review for essay questions should be on major issues and controversies, studying for multiple-choice, true–false, and matching questions requires more attention to the details. Almost anything is fair game for multiple-choice, true–false, and matching questions, so you can't afford to overlook anything when studying. It's a good idea to write down important facts on index cards: They're portable and available all the time, and the act of creating them helps drive the material into your memory. Furthermore, you can shuffle them and test yourself repeatedly until you've mastered the material.

- **Short-answer and fill-in questions.** Short-answer and fill-in questions are similar to essays in that they require you to recall key pieces of information rather than—as is the case with multiple-choice, true–false, and matching questions—finding it on the page in front of you. However, short-answer and fill-in questions typically don't demand that you integrate or compare different types of information. Consequently, the focus of your study should be on the recall of specific, detailed information.

Test Yourself. Once you feel you've mastered the material, test yourself on it. There are several ways to do this. Often textbooks are accompanied by Web sites that offer automatically scored practice tests and quizzes. (*Psychology and Your Life* does: Go to **www.mhhe.com/psychlife** to try one!) You can also create a test for yourself, in writing, making its form as close as possible to what you expect the actual test to be. For instance, if your instructor has told you the classroom test will be primarily made up of short-answer questions, your test should reflect that. Again, use the learning outcomes within each module to guide you.

You might also construct a test and administer it to a classmate or a member of your study group. In turn, you could take a test that someone else has constructed. Constructing and taking practice tests are excellent ways of studying the material and cementing it into memory.

Deal with Test Anxiety. What does the anticipation of a test do to you? Do you feel shaky? Is there a knot in your stomach? Do you grit your teeth? *Test anxiety* is a temporary condition characterized by fears and concerns about test taking. Almost everyone experiences it to some degree, although for some people it's more of a problem than for others. You'll never eliminate test anxiety completely, nor do you want to. A little bit of nervousness can energize us, making us more attentive and vigilant. Like any competitive event, testing can motivate us to do our best.

On the other hand, for some students, anxiety can spiral into the kind of paralyzing fear that makes their mind go blank. There are several ways to keep this from happening to you:

1. **Prepare thoroughly.** The more you prepare, the less test anxiety you'll feel. Good preparation can give you a sense of control and mastery, and it will prevent test anxiety from overwhelming you.

2. **Take a realistic view of the test.** Remember that your future success does not hinge on your performance on any single exam. Think of the big picture: Put the task ahead in context, and remind yourself of all the hurdles you've passed so far.

3. **Visualize success.** Think of an image of your instructor handing back your test marked with a big "A." Or imagine your instructor congratulating you on your fine performance the day after the test. Positive visualizations that highlight your potential success can help replace images of failure that may fuel test anxiety.

What if these strategies don't work? If your test anxiety is so great that it's getting in the way of your success, make use of your college's resources. Most provide a learning resource center or a counseling center that can provide you with personalized help.

Form a Study Group. *Study groups* are small, informal groups of students who work together to learn course material and study for a test. Forming such a group can be an excellent way to prepare for any kind of test. Some study groups are formed for particular tests, whereas others meet consistently throughout the term. The typical study group meets a week or two before a test and plans a strategy for studying. Members share their understanding of what will be on the test, based on what an instructor has said in class and on their review of notes and text material. Together, they develop a list of review questions to guide their individual study. The group then breaks up, and the members study on their own. If your class meets online, use e-mail or another means to have discussions with your classmates. Ask your instructor if there is a way for you to hold these online discussions through your school.

A few days before the test, members of the study group meet again. They discuss answers to the review questions, go over the material, and share any new insights they may have about the upcoming test. They may also quiz one another about the material to identify any weaknesses or gaps in their knowledge.

Study groups can be extremely powerful tools because they help accomplish several things:

- They help members organize and structure the material to approach their studying in a systematic and logical way.

- They allow students to share different perspectives on the material.

- They make it more likely that students will not overlook any potentially important information.

- They force members to rethink the course material, explaining it in words that other group members will understand. This helps both understanding and recall of the information when it is needed on the test.

- Finally, they help motivate members to do their best. When you're part of a study group, you're no longer working just for yourself; your studying also benefits the other study group members. Not wanting to let down your classmates in a study group may encourage you to put in your best effort.

Some Final Comments

We have discussed numerous techniques for increasing your study, classroom, and test effectiveness. But you need not feel tied to a specific strategy. You might want to combine other elements to create your own study system. Additional learning tips and strategies for critical thinking are presented throughout *Psychology and Your Life*.

Whatever learning strategies you use, you will maximize your understanding of the material in this book and master techniques that will help you learn and think critically in all of your academic endeavors. More important, you will optimize your understanding of the field of psychology. It is worth the effort: The excitement, challenges, and promise that psychology holds for you are significant.

Robert S. Feldman

PSYCHOLOGY

and your life

INTRODUCTION TO
PSYCHOLOGY

CHAPTER OUTLINE

A Gift of Life

It was every subway rider's nightmare, times two.

Who has ridden along New York's 656 miles of subway lines and not wondered: "What if I fell to the tracks as a train came in? What would I do?"

And who has not thought: "What if someone else fell? Would I jump to the rescue?"

Wesley Autrey, a 50-year-old construction worker and navy veteran, faced both those questions in a flashing instant yesterday and got his answers almost as quickly.

Mr. Autrey was waiting for the downtown local at 137th Street and Broadway in Manhattan around 12:45 P.M. He was taking his two daughters, Syshe, 4, and Shuqui, 6, home before work.

Nearby, a man collapsed, his body convulsing. Mr. Autrey and two women rushed to help, he said. The man, Cameron Hollopeter, 20, managed to get up, but then stumbled to the platform edge and fell to the tracks, between the two rails.

The headlights of the No. 1 train appeared. "I had to make a split decision," Mr. Autrey said.

So he made one, and leapt.

Mr. Autrey lay on Mr. Hollopeter, his heart pounding, pressing him down in a space roughly a foot deep. The train's brakes screeched, but it could not stop in time.

Five cars rolled overhead before the train stopped, the cars passing inches from his head, smudging his blue knit cap with grease. Mr. Autrey heard onlookers' screams. "We're O.K. down here," he yelled, "but I've got two daughters up there. Let them know their father's O.K." He heard cries of wonder, and applause. . . .

"I don't feel like I did something spectacular; I just saw someone who needed help," Mr. Autrey said. "I did what I felt was right." (Buckley, 2007, p. 1) ∎

looking AHEAD

Wesley Autrey's extraordinarily brave behavior illustrates the best of human nature. It also gives rise to a host of intriguing questions. For example,

- How did Autrey make the split-second decision to give aid to the man who fell onto the tracks? Would he have made the same decision if he had more time to think about it?
- What physical and biological changes occurred when Autrey leapt onto the tracks?
- What emotions did Autrey experience as the subway car hurtled by above him?
- What memories will Autrey's children have when they think back to the frightening spectacle of the subway passing over their father, and will it affect their later lives?
- Why was Autrey the only one who offered help even though dozens of others witnessed the event?

As we'll soon see, psychology addresses questions like these—and many, many more. In this chapter, we begin our examination of psychology, the different types of psychologists, and the various roles that psychologists play.

》》 》

Psychologists at Work

1.1 Define the science of psychology.

1.2 Describe the subfields of psychology.

1.3 List the major specialties for working in the field of psychology.

Psychology The scientific study of behavior and mental processes.

psych2.0
WWW.MHHE.COM/PSYCHLIFE

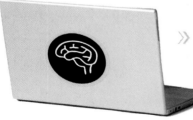

Multiple Causes of Behavior

» LO 1 What Is Psychology?

Psychology is the scientific study of behavior and mental processes. The phrase *behavior and mental processes* means many things: it encompasses not just what people do but also their thoughts, emotions, perceptions, reasoning processes, memories, and even the biological activities that maintain bodily functioning.

Psychologists try to describe, predict, and explain human behavior and mental processes, as well as helping to change and improve the lives of people and the world in which they live. They use scientific methods to find answers that are far more valid and legitimate than those resulting from intuition and speculation, which are often inaccurate. Test your own knowledge of psychology by completing the accompanying Try It! feature.

The questions in the Try It! provide just a hint of the topics that we will encounter in the study of psychology. Our discussions will take us through the range of what is known about behavior and mental processes.

» LO 2 The Subfields of Psychology: Psychology's Family Tree

As the study of psychology has grown, it has given rise to a number of subfields (described in Figure 1). One way to identify the key subfields is to look at some of the basic questions about behavior that they address.

Psychological Truths?

To test your knowledge of psychology, try answering the following questions:

1. Infants love their mothers primarily because their mothers fulfill their basic biological needs, such as providing food. True or false? _____

2. Geniuses generally have poor social adjustment. True or false? _____

3. The best way to ensure that a desired behavior will continue after training is completed is to reward that behavior every single time it occurs during training rather than rewarding it only periodically. True or false? _____

4. People with schizophrenia have at least two distinct personalities. True or false? _____

5. Parents should do everything they can to ensure children have high self-esteem and a strong sense that they are highly competent. True or false? _____

6. Children's IQ scores have little to do with how well they do in school. True or false? _____

7. Frequent masturbation can lead to mental illness. True or false? _____

8. Once people reach old age, their leisure activities change radically. True or false? _____

9. Most people would refuse to give painful electric shocks to other people. True or false? _____

10. People who talk about suicide are unlikely to actually try to kill themselves. True or false? _____

Scoring

The truth about each of these items is that they are all false. Based on psychological research, each of these "facts" have been proven untrue. You will learn the reasons why as we explore what psychologists have discovered about human behavior. (adapted from Lamal, 1979)

What Are the Biological Foundations of Behavior?

In the most fundamental sense, people are biological organisms. *Behavioral neuroscience* is the subfield of psychology that mainly examines how the brain and the nervous system—but other biological processes as well—determine behavior. Thus, neuroscientists consider how our bodies influence our behavior. For example, they may examine the link between specific sites in the brain and the muscular tremors of people affected by Parkinson's disease or attempt to determine how our emotions are related to physical sensations.

How Do People Sense, Perceive, Learn, and Think about the World?

If you have ever wondered why you are susceptible to optical illusions, how your body registers pain, or how to make the most of your study time, an experimental psychologist can answer your questions. *Experimental psychology* is the branch of psychology that studies the processes of sensing, perceiving, learning, and thinking about the world. (The term *experimental psychologist* is somewhat misleading: psychologists in every specialty area use experimental techniques.)

STUDY ALERT

It is important to know the different subfields of psychology in part because we can look at the same behavior in multiple ways.

Several subspecialties of experimental psychology have become specialties in their own right. One is *cognitive psychology,* which focuses on higher mental processes, including thinking, memory, reasoning, problem solving, judging, decision making, and language.

Subfield	Description
Behavioral genetics	*Behavioral genetics* studies the inheritance of traits related to behavior
Behavioral neuroscience	*Behavioral neuroscience* examines the biological basis of behavior
Clinical psychology	*Clinical psychology* deals with the study, diagnosis, and treatment of psychological disorders
Clinical neuropsychology	*Clinical neuropsychology* unites the areas of biopsychology and clinical psychology, focusing on the relationship between biological factors and psychological disorders
Cognitive psychology	*Cognitive psychology* focuses on the study of higher mental processes
Counseling psychology	*Counseling psychology* focuses primarily on educational, social, and career adjustment problems
Cross-cultural psychology	*Cross-cultural psychology* investigates the similarities and differences in psychological functioning in and across various cultures and ethnic groups
Developmental psychology	*Developmental psychology* examines how people grow and change from the moment of conception through death
Educational psychology	*Educational psychology* is concerned with teaching and learning processes, such as the relationship between motivation and school performance
Environmental psychology	*Environmental psychology* considers the relationship between people and their physical environment
Evolutionary psychology	*Evolutionary psychology* considers how behavior is influenced by our genetic inheritance from our ancestors
Experimental psychology	*Experimental psychology* studies the processes of sensing, perceiving, learning, and thinking about the world
Forensic psychology	*Forensic psychology* focuses on legal issues, such as determining the accuracy of witness memories
Health psychology	*Health psychology* explores the relationship between psychological factors and physical ailments or disease
Industrial/ organizational psychology	*Industrial/organizational psychology* is concerned with the psychology of the workplace
Personality psychology	*Personality psychology* focuses on the consistency in people's behavior over time and the traits that differentiate one person from another
Program evaluation	*Program evaluation* focuses on assessing large-scale programs, such as the Head Start preschool program, to determine whether they are effective in meeting their goals
Psychology of women	*Psychology of women* focuses on issues such as discrimination against women and the causes of violence against women
School psychology	*School psychology* is devoted to counseling children in elementary and secondary schools who have academic or emotional problems
Social psychology	*Social psychology* is the study of how people's thoughts, feelings, and actions are affected by others
Sport psychology	*Sport psychology* applies psychology to athletic activity and exercise

FIGURE 1 The major subfields of psychology.

What Are the Sources of Change and Stability in Behavior Across the Life Span?

A baby producing her first smile . . . taking her first step . . . saying her first word. These universal milestones in development are also singularly special and unique for each person. *Developmental psychology* studies how people grow and change from the moment of conception through death. *Personality psychology* focuses on the consistency in people's behavior over time and the traits that differentiate one person from another.

How Do Psychological Factors Affect Physical and Mental Health?

Frequent depression, stress, and fears that prevent people from carrying out their normal activities are topics that would interest a health psychologist, a clinical psychologist, and a counseling psychologist. *Health psychology* explores the relationship between psychological factors and physical ailments or disease. For example, health psychologists are interested in assessing how long-term stress (a psychological factor) can affect physical health and in identifying ways to promote behavior that brings about good health.

Clinical psychology deals with the study, diagnosis, and treatment of psychological disorders. Clinical psychologists are trained to diagnose and treat problems that range from the crises of everyday life, such as unhappiness over the breakup of a relationship, to more extreme conditions, such as profound, lingering depression.

Like clinical psychologists, counseling psychologists deal with people's psychological problems, but the problems they deal with are more specific. *Counseling psychology* focuses primarily on educational, social, and career adjustment problems. Many large business organizations employ counseling psychologists to help employees with work-related problems.

Some clinical and counseling psychologists specialize in *forensic psychology,* which applies psychology to the criminal justice system and legal issues. For example, forensic psychologists may be asked to examine people accused of crimes to determine if they are competent to stand trial or have psychological disorders.

How Do Our Social Networks Affect Behavior?

Our complex networks of social interrelationships are the focus for a number of subfields of psychology. For example, *social psychology* is the study of how people's thoughts, feelings, and actions are affected by others. Social psychologists concentrate on such diverse topics as human aggression, liking and loving, persuasion, and conformity.

Cross-cultural psychology investigates the similarities and differences in psychological functioning in and across various cultures and ethnic groups. For example, cross-cultural psychologists examine how cultures differ in their use of punishment during child rearing.

Expanding Psychology's Frontiers

The boundaries of the science of psychology are constantly growing. Three newer members of the field's family tree—evolutionary psychology, behavioral genetics, and clinical neuropsychology—have sparked particular excitement, and debate, within psychology.

> *The boundaries of the science of psychology are constantly growing.*

Evolutionary Psychology. *Evolutionary psychology* considers how behavior is influenced by our genetic inheritance from our ancestors. The evolutionary approach suggests that the chemical coding of information in our cells not only determines traits such as hair color and race but also holds the key to understanding a broad variety of behaviors that helped our ancestors survive and reproduce.

For example, evolutionary psychologists suggest that behavior such as shyness, jealousy, and cross-cultural similarities in qualities desired in potential mates are at least partially determined by genetics, presumably because such behavior helped increase the survival rate of humans' ancient relatives (Buss, 2003; Sefcek, Brumbach, & Vasquez, 2007).

Behavioral Genetics. Another rapidly growing area in psychology focuses on the biological mechanisms, such as genes and chromosomes, that enable inherited behavior to unfold. *Behavioral genetics* seeks to understand how we might inherit certain behavioral traits and how the environment influences whether we actually display such traits (Rende, 2007; Moffitt & Caspi, 2007).

Clinical Neuropsychology. *Clinical neuropsychology* unites the areas of neuroscience and clinical psychology: it focuses on the origin of psychological disorders in biological factors. Building on advances in our understanding of the structure and chemistry of the brain, this specialty has already led to promising new treatments for psychological disorders as well as debates over the use of medication to control behavior.

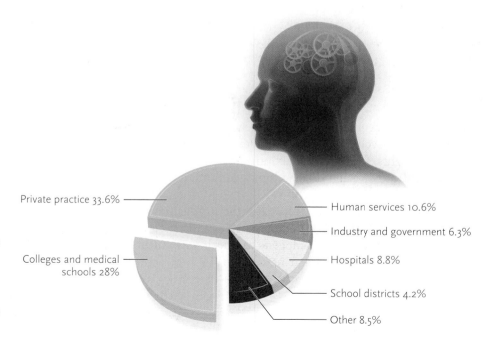

FIGURE 2 The breakdown of where U.S. psychologists (who have a Ph.D. or Psy.D. degree) work (APA, 2007). Why do you think so many psychologists work in college and university settings?

Private practice 33.6%

Colleges and medical schools 28%

Human services 10.6%

Industry and government 6.3%

Hospitals 8.8%

School districts 4.2%

Other 8.5%

Working at Psychology

Help Wanted: Instructor at a growing career college. Teach courses in introductory psychology and courses in specialty areas of cognitive psychology, perception, and learning. Strong commitment to quality teaching necessary.

. . .

Help Wanted: Industrial-organizational consulting psychologist. International firm seeks psychologists for full-time career positions as consultants to management. Candidates must have the ability to establish a rapport with senior business executives and help them find innovative and practical solutions to problems concerning people and organizations.

. . .

Help Wanted: Clinical psychologist. Ph.D., internship experience, and license required. Comprehensive clinic seeks psychologist to work with children and adults providing individual and group therapy, psychological evaluations, crisis intervention, and development of behavior treatment plans on multidisciplinary team.

As these job ads suggest, psychologists are employed in a variety of settings. Many doctoral-level psychologists are employed by institutions of higher learning (universities and colleges) or are self-employed, usually working as private practitioners treating clients (see Figure 2). Other work sites include hospitals, clinics, mental health centers, counseling centers, government human-services organizations, and schools (APA, 2007).

Psychologists: A Portrait

Although there is no "average" psychologist in terms of personal characteristics, we can draw a statistical portrait of the field. There are close to 300,000 psychologists working today in the United States—about half are men and half are women. But that's changing. Predictions are that by 2010 women will outnumber men in the field. Right now, almost three-fourths of new psychology doctorate degrees are earned by women (Frincke & Pate, 2004; Cynkar, 2007).

The vast majority of psychologists in the United States are white, with only 6 percent of all psychologists being members of racial minority groups. The underrepresentation of racial and ethnic minorities among psychologists is troubling for several reasons. First, the field of psychology is diminished by a lack of the diverse perspectives and talents that minority-group members can provide. Furthermore, minority-group psychologists serve as role models for members of minority communities, and their underrepresentation in the profession might deter other minority-group members from entering the field. Finally, because members of minority groups often prefer to receive psychological therapy from treatment providers of their own race or

B. D. Wong is well known for playing forensic psychologist Dr. George Huang on *Law and Order: Special Victims Unit*. As an Asian American psychologist, Wong's character represents a minority group that is relatively rare among psychologists. Why do you believe certain ethnic and racial groups are underrepresented in the field of psychology?

STUDY ALERT

Be able to differentiate the difference between a Ph.D. (doctor of philosophy) and Psy.D. (doctor of psychology), as well as the difference between psychologists and psychiatrists.

ethnic group, the rarity of minority psychologists can discourage some members of minority groups from seeking treatment (Jenkins et al., 2003; Bryant et al., 2005).

The Education of a Psychologist

How do people become psychologists? The most common route is a long one. Most psychologists have a doctorate, either a *Ph.D.* (doctor of philosophy) or, less frequently, a *Psy.D.* (doctor of psychology). The Ph.D. is a research degree that requires a dissertation based on an original investigation. The Psy.D. is obtained by psychologists who wish to focus on the treatment of psychological disorders. (Psychologists are distinct from psychiatrists, who are physicians who specialize in the treatment of psychological disorders.)

About a third of the people working in the field of psychology have a master's degree as their highest degree, which they earn after two or three years of graduate work. These individuals teach, conduct research, work in specialized programs dealing with drug abuse or crisis intervention, or—depending on state regulations—may provide therapy. Some work in universities, government, and business, collecting and analyzing data.

RECAP

Define the science of psychology.

- Psychology is the scientific study of behavior and mental processes, encompassing not just what people do but their biological activities, feelings, perceptions, memory, reasoning, and thoughts. (p. 4)

Describe the subfields of psychology.

- Behavioral neuroscientists focus on the biological basis of behavior, and experimental psychologists study the processes of sensing, perceiving, learning, and thinking about the world. (p. 6)
- Cognitive psychology, an outgrowth of experimental psychology, studies higher mental processes, including memory, knowing, thinking, reasoning, problem solving, judging, decision making, and language. (p. 6)
- Developmental psychologists study how people grow and change throughout the life span. (p. 6)
- Personality psychologists consider the consistency and change in an individual's behavior, as well as the individual differences that distinguish one person's behavior from another's. (p. 6)
- Health psychologists study psychological factors that affect physical disease, while

clinical psychologists consider the study, diagnosis, and treatment of abnormal behavior. Counseling psychologists focus on educational, social, and career adjustment problems. Forensic psychologists apply psychology to the criminal justice system and legal issues. (p. 6)

- Social psychology is the study of how people's thoughts, feelings, and actions are affected by others. (p. 6)
- Cross-cultural psychology examines the similarities and differences in psychological functioning among various cultures. (p. 6)
- Other increasingly important fields are evolutionary psychology, behavioral genetics, and clinical neuropsychology. (p. 6)

Where do psychologists work?

- Psychologists are employed in a variety of settings. Although the primary sites of employment are private practice and colleges, many psychologists are found in hospitals, clinics, community mental health centers, and counseling centers. (p. 9)

EVALUATE

1. Match each subfield of psychology with the issues or questions posed below.

   a. Behavioral neuroscience

   b. Experimental psychology

   c. Cognitive psychology

   d. Developmental psychology

   e. Personality psychology

   f. Health psychology

   g. Clinical psychology

   h. Counseling psychology

   i. Social psychology

   j. Industrial psychology

   1. Joan, an older student returning to college, is overwhelmed by the demands of studying while working at a full-time job. She needs to learn better organizational skills and work habits.
   2. At what age do children generally begin to acquire an emotional attachment to their fathers?
   3. During an election campaign, a politician devises strategies to change people's attitudes and persuade them to vote for her.
   4. What chemicals are released in the human body as a result of a stressful event? What are their effects on behavior?
   5. Luis is unique in his manner of responding to crisis situations, with an even temperament and a positive outlook.
   6. Janetta's job is demanding and stressful. She wonders if her lifestyle is making her more prone to certain illnesses, such as cancer and heart disease.
   7. A psychologist is intrigued by the fact that some people are much more sensitive to painful stimuli than others are.
   8. A strong fear of crowds leads a young woman to seek treatment for her problem.
   9. What mental strategies are involved in solving complex word problems?
   10. Jessica is asked to develop a management strategy that will encourage safer work practices in an assembly plant.

RETHINK

Do you think intuition and common sense are sufficient for understanding why people act the way they do? In what ways is a scientific approach appropriate for studying human behavior?

Answers to Evaluate Question 1. a-4, b-7, c-9, d-2, e-5, f-6, g-8, h-1, i-3, j-10

[KEY TERMS]

Psychology *p. 4*

A Science Evolves
The Past, the Present, and the Future

LEARNING OUTCOMES

2.1 Explain the roots of psychology.

2.2 Discuss today's perspectives on psychology.

2.3 Apply psychology to your life.

2.4 Summarize psychology's key issues and controversies.

psych2.0
WWW.MHHE.COM/PSYCHLIFE

Key Milestones of Psychology

Seven thousand years ago, people assumed that psychological problems were caused by evil spirits. To allow those spirits to escape from a person's body, ancient healers chipped a hole in a patient's skull with crude instruments—a procedure called *trephining*.

• • •

According to the seventeenth-century philosopher Descartes, nerves were hollow tubes through which "animal spirits" conducted impulses in the same way that water is transmitted through a pipe. When a person put a finger too close to a fire, heat was transmitted to the brain through the tubes.

• • •

Franz Josef Gall, an eighteenth-century physician, argued that a trained observer could discern intelligence, moral character, and other basic personality characteristics from the shape and number of bumps on a person's skull. His theory gave rise to the field of *phrenology*, employed by hundreds of practitioners in the nineteenth century.

Although these explanations might sound far-fetched, in their own times they represented the most advanced thinking about what might be called the psychology of the era. Our understanding of behavior has progressed tremendously since the eighteenth century, but most of the advances have been recent. As sciences go, psychology is one of the new kids on the block. (For highlights in the development of the field, see Figure 1 on pages 14 and 15.)

» LO1 The Roots of Psychology

The formal beginning of psychology as a scientific discipline is generally considered to be in the late nineteenth century, when, in Leipzig, Germany, Wilhelm Wundt established the first experimental laboratory devoted to psychological phenomena. At about the same time, William James was setting up his laboratory in Cambridge, Massachusetts.

When Wundt set up his laboratory in 1879, his aim was to study the building blocks of the mind. He considered psychology to be the study of conscious experience. His perspective, which came to be known as **structuralism,** focused on uncovering the fundamental mental components of perception, consciousness, thinking, emotions, and other kinds of mental states and activities.

To determine how basic sensory processes shape our understanding of the world, Wundt and other structuralists used a procedure called **introspection,** in which they presented people with a stimulus—such as a bright green object or a sentence printed on a card—and asked them to describe, in their own words and in as much detail as they could, what they were experiencing. Wundt argued that by analyzing their reports, psychologists could come to a better understanding of the structure of the mind.

Over time, psychologists challenged Wundt's approach. They became increasingly dissatisfied with the assumption that introspection could reveal the structure of the mind. Introspection was not a truly scientific technique, because there were few ways an outside observer could confirm the accuracy of others' introspections. Moreover, people had difficulty describing some kinds of inner experiences, such as emotional responses. Those drawbacks led to the development of new approaches, which largely replaced structuralism.

The perspective that replaced structuralism is known as functionalism. Rather than focusing on the mind's structure, **functionalism** concentrated on what the mind *does* and how behavior *functions.* Functionalists, whose perspective became prominent in the early 1900s, asked what role behavior plays in allowing people to adapt to their environments. For example, a functionalist might examine the function of the emotion of fear in preparing us to deal with emergency situations. Led by the American psychologist William James, the functionalists examined how behavior allows people to satisfy their needs and how our "stream of consciousness" permits us to adapt to our environment.

Another important reaction to structuralism was the development of gestalt psychology in the early 1900s. **Gestalt psychology** emphasizes how perception is organized. Instead of considering the individual parts that make up thinking, gestalt psychologists took the opposite tack, studying how people consider individual elements together as units or wholes. Led by German scientists such as Hermann Ebbinghaus and Max Wertheimer, gestalt psychologists proposed that "The

> *Over time, psychologist challenged Wundt's approach. They became increasingly dissatisfied with the assumption that introspection could reveal the structure of the mind.*

Structuralism Wundt's approach, which focuses on uncovering the fundamental mental components of consciousness, thinking, and other kinds of mental states and activities.

Introspection A procedure used to study the structure of the mind in which subjects are asked to describe in detail what they are experiencing when they are exposed to a stimulus.

Functionalism An early approach to psychology that concentrated on what the mind does—the functions of mental activity—and the role of behavior in allowing people to adapt to their environments.

Gestalt (geh SHTALLT) psychology An approach to psychology that focuses on the organization of perception and thinking in a "whole" sense rather than on the individual elements of perception.

I ♥ Structuralism

Wilhelm Wundt

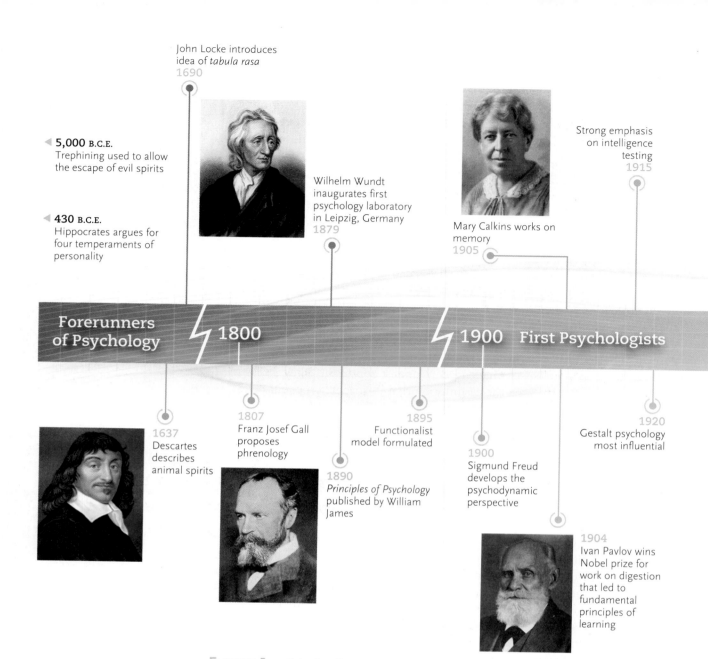

5,000 B.C.E.
Trephining used to allow the escape of evil spirits

430 B.C.E.
Hippocrates argues for four temperaments of personality

John Locke introduces idea of *tabula rasa*
1690

Wilhelm Wundt inaugurates first psychology laboratory in Leipzig, Germany
1879

Mary Calkins works on memory
1905

Strong emphasis on intelligence testing
1915

Forerunners of Psychology   **1800**   **1900**   **First Psychologists**

1637
Descartes describes animal spirits

1807
Franz Josef Gall proposes phrenology

1890
Principles of Psychology published by William James

1895
Functionalist model formulated

1900
Sigmund Freud develops the psychodynamic perspective

1904
Ivan Pavlov wins Nobel prize for work on digestion that led to fundamental principles of learning

1920
Gestalt psychology most influential

FIGURE 1   This timeline illustrates the major milestones in the development of psychology.

Anna Freud

whole is different from the sum of its parts," meaning that our perception, or understanding, of objects is greater and more meaningful than the individual elements that make up our perceptions. Gestalt psychologists have made substantial contributions to our understanding of perception.

Women in Psychology: Founding Mothers

As in many scientific fields, social prejudices hindered women's participation in the early development of psychology. For example, many universities would not even admit women to their graduate psychology programs in the early 1900s.

Despite the hurdles they faced, women made notable contributions to psychology, although their impact on the field was largely overlooked until recently. For example, Margaret Floy Washburn (1871–1939) was the first woman to receive a doctorate in psychology, and she did important work on

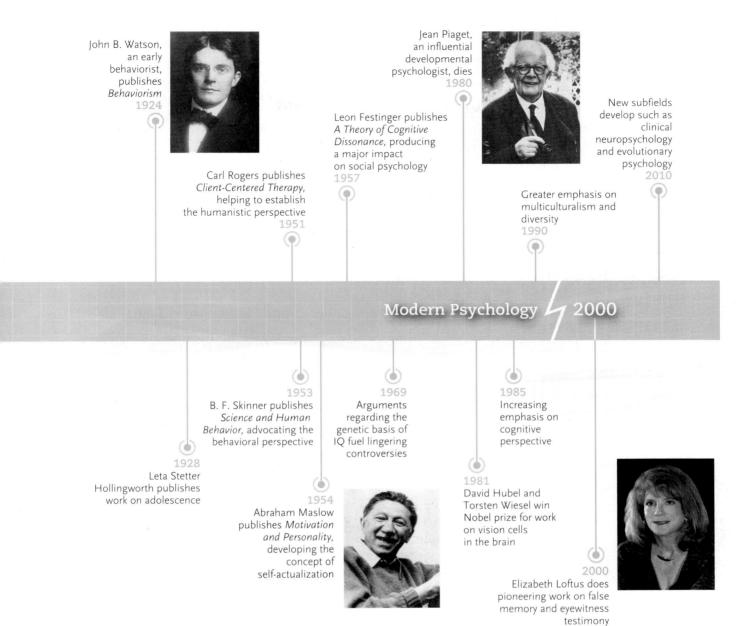

John B. Watson, an early behaviorist, publishes *Behaviorism*
1924

Carl Rogers publishes *Client-Centered Therapy*, helping to establish the humanistic perspective
1951

Leon Festinger publishes *A Theory of Cognitive Dissonance*, producing a major impact on social psychology
1957

Jean Piaget, an influential developmental psychologist, dies
1980

New subfields develop such as clinical neuropsychology and evolutionary psychology
2010

Greater emphasis on multiculturalism and diversity
1990

Modern Psychology 2000

1928
Leta Stetter Hollingworth publishes work on adolescence

1953
B. F. Skinner publishes *Science and Human Behavior*, advocating the behavioral perspective

1954
Abraham Maslow publishes *Motivation and Personality*, developing the concept of self-actualization

1969
Arguments regarding the genetic basis of IQ fuel lingering controversies

1981
David Hubel and Torsten Wiesel win Nobel prize for work on vision cells in the brain

1985
Increasing emphasis on cognitive perspective

2000
Elizabeth Loftus does pioneering work on false memory and eyewitness testimony

animal behavior. Leta Stetter Hollingworth (1886–1939) was one of the first psychologists to focus on child development and on women's issues. She collected data to refute the view, popular in the early 1900s, that women's abilities periodically declined during parts of the menstrual cycle (Hollingworth, 1943/1990; Denmark & Fernandez, 1993; Furumoto & Scarborough, 2002).

Mary Calkins (1863–1930), who studied memory in the early part of the twentieth century, became the first female president of the American Psychological Association. Karen Horney (pronounced "HORN-eye") (1885–1952) focused on the social and cultural factors behind personality, and June Etta Downey (1875–1932) spearheaded the study of personality traits and became the first woman to head a psychology department at a state university. Anna Freud (1895–1982), the daughter of Sigmund Freud, also made notable contributions to the treatment of abnormal behavior, and Mamie Phipps Clark (1917–1983) carried out pioneering work on how children of color grew to recognize racial differences (Horney, 1937; Stevens & Gardner, 1982; Lal, 2002).

» LO₂ Today's Perspectives

The men and women who laid the foundations of psychology shared a common goal: to explain and understand behavior using scientific methods. Seeking to achieve the same goal, the tens of thousands of psychologists who followed those early pioneers embraced—and often rejected—a variety of broad perspectives.

The perspectives of psychology offer distinct outlooks and emphasize different factors. Just as we can use more than one map to find our way around a particular region—for instance, a map that shows roads and highways and another map that shows major landmarks—psychologists developed a variety of approaches to understanding behavior. When considered jointly, the different perspectives provide the means to explain behavior in its amazing variety.

Today, the field of psychology includes five major perspectives (summarized in Figure 2). These broad perspectives emphasize different aspects of behavior and mental processes, and each takes our understanding of behavior in a somewhat different direction.

The Neuroscience Perspective: Blood, Sweat, and Fears

Neuroscience perspective The approach that views behavior from the perspective of the brain, the nervous system, and other biological functions.

When we get down to the basics, humans are animals made of skin and bones. The **neuroscience perspective** considers how people and nonhumans function biologically: how individual nerve cells are joined together, how the inheritance of certain characteristics from parents and other ancestors influences behavior, how the functioning of the body affects hopes and fears, which behaviors are instinctual, and so forth. Even more complex kinds of behaviors, such as a baby's response to strangers, are viewed as having critical biological components by psychologists who embrace the neuroscience perspective. This perspective includes the study of heredity and evolution, which considers how heredity may influence behavior; and behavioral neuroscience, which examines how the brain and the nervous system affect behavior.

Because every behavior ultimately can be broken down into its biological components, the neuroscience perspective has broad appeal. Psychologists who subscribe to this perspective have made major contributions to the understanding and betterment of human life, ranging from cures for certain types of deafness to drug treatments for people with severe mental disorders.

Neuroscience
Views behavior from the perspective of biological functioning

Behavioral
Focuses on observable behavior

Psychodynamic
Believes behavior is motivated by inner, unconscious forces over which a person has little control

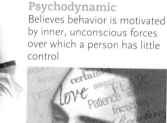

Cognitive
Examines how people understand and think about the world

Humanistic
Contends that people can control their behavior and that they naturally try to reach their full potential

FIGURE 2   The major perspectives of psychology.

Furthermore, advances in methods for examining the anatomy and functioning of the brain have permitted the neuroscientific perspective to extend its influence across a broad range of subfields in psychology. (We'll see examples of these methods in the *Neuroscience and Your Life* feature in future chapters.)

The Psychodynamic Perspective: Understanding the Inner Person

To many people who have never taken a psychology course, psychology begins and ends with the psychodynamic perspective. Proponents of the **psychodynamic perspective** argue that behavior is motivated by inner forces and conflicts about which we have little awareness or control. They view dreams and slips of the tongue as indications of what a person is truly feeling within a seething cauldron of unconscious psychic activity.

The origins of the psychodynamic view are linked to one person: Sigmund Freud. Freud was a Viennese physician in the early 1900s whose ideas about unconscious determinants of behavior had a revolutionary effect on twentieth-century thinking, not just in psychology but in related fields as well. Although some of the original Freudian principles have been roundly criticized, the contemporary psychodynamic perspective has provided a means not only to understand and treat some kinds of psychological disorders but also to understand everyday phenomena such as prejudice and aggression.

The Behavioral Perspective: Observing the Outer Person

Whereas the neuroscience and psychodynamic approaches look inside the organism to determine the causes of its behavior, the behavioral perspective takes a very different approach. The **behavioral perspective** grew out of a rejection of psychology's early emphasis on the inner workings of the mind. Instead, behaviorists suggested that the field should focus on observable behavior that can be measured objectively.

John B. Watson was the first major American psychologist to advocate a behavioral approach. Working in the 1920s, Watson believed that one could gain a complete understanding of behavior by studying and modifying the environment in which people operate. In fact, Watson thought that it was possible to produce any desired type of behavior by controlling a person's environment.

The behavioral perspective was championed by B. F. Skinner, a pioneer in the field. Much of our understanding of how people learn new behaviors is based on the behavioral perspective. As we will see, the behavioral perspective crops up along every byway of psychology. Along with its influence in the area of learning processes, this perspective has made contributions in such diverse areas as treating mental disorders, curbing aggression, resolving sexual problems, and ending drug addiction.

The Cognitive Perspective: Identifying the Roots of Understanding

Efforts to understand behavior lead some psychologists straight into the mind. Evolving in part from structuralism and in part as a reaction to behaviorism, which focused so heavily on observable behavior and the environment, the **cognitive perspective** focuses on how people think, understand, and know about the world. The emphasis is on learning how people comprehend and represent the outside world within themselves and how our ways of thinking about the world influence our behavior.

Psychodynamic perspective The approach based on the view that behavior is motivated by unconscious inner forces over which the individual has little control.

Behavioral perspective The approach that suggests that observable, measurable behavior should be the focus of study.

Cognitive perspective The approach that focuses on how people think, understand, and know about the world.

Sigmund Freud

Many psychologists who adhere to the cognitive perspective compare human thinking to the workings of a computer, which takes in information and transforms, stores, and retrieves it. In their view, thinking is *information processing*.

Psychologists who rely on the cognitive perspective ask questions ranging from how people make decisions to whether a person can watch television and study at the same time. The common elements that link cognitive approaches are an emphasis on how people understand and think about the world and an interest in describing the patterns and irregularities in the operation of our minds.

The Humanistic Perspective: The Unique Qualities of the Human Species

Humanistic perspective The approach that suggests that all individuals naturally strive to grow, develop, and be in control of their lives and behavior.

Rejecting the view that behavior is determined largely by automatically unfolding biological forces, unconscious processes, or the environment, the **humanistic perspective** instead suggests that all individuals naturally strive to grow, develop, and be in control of their lives and behavior. Humanistic psychologists maintain that each of us has the capacity to seek and reach fulfillment.

According to Carl Rogers and Abraham Maslow, who were central figures in the development of the humanistic perspective, people will strive to reach their full potential if they are given the opportunity. The emphasis of the humanistic perspective is on *free will*, the ability to freely make decisions about one's own behavior and life. The notion of free will stands in contrast to *determinism*, which sees behavior as caused, or determined, by things beyond a person's control.

The humanistic perspective assumes that people have the ability to make their own choices about their behavior rather than relying on societal standards. More than any other approach, it stresses the role of psychology in enriching people's lives and helping them achieve self-fulfillment. By reminding psychologists of their commitment to the individual person in society, the humanistic perspective has been an important influence.

» LO3 Psychology and Your Life

It is important not to let the abstract qualities of the broad approaches we have discussed lull you into thinking that they are purely theoretical: these perspectives underlie ongoing work of a practical nature, as we will discuss throughout this book. For example, these are a sampling of some of the real-world problems that psychology is addressing:

- **What are the causes of terrorism?** What motivates suicide bombers? Are they psychologically disordered, or can their behavior be seen as a rational response to a particular system of beliefs? Psychologists are gaining an

From the perspective of . . .

A HEALTH CARE WORKER   How can a basic understanding of psychology improve your job performance in the health care industry? In criminal justice? In your chosen career path?

During a November NBA game between Pacers and Pistons players and seven fans charged with assault after a brawl instigated by a thrown plastic cup of beer. As we can see from this security video, the incident highlights how quickly aggression can escalate.

understanding of the factors that lead people to embrace suicide and to engage in terrorism to further a cause in which they deeply believe.

- **Why is aggression so prevalent, and how can more humane and peaceful alternatives be promoted?** Aggression, whether on the playground or the battlefield, is arguably the world's greatest problem. Psychologists have sought to understand how aggression begins in childhood and how it may be prevented. For example, Brad Bushman and Craig Anderson have been looking at the ways in which violent video games may result in heightened violence on the part of those who play those games. They have found that people who play such games have an altered view of the world, seeing it as a more violent place. In addition, they are more apt to respond with aggression to others even when provoked only minimally (Bushman & Anderson, 2001, 2002; Crawford, 2002; Konijn, Bijvank, & Bushman, 2007).

- **Why do eyewitnesses to crimes often remember the events inaccurately, and how can we increase the precision of eyewitness accounts?** Psychologists' research has come to an important conclusion: eyewitness testimony in criminal cases is often inaccurate and biased. Memories of crimes are often clouded by emotion, and the questions asked by police investigators often elicit inaccurate responses. Work by psychologists has been used to provide national guidelines for obtaining more accurate memories during criminal investigations (Kassin, 2005; Busey & Loftus, 2007).

- **Does using a cell phone really impair people's driving ability?** Several states have enacted controversial laws banning cell phone usage while driving. Although many people feel that they are perfectly able to talk and drive at the same time, psychological research on attention tells a different story: merely talking on a cell phone—whether hands-free or not—impairs people's driving about as much as if they were legally drunk. The problem, of course, is that drivers' attention is taken away from the road and focused instead on the conversation (Strayer et al., 2005; Taggi et al., 2007).

- **What are the roots of obesity, and how can healthier eating and better physical fitness be encouraged?** Why are some people more predisposed to obesity than others are? What might be some social factors at play in the rising rate of obesity in childhood? As we'll discuss in Module 23, obesity is a complex problem with biological, psychological, and social underpinnings. Approaches to treating obesity therefore must take many factors into account in order to be successful. There is no magic bullet providing a quick fix, but psychologists recommend a number of strategies that help make weight-loss goals more achievable (Puhl & Latner, 2007).

These topics represent just a few of the issues that psychologists address on a daily basis. To further explore the many ways that psychology has an impact on everyday life, check out the Psychology Matters Web site of the American Psychological Association, which features psychological applications in everyday life, at www.psychologymatters.org.

» LO4 Psychology's Key Issues and Controversies

psych2.0

WWW.MHHE.COM/PSYCHLIFE

Key Issues in Psychology

As you consider the many topics and perspectives that make up psychology, ranging from a narrow focus on minute biochemical influences on behavior to a broad focus on social behaviors, you might find yourself thinking that the discipline lacks cohesion. However, the field is more unified than a first glimpse might suggest. For one thing, no matter what topical area a psychologist specializes in, he or she will rely primarily on one of the five major perspectives. For example, a developmental psychologist who specializes in the study of children could make use of the cognitive perspective or the psychodynamic perspective or any of the other major perspectives.

Psychologists also agree on what the key issues of the field are (see Figure 3). Although there are major arguments regarding how best to address and resolve the key issues, psychology is a unified science because psychologists of all

Issue	Neuroscience	Cognitive	Behavioral	Humanistic	Psychodynamic
Nature (heredity) vs. nurture (environment)	Nature (heredity)	Both	Nurture (environment)	Nurture (environment)	Nature (heredity)
Conscious vs. unconscious determinants of behavior	Unconscious	Both	Conscious	Conscious	Unconscious
Observable behavior vs. internal mental processes	Internal emphasis	Internal emphasis	Observable emphasis	Internal emphasis	Internal emphasis
Free will vs. determinism	Determinism	Free will	Determinism	Free will	Determinism
Individual differences vs. universal principles	Universal emphasis	Individual emphasis	Both	Individual emphasis	Universal emphasis

FIGURE 3 Key issues in psychology and the positions taken by psychologists subscribing to the five major perspectives of psychology.

perspectives agree that the issues must be addressed if the field is going to advance. As you contemplate these key issues, try not to think of them in "either/or" terms. Instead, consider the opposing viewpoints on each issue as the opposite ends of a continuum, with the positions of individual psychologists typically falling somewhere between the two ends.

Nature (heredity) versus nurture (environment) is one of the major issues that psychologists address. How much of people's behavior is due to their genetically determined nature (heredity), and how much is due to nurture, the influences of the physical and social environment in which a child is raised? Furthermore, what is the interplay between heredity and environment? These questions have deep philosophical and historical roots, and they are involved in many topics in psychology. Psychologists agree that neither nature nor nurture alone is the sole determinant of behavior; rather, it is a combination of the two. In a sense, then, the real controversy involves how much of our behavior is caused by heredity and how much is caused by environmental influences.

A second major question addressed by psychologists concerns *conscious versus unconscious causes of behavior.* How much of our behavior is produced by forces of which we are fully aware, and how much is due to unconscious activity—mental processes that are not accessible to the conscious mind? This question represents one of the great controversies in the field of psychology. For example, clinical psychologists adopting a psychodynamic perspective argue that psychological disorders are brought about by unconscious factors, whereas psychologists employing the cognitive perspective suggest that psychological disorders largely are the result of faulty thinking processes.

The next issue is *observable behavior versus internal mental processes.* Should psychology concentrate solely on behavior that can be seen by outside observers, or should it focus on unseen thinking processes? Some psychologists, particularly those relying on the behavioral perspective, contend that the only legitimate source of information for psychologists is behavior that can be observed directly. Other psychologists, building on the cognitive perspective, argue that what goes on inside a person's mind is critical to understanding behavior, and so we must concern ourselves with mental processes.

Free will versus determinism is another key issue. How much of our behavior is a matter of **free will** (choices made freely by an individual), and how much is subject to **determinism,** the notion that behavior is largely produced by factors beyond people's willful control? An issue long debated by philosophers, the free-will/determinism argument is also central to the field of psychology (Dennett, 2003; Cary, 2007).

For example, some psychologists who specialize in psychological disorders argue that people make intentional choices and that those who display so-called abnormal behavior should be considered responsible for their actions. Other psychologists disagree and contend that such individuals are the victims of forces beyond their control. The position psychologists take on this issue has important implications for the way they treat psychological disorders, especially in deciding whether treatment should be forced on people who don't want it.

Free will The idea that behavior is caused primarily by choices that are made freely by the individual.

Determinism The idea that people's behavior is produced primarily by factors outside of their willful control.

You could argue this man was the victim of determinism because his friend turned him in for theft. Or you could argue he exercised free will by stealing in the first place.

The last of the key issues concerns *individual differences versus universal principles.* How much of our behavior is a consequence of our unique and special qualities, and how much reflects the culture and society in which we live? How much of our behavior is universally human? Psychologists who rely on the neuroscience perspective tend to look for universal principles of behavior, such as how the nervous system operates or the way certain hormones automatically prime us for sexual activity. Such psychologists concentrate on the similarities in our behavioral destinies despite vast differences in our upbringing. In contrast, psychologists who employ the humanistic perspective focus more on the uniqueness of every individual. They consider every person's behavior a reflection of distinct and special individual qualities.

The question of the degree to which psychologists can identify universal principles that apply to all people has taken on new significance in light of the tremendous demographic changes now occurring in the United States and around the world. These changes raise new and critical issues for the discipline of psychology in the twenty-first century.

RECAP

Explain the roots of psychology.

- Wilhelm Wundt laid the foundation of psychology in 1879, when he opened his laboratory in Germany. (p. 13)
- Early perspectives that guided the work of psychologists were structuralism, functionalism, and gestalt theory. (p. 13)

Discuss today's perspectives on psychology.

- The neuroscience approach focuses on the biological components of the behavior of people and animals. (p. 16)
- The psychodynamic perspective suggests that powerful, unconscious inner forces and conflicts about which people have little or no awareness are the primary determinants of behavior. (p. 17)
- The behavioral perspective de-emphasizes internal processes and concentrates instead on observable, measurable behavior, suggesting that understanding and control of a person's environment are sufficient to fully explain and modify behavior. (p. 17)

- Cognitive approaches to behavior consider how people know, understand, and think about the world. (p. 17)
- The humanistic perspective emphasizes that people are uniquely inclined toward psychological growth and higher levels of functioning and that they will strive to reach their full potential. (p. 18)

Apply psychology to your life.

- Psychologists study a variety of topics related to the real world and everyday life, including ways to reduce aggression, eyewitness testimony in trials, and the way that cell phone use impairs driving. (p. 18)

Summarize psychology's key issues and controversies.

- Psychology's key issues and controversies center on how much of human behavior is a product of nature or nurture, conscious or unconscious thoughts, observable actions or internal mental processes, free will or determinism, and individual differences or universal principles. (p. 20)

EVALUATE

1. Wundt described psychology as the study of conscious experience, a perspective he called _____.

2. Early psychologists studied the mind by asking people to describe what they were experiencing when exposed to various stimuli. This procedure was known as _____.

3. The statement "In order to study human behavior, we must consider the whole of perception rather than its component parts" might be made by a person subscribing to which perspective of psychology?

4. Jeanne's therapist asks her to recount a violent dream she recently experienced in order to gain insight into the unconscious forces affecting her behavior. Jeanne's therapist is working from a _____ perspective.

5. "It is behavior that can be observed that should be studied, not the suspected inner workings of the mind." This statement was most likely made by someone with which perspective?
   a. Cognitive perspective
   b. Neuroscience perspective
   c. Humanistic perspective
   d. Behavioral perspective

6. "My therapist is wonderful! She always points out my positive traits. She dwells on my uniqueness and strength as an individual. I feel much more confident about myself—as if I'm really growing and reaching my potential." The therapist being described most likely follows a _____ perspective.

7. In the nature-nurture issue, nature refers to heredity, and nurture refers to the _____.

RETHINK

Focusing on one of the five major perspectives in use today (i.e., neuroscience, psychodynamic, behavioral, cognitive, and humanistic), can you describe the kinds of research questions and studies that researchers using that perspective might pursue?

Answers to Evaluate Questions 1. structuralism; 2. introspection; 3. gestalt; 4. psychodynamic; 5. d; 6. humanistic; 7. environment

[KEY TERMS]

Structuralism *p. 13*

Introspection *p. 13*

Functionalism *p. 13*

Gestalt (geh SHTALLT) psychology *p. 13*

Neuroscience perspective *p. 16*

Psychodynamic perspective *p. 16*

Behavioral perspective *p. 16*

Cognitive perspective *p. 17*

Humanistic perspective *p. 18*

Free will *p. 21*

Determinism *p. 21*

Research in Psychology

LEARNING OUTCOMES

3.1 Define the scientific method, and list the steps involved.

3.2 Describe how psychologists use research to answer questions of interest.

3.3 Summarize the descriptive research method used by psychologists.

3.4 Summarize the experimental research method used by psychologists.

Scientific method The approach through which psychologists systematically acquire knowledge and understanding about behavior and other phenomena of interest.

Theories Broad explanations and predictions concerning phenomena of interest.

Hypothesis A prediction, stemming from a theory, stated in a way that allows it to be tested.

Operational definition The translation of a hypothesis into specific, testable procedures that can be measured and observed.

» LO1 The Scientific Method

"Birds of a feather flock together" . . . or "opposites attract"? "Two heads are better than one" . . . or "if you want a thing done well, do it yourself"? "The more the merrier" . . . or "two's company, three's a crowd"?

If we were to rely on common sense to understand behavior, we'd have considerable difficulty—especially because commonsense views are often contradictory. In fact, one of the major undertakings for the field of psychology is to develop suppositions about behavior and to determine which of those suppositions are accurate. Psychologists—as well as scientists in other disciplines—meet the challenge of posing appropriate questions and properly answering them by relying on the scientific method. The **scientific method** is the approach used by psychologists to systematically acquire knowledge and understanding about behavior and other phenomena of interest. As illustrated in Figure 1, it consists of four main steps: (1) identifying questions of interest, (2) formulating an explanation, (3) carrying out research designed to support or refute the explanation, and (4) communicating the findings.

Theories: Specifying Broad Explanations

Psychologists ask questions about the nature and causes of behavior. They may wish to explore explanations for everyday behaviors or for various phenomena. They may also pose questions that build on findings from their previous research or from research carried out by other psychologists. Or they may produce new questions that are based on curiosity, creativity, or insight.

Once a question has been identified, the next step in the scientific method is to develop a theory to explain the observed phenomenon. **Theories** are broad explanations and predictions concerning phenomena of interest. They provide a framework for understanding the relationships among a set of otherwise unorganized facts or principles.

All of us have developed our own informal theories of human behavior, such as "People are basically good" or "People's behavior is usually motivated by self-interest." However, psychologists' theories are more formal and focused.

They are established on the basis of a careful study of the psychological literature to identify earlier relevant research and previously formulated theories, as well as psychologists' general knowledge of the field (Sternberg & Beall, 1991; McGuire, 1997).

Hypotheses: Crafting Testable Predictions

Once a theory is formed, the next step is to test it. To do this, psychologists need to create a hypothesis. A **hypothesis** is a prediction stated in a way that allows it to be tested. Hypotheses stem from theories; they help test the underlying soundness of theories.

In the same way that we develop our own broad theories about the world, we also construct hypotheses about events and behavior. Those hypotheses can range from trivialities (such as why a supervisor wears those weird shirts) to more meaningful matters (such as what is the best way to save money for retirement). Although we rarely test these hypotheses systematically, we do try to determine whether they are right. Perhaps we try comparing two strategies: putting our retirement savings in a 401(k) plan or managing how it is invested ourselves. By assessing which approach yields better returns, we have created a way to compare the two strategies.

A hypothesis must be restated in a way that will allow it to be tested, which involves creating an operational definition. An **operational definition** is the translation of a hypothesis into specific, testable procedures that can be measured and observed.

There is no single way to go about devising an operational definition for a hypothesis; it depends on logic, the equipment and facilities available, the psychological perspective being employed, and ultimately the creativity of the researcher. For example, one researcher might develop a hypothesis in which she uses as an operational definition of "fear" an increase in heart rate. In contrast, another psychologist might use as an operational definition of "fear" a written response to the question "How much fear are you experiencing at this moment?"

FIGURE 1   The scientific method, which encompasses the process of identifying, asking, and answering questions, is used by psychologists, and by researchers from every other scientific discipline, to come to an understanding about the world. What do you think are the advantages of this method?

STUDY ALERT

Understanding the distinction between theory and hypothesis is important. Remember that a theory is a broad explanation, while a hypothesis is a more narrow prediction that can be tested.

In short, the scientific method, with its emphasis on theories and hypotheses, helps psychologists pose appropriate questions. With properly stated questions in hand, psychologists then can choose from a variety of research methods to find answers.

» LO 2 Psychological Research

Research—systematic inquiry aimed at the discovery of new knowledge—is a central ingredient of the scientific method in psychology. It provides the key to understanding the degree to which hypotheses (and the theories behind them) are accurate.

All of us carry out elementary forms of research on our own.

Just as we can apply different theories and hypotheses to explain the same phenomena, we can use a number of alternative methods to conduct research.

As we consider the major tools psychologists use to conduct research, keep in mind that their relevance extends beyond testing and evaluating hypotheses in psychology. All of us carry out elementary forms of research on our own. For instance, a supervisor might evaluate an employee's performance; a physician might systematically test the effects of different doses of a drug on a patient; a salesperson might compare different persuasive strategies. Each of these situations draws on the research practices we are about to discuss.

» LO 3 Descriptive Research

psych2.0
WWW.MHHE.COM/PSYCHLIFE

The Scientific Method

Let's begin by considering several types of **descriptive research** designed to systematically investigate a person, group, or patterns of behavior. These methods include archival research, naturalistic observation, survey research, and case studies.

Archival Research

In **archival research,** existing data, such as census documents, college records, and newspaper clippings, are examined to test a hypothesis. For example, college records may be used to determine if there are gender differences in academic performance.

Archival research is a relatively inexpensive means of testing a hypothesis because someone else has already collected the basic data; however, records with the necessary information often do not exist. In these instances, researchers often turn to another research method: naturalistic observation.

Naturalistic Observation

In **naturalistic observation,** the investigator observes some naturally occurring behavior and does not make a change in the situation. For example, a researcher investigating helping behavior might observe the kind of help given to victims in a high-crime area of a city. The important point to remember about naturalistic observation is that the researcher simply records what occurs, making no modification in the situation that is being observed (Schutt, 2001; Moore, 2002; Rusting, 2006).

Although the advantage of naturalistic observation is obvious—we get a sample of what people do in their "natural habitat"—there is also an

Descriptive research An approach to research designed to systematically investigate a person, group, or patterns of behavior.

Archival research Research in which existing data, such as census documents, college records, and newspaper clippings, are examined to test a hypothesis.

Naturalistic observation Research in which an investigator simply observes some naturally occurring behavior and does not make a change in the situation.

important drawback: the inability to control any of the factors of interest. For example, we might find so few naturally occurring instances of helping behavior that we would be unable to draw any conclusions. Because naturalistic observation prevents researchers from making changes in a situation, they must wait until the appropriate conditions occur. Furthermore, if people know they are being watched, they may alter their reactions and produce behavior that is not truly representative.

Survey Research

There is no more straightforward way of finding out what people think, feel, and do than asking them directly. For this reason, surveys are an important research method. In **survey research,** a *sample* of people chosen to represent a larger group of interest (a *population*) is asked a series of questions about their behavior, thoughts, or attitudes. Survey methods have become so sophisticated that even with a very small sample researchers are able to infer with great accuracy how a larger group would respond. For instance, a sample of just a few thousand voters is sufficient to predict within one or two percentage points who will win a presidential election—if the representative sample is chosen with care (Sommer & Sommer, 2001; Groves et al., 2004; Igo, 2006).

However, survey research has several potential pitfalls. For one thing, if the sample of people who are surveyed is not representative of the broader population of interest, the results of the survey will have little meaning. For instance, if a sample of voters in a town only includes Republicans, it would hardly be useful for predicting the results of an election in which both Republicans and Democrats are voting (Dale, 2006). In addition, survey respondents may not want to admit to holding socially undesirable attitudes. (Most racists know they are racists and might not want to admit it.)

The Case Study

When a terrorist drove his car into a Scotland airport in 2007, many people wondered what it was about his personality or background that might have led to his behavior. To answer this question, psychologists might conduct a case study. In contrast to a survey, in which many people are studied, a **case study** is an in-depth, intensive investigation of a single individual or a small group. Case studies often include *psychological testing,* a procedure in which a carefully designed set of questions is used to gain some insight into the personality of the individual or group (Gass et al., 2000; Addus, Chen, & Khan, 2007).

When case studies are used as a research technique, the goal is often not only to learn about the few individuals being examined but also to use the insights gained from the study to improve our understanding of people in general. Sigmund Freud developed his theories through case studies of individual patients. Similarly, case studies of the London bombers might help identify others who are prone to violence.

The drawback to case studies? If the individuals examined are unique in certain ways, it is impossible to make valid generalizations to a larger population.

Dian Fossey, a pioneer in the study of endangered mountain gorillas in their native habitat, relied on naturalistic observation for her research. What are the advantages and disadvantages of this approach?

psych2.0
WWW.MHHE.COM/PSYCHLIFE

Naturalistic Observation

Survey research Research in which people chosen to represent a larger population are asked a series of questions abut their behavior, thoughts, or attitudes.

Case study An in-depth, intensive investigation of an individual or small group of people.

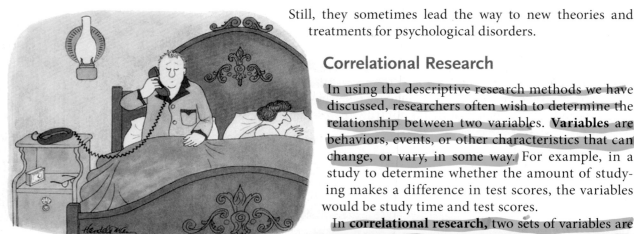

"This is the New York 'Times' Business Poll again, Mr. Landau. Do you feel better or worse about the economy than you did twenty minutes ago?"

psych2.0

WWW.MHHE.COM/PSYCHLIFE

Correlation

Many studies show that the observation of violence in the media is associated with aggression in viewers. The *Grand Theft Auto* series of video games has become a lighting rod for controversy due to its highly violent content. Can we conclude that the observation of violence causes aggression?

Still, they sometimes lead the way to new theories and treatments for psychological disorders.

Correlational Research

In using the descriptive research methods we have discussed, researchers often wish to determine the relationship between two variables. **Variables** are behaviors, events, or other characteristics that can change, or vary, in some way. For example, in a study to determine whether the amount of studying makes a difference in test scores, the variables would be study time and test scores.

In **correlational research,** two sets of variables are examined to determine whether they are associated, or "correlated." The strength and direction of the relationship between the two variables are represented by a mathematical statistic known as a *correlation.*

A *positive correlation* indicates that as the value of one variable increases, we can predict that the value of the other variable will also increase. For example, if we predict that the more years of education that employees have, the higher their income will be and that the fewer years of education they have, the lower their income will be, we are expecting to find a positive correlation. (Higher values of the variable "years of education" would be associated with higher values of the variable "income," and lower values of "years of education" would be associated with lower values of "income.")

In contrast, a *negative correlation* tells us that as the value of one variable increases, the value of the other decreases. For instance, we might predict that as the years of education increases, the number of work-related injuries decreases. Here we are expecting a negative correlation. More education is associated with less work injury, and less work injury is associated with more education. Of course, it's quite possible that little or no relationship exists between two variables. For instance, we would probably not expect to find a relationship between number of years of education and height; knowing how educated someone is does not tell us anything about how tall he or she is.

When two variables are strongly correlated with each other, it is tempting to assume that one variable causes the other. For example, if we find that more education is associated with higher income, we might guess that more studying *causes* higher income. Although this is not a bad guess, it remains just a guess—because finding that two variables are correlated does not mean that there is a causal relationship between them. The strong correlation suggests that knowing how many years of education a person has can help us predict how much money that person earns, but it does not mean that education causes the income. It might be, for instance, that people who are from affluent families can better afford to go to college, and that affluence, not education, predicts income. The mere fact that two variables occur together does not mean that one causes the other (see Figure 2).

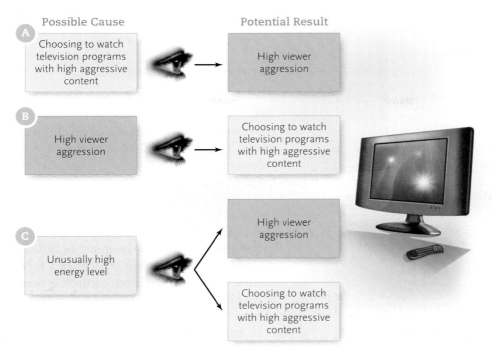

Possible Cause   Potential Result

A Choosing to watch television programs with high aggressive content → High viewer aggression

B High viewer aggression → Choosing to watch television programs with high aggressive content

C Unusually high energy level → High viewer aggression / Choosing to watch television programs with high aggressive content

FIGURE 2 If we find that frequent viewing of television programs with aggressive content is associated with high levels of aggressive behavior, we might cite several plausible causes, as suggested in this figure. For example, choosing to watch shows with aggressive content could produce aggression (a); or being a highly aggressive person might cause one to choose to watch televised aggression (b); or having a high energy level might cause a person to both choose to watch aggressive shows and act aggressively (c). Correlational findings, then, do not permit us to determine causality. Can you think of a way to study the effects of televised aggression on aggressive behavior that is not correlational?

The inability of correlational research to demonstrate cause-and-effect relationships is a crucial drawback to its use. There is, however, an alternative technique that does establish causality: the experiment.

» LO4 Experimental Research

The *only* way psychologists can establish cause-and-effect relationships through research is by carrying out an experiment. In a formal **experiment,** the researcher investigates the relationship between two (or more) variables by deliberately changing one variable in a controlled situation and observing the effects of that change on other aspects of the situation. In an experiment, then, the conditions are created and controlled by the researcher, who deliberately makes a change in those conditions in order to observe the effects of that change.

The change that the researcher deliberately makes in an experiment is called the **experimental manipulation.** Experimental manipulations are used to detect relationships between different variables. Experimenters must manipulate at least one variable in order to observe the effects of the manipulation on another variable while keeping other factors in the situation constant. However, the manipulation cannot be viewed by itself, in isolation; if a cause-and-effect relationship is to be established, the effects of the manipulation must be

Variables Behaviors, events, or other characteristics that can change, or vary, in some way.

Correlational research Research in which the relationship between two sets of variables is examined to determine whether they are associated, or "correlated."

Experiment The investigation of the relationship between two (or more) variables by deliberately producing a change in one variable in a situation and observing the effects of that change on other aspects of the situation.

Experimental manipulation The change that an experimenter deliberately produces in a situation.

"What if these guys in white coats who bring us food are, like, studying us and we're part of some kind of big experiment?"

> By employing both experimental and control groups in an experiment, researchers are able to rule out the possibility that something other than the experimental manipulation produced the results observed in the experiment.

Treatment The manipulation implemented by the experimenter.

Experimental group Any group participating in an experiment that receives a treatment.

Control group A group participating in an experiment that receives no treatment.

Independent variable The variable that is manipulated by an experimenter.

Dependent variable The variable that is measured and is expected to change as a result of changes caused by the experimenter's manipulation of the independent variable.

Random assignment to condition A procedure in which participants are assigned to different experimental groups or "conditions" on the basis of chance and chance alone.

compared with the effects of no manipulation or a different kind of manipulation.

Experimental Groups and Control Groups

Experimental research requires, then, that the responses of at least two groups be compared. One group will receive some special **treatment**—the manipulation implemented by the experimenter—and another group will receive either no treatment or a different treatment. Any group that receives a treatment is called an **experimental group;** a group that receives no treatment is called a **control group.** (In some experiments there are multiple experimental and control groups, each of which is compared with another group.)

By employing both experimental and control groups in an experiment, researchers are able to rule out the possibility that something other than the experimental manipulation produced the results observed in the experiment. Without a control group, we couldn't be sure that some other variable, such as the temperature at the time we were running the experiment, the color of the experimenter's hair, or even the mere passage of time, wasn't causing the changes observed.

For example, consider a medical researcher who thinks she has invented a medicine that cures the common cold. To test her claim, she gives the medicine one day to a group of 20 people who have colds and finds that 10 days later all of them are cured.

Eureka? Not so fast. An observer viewing this flawed study might reasonably argue that the people would have gotten better even without the medicine. What the researcher obviously needed was a control group consisting of people with colds who *don't* get the medicine and whose health is also checked 10 days later. Only if there is a significant difference between experimental and control groups can the effectiveness of the medicine be assessed. Through the use of control groups, then, researchers can isolate specific causes for their findings—and draw cause-and-effect inferences.

Independent and Dependent Variables

The **independent variable** is the condition that is manipulated by an experimenter. (You can think of the independent variable as being independent of the actions of those taking part in an experiment; it is controlled by the experimenter.) The **dependent variable** is the variable that is measured and is expected to change as a result of changes caused by the experimenter's manipulation of the independent variable. The dependent variable is dependent on the actions of the *participants* or *subjects*—the people taking part in the experiment. For example, whether people with colds are given medicine or not would be an independent variable, and whether they remained sick or got better 10 days later would be a dependent variable. *All* true experiments in psychology have an independent variable and a dependent variable.

Random Assignment of Participants

To make an experiment a valid test of the hypothesis, a final step must be added to the design: properly assigning participants to a particular experimental group.

The significance of this step becomes clear when we examine various alternative procedures. For example, the experimenters might assign just males to the experimental group and just females to the control group. If they had done this, however, any differences they found in the dependent variable could not be attributed with any certainty solely to the independent variable, because the differences might just as well have been due to gender. A more reasonable procedure would be to ensure that each group had roughly equal numbers of men and women; then the researchers would be able to make comparisons between groups with considerably more accuracy.

The problem becomes a bit more tricky, though, when we consider other participant characteristics besides gender. How can we ensure that participants in each experimental group will be equally intelligent, extroverted, cooperative, and so forth, when the list of characteristics—any one of which could be important—is potentially endless?

The solution is a simple but elegant procedure called **random assignment to condition**: participants are assigned to different experimental groups or "conditions" on the basis of chance and chance alone. The experimenter might, for instance, flip a coin for each participant and assign a participant to one group when "heads" came up, and to the other group when "tails" came up. The advantage of this technique is that there is an equal chance that participant characteristics will be distributed across the various groups. When a researcher uses random assignment—which in practice is usually carried out using computer-generated random numbers—chances are that each of the groups will have approximately the same proportion of intelligent people, cooperative people, extroverted people, males and females, and so on.

Figure 3 provides another example of an experiment. Like all experiments, it includes the following set of key elements, which are important to keep in mind as you consider whether a research study is truly an experiment:

- An independent variable, the variable that is manipulated by the experimenter.
- A dependent variable, the variable that is measured by the experimenter and that is expected to change as a result of the manipulation of the independent variable.
- A procedure that randomly assigns participants to different experimental groups or "conditions" of the independent variable.
- A hypothesis that predicts the effect the independent variable will have on the dependent variable.

In this experiment, preschoolers' reactions to the puppet are monitored. Can you think of a hypothesis that might be tested in this way?

psych2.0
WWW.MHHE.COM/PSYCHLIFE

Independent and Dependent Variables

STUDY ALERT

To remember the difference between dependent and independent variables, recall that a hypothesis predicts how a dependent variable *depends* on the manipulation of the independent variable.

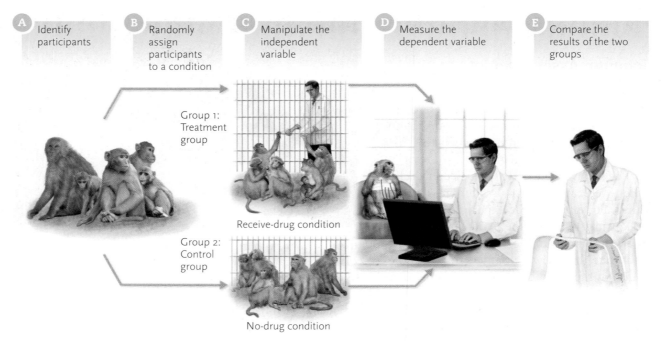

Group 1: Treatment group

Receive-drug condition

Group 2: Control group

No-drug condition

FIGURE 3 In this depiction of a study investigating the effects of the drug propranolol on stress, we can see the basic elements of all true experiments. The participants in the experiment were monkeys, who were randomly assigned to one of two groups. Monkeys assigned to the treatment group were given propranolol, hypothesized to prevent heart disease, whereas those in the control group were not given the drug. Administration of the drugs, then, was the independent variable.

All the monkeys were given a high-fat diet that was the human equivalent of two eggs with bacon every morning, and they occasionally were reassigned to different cages to provide a source of stress. To determine the effects of the drug, the monkeys' heart rates and other measures of heart disease were assessed after 26 months. These measures constituted the dependent variable. (The results? As hypothesized, monkeys that received the drug showed lower heart rates and fewer symptoms of heart disease than those who did not.) (Based on a study by Kaplan & Manuck, 1989.)

Only if each of these elements is present can a research study be considered a true experiment in which cause-and-effect relationships can be determined. (For a summary of the different types of research that we've discussed, see Figure 4.)

Of course, one experiment alone does not forever resolve a question about human behavior. Psychologists require that findings undergo **replication,** or be repeated, sometimes using other procedures, in other settings, with other groups of participants, before full confidence can be placed in the results of any single experiment. A procedure called *meta-analysis* permits psychologists to combine the results of many separate studies into one overall conclusion (Peterson & Brown, 2005; Tenenbaum & Ruck, 2007).

Replication The repetition of research, sometimes using other procedures, settings, and groups of participants, to increase confidence in prior findings.

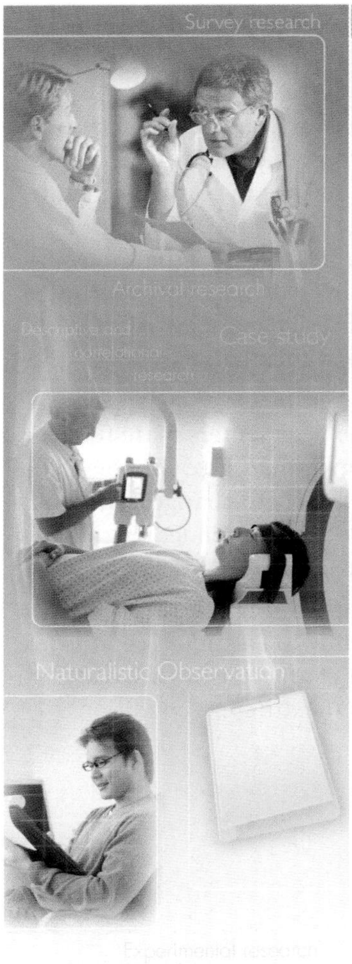

	Research Method	Description	Advantages	Shortcomings
	Descriptive and correlational research	Researcher observes a previously existing situation but does not make a change in the situation	Offers insight into relationships between variables	Cannot determine causality
	Archival research	Examines existing data to confirm hypothesis	Ease of data collection because data already exist	Dependent on availability of data
	Naturalistic observation	Observation of naturally occurring behavior, without making a change in the situation	Provides a sample of people in their natural environment	Cannot control the "natural habitat" being observed
	Survey research	A sample is chosen to represent a larger population and asked a series of questions	A small sample can be used to infer attitudes and behavior of a larger population	Sample may not be representative of the larger population; participants may not provide accurate responses to survey questions
	Case study	Intensive investigation of an individual or small group	Provides a thorough, in-depth understanding of participants	Results may not be generalizable beyond the sample
	Experimental research	Investigator produces a change in one variable to observe the effects of that change on other variables	Experiments offer the only way to determine cause-and-effect relationship	To be valid, experiments require random assignment of participants to conditions, well-conceptualized independent and dependent variables, and other careful controls

FIGURE 4   Research strategies.

RECAP

Define the scientific method, and list the steps involved.

- The scientific method is the approach psychologists use to understand behavior. It consists of four steps: identifying questions of interest, formulating an explanation, carrying out research that is designed to support or refute the explanation, and communicating the findings. (p. 24)

- To test a hypothesis, researchers must formulate an operational definition, which translates the abstract concepts of the hypothesis into the actual procedures used in the study. (p. 25)

Describe how psychologists use research to answer questions of interest.

- Research in psychology is guided by theories (broad explanations and predictions regarding phenomena of interest) and hypotheses (theory-based predictions stated in a way that allows them to be tested). (p. 25)

- Archival research uses existing records, such as old newspapers or other documents, to test a hypothesis. In naturalistic observation, the investigator acts mainly as an observer, making no change in a naturally occurring situation. In survey research, people are asked a series of questions about their behavior, thoughts, or attitudes. The case study is an in-depth interview and examination of one person or group. (p. 26)

- These descriptive research methods rely on correlational techniques, which describe associations between variables but cannot determine cause-and-effect relationships. (p. 28)

- In a formal experiment, the relationship between variables is investigated by deliberately producing a change—called the experimental manipulation—in one variable and observing changes in the other variable. (p. 29)

- In an experiment, at least two groups must be compared to assess cause-and-effect relationships. The group receiving the treatment (the special procedure devised by the experimenter) is the experimental group; the second group (which receives no treatment) is the control group. There also may be multiple experimental groups, each of which is subjected to a different procedure and then compared with the others. (p. 30)

- The variable that experimenters manipulate is the independent variable. The variable that they measure and expect to change as a result of manipulation of the independent variable is called the dependent variable. (p. 30)

- In a formal experiment, participants must be assigned randomly to treatment conditions, so that participant characteristics are distributed evenly across the different conditions. (p. 31)

E V A L U A T E

1. An explanation for a phenomenon of interest is known as a _____.

2. To test this explanation, a researcher must state it in terms of a testable question known as a _____.

3. An experimenter is interested in studying the relationship between hunger and aggression. She decides that she will measure aggression by counting the number of times a participant will hit a punching bag. In this case, her _____ definition of aggression is the number of times the participant hits the bag.

4. Match the following forms of research to their definition:

   1. Archival research
   2. Naturalistic observation
   3. Survey research
   4. Case study

   a. Directly asking a sample of people questions about their behavior.
   b. Examining existing records to test a hypothesis.
   c. Looking at behavior in its true setting without intervening in the setting.
   d. Doing an in-depth investigation of a person or small group.

5. Match each of the following research methods with its primary disadvantage:

   1. Archival research
   2. Naturalistic observation
   3. Survey research
   4. Case study

   a. The researcher may not be able to generalize to the population at large.
   b. People's behavior can change if they know they are being watched.
   c. The data may not exist or may be unusable.
   d. People may lie in order to present a good image.

6. A psychologist wants to study the effect of attractiveness on willingness to help a person with a math problem. Attractiveness would be the _____ variable, and the amount of helping would be the _____ variable.

7. The group in an experiment that receives no treatment is called the _____ group.

RETHINK

Can you describe how a researcher might use naturalistic observation, case studies, and survey research to investigate gender differences in aggressive behavior at the workplace? First state a hypothesis and then describe your research approaches. What positive and negative features does each method have?

[KEY TERMS]

Scientific method *p. 24*

Theories *p. 24*

Hypothesis *p. 24*

Operational definition *p. 25*

Descriptive research *p. 26*

Archival research *p. 26*

Naturalistic observation *p. 26*

Survey research *p. 27*

Case study *p. 27*

Variables *p. 28*

Correlational research *p. 28*

Experiment *p. 29*

Experimental manipulation *p. 29*

Treatment *p. 30*

Experimental group *p. 30*

Control group *p. 30*

Independent variable *p. 30*

Dependent variable *p. 30*

Random assignment to condition *p. 31*

Replication *p. 32*

Research Challenges

Exploring the Process

LEARNING OUTCOMES

4.1 Explain the major ethical issues that confront psychologists conducting research.

4.2 Discuss the issues related to testing on animals.

4.3 Identify threats to experimental validity.

psych2.0

WWW.MHHE.COM/PSYCHLIFE

Ethical Dilemmas

Informed consent A document signed by participants affirming that they have been told the basic outlines of the study and are aware of what their participation will involve.

STUDY ALERT

Because protection of participants is so essential, it is important to understand the key ethical guidelines that underlie research.

You probably realize by now that there are few simple formulas for psychological research. Psychologists must make choices about the type of study to conduct, the measures to take, and the most effective way to analyze the results. Even after they have made these essential decisions, they must still consider several critical issues. We turn first to the most fundamental of these issues: ethics.

» LO1 The Ethics of Research

Because research has the potential to violate the rights of participants, psychologists are expected to adhere to a strict set of ethical guidelines aimed at protecting participants (American Psychological Association, 2002). Those guidelines involve the following safeguards:

- Protection of participants from physical and mental harm
- The right of participants to privacy regarding their behavior
- The assurance that participation in research is completely voluntary
- The necessity of informing participants about the nature of procedures before their participation in the experiment

All experiments must be reviewed by an independent panel before being conducted, including the minority of studies that involve deception (Smith, 2003; Fisher et al., 2002; Fisher, 2003).

One of psychologists' key ethical principles is **informed consent.** Before participating in an experiment, the participants must sign a document affirming that they have been told the basic outlines of the study and are aware of what their participation will involve, what risks the experiment may hold, and the fact that their participation is purely voluntary and they may terminate it at any time. Furthermore, after participation in a study, they must be given a debriefing in which they receive an explanation of the study and the procedures that were involved. The only time informed consent and a debriefing can be eliminated is in experiments in which the risks are minimal, as in a purely observational study in a public place (Koocher, Norcross, & Hill, 2005; Fallon, 2006; Barnett, Wise, & Johnson-Greene, 2007).

EXPLORING diversity

Choosing Participants Who Represent the Scope of Human Behavior

College students are used so frequently in experiments that psychology has been called—somewhat contemptuously—the "science of the behavior of the college sophomore." Using college students as participants has both advantages and drawbacks. The big benefit is that because most research occurs in university settings, college students are readily available. Typically, they cost the researcher very little: they participate for either extra course credit or a relatively small payment.

The problem is that college students may not represent the general population adequately. They tend to be younger and better educated than a significant percentage of the rest of the population of the United States. Compared with older adults, their attitudes are likely to be less well formed, and they are more apt to be influenced by authority figures and peers (Martin & Hull, 2007).

College students are also disproportionately white and middle class. However, even in research that does not involve college students, participants tend to be white, middle-class participants; the use of African Americans, Latinos, Asians, and other minorities as participants is low (Graham, 1992; Guthrie, 1998). Because psychology is a science that purports to explain human behavior in general, something is therefore amiss. Consequently, psychological researchers have become increasingly sensitive to the importance of using participants who are fully representative of the general population. Furthermore, the National Institute of Mental Health and the National Science Foundation—the primary U.S. funding sources for psychological research—now require that experiments address issues of diverse populations (Carpenter, 2002; Lindley, 2006).

Although readily available and widely used as research participants, college students may not represent the population at large. What are some advantages and drawbacks of using college students as subjects?

» LO2 Should Animals Be Used in Research?

Like those who work with humans, researchers who use nonhuman animals in experiments have their own set of exacting guidelines to ensure that the animals do not suffer. Specifically, researchers must make every effort to minimize discomfort, illness, and pain. Procedures that subject animals to distress are permitted only when an alternative procedure is unavailable and when the research is justified by its prospective value. Moreover, researchers strive to avoid causing physical discomfort, but they are also required to promote the *psychological* well-being of some species of research animals, such as primates (Rusche, 2003; Lutz & Novak, 2005; Auer et al., 2007).

Research involving animals is controversial, but when conducted within ethical guidelines, yields significant benefits for humans.

> *Is it really possible to learn about human behavior from the results of research employing rats, gerbils, and pigeons?*

But why should animals be used for research in the first place? Is it really possible to learn about human behavior from the results of research employing rats, gerbils, and pigeons?

The answer is that psychological research that does employ nonhumans is designed to answer questions different from those posed in research with humans. For example, the shorter life span of animals (rats live an average of two years) allows researchers to learn about the effects of aging in a relatively short time frame. It is also possible to provide greater experimental control over non-humans and to carry out procedures that might not be possible with people. For example, some studies require large numbers of participants that share similar backgrounds or have been exposed to particular environments—conditions that could not practically be met with human beings.

» LO3 Threats to Experimental Validity: Avoiding Experimental Bias

Experimental bias Factors that distort how the independent variable affects the dependent variable in an experiment.

Even the best-laid experimental plans are susceptible to **experimental bias**—factors that distort the way the independent variable affects the dependent variable in an experiment. One of the most common forms of experimental bias is *experimenter expectations*: an experimenter unintentionally transmits cues to participants about the way they are expected to behave in a given experimental condition. The danger is that those expectations will bring about an "appropriate" behavior—one that otherwise might not have occurred (Rosenthal, 2002, 2003).

A related problem is *participant expectations* about appropriate behavior. If you have ever been a participant in an experiment, you know that you quickly develop guesses about what is expected of you. In fact, it is typical for people to develop their own hypotheses about what the experimenter hopes to learn from the study. If participants form their own hypotheses, it may be the participant's expectations, rather than the experimental manipulation, that produce an effect.

To guard against participant expectations biasing the results of an experiment, the experimenter may try to disguise the true purpose of the experiment. Participants who do not know that helping behavior is being studied, for example, are more apt to act in a "natural" way than they would if they knew.

Sometimes it is impossible to hide the actual purpose of research; when that is the case, other techniques are available to prevent bias. Suppose you were interested in testing the ability of a new drug to alleviate the symptoms of severe depression. If you simply gave the drug to half your participants and not to the other half, the participants who were given the drug might report feeling less depressed merely because they knew they were getting a drug. Similarly, the participants who got nothing might report feeling no better because they knew that they were in a no-treatment control group.

To solve this problem, psychologists typically use a procedure in which all the participants receive a treatment, but those in the control group receive only a **placebo,** a false treatment, such as a pill, "drug," or other substance, that has no significant chemical properties or active ingredient. Because members of both groups are kept in the dark about whether they are getting a real or a false treatment, any differences in outcome can be attributed to the quality of the drug and not to the possible psychological effects of being administered a pill or other substance (Rajagopal, 2006; Crum & Langer, 2007).

> **Placebo** A false treatment, such as a pill, "drug," or other substance, without any significant chemical properties or active ingredient.

However, there is one more safeguard that a careful researcher must apply in an experiment such as this one. To overcome the possibility that *experimenter* expectations will affect the participant, the person who administers the drug shouldn't know whether it is actually the true drug or the placebo. By keeping both the participant and the experimenter who interacts with the participant "blind" to the nature of the drug that is being administered, researchers can more accurately assess the effects of the drug. This method is known as the *double-blind procedure.*

becoming an *informed consumer*
OF PSYCHOLOGY
Thinking Critically About Research

If you were about to purchase an automobile, it is unlikely that you would stop at the nearest car dealership and drive off with the first car a salesperson recommended. Instead, you would probably mull over the purchase, read about automobiles, consider the alternatives, talk to others about their experiences, and ultimately put in a fair amount of thought before you made such a major purchase.

In contrast, many of us are considerably less conscientious when we expend our intellectual, rather than financial, assets. People often jump to conclusions on the basis of incomplete and inaccurate information, and only rarely do they take the time to critically evaluate the research and data to which they are exposed.

Because the field of psychology is based on an accumulated body of research, it is crucial to scrutinize thoroughly the methods, results, and claims of researchers. Several basic questions can help us sort through what is valid and what is not. Among the most important questions to ask are the following:

- *What was the purpose of the research?* Research studies should evolve from a clearly specified theory. Furthermore, we must take into account the specific hypothesis that is being tested. Unless we know what hypothesis is being examined, it is not possible to judge how successful a study has been.

- *How well was the study conducted?* Consider who the participants were, how many were involved, what methods were employed, and what problems the researcher encountered in collecting the data. There are important differences, for example, between a case study that reports the anecdotes of a handful of respondents and a survey that collects data from several thousand people.

- *Are the results presented fairly?* It is necessary to assess statements on the basis of the actual data they reflect and their logic. For instance, when the manufacturer of car X boasts that "no other car has a better safety record than car X," this does not mean that car X is safer than every other car. It just means that no other car has been proved safer, though many other cars could be just as safe as car X. Expressed in the latter fashion, the finding doesn't seem worth bragging about.

These three basic questions can help you assess the validity of research findings you come across—both within and outside the field of psychology. The more you know how to evaluate research in general, the better you will be able to assess what the field of psychology has to offer.

RECAP

Explain the major ethical issues that confront psychologists conducting research.

- One of the key ethical principles followed by psychologists is that of informed consent. Participants must be informed, before participation, about the basic outline of the experiment and the risks and potential benefits of their participation. (p. 36)

Discuss the issues related to testing on animals.

- Although the use of college students as participants has the advantage of easy availability, there are drawbacks, too. For instance, students do not necessarily represent the population as a whole. The use of nonhuman animals as participants may also have costs in terms of the ability to generalize to humans, although the benefits of using animals in research have been profound. (p. 37)

Identify threats to experimental validity.

- Experiments are subject to a number of biases, or threats. Experimenter expectations can produce bias when an experimenter unintentionally transmits cues to participants about her or his expectations regarding their behavior in a given experimental condition. Participant expectations can also bias an experiment. Among the tools experimenters use to help eliminate bias are placebos and double-blind procedures. (p. 38)

EVALUATE

1. Ethical research begins with the concept of informed consent. Before signing up to participate in an experiment, participants should be informed of which of the following?
   a. The procedure of the study, stated generally.
   b. The risks that may be involved.
   c. Their right to withdraw at any time.
   d. All of the above.

2. List three benefits of using animals in psychological research.

3. Deception is one means experimenters can use to try to eliminate participants' expectations. True or false?

4. A false treatment, such as a pill, that has no significant chemical properties or active ingredient, is known as a _____.

5. According to a report, a study has shown that men differ from women in their preference for ice cream flavors. This study was based on a sample of two men and three women. What might be wrong with this study?

RETHINK

A researcher strongly believes that physicians tend to show female nurses less attention and respect than they show male nurses. She sets up an experimental study involving observations of health clinics in different conditions. In explaining the study to the physicians and nurses who will participate, what steps should the researcher take to eliminate experimental bias based on both experimenter expectations and participant expectations?

[KEY TERMS]

Informed consent *p. 36*   Placebo *p. 39*

Experimental bias *p. 38*

looking BACK

Psychology on the Web

1. Practice using several search strategies to find information on the Web about one of the key issues in psychology (e.g., free will versus determinism, nature versus nurture, or conscious versus unconscious determinants of behavior), using (a) a general-purpose search engine (such as Google at www.google .com) and (b) a more specialized search engine (such as Yahoo's Psychology section, under the "Social Science" heading, at www.yahoo.com). Summarize and then compare the kinds of information you have found through each strategy.

2. Search the Web for discussions of youth violence and try to find (a) an article in the general news media, (b) information from a psychological point of view (e.g., experimental information or recommendations for parents from a professional organization), and (c) political opinion or debate about how to address the issue of youth violence.

the case of... CONFUSION

Alexis Dempsey had often wished that she could understand herself better. But the fight with her boyfriend the previous night really made her wonder what was driving her behavior. For no real reason at all, she had gotten annoyed with him at a party and had begun to criticize him. When he responded by asking her what her problem was, she had gotten really angry. She shouted at him that he was a total loser and that she didn't want to see him again. She stormed out of the party and had gone home.

By the time she reached home, though, she was miserable. She really did like her boyfriend, and she didn't want to end the relationship. She wondered why she'd gotten into the fight and why, in generally, she was acting more and more aggressively with others. She wished she could find a way to reduce her combativeness and strengthen her relationships with important people in her life. She has gotten some random insights from browsing the Web and looking at some of the self-help books her local bookstore, but mostly she ended up being confused.

1. What subfields of psychology might be of greatest relevance to Alexis's problem, and why?

2. If Alexis were to seek practical advice about making changes in her own life, which perspectives on psychology do you think would be most helpful, and why?

3. What do you think about Alexis's strategy of surfing the Web and looking at self-help books at the bookstore to better understand herself? What are the dangers of this approach?

4. What advice would *you* give Alexis to help her solve her problem?

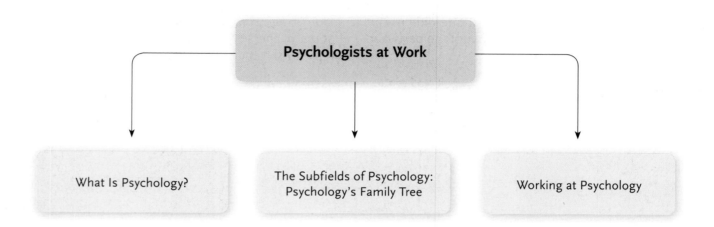

Psychologists at Work

What Is Psychology?

The Subfields of Psychology: Psychology's Family Tree

Working at Psychology

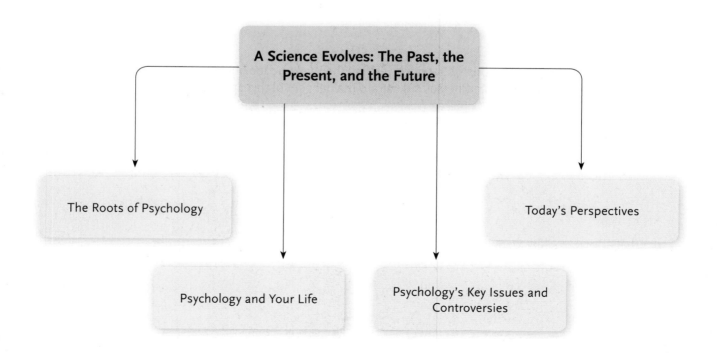

A Science Evolves: The Past, the Present, and the Future

The Roots of Psychology

Psychology and Your Life

Psychology's Key Issues and Controversies

Today's Perspectives

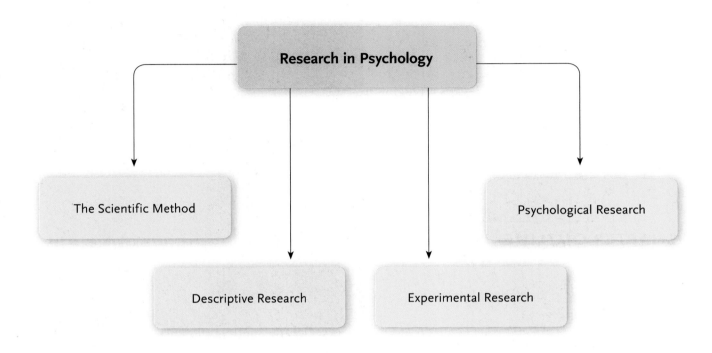

Research in Psychology

- The Scientific Method
- Descriptive Research
- Experimental Research
- Psychological Research

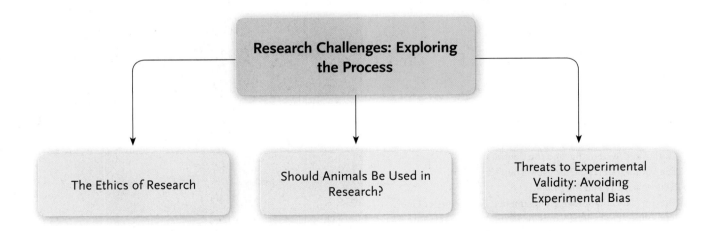

Research Challenges: Exploring the Process

- The Ethics of Research
- Should Animals Be Used in Research?
- Threats to Experimental Validity: Avoiding Experimental Bias

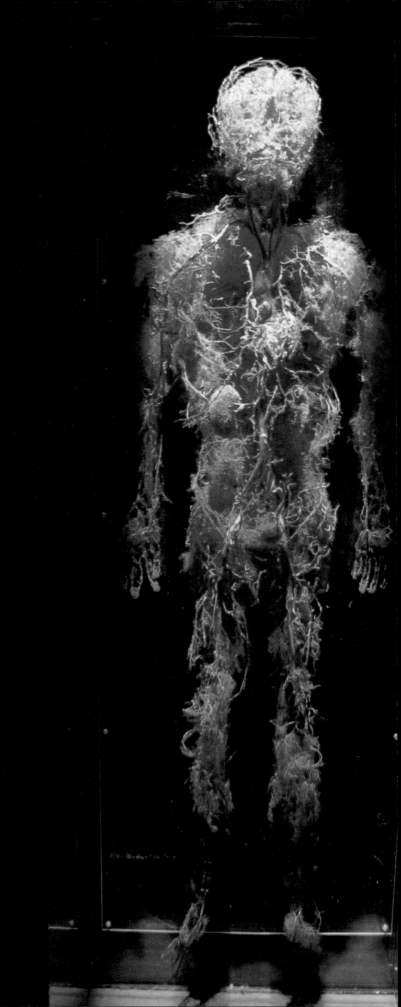

CHAPTER 2

The Deepest Cut

Wendy Nissley carried her two-year-old daughter, Lacy, into O.R. 12 at Johns Hopkins Hospital to have half of her brain removed. Lacy suffers from a rare malformation of the brain, known as hemimegalencephaly, in which one hemisphere grows larger than the other. The condition causes seizures, and Lacy was having so many—up to forty in a day—that at an age when other toddlers were trying out sentences, she could produce only a few language-like sounds. As long as Lacy's malformed right hemisphere was attached to the rest of her brain, it would prevent her left hemisphere from functioning normally. So Lacy's parents had brought her to Johns Hopkins for a hemispherectomy, which is probably the most radical procedure in neurosurgery. (Kenneally, 2006, p. 36) ■

NEUROSCIENCE AND **BEHAVIOR**

It took nearly a day, but the surgery to remove half of Lacy's brain was a success. Within a few months, Lacy was crawling and beginning to speak. Although the long-term effects of the radical operation are still unclear, it brought substantial improvement to Lacy's life.

The ability of surgeons to identify and remove damaged portions of the brain is little short of miraculous. The greater miracle, though, is the brain itself. An organ roughly half the size of a loaf of bread, the brain controls our behavior through every waking and sleeping moment. Our movements, thoughts, hopes, aspirations, dreams—our very awareness that we are human—all depend on the brain and the nerves that extend throughout the body, constituting the nervous system.

Because of the importance of the nervous system in controlling behavior, and because humans at their most basic level are biological beings, many researchers in psychology and other fields as diverse as computer science, zoology, and medicine have made the biological underpinnings of behavior their specialty. These experts collectively are called *neuroscientists* (Beatty, 2000; Posner & DiGirolamo, 2000; Gazzaniga, Ivry, & Mangun, 2002; Cartwright, 2006).

Psychologists who specialize in considering the ways in which the biological structures and functions of the body affect behavior are known as **behavioral neuroscientists** (or *biopsychologists*). They seek to answer several key questions: How does the brain control the voluntary and involuntary functioning of the body? How does the brain communicate with other parts of the body? What is the physical structure of the brain, and how does this structure affect behavior? Are psychological disorders caused by biological factors, and how can such disorders be treated?

Behavioral neuroscientists Psychologists who specialize in considering the ways in which the biological structures and functions of the body affect behavior.

As you consider the biological processes that we'll discuss in this chapter, it is important to keep in mind why behavioral neuroscience is an essential part of psychology: our understanding of human behavior requires knowledge of the brain and other parts of the nervous system. Biological factors are central to our sensory experiences, states of consciousness, motivation and emotion, development throughout the life span, and physical and psychological health. Furthermore, advances in behavioral neuroscience have led to the creation of drugs and other treatments for psychological and physical disorders. In short, we cannot understand behavior without understanding our biological makeup (Plomin, 2003a; Compagni & Manderscheid, 2006; Plomin et al., 2008).

looking
AHEAD

Neurons

The Basic Elements of Behavior

The nervous system is the pathway for the instructions that permit our bodies to carry out everyday activities such as scratching an itch as well as more remarkable skills like climbing to the top of Mount Everest. Here we will look at the structure and function of neurons, the cells that make up the nervous system, including the brain.

» LO 1 The Structure of the Neuron

Playing the piano, driving a car, or hitting a tennis ball depend, at one level, on exact muscle coordination. But if we consider *how* the muscles can be activated so precisely, we see that there are more fundamental processes involved. For the muscles to produce the complex movements that make up any meaningful physical activity, the brain has to provide the right messages to them and coordinate those messages.

Such messages—as well as those which enable us to think, remember, and experience emotion—are passed through specialized cells called neurons. **Neurons,** or nerve cells, are the basic elements of the nervous system. Their quantity is staggering—perhaps as many as 1 *trillion* neurons throughout the body are involved in the control of behavior (Boahen, 2005).

Although there are several types of neurons, they all have a similar structure, as illustrated in Figure 1. In contrast to most other cells, however, neurons have a distinctive feature: the ability to communicate with other cells and transmit information across relatively long distances. Many of the body's neurons receive signals from the environment or relay the nervous system's messages to muscles and other target cells, but the vast majority of neurons communicate only with other neurons in the elaborate information system that regulates behavior.

As you can see in Figure 1, a neuron has a cell body with a cluster of fibers called **dendrites** at one end. Those fibers, which look like the twisted branches of a tree, receive messages from other neurons. On the opposite of the cell body is a long, slim, tubelike extension called an **axon.** The axon carries messages received by the dendrites to other neurons. The axon is considerably longer than the rest of the neuron. Although most axons are several

Neurons Nerve cells, the basic elements of the nervous system.

Dendrites A cluster of fibers at one end of the neuron that receives messages from other neurons.

Axon The part of the neuron that carries messages destined for other neurons.

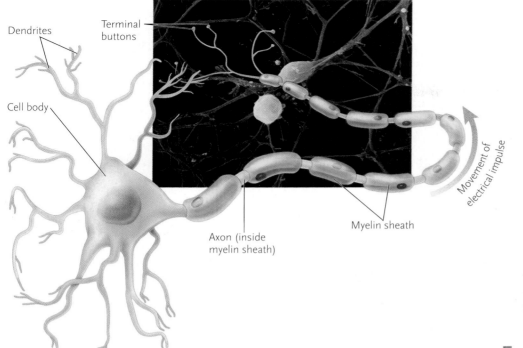

Dendrites

Terminal buttons

Cell body

Axon (inside myelin sheath)

Myelin sheath

Movement of electrical impulse

FIGURE 1 The primary components of the specialized cell called the neuron, the basic element of the nervous system (Van De Graaff, 2000). A neuron, like most types of cells in the body, has a cell body and a nucleus, but it also contains structures that carry messages: the dendrites, which receive messages from other neurons, and the axon, which carries messages to other neurons or body cells. In this neuron, as in most neurons, the axon is protected by the sausagelike myelin sheath. What advantages does the treelike structure of the neuron provide?

millimeters in length, some are as long as three feet. Axons end in small bulges called **terminal buttons,** which send messages to other neurons.

The messages that travel through a neuron are electrical in nature. Although there are exceptions, those electrical messages, or *impulses,* generally move across neurons in one direction only, as if they were traveling on a one-way street. Impulses follow a route that begins with the dendrites, continues into the cell body, and leads ultimately along the tubelike extension, the axon, to adjacent neurons.

To prevent messages from short-circuiting one another, axons must be insulated in some fashion (just as electrical wires must be insulated). Most axons are insulated by a **myelin sheath,** a protective coating of fat and protein that wraps around the axon like links of sausage.

Terminal buttons Small bulges at the end of the axons that send messages to other neurons.

Myelin sheath A protective coat of fat and protein that wraps around the axon.

All-or-none law The rule that neurons are either on or off.

Resting state The state in which there is a negative electrical charge of about −70 millivolts within a neuron.

» LO2 How Neurons Fire

Like a gun, neurons either fire—that is, transmit an electrical impulse along the axon—or don't fire. There is no in-between stage, just as pulling harder on a gun trigger doesn't make the bullet travel faster. Similarly, neurons follow an **all-or-none law:** they are either on or off, with nothing in between the on state and the off state. Once there is enough force to pull the trigger, a neuron fires.

Before a neuron is triggered—that is, when it is in a **resting state**—it has a negative electrical charge of about −70 millivolts. When a message arrives at a neuron, gates along the cell membrane open briefly to allow positively charged ions to rush in at rates as high as 100 million ions per second. The sudden arrival of these positive ions causes the charge within the nearby part of the cell to change momentarily from negative to positive. When the positive charge reaches a critical level, the "trigger" is pulled, and an electrical impulse, known as an action potential, travels along the axon of the neuron (see Figure 2).

psych2.0
WWW.MHHE.COM/PSYCHLIFE

Neurons

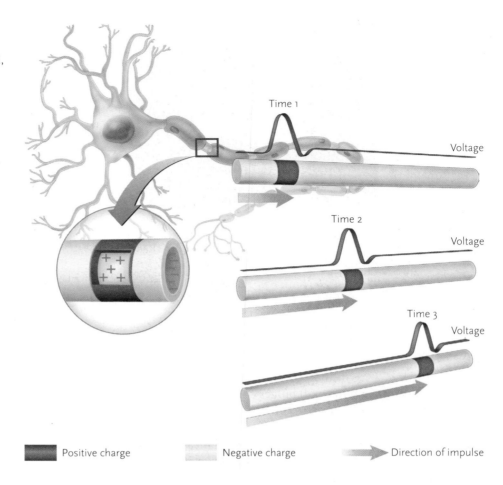

FIGURE 2 Movement of the action potential across the axon. Just before Time 1, positively charged ions enter the cell membrane, changing the charge in the nearby part of the neuron from negative to positive and triggering an action potential. The action potential travels along the axon, as illustrated in the changes occurring from Time 1 to Time 3 (from top to bottom in this drawing). Immediately after the action potential has passed through a section of the axon, positive ions are pumped out, restoring the charge in that section to negative.

Time 1 — Voltage

Time 2 — Voltage

Time 3 — Voltage

▬ Positive charge ▭ Negative charge ➔ Direction of impulse

Action potential An electric nerve impulse that travels through a neuron when it is set off by a "trigger," changing the neuron's charge from negative to positive.

Mirror neurons Neurons that fire when a person enacts a particular behavior and also when a person views others' behavior.

The **action potential** moves from one end of the axon to the other like a flame moving along a fuse. Just after an action potential has occurred, a neuron cannot fire again immediately no matter how much stimulation it receives. It is as if the gun has to be reloaded after each shot. Eventually, though, the neuron is ready to fire once again.

Neurons differ not only in terms of how quickly an impulse moves along the axon but also in their potential rate of firing. Some neurons are capable of firing as many as a thousand times per second; others fire at much slower rates. The intensity of a stimulus determines how much of a neuron's potential firing rate is reached. A strong stimulus, such as a bright light or a loud sound, leads to a higher rate of firing than a less intense stimulus does. Thus, even though all impulses move at the same strength or speed through a particular axon—because of the all-or-none law—there is variation in the frequency of impulses, providing a mechanism by which we can distinguish the tickle of a feather from the weight of someone standing on our toes.

Although all neurons operate through the firing of action potentials, there is significant specialization among different types of neurons. For example, in the last decade, neuroscientists have discovered the existence of **mirror neurons,** neurons that fire not only when a person enacts a particular behavior, but also when a person simply observes *another* individual carrying out the same behavior (Lepage & Theoret, 2007; Schulte-Ruther et al., 2007).

Mirror neurons may help explain how (and why) humans have the capacity to understand others' intentions. Specifically, mirror neurons may fire when we view others' behavior, helping us to predict what their goals are and what they may do next (Oberman, Pineda, & Ramachandran, 2007; Triesch, Jasso, & Deák, 2007).

> *Mirror neurons may help explain how (and why) humans have the capacity to understand others' intentions.*

» LO3 Where Neurons Connect to One Another: Bridging the Gap

If you have looked inside a computer, you've seen that each part is physically connected to another part. In contrast, evolution has produced a neural transmission system that at some points has no need for a structural connection between its components. Instead, a chemical connection bridges the gap, known as a synapse, between two neurons (see Figure 3). The **synapse** is the space between two neurons where the axon of a sending neuron

> **Synapse** The space between two neurons where the axon of a sending neuron communicates with the dendrites of a receiving neuron by using chemical messages.

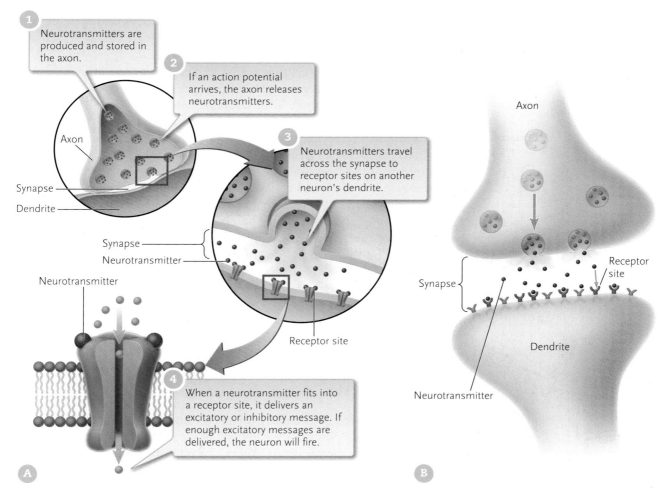

1. Neurotransmitters are produced and stored in the axon.

2. If an action potential arrives, the axon releases neurotransmitters.

3. Neurotransmitters travel across the synapse to receptor sites on another neuron's dendrite.

4. When a neurotransmitter fits into a receptor site, it delivers an excitatory or inhibitory message. If enough excitatory messages are delivered, the neuron will fire.

Axon
Synapse
Dendrite
Synapse
Neurotransmitter
Neurotransmitter
Receptor site

Axon
Synapse
Receptor site
Dendrite
Neurotransmitter

A

B

FIGURE 3   (A) A synapse is the junction between an axon and a dendrite. The gap between the axon and the dendrite is bridged by chemicals called neurotransmitters (Mader, 2000). (B) Just as the pieces of a jigsaw puzzle can fit in only one specific location in a puzzle, each kind of neurotransmitter has a distinctive configuration that allows it to fit into a specific type of receptor cell (Johnson, 2000). Why is it advantageous for axons and dendrites to be linked by temporary chemical bridges rather than by the hard wiring typical of a radio connection or telephone hookup?

Neurotransmitters Chemicals that carry messages across the synapse to the dendrite (and sometimes the cell body) of a receiver neuron.

Excitatory messages Chemical messages that make it more likely that a receiving neuron will fire and an action potential will travel down its axon.

Inhibitory messages Chemical messages that prevent or decrease the likelihood that a receiving neuron will fire.

Reuptake The reabsorption of neurotransmitters by a terminal button.

psych2.0
WWW.MHHE.COM/PSYCHLIFE

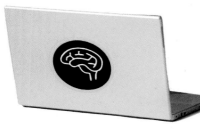

Messages Traveling between Neurons

communicates with the dendrites of a receiving neuron by using chemical messages (Fanselow & Poulos, 2005; Dean & Dresbach, 2006).

When a nerve impulse comes to the end of the axon and reaches a terminal button, the terminal button releases a chemical courier called a neurotransmitter. **Neurotransmitters** are chemicals that carry messages across the synapse to a dendrite (and sometimes the cell body) of a receiving neuron. The chemical mode of message transmission that occurs between neurons is strikingly different from the means by which communication occurs inside neurons: although messages travel in electrical form *within* a neuron, they move *between* neurons through a chemical transmission system.

There are several types of neurotransmitters, and not all neurons are capable of receiving the chemical message carried by a particular neurotransmitter. In the same way that a jigsaw puzzle piece can fit in only one specific location in a puzzle, each kind of neurotransmitter has a distinctive configuration that allows it to fit into a specific type of receptor site on the receiving neuron (see Figure 3B). It is only when a neurotransmitter fits precisely into a receptor site that successful chemical communication is possible.

If a neurotransmitter does fit into a site on the receiving neuron, the chemical message it delivers is basically one of two types: excitatory or inhibitory. **Excitatory messages** make it more likely that a receiving neuron will fire and an action potential will travel down its axon. **Inhibitory messages,** in contrast, do just the opposite; they provide chemical information that prevents or decreases the likelihood that the receiving neuron will fire.

Because the dendrites of a neuron receive both excitatory and inhibitory messages simultaneously, the neuron must integrate the messages by using a kind of chemical calculator. Put simply, if the excitatory messages ("fire!") outnumber the inhibitory ones ("don't fire!"), the neuron fires. In contrast, if the inhibitory messages outnumber the excitatory ones, nothing happens, and the neuron remains in its resting state (Mel, 2002; Flavell et al., 2006).

If neurotransmitters remained at the site of the synapse, receiving neurons would be awash in a continual chemical bath, producing constant stimulation or constant inhibition of the receiving neurons—and effective communication across the synapse would no longer be possible. To solve this problem, neurotransmitters are either deactivated by enzymes or—more commonly—reabsorbed by the terminal button in an example of chemical recycling called **reuptake.** Like a vacuum cleaner sucking up dust, neurons reabsorb the neurotransmitters that are now clogging the synapse. All this activity occurs at lightning speed (Helmuth, 2000; Holt & Jahn, 2004).

» LO4 Neurotransmitters: Multitalented Chemical Couriers

Neurotransmitters are a particularly important link between the nervous system and behavior. Not only are they important for maintaining vital brain and body functions, a deficiency or an excess of a neurotransmitter can produce severe behavior disorders. More than a hundred chemicals have been found to act as neurotransmitters, and neuroscientists believe that more may ultimately be identified (Penney, 2000; Schmidt, 2006).

Neurotransmitters vary significantly in terms of how strong their concentration must be to trigger a neuron to fire. Furthermore, the effects of a particular neurotransmitter vary, depending on the area of the nervous system in

Dopamine Pathways	Name	Location	Effect	Function
	Acetylcholine (ACh)	Brain, spinal cord, peripheral nervous system, especially some organs of the parasympathetic nervous system	Excitatory in brain and autonomic nervous system; inhibitory elsewhere	Muscle movement, cognitive functioning
	Glutamate	Brain, spinal cord	Excitatory	Memory
	Gamma-amino butyric acid (GABA)	Brain, spinal cord	Main inhibitory neurotransmitter	Eating, aggression, sleeping
Serotonin Pathways	Dopamine (DA)	Brain	Inhibitory or excitatory	Muscle disorders, mental disorders, Parkinson's disease
	Serotonin	Brain, spinal cord	Inhibitory	Sleeping, eating, mood, pain, depression
	Endorphins	Brain, spinal cord	Primarily inhibitory, except in hippocampus	Pain suppression, pleasurable feelings, appetites, placebos

FIGURE 4   Some major neurotransmitters.

which it is produced. The same neurotransmitter, then, can act as an excitatory message to a neuron located in one part of the brain and can inhibit firing in neurons located in another part. (The major neurotransmitters and their effects are described in Figure 4.)

One of the most common neurotransmitters is *acetylcholine* (or *ACh*, its chemical symbol), which is found throughout the nervous system. ACh is

Michael J. Fox, who suffers from Parkinson's disease, like Muhammad Ali, has become a strong advocate for research into the disorder. The pair is seen here asking Congress for additional funds for Parkinson's research.

involved in our every move, because—among other things—it transmits messages relating to our skeletal muscles. ACh is also involved in memory capabilities, and diminished production of ACh may be related to Alzheimer's disease (Mohapel et al., 2005).

Another major neurotransmitter is *dopamine (DA)*, which is involved in movement, attention, and learning. The discovery that certain drugs can have a significant effect on dopamine release has led to the development of effective treatments for a wide variety of physical and mental ailments. For instance, Parkinson's disease, from which actor Michael J. Fox suffers, is caused by a deficiency of dopamine in the brain. Techniques for increasing the production of dopamine in

From the perspective of . . .

A HEALTH CARE PROVIDER How might your understanding of the nervous system help you explain the symptoms of Parkinson's disease to a patient with the disorder?

Parkinson's patients are proving effective (Kaasinen & Rinne, 2002; Willis, 2005; Iversen & Iversen, 2007).

In other instances, *over*production of dopamine produces negative consequences. For example, researchers have hypothesized that schizophrenia and some other severe mental disturbances are affected or perhaps even caused by the presence of unusually high levels of dopamine. Drugs that block the reception of dopamine reduce the symptoms displayed by some people diagnosed with schizophrenia (Baumeister & Francis, 2002; Bolonna & Kerwin, 2005; Olijslagers, Werkman, & McCreary, 2006).

RECAP

Explain the structure of a neuron.

- A neuron has a cell body (which contains a nucleus) with a cluster of fibers called dendrites, which receive messages from other neurons. On the opposite end of the cell body is a tubelike extension, an axon, which ends in a small bulge called a terminal button. Terminal buttons send messages to other neurons. (p. 48)

Describe how neurons fire.

- Most axons are insulated by a coating called the myelin sheath. When a neuron receives a message to fire, it releases an action potential, an electrical charge that travels through the axon. Neurons operate according to an all-or-none law: Either they are at rest, or an action potential is moving through them. There is no in-between state. (p. 49)

Summarize how messages travel from one neuron to another.

- Once a neuron fires, nerve impulses are carried to other neurons through the production of chemical substances, neurotransmitters, that actually bridge the gaps—known as synapses—between neurons. Neurotransmitters may be either excitatory, telling other neurons to fire, or inhibitory, preventing or decreasing the likelihood of other neurons firing. (p. 52)

Identify neurotransmitters.

- Neurotransmitters are an important link between the nervous system and behavior. Common neurotransmitters include the following: *acetylcholine,* which transmits messages relating to our muscles and is involved in memory capabilities; *glutamate,* which plays a role in memory; *gamma-amino butyric acid (GABA),* which moderates behaviors from eating to aggression; *dopamine,* which is involved in movement, attention, and learning; *serotonin,* which is associated with the regulation of sleep, eating, mood, and pain; and *endorphins,* which seem to be involved in the brain's effort to deal with pain and elevate mood. (p. 53)

E V A L U A T E

1. The _____ is the fundamental element of the nervous system.

2. Neurons receive information through their _____ and send messages through their _____.

3. Just as electrical wires have an outer coating, axons are insulated by a coating called the _____ _____.

4. The gap between two neurons is bridged by a chemical connection called a _____.

5. Endorphins are one kind of _____, the chemical "messengers" between neurons.

R E T H I N K

How might psychologists use drugs that mimic the effects of neurotransmitters to treat psychological disorders?

Answers to Evaluate Questions 1. neuron; 2. dendrites, axons; 3. myelin sheath; 4. synapse; 5. neurotransmitter

[K E Y   T E R M S]

Behavioral neuroscientists (or biopsychologists) *p. 47*

Neurons *p. 48*

Dendrites *p. 48*

Axon *p. 48*

Terminal buttons *p. 49*

Myelin sheath *p. 49*

All-or-none law *p. 49*

Resting state *p. 49*

Action potential *p. 50*

Mirror neurons *p. 50*

Synapse *p. 51*

Neurotransmitters *p. 52*

Excitatory messages *p. 52*

Inhibitory messages *p. 52*

Reuptake *p. 52*

The Nervous System and the Endocrine System

Communicating within the Body

The complexity of the nervous system is astounding. Estimates of the number of connections between neurons within the brain fall in the neighborhood of 10 quadrillion—a 1 followed by 16 zeros. Furthermore, connections among neurons are not the only means of communication within the body; as we'll see, the endocrine system, which secretes chemical messages that circulate through the blood, also communicates messages that influence behavior and many aspects of biological functioning (Kandel, Schwartz, & Jessell, 2000; Forlenza & Baum, 2004; Boahen, 2005).

Central nervous system (CNS) The part of the nervous system that includes the brain and spinal cord.

Spinal cord A bundle of neurons that leaves the brain and runs down the length of the back and is the main means of transmitting messages between the brain and the body.

» LO 1 The Nervous System

The human nervous system has both logic and elegance. We turn now to a discussion of its basic structures.

Central and Peripheral Nervous Systems

As you can see from the schematic representation in Figure 1, the nervous system is divided into two main parts: the central nervous system and the peripheral nervous system. The **central nervous system (CNS)** is composed of the brain and spinal cord. The **spinal cord,** which is about the thickness of a pencil, contains a bundle of neurons that leaves the brain and runs down the length of the back (see Figure 2). As you can see in Figure 1, the spinal cord is the primary means for transmitting messages between the brain and the rest of the body.

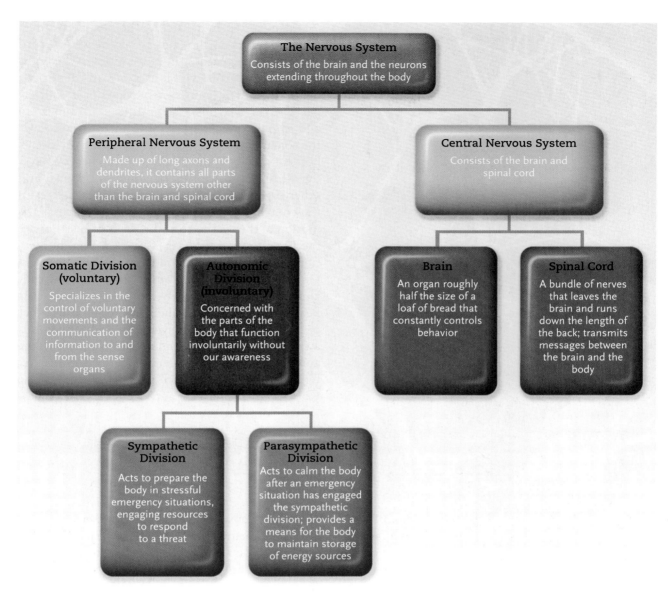

The Nervous System
Consists of the brain and the neurons extending throughout the body

Peripheral Nervous System
Made up of long axons and dendrites, it contains all parts of the nervous system other than the brain and spinal cord

Central Nervous System
Consists of the brain and spinal cord

Somatic Division (voluntary)
Specializes in the control of voluntary movements and the communication of information to and from the sense organs

Autonomic Division (involuntary)
Concerned with the parts of the body that function involuntarily without our awareness

Brain
An organ roughly half the size of a loaf of bread that constantly controls behavior

Spinal Cord
A bundle of nerves that leaves the brain and runs down the length of the back; transmits messages between the brain and the body

Sympathetic Division
Acts to prepare the body in stressful emergency situations, engaging resources to respond to a threat

Parasympathetic Division
Acts to calm the body after an emergency situation has engaged the sympathetic division; provides a means for the body to maintain storage of energy sources

FIGURE 1   A schematic diagram of the relationship of the parts of the nervous system.

However, the spinal cord is not just a communication channel. It also controls some simple behaviors on its own, without any help from the brain. An example is the way the knee jerks forward when it is tapped with a rubber hammer. This behavior is a type of **reflex,** an automatic, involuntary response to an incoming stimulus. A reflex is also at work when you touch a hot stove and immediately withdraw your hand. Although the brain eventually analyzes and reacts to the situation ("Ouch—hot stove—pull away!"), the initial withdrawal is directed only by neurons in the spinal cord.

Three kinds of neurons are involved in reflexes. **Sensory (afferent) neurons** transmit information from the perimeter of the body to the central nervous system. **Motor (efferent) neurons** communicate information from the nervous system to muscles and glands. **Interneurons** connect sensory and motor neurons, carrying messages between the two.

Reflex An automatic, involuntary response to an incoming stimulus.

psych2.0
WWW.MHHE.COM/PSYCHLIFE

Organization of the Nervous System

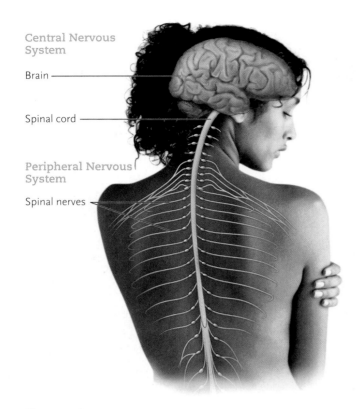

Central Nervous System

Brain

Spinal cord

Peripheral Nervous System

Spinal nerves

FIGURE 2   The central nervous system, consisting of the brain and spinal cord, and the peripheral nervous system.

Sensory (afferent) neurons Neurons that transmit information from the perimeter of the body to the central nervous system.

Motor (efferent) neurons Neurons that communicate information from the nervous system to muscles and glands.

Interneurons Neurons that connect sensory and motor neurons, carrying messages between the two.

Peripheral nervous system The part of the nervous system that includes the autonomic and somatic subdivisions; made up of neurons with long axons and dendrites, it branches out from the spinal cord and brain and reaches the extremities of the body.

Somatic division The part of the peripheral nervous system that specializes in the control of voluntary movements and the communication of information to and from the sense organs.

Autonomic division The part of the peripheral nervous system that controls involuntary movement of the heart, glands, lungs, and other organs.

As suggested by its name, the **peripheral nervous system** branches out from the spinal cord and brain and reaches the extremities of the body. Made up of neurons with long axons and dendrites, the peripheral nervous system encompasses all the parts of the nervous system other than the brain and spinal cord. There are two major divisions—the somatic division and the autonomic division—both of which connect the central nervous system with the sense organs, muscles, glands, and other organs. The **somatic division** specializes in the control of voluntary movements—such as the motion of the eyes to read this sentence or those of the hand to turn this page—and the communication of information to and from the sense organs. On the other hand, the **autonomic division** controls the parts of the body that keep us alive—the heart, blood vessels, glands, lungs, and other organs that function involuntarily without our awareness. As you are reading at this moment, the autonomic division of the peripheral nervous system is pumping blood through your body, pushing your lungs in and out, and overseeing the digestion of your last meal.

Activating the Divisions of the Autonomic Nervous System

The autonomic division plays a particularly crucial role during emergencies. Suppose that as you are reading in bed you suddenly sense that someone is outside your bedroom window. As you look up, you see the glint of an object that might be a knife. As confusion and fear overcome you, what happens to your body? If you are like most people, you react immediately on a physiological level. Your heart rate increases, you begin to sweat, and you develop goose bumps all over your body.

The physiological changes that occur during a crisis result from the activation of one of the two parts of the autonomic nervous system: the **sympathetic division.** The sympathetic division acts to prepare the body for action in stressful situations by engaging all of the organism's resources to run away or confront the threat. This response is often called the "fight-or-flight" response.

In contrast, the **parasympathetic division** acts to calm the body after the emergency has ended. When you find, for instance, that the stranger at the window is actually your boyfriend who has lost his keys and is climbing in the window to avoid waking you, your parasympathetic division begins to predominate, lowering your heart rate, stopping your sweating, and returning your body to the state it was in before you became alarmed. The parasympathetic division also directs the body to store energy for use in emergencies. The sympathetic and parasympathetic divisions work together to regulate many functions of the body (see Figure 3).

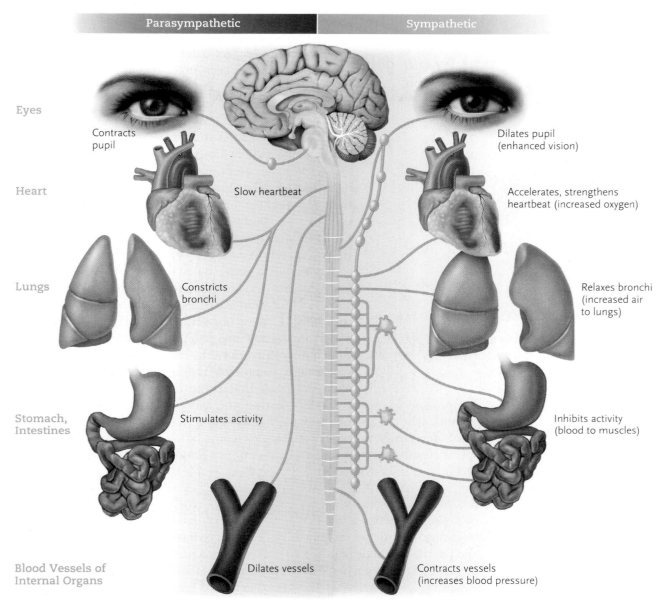

Parasympathetic	Sympathetic

Eyes
Contracts pupil — Dilates pupil (enhanced vision)

Heart
Slow heartbeat — Accelerates, strengthens heartbeat (increased oxygen)

Lungs
Constricts bronchi — Relaxes bronchi (increased air to lungs)

Stomach, Intestines
Stimulates activity — Inhibits activity (blood to muscles)

Blood Vessels of Internal Organs
Dilates vessels — Contracts vessels (increases blood pressure)

FIGURE 3   The major functions of the autonomic nervous system. The sympathetic division acts to prepare certain organs of the body for stressful situations, and the parasympathetic division acts to calm the body after the emergency has passed. Can you explain why each response of the sympathetic division might be useful in an emergency? *(Source: Adapted from Passer & Smith, 2001.)*

Behavioral Genetics

Our personality and behavioral habits are affected in part by our genetic and evolutionary heritage. **Behavioral genetics** studies the effects of heredity on behavior. Behavioral genetics researchers are finding increasing evidence that cognitive abilities, personality traits, sexual orientation, and psychological disorders are determined to some extent by genetic factors (Reif & Lesch, 2003; Viding et al., 2005; Ilies, Arvey, & Bouchard, 2006).

Behavioral genetics lies at the heart of the nature-nurture question, one of the key issues in the study of psychology. Although no one would argue that our behavior is determined *solely* by inherited factors, evidence

Sympathetic division The part of the autonomic division of the nervous system that acts to prepare the body for action in stressful situations, engaging all the organism's resources to respond to a threat.

Parasympathetic division The part of the autonomic division of the nervous system that acts to calm the body after an emergency or a stressful situation has ended.

Behavioral genetics The study of the effects of heredity on behavior.

Our personality and behavioral habits are affected in part by our genetic and evolutionary heritage.

Genetic testing can be done to determine potential risks to an unborn child based on family history of illnesses.

collected by behavioral geneticists does suggest that our genetic inheritance predisposes us to respond in particular ways to our environment, and even to seek out particular kinds of environments. For instance, research indicates that genetic factors may be related to such diverse behaviors as level of family conflict, schizophrenia, learning disabilities, and general sociability (Harlaar et al., 2005; Moffitt & Caspi, 2007).

Furthermore, important human characteristics and behaviors are related to the presence (or absence) of particular *genes,* the inherited material that controls the transmission of traits. For example, researchers have found evidence that novelty-seeking behavior is determined, at least in part, by a certain gene.

As we will consider later in the book when we discuss human development, researchers have identified some 25,000 individual genes, each of which appears in a specific sequence on a particular *chromosome,* a rod-shaped structure that transmits genetic information across generations. In 2003, after a decade of effort, researchers identified the sequence of the 3 billion chemical pairs that make up human *DNA,* the basic component of genes. Understanding the basic structure of the human *genome*—the "map" of humans' total genetic makeup—brings scientists a giant step closer to understanding the contributions of individual genes to specific human structures and functioning (Plomin et al., 2003; Plomin & McGuffin, 2003; Andreasen, 2005).

Behavioral Genetics, Gene Therapy, and Genetic Counseling. Behavioral genetics also holds the promise of developing new diagnostic and treatment techniques for genetic deficiencies that can lead to physical and psychological difficulties. In *gene therapy,* scientists inject genes meant to cure a particular disease into a patient's bloodstream. When the genes arrive at the site of defective genes that are producing the illness, they trigger the production of chemicals that can treat the disease (Rattazzi, LaFuci, & Brown, 2004; Jaffé, Prasad, & Larcher, 2006; Plomin et al., 2008).

The number of diseases that can be treated through gene therapy is growing, as we will see when we discuss human development. For example, gene therapy is now being used in experimental trials involving people with certain forms of cancer, leukemia, and blindness (Nakamura et al., 2004; Wagner et al., 2004; Hirschler, 2007).

STUDY ALERT

The endocrine system produces hormones, chemicals that circulate through the blood via the bloodstream.

From the perspective of . . .

A PHYSICIAN'S ASSISTANT How valuable would an understanding of the brain and neurosystem be in your job as a physician's assistant?

Advances in behavioral genetics also have led to the development of a profession that did not exist several decades ago: genetic counseling. Genetic counselors help people deal with issues related to inherited disorders. For example, genetic counselors provide advice to prospective parents about the potential risks in a future pregnancy, based on their family history of birth defects and hereditary illnesses. In addition, the counselor will consider the parents' age and problems with children they already have. They also can take blood, skin, and urine samples to examine specific chromosomes.

> **Endocrine system** A chemical communication network that sends messages throughout the body via the bloodstream.
>
> **Hormones** Chemicals that circulate through the blood and regulate the functioning or growth of the body.
>
> **Pituitary gland** The major component of the endocrine system, or "master gland," which secretes hormones that control growth and other parts of the endocrine system.

» LO2 The Endocrine System: Of Chemicals and Glands

Another of the body's communication systems, the **endocrine system** is a chemical communication network that sends messages throughout the body via the bloodstream. Its job is to secrete **hormones,** chemicals that circulate through the blood and regulate the functioning or growth of the body. It also influences—and is influenced by—the functioning of the nervous system.

As chemical messengers, hormones are like neurotransmitters, although their speed and mode of transmission are quite different. Whereas neural messages are measured in thousandths of a second, hormonal communications may take minutes to reach their destination. Furthermore, neural messages move through neurons in specific lines (like a signal carried by wires strung along telephone poles), whereas hormones travel throughout the body, similar to the way radio waves are transmitted across the entire landscape. Just as radio waves evoke a response only when a radio is tuned to the correct station, hormones flowing through the bloodstream activate only those cells which are receptive and "tuned" to the appropriate hormonal message.

A key component of the endocrine system is the tiny **pituitary gland.** The pituitary gland has sometimes been called the "master gland" because it controls the functioning of the rest of the endocrine system. But the pituitary gland is more than just the taskmaster of other glands; it has important functions in its own right. For instance, hormones secreted by the pituitary gland control growth. Extremely short people and unusually tall ones usually have pituitary gland abnormalities. Other endocrine glands, shown in Figure 4, affect emotional reactions, sexual urges, and energy levels.

Although hormones are produced naturally by the endocrine system, there are a variety of artificial hormones that people may choose to take. For example, physicians sometimes prescribe hormone replacement therapy (HRT) to treat symptoms of menopause in older women. Other artificial hormones can be harmful. For example, some athletes use testosterone, a male hormone, and drugs known as *steroids,* which act like testosterone. For athletes and others who want to bulk up their appearance, steroids provide a way to add muscle weight and increase strength. However, these drugs can lead to heart attacks, strokes, cancer, and even violent behavior, making them extremely dangerous (Kolata, 2002; Arangure, 2005; Klötz, Garle, & Granath, 2006; Pagonis, Angelopoulos, & Koukoulis, 2006).

psych2.0
WWW.MHHE.COM/PSYCHLIFE

The Endocrine System

Steroids can provide added muscle strength, but they have dangerous side effects. A number of well-known athletes have been accused of using the drugs illegally. Jose Conseco is one of the few major league baseball players to admit steroid use.

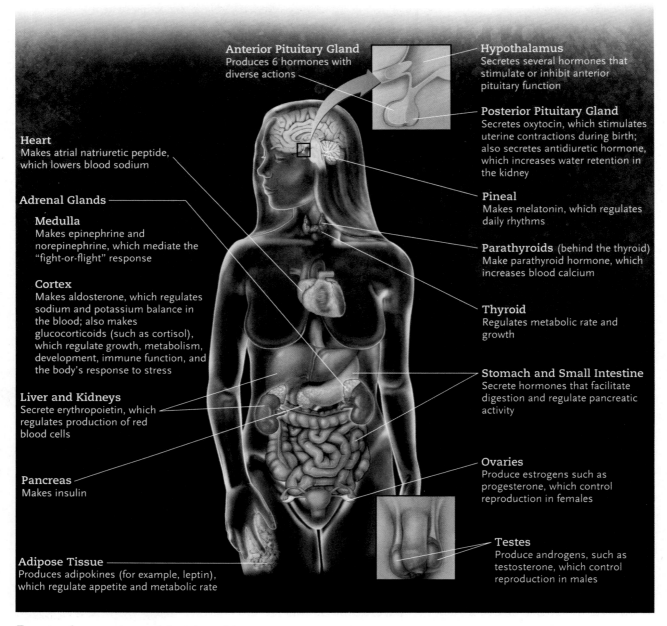

Anterior Pituitary Gland
Produces 6 hormones with diverse actions

Hypothalamus
Secretes several hormones that stimulate or inhibit anterior pituitary function

Posterior Pituitary Gland
Secretes oxytocin, which stimulates uterine contractions during birth; also secretes antidiuretic hormone, which increases water retention in the kidney

Heart
Makes atrial natriuretic peptide, which lowers blood sodium

Pineal
Makes melatonin, which regulates daily rhythms

Adrenal Glands

Medulla
Makes epinephrine and norepinephrine, which mediate the "fight-or-flight" response

Parathyroids (behind the thyroid)
Make parathyroid hormone, which increases blood calcium

Cortex
Makes aldosterone, which regulates sodium and potassium balance in the blood; also makes glucocorticoids (such as cortisol), which regulate growth, metabolism, development, immune function, and the body's response to stress

Thyroid
Regulates metabolic rate and growth

Stomach and Small Intestine
Secrete hormones that facilitate digestion and regulate pancreatic activity

Liver and Kidneys
Secrete erythropoietin, which regulates production of red blood cells

Ovaries
Produce estrogens such as progesterone, which control reproduction in females

Pancreas
Makes insulin

Testes
Produce androgens, such as testosterone, which control reproduction in males

Adipose Tissue
Produces adipokines (for example, leptin), which regulate appetite and metabolic rate

FIGURE 4 Location and function of the major endocrine glands. The pituitary gland controls the functioning of the other endocrine glands and in turn is regulated by the brain. Steroids can provide added muscle and strength, but they have dangerous side effects. *(Source: Adapted from Brooker et al, 2008, p.1062)*

RECAP

Explain how the structures of the nervous system are linked together.

- The nervous system is made up of the central nervous system (the brain and spinal cord) and the peripheral nervous system. The peripheral nervous system is made up of the somatic division, which controls voluntary movements and the communication of information to and from the sense organs, and the autonomic division, which controls involuntary functions such as those of the heart, blood vessels, and lungs. (p. 56)

- The autonomic division of the peripheral nervous system is further subdivided into the sympathetic and parasympathetic divisions. The sympathetic division prepares the body in emergency situations, and the parasympathetic division helps the body return to its typical resting state. (p. 58)

- Behavioral genetics examines the hereditary basis of human personality traits and behavior. (p. 59)

Describe the operation of the endocrine system and how it affects behavior.

- The endocrine system secretes hormones, chemicals that regulate the functioning of the body, via the bloodstream. The pituitary gland secretes growth hormones and influences the release of hormones by other endocrine glands, and in turn is regulated by the hypothalamus. (p. 61)

EVALUATE

1. If you put your hand on a red-hot piece of metal, the immediate response of pulling it away would be an example of a(n) _____.

2. The central nervous system is composed of the _____ and _____.

3. In the peripheral nervous system, the _____ division controls voluntary movements, whereas the _____ division controls organs that keep us alive and function without our awareness.

4. Maria saw a young boy run into the street and get hit by a car. When she got to the fallen child, she was in a state of panic. She was sweating, and her heart was racing. Her biological state resulted from the activation of what division of the nervous system?
   a. Parasympathetic
   b. Central
   c. Sympathetic

RETHINK

In what ways is the "fight-or-flight" response helpful to humans in emergency situations?

Answers to Evaluate Questions 1. reflex; 2. brain, spinal cord; 3. somatic, autonomic; 4. sympathetic

[KEY TERMS]

Central nervous system (CNS) *p. 56*

Spinal cord *p. 56*

Reflex *p. 57*

Sensory (afferent) neurons *p. 57*

Motor (efferent) neurons *p. 57*

Interneurons *p. 57*

Peripheral nervous system *p. 58*

Somatic division *p. 58*

Autonomic division *p. 58*

Sympathetic division *p. 58*

Parasympathetic division *p. 58*

Behavioral genetics *p. 59*

Endocrine system *p. 61*

Hormones *p. 61*

Pituitary gland *p. 61*

The Brain

7.1 Illustrate how researchers identify the major parts and functions of the brain.

7.2 Describe the central core of the brain.

7.3 Describe the limbic system of the brain.

7.4 Describe the cerebral cortex of the brain.

7.5 Recognize neuroplasticity and its implications.

7.6 Explain how the two hemispheres of the brain operate interdependently and the implications for human behavior.

It is not much to look at. Soft, spongy, mottled, and pinkish-gray in color, it hardly can be said to possess much in the way of physical beauty. Despite its physical appearance, however, it ranks as the greatest natural marvel that we know and has a beauty and sophistication all its own.

The object to which this description applies: the brain. The brain is responsible for our loftiest thoughts—and our most primitive urges. It is the overseer of the intricate workings of the human body. Many billions of neurons make up a structure weighing just three pounds in the average adult. However, it is not the number of cells that is the most astounding thing about the brain but its ability to allow the human intellect to flourish by guiding our behavior and thoughts.

We turn now to a consideration of the particular structures of the brain and the primary functions to which they are related. However, a caution is in order. Although we'll discuss specific areas of the brain in relation to specific behaviors, this approach is an oversimplification. No simple one-to-one correspondence exists between a distinct part of the brain and a particular behavior. Instead, behavior is produced by complex interconnections among sets of neurons in many areas of the brain: our behavior, emotions, thoughts, hopes, and dreams are produced by a variety of neurons throughout the nervous system working in concert.

» LO1 Studying the Brain's Structure and Functions: Spying on the Brain

Remember that EEG, fMRI, PET, and TMS differ in terms of whether they examine brain *structures* or brain *functioning*.

Modern brain-scanning techniques provide a window into the living brain. Using these techniques, investigators can take a "snapshot" of the internal workings of the brain without having to cut open a person's skull. The most important scanning techniques, illustrated in Figure 1, are the electroencephalogram (EEG), positron emission tomography (PET), functional magnetic resonance imaging (fMRI), and transcranial magnetic stimulation imaging (TMS).

The *electroencephalogram (EEG)* records electrical activity in the brain through electrodes placed on the outside of the skull. Although traditionally the EEG could produce only a graph of electrical wave patterns, new techniques are now used to transform the brain's electrical activity into a pictorial representation of the brain that allows more precise diagnosis of disorders such as epilepsy and learning disabilities.

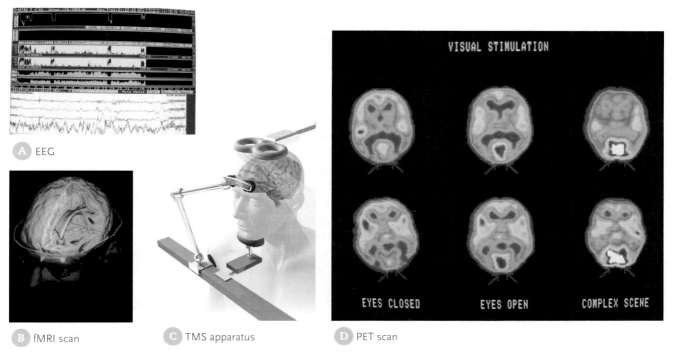

(A) EEG

(B) fMRI scan

(C) TMS apparatus

(D) PET scan

VISUAL STIMULATION

EYES CLOSED   EYES OPEN   COMPLEX SCENE

FIGURE 1   Brain scans produced by different techniques. (A) A computer-produced EEG image. (B) The fMRI scan uses a magnetic field to provide a detailed view of brain activity on a moment-by-moment basis. (C) Transcranial magnetic stimulation (TMS), the newest type of scan, produces a momentary disruption in an area of the brain, allowing researchers to see what activities are controlled by that area. TMS also has the potential to treat some psychological disorders. (D) The PET scan displays the functioning of the brain at a given moment.

Positron emission tomography (PET) scans show biochemical activity within the brain at a given moment. PET scans begin with the injection of a radioactive (but safe) liquid into the bloodstream, which makes its way to the brain. By locating radiation within the brain, a computer can determine which are the more active regions, providing a striking picture of the brain at work.

Functional magnetic resonance imaging (fMRI) scans provide a detailed, three-dimensional computer-generated image of brain structures and activity by aiming a powerful magnetic field at the body. With fMRI scanning, it is possible to produce vivid, detailed images of the functioning of the brain.

Transcranial magnetic stimulation (TMS) is one of the newest types of scan. By exposing a tiny region of the brain to a strong magnetic field, TMS causes a momentary interruption of electrical activity. Researchers then are able to note the effects of this interruption on normal brain functioning. The procedure is sometimes called a "virtual lesion" because it produces effects analogous to what would occur if areas of the brain were physically cut. The enormous advantage of TMS, of course, is that the virtual cut is only temporary.

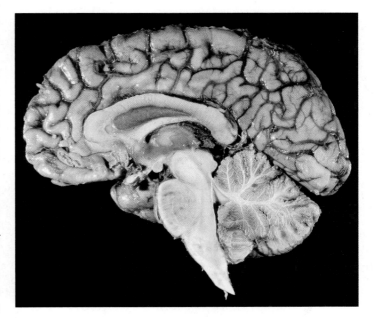

The brain (shown here in cross section) may not be much to look at, but it represents one of the great marvels of human development. Why do most scientist believe that it will be difficult, if not impossible, to duplicate the brain's abilities?

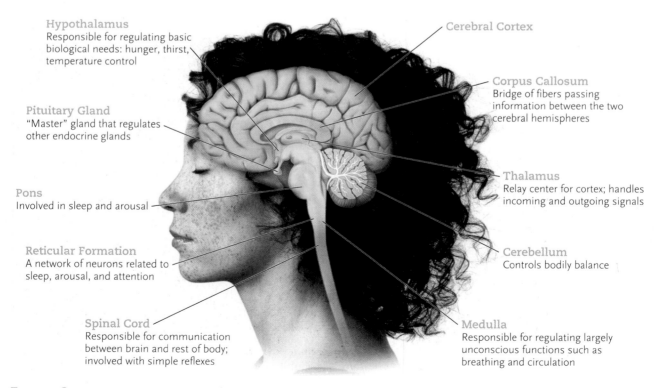

Cerebral cortex
(the "new brain")

Central core
(the "old brain")

FIGURE 2 The major divisions of the brain: the cerebral cortex and the central core. *(Source: Seeley, Stephens, & Tate, 2000.)*

Central core The "old brain," which controls basic functions such as eating and sleeping and is common to all vertebrates.

Cerebellum (ser uh BELL um) The part of the brain that controls bodily balance.

» LO2 The Central Core: Our "Old Brain"

Although the capabilities of the human brain far exceed those of the brain of any other species, humans share some basic functions, such as breathing, eating, and sleeping, with more primitive animals. Not surprisingly, those activities are directed by a relatively primitive part of the brain. A portion of the brain known as the **central core** (see Figure 2) is quite similar in all vertebrates (species with backbones). The central core is sometimes referred to as the "old brain" because its evolution can be traced back some 500 million years to primitive structures found in nonhuman species.

If we were to move up the spinal cord from the base of the skull to locate the structures of the central core of the brain, the first part we would come to would be the *hindbrain*, which contains the medulla, pons, and cerebellum (see Figure 3). The *medulla* controls a number of critical body functions, the most important of which are breathing and heartbeat. The *pons* comes next, joining the two halves of the cerebellum, which lies adjacent to it. Containing large bundles of nerves, the pons acts as a transmitter of motor information, coordinating muscles and integrating movement between the right and left halves of the body. It is also involved in regulating sleep.

The **cerebellum** is found just above the medulla and behind the pons. Without the help of the cerebellum we would be unable to walk a straight line without staggering and lurching forward, for it is the job of the cerebellum to control bodily balance. It constantly monitors feedback from the muscles to coordinate their placement, movement, and tension. In fact, drinking too much alcohol seems to depress the activity of the cerebellum, leading to the unsteady gait and movement characteristic of drunkenness.

Hypothalamus
Responsible for regulating basic biological needs: hunger, thirst, temperature control

Pituitary Gland
"Master" gland that regulates other endocrine glands

Pons
Involved in sleep and arousal

Reticular Formation
A network of neurons related to sleep, arousal, and attention

Spinal Cord
Responsible for communication between brain and rest of body; involved with simple reflexes

Cerebral Cortex

Corpus Callosum
Bridge of fibers passing information between the two cerebral hemispheres

Thalamus
Relay center for cortex; handles incoming and outgoing signals

Cerebellum
Controls bodily balance

Medulla
Responsible for regulating largely unconscious functions such as breathing and circulation

FIGURE 3 The major structures in the brain. *(Source: Johnson, 2000.)*

The cerebellum is also involved in several intellectual functions, ranging from the analysis and coordination of sensory information to problem solving (Bower & Parsons, 2004; Paquier & Mariën, 2005; Vandervert, Schimpf, & Liu, 2007).

The **reticular formation** extends from the medulla through the pons, passing through the middle section of the brain—or *midbrain*—and into the front-most part of the brain, called the *forebrain*. Like an ever-vigilant guard, the reticular formation is made up of groups of nerve cells that can activate other parts of the brain immediately to produce general bodily arousal. If, for example, we are startled by a loud noise, the reticular formation can prompt a heightened state of awareness to determine whether a response is necessary. The reticular formation serves a different function when we are sleeping, seeming to filter out background stimuli to allow us to sleep undisturbed.

Hidden within the forebrain, the **thalamus** acts primarily as a relay station for information about the senses. Messages from the eyes, ears, and skin travel to the thalamus to be communicated upward to higher parts of the brain. The thalamus also integrates information from higher parts of the brain, sorting it out so that it can be sent to the cerebellum and medulla.

The **hypothalamus** is located just below the thalamus. Although tiny—about the size of a fingertip—the hypothalamus plays an extremely important role. One of its major functions is to maintain *homeostasis,* a steady internal environment for the body. The hypothalamus helps provide a constant body temperature and monitors the amount of nutrients stored in the cells. A second major function is equally important: the hypothalamus produces and regulates behavior that is critical to the basic survival of the species, such as eating, self-protection, and sex.

> Like an ever-vigilant guard, the reticular formation is made up of groups of nerve cells that can activate other parts of the brain immediately to produce general bodily arousal.

Reticular formation The part of the brain extending from the medulla through the pons and made up of groups of nerve cells that can immediately activate other parts of the brain to produce general bodily arousal.

Thalamus The part of the brain located in the middle of the central core that acts primarily to relay information about the senses.

Hypothalamus A tiny part of the brain, located below the thalamus, that maintains homeostasis and produces and regulates vital behavior, such as eating, drinking, and sexual behavior.

Limbic system The part of the brain that controls eating, aggression, and reproduction.

» LO3 The Limbic System: Beyond the Central Core

The **limbic system** of the brain consists of a series of doughnut-shaped structures that include the *amygdala* and *hippocampus,* the limbic system borders the top of the central core and has connections with the cerebral cortex (see Figure 4). The structures of the limbic system jointly control a variety of basic functions relating to emotions and self-preservation, such as eating, aggression, and reproduction. Injury to the limbic system can produce striking changes in behavior. For example, injury to the amygdala, which is involved in fear and aggression, can turn animals that are usually docile and tame into belligerent savages. Conversely, animals that are usually wild and uncontrollable may become meek and obedient following injury to the amygdala (Bedard & Persinger, 1995; Gontkovsky, 2005).

The limbic system is involved in several important functions, including

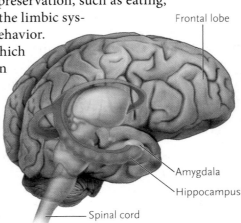

Frontal lobe

Amygdala

Hippocampus

Spinal cord

FIGURE 4 The limbic system consists of a series of doughnut-shaped structures that are involved in self-preservation, learning, memory, and the experience of pleasure.

self-preservation, learning, memory, and the experience of pleasure. These functions are hardly unique to humans; in fact, the limbic system is sometimes referred to as the "animal brain" because its structures and functions are so similar to those of other mammals. To identify the part of the brain that provides the complex and subtle capabilities that are uniquely human, we need to turn to another structure—the cerebral cortex.

» LO 4 The Cerebral Cortex: Our "New Brain"

Cerebral cortex The "new brain," responsible for the most sophisticated information processing in the brain; contains four lobes.

Lobes The four major sections of the cerebral cortex: frontal, parietal, temporal, and occipital.

Motor area The part of the cortex that is largely responsible for the body's voluntary movement.

As we have proceeded up the spinal cord and into the brain, our discussion has centered on areas of the brain that control functions similar to those found in less sophisticated organisms. But where, you may be asking, are the portions of the brain that enable humans to do what they do best and that distinguish humans from all other animals? Those unique features of the human brain—indeed, the very capabilities that allow you to come up with such a question in the first place—are embodied in the ability to think, evaluate, and make complex judgments. The principal location of these abilities, along with many others, is the **cerebral cortex.**

But where, you may be asking, are the portions of the brain that enable humans to do what they do best and that distinguish humans from all other animals?

The cerebral cortex is referred to as the "new brain" because of its relatively recent evolution. It consists of a mass of deeply folded, rippled, convoluted tissue. Although only about one-twelfth of an inch thick, it would, if flattened out, cover an area more than two feet square. This configuration allows the surface area of the cortex to be considerably greater than it would be if it were smoother and more uniformly packed into the skull. The uneven shape also permits a high level of integration of neurons, allowing sophisticated information processing.

psych2.0
WWW.MHHE.COM/PSYCHLIFE

The Brain

The cortex has four major sections called **lobes.** If we take a side view of the brain, the *frontal lobes* lie at the front center of the cortex and the *parietal lobes* lie behind them. The *temporal lobes* are found in the lower center portion of the cortex, with the *occipital lobes* lying behind them. These four sets of lobes are physically separated by deep grooves called *sulci.* Figure 5 shows the four areas.

Another way to describe the brain is in terms of the functions associated with a particular area. Figure 5 also shows the specialized regions within the lobes related to specific functions and areas of the body. Three major areas are known: the motor areas, the sensory areas, and the association areas. Although we will discuss these areas as though they were separate and independent, keep in mind that this is an oversimplification. In most instances, behavior is influenced simultaneously by several structures and areas within the brain, operating interdependently.

The Motor Area of the Cortex

If you look at the frontal lobe in Figure 5, you will see a shaded portion labeled **motor area.** This part of the cortex is largely responsible for the body's voluntary movement. Every portion of the motor area corresponds to a specific locale within the body. If we were to insert an electrode into a particular part of the motor area of the cortex and apply mild electrical stimulation, there would be involuntary

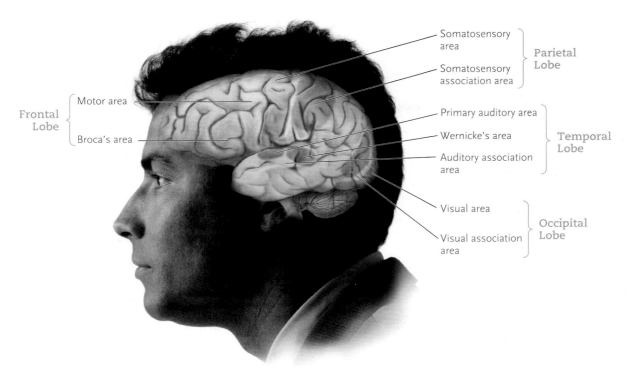

FIGURE 5   The cerebral cortex of the brain. The major physical structures of the cerebral cortex are called lobes. This figure also illustrates the functions associated with particular areas of the cerebral cortex. Are any areas of the cerebral cortex present in nonhuman animals?

movement in the corresponding part of the body. If we moved to another part of the motor area and stimulated it, a different part of the body would move.

The motor area is so well mapped that researchers have identified the amount and relative location of cortical tissue used to produce movement in specific parts of the human body. For example, the control of movements that are relatively large scale and require little precision, such as the movement of a knee or a hip, is centered in a very small space in the motor area. In contrast, movements that must be precise and delicate, such as facial expressions and finger movements, are controlled by a considerably larger portion of the motor area.

The Sensory Area of the Cortex

Given the one-to-one correspondence between the motor area and body location, it is not surprising to find a similar relationship between specific portions of the cortex and the senses. The **sensory area** of the cortex includes three regions: one that corresponds primarily to body sensations (including touch and pressure), one relating to sight, and a third relating to sound. For instance, the *somatosensory area* in the parietal lobe encompasses specific locations associated with the ability to perceive touch and pressure in a particular area of the body. As with the motor area, the amount of brain tissue related to a particular location on the body determines the degree of sensitivity of that location: the greater the area devoted to a specific area of the body within the cortex, the more sensitive that area of the body. As you can see from the weird-looking individual in Figure 6, parts such as the fingers are related to proportionally more area in the somatosensory area and are the most sensitive.

The senses of sound and sight are also represented in specific areas of the cerebral cortex. An *auditory area* located in the temporal lobe is responsible for

Sensory area The site in the brain of the tissue that corresponds to each of the senses, with the degree of sensitivity related to the amount of tissue allocated to that sense.

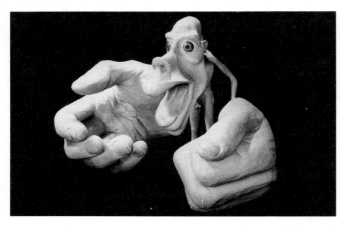

FIGURE 6 The greater the amount of tissue in the somatosensory area of the brain that is related to a specific body part, the more sensitive is that body part. If the size of our body parts reflected the corresponding amount of brain tissue, we would look like this strange creature.

the sense of hearing. If the auditory area is stimulated electrically, a person will hear sounds such as clicks or hums. It also appears that particular locations within the auditory area respond to specific pitches (Hudspeth, 2000; Brown & Martinez, 2007).

The visual area in the cortex, located in the occipital lobe, responds in the same way to electrical stimulation. Stimulation by electrodes produces the experience of flashes of light or colors, suggesting that the raw sensory input of images from the eyes is received in this area of the brain and transformed into meaningful stimuli. The visual area provides another example of how areas of the brain are intimately related to specific areas of the body: specific structures in the eye are related to a particular part of the cortex—with, as you might guess, more area of the brain given to the most sensitive portions of the retina (Wurtz & Kandel, 2000; Stenbacka & Vanni, 2007).

The Association Areas of the Cortex

Association areas One of the major regions of the cerebral cortex; the site of the higher mental processes, such as thought, language, memory, and speech.

In a freak accident in 1848, an explosion drove a 3-foot-long iron bar completely through the skull of railroad worker Phineas Gage, where it remained after the accident. Amazingly, Gage survived, and, despite the rod lodged through his head, a few minutes later seemed to be fine.

But he wasn't. Before the accident, Gage was hardworking and cautious. Afterward, he became irresponsible, drank heavily, and drifted from one wild scheme to another. In the words of one of his physicians, he was "no longer Gage" (Harlow, 1869, p. 14).

What had happened to the old Gage? Although there is no way of knowing for sure, we can speculate that the accident may have injured the region of Gage's cerebral cortex known as the **association areas,** which generally are considered to be the site of higher mental processes such as thinking, language, memory, and speech (Rowe et al., 2000).

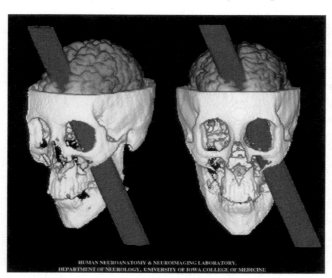

A model of the injury sustained by Phineas Gage.

The association areas make up a large portion of the cerebral cortex and consist of the sections that are not directly involved in either sensory processing or directing movement. The association areas control *executive functions,* which are abilities relating to planning, goal setting, judgment, and impulse control.

Much of our understanding of the association areas comes from patients who, like Phineas Gage, have suffered some type of brain injury. For example, when parts of the association areas are damaged, people undergo personality changes that affect their ability to make moral judgments and process emotions. At the same time, people with damage in those areas can still be capable of reasoning logically, performing calculations, and recalling information (Damasio, 1999).

» LO5 Neuroplasticity and the Brain

"Shortly after he was born, Jacob Stark's arms and legs started jerking every 20 minutes. Weeks later he could not focus his eyes on his mother's face. The diagnosis: uncontrollable epileptic seizures involving his entire brain.

His mother, Sally Stark, recalled: "When Jacob was two and a half months old, they said he would never learn to sit up, would never be able to feed himself. . . . They told us to take him home, love him and find an institution." (Blakeslee, 1992, p. C3)

Instead, Jacob had brain surgery when he was 5 months old in which physicians removed 20 percent of his brain. The operation was a complete success. Three years later Jacob seemed normal in every way, with no sign of seizures.

The surgery that helped Jacob was based on the premise that the diseased part of his brain was producing seizures throughout the brain. Surgeons reasoned that if they removed the misfiring portion, the remaining parts of the brain, which appeared intact in PET scans, would take over. They correctly bet that Jacob could still lead a normal life after surgery, particularly because the surgery was being done at so young an age.

The success of Jacob's surgery illustrates that the brain has the ability to shift functions to different locations after injury to a specific area or in cases of surgery. But equally encouraging are some new findings about the *regenerative* powers of the brain and nervous system.

Scientists have learned in recent years that the brain continually reorganizes itself in a process termed **neuroplasticity.** Although for many years conventional wisdom held that no new brain cells are created after childhood, new research finds otherwise. Not only do the interconnections between neurons become more complex throughout life, but it now appears that new neurons are also created in certain areas of the brain during adulthood—a process called *neurogenesis.* In fact, new neurons may become integrated with existing neural connections after some kinds of brain injury during adulthood (Bhardwaj et al., 2006; Jang, You, & Ahn, 2007; Poo & Isaacson, 2007).

The ability of neurons to renew themselves during adulthood has significant implications for the potential treatment of disorders of the nervous system. For example, drugs that trigger the development of new neurons might be used to counter diseases like Alzheimer's that are produced when neurons die (Steiner, Wolf, & Kempermann, 2006; Tsai, Tsai, & Shen, 2007).

Neuroplasticity Changes in the brain that occur throughout the life span relating to the addition of new neurons, new interconnections between neurons, and the reorganization of information-processing areas.

» LO6 The Specialization of the Hemispheres: Two Brains or One?

The most recent development, at least in evolutionary terms, in the organization and operation of the human brain probably occurred in the last million years: a specialization of the functions controlled by the left and right sides of the brain (McManus, 2004; Sun et al., 2005).

The brain is divided into two roughly mirror-image halves. Just as we have two arms, two legs, and two lungs, we have a left brain and a right brain. Because of the way nerves in the brain are connected to the rest of the body, these symmetrical left and right halves, called **hemispheres,** control motion

It's likely that Vincent Van Gogh created *Wheat Field with Cypresses* by relying primarily on right hemisphere brain processing. What are some functions that might involve both hemispheres?

Hemispheres Symmetrical left and right halves of the brain that control the side of the body opposite to their location.

Lateralization The dominance of one hemisphere of the brain in specific functions, such as language.

psych2.0

Hemispheres of the Brain

in—and receive sensation from—the side of the body opposite their location. The left hemisphere of the brain, then, generally controls the right side of the body, and the right hemisphere controls the left side of the body. Thus, damage to the right side of the brain is typically indicated by functional difficulties in the left side of the body.

Despite the appearance of similarity between the two hemispheres of the brain, they are somewhat different in the functions they control and in the ways they control them. Certain behaviors are more likely to reflect activity in one hemisphere than in the other; that is, the brain exhibits **lateralization.**

For example, for most people, language processing occurs more in the left side of the brain. In general, the left hemisphere concentrates more on tasks that require verbal competence, such as speaking, reading, thinking, and reasoning. In addition, the left hemisphere tends to process information sequentially, one bit at a time (Turkewitz, 1993; Banich & Heller, 1998; Hines, 2004).

The right hemisphere has its own strengths, particularly in nonverbal areas such as the understanding of spatial relationships, recognition of patterns and drawings, music, and emotional expression. The right hemisphere tends to process information globally, considering it as a whole (Ansaldo, Arguin, & RochLocours, 2002; Holowka & Petitto, 2002).

On the other hand, the differences in specialization between the hemispheres are not great, and the degree and nature of lateralization vary from one person to another. (To get a rough sense of your own degree of lateralization, complete the questionnaire in the *Try It!* box.) If, like most people, you are right-handed, the control of language is probably concentrated more in your left hemisphere. By contrast, if you are among the 10 percent of people who are left-handed or are ambidextrous (you use both hands interchangeably), it is much more likely that the language centers of your brain are located more in the right hemisphere or are divided equally between the left and right hemispheres.

Furthermore, the two hemispheres of the brain function in tandem. It is a mistake to think of particular kinds of information as being processed solely in the right or the left hemisphere. The hemispheres work interdependently in deciphering, interpreting, and reacting to the world.

Researchers also have unearthed evidence that there may be subtle differences in brain lateralization patterns between males and females and members of different cultures, as we see next.

EXPLORING diversity

Human Diversity and the Brain

The interplay of biology and environment in behavior is particularly clear when we consider evidence suggesting that even in brain structure and function there are both sex and cultural differences. Let's consider sex first. Accumulating evidence seems to show intriguing differences in males' and females' brain

Assessing Brain Lateralization

To get a rough sense of your own preferences in terms of brain lateralization, complete the following questionnaire.

1. I often talk about my and others' feelings of emotion. True_____ False_____

2. I am an analytical person. True_____ False_____

3. I methodically solve problems. True_____ False_____

4. I'm usually more interested in people and feelings than objects and things. True_____ False_____

5. I see the big picture, rather than thinking about projects in terms of their individual parts. True_____ False_____

6. When planning a trip, I like every detail in my itinerary worked out in advance. True_____ False_____

7. I tend to be independent and work things out in my head. True_____ False_____

8. When buying a new car, I prefer style over safety. True_____ False_____

9. I would rather hear a lecture than read a textbook. True_____ False_____

10. I remember names better than faces. True_____ False_____

Scoring

Give yourself 1 point for each of the following responses: 1. False; 2. True; 3. True; 4. False; 5. False; 6. True; 7. True; 8. False; 9. False; 10. True. Maximum score is 10, and minimum score is 0.

The higher your score, the more your responses are consistent with people who are left-brain oriented, meaning that you have particular strength in tasks that require verbal competence, analytic thinking, and processing of information sequentially, one bit of information at a time.

The lower your score, the more your responses are consistent with a right-brain orientation, meaning that you have particular strengths in nonverbal areas, recognition of patterns, music, and emotional expression, and process information globally.

Remember, though, that this is only a rough estimate of your processing preferences, and that all of us have strengths in both hemispheres of the brain.

Source: Adapted in part from Morton, 2003.

lateralization and weight (Boles, 2005; Clements, 2006).

For instance, most males tend to show greater lateralization of language in the left hemisphere. For them, language is clearly relegated largely to the left side of the brain. In contrast, women display less lateralization, with language abilities apt to be more evenly divided between the two hemispheres. Such differences in brain lateralization may account, in part, for the superiority often displayed by females

The interplay of biology and environment in behavior is particularly clear when we consider evidence suggesting that even in brain structure and function there are both sex and cultural differences.

on certain measures of verbal skills, such as the onset and fluency of speech (Frings et al., 2006; Petersson et al., 2007).

Other research suggests that men's brains are somewhat bigger than women's brains even after taking differences in body size into account. In contrast, part of the *corpus callosum*, a bundle of fibers that connects the hemispheres of the brain, is proportionally larger in women than in men (Cahill, 2005; Luders et al., 2006; Smith et al., 2007).

From the perspective of . . .

AN OFFICE WORKER Could personal differences in people's specialization of right and left hemispheres be related to occupational success? For example, might a designer who relies on spatial skills have a different pattern of hemispheric specialization than a paralegal?

Men and women also may process information differently. For example, in one study, fMRI brain scans of men making judgments discriminating real from false words showed activation of the left hemisphere, of the brain, whereas women used areas on both sides of the brain (Rossell et al., 2002).

The meaning of such sex differences is far from clear. Consider one possibility related to differences in the proportional size of the corpus callosum. Its greater size in women may permit stronger connections to develop between the parts of the brain that control speech. In turn, this would explain why speech tends to emerge slightly earlier in girls than in boys.

Before we rush to such a conclusion, though, it is important to consider an alternative hypothesis: the reason verbal abilities emerge earlier in girls may be that infant girls receive greater encouragement to talk than do infant boys. In turn, this greater early experience may foster the growth of certain parts of the brain. Hence, physical brain differences may be a *reflection* of social and environmental influences rather than a *cause* of the differences in men's and women's behavior. At this point, it is impossible to know which of these alternative hypotheses is correct.

The Split Brain: Exploring the Two Hemispheres

The patient, V.J., had suffered severe seizures. By cutting her corpus callosum, the fibrous portion of the brain that carries messages between the hemispheres, surgeons hoped to create a firebreak to prevent the seizures from spreading. The operation did decrease the frequency and severity of V.J.'s attacks. But V.J. developed an unexpected side effect: She lost the ability to write at will, although she could read and spell words aloud. (Strauss, 1998, p. 287)

People like V.J., whose corpus callosum has been surgically cut to stop seizures and who are called *split-brain patients*, offer a rare opportunity for researchers investigating the independent functioning of the two hemispheres of the brain. For example, psychologist Roger Sperry—who won the Nobel Prize for his work—developed a number of ingenious techniques for studying how each hemisphere operates (Sperry, 1982; Gazzaniga, 1998; Savazzi et al., 2007).

In one experimental procedure, blindfolded patients touched an object with their right hand and were asked to name it (see Figure 7). Because the right side of the body corresponds to the language-oriented left side of the brain, split-brain patients were able to name it. However, if blindfolded patients touched the object with their left hand, they were unable to name it aloud, even though the information had registered in their brains: when the blindfold was removed, patients could identify the object they had touched. Information can be learned and remembered, then, using only the right side of the brain. (By the way, unless you've had a split-brain operation, this experiment won't work with you, because the bundle of fibers connecting the two hemispheres of a normal brain immediately transfers the information from one hemisphere to the other.)

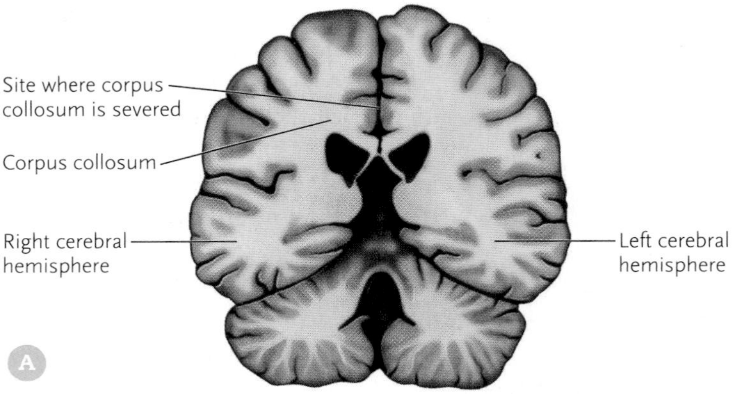

It is clear from experiments like this one that the right and left hemispheres of the brain specialize in handling different sorts of information. At the same time, it is important to realize that both hemispheres are capable of understanding, knowing, and being aware of the world, in somewhat different ways. The two hemispheres, then, should be regarded as different in terms of the efficiency with which they process certain kinds of information, rather than as two entirely separate brains. The hemispheres work interdependently to allow the full range and richness of thought of which humans are capable.

Site where corpus collosum is severed
Corpus collosum
Right cerebral hemisphere
Left cerebral hemisphere

A

Screen prevents test subject from seeing objects

B

FIGURE 7 The hemispheres of the brain. (A) The corpus callosum connects the cerebral hemispheres of the brain. (B) A split-brain patient is tested by touching objects behind a screen. Patients could name objects when they touched it with their right hand, but couldn't if they touched with their left hand. If a split-brain patient with her eyes closed was given a pencil to hold and called it a pencil, what hand was the pencil in? *(Source: Brooker, Widmaier, Graham, & Stilling, 2008, p. 943.)*

becoming an *informed consumer*
OF PSYCHOLOGY

Learning to Control Your Heart—and Mind—
through Biofeedback

When Tammy DeMichael was involved in a horrific car accident that broke her neck and crushed her spinal cord, experts told her that she was doomed to be a quadriplegic for the rest of her life, unable to move from the neck down. But they were wrong. Not only did she regain the use of her arms, but she was able to walk 60 feet with a cane (Morrow & Wolff, 1991; Hess et al., 2000).

Biofeedback A procedure in which a person learns to control through conscious thought the internal physiological processes such as blood pressure, heart and respiration rate, skin temperature, sweating, and the constriction of particular muscles.

The key to DeMichael's astounding recovery: biofeedback. **Biofeedback** is a procedure in which a person learns to control through conscious thought internal physiological processes such as blood pressure, heart and respiration rate, skin temperature, sweating, and the constriction of particular muscles. Although it traditionally had been thought that the heart rate, respiration rate, blood pressure, and other bodily functions are under the control of parts of the brain over which we have no influence, psychologists have discovered that these responses are actually susceptible to voluntary control (Nagai et al., 2004; Cho et al., 2007).

In biofeedback, a person is hooked up to electronic devices that provide continuous feedback relating to the physiological response in question. For instance, a person interested in controlling headaches through biofeedback might have electronic sensors placed on certain muscles on her head and learn to control the constriction and relaxation of those muscles. Later, when she felt a headache starting, she could relax the relevant muscles and abort the pain (Andrasik, 2007).

In DeMichael's case, biofeedback was effective because not all of the nervous system's connections between the brain and her legs were severed. Through biofeedback, she learned how to send messages to specific muscles, "ordering" them to move. Although it took more than a year, DeMichael was successful in restoring a large degree of her mobility.

Although the control of physiological processes through the use of biofeedback is not easy to learn, it has been employed with success in a variety of ailments, including emotional problems (such as anxiety, depression, phobias, tension headaches, insomnia, and hyperactivity), physical illnesses with a psychological component (such as asthma, high blood pressure, ulcers, muscle spasms, and migraine headaches), and physical problems (such as DeMichael's injuries, strokes, cerebral palsy, and curvature of the spine) (Cho et al., 2007; Morone & Greco, 2007).

RECAP

Illustrate how researchers identify the major parts and functions of the brain.

- Brain scans take a "snapshot" of the internal workings of the brain without having to cut surgically into a person's skull. Major brain-scanning techniques include the electroencephalogram (EEG), positron emission tomography (PET), functional magnetic resonance imaging (fMRI), and transcranial magnetic stimulation imaging (TMS). (p. 64)

Describe the central core of the brain.

- The central core of the brain is made up of the medulla (which controls functions such as breathing and the heartbeat), the pons (which coordinates the muscles and the two sides of the body), the cerebellum (which controls balance), the reticular formation (which acts

to heighten awareness in emergencies), the thalamus (which communicates sensory messages to and from the brain), and the hypothalamus (which maintains homeostasis, or body equilibrium, and regulates behavior related to basic survival). The functions of the central core structures are similar to those found in other vertebrates. This central core is sometimes referred to as the "old brain." Increasing evidence also suggests that male and female brains may differ in structure in minor ways. (p. 66)

Describe the limbic system of the brain.

- The limbic system, found on the border of the "old" and "new" brains, is associated with eating, aggression, reproduction, and the experiences of pleasure and pain. (p. 67)

Describe the cerebral cortex of the brain.

- The cerebral cortex—the "new brain"—has areas that control voluntary movement (the motor area); the senses (the sensory area); and thinking, reasoning, speech, and memory (the association areas). (p. 68)

Recognize neuroplasticity and its implications.

- Neuroplasticity refers to changes in the brain relating to the addition of new neurons, new interconnections between neurons, and the reorganization of information-processing areas (p. 71)

Explain how the two hemispheres of the brain operate interdependently and the implications for human behavior.

- The brain is divided into left and right halves, or hemispheres, each of which generally controls the opposite side of the body. (p. 71)
- The left hemisphere specializes in verbal tasks, such as logical reasoning, speaking, and reading (p. 71)
- The right side of the brain specializes in nonverbal tasks, such as spatial perception, pattern recognition, and emotional expression. (p. 71)

EVALUATE

1. Match the name of each brain scan with the appropriate description:
   a. EEG
   b. fMRI
   c. PET

   1. By locating radiation within the brain, a computer can provide a striking picture of brain activity.
   2. Electrodes placed around the skull record the electrical signals transmitted through the brain.
   3. Provides a three-dimensional view of the brain by aiming a magnetic field at the body.

2. Match the portion of the brain with its function:
   a. Medulla
   b. Pons
   c. Cerebellum
   d. Reticular formation

   1. Maintains breathing and heartbeat.
   2. Controls bodily balance.
   3. Coordinates and integrates muscle movements.
   4. Activates other parts of the brain to produce general bodily arousal.

3. A surgeon places an electrode on a portion of your brain and stimulates it. Immediately, your right wrist involuntarily twitches. The doctor has most likely stimulated a portion of the _____ area of your brain.

4. Each hemisphere controls the _____ side of the body.

5. Nonverbal realms, such as emotions and music, are controlled primarily by the _____ hemisphere of the brain, whereas the _____ hemisphere is more responsible for speaking and reading.

RETHINK

Before sophisticated brain-scanning techniques were developed, behavioral neuroscientists' understanding of the brain was based largely on the brains of people who had died. What limitations would this pose, and in what areas would you expect the most significant advances once brain-scanning techniques became possible?

Answers to Evaluate Questions 1. a-2, b-3, c-1; 2. a-1, b-3, c-2, d-4; 3. motor; 4. opposite; 5. right, left

[KEY TERMS]

looking BACK

Psychology on the Web

1. Biofeedback research is continuously changing and being applied to new areas of human functioning. Find at least two Web sites that discuss recent research on biofeedback and summarize the research and any findings it has produced. Include in your summary your best estimate of future applications of this technique.

2. Find one or more Web sites on Parkinson's disease and learn more about this topic. Specifically, find reports of new treatments for Parkinson's disease that do not involve the use of fetal tissue. Write a summary of your findings.

the case of... THE FALLEN ATHLETE

Since he was a boy, Tim Levesque has always loved sports. From football and basketball in high school through rugby in college, Tim enjoyed the hours of training, the satisfaction of mastering complex plays, and especially the thrill of facing challenging competitors. He remained physically active in the years that followed and spent many evenings and weekends coaching his son Adam's Little League baseball team. He continued to challenge himself to learn new skills, as when he took up bowling and practiced regularly until he was good enough to join a league.

Six months ago, Tim suffered a stroke while he was taking his morning jog. Immediately afterward, much of the right side of Tim's body was paralyzed and he was having great difficulty trying to talk. When Adam saw him in the hospital, he barely recognized his strong, active father now lying weak and incapacitated in a hospital bed. Although his physicians could not give him a clear prognosis, Tim was determined to regain his strength and mobility and fully resume his active lifestyle.

Today Tim has not quite reached his goal, but he has made a remarkable recovery. He is out of the hospital and receiving regular physical therapy. His speech has returned with only occasional difficulty, and he is able to walk and move well enough to return to work. He can't quite manage to roll a 12-pound bowling ball with the ease and accuracy as he previously could, but that doesn't bother him much. What really excites Tim is the ever increasing likelihood that he'll be back to coach Adam's team next season.

1. Is there any evidence to suggest which hemisphere of Tim's brain suffered damage during his stroke?

2. What imaging technology would best reveal the location and extent of damage to Tim's brain produced by his stroke, and why?

3. If physicians did not have any means of viewing the damage to Tim's brain directly, what other clues might they have to the location of the damage? Where might the damage be if Tim had lost his vision after the stroke? Where might it be if he lost sensation on the left side of his body? Where might it be if his personality suddenly changed?

4. Explain how the endocrine system played a role in keeping Tim's body performing optimally whether he was exercising strenuously or relaxing. How might Tim have been able to manipulate his endocrine system function to enhance his athletic performance, if he so chose? What might be some risks of doing so?

5. Describe the brain phenomena that are chiefly responsible for Tim's recovery of lost speech and motor functions. How likely do you think Tim is to completely return to his prestroke level of functioning, and why?

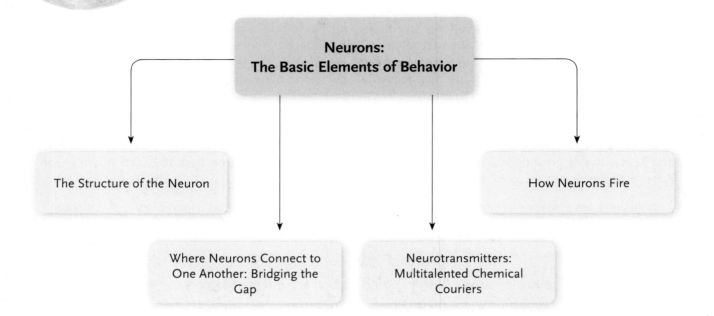

Neurons:
The Basic Elements of Behavior

The Structure of the Neuron

Where Neurons Connect to One Another: Bridging the Gap

Neurotransmitters: Multitalented Chemical Couriers

How Neurons Fire

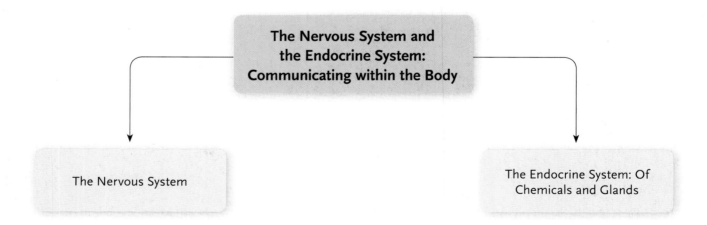

The Nervous System and the Endocrine System: Communicating within the Body

The Nervous System

The Endocrine System: Of Chemicals and Glands

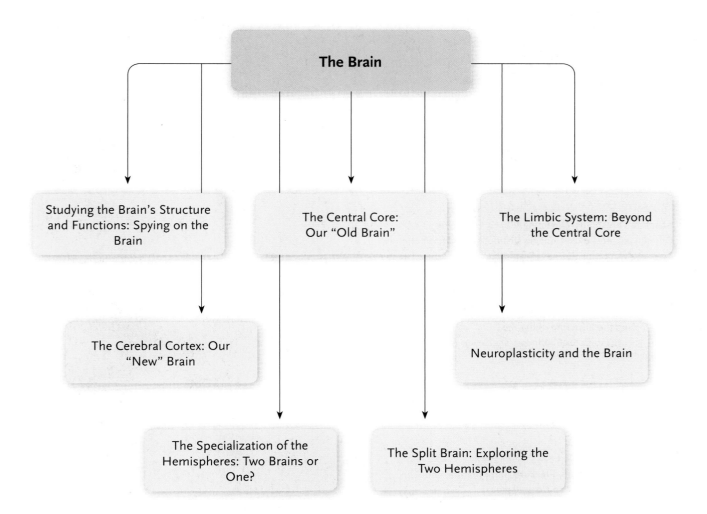

The Brain

Studying the Brain's Structure and Functions: Spying on the Brain

The Central Core: Our "Old Brain"

The Limbic System: Beyond the Central Core

The Cerebral Cortex: Our "New" Brain

Neuroplasticity and the Brain

The Specialization of the Hemispheres: Two Brains or One?

The Split Brain: Exploring the Two Hemispheres

CHAPTER

3

SENSATION

Only Blank Faces

Several years ago, when Margaret Mitchell picked up her son Duncan from his Seattle school, he looked at her curiously and asked, "Are you my mommy?"

Ms. Mitchell, an attorney by training, was taken aback. When she answered, "Yes, I'm your mommy," he recognized her voice and was reassured.

A short while later, Duncan, then 4 years old, was diagnosed with prosopagnosia, a selective developmental condition often referred to as "faceblindness." Although his eyesight is perfectly fine, he can't always identify people by their faces. In school, for instance, Duncan has trouble matching the faces and names of teachers and pupils.

Like many other prosopagnosics, Duncan, now 8, has a memory that functions normally in other ways. He can visually distinguish between cars and houses and toys. He knows his dog and cat and other neighborhood pets. He's a sociable child and likes being around people. But the frustration of not being able to discern faces has made everyday life, from attending school to making friends, unbearably difficult. His parents engineer much of his social life around one-on-one playdates so he can try to remember classmates. (Tesoriero, 2007, p. A1) ■

AND PERCEPTION

looking AHEAD

People with faceblindness such as Duncan Mitchell can see faces, of course. They see the parts that make up a facial configuration—an oval shape with two eyes, a nose, and a mouth. But they lack the specialized processing ability most of us take for granted that allows us to detect the subtle differences that make each individual face unique. Although they can detect face-related information just fine, prosopagnosics have difficulty with finding that information meaningful—with seeing that face as a friend or foe.

Disorders such as faceblindness illustrate how much we depend on our senses to function normally. Our senses offer a window to the world, providing us with not only an awareness, understanding, and appreciation of the world's beauty, but alerting us to its dangers. Our senses enable us to feel the gentlest of breezes, see flickering lights miles away, and hear the soft murmuring of distant songbirds.

In the next four modules, we focus on the field of psychology that is concerned with the ways our bodies take in information through the senses and the ways we interpret that information. We will explore both sensation and perception. Sensation encompasses the processes by which our sense organs receive information from the environment. Perception is the brain's and the sense organs' sorting out, interpretation, analysis, and integration of stimuli.

Although perception clearly represents a step beyond sensation, in practice it is sometimes difficult to find the precise boundary between the two. The primary difference is that sensation can be thought of as an organism's first encounter with a raw sensory stimulus, whereas perception is the process by which that stimulus is interpreted, analyzed, and integrated with other sensory information. For example, if we were considering sensation, we might ask about the loudness of a ringing fire alarm. If we were considering perception, we might ask whether someone recognizes the ringing sound as an alarm and identifies its meaning.

To a psychologist interested in understanding the causes of behavior, sensation and perception are fundamental topics because so much of our behavior is a reflection of how we react to and interpret stimuli from the world around us. The areas of sensation and perception deal with a wide range of questions—among them, how we respond to the characteristics of physical stimuli; what processes enable us to see, hear, and experience pain; why visual illusions fool us; and how we distinguish one person from another.

Sensing the World Around Us

LEARNING OUTCOMES

8.1 Define absolute thresholds.

8.2 Explain the difference threshold and Weber's law.

8.3 Discuss sensory adaptation.

Sensation The activation of the sense organs by a source of physical energy.

Perception The sorting out, interpretation, analysis, and integration of stimuli by the sense organs and brain.

Stimulus Energy that produces a response in a sense organ.

STUDY ALERT

Remember that sensation refers to the activation of the sense organs (a physical response), while perception refers to how stimuli are interpreted (a psychological response).

As Isabel sat down to Thanksgiving dinner, her husband carried the turkey in on a tray and placed it squarely in the center of the table. The noise level, already high from the talking and laughter of family members, grew louder still. As Isabel picked up her fork, the smell of the turkey reached her and she felt her stomach growl hungrily. The sight and sound of her family around the table, along with the smells and tastes of the holiday meal, triggered happy childhood memories and put Isabel in a relaxed, contented mood.

Put yourself in this setting and consider how different it might be if any one of your senses was not functioning. What if you were blind and unable to see the faces of your family members or the welcome shape of the golden-brown turkey? What if you had no sense of hearing and could not listen to the conversations of family members or were unable to feel your stomach growl, smell the dinner, or taste the food? Clearly, you would experience the dinner very differently than would someone whose sensory apparatus was intact.

Moreover, the sensations mentioned above barely scratch the surface of sensory experience. Although perhaps you were taught, as I was, that there are just five senses—sight, sound, taste, smell, and touch—that enumeration is too modest. Human sensory capabilities go well beyond the basic five senses. For example, we are sensitive not merely to touch but to a considerably wider set of stimuli—pain, pressure, temperature, and vibration, to name a few.

To consider how psychologists understand the senses and, more broadly, sensation and perception, we first need a basic working vocabulary. In formal terms, **sensation** is the activation of the sense organs by a source of physical energy. **Perception** is the sorting out, interpretation, analysis, and integration of stimuli carried out by the sense organs and brain. A **stimulus** is any passing source of physical energy that produces a response in a sense organ.

Human sensory capabilities go well beyond the basic five senses.

Stimuli vary in both type and intensity. Different types of stimuli activate different sense organs. For instance, we can differentiate light stimuli (which activate the sense of sight and allow us to see the colors of a tree in autumn) from sound stimuli (which, through the sense of hearing, permit us to hear the sounds of an orchestra).

How intense a light stimulus needs to be before it can be detected and how much perfume a person must wear before it is noticed by others are questions related to stimulus intensity.

The issue of how the intensity of a stimulus influences our sensory responses is considered in a branch of psychology known as psychophysics. **Psychophysics** is the study of the relationship between the physical aspects of stimuli and our psychological experience of them. Psychophysics played a central role in the development of the field of psychology, and many of the first psychologists studied issues related to psychophysics (Gardner, 2005; Hock & Ploeger, 2006).

Psychophysics The study of the relationship between the physical aspects of stimuli and our psychological experience of them.

Absolute threshold The smallest intensity of a stimulus that must be present for the stimulus to be detected.

» LO1 Absolute Thresholds: Detecting What's Out There

Just when does a stimulus become strong enough to be detected by our sense organs? The answer to this question requires an understanding of the concept of absolute threshold. An **absolute threshold** is the smallest intensity of a stimulus that must be present for it to be detected (Aazh & Moore, 2007).

Our senses are extremely responsive to stimuli. For example, the sense of touch is so sensitive that we can feel a bee's wing falling on our cheeks when it is dropped from a distance of one centimeter. Test your knowledge of the absolute thresholds of other senses by completing the questionnaire in Figure 1.

Of course, the absolute thresholds we have been discussing are measured under ideal conditions. Normally our senses cannot detect stimulation quite as well because of the presence of noise. *Noise,* as defined by psychophysicists, is background stimulation that interferes with the perception of other stimuli. Hence, noise refers not just to auditory stimuli, as the word suggests, but also to unwanted stimuli that interfere with other senses.

Crowded conditions, sounds, and sights can all be considered noise that interferes with sensation. Can you think of other examples of noise that is not auditory in nature?

Q How Sensitive Are You?

To test your awareness of the capablities of your senses, answer the following questions:

1. How far can a candle flame be seen on a clear, dark night?
   a. From a distance of 10 miles _____
   b. From a distance of 30 miles _____

2. How far can the ticking of a watch be heard under quiet conditions?
   a. From 5 feet away _____
   b. From 20 feet away _____

3. How much sugar is needed to allow it to be detected when dissolved in 2 gallons of water?
   a. 2 tablespoons _____
   b. 1 teaspoon _____

4. Over what area can a drop of perfume be detected?
   a. A 5-foot by 5-foot area _____
   b. A 3-room apartment _____

Scoring: In each case, the answer is b, illustrating the tremendous sensitivity of our senses.

FIGURE 1 This test can shed some light on how sensitive the human senses are. *(Source: Galanter, 1962.)*

» LO2 Difference Thresholds: Noticing Distinctions between Stimuli

Difference threshold (just noticeable difference) The smallest level of added or reduced stimulation required to sense that a change in stimulation has occurred.

Weber's law A basic law of psychophysics stating that a just noticeable difference is in constant proportion to the intensity of an initial stimulus.

STUDY ALERT

Remember that Weber's law holds for every type of sensory stimuli: vision, sound, taste, etc.

Weber's law helps explain why a person in a quiet room is more startled by the ringing of a telephone than is a person in an already noisy room.

psych2.0
WWW.MHHE.COM/PSYCHLIFE

Weber's law, in which you can conduct an experiment on your ability to discern differences in sound levels.

Suppose you wanted to choose the six best apples from a supermarket display—the biggest, reddest, and sweetest apples. One approach would be to compare one apple with another systematically until you were left with a few so similar that you could not tell the difference between them. At that point, it wouldn't matter which ones you chose.

Psychologists have discussed this comparison problem in terms of the **difference threshold,** the smallest level of added (or reduced) stimulation required to sense that a *change* in stimulation has occurred). Thus, the difference threshold is the minimum change in stimulation required to detect the difference between two stimuli, and so it also is called a **just noticeable difference** (Nittrouer & Lowenstein, 2007).

The stimulus value that constitutes a just noticeable difference depends on the initial intensity of the stimulus. The relationship between changes in the original value of a stimulus and the degree to which a change will be noticed forms one of the basic laws of psychophysics: Weber's law. **Weber's law** (with *Weber* pronounced "vay-ber") states that a just noticeable difference is a *constant proportion* of the intensity of an initial stimulus.

For example, Weber found that the just noticeable difference for weight is 1:50. Consequently, it takes a 1-ounce increase in a 50-ounce weight to produce a noticeable difference, and it would take a 10-ounce increase to produce a noticeable difference if the initial weight were 500 ounces. In both cases, the same proportional increase is necessary to produce a just noticeable difference—1:50 = 10:500. Similarly, the just noticeable difference distinguishing changes in loudness between sounds is larger for sounds that are initially loud than it is for sounds that are initially soft, but the *proportional* increase remains the same.

Weber's law helps explain why a person in a quiet room is more startled by the ringing of a telephone than is a person in an already noisy room. To produce the same amount of reaction in a noisy room, a telephone ring might have to approximate the loudness of cathedral bells. Similarly, when the moon is visible during the late afternoon, it appears relatively dim—yet against a dark night sky, it seems quite bright.

From the perspective of . . .

A SOFTWARE DESIGNER How might you use principles of psychophysics to direct the software user's attention?

» LO2 Sensory Adaptation: Turning Down Our Responses

You enter a movie theater, and the smell of popcorn is everywhere. A few minutes later, though, you barely notice the smell. The reason you acclimate to the odor is sensory adaptation. **Adaptation** is an adjustment in sensory capacity after prolonged exposure to unchanging stimuli. Adaptation occurs as people become accustomed to a stimulus and change their frame of reference. In a sense, our brain mentally turns down the volume of the stimulation it's experiencing (Calin-Jageman & Fischer, 2007).

One example of adaptation is the decrease in sensitivity that occurs after repeated exposure to a strong stimulus. If you were to hear a loud tone over and over again, eventually it would begin to sound softer. Similarly, although jumping into a cold lake may be temporarily unpleasant, eventually we probably would get used to the temperature.

This apparent decline in sensitivity to sensory stimuli is due to the inability of the sensory nerve receptors to fire off messages to the brain indefinitely. Because these receptor cells are most responsive to *changes* in stimulation, constant stimulation is not effective in producing a sustained reaction.

When Lizeth began working as a pharmacy assistant, she was overwhelmed by the smells in the pharmacy. Now that she has been in her job for a few months, she no longer notices.

Adaptation An adjustment in sensory capacity after prolonged exposure to unchanging stimuli.

R E C A P

Define absolute thresholds.

- Sensation is the activation of the sense organs by any source of physical energy. In contrast, perception is the process by which we sort out, interpret, analyze, and integrate stimuli to which our senses are exposed. (p. 84)

- Psychophysics studies the relationship between the physical nature of stimuli and the sensory responses they evoke. (p. 85)

- The absolute threshold is the smallest amount of physical intensity at which a stimulus can be detected. Under ideal conditions absolute thresholds are extraordinarily sensitive, but the presence of noise (background stimuli that interfere with other stimuli) reduces detection capabilities. (p. 85)

Explain the difference threshold and Weber's law.

- The difference threshold, or just noticeable difference, is the smallest change in the level of stimulation required to sense that a change has occurred. According to Weber's law, a just noticeable difference is a constant proportion of the intensity of an initial stimulus. (p. 86)

Discuss sensory adaptation.

- Sensory adaptation occurs when we become accustomed to a constant stimulus and change our evaluation of it. Repeated exposure to a stimulus results in an apparent decline in sensitivity to it. (p. 87)

1. _____ is the stimulation of the sense organs; _____ is the sorting out, interpretation, analysis, and integration of stimuli by the sense organs and the brain.

2. The term *absolute threshold* refers to the _____ intensity of a stimulus that must be present for the stimulus to be detected.

3. Weber discovered that for a difference between two stimuli to be perceptible, the stimuli must differ by at least a _____ proportion.

4. After completing a very difficult rock climb in the morning, Carmella found the afternoon climb unexpectedly easy. This case illustrates the phenomenon of _____.

R E T H I N K

Do you think it is possible to have sensation without perception? Is it possible to have perception without sensation?

Answers to Evaluate Questions 1. sensation; perception; 2. smallest; 3. constant; 4. adaptation

[K E Y T E R M S]

Sensation *p. 84*

Perception *p. 84*

Stimulus *p. 84*

Psychophysics *p. 85*

Absolute threshold *p. 85*

Difference threshold (just noticeable difference) *p. 86*

Weber's law *p. 86*

Adaptation *p. 87*

Vision
Shedding Light on the Eye

If, as poets say, the eyes provide a window to the soul, they also provide us with a window to the world. Our visual capabilities permit us to admire and react to scenes ranging from the beauty of a sunset, to the configuration of a lover's face, to the words written on the pages of a book.

Vision starts with light, the physical energy that stimulates the eye. Light is a form of electromagnetic radiation waves, which, as shown in Figure 1, are measured in wavelengths. The sizes of wavelengths correspond to different types of energy. The range of wavelengths that humans are sensitive to—called the *visual spectrum*—is relatively small.

Vision starts with light, the physical energy that stimulates the eye. Light waves coming from some object outside the body (such as the butterfly in Figure 2) are sensed by the only organ that is capable of responding to the visible spectrum: the eye. Our eyes convert light to a form that can be used by the neurons that serve as messengers to the brain. The neurons themselves take up a relatively small percentage of the total eye. Most of the eye is a mechanical device that is similar in many respects to a traditional, nondigital electronic camera that uses film, as you can see in Figure 2.

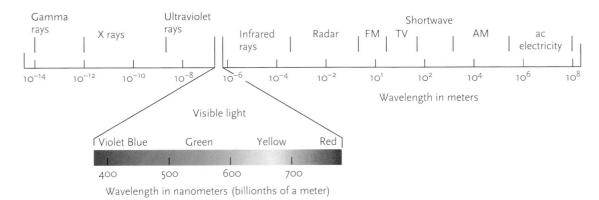

FIGURE 1 The visible spectrum—the range of wavelengths to which people are sensitive—is only a small part of the kinds of wavelengths present in our environment. Is it a benefit or disadvantage to our everyday lives that we aren't more sensitive to a broader range of visual stimuli? Why?

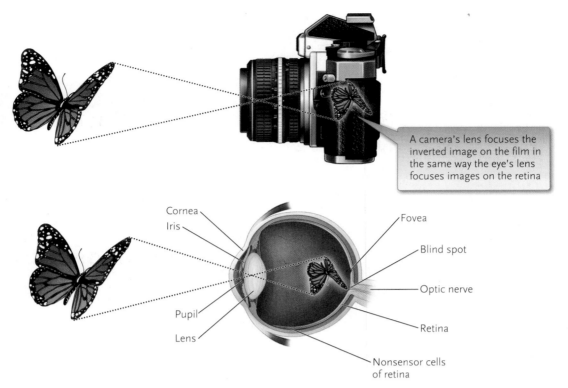

A camera's lens focuses the inverted image on the film in the same way the eye's lens focuses images on the retina

Cornea
Iris
Fovea
Blind spot
Optic nerve
Pupil
Retina
Lens
Nonsensor cells of retina

FIGURE 2 Although human vision is far more complicated than the most sophisticated camera, in some ways basic visual processes are analogous to those used in traditional, nondigital photography.

> *Despite the similarities between the eye and a traditional camera, vision involves processes that are far more complex and sophisticated than those of any camera.*

Despite the similarities between the eye and a traditional camera, vision involves processes that are far more complex and sophisticated than those of any camera. Furthermore, once an image reaches the neuronal receptors of the eye, the eye/camera analogy ends, for the processing of the visual image in the brain is more reflective of a computer than it is of a camera.

» LO1 Illuminating the Structure of the Eye

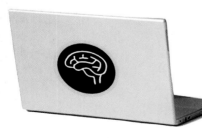

psych2.0
WWW.MHHE.COM/PSYCHLIFE

How Vision Operates

The ray of light being reflected off the butterfly in Figure 2 first travels through the *cornea,* a transparent, protective window. The cornea, because of its curvature, bends (or *refracts*) light as it passes through to focus it more sharply. After moving through the cornea, the light traverses the pupil. The *pupil* is a dark hole in the center of the *iris,* the colored part of the eye, which in humans ranges from a light blue to a dark brown. The size of the pupil opening depends on the amount of light in the environment. The dimmer the surroundings are, the more the pupil opens to allow more light to enter.

Once light passes through the pupil, it enters the *lens,* which is directly behind the pupil. The lens acts to bend the rays of light so that they are properly

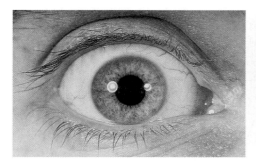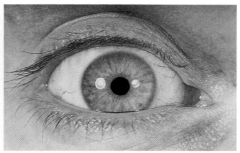

Like the automatic lighting system on a camera, the pupil in the human eye expands to let in more light (left) and contracts to block out light (right). Can humans adjust their ears to let in more or less sound in a similar manner?

focused on the rear of the eye. The lens focuses light by changing its own thickness, a process called *accommodation:* It becomes flatter when viewing distant objects and rounder when looking at closer objects.

Reaching the Retina

Having traveled through the pupil and lens, our image of the butterfly finally reaches its ultimate destination in the eye—the **retina.** Here the electromagnetic energy of light is converted to electrical impulses for transmission to the brain. It is important to note that because of the physical properties of light, the image has reversed itself in traveling through the lens, and it reaches the retina upside down (relative to its original position). Although it might seem that this reversal would cause difficulties in understanding and moving about the world, this is not the case. The brain interprets the image in terms of its original position.

The retina consists of a thin layer of nerve cells at the back of the eyeball (see Figure 3). There are two kinds of light-sensitive receptor cells in the retina. The names they have been given describe their shapes: rods and cones. **Rods** are thin, cylindrical receptor cells that are highly sensitive to light. **Cones** are cone-shaped, light-sensitive receptor cells that are responsible for sharp focus and color perception, particularly in bright light. The rods and cones are distributed unevenly throughout the retina. Cones are concentrated on the part of the retina called the *fovea.* The fovea is a particularly sensitive region of the retina. If you want to focus on something of particular interest, you will automatically try to center the image on the fovea to see it more sharply.

The rods and cones are not only structurally dissimilar but they also play distinctly different roles in vision. Cones are primarily responsible for the sharply focused perception of color, particularly in brightly lit situations; rods are related to vision in dimly lit situations and are largely insensitive to color and to details as sharp as those the cones are capable of recognizing. The rods play a key role in *peripheral vision*—seeing objects that are outside the main center of focus—and in night vision.

Sending the Message from the Eye to the Brain

When light energy strikes the rods and cones, it triggers a neural response that moves out of the back of the eyeball and into the brain through a bundle of ganglion axons called the **optic nerve.**

Retina The part of the eye that converts the electromagnetic energy of light to electrical impulses for transmission to the brain.

Rods Thin, cylindrical receptor cells in the retina that are highly sensitive to light.

Cones Cone-shaped, light-sensitive receptor cells in the retina that are responsible for sharp focus and color perception, particularly in bright light.

Optic nerve A bundle of ganglion axons that carry visual information to the brain.

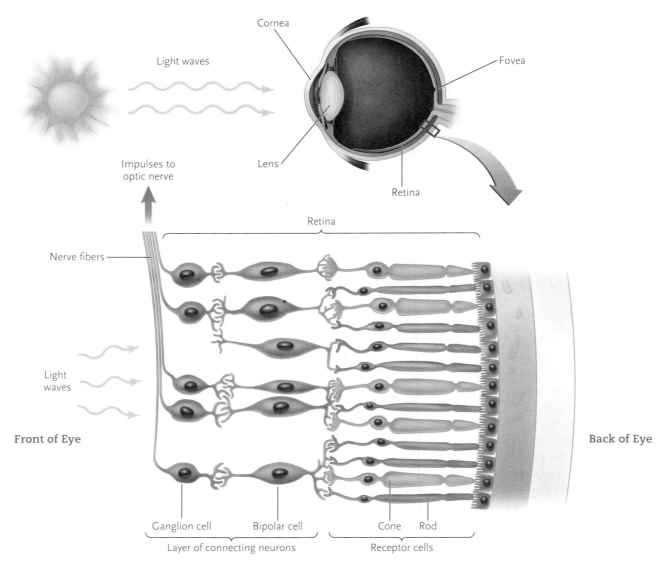

FIGURE 3 The basic cells of the eye. Light entering the eye travels through the ganglion and bipolar cells and strikes the light-sensitive rods and cones located at the back of the eye. The rods and cones then transmit nerve impulses to the brain via the bipolar and ganglion cells. *(Source: Shier, Butler, & Lewis, 2000.)*

FIGURE 4 To find your blind spot, close your right eye and look at the haunted house with your left eye. You will see the ghost on the periphery of your vision. Now, while staring at the house, move the page toward you. When the book is about a foot from your eye, the ghost will disappear. At this moment, the image of the ghost is falling on your blind spot. But also notice how, when the page is at that distance, not only does the ghost seem to disappear, but the line seems to run continuously through the area where the ghost used to be. This shows how we automatically compensate for missing information by using nearby material to complete what is unseen. That's the reason you never notice the blind spot. What is missing is replaced by what is seen next to the blind spot. Can you think of any advantages that this tendency to provide missing information gives humans as a species?

Because the opening for the optic nerve passes through the retina, there are no rods or cones in the area, and that creates a blind spot. Normally, however, this absence of nerve cells does not interfere with vision because you automatically compensate for the missing part of your field of vision. (To find your blind spot, see Figure 4.)

Once beyond the eye itself, the neural impulses relating to the image move through the *optic nerve.* As the optic nerve leaves the eyeball, its path does not take the most direct route to the part of the brain right behind the eye. Instead, the optic nerves from each eye meet at a point roughly between the two eyes—called the *optic chiasm* (pronounced ki-asm)—where each optic nerve then splits.

When the optic nerves split, the nerve impulses coming from the right half of each retina are sent to the right side of the brain, and the impulses arriving from the left half of each retina are sent to the left side of the brain. Because the image on the retinas is reversed and upside down, however, those images coming from the right half of each retina actually originated in the field of vision to the person's left, and the images coming from the left half of each retina originated in the field of vision to the person's right (see Figure 5).

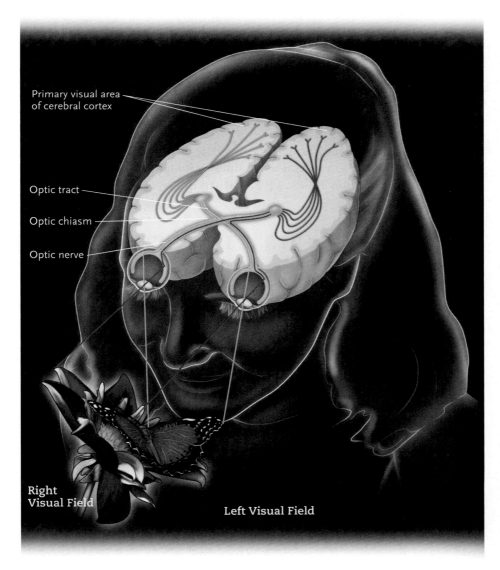

Primary visual area of cerebral cortex

Optic tract

Optic chiasm

Optic nerve

Right Visual Field

Left Visual Field

FIGURE 5   Because the optic nerve coming from each eye splits at the optic chiasm, the image to a person's right is sent to the left side of the brain and the image to the person's left is transmitted to the right side of the brain. *(Source: Mader, 2000.)*

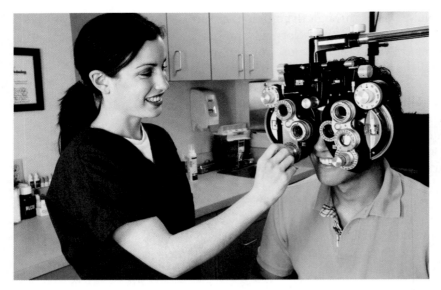

Most of us rarely think of our own vision, but optometrists and their assistants focus on it daily. What are some other careers that have a sensory focus?

Feature detection The activation of neurons in the cortex by visual stimuli of specific shapes or patterns.

Processing the Visual Message

Most processing of visual images takes place in the visual cortex of the brain, and it is here that the most complex kinds of processing occur. Many neurons in the cortex are extraordinarily specialized, being activated only by visual stimuli of a particular shape or pattern—a process known as **feature detection.** Researchers have found that some cells are activated only by lines of a particular width, shape, or orientation. Other cells are activated only by moving, as opposed to stationary, stimuli (Hubel & Wiesel, 2004; Pelli, Burns, & Farell, 2006).

More recent work has added to our knowledge of the complex ways in which visual information coming from individual neurons is combined and processed. Different parts of the brain process nerve impulses in several individual systems simultaneously. For instance, one system relates to shapes, one to colors, and others to movement, location, and depth. Furthermore, different parts of the brain are involved in the perception of specific *kinds* of stimuli, showing distinctions, for example, between the perception of human faces, animals, and inanimate stimuli. The brain's integration of visual information does not occur in any single step or location in the brain but instead is a process that occurs on several levels simultaneously (Winston, O'Doherty, & Kilner, 2006; Werblin & Roska, 2007; Werner, Pinna, & Spillmann, 2007).

» LO 2 Color Vision and Color Blindness: The Seven-Million-Color Spectrum

Although the range of wavelengths to which humans are sensitive is relatively narrow, at least in comparison with the entire electromagnetic spectrum, the portion to which we are capable of responding allows us great flexibility in sensing the world. Nowhere is this clearer than in terms of the number of colors we can discern (Bruce, Green, & Georgeson, 1997; Rabin, 2004).

Although the variety of colors that people are generally able to distinguish is vast, there are certain individuals whose ability to perceive color is quite limited—the color-blind. Interestingly, the condition of these individuals has provided some of the most important clues to understanding how color vision operates (Neitz, Neitz, & Kainz, 1996; Bonnardel, 2006).

A person with normal color vision is capable of distinguishing no less than 7 million different colors, but approximately 50 men or 1 in 5,000 women are color-blind. For most people with color blindness, the world looks quite dull. Red fire engines appear yellow, green grass seems yellow, and the three colors of a traffic light all look yellow. In fact, in the most common form of color blindness, all red and green objects are seen as yellow. There are other forms of color blindness as well, but they are quite rare. In yellow-blue blindness, people are unable to tell the difference between yellow and blue, and in the most extreme case an individual perceives no color at all. To such a person the world looks something like the picture on a black-and-white television set.

Explaining Color Vision

To understand why some people are color-blind, we need to consider the basics of color vision. There are two processes

From the perspective of . . .

A GRAPHIC DESIGNER How might you market your products similarly or differently to those who are color-blind versus those who have normal color vision?

involved. The first process is explained by the **trichromatic theory of color vision.** This theory suggests that there are three kinds of cones in the retina, each of which responds primarily to a specific range of wavelengths. One is most responsive to blue-violet colors, one to green, and the third to yellow-red (Brown & Wald, 1964). According to trichromatic theory, perception of color is influenced by the relative strength with which each of the three kinds of cones is activated. If we see a blue sky, the blue-violet cones are primarily triggered, and the others show less activity.

However, there are aspects of color vision that the trichromatic theory is less successful at explaining. For example, the theory does not explain what happens after you stare at something like the flag shown in Figure 6 for about a minute. Try this yourself and then look at a blank white page: you'll see an image of the traditional red, white, and blue U.S. flag. Where there was

Trichromatic theory of color and vision The theory that there are three kinds of cones in the retina, each of which responds primarily to a specific range of wavelengths.

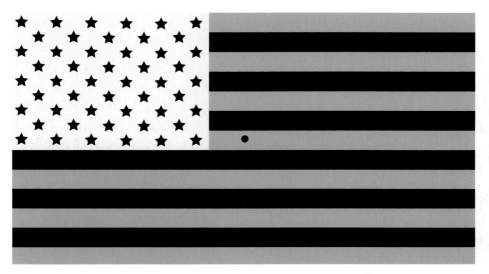

FIGURE 6 Stare at the dot in this flag for about a minute and then look at a piece of plain white paper. What do you see? Most people see an afterimage that converts the colors in the figure into the traditional red, white, and blue U.S. flag. If you have trouble seeing it the first time, blink once and try again.

yellow, you'll see blue, and where there were green and black, you'll see red and white.

The phenomenon you have just experienced is called an *afterimage*. It occurs because activity in the retina continues even when you are no longer staring at the original picture. However, it also demonstrates that the trichromatic theory does not explain color vision completely. Why should the colors in the afterimage be different from those in the original?

Because trichromatic processes do not provide a full explanation of color vision, alternative explanations have been proposed. According to the **opponent-process theory of color vision,** receptor cells are linked in pairs, working in opposition to each other. Specifically, there is a blue-yellow pairing, a red-green pairing, and a black-white pairing. If an object reflects light that contains more blue than yellow, it will stimulate the firing of the cells sensitive to blue, simultaneously discouraging or inhibiting the firing of receptor cells sensitive to yellow—and the object will appear blue. If, in contrast, a light contains more yellow than blue, the cells that respond to yellow will be stimulated to fire while the blue ones are inhibited, and the object will appear yellow (D. N. Robinson, 2007).

The opponent-process theory provides a good explanation for afterimages. When we stare at the yellow in the figure, for instance, our receptor cells for the yellow component of the yellow-blue pairing become fatigued and are less able to respond to yellow stimuli. In contrast, the receptor cells for the blue part of the pair are not tired, because they are not being stimulated. When we look at a white surface, the light reflected off it would normally stimulate both the yellow and the blue receptors equally. But the fatigue of the yellow receptors prevents this from happening. They temporarily do not respond to the yellow, which makes the white light appear to be blue. Because the other colors in the figure do the same thing relative to their specific opponents, the afterimage produces the opponent colors—for a while. The afterimage lasts only a short time, because the fatigue of the yellow receptors is soon overcome, and the white light begins to be perceived more accurately.

Both opponent processes and trichromatic mechanisms are at work in allowing us to see color. However, they operate in different parts of the visual sensing system. Trichromatic processes work within the retina itself, whereas opponent mechanisms operate both in the retina and at later stages of neuronal processing (Gegenfurtner, 2003; Chen, Zhou, & Gong, 2004; Baraas, Foster, & Amano, 2006).

RECAP

Explain the basic structure of the eye.

- Vision depends on sensitivity to light that is either reflected off objects or produced by an energy source. The eye shapes the light into an image that is transformed into nerve impulses and interpreted by the brain. (p. 89)

- As light enters the eye, it passes through the cornea, pupil, and lens and ultimately reaches the retina, where the electromagnetic energy of light is converted to nerve impulses for transmission to the brain. These impulses leave the eye via the optic nerve. (p. 90)

- The visual information gathered by the rods and cones is transferred through the optic nerve, which leads to the optic chiasm—the point where the optic nerve splits. (p. 93)

Compare and contrast color vision with color blindness.

- Color vision seems to be based on two processes described by the trichromatic theory and the opponent-process theory. (p. 95)

- The trichromatic theory suggests that there are three kinds of cones in the retina, each of which is responsive to a certain range of colors. The opponent-process theory presumes pairs of different types of cells in the eye that work in opposition to each other. (p. 95)

EVALUATE

1. Light entering the eye first passes through the _____, a protective window.

2. The structure that converts light into usable neural messages is called the _____.

3. A woman with blue eyes could be described as having blue pigment in her _____.

4. What is the process by which the thickness of the lens is changed in order to focus light properly?

5. The proper sequence of structures that light passes through in the eye is the _____, _____, _____, and _____.

6. Match each type of visual receptor with its function.
   a. Rods   1. Used for dim light, largely insensitive to color.
   b. Cones   2. Detect color, good in bright light.

7. _____ theory states that there are three types of cones in the retina, each of which responds primarily to a different color.

RETHINK

If the eye had a second lens that "unreversed" the image hitting the retina, do you think there would be changes in the way people perceive the world?

Answers to Evaluate Questions 1. cornea; 2. retina; 3. iris; 4. accommodation; 5. cornea, pupil, lens, retina; 6. a-1, b-2; 7. trichromatic

[KEY TERMS]

Retina *p. 91*
Rods *p. 91*
Cones *p. 91*
Optic nerve *p. 91*

Feature detection *p. 94*
Trichromatic theory of color vision *p. 95*
Opponent-process theory of color vision *p. 96*

Hearing and the Other Senses

The blastoff was easy compared with what the astronaut was experiencing now: space sickness. The constant nausea and vomiting were enough to make him wonder why he had worked so hard to become an astronaut. Even though he had been warned that there was a two-thirds chance that his first experience in space would cause these symptoms, he wasn't prepared for how terribly sick he really felt.

Whether or not the astronaut wishes he could head right back to the earth, his experience, a major problem for space travelers, is related to a basic sensory process: the sense of motion and balance. This sense allows people to navigate their bodies through the world and keep themselves upright without falling. Along with hearing—the process by which sound waves are translated into understandable and meaningful forms—the sense of motion and balance resides in the ear.

» LO1 Sensing Sound

Sound The movement of air molecules brought about by a source of vibration.

Eardrum The part of the ear that vibrates when sound hits it.

Cochlea (KOKE lee uh) A coiled tube in the ear filled with fluid that vibrates in response to sound.

Basilar membrane A vibrating structure that runs through the center of the cochlea, dividing it into an upper chamber and a lower chamber and containing sense receptors for sound.

Hair cells Tiny cells covering the basilar membrane that, when bent by vibrations entering the cochlea, transmit neural messages to the brain.

Although many of us think primarily of the outer ear when we speak of the ear, that structure is only one simple part of the whole. The outer ear acts as a reverse megaphone, designed to collect and bring sounds into the internal portions of the ear (see Figure 1). The location of the outer ears on different sides of the head helps with *sound localization,* the process by which we identify the direction from which a sound is coming. Wave patterns in the air enter each ear at a slightly different time, and the brain uses the discrepancy as a clue to the sound's point of origin. In addition, the two outer ears delay or amplify sounds of particular frequencies to different degrees.

Sound is the movement of air molecules brought about by a source of vibration. Sounds, arriving at the outer ear in the form of wavelike vibrations, are funneled into the *auditory canal,* a tube-like passage that leads to the eardrum. The **eardrum** is aptly named because it operates like a miniature drum, vibrating when sound waves hit it. The more intense the sound, the more the eardrum vibrates. These vibrations are then transferred into the *middle ear,* a tiny chamber containing three bones (the *hammer,* the

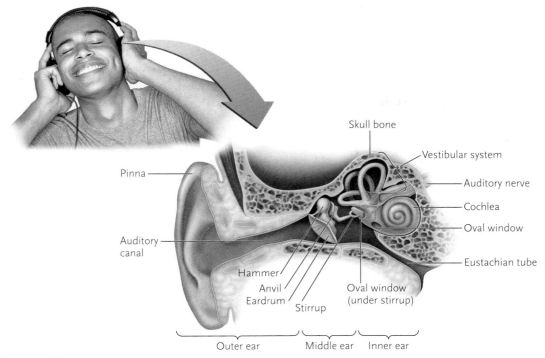

FIGURE 1   The major parts of the ear. *(Source: Brooker et al., 2008, p. 956.)*

anvil, and the *stirrup)* that transmit vibrations to the oval window, a thin membrane leading to the inner ear.

The *inner ear* is the portion of the ear that changes the sound vibrations into a form in which they can be transmitted to the brain. (As you will see, it also contains the organs that allow us to locate our position and determine how we are moving through space.) When sound enters the inner ear through the oval window, it moves into the **cochlea,** a coiled tube that looks something like a snail and is filled with fluid that vibrates in response to sound. Inside the cochlea is the **basilar membrane,** a structure that runs through the center of the cochlea, dividing it into an upper chamber and a lower chamber. The basilar membrane is covered with **hair cells.** When the hair cells are bent by the vibrations entering the cochlea, the cells send a neural message to the brain (Cho, 2000; Zhou, Liu, & Davis, 2005).

When an auditory message leaves the ear, it is transmitted to the auditory cortex of the brain through a complex series of neural interconnections. As the message is transmitted, it is communicated through neurons that respond to specific types of sounds. Within the auditory cortex itself, there are neurons that respond selectively to very specific sorts of sound features, such as clicks and whistles. Some neurons respond only to a specific pattern of sounds, such as a steady tone but not an intermittent one. Furthermore, specific neurons transfer information about a sound's location through their particular pattern of firing (Middlebrooks et al., 2005; Wang et al., 2005; Tervaniemi, Jacobsen, & Röttger, 2006).

Neighboring cells in the auditory cortex of the brain are responsive to similar frequencies. The auditory cortex, then, provides us with a "map" of sound frequencies, just as the visual cortex furnishes a representation of the visual field. In addition, because of the asymmetry in the two hemispheres of the brain (which we discussed in the last chapter), the left and right ears process sound differently.

psych2.0
WWW.MHHE.COM/PSYCHLIFE

The operation of the auditory sensory system.

The right ear reacts more to speech, while the left ear responds more to music (Sininger & Cone-Wesson, 2004, 2006).

Balance: The Ups and Downs of Life

Semicircular canals Three tubelike structures of the inner ear containing fluid that sloshes through them when the head moves, signaling rotational or angular movement to the brain.

Several structures of the ear are related more to our sense of balance than to our hearing. The **semicircular canals** of the inner ear (refer to Figure 1) consist of three tubes containing fluid that sloshes through them when the head moves, signaling rotational or angular movement to the brain. The pull on our bodies caused by the acceleration of forward, backward, or up-and-down motion, as well as the constant pull of gravity, is sensed by the *otoliths*, tiny, motion-sensitive crystals in the semicircular canals. When we move, these crystals shift like sands on a windy beach. The brain's inexperience in interpreting messages from the weightless otoliths is the cause of the space sickness commonly experienced by two-thirds of all space travelers (Flam, 1991; Stern & Koch, 1996).

» LO2 Smell and Taste

Until he bit into a piece of raw cabbage on that February evening . . . , Raymond Fowler had not thought much about the sense of taste. The cabbage, part of a pasta dish he was preparing for his family's dinner, had an odd, burning taste, but he did not pay it much attention. Then a few minutes later, his daughter handed him a glass of cola, and he took a swallow. "It was like sulfuric acid," he said. "It was like the hottest thing you could imagine boring into your mouth." (Goode, 1999, pp. D1–D2)

It was evident that something was very wrong with Fowler's sense of taste. After extensive testing, it became clear that he had damaged the nerves involved in his sense of taste, probably because of a viral infection or a medicine he was taking. (Luckily for him, a few months later his sense of taste returned to normal.)

Even without disruptions in our ability to perceive the world such as those experienced by Fowler, we all know the important roles that taste and smell play. We'll consider these two senses next.

Smell

Although many animals have keener abilities to detect odors than we do, the human sense of smell (*olfaction*) permits us to detect more than 10,000 separate smells. We also have a good memory for smells, and long-forgotten events and memories can be brought back with the mere whiff of an odor associated with a memory (DiLorenzo & Youngentob, 2003; Stevenson & Case, 2005; Willander & Larsson, 2006).

More than 1,000 types of receptor cells, known as *olfactory cells,* are spread across the nasal cavity. The cells are specialized to react to particular odors. Do you think it is possible to "train" the nose to pick up a greater number of odors?

Results of "sniff tests" have shown that women generally have a better sense of smell than men do (Herz & Engen, 1996). People also have the ability to distinguish males from females on the basis of smell alone. In one experiment, blindfolded students who were asked to sniff the breath of a female or male volunteer who was hidden from view were able to distinguish the sex of the donor at better than chance levels. People can also distinguish happy from sad emotions by sniffing underarm smells, and women are able to identify their babies solely on the basis of smell just a few hours after birth (Doty et al., 1982; Haviland-Jones & Chen, 1999).

The sense of smell is sparked when the molecules of a substance enter the nasal passages and meet *olfactory cells,* the receptor neurons of the nose, which are spread across the nasal cavity. More than 1,000 separate types of receptors have been identified on those cells so far. Each of these receptors is so specialized that it responds only to a small band of different odors. The responses of the separate olfactory cells are then transmitted to the brain, where they are combined into recognition of a particular smell (Marshall, Laing, & Jinks, 2006; Murphy et al., 2004; Zou & Buck, 2006).

Taste

The sense of taste (*gustation*) involves receptor cells that respond to four basic stimulus qualities: sweet, sour, salty, and bitter. Although the specialization of the receptor cells leads them to respond most strongly to a particular type of taste, they also are capable of responding to other tastes as well. Ultimately, every taste is simply a combination of the basic flavor qualities, in the same way that the primary colors blend into a vast variety of shades and hues (DiLorenzo & Youngentob, 2003; Yeomans, Tepper, & Ritezschel, 2007).

The sense of taste (gustation) involves receptor cells that respond to four basic stimulus qualities: sweet, sour, salty, and bitter.

The receptor cells for taste are located in roughly 10,000 *taste buds,* which are distributed across the tongue and other parts of the mouth and throat. The taste buds wear out and are replaced every 10 days or so. That's a good thing, because if our taste buds weren't constantly reproducing, we'd lose the ability to taste after we'd accidentally burned our tongues.

The sense of taste differs significantly from one person to another, largely as a result of genetic factors. Some people, dubbed "supertasters," are highly sensitive to taste; they have twice as many taste receptors as "nontasters," who are relatively insensitive to taste. Supertasters (who, for unknown reasons, are more likely to be female than male) find sweets sweeter, cream creamier, and spicy dishes spicier, and weaker concentrations of flavor are enough to satisfy any cravings they may have. In contrast, because they aren't so sensitive to taste, nontasters may seek out relatively sweeter and fattier foods in order to maximize the taste. As a consequence, they may be prone to obesity (Bartoshuk, 2000; Snyder, Fast, & Bartoshuk, 2004; Pickering & Gordon, 2006).

Are you a supertaster? To find out, complete the accompanying Try It! questionnaire.

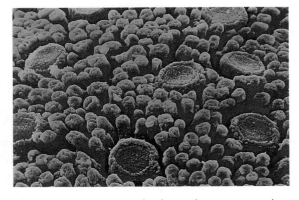

There are 10,000 taste buds on the tongue and other parts of the mouth. Taste buds wear out and are replaced every 10 days. What would happen if taste buds were not generated?

Take a Taste Test

1. **Taste Bud Count**

   Punch a hole with a standard hole punch in a square of wax paper. Paint the front of your tongue with a cotton swab dipped in blue food coloring. Put wax paper on the tip of your tongue, just to the right of center. With a flashlight and magnifying glass, count the number of pink, unstained circles. They contain taste buds.

2. **Sweet Taste**

   Rinse your mouth with water before tasting each sample. Put 1/2 cup sugar in a measuring cup, and then add enough water to make 1 cup. Mix. Coat front half of your tongue, including the tip, with a cotton swab dipped in the solution. Wait a few moments. Rate the sweetness according to the scale shown below.

3. **Salt Taste**

   Put 2 teaspoons of salt in a measuring cup and add enough water to make 1 cup. Repeat the steps listed above, rating how salty the solution is.

   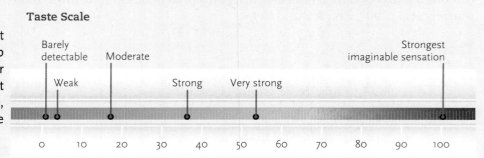

   Taste Scale

4. **Spicy Taste**

   Add 1 teaspoon of Tabasco sauce to 1 cup of water. Apply with a cotton swab to first half inch of the tongue, including the tip. Keep your tongue out of your mouth until the burn reaches a peak, then rate the burn according to the scale.

	Supertasters	**Nontasters**
No. of taste buds	25 on average	10
Sweet rating	56 on average	32
Tabasco	64 on average	31

Average tasters lie in between supertasters and nontasters. Bartoshuk and Lucchina lack the data at this time to rate salt reliably, but you can compare your results with others taking the test.

Source: Bartoshuk & Lucchina, 1997.

» LO3 The Skin Senses: Touch, Pressure, Temperature, and Pain

It started innocently when Jennifer Darling hurt her right wrist during gym class. At first it seemed like a simple sprain. But even though the initial injury healed, the excruciating, burning pain accompanying it did not go away. Instead, it spread to her other arm and then to her legs. The pain, which Jennifer described as similar to "a hot iron on your arm," was unbearable—and never stopped.

The source of Darling's pain turned out to be a rare condition known as "reflex sympathetic dystrophy syndrome," or RSDS for short. For a victim of RSDS, a stimulus as mild as a gentle breeze or the touch of a feather can produce agony. Even bright sunlight or a loud noise can trigger intense pain.

Pain like Darling's can be devastating, yet a lack of pain can be equally bad. If you never experienced pain, for instance, you might not notice that your arm had brushed against a hot pan, and you would suffer a severe burn. Similarly, without the warning sign of abdominal pain that typically accompanies an inflamed appendix, your appendix might eventually rupture, spreading a fatal infection throughout your body.

In fact, all our **skin senses**—touch, pressure, temperature, and pain—play a critical role in survival, making us aware of potential danger to our bodies. Most of these senses operate through nerve receptor cells located at various depths throughout the skin, distributed unevenly throughout the body. For example, some areas, such as the fingertips, have many more receptor cells sensitive to touch and as a consequence are notably more sensitive than other areas of the body (Gardner & Kandel, 2000; see Figure 2).

Probably the most extensively researched skin sense is pain, and with good reason: people consult physicians and take medication for pain more than for any other symptom or condition. Losses to U.S. business productivity due to employee pain is more than $60 billion a year, and overall pain costs $100 billion a year in the United States alone. (Stewart et al., 2003; Pesmen, 2006).

Pain is a response to a great variety of different kinds of stimuli. A light that is too bright can produce pain, and sound that is too loud can be painful. One explanation is that pain is an outcome of cell injury; when a cell is damaged, regardless of the source of damage, it releases a chemical called *substance P* that transmits pain messages to the brain.

Skin senses The senses of touch, pressure, temperature, and pain.

If you choose a profession in the medical field, how will the $100 billion price tag on pain impact your professional life?

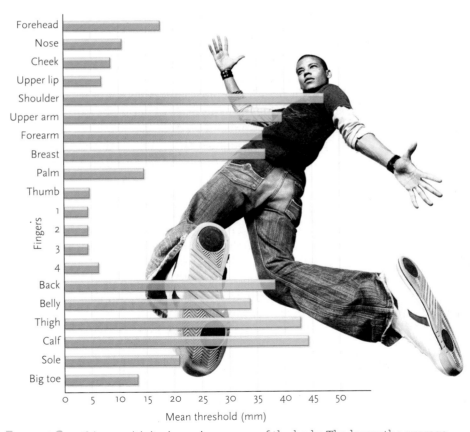

FIGURE 2   Skin sensitivity in various areas of the body. The lower the average threshold is, the more sensitive a body part is. The fingers and thumb, lips, nose, cheeks, and big toe are the most sensitive. Why do you think certain areas are more sensitive than others? (*Source: From D. R. Kenshalo, The Skin Senses, 1968. Courtesy of Charles C Thomas, Publisher, Ltd., Springfield, Illinois.*)

Some people are more susceptible to pain than others. For example, women experience painful stimuli more intensely than men. These gender differences are associated with the production of hormones related to menstrual cycles. In addition, certain genes are linked to the experience of pain, so that we may inherit our sensitivity to pain (Apkarian et al., 2005; Edwards & Fillingim, 2007).

But the experience of pain is not determined by biological factors alone. For example, women report that the pain experienced in childbirth is moderated to some degree by the joyful nature of the situation. In contrast, even a minor stimulus can produce the perception of strong pain if it is accompanied by anxiety (like a visit to the dentist). Clearly, then, pain is a perceptual response that depends heavily on our emotions and thoughts (Hadjistavropoulos, Craig, & Fuchs-Lacelle, 2004; Rollman, 2004; Lang, Sorrell, & Rodgers, 2006).

From the perspective of . . .

A MEDICAL OR DENTAL ASSISTANT   How would you handle a patient who is anxiously awaiting treatment and complaining that her pain is getting worse?

Gate-control theory of pain The theory that particular nerve receptors lead to specific areas of the brain related to pain.

According to the **gate-control theory of pain,** particular nerve receptors in the spinal cord lead to specific areas of the brain related to pain. When these receptors are activated because of an injury or problem with a part of the body, a "gate" to the brain is opened, allowing us to experience the sensation of pain (Melzack & Katz, 2004).

However, another set of neural receptors can, when stimulated, close the "gate" to the brain, thereby reducing the experience of pain. The gate can be shut in two different ways. First, other impulses can overwhelm the nerve pathways relating to pain, which are spread throughout the brain. In this case, nonpainful stimuli compete with and sometimes displace the neural message of pain, thereby shutting off the painful stimulus.

Psychological factors account for the second way a gate can be shut. Depending on an individual's current emotions, interpretation of events, and previous experience, the brain can close a gate by sending a message down the spinal cord to an injured area, producing a reduction in or relief from pain. Thus, soldiers who are injured in battle may experience no pain. The lack of pain probably occurs because a soldier experiences such relief at still being alive that the brain sends a signal to the injury site to shut down the pain gate (Turk, 1994; Gatchel & Weisberg, 2000; Pincus & Morley, 2001).

becoming an *informed consumer* **OF PSYCHOLOGY**

Managing Pain

Are you one of the 50 million people in the United States who suffer from chronic pain? Psychologists and medical specialists have devised several strategies to fight pain. Among the most important approaches are the following:

- *Medication.* Painkilling drugs are the most popular treatment in fighting pain. Drugs range from those which directly treat the source of the pain—such as reducing swelling in painful joints—to those which work on the symptoms. Medication can be in the form of pills, patches, injections, or liquids. In a recent innovation, drugs are pumped directly into the spinal cord (Pesmen, 2006).

- *Nerve and brain stimulation.* Pain can sometimes be relieved when a low-voltage electric current is passed through the specific part of the body that is in pain. In even more severe cases, electrodes can be implanted surgically directly into the brain, or a handheld battery pack can stimulate nerve cells to provide direct relief. This process is known as *transcutaneous electrical nerve stimulation,* or *TENS* (Tugay et al., 2007; Claydon et al., 2008).

- *Light therapy.* One of the newest forms of pain reduction involves exposure to specific wavelengths of red or infrared light. Certain kinds of light increase the production of enzymes that may promote healing (Evcik et al., 2007; Rastad, Ulfberg, & Lindberg, 2008).

- *Hypnosis.* For people who can be hypnotized, hypnosis can greatly relieve pain (Patterson, 2004; Neron & Stephenson, 2007).

- *Biofeedback and relaxation techniques.* Using *biofeedback,* people learn to control "involuntary" functions such as heartbeat and respiration. If the pain involves muscles, as in tension headaches or back pain, sufferers can be trained to relax their bodies systematically (Vitiello, Bonello, & Pollard, 2007).

- *Surgery.* In one of the most extreme methods, nerve fibers that carry pain messages to the brain can be cut surgically. Still, because of the danger that other bodily functions will be affected, surgery is a treatment of last resort, used most frequently with dying patients (Cullinane, Chu, & Mamelak, 2002; Lai, Chen, & Chien, 2007).

- *Cognitive restructuring.* Cognitive treatments are effective for people who continually say to themselves, "This pain will never stop," "The pain is ruining my life," or "I can't take it anymore" and are thereby likely to make their pain even worse. By substituting more positive ways of thinking, people can increase their sense of control—and actually reduce the pain they experience (Spanos, Barber, & Lang, 2005; Bogart et al., 2007).

RECAP

Describe how we sense sound.

- Sound, motion, and balance are centered in the ear. Sounds, in the form of vibrating airwaves, enter through the outer ear and travel through the auditory canal until they reach the eardrum. (p. 98)

- The vibrations of the eardrum are transmitted into the middle ear, which consists of three bones: the hammer, the anvil, and the stirrup. These bones transmit vibrations to the oval window. (p. 98)

- In the inner ear, vibrations move into the cochlea, which encloses the basilar membrane. Hair cells on the basilar membrane change the mechanical energy of sound waves into nerve impulses that are transmitted to the brain. The ear is also involved in the sense of balance and motion. (p. 98)

Discuss smell and taste.

■ Smell depends on olfactory cells (the receptor cells of the nose), and taste is centered in the tongue's taste buds. (p. 101)

Distinguish the skin senses.

■ The skin senses are responsible for the experiences of touch, pressure, temperature, and pain. Gate-control theory suggests that particular nerve receptors, when activated, open a "gate" to specific areas of the brain related to pain, and that another set of receptors closes the gate when stimulated. (p. 104)

■ Among the techniques used frequently to alleviate pain are medication, hypnosis, biofeedback, relaxation techniques, surgery, nerve and brain stimulation, and cognitive therapy. (p. 105)

E V A L U A T E

1. The tubelike passage leading from the outer ear to the eardrum is known as the _____.

2. The purpose of the eardrum is to protect the sensitive nerves underneath it. It serves no purpose in actual hearing. True or false?

3. The three middle ear bones transmit their sound to the _____.

4. The three fluid-filled tubes in the inner ear that are responsible for our sense of balance are known as the _____.

5. Touch, pressure, temperature, and pain are collectively known as our _____.

R E T H I N K

Much research is being conducted on repairing faulty sensory organs through devices such as personal guidance systems and eyeglasses, among others. Do you think that researchers should attempt to improve normal sensory capabilities beyond their "natural" range (for example, make human visual or audio capabilities more sensitive than normal)? What benefits might this ability bring? What problems might it cause?

Answers to Evaluate Questions 1. auditory canal; 2. false; it vibrates when sound waves hit it, and transmits the sound; 3. oval window; 4. semicircular canals; 5. skin senses.

[K E Y   T E R M S]

Sound *p. 98*

Eardrum *p. 98*

Cochlea (KOKE lee uh) *p. 98*

Basilar membrane *p. 98*

Hair cells *p. 98*

Semicircular canals *p. 100*

Skin senses *p. 103*

Gate-control theory of pain *p. 104*

Perceptual Organization
Constructing Our View of the World

Consider the vase shown in Figure 1A for a moment. Or is it a vase? Take another look, and instead you may see the profiles of two people.

Now that an alternative interpretation has been pointed out, you will probably shift back and forth between the two interpretations. Similarly, if you examine the shapes in Figure 1B long enough, you will probably experience a shift in what you're seeing. The reason for these reversals is this: because each figure is two-dimensional, the usual means we employ for distinguishing the *figure* (the object being perceived) from the *ground* (the background or spaces within the object) do not work.

FIGURE 1 When the usual cues we use to distinguish figure from ground are absent, we may shift back and forth between different views of the same figure. If you look at each of these objects long enough, you'll probably experience a shift in what you're seeing. In (A), you can see either a vase or the profiles of two people. (For another example of this, look at the cover of this book!) In (B), the shaded portion of the figure, called a Necker cube, can appear to be either the front or the back of the cube. Finally, in (C), you'll be able to see a face of a woman if you look at the drawing long enough.

A

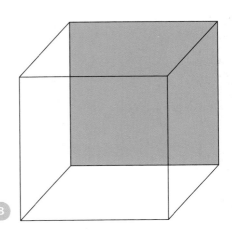

B

C

"I'm turning into my mother."

Understanding this cartoon involves the ability to separate the figure from the ground. If you're having trouble appreciating the humor, stare at the woman on the right, who eventually will be transformed.

Gestalt laws of organization A series of principles that describe how we organize bits and pieces of information into meaningful wholes.

> We do not just passively respond to visual stimuli that happens to fall on our retinas. Instead, we actively try to organize and make sense of what we see.

The fact that we can look at the same figure in more than one way illustrates an important point. We do not just passively respond to visual stimuli that happen to fall on our retinas. Instead, we actively try to organize and make sense of what we see.

We turn now from a focus on the initial response to a stimulus (sensation) to what our minds make of that stimulus—perception. Perception is a constructive process by which we go beyond the stimuli that are presented to us and attempt to construct a meaningful situation.

» LO1 The Gestalt Laws of Organization

Some of the most basic perceptual processes can be described by a series of principles that focus on the ways we organize bits and pieces of information into meaningful wholes. Known as **gestalt laws of organization,** these principles were set forth in the early 1900s by a group of German psychologists who studied patterns, or *gestalts* (Wertheimer, 1923). Those psychologists discovered a number of important principles that are valid for visual (as well as auditory) stimuli, illustrated in Figure 2: closure, proximity, similarity, and simplicity.

Figure 2A illustrates *closure.* We usually group elements to form enclosed or complete figures rather than open ones. We tend to ignore the breaks in Figure 2A and concentrate on the overall form. Figure 2B demonstrates the principle of *proximity:* We perceive elements that are closer together as grouped together. As a result, we tend to see pairs of dots rather than a row of single dots in Figure 2B.

| A | Closure | B | Proximity | C | Similarity | D | Simplicity |

FIGURE 2 Organizing these various bits and pieces of information into meaningful wholes constitutes some of the most basic processes of perception, which are summed up in the gestalt laws of organization. Do you think any other species share this organizational tendency? How might we find out?

Elements that are *similar* in appearance we perceive as grouped together. We see, then, horizontal rows of circles and squares in Figure 2C instead of vertical mixed columns. Finally, in a general sense, the overriding gestalt principle is *simplicity:* When we observe a pattern, we perceive it in the most basic, straightforward manner that we can. For example, most of us see Figure 2D as a square with lines on two sides, rather than as the block letter *W* on top of the letter *M*. If we have a choice of interpretations, we generally opt for the simpler one.

Although gestalt psychology no longer plays a prominent role in contemporary psychology, its legacy endures. One fundamental gestalt principle that remains influential is that two objects considered together form a whole that is different from the simple combination of the objects. Gestalt psychologists argued that the perception of stimuli in our environment goes well beyond the individual elements that we sense. Instead, it represents an active, constructive process carried out within the brain (Humphreys & Müller, 2000; Lehar, 2003; van der Helm, 2006; see Figure 3).

> *Although gestalt psychology no longer plays a prominent role in contemporary psychology, its legacy endures.*

» LO 2 Top-Down and Bottom-Up Processing

Ca- yo- re-d t-is -en-en-e, w-ic- ha- ev-ry -hi-d l-tt-r m-ss-ng? It probably won't take you too long to figure out that it says, "Can you read this sentence, which has every third letter missing?"

If perception were based primarily on breaking down a stimulus into its most basic elements, understanding the sentence, as well as other ambiguous stimuli, would not be possible. The fact that you were probably able to recognize such an imprecise stimulus illustrates that perception proceeds along two different avenues, called top-down processing and bottom-up processing.

In **top-down processing,** perception is guided by higher-level knowledge, experience, expectations, and motivations. You were able to figure out the

> **Top-down processing** Perception that is guided by higher-level knowledge, experience, expectations, and motivations.

FIGURE 3 Although at first it is difficult to distinguish anything in this drawing, keep looking, and eventually you'll probably be able to see the figure of a dog (James, 1966). The dog represents a gestalt, or perceptual whole, which is something greater than the sum of the individual elements.

A B C D E F
IO II I2 I3 I4

FIGURE 4 The power of context is shown in this figure. Note how the B and the 13 are identical. *(Source: Coren & Ward, 1989.)*

meaning of the sentence with the missing letters because of your prior reading experience, and because written English contains redundancies. Not every letter of each word is necessary to decode its meaning. Moreover, your expectations played a role in your being able to read the sentence. You were probably expecting a statement that had *something* to do with psychology, not a recipe for meatloaf.

Top-down processing is illustrated by the importance of context in determining how we perceive objects. Look, for example, at Figure 4. Most of us perceive that the first row consists of the letters *A* through *F*, while the second contains the numbers 10 through 14. But take a more careful look and you'll see that the "B" and the "13" are identical. Clearly, our perception is affected by our expectations about the two sequences—even though the two stimuli are exactly the same.

However, top-down processing cannot occur on its own. Even though top-down processing allows us to fill in the gaps in ambiguous and out-of-context stimuli, we would be unable to perceive the meaning of such stimuli without bottom-up processing. **Bottom-up processing** consists of the progression of recognizing and processing information from individual components of a stimulus and moving to the perception of the whole. We would make no headway in our recognition of the sentence without being able to perceive the individual shapes that make up the letters. Some perception, then, occurs at the level of the patterns and features of each of the separate letters.

Bottom-up processing Perception that consists of the progression of recognizing and processing information from individual components of a stimuli and moving to the perception of the whole.

Top-down and bottom-up processing occur simultaneously, and interact with each other, in our perception of the world around us. Bottom-up processing permits us to process the fundamental characteristics of stimuli, whereas top-down processing allows us to bring our experience to bear on perception. As we learn more about the complex processes involved in perception, we are developing a better understanding of how the brain continually interprets information from the senses and permits us to make responses appropriate to the environment (Buschman & Miller, 2007).

» LO3 Perceptual Constancy

Consider what happens as you finish a conversation with a friend and she begins to walk away from you. As you watch her walk down the street, the image on your retina becomes smaller and smaller. Do you wonder why she is shrinking?

Of course not. Despite the very real change in the size of the retinal image, you factor into your thinking the knowledge that your friend is moving farther away from you because of perceptual constancy. *Perceptual constancy* is a phenomenon in which physical objects are perceived as unvarying and consistent despite changes in their appearance or in the physical environment.

In some cases, though, our application of perceptual constancy can mislead us. One good example of this involves the rising moon. When the moon first appears at night, close to the horizon, it seems to be huge—much larger than when it is high in the sky later in the evening. You may have thought that the apparent change in the size of the moon was caused by the moon's being physically closer to the earth when it first appears. In fact, though, this is not

When the moon is near the horizon, we do not see it by itself, and perceptual constancy leads us to take into account a misleading sense of distance.

the case at all: the actual image of the moon on our retina is the same, whether it is low or high in the sky.

Instead, the moon appears to be larger when it is close to the horizon primarily because of the phenomenon of perceptual constancy. When the moon is near the horizon, the perceptual cues of intervening terrain and objects such as trees on the horizon produce a misleading sense of distance. The phenomenon of perceptual constancy leads us to take that assumed distance into account when we view the moon, and it leads us to misperceive the moon as relatively large.

In contrast, when the moon is high in the sky, we see it by itself, and we don't try to compensate for its distance from us. In this case, then, perceptual constancy leads us to perceive it as relatively small. To demonstrate perceptual constancy for yourself, try looking at the moon when it is relatively low on the horizon through a paper-towel tube; the moon suddenly will appear to "shrink" back to normal size (Coren, 1992; Ross & Plug, 2002; Imamura & Nakamizo, 2006). Perceptual constancy applies not just to size (as with the moon illusion) but to shape and color as well. For example, despite the varying images on the retina as an airplane approaches, flies overhead, and disappears, we do not perceive the airplane as changing shape (Redding, 2002; Wickelgren, 2004).

» LO 4 Depth Perception: Translating 2-D to 3-D

As sophisticated as the retina is, the images projected onto it are flat and two-dimensional. Yet the world around us is three-dimensional, and we perceive it that way. How do we make the transformation from 2-D to 3-D?

The ability to view the world in three dimensions and to perceive distance—a skill known as **depth perception**—is due largely to the fact that we have two eyes. Because there is a certain distance between the eyes, a slightly

Depth perception The ability to view the world in three dimensions and to perceive distance.

Our perception makes the dog biscuits appear huge. How would we function if we were not able to make that distinction?

different image reaches each retina. The brain integrates the two images into one composite view, but it also recognizes the difference in images and uses it to estimate the distance of an object from us. The difference in the images seen by the left eye and the right eye is known as *binocular disparity.*

To get a sense of binocular disparity for yourself, hold a pencil at arm's length and look at it first with one eye and then with the other. There is little difference between the two views relative to the background. Now bring the pencil just six inches away from your face, and try the same thing. This time you will perceive a greater difference between the two views.

The fact that the discrepancy between the images in the two eyes varies according to the distance of objects that we view provides us with a means of determining distance. If we view two objects and one is considerably closer to us than the other is, the retinal disparity will be relatively large and we will have a greater sense of depth between the two. However, if the two objects are a similar distance from us, the retinal disparity will be minor, and we will perceive them as being a similar distance from us.

In some cases, certain cues permit us to obtain a sense of depth and distance with just one eye. These cues are known as *monocular cues.* One monocular cue—*motion parallax*— is the change in position of an object on the retina caused by movement of your body relative to the object. For example, suppose you are a passenger in a

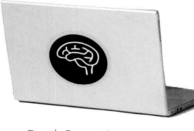

psych2.0
WWW.MHHE.COM/PSYCHLIFE

Depth Perception

From the perspective of . . .

A COMPUTER GAME DESIGNER What are some techniques you might use to produce the appearance of three-dimensional terrain on a two-dimensional computer screen? What are some techniques you might use to suggest motion?

moving car, and you focus your eye on a stable object such as a tree. Objects that are closer than the tree will appear to move backward, and the nearer the object is, the more quickly it will appear to move. In contrast, objects beyond the tree will seem to move at a slower speed, but in the same direction as you are. Your brain is able to use these cues to calculate the relative distances of the tree and other objects.

Similarly, experience has taught us that if two objects are the same size, the one that makes a smaller image on the retina is farther away than is the one that provides a larger image—an example of the monocular cue of *relative size*. The quality of the image on the retina also helps us judge distance. The monocular cue of *texture gradient* provides information about distance because the details of things that are far away are less distinct (Proffitt, 2006).

Finally, anyone who has ever seen railroad tracks that seem to join together in the distance knows that distant objects appear to be closer together than are nearer ones, a phenomenon called linear perspective. People use *linear perspective* as a monocular cue in estimating distance, allowing the two-dimensional image on the retina to record the three-dimensional world (Bruce et al., 1997; Dobbins et al., 1998; Shimono & Wade, 2002; Bruggeman, Yonas, & Konczak, 2007).

» LO5 Motion Perception: As the World Turns

When a batter tries to hit a pitched ball, the most important factor is the motion of the ball. How is a batter able to judge the speed and location of a target that is moving at some 90 miles per hour?

The answer rests in part on several cues that provide us with relevant information about the perception of motion. For one thing, the movement of an object across the retina is typically perceived relative to some stable, unmoving background. Moreover, if the stimulus is heading toward us, the image on the retina will expand in size, filling more and more of the visual field. In such cases, we assume that the stimulus is approaching—not that it is an expanding stimulus viewed at a constant distance.

It is not, however, just the movement of images across the retina that brings about the perception of motion. If it were, we would perceive the world as moving every time we moved our heads. Instead, one of the critical things we learn about perception is to factor information about our own head and eye movements along with information about changes in the retinal image.

» LO6 Perceptual Illusions: The Deceptions of Perceptions

If you look carefully at the Parthenon, one of the most famous buildings of ancient Greece, still standing at the top of an Athens hill, you'll see that it was built with a bulge on one side. If it didn't have that bulge—and quite a few other "tricks" like it, such as columns that incline inward—it would look as if it were crooked and about to fall down. Instead, it appears to stand completely straight, at right angles to the ground.

The fact that the Parthenon appears to be completely upright is the result of a series of visual illusions. **Visual illusions** are physical stimuli that

Visual illusions Physical stimuli that consistently produce errors in perception.

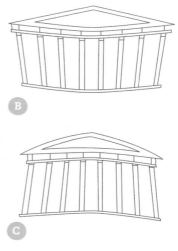

FIGURE 5 In building the Parthenon, the Greeks constructed an architectural wonder that looks perfectly straight, with right angles at every corner, as in (A). However, if it had been built with completely true right angles, it would have looked as it does in (B). To compensate for this illusion, the Parthenon was designed to have a slight upward curvature, as shown in (C). *(Source: Coren & Ward, 1989, p. 5.)*

consistently produce errors in perception. In the case of the Parthenon, the building appears to be completely square, as illustrated in Figure 5A. However, if it had been built that way, it would look to us as it does in Figure 5B. The reason for this is an illusion that makes right angles placed above a line appear as if they were bent. To offset the illusion, the Parthenon was constructed as in Figure 5C, with a slight upward curvature.

The *Müller-Lyer illusion* (illustrated in Figure 6) has fascinated psychologists for decades. Although the two lines are the same length, the one with the arrow tips pointing inward (Figure 6A, right) appears to be longer than the one with the arrow tips pointing outward (Figure 6A, left).

Although all kinds of explanations for visual illusions have been suggested, most concentrate either on the physical operation of the eye or on our misinterpretation of the visual stimulus. For example, one explanation for the Müller-Lyer illusion is that eye movements are greater when the arrow tips point inward, making us perceive the line as longer than it is when the arrow tips face outward. In contrast, a different explanation for the illusion suggests that we unconsciously attribute particular significance to each of the lines (Gregory, 1978; Redding & Hawley, 1993). When we see the line on the right in Figure 6A, we tend to perceive it as if it were the inside corner of a room extending away from us, as illustrated in Figure 6C. In contrast, when we view the line on the left in Figure 6A, we perceive it as the relatively close outside corner of a rectangular object such as the building corner in Figure 6B. Because previous experience leads us to assume that the outside corner is closer than the inside corner, we make the further assumption that the inside corner must therefore be larger.

Despite the complexity of the latter explanation, a good deal of evidence supports it. For instance, cross-cultural studies show that people raised in areas where there are few right angles—such as the Zulu in Africa—are much less susceptible to the illusion than are people who grow up where most structures are built using right angles and rectangles (Segall, Campbell, & Herskovits, 1966).

psych2.0

WWW.MHHE.COM/PSYCHLIFE

Understand the reasons we are susceptible to visual illustrations.

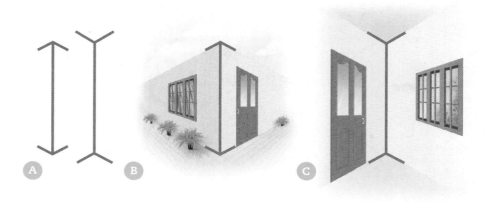

FIGURE 6 In the Müller-Lyer illusion (A), the vertical line on the right appears longer than the one on the left. One explanation for the Müller-Lyer illusion suggests that the line with arrow points directed inward is to be interpreted as the inside corner of a rectangular room extending away from us (C), and the line with arrow points directed outward is viewed as the relatively close corner of a rectangular object, such as the building corner in (B), Our previous experience with distance cues leads us to assume that the outside corner is closer than the inside corner and that the inside corner must therefore be longer.

EXPLORING diversity

Culture and Perception

As the example of the Zulu indicates, the culture in which we are raised has clear consequences for how we perceive the world. Consider the drawing in Figure 7. Sometimes called the "devil's tuning fork," it is likely to produce a mind-boggling effect, as the center tine of the fork alternates between appearing and disappearing.

Now try to reproduce the drawing on a piece of paper. Chances are that the task is nearly impossible for you—unless you are a member of an African tribe with little exposure to Western cultures. For such individuals, the task is simple; they have no trouble reproducing the figure. The reason is that Westerners automatically interpret the drawing as something that cannot exist in three dimensions, and they therefore are inhibited from reproducing it. The African tribal members, in contrast, do not make the assumption that the figure is "impossible" and instead view it in two dimensions, a perception that enables them to copy the figure with ease (Deregowski, 1973).

Cultural differences are also reflected in depth perception. A Western viewer of Figure 8 would interpret the hunter in the drawing as aiming for the antelope in the foreground, while an elephant stands under the tree in the background. A member of an isolated African tribe, however, interprets the scene very differently by assuming that the hunter is aiming at the elephant. Westerners use the difference in sizes between the two animals as a cue that the elephant is farther away than the antelope (Hudson, 1960).

The misinterpretations created by visual illusions are ultimately due, then, to errors in both fundamental visual processing and the way the

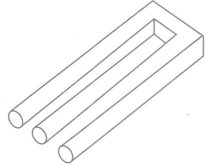

FIGURE 7 The "devil's tuning fork" has three prongs . . . . or does it have two?

FIGURE 8   Is the man aiming for the elephant or the antelope? Westerners assume that the differences in size between the two animals indicate that the elephant is farther away, and therefore the man is aiming for the antelope. In contrast, members of some African tribes, not used to depth cues in two-dimensional drawings, assume that the man is aiming for the elephant. (The drawing is based on Deregowski, 1973.) Do you think Westerners, who view the picture in three dimensions, could explain what they see to someone who views the scene in two dimensions and eventually get that person to view it in three dimensions?

brain interprets the information it receives. But visual illusions, by illustrating something fundamental about perception, become more than mere psychological curiosities. There is a basic connection between our prior knowledge, needs, motivations, and expectations about how the world is put together and the way we perceive it. Our view of the world is very much an outcome, then, of fundamental psychological factors. Furthermore, each person perceives the environment in a way that is unique and special (Knoblich & Sebanz, 2006; Repp & Knoblich, 2007).

RECAP

Explain the gestalt laws of organization.

- Perception is a constructive process in which people go beyond the stimuli that are physically present and try to construct a meaningful interpretation. (p. 108)

- The gestalt laws of organization are used to describe the way in which we organize bits and pieces of information into meaningful wholes, known as gestalts, through closure, proximity, similarity, and simplicity. (p. 108)

Identify top-down and bottom-up processing.

- In top-down processing, perception is guided by higher-level knowledge, experience, expectations, and motivations. In bottom-up processing, perception consists of the progression of recognizing and processing information from individual components of a stimuli and moving to the perception of the whole. (p. 109)

Define perceptual constancy.

- Perceptual constancy permits us to perceive stimuli as unvarying in size, shape, and color despite changes in the environment or the appearance of the objects being perceived. (p. 110)

Explain depth perception.

- Depth perception is the ability to perceive distance and view the world in three dimensions even though the images projected on our retinas are two-dimensional. We are able to judge depth and distance as a result of binocular disparity and monocular cues, such as motion parallax, the relative size of images on the retina, and linear perspective. (p. 111)

Relate motion perception to daily life.

- Motion perception depends on cues such as the perceived movement of an object across the retina and information about how the head and eyes are moving. (p. 113)

Determine the importance of perceptual illusions.

- Visual illusions are physical stimuli that consistently produce errors in perception, causing judgments that do not reflect the physical reality of a stimulus accurately. One of the best-known illusions is the Müller-Lyer illusion. (p. 113)
- Visual illusions are usually the result of errors in the brain's interpretation of visual stimuli. Furthermore, culture clearly affects how we perceive the world. (p. 114)

EVALUATE

1. Match each of the following organizational laws with its meaning:

   a. Closure   1. Elements close together are grouped together.

   b. Proximity   2. Patterns are perceived in the most basic, direct manner possible.

   c. Similarity   3. Groupings are made in terms of complete figures.

   d. Simplicity   4. Elements similar in appearance are grouped together.

2. Processing that involves higher functions such as expectations and motivations is known as _____, whereas processing that recognizes the individual components of a stimulus is known as _____.

3. When a car passes you on the road and appears to shrink as it gets farther away, the phenomenon of _____ permits you to realize that the car is not in fact getting smaller.

4. _____ is the ability to view the world in three dimensions instead of two.

5. The brain makes use of a phenomenon known as _____, or the difference in the images the two eyes see, to give three dimensions to sight.

6. Match the monocular cues with their definitions.

   a. Relative size   1. Straight lines seem to join together as they become more distant.

   b. Linear perspective   2. An object changes position on the retina as the head moves.

   c. Motion parallax   3. If two objects are the same size, the one producing the smaller retinal image is farther away.

RETHINK

In what ways do painters represent three-dimensional scenes in two dimensions on a canvas? Do you think artists in non-Western cultures use the same or different principles to represent three-dimensionality? Why?

[KEY TERMS]

Gestalt laws of organization *p. 108*

Top-down processing *p. 109*

Bottom-up processing *p. 110*

Depth perception *p. 111*

Visual illusions *p. 113*

looking BACK

Psychology on the Web

1. Select one topic of personal interest to you that was mentioned in this set of modules (for instance, cochlear implants, visual illusions). Find one "serious" or scientific Web site and one "popular" or commercial Web site with information about the chosen topic. Compare the type, level, and reliability of the information that you find on each site. Write a summary of your findings.

2. Are there more gestalt laws of organization than the four we've considered (closure, proximity, similarity, and simplicity)? Find the answer to this question on the Web and write a summary of any additional gestalt laws you find.

the case of...
THE CAUTIOUS PILOT

Captain Kevin Mueller has been flying private and commercial aircraft for almost 30 years. His flight from Boston to Dallas on the night of November 4 was as routine as any other; Mueller and his copilot had run through their preflight routine in the darkness of the cockpit and, after a 20-minute delay, were cleared for takeoff. Halfway through the flight, Captain Mueller noticed something unusual out of the corner of his eye: a point of light that was initially very faint but growing brighter. It stood out against the backdrop of terrestrial light sources because it appeared to be much closer, and possibly moving. Knowing that no other aircraft were operating in the area, Mueller focused his attention on the mysterious light source, concerned only with whether it might pose a threat to the safety of his passengers and crew.

When at last Mueller still couldn't make out what the mysterious object was after observing it for several minutes, he decided to take no chances. He rapidly increased altitude to put more distance between his aircraft and the object, which eventually faded from view and did not return. A later investigation could make no determination of what Mueller saw, but concluded that he acted appropriately to protect his passengers.

1. Why would Captain Mueller and his copilot sit in darkness before taking off on a night flight?

2. Why would the mysterious object have first appeared to Mueller in his peripheral vision?

3. What cues might Captain Mueller have used to determine that the mysterious object was much closer to his aircraft than any light source on the ground? Why might it have been difficult to determine whether the object was actually moving?

4. Even though many of the passengers were awake and looking out their windows, only Captain Mueller and his copilot noticed anything amiss. Why might the passengers have failed to notice the object when it was so obvious to the pilots?

5. Several of the passengers did, however, notice when Captain Mueller changed altitude despite having no visual cues as a reference. Describe the sense that allowed these passengers to detect the aircraft's motion.

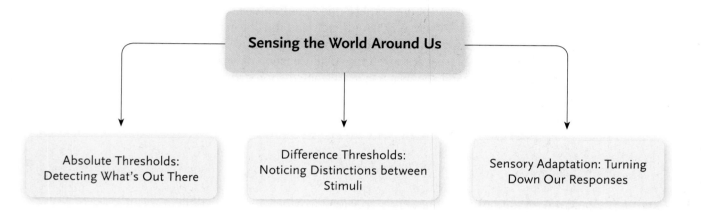

Sensing the World Around Us

Absolute Thresholds: Detecting What's Out There

Difference Thresholds: Noticing Distinctions between Stimuli

Sensory Adaptation: Turning Down Our Responses

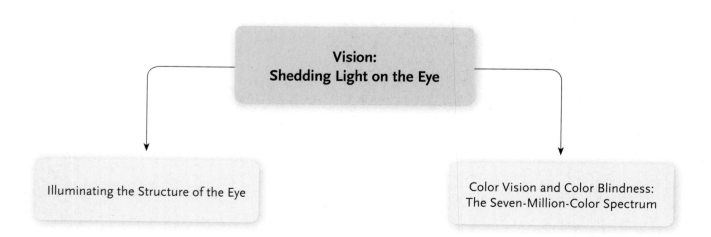

Vision: Shedding Light on the Eye

Illuminating the Structure of the Eye

Color Vision and Color Blindness: The Seven-Million-Color Spectrum

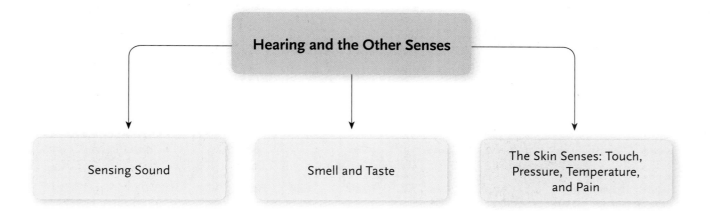

Hearing and the Other Senses

Sensing Sound

Smell and Taste

The Skin Senses: Touch, Pressure, Temperature, and Pain

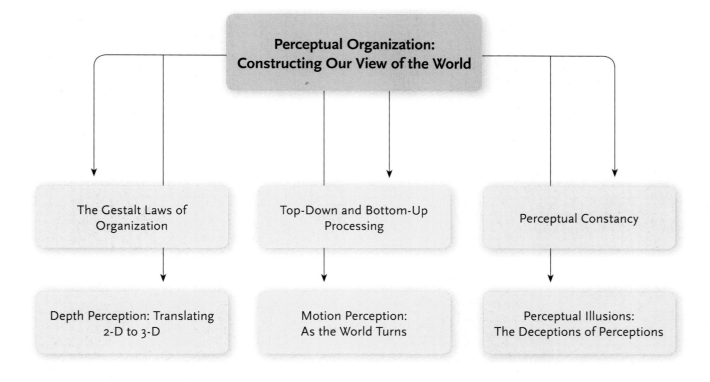

Perceptual Organization: Constructing Our View of the World

The Gestalt Laws of Organization

Top-Down and Bottom-Up Processing

Perceptual Constancy

Depth Perception: Translating 2-D to 3-D

Motion Perception: As the World Turns

Perceptual Illusions: The Deceptions of Perceptions

Nodding Off

Martha Yasso was tired all the time—so tired that whenever her 3-year-old son went down for a nap, she grabbed the chance to rest as well. But even with those precious extra minutes of sleep, she was still so exhausted by late afternoon that she could barely keep her eyes open. One day last fall, as her son played in the den of their New York home, Yasso's eyelids got heavier and heavier. Just before she nodded off completely, she felt her son's hands on her face. He was shouting, "Mama, Mama! Wake up!" That was the turning point. . . . She called her doctor, who referred her to the NYU Sleep Disorders Center. After a night in the sleep lab, with electrodes monitoring her brain waves, breathing and movements, Yasso finally understood what was behind her overwhelming fatigue. NYU pulmonologist Ana Krieger told Yasso that during the eight hours she thought she was asleep, she had actually awakened 245 times. "That number shocked me," Yasso says. "But it also explained a lot." (Kantrowitz, 2006, p. 51) ▪

looking AHEAD

Martha Yasso was suffering from a sleep disorder known as *sleep apnea,* which is characterized by constricted breathing during sleep that forces the sleeper to wake up momentarily—sometimes as many as hundreds of times each night. Fortunately, Martha was able to find rest with an electronic device that helps to keep her airway open while she sleeps.

For most of us, sleep occurs naturally. In this and the following modules we'll consider a range of topics about sleep and, more broadly, states of consciousness. **Consciousness** is the awareness of the sensations, thoughts, and feelings being experienced at a given moment. Unobservable to outsiders, consciousness is our subjective understanding of both the environment around us and our private internal world.

In *waking consciousness,* we are awake and aware of our thoughts, emotions, and perceptions. All other states of consciousness are considered *altered states of consciousness.* Among these, sleeping and dreaming occur naturally; drug use and hypnosis, in contrast, are methods of deliberately altering one's state of consciousness.

Because consciousness is so personal a phenomenon, psychologists were sometimes reluctant to study it. After all, who can say that your consciousness is similar to or, for that matter, different from anyone else's? Contemporary psychologists reject the view that the study of consciousness is unsuitable for the field of psychology. Instead, they argue that several approaches permit the scientific study of consciousness. For example, behavioral neuroscientists can measure brain-wave patterns under conditions of consciousness ranging from sleep to waking to hypnotic trances. And new understanding of the chemistry of drugs such as marijuana and alcohol has provided insights into the way they produce their pleasurable—as well as adverse—effects (Damasio, 2003; Mosher & Akins, 2007).

Whatever state of consciousness we are in—be it waking, sleeping, hypnotic, or drug induced—the complexities of consciousness are profound.

>> >>

Sleep and Dreams

Mike Trevino, 29, slept nine hours in nine days in his quest to win a 3,000-mile, cross-country bike race. For the first 38 hours and 646 miles, he skipped sleep entirely. Later he napped—with no dreams he can remember—for no more than 90 minutes a night. Soon he began to imagine that his support crew was part of a bomb plot. "It was almost like riding in a movie. I thought it was a complex dream, even though I was conscious," says Trevino, who finished second. (Springen, 2004, p. 47)

Trevino's case is unusual—in part because he was able to function with so little sleep for so long—and it raises a host of questions about sleep and dreams. Can we live without sleep? What is the meaning of dreams? More generally, what is sleep?

Although sleeping is a state that we all experience, there are still many unanswered questions about sleep that remain, along with a considerable number of myths. Test your knowledge of sleep and dreams by answering the questionnaire in Figure 1.

» LO1 The Stages of Sleep

Consciousness The awareness of the sensations, thoughts, and feelings being experienced at a given moment.

Most of us consider sleep a time of tranquility when we set aside the tensions of the day and spend the night in uneventful slumber. However, a closer look at sleep shows that a good deal of activity occurs throughout the night, and that what at first appears to be a unitary state is, in fact, quite diverse.

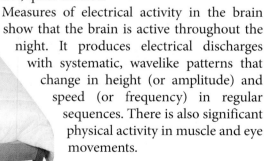

Measures of electrical activity in the brain show that the brain is active throughout the night. It produces electrical discharges with systematic, wavelike patterns that change in height (or amplitude) and speed (or frequency) in regular sequences. There is also significant physical activity in muscle and eye movements.

Q Sleep Quiz

Although sleeping is something we all do for a significant part of our lives, myths and misconceptions about the topic abound. To test your own knowledge of sleep and dreams, try answering the following questions before reading further.

1. Some people never dream. *True or false?*

2. Most dreams are caused by bodily sensations such as an upset stomach. *True or false?*

3. It has been proved that people need eight hours of sleep to maintain mental health. *True or false?*

4. When people do not recall their dreams, it is probably because they are secretly trying to forget them. *True or false?*

5. Depriving someone of sleep will invariably cause the individual to become mentally imbalanced. *True or false?*

6. If we lose some sleep we will eventually make up all the lost sleep the next night or another night. *True or false?*

7. No one has been able to go for more than 48 hours without sleep. *True or false?*

8. Everyone is able to sleep and breathe at the same time. *True or false?*

9. Sleep enables the brain to rest because little brain activity takes place during sleep. *True or false?*

10. Drugs have been proved to provide a long-term cure for sleeplessness. *True or false?*

Scoring: This is an easy set of questions to score, for every item is false. But don't lose any sleep if you missed them; they were chosen to represent the most common myths regarding sleep.

Stage 1 sleep The stage of transition between wakefulness and sleep, characterized by relatively rapid, low-amplitude brain waves.

Stage 2 sleep A sleep deeper than that of stage 1, characterized by a slower, more regular wave pattern, along with momentary interruptions of sleep spindles.

Stage 3 sleep A sleep characterized by slow brain waves, with greater peaks and valleys in the wave pattern than in stage 2 sleep.

psych2.0
WWW.MHHE.COM/PSYCHLIFE

Sleep Stages

People progress through a series of distinct stages of sleep during a night's rest—known as *stage 1* through *stage 4* and *REM sleep*—moving through the stages in cycles lasting about 90 minutes. Each of these sleep stages is associated with a unique pattern of brain waves, which you can see in Figure 2.

When people first go to sleep, they move from a waking state in which they are relaxed with their eyes closed into **stage 1 sleep,** which is characterized by relatively rapid, low-amplitude brain waves. This is actually a stage of transition between wakefulness and sleep and lasts only a few minutes. During stage 1, images sometimes appear, as if we were viewing still photos, although this is not true dreaming, which occurs later in the night.

As sleep becomes deeper, people enter **stage 2 sleep,** which is characterized by a slower, more regular wave pattern. However, there are also momentary interruptions of sharply pointed, spiky waves that are called, because of their configuration, *sleep spindles*. It becomes increasingly difficult to awaken a person from sleep as stage 2 progresses.

As people drift into **stage 3 sleep,** the brain waves become slower, with higher peaks and lower valleys in the wave pattern. By the time sleepers arrive

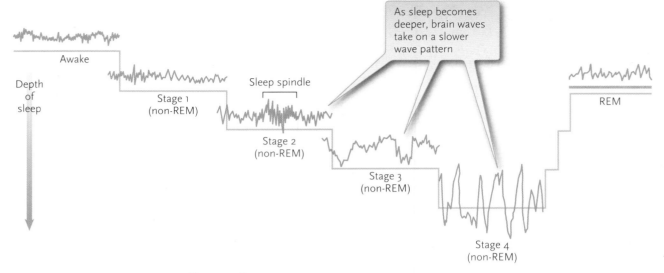

FIGURE 2   Brain-wave patterns (measured by an EEG apparatus) vary significantly during the different stages of sleep (Hobson, 2007). As sleep moves from stage 1 through stage 4, brain waves become slower.

Stage 4 sleep The deepest stage of sleep, during which we are least responsive to outside stimulation.

at **stage 4 sleep,** the pattern is even slower and more regular, and people are least responsive to outside stimulation.

As you can see in Figure 3, stage 4 sleep is most likely to occur during the early part of the night. In the first half of the night, sleep is dominated by

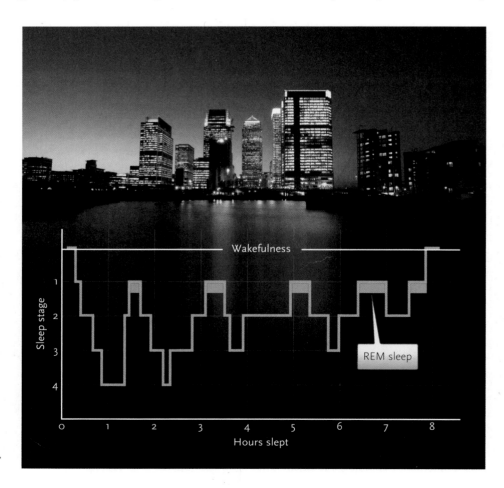

FIGURE 3   During the night, the typical sleeper passes through all four stages of sleep and several REM periods. *(Source: Hartmann, 1967.)*

stages 3 and 4. The second half is characterized by stages 1 and 2—as well as a fifth stage during which dreams occur.

» LO2 REM Sleep: The Paradox of Sleep

Several times a night, when sleepers have cycled back to a shallower state of sleep, something curious happens. Their heart rate increases and becomes irregular, their blood pressure rises, their breathing rate increases, and males—even male infants—have erections. Most characteristic of this period is the back-and-forth movement of their eyes, as if they were watching an action-filled movie. This period of sleep is called **rapid eye movement,** or **REM, sleep** and contrasts with stages 1 through 4, which are collectively labeled *non-REM* (or *NREM*) sleep. REM sleep occupies a little over 20 percent of adults' total sleeping time.

Paradoxically, while all this activity is occurring, the major muscles of the body appear to be paralyzed. In addition, and most important, REM sleep is usually accompanied by dreams, which—whether or not people remember them—are experienced by *everyone* during some part of the night. Although some dreaming occurs in non-REM stages of sleep, dreams are most likely to occur in the REM period, where they are the most vivid and easily remembered (Titone, 2002; Conduit, Crewther, & Coleman, 2004; Lu et al., 2006).

There is good reason to believe that REM sleep plays a critical role in everyday human functioning. People deprived of REM sleep—by being awakened every time they begin to display the physiological signs of that stage—show a *rebound effect* when allowed to rest undisturbed. With this rebound effect, REM-deprived sleepers spend significantly more time in REM sleep than they normally would.

Rapid eye movement (REM) sleep Sleep occupying 20 percent of an adult's sleep time, characterized by increased heart rate, blood pressure, and breathing rate; erections (in males); eye movements; and the experience of dreaming.

 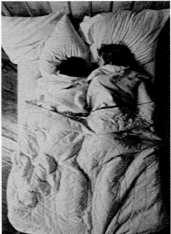 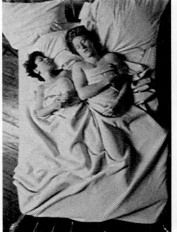 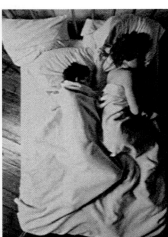

People progress through four distinct stages of sleep during a night's rest spread over cycles lasting about 90 minutes. REM sleep, which occupies only 20 percent of adults' sleeping time, occurs in stage 1 sleep. These photos, taken at different times of night, show the synchronized patterns of a couple accustomed to sleeping in the same bed.

» LO3 Why Do We Sleep, and How Much Sleep Is Necessary?

> *Sleep is a requirement for normal human functioning, although, surprisingly, we don't know exactly why.*

Sleep is a requirement for normal human functioning, although, surprisingly, we don't know exactly why. It is reasonable to expect that our bodies would require a tranquil "rest and relaxation" period to revitalize themselves, and experiments with rats show that total sleep deprivation results in death. But why?

Some researchers, using an evolutionary perspective, suggest that sleep permitted our ancestors to conserve energy at night, a time when food was relatively hard to come by. Others suggest that the reduced activity of the brain during non-REM sleep may give neurons in the brain a chance to repair themselves. Another hypothesis suggests that the onset of REM sleep stops the release of neurotransmitters called *monoamines,* and so permits receptor cells to get some necessary rest and to increase their sensitivity during periods of wakefulness. Still, these explanations remain speculative (Porkka-Heiskanen et al., 1997; Siegel, 2003; McNamara, 2004; Steiger, 2007).

Scientists have also been unable to establish just how much sleep is absolutely required. Most people today sleep between seven and eight hours each night, which is three hours a night *less* than people slept a hundred years ago. In addition, there is wide variability among individuals, with some people needing as little as three hours of sleep (see Figure 4). Sleep requirements also vary over the course of a lifetime: as they age, people generally need less and less sleep.

People who participate in sleep deprivation experiments, in which they are kept awake for stretches as long as 200 hours, show no lasting effects. It's no fun—they feel weary and irritable, can't concentrate, and show a loss of creativity, even after only minor deprivation. They also show a decline in logical reasoning ability. However, after being allowed to sleep normally, they bounce back quickly and are able to perform at predeprivation levels after just a few days (Dinges et al., 1997; Veasey et al., 2002; McClelland & Pilcher, 2007).

In short, as far as we know, most people suffer no permanent consequences of such temporary sleep deprivation. But—and this is an important but—a lack of sleep can make us feel edgy, slow our reaction time, and lower our performance on academic and physical tasks. In addition, we put ourselves, and others, at risk when we carry out routine activities, such

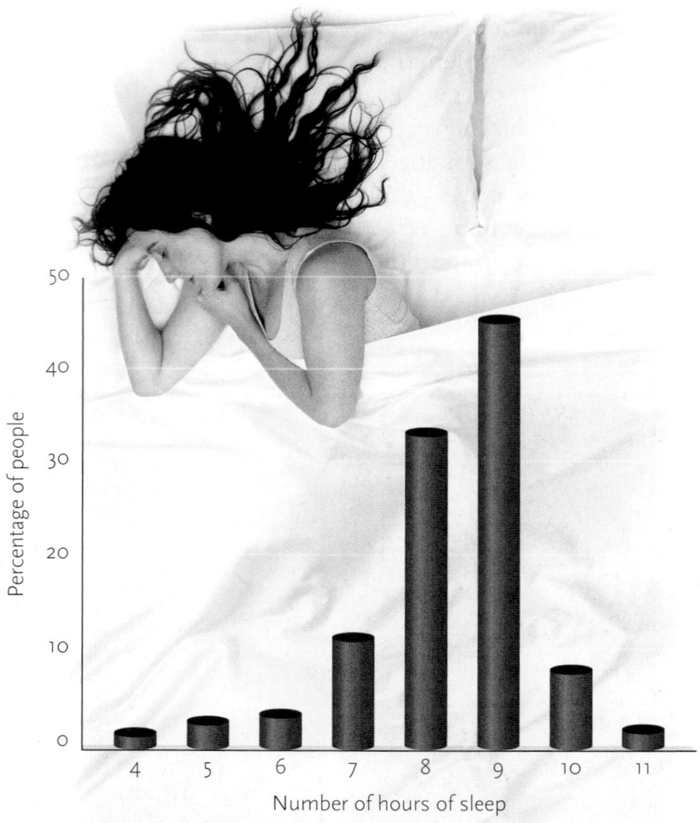

FIGURE 4 Although most people report sleeping between eight and nine hours per night, the amount varies a great deal (Borbely, 1986). Where would you place yourself on this graph, and why do you think you need more or less sleep than others?

as driving, when we're very sleepy (Stickgold, Winkelman, & Wehrwein, 2004; Philip et al., 2005; Anderson & Home, 2006).

» LO4 The Function and Meaning of Dreaming

The average person experiences 150,000 dreams by the age of 70. They typically encompass everyday events such as going to the supermarket, working at the office, and preparing a meal. Students dream about going to class; professors dream about lecturing. Dental patients dream of getting their teeth drilled; dentists dream of drilling the wrong tooth. The English have tea with the queen in their dreams; in the United States, people go to a bar with the president (Domhoff, 1996; Schredl & Piel, 2005; Taylor & Bryant, 2007). Figure 5 shows the most common themes found in people's dreams.

But what, if anything, do all these dreams mean? Whether dreams have a specific significance and function is a question that scientists have considered for many years, and they have developed the three alternative theories discussed next (and summarized in Figure 6).

Do Dreams Represent Unconscious Wish Fulfillment?

Sigmund Freud viewed dreams as a guide to the unconscious (Freud, 1900). In his **unconscious wish fulfillment theory,** he proposed that dreams represent unconscious wishes that dreamers desire to see fulfilled. However, because these wishes are threatening to the dreamer's conscious awareness,

> **Unconscious wish fulfillment theory** Sigmund Freud's theory that dreams represent unconscious wishes that dreamers desire to see fulfilled.

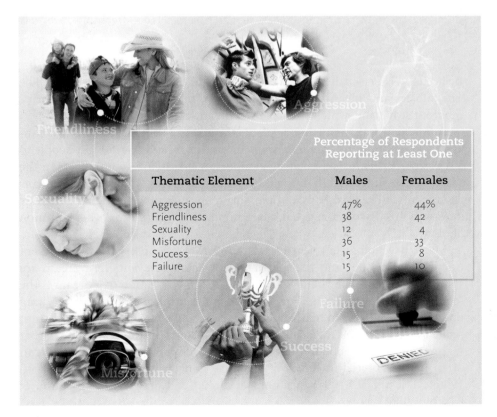

Thematic Element	Percentage of Respondents Reporting at Least One	
	Males	Females
Aggression	47%	44%
Friendliness	38	42
Sexuality	12	4
Misfortune	36	33
Success	15	8
Failure	15	10

FIGURE 5 Although dreams tend to be subjective to the person having them, there are common elements that frequently occur in everyone's dreams. Why do you think so many common dreams are unpleasant and so few are pleasant? Do you think this tells us anything about the function of dreams? *(Source: Domhoff & Schneider, 1999.)*

Theory	Basic Explanation	Meaning of Dreams	Is Meaning of Dream Disguised?
Unconscious wish fulfillment theory (Freud)	Dreams represent unconscious wishes the dreamer wants to fulfill	Latent content reveals unconscious wishes	Yes, by manifest content of dreams
Dreams-for-survival theory	Information relevant to daily survival is reconsidered and reprocessed	Clues to everyday concerns about survival	Not necessarily
Activation-synthesis theory	Dreams are the result of random activation of various memories, which are tied together in a logical story line	Dream scenario that is constructed is related to dreamer's concerns	Not necessarily

FIGURE 6   Three theories of dreams. Researchers have yet to agree on the fundamental meaning of dreams, and so several theories about dreaming have emerged.

STUDY ALERT

Use Figure 6 to learn the differences between the three main explanations of dreaming.

Latent content of dreams According to Freud, the "disguised" meanings of dreams, hidden by more obvious subjects.

Manifest content of dreams According to Freud, the apparent story line of dreams.

the actual wishes—called the **latent content of dreams**—are disguised. The true subject and meaning of a dream, then, may have little to do with its apparent story line, which Freud called the **manifest content of dreams.**

To Freud, it was important to pierce the armor of a dream's manifest content to understand its true meaning. To do this, Freud tried to get people to discuss their dreams, associating symbols in the dreams with events in the past. He also suggested that certain common symbols with universal meanings appear in dreams. For example, to Freud, dreams in which a person is flying symbolize a wish for sexual intercourse. (See Figure 7 for other common symbols.)

Many psychologists reject Freud's view that dreams typically represent unconscious wishes and that particular objects and events in a dream are symbolic. Instead, they believe that the direct, overt action of a dream is the focal point of its meaning. For example, a dream in which we are walking down a long hallway to take an exam for which we haven't studied does not relate to unconscious, unacceptable wishes. Instead, it simply may mean that we are concerned about an impending test. Even more complex dreams can often be interpreted in terms of everyday concerns and stress (Domhoff, 1996; Nikles et al., 1998; Picchioni et al., 2002; Cartwright, Agargum, & Kirkby, 2006).

Dreams-for-Survival Theory

According to the **dreams-for-survival theory,** dreams permit information that is critical for our daily survival to be reconsidered and reprocessed during sleep. Dreaming is seen as an inheritance from our animal ancestors, whose small brains were unable to sift sufficient information during waking hours. Consequently, dreaming provided a mechanism that permitted the processing of information 24 hours a day.

According to this theory, dreams represent concerns about our daily lives, illustrating our uncertainties, indecisions, ideas, and desires. Dreams are seen, then, as consistent with everyday living. Rather than being disguised wishes, as Freud suggested, they represent key concerns growing out of our daily experiences (Winson, 1990; Ross, 2006).

Research supports the dreams-for-survival theory, suggesting that certain dreams permit people to focus on and consolidate memories, particularly dreams that pertain to "how-to-do-it" memories related to motor skills. For example, rats seem to dream about mazes that they learned to run through during the day, at least according to the patterns of brain activity that appear while they are sleeping (Kenway & Wilson, 2001; Stickgold et al., 2001; Kuriyama, Stickgold, & Walker, 2004; C. Smith, 2006).

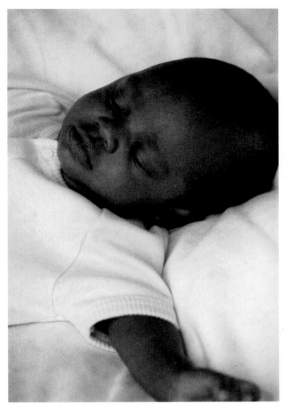

Sleep is important to general well being at any age. Do you feel you get enough sleep?

Activation-Synthesis Theory

According to psychiatrist J. Allan Hobson, who proposed **activation-synthesis theory,** the brain produces random electrical energy during REM sleep, possibly as a result of changes in the production of particular neurotransmitters. This electrical energy randomly stimulates memories lodged in various portions of the brain. Because we have a need to make sense of our world even while asleep, the brain takes these chaotic memories and weaves them into a logical story line, filling in the gaps to produce a rational scenario (Porte & Hobson, 1996; Hobson, 2005).

However, Hobson does not entirely reject the view that dreams reflect unconscious wishes. He suggests that the particular scenario a dreamer produces is not random but instead is a clue to the dreamer's fears, emotions, and concerns. Hence, what starts out as a random process culminates in something meaningful.

Dreams-for-survival theory The theory suggesting that dreams permit information that is critical for our daily survival to be reconsidered and reprocessed during sleep.

Activation-synthesis theory J. Allan Hobson's theory that the brain produces random electrical energy during REM sleep that stimulates memories lodged in various portions of the brain.

Symbol (Manifest Content of Dream)	Interpretation (Latent Content)
Climbing up a stairway, crossing a bridge, riding an elevator, flying in an airplane, walking down a long hallway, entering a room, train traveling through a tunnel	Sexual intercourse
Apples, peaches, grapefruits	Breasts
Bullets, fire, snakes, sticks, umbrellas, guns, hoses, knives	Male sex organs
Ovens, boxes, tunnels, closets, caves, bottles, ships	Female sex organs

FIGURE 7 According to Freud, dreams contain common symbols with universal meanings.

» LO5 Sleep Disturbances: Slumbering Problems

Some people are simply unable to fall asleep easily, or they go to sleep readily but wake up frequently during the night.

At one time or another, almost all of us have difficulty sleeping—a condition known as *insomnia*. It could be due to a particular situation, such as the breakup of a relationship, concern about a test score, or the loss of a job. Some cases of insomnia, however, have no obvious cause. Some people are simply unable to fall asleep easily, or they go to sleep readily but wake up frequently during the night. Insomnia is a problem that afflicts as many as one-third of all people (American Insomnia Association, 2005; Bains, 2006; Cooke & Ancoli-Israel, 2006).

Other sleep problems are less common than insomnia, although they are still widespread. For instance, some 20 million people suffer from sleep apnea, the disorder from which the mother in the chapter opening story suffered. *Sleep apnea* is a condition in which a person has difficulty breathing while sleeping. The result is disturbed, fitful sleep, as the person is constantly reawakened when the lack of oxygen becomes great enough to trigger a waking response. Some people with apnea wake as many as 500 times during the course of a night, although they may not even be aware that they have wakened. Not surprisingly, such disturbed sleep results in extreme fatigue the next day. Sleep apnea also may play a role in *sudden infant death syndrome (SIDS),* a mysterious killer of seemingly normal infants who die while sleeping (Rambaud & Guilleminault, 2004; Gami et al., 2005; Aloia, Smith, & Arnedt, 2007).

From the perspective of . . .

A LAW ENFORCEMENT OFFICER What impact would an irregular sleep schedule have on your job performance? What would you do to ensure you were getting enough rest?

Night terrors are sudden awakenings from non-REM sleep that are accompanied by extreme fear, panic, and strong physiological arousal. Usually occurring in stage 4 sleep, night terrors may be so frightening that a sleeper awakens with a shriek. Although night terrors initially produce great agitation, victims usually can get back to sleep fairly quickly. They occur most frequently in children between the ages of 3 and 8 (Lowe, Humphreys, & Williams, 2007).

Narcolepsy is uncontrollable sleeping that occurs for short periods while a person is awake. No matter what the activity—holding a heated conversation, exercising, or driving—a narcoleptic will suddenly fall asleep. People with narcolepsy go directly from wakefulness to REM sleep, skipping the other stages.

The causes of narcolepsy are not known, although there could be a genetic component because narcolepsy runs in families (Mahmood & Black, 2005; Ervik et al., 2006).

We know relatively little about sleeptalking and sleepwalking, two sleep disturbances that are usually harmless. Both occur during stage 4 sleep and are more common in children than in adults. Sleeptalkers and sleepwalkers usually have a vague consciousness of the world around them, and a sleepwalker may be able to walk with agility around obstructions in a crowded room. Unless a sleepwalker wanders into a dangerous environment, sleepwalking typically poses little risk (Guilleminault et al., 2005; Lee-Chiong, 2006).

» LO6 Circadian Rhythms: Life Cycles

The fact that we cycle back and forth between wakefulness and sleep is one example of the body's circadian rhythms. **Circadian rhythms** (from the Latin *circa diem,* or "around the day") are biological processes that occur regularly on approximately a 24-hour cycle. Sleeping and waking, for instance, occur naturally to the beat of an internal pacemaker that works on a cycle of about 24 hours. Several other bodily functions, such as body temperature, hormone production, and blood pressure, also follow circadian rhythms (Saper et al., 2005; Beersma & Gordijn, 2007; Blatter & Cajochen, 2007). Circadian cycles are complex, and they involve a variety of behaviors (see Figure 8).

Circadian rhythms Biological processes that occur regularly on approximately a 24-hour cycle.

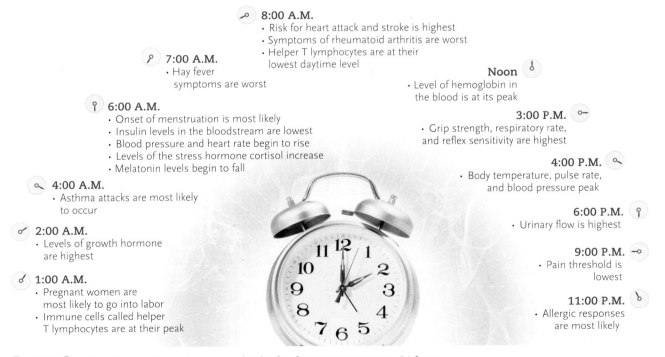

8:00 A.M.
• Risk for heart attack and stroke is highest
• Symptoms of rheumatoid arthritis are worst
• Helper T lymphocytes are at their lowest daytime level

7:00 A.M.
• Hay fever symptoms are worst

Noon
• Level of hemoglobin in the blood is at its peak

6:00 A.M.
• Onset of menstruation is most likely
• Insulin levels in the bloodstream are lowest
• Blood pressure and heart rate begin to rise
• Levels of the stress hormone cortisol increase
• Melatonin levels begin to fall

3:00 P.M.
• Grip strength, respiratory rate, and reflex sensitivity are highest

4:00 P.M.
• Body temperature, pulse rate, and blood pressure peak

4:00 A.M.
• Asthma attacks are most likely to occur

6:00 P.M.
• Urinary flow is highest

2:00 A.M.
• Levels of growth hormone are highest

9:00 P.M.
• Pain threshold is lowest

1:00 A.M.
• Pregnant women are most likely to go into labor
• Immune cells called helper T lymphocytes are at their peak

11:00 P.M.
• Allergic responses are most likely

FIGURE 8 Day times, night times: regular body changes over every 24-hour period. Over the course of the day, our circadian rhythms produce a wide variety of effects. *(Source: Young, 2000.)*

becoming an *informed consumer*
OF PSYCHOLOGY

Sleeping Better

Do you have trouble sleeping? You're not alone—70 million people in the United States have sleep problems. For those of us who spend hours tossing and turning in bed, psychologists studying sleep disturbances have a number of suggestions for overcoming insomnia (Edinger et al., 2001; Benca, 2005; Finley & Cowley, 2005). Here are some ideas.

- *Exercise during the day (at least six hours before bedtime) and avoid naps.* Not surprisingly, it helps to be tired before going to sleep! Moreover, learning systematic relaxation techniques and biofeedback can help you unwind from the day's stresses and tensions.

- *Choose a regular bedtime and stick to it.* Adhering to a habitual schedule helps your internal timing mechanisms regulate your body more effectively.

- *Avoid drinks with caffeine after lunch.* The effects of beverages such as coffee, tea, and some soft drinks can linger for as long as 8 to 12 hours after they are consumed.

- *Drink a glass of warm milk at bedtime.* Your grandparents were right when they dispensed this advice: milk contains the chemical tryptophan, which helps people fall asleep.

- *Avoid sleeping pills.* Even though 25 percent of U.S. adults report having taken medication for sleep in the previous year, in the long run sleep medications can do more harm than good because they disrupt the normal sleep cycle.

- *Try* not *to sleep.* This approach works because people often have difficulty falling asleep because they are trying so hard. A better strategy is to go to bed only when you feel tired. If you don't get to sleep within 10 minutes, leave the bedroom and do something else, returning to bed only when you feel sleepy. Continue this process all night if necessary. But get up at your usual hour in the morning, and don't take any naps during the day. After three or four weeks, most people become conditioned to associate their beds with sleep—and fall asleep rapidly at night (Sloan et al., 1993; Ubell, 1993; Smith, 2001).

For long-term problems with sleep, you might consider visiting a sleep disorders center. For information on accredited clinics, consult the American Academy of Sleep Medicine at www.aasmnet.org.

RECAP

- Consciousness is a person's awareness of the sensations, thoughts, and feelings at a given moment. Waking consciousness can vary from more active to more passive states. (p. 123)
- Altered states of consciousness include naturally occurring sleep and dreaming, as well as hypnotic and drug-induced states. (p. 123)

Summarize the stages of sleep.

- Using the electroencephalogram, or EEG, to study sleep, scientists have found that the brain is active throughout the night, and that sleep proceeds through a series of stages identified by unique patterns of brain waves. (p. 124)

Explain REM sleep.

- REM (rapid eye movement) sleep is characterized by an increase in heart rate, a rise in blood pressure, an increase in the rate of breathing, and, in males, erections. Dreams occur during this stage. (p. 127)

Explain why we sleep.

- Sleep is a requirement for normal functioning, although it is not yet known why it is necessary. (p. 128)
- There is great variability regarding how much people sleep. (p. 128)

Differentiate the explanations of dreaming.

- Freud suggests dreams have both a manifest content (the story line) and a latent content (the true meaning). (p. 130)

- The dreams-for-survival theory suggests that information relevant to daily survival is reconsidered and reprocessed in dreams. (p. 131)
- The activation-synthesis theory proposes that dreams are a result of random electrical energy that stimulates different memories, which then are woven into a coherent story line. (p. 131)

State the impact of sleep disturbances.

- Insomnia is a sleep disorder characterized by difficulty sleeping. Sleep apnea is a condition in which people have difficulty sleeping and breathing at the same time. People with narcolepsy have an uncontrollable urge to sleep. Sleepwalking and sleeptalking are relatively harmless. (p. 132)
- Psychologists and sleep researchers advise people with insomnia to increase exercise during the day, avoid caffeine and sleeping pills, drink a glass of warm milk before bedtime, and try to avoid going to sleep. (p. 134)

Explain circadian rhythms.

- Circadian rhythms are biological processes that occur regularly on approximately a 24-hour cycle. (p. 133)
- Sleep, wakefulness, body temperature, and other bodily functions follow circadian rhythms. (p. 133)

EVALUATE

1. _____ is the term used to describe our understanding of the world external to us, as well as our own internal world.

2. A great deal of neural activity goes on during sleep. True or false?

3. Dreams occur in _____ sleep.

4. _____ _____ are internal bodily processes that occur on a daily cycle.

5. Freud's theory of unconscious _____ _____ states that the actual wishes an individual expresses in dreams are disguised because they are threatening to the person's conscious awareness.

6. Match the theory of dreaming with its definition.

   1. Activation-synthesis theory
   2. Dreams-for-survival theory
   3. Unconscious theory wish fulfillment

   a. Dreams permit important information to be reprocessed during sleep.
   b. The manifest content of dreams disguises the latent content of the dreams.
   c. Electrical energy stimulates random memories, which are woven together to produce dreams.

RETHINK

Suppose that a new "miracle pill" will allow a person to function with only one hour of sleep per night. However, because a night's sleep is so short, a person who takes the pill will never dream again. Knowing what you do about the functions of sleep and dreaming, what would be some advantages and drawbacks of such a pill from a personal standpoint? Would you take such a pill?

Answers to Evaluate Questions 1. consciousness; 2. true; 3. REM; 4. circadian rhythms; 5. wish fulfillment; 6. 1-c, 2-a, 3-b

[KEY TERMS]

Consciousness *p. 124*

Stage 1 sleep *p. 125*

Stage 2 sleep *p. 125*

Stage 3 sleep *p. 125*

Stage 4 sleep *p. 126*

Rapid eye movement (REM) sleep *p. 127*

Unconscious wish fulfillment theory *p. 129*

Latent content of dreams *p. 130*

Manifest content of dreams *p. 130*

Dreams-for-survival theory *p. 131*

Activation-synthesis theory *p. 131*

Circadian rhythms *p. 133*

Hypnosis and Meditation

You are feeling relaxed and drowsy. You are getting sleepier. Your body is becoming limp. Your eyelids are feeling heavier. Your eyes are closing; you can't keep them open anymore. You are totally relaxed. Now, place your hands above your head. But you will find they are getting heavier and heavier—so heavy you can barely keep them up. In fact, although you are straining as hard as you can, you will be unable to hold them up any longer.

An observer watching the above scene would notice a curious phenomenon occurring. Many of the people listening to the voice are dropping their arms to their sides. The reason for this strange behavior? Those people have been hypnotized.

» LO1 Hypnosis: A Trance-Forming Experience?

People under **hypnosis** are in a trancelike state of heightened susceptibility to the suggestions of others. In some respects, it appears that they are asleep. Yet other aspects of their behavior contradict this notion, for people are attentive to the hypnotist's suggestions and may carry out bizarre or silly suggestions.

Despite their compliance when hypnotized, people do not lose all will of their own. They will not perform antisocial behaviors, and they will not carry out self-destructive acts. People will not reveal hidden truths about themselves, and they are capable of lying. Moreover, people cannot be hypnotized against their will—despite popular misconceptions (Gwynn & Spanos, 1996; Raz, 2007).

There are wide variations in people's susceptibility to hypnosis. About 5 to 20 percent of the population cannot be hypnotized at all, and some 15 percent are very easily hypnotized. Most people fall somewhere in between. Moreover, the ease with which a person is hypnotized is related to a number of other characteristics. People who are hypnotized readily are also easily absorbed while reading books or listening to music, becoming unaware of what is happening around them, and they often spend an unusual amount of time daydreaming. In sum, then, they show a high ability to concentrate and to become completely absorbed in what they are doing (Kirsch & Braffman, 2001; Rubichi et al., 2005; Benham, Woody, & Wilson, 2006).

> **Hypnosis** A trancelike state of heightened susceptibility to the suggestions of others.

psych2.0
WWW.MHHE.COM/PSYCHLIFE

Hypnosis

Despite common misconceptions, people cannot be hypnotized against their will, nor do they lose all will of their own. Why, then, do people sometimes behave so unusually when asked to by a hypnotist?

A Different State of Consciousness?

The question of whether hypnosis is a state of consciousness that is qualitatively different from normal waking consciousness is controversial. Some psychologists believe that hypnosis represents a state of consciousness that differs significantly from other states. In this view, the high suggestibility, increased ability to recall and construct images, and acceptance of suggestions that clearly contradict reality suggest it is a different state. Moreover, changes in electrical activity in the brain are associated with hypnosis, supporting the position that hypnosis is a state of consciousness different from normal waking (Hilgard, 1992; Kallio & Revonsuo, 2003; Fingelkurts, Fingelkurts, & Kallio, 2007).

STUDY ALERT

The question of whether hypnosis represents a different state of consciousness or is similar to normal waking consciousness is a key issue.

On the other side of the controversy are psychologists who reject the notion that hypnosis is a state significantly different from normal waking consciousness. They argue that altered brain-wave patterns are not sufficient to demonstrate a qualitative difference because no other specific physiological changes occur when people are in trances. Furthermore, little support exists for the contention that adults can recall memories of childhood events accurately while hypnotized. That lack of evidence suggests that there is nothing qualitatively special about the hypnotic trance (Lynn et al., 2003; Lynn, Fassler, & Knox, 2005; Hongchun & Ming, 2006).

There is increasing agreement that the controversy over the nature of hypnosis has led to extreme positions on both sides of the issue. More recent approaches suggest that the hypnotic state may best be viewed as lying along a continuum in which hypnosis is neither a totally different state of consciousness nor totally similar to normal waking consciousness (Lynn et al., 2000; Kihlstrom, 2005b; Jamieson, 2007).

From the perspective of . . .

A RETAIL OR RESTAURANT SUPERVISOR Would you allow (or even encourage) employees to engage in meditation during the workday? Why or why not?

» LO2 Meditation: Regulating Our Own State of Consciousness

When traditional practitioners of the ancient Eastern religion of Zen Buddhism want to achieve greater spiritual insight, they turn to a technique that has been used for centuries to alter their state of consciousness. This technique is called meditation.

Meditation is a learned technique for refocusing attention that brings about an altered state of consciousness. Meditation typically consists of the repetition of a *mantra*—a sound, word, or syllable—over and over. In other forms of meditation, the focus is on a picture, flame, or specific part of the body. Regardless of the nature of the particular initial stimulus, the key to the procedure is concentrating on it so thoroughly that the meditator becomes unaware of any outside stimulation and reaches a different state of consciousness.

Meditation A learned technique for refocusing attention that brings about an altered state of consciousness.

After meditation, people report feeling thoroughly relaxed. They sometimes relate that they have gained new insights into themselves and the problems they are facing. The long-term practice of meditation may even improve health because of the biological changes it produces. For example, during meditation, oxygen usage decreases, heart rate and blood pressure decline, and brain-wave patterns change (Arambula et al., 2001; Barnes et al., 2004; Lee, Ahn, & Lee, 2007; see Figure 1).

Anyone can meditate by following a few simple procedures. The fundamentals include sitting in a quiet room with the eyes closed, breathing deeply and rhythmically, and repeating a word or sound—such as the word *one*—over and over. Practiced twice a day for 20 minutes, the technique is effective in bringing about relaxation (Benson et al., 1994; Aftanas & Golosheykin, 2005).

Meditation is a means of altering consciousness that is practiced in many different cultures, though it can take different forms and serve different purposes across cultures. In fact, one impetus for the study of consciousness is the realization that people in many different cultures routinely seek ways to alter their states of consciousness (Walsh & Shapiro, 2006).

STUDY ALERT

Remember that although there are several alternate techniques used in meditation, they are all designed to bring about an altered state of consciousness in which attention is refocused.

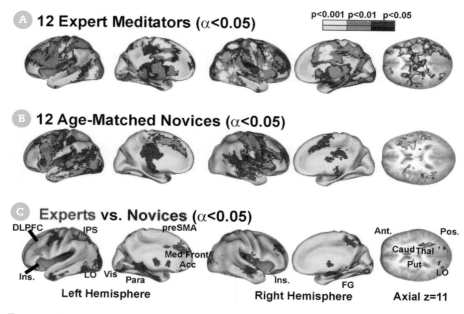

A 12 Expert Meditators (α<0.05)

p<0.001 p<0.01 p<0.05

B 12 Age-Matched Novices (α<0.05)

C Experts vs. Novices (α<0.05)

DLPFC IPS preSMA Ant. Pos.

Med Front CaudThal
Acc Put

Ins. LO Vis Ins. LO
Para FG

Left Hemisphere Right Hemisphere Axial z=11

FIGURE 1   Neural correlates of attentional expertise in long-term mediation practitioners. These fMRI brain scans show the regions of brain activation in (A) expert meditators who had between 10,000 and 54,000 hours of practice in meditating, (B) novice meditators who had no experience mediating, and (C) the comparison between the two. In (C), red hues show greater activation in the experts, and blue hues show greater activation for the novices.

EXPLORING diversity

Cross-Cultural Routes to Altered States of Consciousness

A group of Native American Sioux men sit naked in a steaming sweat lodge as a medicine man throws water on sizzling rocks to send billows of scalding steam into the air.

Aztec priests smear themselves with a mixture of crushed poisonous herbs, hairy black worms, scorpions, and lizards. Sometimes they drink the potion.

During the sixteenth century, a devout Hasidic Jew lies across the tombstone of a celebrated scholar. As he murmurs the name of God repeatedly, he seeks to be possessed by the soul of the dead wise man's spirit. If successful, he will attain a mystical state, and the deceased's words will flow out of his mouth.

Each of these rituals has a common goal: suspension from the bonds of everyday awareness and access to an altered state of consciousness. Although they may seem exotic from the vantage point of many Western cultures, these rituals represent an apparently universal effort to alter consciousness (Fine, 1994; Bartocci, 2004; Irwin, 2006).

Some scholars suggest that the quest to alter consciousness represents a basic human desire (Siegel, 1989). Whether or not one accepts such an extreme view, it is clear that variations in states of consciousness share some basic characteristics across a variety of cultures. One is an alteration in thinking, which may become shallow, illogical, or otherwise different from normal. In addition, people's sense of time can become disturbed, and their perceptions of the physical world and of themselves may change. They may lose self-control, doing things that they would never otherwise do. Finally, they may feel a sense of *ineffability*—the inability to understand an experience rationally or describe it in words (Martindale, 1981; Finkler, 2004; Travis, 2006).

RECAP

Define hypnosis.

- Hypnosis produces a state of heightened susceptibility to the suggestions of the hypnotist. Under hypnosis, significant behavioral changes occur, including increased concentration and suggestibility, heightened ability to recall and construct images, lack of initiative, and acceptance of suggestions that clearly contradict reality. (p. 137)

Describe the effects of meditation.

- Meditation is a learned technique for refocusing attention that brings about an altered state of consciousness. (p. 139)
- Different cultures have developed their own unique ways to alter states of consciousness. (p. 140)

EVALUATE

1. _____ is a state of heightened susceptibility to the suggestions of others.
2. A friend tells you, "I once heard of a person who was murdered by being hypnotized and then told to jump from the Golden Gate Bridge!" Could such a thing have happened? Why or why not?
3. _____ is a learned technique for refocusing attention to bring about an altered state of consciousness.
4. Leslie repeats a unique sound, known as a _____, when she engages in meditation.

RETHINK

Why do you think people in almost every culture use psychoactive drugs and search for altered states of consciousness?

Answers to Evaluate Questions 1. hypnosis; 2. no; people who are hypnotized cannot be made to perform self-destructive acts; 3. meditation; 4. mantra

[KEY TERMS]

Hypnosis *p. 137*

Meditation *p. 139*

Drug Use
The Highs and Lows of Consciousness

LEARNING OUTCOMES

14.1 Explain the effects of stimulants.

14.2 Explain the effects of depressants.

14.3 Explain the effects of narcotics.

14.4 Explain the effects of hallucinogens.

Drugs of one sort or another are a part of almost everyone's life. From infancy on, most people take vitamins, aspirin, cold-relief medicine, and the like, and surveys find that 80 percent of adults in the United States have taken an over-the-counter pain reliever in the last six months. However, these drugs rarely produce an altered state of consciousness (Dortch, 1996).

In contrast, some substances, known as psychoactive drugs, lead to an altered state of consciousness. **Psychoactive drugs** influence a person's emotions, perceptions, and behavior. Yet even this category of drugs is common in most of our lives. If you have ever had a cup of coffee or sipped a beer, you have taken a psychoactive drug. A large number of individuals have used more potent—and dangerous—psychoactive drugs than coffee and beer (see Figure 1);

Psychoactive drugs Drugs that influence a person's emotions, perceptions, and behavior.

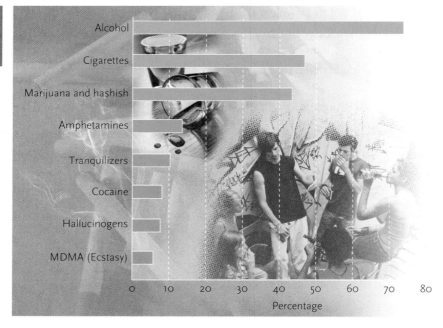

FIGURE 1   How many teenagers use drugs? The results of the most recent comprehensive survey of 14,000 high school seniors across the United States show the percentage of respondents who have used various substances for nonmedical purposes at least once (Johnston et al., 2007). Can you think of any reasons why teenagers—as opposed to older people—might be particularly likely to use drugs?

for instance, surveys find that 41 percent of high school seniors have used an illegal drug in the last year. In addition, 30 percent report having been drunk on alcohol. The figures for the adult population are even higher (Johnston et al., 2007).

Of course, drugs vary widely in the effects they have on users, in part because they affect the nervous system in very different ways. Some drugs alter the limbic system, and others affect the operation of specific neurotransmitters across the synapses of neurons. For example, some drugs block or enhance the release of neurotransmitters, others block the receipt or the removal of a neurotransmitter, and still others mimic the effects of a particular neurotransmitter (see Figure 2).

The most dangerous drugs are addictive. **Addictive drugs** produce a biological or psychological dependence in the user, and withdrawal from them leads to a craving for the drug that, in some cases, may be nearly irresistible. In *biologically based* addictions, the body becomes so accustomed to functioning in the presence of a drug that it cannot function without it. *Psychologically based* addictions are those in which people believe that they need the drug to respond to the stresses of daily living. Although we generally associate addiction with drugs such as heroin, everyday sorts of drugs, such as caffeine (found in coffee) and nicotine (found in cigarettes), have addictive aspects as well (Li, Volkow, & Baler, 2007).

Why do people take drugs in the first place? There are many reasons, ranging from the perceived pleasure of the experience itself, to the escape that a drug-induced high affords from the everyday pressures of life, to an attempt to achieve a religious or spiritual state. In some cases, the motive is simply the thrill of trying something new. Finally, the sense of helplessness

With drug use in teens on the rise, what are some preventative measures parents can use?

Addictive drugs Drugs that produce a biological or psychological dependence in the user so that withdrawal from them leads to a craving for the drug that, in some cases, may be nearly irresistible.

STUDY ALERT

Use Figure 2 to learn the different ways that drugs produce their effects on a biological level.

psych2.0
WWW.MHHE.COM/PSYCHLIFE

Drug Effects

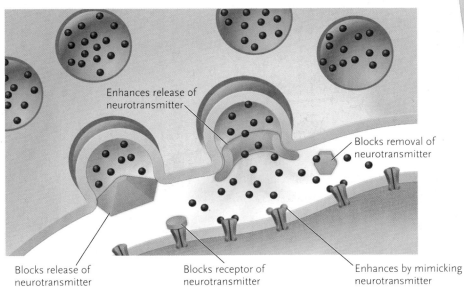

Enhances release of neurotransmitter

Blocks removal of neurotransmitter

Blocks release of neurotransmitter

Blocks receptor of neurotransmitter

Enhances by mimicking neurotransmitter

FIGURE 2 Different drugs affect different parts of the nervous system and brain and each drug functions in one of these specific ways.

experienced by unemployed individuals trapped in lives of poverty may lead them to try drugs as a way of escaping from the bleakness of their lives. Regardless of the forces that lead a person to begin using drugs, drug addiction is among the most difficult of all behaviors to modify, even with extensive treatment (Lemonick, 2000; Mosher & Akins, 2007). There is therefore little disagreement that the best hope for dealing with the overall societal problem of substance abuse is to prevent people from becoming involved with drugs in the first place.

From the perspective of . . .

A Co-worker How could you determine whether your co-worker was addicted to drugs or alcohol? What steps would you take to help him or her? As an employee, what are the limits to which you could get involved?

» LO1 Stimulants: Drug Highs

Stimulants Drugs that have an arousal effect on the central nervous system, causing a rise in heart rate, blood pressure, and muscular tension.

Does your day not start until you've had your morning cup of coffee? *Caffeine* is one of a number of **stimulants,** drugs whose effect on the central nervous system causes a rise in heart rate, blood pressure, and muscular tension. Caffeine is present in tea, soft drinks, and chocolate as well as coffee (see Figure 3).

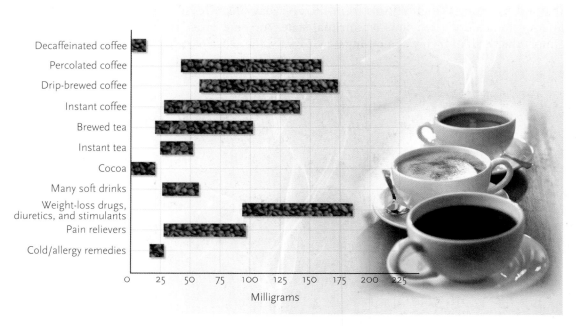

Figure 3 How much caffeine do you consume? This chart shows the range of caffeine found in common foods and drinks (Blakeslee, 1991). The average person in the United States consumes about 200 milligrams of caffeine each day.

Caffeine produces several reactions. The major behavioral effects are an increase in attentiveness and a decrease in reaction time. Caffeine can also bring about an improvement in mood, most likely by mimicking the effects of a natural brain chemical, adenosine. Too much caffeine, however, can result in nervousness and insomnia. People can build up a biological dependence on the drug. Regular users who suddenly stop drinking coffee may experience headaches or depression. Many people who drink large amounts of coffee on weekdays have headaches on weekends because of the sudden drop in the amount of caffeine they are consuming (Juliano & Griffiths, 2004; Satel, 2006; Kendler, Myers, & Gardner, 2006).

Nicotine, found in cigarettes, is another common stimulant. The soothing effects of nicotine help explain why cigarette smoking is addictive. Smokers develop a dependence on nicotine, and those who suddenly stop smoking develop strong cravings for the drug. This is not surprising: nicotine activates neural mechanisms similar to those activated by cocaine, which, as we see next, is also highly addictive (Collins & Izenwasser, 2004; Haberstick, Timberlake, & Ehringer, 2007).

We are not alone in our consumption of coffee. This Starbucks, located in Bangkok, Thailand, indicates that the desire for caffeine may be universal. Why do you think a company like Starbucks can be successful in so many countries and cultures?

Amphetamines

Amphetamines are strong stimulants, such as Dexedrine and Benzedrine, popularly known as speed. In small quantities, amphetamines—which stimulate the central nervous system—bring about a sense of energy and alertness, talkativeness, heightened confidence, and a mood "high." They increase concentration and reduce fatigue. Amphetamines also cause a loss of appetite, increased anxiety, and irritability. When taken over long periods of time, amphetamines can cause feelings of being persecuted by others, as well as a general sense of suspiciousness. People taking amphetamines may lose interest in sex. If taken in too large a quantity, amphetamines overstimulate the central nervous system to such an extent that convulsions and death can occur (Carhart-Harris, 2007).

Regular users who suddenly stop drinking coffee may experience headaches or depression.

Methamphetamine is a white, crystalline drug that U.S. police now say is the most dangerous street drug. "Meth" is highly addictive and relatively cheap, and it produces a strong, lingering high. It has made addicts of people across the social spectrum, ranging from soccer moms to urban professionals to poverty-stricken inner-city residents. After becoming addicted, users take it more and more frequently and in increasing doses. Long-term use of the drug can lead to brain damage (Thompson et al., 2004; Brecht et al., 2008).

Cocaine

Although its use has declined over the last decade, the stimulant *cocaine* and its derivative, *crack,* still represent a serious concern. Cocaine is inhaled or "snorted" through the nose, smoked, or injected directly into the bloodstream. It is rapidly absorbed into the body and takes effect almost immediately.

Drugs	Street Name	Effects	Withdrawal Symptoms	Adverse Overdose Reactions
Stimulants				
Cocaine	Coke, blow, snow, lady, crack	Increased confidence, mood elevation, sense of energy and alertness, decreased appetite, anxiety, irritability, insomnia, transient drowsiness, delayed orgasm	Apathy, general fatigue, prolonged sleep, depression, disorientation, suicidal thoughts, agitated motor activity, irritability, bizarre dreams	Elevated blood pressure, increase in body temperature, face picking, suspiciousness, bizarre and repetitious behavior, vivid hallucinations, convulsions, possible death
Amphetamines				
Benzedrine	Speed			
Dexedrine	Speed			
Depressants				
Alcohol	Booze	Anxiety reduction, impulsiveness, dramatic mood swings, bizarre thoughts, suicidal behavior, slurred speech, disorientation, slowed mental and physical functioning, limited attention span	Weakness, restlessness, nausea and vomiting, headaches, nightmares, irritability, depression, acute anxiety, hallucinations, seizures, possible death	Confusion, decreased response to pain, shallow respiration, dilated pupils, weak and rapid pulse, coma, possible death
Barbiturates				
Nembutal	Yellowjackets, yellows			
Seconal	Reds			
Phenobarbital				
Rohypnol	Roofies, rope, "date-rape drug"	Muscle relaxation, amnesia, sleep	Seizures	Seizures, coma, incapacitation, inability to resist sexual assault
Narcotics				
Heroin	H, hombre, junk, smack, dope, crap, horse	Anxiety and pain reduction, apathy, difficulty in concentration, slowed speech, decreased physical activity, drooling, itching, euphoria, nausea	Anxiety, vomiting, sneezing, diarrhea, lower back pain, watery eyes, runny nose, yawning, irritability, tremors, panic, chills and sweating, cramps	Depressed levels of consciousness, low blood pressure, rapid heart rate, shallow breathing, convulsions, coma, possible death
Morphine	Drugstore dope, cube, first line, mud			
Hallucinogens				
Cannabis	Bhang, kif, ganja, dope, grass, pot, hemp, joint, weed, bone, Mary Jane, reefer	Euphoria, relaxed inhibitions, increased appetite, disoriented behavior	Hyperactivity, insomnia, decreased appetite, anxiety	Severe reactions rare but include panic, paranoia, fatigue, bizarre and dangerous behavior, decreased testosterone over long-term; immune system effects
Marijuana				
Hashish				
Hash oil				
MDMA	Ecstasy	Heightened sense of oneself and insight, feelings of peace, empathy, energy	Depression, anxiety, sleeplessness	Increase in body temperature, memory difficulties
LSD	Acid, quasey, microdot, white lightning	Heightened aesthetic responses; vision and depth distortion; heightened sensitivity to faces and gestures; magnified feelings; paranoia, panic, euphoria	Not reported	Nausea and chills; increased pulse, temperature, and blood pressure; slow, deep breathing; loss of appetite; insomnia; bizarre, dangerous behavior

FIGURE 4 The most commonly used drugs and their effects.

When used in relatively small quantities, cocaine produces feelings of profound psychological well-being, increased confidence, and alertness. Cocaine produces this "high" through the neurotransmitter dopamine. Dopamine is one of the chemicals that transmit between neurons messages that are related to ordinary feelings of pleasure. Normally when dopamine is released, excess amounts of the neurotransmitter are reabsorbed by the releasing neuron. However, when cocaine enters the brain, it blocks reabsorption of leftover dopamine. As a result, the brain is flooded with dopamine-produced pleasurable sensations (Redish, 2004; Jarlais, Arasteh, & Perlis, 2007). Figure 4 provides a summary of the effects of cocaine and other illegal drugs.

However, there is a steep price for the pleasurable effects of cocaine. The brain may become permanently rewired, triggering a psychological and physical addiction in which users grow obsessed with obtaining the drug. Over time, users deteriorate mentally and physically. In extreme cases, cocaine can cause hallucinations—a common one is of insects crawling over one's body. Ultimately, an overdose of cocaine can lead to death (Carpenter, 2001; Nestler, 2001; George & Moselhy, 2005; Paulozzi, 2006).

STUDY ALERT

Figure 4, which summarizes the different categories of drugs (stimulants, depressants, narcotics, and hallucinogens), will help you learn the effects of particular drugs.

» LO2 Depressants: Drug Lows

In contrast to the initial effect of stimulants, which is an increase in arousal of the central nervous system, the effect of **depressants** is to impede the nervous system by causing neurons to fire more slowly. Small doses result in at least temporary feelings of *intoxication*—drunkenness—along with a sense of euphoria and joy. When large amounts are taken, however, speech becomes slurred and muscle control becomes disjointed, making motion difficult. Ultimately, heavy users may lose consciousness entirely.

Depressants Drugs that slow down the nervous system.

Alcohol

The most common depressant is alcohol, which is used by more people than is any other drug. Based on liquor sales, the average person over the age of 14 drinks 2 1/2 gallons of pure alcohol over the course of a year. This works out to more than 200 drinks per person. Although alcohol consumption has declined steadily over the last decade, surveys show that more than three-fourths of college students indicate that they have had a drink within the last 30 days (Jung, 2002; Midanik, Tam, & Weisner, 2007).

FIGURE 5 Drinking habits of college students (Wechsler et al., 2002). For men, binge drinking was defined as consuming five or more drinks in one sitting; for women, the total was four or more.

Generally, women are typically somewhat lighter drinkers than men—although the gap between the sexes is narrowing for older women and has closed completely for teenagers. Women are more susceptible to the effects of alcohol, and alcohol abuse may harm the brains of women more than those of men (Wuethrich, 2001; Mann et al., 2005; Mancinelli, Binetti, & Ceccanti, 2007).

Although alcohol is a depressant, most people claim that it increases their sense of sociability and well-being. The discrepancy between the actual and the perceived effects of alcohol lies in the initial effects it produces in the majority of individuals who use it: release of tension and stress, feelings of happiness, and loss of inhibitions (Steele & Josephs, 1990; Sayette, 1993).

As the dose of alcohol increases, however, the depressive effects become more pronounced (see Figure 6). People may feel emotionally and physically unstable. They also show poor judgment and may act aggressively. Moreover, memory is impaired, brain processing of spatial information is diminished, and speech becomes slurred and incoherent. Eventually they may fall into a stupor and pass out. If they drink enough alcohol in a short time, they may die of alcohol poisoning (Zeigler et al., 2005; Thatcher & Clark, 2006).

Although most people fall into the category of casual users, 14 million people in the United States—1 in every 13 adults—have a drinking problem. *Alcoholics,* people with alcohol-abuse problems, come to rely on alcohol and continue to drink even though it causes serious difficulties. In addition, they become increasingly immune to the effects of alcohol. Consequently, alcoholics must drink progressively more to experience the initial positive feelings that alcohol produces.

In some cases of alcoholism, people must drink constantly in order to feel well enough to function in their daily lives. In other cases, though, people drink inconsistently, but occasionally go on binges in which they consume large quantities of alcohol.

Cedric Benson was released from the Chicago Bears after being arrested on suspicions of DUI twice in two months. Despite the charges being dropped, the damage was done to his career. Why do you think he was willing to put his career in jeopardy by continuing his rash behavior?

It is not clear why certain people become alcoholics and develop a tolerance for alcohol, whereas others do not. There may be a genetic cause, although the question whether there is a specific inherited gene that produces alcoholism is controversial. What is clear is that the chances of becoming an alcoholic are considerably higher if alcoholics are present in earlier generations of a person's family. However, not all alcoholics have close relatives who are alcoholics. In these cases, environmental stressors are suspected of playing a larger role (Whitfield et al., 2004; Nurnberger & Bierut, 2007; Zimmerman, Blomeyer, & Laucht, 2007).

Number of Drinks Consumed in Two Hours		Alcohol in Blood (Percentage)	Typical Effects
	②	0.05	Judgment, thought, and restraint weakened; tension released, giving carefree sensation
	③	0.08	Tensions and inhibitions of everyday life lessened; cheerfulness
	④	0.10	Voluntary motor action affected, making hand and arm movements, walk, and speech clumsy
	⑦	0.20	Severe impairment—staggering, loud, incoherent, emotionally unstable, 100 times greater traffic risk; exuberance and aggressive inclinations magnified
	⑨	0.30	Deeper areas of brain affected, with stimulus-response and understanding confused; stuporous; blurred vision
	⑫	0.40	Incapable of voluntary action; sleepy, difficult to arouse; equivalent of surgical anesthesia
	⑮	0.50	Comatose; centers controlling breathing and heartbeat anesthetized; death increasingly probable

Note: A drink refers to a typical 12-ounce bottle of beer, a 1.5-ounce shot of hard liquor, or a 5-ounce glass of wine.

FIGURE 6   The effects of alcohol. The quantities represent only rough benchmarks; the effects vary significantly depending on an individual's weight, height, recent food intake, genetic factors, and even psychological state.

To determine your own drinking style, complete the Try It! on page 150.

Barbiturates

Barbiturates, which include drugs such as Nembutal®, Seconal®, and phenobarbital, are another form of depressant. Frequently prescribed by physicians to induce sleep or reduce stress, barbiturates produce a sense of relaxation. Yet they too are psychologically and physically addictive and, when combined with alcohol, can be deadly, since such a combination relaxes the muscles of the diaphragm to such an extent that the user stops breathing.

Rohypnol

Rohypnol is sometimes called the "date rape drug," because when it is mixed with alcohol, it can prevent victims from resisting sexual assault. Sometimes people who are unknowingly given the drug are so incapacitated that they have no memory of the assault.

Even legal drugs, when used improperly, can lead to addiction.

Consider Your Drinking Style

If you drink alcohol, do you have a style of use that is safe and responsible? Read the statements below and rate the extent to which you agree with them, using the following scale:

1 = Strongly disagree

2 = Disagree

3 = Neutral

4 = Agree

5 = Strongly agree

	1	2	3	4	5
1. I usually drink alcohol a few times a week.	___	___	___	___	___
2. I sometimes go to class after I've been drinking alcohol.	___	___	___	___	___
3. I frequently drink when I'm alone.	___	___	___	___	___
4. I have driven while under the influence of alcohol.	___	___	___	___	___
5. I've used a fake ID card to purchase alcohol.	___	___	___	___	___
6. I'm a totally different person when I'm drinking alcohol.	___	___	___	___	___
7. I often drink so much that I feel drunk.	___	___	___	___	___
8. I wouldn't want to go to party where alcohol wasn't being served.	___	___	___	___	___
9. I avoid people who don't like to drink alcohol.	___	___	___	___	___
10. I sometimes urge others to drink more alcohol.	___	___	___	___	___

Scoring

The lower your score (i.e., the more 1s and 2s), the better able you are to control your alcohol consumption and the more likely it is that your alcohol use is responsible. The higher your score (i.e., the more 4s and 5s), the greater is your use and reliance on alcohol, and the more likely it is that your alcohol consumption may be reckless. If your score is over 40, you may have an alcohol problem and should seek professional help to control your alcohol usage.

» LO3 Narcotics: Relieving Pain and Anxiety

Narcotics Drugs that increase relaxation and relieve pain and anxiety.

Hallucinogen A drug that is capable of producing hallucinations, or changes in the perceptual process.

Narcotics are drugs that increase relaxation and relieve pain and anxiety. Two of the most powerful narcotics, *morphine* and *heroin,* are derived from the poppy seed pod. Although morphine is used medically to control severe pain, heroin is illegal in the United States. This has not prevented its widespread use.

Heroin users usually inject the drug directly into their veins with a hypodermic needle. The immediate effect has been described as a "rush" of positive feeling, similar in some respects to a sexual orgasm—and just as difficult to describe. After the rush, a heroin user experiences a sense of well-being and peacefulness that lasts three to five hours. When the effects of the drug wear off, however, the user feels extreme anxiety and a desperate desire to repeat the experience. Moreover, larger amounts of heroin are needed each time to produce the same pleasurable effect. These last two properties are all the ingredients necessary for biological and psychological addiction: the user is constantly either shooting up or attempting to obtain ever-increasing amounts of the drug. Eventually, the life of the addict revolves around heroin.

The use of heroin creates a cycle of biological and physical dependence. Combined with the strong positive feelings produced by the drug, this makes heroin addiction especially difficult to cure.

Because of the powerful positive feelings the drug produces, heroin addiction is particularly difficult to cure. One treatment that has shown some success is the use of methadone. *Methadone* is a synthetic chemical that satisfies a heroin user's physiological cravings for the drug without providing the "high" that accompanies heroin. When heroin users are placed on regular doses of methadone, they may be able to function relatively normally. The use of methadone has one substantial drawback, however: although it removes the psychological dependence on heroin, it replaces the biological addiction to heroin with a biological addiction to methadone (Amato et al., 2005; Verdejo, Toribio, & Orozco, 2005; Joe, Flynn, & Broome, 2007).

» LO4 Hallucinogens: Psychedelic Drugs

What do mushrooms, jimsonweed, and morning glories have in common? Besides being fairly common plants, each can be a source of a powerful **hallucinogen,** a drug that is capable of producing hallucinations, or changes in the perceptual process.

Marijuana

The most common hallucinogen in widespread use today is *marijuana,* whose active ingredient—tetrahydrocannabinol (THC)—is found in a common weed, cannabis. Marijuana is typically smoked in cigarettes or pipes, although it can be cooked and eaten. Just over 31 percent of high school seniors and 12 percent of eighth-graders report having used marijuana in the last year (Johnston et al., 2007; see Figure 7).

The effects of marijuana vary from person to person, but they typically consist of feelings of euphoria and general well-being. Sensory experiences seem

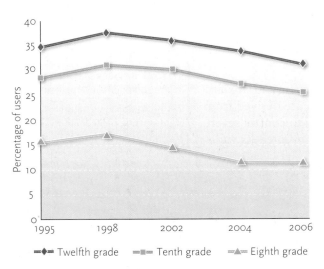

FIGURE 7 Although the level of marijuana use has declined slightly in recent years, overall the absolute number of teenagers who have used the drug in the last year remains relatively high. *(Source: Johnston et al., 2007.)*

> *Although marijuana does not seem to produce addiction by itself, some evidence suggests that there are similarities in the way marijuana and drugs such as cocaine and heroin affect the brain.*

In recent years the use of Ecstasy has been romanticized in connection with club hopping and raves. What are the potential consequences of idealizing such a harmful drug?

more vivid and intense, and a person's sense of self-importance seems to grow. Memory may be impaired, causing the user to feel pleasantly "spaced out." However, the effects are not universally positive. Individuals who use marijuana when they feel depressed can end up even more depressed, because the drug tends to magnify both good and bad feelings.

There are risks associated with long-term, heavy marijuana use. Although marijuana does not seem to produce addiction by itself, some evidence suggests that there are similarities in the way marijuana and drugs such as cocaine and heroin affect the brain. Furthermore, there is some evidence that heavy use at least temporarily decreases the production of the male sex hormone testosterone, potentially affecting sexual activity and sperm count (Block et al., 2000; Iversen, 2000; Lane, Cherek, & Tcheremissine, 2007).

In addition, marijuana smoked during pregnancy may have lasting effects on children who are exposed prenatally, although the results are inconsistent. Heavy use also affects the ability of the immune system to fight off germs and increases stress on the heart, although it is unclear how strong these effects are. There is one unquestionably negative consequence of smoking marijuana: the smoke damages the lungs much the way cigarette smoke does, producing an increased likelihood of developing cancer and other lung diseases (Cornelius et al., 1995; Julien, 2001).

Despite the possible dangers of marijuana use, there is little scientific evidence for the popular belief that users "graduate" from marijuana to more dangerous drugs. Furthermore, the use of marijuana is routine in certain cultures. For instance, some people in Jamaica habitually drink a marijuana-based tea related to religious practices. In addition, marijuana has several medical uses; it can be used to prevent nausea from chemotherapy, treat some AIDS symptoms, and relieve muscle spasms for people with spinal cord injuries. In fact, several states have made the use of the drug legal if it is prescribed by a physician—although it remains illegal under U.S. federal law (National Academy of Sciences, 1999; Iversen, 2004; Seamon et al., 2007).

MDMA (Ecstasy) and LSD

MDMA ("Ecstasy") and *lysergic acid diethylamide (LSD,* or *"acid")* fall into the category of hallucinogens. Both drugs affect the operation of the neurotransmitter serotonin in the brain, causing an alteration in brain-cell activity and perception (Aghajanian, 1994; Cloud, 2000; Buchert et al., 2004).

Ecstasy users report a sense of peacefulness and calm. People on the drug report experiencing increased empathy and connection with others, as well as feeling more relaxed, yet energetic. Although the data are not conclusive, some researchers have found declines in memory and performance on intellectual tasks, and such findings suggest that there may be long-term changes in serotonin receptors in the brain (Parrott, 2002; Montgomery et al., 2005; El-Mallakh & Abraham, 2007).

LSD, which is structurally similar to serotonin, produces vivid hallucinations. Perceptions of colors, sounds, and shapes are altered so much that even the most mundane experience—such as looking at the knots in a wooden table—can seem moving and exciting. Time perception is distorted, and objects and people may be viewed in a new way, with some users reporting that LSD increases their understanding of the world. For others, however, the experience brought on by LSD can be terrifying, particularly if users have had emotional difficulties in the past. Furthermore, people occasionally experience flashbacks, in which they hallucinate long after they initially used the drug (Baruss, 2003; Wu, Schlenger, & Galvin, 2006).

becoming an *informed consumer*
OF PSYCHOLOGY

Identifying Drug and Alcohol Problems

In a society bombarded with commercials for drugs that are guaranteed to do everything from curing the common cold to giving new life to "tired blood," it is no wonder that drug-related problems are a major social issue. Yet many people with drug and alcohol problems deny they have them, and even close friends and family members may fail to realize when occasional social use of drugs or alcohol has turned into abuse.

Certain signs, however, indicate when use becomes abuse (Archambault, 1992; National Institute on Drug Abuse, 2000). Among them are the following:

- Always getting high to have a good time
- Being high more often than not
- Getting high to get oneself going
- Going to work while high
- Missing or being unprepared for work because you were high
- Feeling bad later about something you said or did while high
- Driving a car while high
- Coming in conflict with the law because of drugs
- Doing something while high that you wouldn't do otherwise
- Being high in nonsocial, solitary situations
- Being unable to stop getting high
- Feeling a need for a drink or a drug to get through the day
- Becoming physically unhealthy

> *Because drug and alcohol dependence are almost impossible to cure on one's own, people who suspect that they have a problem should seek immediate attention from a psychologist, physician, or counselor.*

- Failing on the job
- Thinking about liquor or drugs all the time
- Avoiding family or friends while using liquor or drugs

Any combination of these symptoms should be sufficient to alert you to the potential of a serious drug problem. Because drug and alcohol dependence are almost impossible to cure on one's own, people who suspect that they have a problem should seek immediate attention from a psychologist, physician, or counselor.

You can also get help from national hotlines. For alcohol difficulties, call the National Council on Alcoholism at (800) 622-2255. For drug problems, call the National Institute on Drug Abuse at (800) 662-4357. You can also check your telephone book for a local listing of Alcoholics Anonymous or Narcotics Anonymous. Finally, check out the Web sites of the National Institute on Alcohol Abuse and Alcoholism (www.niaaa.nih.gov) and the National Institute on Drug Abuse (www.nida.nih.gov).

RECAP

Explain the effects of stimulants.

- Drugs can produce an altered state of consciousness. However, they vary in how dangerous they are and in whether they are addictive. (p. 142)
- Stimulants cause arousal in the central nervous system. Two common stimulants are caffeine and nicotine. More dangerous are cocaine and amphetamines, which in large quantities can lead to convulsions and death. (p. 144)

Explain the effects of depressants.

- Depressants decrease arousal in the central nervous system. They can cause intoxication along with feelings of euphoria. The most common depressants are alcohol and barbiturates. (p. 147)
- Alcohol is the most frequently used depressant. Its initial effects of released tension and positive feelings yield to depressive effects as the dose of alcohol increases. Both heredity and environmental stressors can lead to alcoholism. (p. 147)

Explain the effects of narcotics.

- Morphine and heroin are narcotics, drugs that produce relaxation and relieve pain and anxiety. Because of their addictive qualities, morphine and heroin are particularly dangerous. (p. 151)

Explain the effects of hallucinogens.

- Hallucinogens are drugs that produce hallucinations or other changes in perception. The most frequently used hallucinogen is marijuana, which has several long-term risks. Two other hallucinogens are LSD and Ecstasy. (p. 151)
- A number of signals indicate when drug use becomes drug abuse. A person who suspects that he or she has a drug problem should get professional help. People are almost never capable of solving drug problems on their own. (p. 153)

EVALUATE

1. Drugs that affect a person's consciousness are referred to as _____.
2. Match the type of drug to an example of that type.
   1. Narcotic—a pain reliever   a. LSD
   2. Amphetamine—a strong stimulant   b. Heroin
   3. Hallucinogen—capable of producing hallucinations c. Dexedrine® or speed
3. Classify each drug listed as a stimulant (S), depressant (D), hallucinogen (H), or narcotic (N).
   1. Nicotine
   2. Cocaine
   3. Alcohol
   4. Morphine
   5. Marijuana
4. The effects of LSD can recur long after the drug has been taken. True or false?
5. _____ is a drug that has been used to cure people of heroin addiction.

RETHINK

Why have drug education campaigns largely been ineffective in stemming the use of illegal drugs? Should the use of certain now-illegal drugs be made legal? Would it be more effective to stress reduction of drug use rather than a complete prohibition of drug use?

Answers to Evaluate Questions 1. psychoactive; 2. 1-b, 2-c, 3-a; 3. 1-S, 2-S, 3-D, 4-N, 5-H; 4. true; 5. methadone

KEY TERMS

Psychoactive drugs *p. 142*   Depressants *p. 147*
Addictive drugs *p. 143*   Narcotics *p. 151*
Stimulants *p. 144*   Hallucinogen *p. 151*

«« «« looking
BACK

Psychology on the Web

1. Find a resource on the Web that interprets dreams and another that reports the results of scientific dream research. Compare the nature and content of the two sites in terms of the topics covered, the reliability of information provided, and the promises made about the use of the site and its information. Write a summary of what you found.

2. There is considerable debate about the effectiveness of D.A.R.E., the Drug Abuse Resistance Education program. Find a discussion of both sides of the issue on the Web and summarize the arguments on each side. State your own preliminary conclusions about the D.A.R.E. program.

the case of . . .
THE WOMAN WHO DREAMS OF STRESS

Arlene Amarosi, a working mother, has been under a lot of stress this year. She has been having difficulty getting to sleep and often lies in bed staring at the ceiling while worrying about her problems. As a result, she's often tired throughout her workday and relies on coffee and caffeinated energy drinks to keep her going.

Lately Arlene's sleep has been disturbed even more often than usual. Several times over the past week she has been awakened by disturbing dreams. In these dreams she is always at work, struggling to keep up with an impossible workload. She is struggling with the new software that her company recently trained her to use, but no matter how fast she goes, she can't keep up with the workflow. The dream ends when Arlene wakes up in a panic. It often takes Arlene hours to get back to sleep, and she has been feeling even more tired than usual during work.

1. Arlene is worried that her recent dream experiences indicate that something is wrong with her. If you were Arlene's friend and wanted to reassure her, how would you help her to understand the normal experience of sleep and dreams?

2. Which theory of dreaming seems to best explain Arlene's disturbing dreams, and why?

3. How might meditation help Arlene?

4. If you were Arlene's health care provider, how would you advise her to overcome her insomnia?

5. What are some effects on Arlene of her high caffeine intake? What would happen if she just suddenly stopped drinking coffee and energy drinks? How would you advise her to modify her caffeine use?

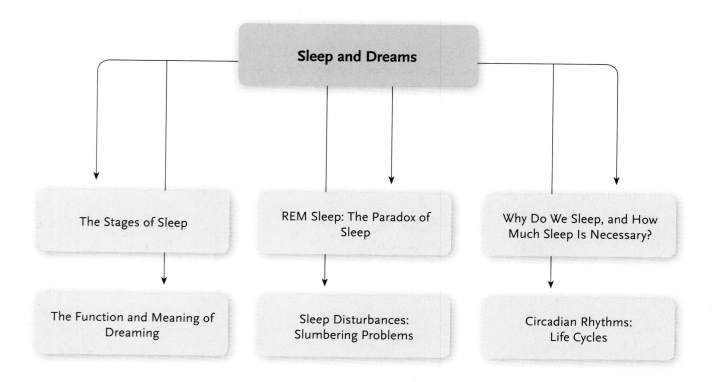

Sleep and Dreams

The Stages of Sleep

REM Sleep: The Paradox of Sleep

Why Do We Sleep, and How Much Sleep Is Necessary?

The Function and Meaning of Dreaming

Sleep Disturbances: Slumbering Problems

Circadian Rhythms: Life Cycles

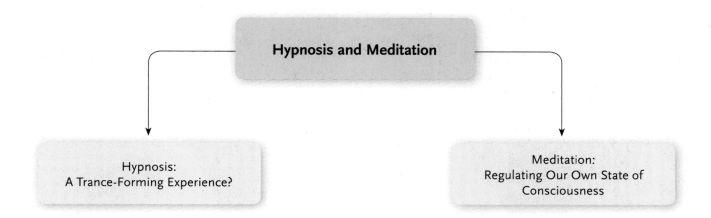

Hypnosis and Meditation

Hypnosis:
A Trance-Forming Experience?

Meditation:
Regulating Our Own State of
Consciousness

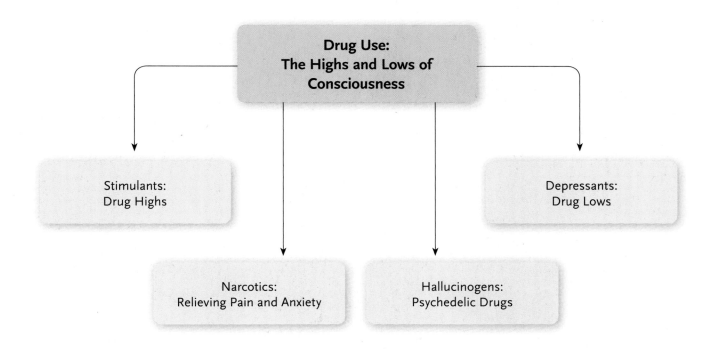

Drug Use:
The Highs and Lows of
Consciousness

Stimulants:
Drug Highs

Narcotics:
Relieving Pain and Anxiety

Hallucinogens:
Psychedelic Drugs

Depressants:
Drug Lows

LEARNING

A Four-Legged Co-Worker

Declan lies on his back wanting his belly scratched. The eight-year-old black Labrador cross swings his legs in the air for a few minutes before resigning himself to chewing on someone's shoe.

In the office he behaves like any pet dog, but in the field he is like a tornado—focused on finding illegal drugs being smuggled. Declan is a drug-detector dog for the Customs Service and has been busting drug smugglers with his handler, Kevin Hattrill, for eight years.

Airport passengers look on with curiosity as Declan darts around people and their luggage. Within minutes he sniffs out a person of interest, who is taken away and questioned by airport authorities.

Dogs like Declan are trained to detect illegal drugs, such as cannabis, methamphetamine, and cocaine, or explosives. Hattrill said the dogs were dual response-trained when they detected something. "If the odor is around a passenger, they are trained to sit beside them. If it's around cargo, they are trained to scratch. When they detect something, their whole temperament will change.

"The dogs can screen up to 300 people within 10 to 15 minutes at the airport. Nothing else can do that." (McKenzie-McLean, 2006, p. 7) ■

looking AHEAD

Declan's expertise did not just happen, of course. It is the result of painstaking training procedures—the same ones that are at work in each of our lives, illustrated by our ability to read a book, drive a car, play poker, study for a test, or perform any of the numerous activities that make up our daily routine. Like Declan, each of us must acquire and then refine our skills and abilities through learning.

Learning is a fundamental topic for psychologists and plays a central role in almost every specialty area of psychology. For example, a developmental psychologist might inquire, "How do babies learn to distinguish their mothers from other people?" whereas a clinical psychologist might wonder, "Why do some people learn to be afraid when they see a spider?"

Psychologists have approached the study of learning from several angles. Among the most fundamental are studies of the type of learning that is illustrated in responses ranging from a dog salivating when it hears its owner opening a can of dog food to the emotions we feel when our national anthem is played. Other theories consider how learning is a consequence of rewarding circumstances. Finally, several other approaches focus on the cognitive aspects of learning, or the thought processes that underlie learning.

Classical Conditioning

LEARNING OUTCOMES

15.1 Describe the basics of classical conditioning and how they relate to learning.

15.2 Give examples of applying conditioning principles to human behavior.

15.3 Explain extinction.

15.4 Discuss stimulus generalization and discrimination.

Learning A relatively permanent change in behavior brought about by experience.

Does the mere sight of the golden arches in front of McDonald's make you feel pangs of hunger and think about hamburgers? If it does, you are displaying an elementary form of learning called classical conditioning. *Classical conditioning* helps explain such diverse phenomena as crying at the sight of a bride walking down the aisle, fearing the dark, and falling in love.

Classical conditioning is one of a number of different types of learning that psychologists have identified, but a general definition encompasses them all: **learning** is a relatively permanent change in behavior that is brought about by experience.

We are primed for learning from the beginning of life. Infants exhibit a primitive type of learning called habituation. *Habituation* is the decrease in response to a stimulus that occurs after repeated presentations of the same stimulus. For example, young infants may initially show interest in a novel stimulus, such as a brightly colored toy, but they will soon lose interest if they see the same toy over and over. (Adults exhibit habituation, too: newlyweds soon stop noticing that they are wearing a wedding ring.) Habituation permits us to ignore things that have stopped providing new information.

Most learning is considerably more complex than habituation, and the study of learning has been at the core of the field of psychology. Although philosophers since the time of Aristotle have speculated on the foundations of learning, the first systematic research on learning was done at the beginning of the twentieth century, when Ivan Pavlov (does the name ring a bell?) developed the framework for learning called classical conditioning.

» LO1 The Basics of Classical Conditioning

In the early twentieth century, Ivan Pavlov, a famous Russian physiologist, had been studying the secretion of stomach acids and salivation in dogs in response to the ingestion of varying amounts and kinds of food. While doing that he observed a curious phenomenon: sometimes stomach secretions and salivation would begin in the dogs when they had not yet eaten any food. The mere sight of the experimenter who normally brought the food, or even the sound of the experimenter's footsteps, was enough to produce salivation in the dogs.

Ivan Pavlov (center) developed the principles of classical conditioning.

Pavlov's genius lay in his ability to recognize the implications of this discovery. He saw that the dogs were responding not only on the basis of a biological need (hunger), but also as a result of learning—or, as it came to be called, classical conditioning. **Classical conditioning** is a type of learning in which a neutral stimulus (such as the experimenter's footsteps) comes to elicit a response after being paired with a stimulus (such as food) that naturally brings about that response.

To demonstrate classical conditioning, Pavlov (1927) attached a tube to the salivary gland of a dog, allowing allow him to measure precisely the dog's salivation. He then rang a bell and, just a few seconds later, presented the dog with meat. This pairing occurred repeatedly and was carefully planned so that, each time, exactly the same amount of time elapsed between the presentation of the bell and the meat. At first the dog would salivate only when the meat was presented, but soon it began to salivate at the sound of the bell. In fact, even when Pavlov stopped presenting the meat, the dog still salivated after hearing the sound. The dog had been classically conditioned to salivate to the bell.

As you can see in Figure 1, the basic processes of classical conditioning that underlie Pavlov's discovery are straightforward, although the terminology he chose is not simple. Consider first the diagram in Figure 1A. Before conditioning, there are two unrelated stimuli: the ringing of a bell and meat. We know that normally the ringing of a bell does not lead to salivation but to some irrelevant response, such as pricking up the ears or perhaps a startle reaction. The bell is therefore called the **neutral stimulus** because it is a stimulus that, before conditioning, does not naturally bring about the response in which we are interested. We also have meat, which naturally causes a dog to salivate—the response we are interested in conditioning. The meat is considered an **unconditioned stimulus,** or **UCS,** because food placed in a dog's mouth automatically causes salivation to occur. The response that the meat elicits (salivation) is called an **unconditioned response,** or **UCR**—a natural, innate, reflexive response that is not associated with previous learning. Unconditioned responses are always brought about by the presence of unconditioned stimuli.

Figure 1B illustrates what happens during conditioning. The bell is rung just before each presentation of the meat. The goal of conditioning is for the dog to associate the bell with the unconditioned stimulus (meat) and therefore to bring about the same sort of response as the unconditioned stimulus. After a number of pairings of the bell and meat, the bell alone causes the dog to salivate.

Classical conditioning A type of learning in which a neutral stimulus comes to bring about a response after it is paired with a stimulus that naturally brings about that response.

Neutral stimulus A stimulus that, before conditioning, does not naturally bring about the response of interest.

Unconditioned stimulus (UCS) A stimulus that naturally brings about a particular response without having been learned.

Unconditioned response (UCR) A response that is natural and needs no training (e.g., salivation at the smell of food).

STUDY ALERT

Figure 1 (on the next page) can help you learn and understand the process (and terminology) of classical conditioning, which can be confusing.

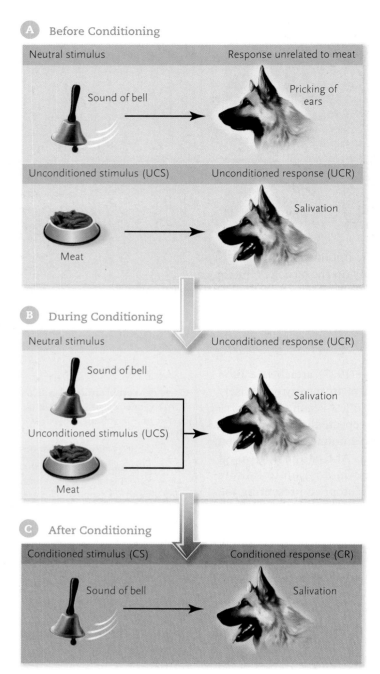

A Before Conditioning

Neutral stimulus · Response unrelated to meat

Sound of bell → Pricking of ears

Unconditioned stimulus (UCS) · Unconditioned response (UCR)

Meat → Salivation

B During Conditioning

Neutral stimulus · Unconditioned response (UCR)

Sound of bell

Unconditioned stimulus (UCS)

Meat → Salivation

C After Conditioning

Conditioned stimulus (CS) · Conditioned response (CR)

Sound of bell → Salivation

FIGURE 1 The basic process of classical conditioning. (A) Before conditioning, the ringing of a bell does not bring about salivation—making the bell a neutral stimulus. In contrast, meat naturally brings about salivation, making the meat an unconditioned stimulus and salivation an unconditioned response. (B) During conditioning, the bell is rung just before the presentation of the meat. (C) Eventually, the ringing of the bell alone brings about salivation. We now can say that conditioning has been accomplished: the previously neutral stimulus of the bell now is a conditioned stimulus that brings about the conditioned response of salivation.

When conditioning is complete, the bell has evolved from a neutral stimulus to what is now called a **conditioned stimulus,** or **CS.** At this time, salivation that occurs as a response to the conditioned stimulus (bell) is considered a **conditioned response,** or **CR.** This situation is depicted in Figure 1C. After conditioning, then, the conditioned stimulus evokes the conditioned response.

The sequence and timing of the presentation of the unconditioned stimulus and the conditioned stimulus are particularly important. Like a malfunctioning warning light at a railroad crossing that goes on after the train has passed by, a neutral stimulus that *follows* an unconditioned stimulus has little chance of becoming a conditioned stimulus. However, just as a warning light works best if it goes on right before a train passes, a neutral stimulus that is presented *just before* the unconditioned stimulus is most apt to result in successful conditioning (Bitterman, 2006).

Although the terminology Pavlov used to describe classical conditioning may seem confusing, the following summary can help make the relationships between stimuli and responses easier to understand and remember:

- Conditioned = learned.

- Unconditioned = not learned.

- An *un*conditioned stimulus leads to an *un*conditioned response.

- *Un*conditioned stimulus–*un*conditioned response pairings are *un*learned and *un*trained.

- During conditioning, a previously neutral stimulus is transformed into the conditioned stimulus.

- A conditioned stimulus leads to a conditioned response, and a conditioned stimulus–conditioned response pairing is a consequence of learning and training.

- An unconditioned response and a conditioned response are similar (such as salivation in Pavlov's experiment), but the unconditioned response occurs naturally, whereas the conditioned response is learned.

» LO2 Applying Conditioning Principles to Human Behavior

Although the initial conditioning experiments were carried out with animals, classical conditioning principles were soon found to explain many aspects of everyday human behavior. Recall, for instance, the earlier illustration of how people may experience hunger pangs at the sight of McDonald's golden arches. The cause of this reaction is classical conditioning: the previously neutral arches have become associated with the food inside the restaurant (the unconditioned stimulus), causing the arches to become a conditioned stimulus that brings about the conditioned response of hunger.

Emotional responses are especially likely to be learned through classical conditioning processes. For instance, how do some of us develop fears of mice, spiders, and other creatures that are typically harmless? In a now infamous case study, psychologist John B. Watson and colleague Rosalie Rayner (1920) showed that classical conditioning was at the root of such fears by conditioning an 11-month-old infant named Albert to be afraid of rats. "Little Albert," like most infants, initially was frightened by loud noises but had no fear of rats.

In the study, the experimenters sounded a loud noise just as they showed Little Albert a rat. The noise (the unconditioned stimulus) evoked fear (the unconditioned response). However, after just a few pairings of noise and rat, Albert began to show fear of the rat by itself, bursting into tears when he saw it. The rat, then, had become a CS that brought about the CR, fear. Furthermore, the effects of the conditioning lingered: five days later, Albert reacted with fear not only when shown a rat, but when shown objects that looked similar to the white, furry rat, including a white rabbit, a white sealskin coat, and even a white Santa Claus mask. (By the way, we don't know what happened to the unfortunate Little Albert. Watson, the experimenter, has been condemned for using ethically questionable procedures that could never be conducted today.)

Emotional responses are especially likely to be learned through classical conditioning processes.

Learning by means of classical conditioning also occurs during adulthood. For example, you may not go to a dentist as often as you should because of prior associations of dentists with pain. On the other hand, classical conditioning also accounts for pleasant experiences. For instance, you may have a particular fondness for the smell of a certain perfume or aftershave lotion because the feelings and thoughts of an early love come rushing back whenever you encounter it. Classical conditioning, then, explains many of the reactions we have to stimuli in the world around us.

» LO3 Extinction

What do you think would happen if a dog that had become classically conditioned to salivate at the ringing of a bell never again received food when the bell was rung? The answer lies in one of the basic phenomena of learning: extinction. **Extinction** occurs when a previously conditioned response decreases in frequency and eventually disappears.

To produce extinction, one needs to end the association between conditioned stimuli and unconditioned stimuli. For instance, if we had trained a dog to salivate (the conditioned response) at the ringing of a bell (the conditioned

Conditioned stimulus (CS) A once-neutral stimulus that has been paired with an unconditioned stimulus to bring about a response formerly caused only by the unconditioned stimulus.

Conditioned response (CR) A response that, after conditioning, follows a previously neutral stimulus (e.g., salivation at the ringing of a bell).

Extinction A basic phenomenon of learning that occurs when a previously conditioned response decreases in frequency and eventually disappears.

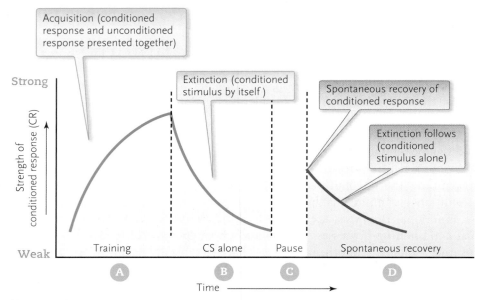

FIGURE 2   Acquisition, extinction, and spontaneous recovery of a classically conditioned response. A conditioned response (CR) gradually increases in strength during training (A). However, if the conditioned stimulus is presented by itself enough times, the conditioned response gradually fades, and extinction occurs (B). After a pause (C) in which the conditioned stimulus is not presented, spontaneous recovery can occur (D). However, extinction typically reoccurs soon after.

Spontaneous recovery The reemergence of an extinguished conditioned response after a period of rest and with no further conditioning.

stimulus), we could produce extinction by repeatedly ringing the bell but *not* providing meat. At first the dog would continue to salivate when it heard the bell, but after a few such instances, the amount of salivation would probably decline, and the dog would eventually stop responding to the bell altogether.

At that point, we could say that the response had been extinguished. In sum, extinction occurs when the conditioned stimulus is presented repeatedly without the unconditioned stimulus (see Figure 2).

> *Once a conditioned response has been extinguished, has it vanished forever? Not necessarily.*

Once a conditioned response has been extinguished, has it vanished forever? Not necessarily. Pavlov discovered this phenomenon when he returned to his dog a few days after the conditioned behavior had seemingly been extinguished. If he rang a bell, the dog once again salivated—an effect known as **spontaneous recovery,** or the reemergence of an extinguished conditioned response after a period of rest and with no further conditioning.

Spontaneous recovery helps explain why it is so hard to overcome drug addictions. For example, cocaine addicts who are thought to be "cured" can experience an irresistible impulse to use the drug again if they are subsequently confronted by a stimulus with strong connections to the drug, such as a white powder (DiCano & Everitt, 2002; Rodd et al., 2004; Plowright, Simonds, & Butler, 2006).

From the perspective of . . .

A VETERINARY ASSISTANT   How might knowledge of classical conditioning be useful in your career?

» LO4 Generalization and Discrimination

Despite differences in color and shape, to most of us a rose is a rose is a rose. The pleasure we experience at the beauty, smell, and grace of the flower is similar for different types of roses. Pavlov noticed a similar phenomenon. His dogs often salivated not only at the ringing of the bell that was used during their original conditioning but at the sound of a buzzer as well.

Such behavior is the result of stimulus generalization. **Stimulus generalization** occurs when a conditioned response follows a stimulus that is similar to the original conditioned stimulus. The greater the similarity between two stimuli, the greater the likelihood of stimulus generalization. Little Albert, who, as we mentioned earlier, was conditioned to be fearful of white rats, grew afraid of other furry white things as well. However, according to the principle of stimulus generalization, it is unlikely that he would have been afraid of a black dog, because its color would have differentiated it sufficiently from the original fear-evoking stimulus.

The greater the similarity between two stimuli, the greater the likelihood of stimulus generalization.

On the other hand, **stimulus discrimination** occurs if two stimuli are sufficiently distinct from each other that one evokes a conditioned response but the other does not. Stimulus discrimination provides the ability to differentiate between stimuli. For example, my dog, Cleo, comes running into the kitchen when she hears the sound of the electric can opener, which she has learned is used to open her dog food when her dinner is about to be served. She does not bound into the kitchen at the sound of the food processor, although it sounds similar. In other words, she discriminates between the stimuli of can opener and food processor. Similarly, our ability to discriminate between the behavior of a growling dog and that of one whose tail is wagging can lead to adaptive behavior—avoiding the growling dog and petting the friendly one.

Stimulus generalization Occurs when a conditioned response follows a stimulus that is similar to the original conditioned stimulus; the more similar the two stimuli are, the more likely generalization is to occur.

Stimulus discrimination The process that occurs if two stimuli are sufficiently distinct from each other that one evokes a conditioned response but the other does not; the ability to differentiate between stimuli.

Because of a previous unpleasant experience, a person may expect a similar occurrence when faced with a comparable situation in the future, a process known as stimulus generalization. Can you think of ways this process is used in everyday life?

RECAP

Describe the basics of classical conditioning and how they relate to learning.

- One major form of learning is classical conditioning, which occurs when a neutral stimulus—one that normally brings about no relevant response—is repeatedly paired with a stimulus (called an unconditioned stimulus) that brings about a natural, untrained response. (p. 163)

- After repeated pairings, the neutral stimulus elicits the same response that the unconditioned stimulus brings about. When this occurs, the neutral stimulus has become a conditioned stimulus, and the response a conditioned response. (p. 164)

Give examples of applying conditioning principles to human behavior.

- Examples of classical conditioning include the development of emotions and fears. (p. 165)

Explain extinction.

- Learning is not always permanent. Extinction occurs when a previously learned response decreases in frequency and eventually disappears. (p. 166)

Discuss stimulus generalization and discrimination.

- Stimulus generalization is the tendency for a conditioned response to follow a stimulus that is similar to, but not the same as, the original conditioned stimulus. The converse phenomenon, stimulus discrimination, occurs when an organism learns to distinguish between stimuli. (p. 167)

EVALUATE

1. _____ involves changes brought about by experience.

2. _____ is the name of the scientist responsible for discovering the learning phenomenon known as _____ conditioning, in which an organism learns a response to a stimulus to which it normally would not respond.

Refer to the passage below to answer questions 3 through 5:

The last three times little Theresa visited Dr. Lopez for checkups, he administered a painful preventive immunization shot that left her in tears. Today, when her mother takes her for another checkup, Theresa begins to sob as soon as she comes face-to-face with Dr. Lopez, even before he has a chance to say hello.

3. The painful shot that Theresa received during each visit was a(n) _____ _____ that elicited the _____ _____ , her tears.

4. Dr. Lopez is upset because his presence has become a _____ _____ for Theresa's crying.

5. Fortunately, Dr. Lopez gave Theresa no more shots for quite some time. Over that period she gradually stopped crying and even came to like him. _____ had occurred.

RETHINK

How likely is it that Little Albert, Watson's experimental subject, went through life afraid of Santa Claus? Describe what could have happened to prevent his continual dread of Santa.

[KEY TERMS]

Learning *p. 162*

Classical conditioning *p. 163*

Neutral stimulus *p. 163*

Unconditioned stimulus (UCS) *p. 163*

Unconditioned response (UCR) *p. 163*

Conditioned stimulus (CS) *p. 165*

Conditioned response (CR) *p. 165*

Extinction *p. 165*

Spontaneous recovery *p. 166*

Stimulus generalization *p. 167*

Stimulus discrimination *p. 167*

Operant Conditioning

Operant conditioning Learning in which a voluntary response is strengthened or weakened, depending on its favorable or unfavorable consequences.

Very good . . . What a clever idea . . . Fantastic . . . I agree . . . Thank you . . . Excellent . . . Super . . . Right on . . . This is the best paper you've ever written; you get an A . . . You are really getting the hang of it . . . I'm impressed . . . You're getting a raise . . . Have a cookie . . . You look great . . . I love you . . .

Few of us mind being the recipient of any of the preceding comments. But what is especially noteworthy about them is that each of these simple statements can be used, through a process known as operant conditioning, to bring about powerful changes in behavior and to teach the most complex tasks. Operant conditioning is the basis for many of the most important kinds of human, and animal, learning.

Operant conditioning is learning in which a voluntary response is strengthened or weakened, depending on its favorable or unfavorable consequences. When we say that a response has been strengthened or weakened, we mean that it has been made more or less likely to recur regularly.

Unlike classical conditioning, in which the original behaviors are the natural, biological responses to the presence of a stimulus such as food, water, or pain, operant conditioning applies to voluntary responses, which an organism performs deliberately to produce a desirable outcome. The term *operant* emphasizes this point: the organism *operates* on its environment to produce a desirable result. Operant conditioning is at work when we learn that toiling industriously can bring about a raise or that exercising hard results in a good physique.

» LO1 The Basics of Operant Conditioning

The inspiration for a whole generation of psychologists studying operant conditioning was one of the twentieth century's most influential psychologists, B. F. Skinner (1904–1990). Skinner was interested in specifying how behavior varies as a result of alterations in the environment.

Skinner conducted his research using an apparatus called the Skinner box (shown in Figure 1), a chamber with a highly controlled environment that was used to study operant conditioning processes with laboratory animals. Let's consider what happens to a rat in the typical Skinner box (Pascual & Rodríguez, 2006).

Suppose you want to teach a hungry rat to press a lever that is in its box. At first the rat will wander around the box, exploring the environment in a relatively random fashion. At some point, however, it will probably press the lever by chance, and when it does, it will receive a food pellet. The first time this happens, the rat will not learn the connection between pressing a lever and receiving food and will continue to explore the box. Sooner or later the rat will press the lever again and receive a pellet, and in time the frequency of the pressing response will increase. Eventually, the rat will press the lever continually until it satisfies its hunger, thereby demonstrating that it has learned that the receipt of food is contingent on pressing the lever.

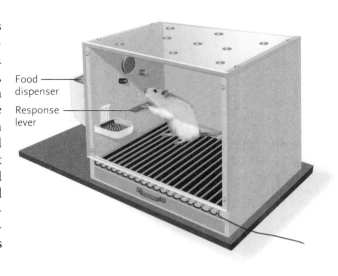

Food dispenser
Response lever

FIGURE 1   B. F. Skinner with a Skinner box used to study operant conditioning. Laboratory rats learn to press the lever in order to obtain food, which is delivered in the tray.

Reinforcement: The Central Concept of Operant Conditioning

Skinner called the process that leads the rat to continue pressing the key "reinforcement." **Reinforcement** is the process by which a stimulus increases the probability that a preceding behavior will be repeated. In other words, pressing the lever is more likely to occur again because of the stimulus of food.

In a situation such as this one, the food is called a reinforcer. A **reinforcer** is any stimulus that increases the probability that a preceding behavior will occur again. Hence, food is a reinforcer because it increases the probability that the behavior of pressing (formally referred to as the *response* of pressing) will take place.

What kind of stimuli can act as reinforcers? Bonuses, toys, and good grades can serve as reinforcers—if they strengthen the probability of the response that occurred before their introduction.

There are two major types of reinforcers. A *primary reinforcer* satisfies some biological need and works naturally, regardless of a person's prior experience. Food for a hungry person, warmth for a cold person, and relief for a person in pain all would be classified as primary reinforcers. A *secondary reinforcer,* in contrast, is a stimulus that becomes reinforcing because of its association with a primary reinforcer. For instance, we know that money is valuable because we have learned that it allows us to obtain other desirable objects, including primary reinforcers such as food and shelter. Money thus becomes a secondary reinforcer.

Reinforcement The process by which a stimulus increases the probability that a preceding behavior will be repeated.

Reinforcer Any stimulus that increases the probability that a preceding behavior will occur again.

> *Bonuses, toys, and good grades can serve as reinforcers—if they strengthen the probability of the response that occurred before their introduction.*

» LO2 Positive Reinforcers, Negative Reinforcers, and Punishment

In many respects, reinforcers can be thought of in terms of rewards; both a reinforcer and a reward increase the probability that a preceding response will occur again. But the term *reward* is limited to *positive* occurrences, and this is where it differs from a reinforcer—for it turns out that reinforcers can be positive or negative.

A **positive reinforcer** is a stimulus *added* to the environment that brings about an increase in a preceding response. If food, water, money, or praise is provided after a response, it is more likely that that response will occur again in the future. The paychecks that workers get at the end of the week, for example, increase the likelihood that they will return to their jobs the following week.

In contrast, a **negative reinforcer** refers to an unpleasant stimulus whose *removal* leads to an increase in the probability that a preceding response will be repeated in the future. For example, if you have an itchy rash (an unpleasant stimulus) that is relieved when you apply a certain brand of ointment, you are more likely to use that ointment the next time you have an itchy rash. Using the ointment, then, is negatively reinforcing, because it removes the unpleasant itch. Negative reinforcement, then, teaches the individual that taking an action removes a negative condition that exists in the environment. Like positive reinforcers, negative reinforcers increase the likelihood that preceding behaviors will be repeated.

Note that negative reinforcement is not the same as punishment. **Punishment** refers to a stimulus that *decreases* the probability that a prior behavior will occur again. Unlike negative reinforcement, which produces an *increase* in behavior, punishment reduces the likelihood of a prior response. If we receive a shock that is meant to decrease a certain behavior, then, we are receiving punishment, but if we are already receiving a shock and do something to stop that shock, the behavior that stops the shock is considered to be negatively reinforced. In the first case, the specific behavior is apt to decrease because of the punishment; in the second, it is likely to increase because of the negative reinforcement.

There are two types of punishment: positive punishment and negative punishment, just as there are positive reinforcement and negative reinforcement. (In both cases, "positive" means adding something, and "negative" means removing something.) *Positive punishment* weakens a response through the application of an unpleasant stimulus. For instance, spanking a child for misbehaving, or spending 10 years in jail for committing a crime, is positive punishment. In contrast, *negative punishment* consists of the removal of something pleasant. For instance, when a teenager is told she is "grounded" and will no longer be able to use the family car because of her poor grades, or when an employee is informed that he has been demoted with a cut in pay because of a poor job evaluation, negative punishment is being administered. Both positive and negative punishment result in a decrease in the likelihood that a prior behavior will be repeated.

The following rules (and the summary in Figure 2) can help you distinguish these concepts from one another:

- Reinforcement *increases* the frequency of the behavior preceding it; punishment *decreases* the frequency of the behavior preceding it.

- The *application* of a *positive* stimulus brings about an increase in the frequency of behavior and is referred to as positive

Positive reinforcer A stimulus added to the environment that brings about an increase in a preceding response.

Negative reinforcer An unpleasant stimulus whose *removal* leads to an increase in the probability that a preceding response will be repeated in the future.

Punishment A stimulus that decreases the probability that a previous behavior will occur again.

From the perspective of . . .

A RETAIL SUPERVISOR How might you use the principles of operant conditioning to change employee behavior involving tardiness, customer service, or store cleanliness?

Intended Result	When Stimulus Is *Added*, the Result Is . . .	When Stimulus Is *Removed* or *Terminated*, the Result Is . . .
Increase in behavior (reinforcement)	**Positive Reinforcement** Example: Giving a raise for good performance Result: *Increase* in response of good performance 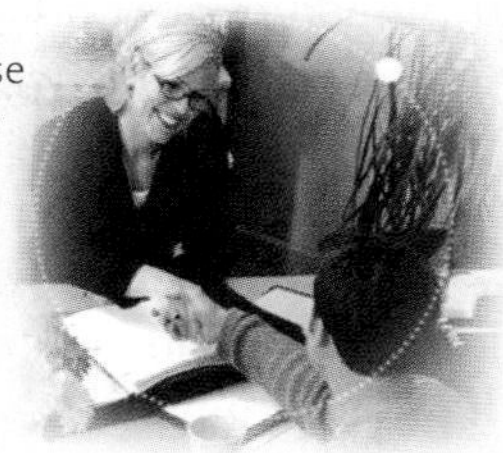	**Negative Reinforcement** Example: Applying ointment to relieve an itchy rash leads to a higher future likelihood of applying the ointment Result: *Increase* in response of using ointment 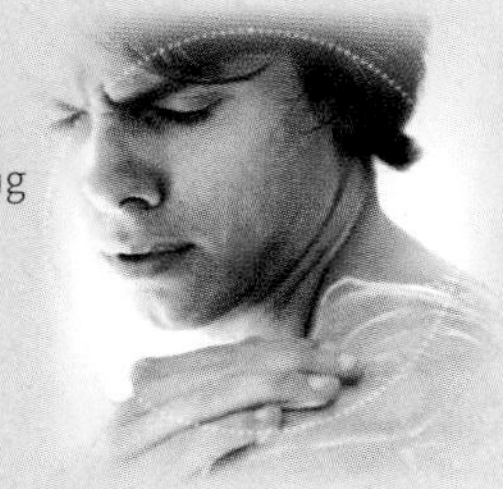
Decrease in behavior (punishment)	**Positive Punishment** Example: Yelling at a teenager when she steals a bracelet Result: *Decrease* in frequency of response of stealing 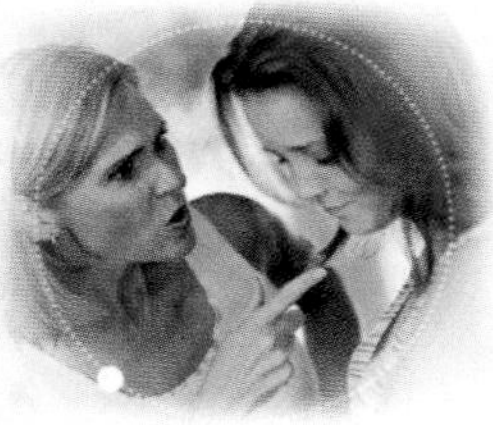	**Negative Punishment** Example: Teenager's access to car restricted by parents due to teenager's breaking curfew Result: *Decrease* in response of breaking curfew 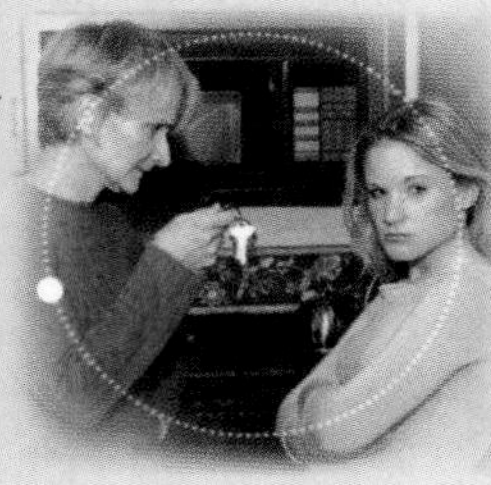

FIGURE 2 Types of reinforcement and punishment.

reinforcement; the *application* of a *negative* stimulus decreases or reduces the frequency of behavior and is called punishment.

- The *removal* of a *negative* stimulus that results in an increase in the frequency of behavior is negative reinforcement; the *removal* of a *positive* stimulus that decreases the frequency of behavior is negative punishment.

STUDY ALERT

The differences between positive reinforcement, negative reinforcement, positive punishment, and negative punishment are tricky, so pay special attention to Figure 2 and the rules in the text.

» LO3 The Pros and Cons of Punishment: Why Reinforcement Beats Punishment

Is punishment an effective way to modify behavior? Punishment often presents the quickest route to changing behavior that, if allowed to continue, might be dangerous to an individual. For instance, a parent may not have a second chance to warn a child not to run into a busy street, and so punishing the first incidence of this behavior may prove to be wise. Moreover, the use of punishment to suppress behavior, even temporarily, provides an opportunity to reinforce a person for subsequently behaving in a more desirable way.

Punishment has several disadvantages that make its routine use questionable.

Punishment has several disadvantages that make its routine use questionable. For one thing, punishment is frequently ineffective, particularly if it is not delivered shortly after the undesired behavior or if the individual is able to leave the setting in which the punishment is being given. An employee who is reprimanded by the boss may quit; a teenager who loses the use of the family car may borrow a friend's car instead. In such instances, the initial behavior that is being punished may be replaced by one that is even less desirable.

Even worse, physical punishment can convey to the recipient the idea that physical aggression is permissible and perhaps even desirable. A father who yells at and hits his son for misbehaving teaches the son that aggression is an appropriate, adult response. The son soon may copy his father's behavior by acting aggressively toward others. In addition, physical punishment is often administered by people who are themselves angry or enraged. It is unlikely that individuals in such an emotional state will be able to think through what they are doing or control carefully the degree of punishment they are inflicting (Baumrind, Larzelere, & Cowan, 2002; Sorbring, Deater-Deckard, & Palmerus, 2006).

In short, the research findings are clear: reinforcing desired behavior is a more appropriate technique for modifying behavior than using punishment (Hiby, Rooney, & Bradshaw, 2004; Sidman, 2006).

» LO4 Schedules of Reinforcement: Timing Life's Rewards

The world would be a different place if poker players never played cards again after the first losing hand, fishermen returned to shore as soon as they missed a catch, or telemarketers never made another phone call after their first hang-up. The fact that such unreinforced behaviors continue, often with great frequency and persistence, illustrates that reinforcement need not be received continually for behavior to be learned and maintained. In fact, behavior that is reinforced only occasionally can ultimately be learned better than can behavior that is always reinforced.

When we refer to the frequency and timing of reinforcement that follows desired behavior, we are talking about **schedules of reinforcement.** Behavior that is reinforced every time it occurs is said to be on a **continuous reinforcement schedule;** if it is reinforced some but not all of the time, it is on a **partial (or intermittent) reinforcement schedule.** Although learning occurs more rapidly under a continuous reinforcement schedule, behavior lasts longer after reinforcement stops when it is learned under a partial reinforcement schedule (Staddon & Cerutti, 2003; Gottlieb, 2004; Casey, Cooper-Brown, & Wacher, 2006).

Why should intermittent reinforcement result in stronger, longer-lasting learning than continuous reinforcement? We can answer the question by examining how we might behave when using a candy vending machine compared with a Las Vegas slot machine. When we use a vending machine, prior experience has taught us that every time we put in the appropriate amount of money, the reinforcement, a candy bar, ought to be delivered. In other words, the schedule of

Schedules of reinforcement Different patterns of frequency and timing of reinforcement following desired behavior.

Continuous reinforcement schedule Reinforcing of a behavior every time it occurs.

Partial (or intermittent) reinforcement schedule Reinforcing of a behavior some but not all of the time.

reinforcement is continuous. In comparison, a slot machine offers intermittent reinforcement. We have learned that after putting in our cash, most of the time we will not receive anything in return. At the same time, though, we know that we will occasionally win something.

Now suppose that, unknown to us, both the candy vending machine and the slot machine are broken, and so neither one is able to dispense anything. It would not be very long before we stopped depositing coins into the broken candy machine. Probably at most we would try only two or three times before leaving the machine in disgust. But the story would be quite different with the broken slot machine. Here, we would drop in money for a considerably longer time, even though there would be no payoff.

In formal terms, we can see the difference between the two reinforcement schedules: partial reinforcement schedules (such as those provided by slot machines) maintain performance longer than do continuous reinforcement schedules (such as those established in candy vending machines) before *extinction*—the disappearance of the conditioned response—occurs.

Certain kinds of partial reinforcement schedules produce stronger and lengthier responding before extinction than do others. Although many different partial reinforcement schedules have been examined, they can most readily be put into two categories: schedules that consider the *number of responses* made before reinforcement is given, called fixed-ratio and variable-ratio schedules, and those that consider the *amount of time* that elapses before reinforcement is provided, called fixed-interval and variable-interval schedules (Svartdal, 2003; Pellegrini et al., 2004; Gottlieb, 2006).

Fixed- and Variable-Ratio Schedules

In a **fixed-ratio schedule,** reinforcement is given only after a specific number of responses. For instance, a rat might receive a food pellet every 10th time it pressed a lever; here, the ratio would be 1:10. Similarly, garment workers are generally paid on fixed-ratio schedules: they receive a specific number of dollars for every blouse they sew. Because a greater rate of production means more reinforcement, people on fixed-ratio schedules are apt to work as quickly as possible (see Figure 3).

In a **variable-ratio schedule,** reinforcement occurs after a varying number of responses rather than after a fixed number. Although the specific number of responses necessary to receive reinforcement varies, the number of responses usually hovers around a specific average. A good example of a variable-ratio schedule is a telephone salesperson's job. She might make a sale during the third, eighth, ninth, and twentieth calls without being successful during any call in between. Although the number of responses that must be made before making a sale varies, it averages out to a 20 percent success rate. Under these circumstances, you might expect that the salesperson would try to make as many calls as possible in as short a time as possible. This is the case with all variable-ratio schedules, which lead to a high rate of response and resistance to extinction.

Fixed-ratio schedule A schedule by which reinforcement is given only after a specific number of responses are made.

Variable-ratio schedule A schedule by which reinforcement occurs after a varying number of responses rather than after a fixed number.

Fixed- and Variable-Interval Schedules: The Passage of Time

In contrast to fixed- and variable-ratio schedules, in which the crucial factor is the number of responses, fixed-*interval* and variable-*interval* schedules focus on the amount of time that has elapsed since a person or animal was rewarded.

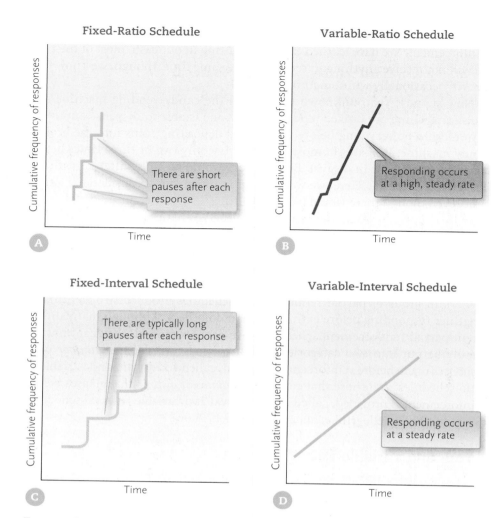

FIGURE 3 Typical outcomes of different reinforcement schedules. (A) In a fixed-ratio schedule, short pauses occur after each response. Because the more responses, the more reinforcement, fixed-ratio schedules produce a high rate of responding. (B) In a variable-ratio schedule, responding also occurs at a high rate. (C) A fixed-interval schedule produces lower rates of responding, especially just after reinforcement has been presented, because the organism learns that a specified time period must elapse between reinforcements. (D) A variable-interval schedule produces a fairly steady stream of responses.

One example of a fixed-interval schedule is a weekly paycheck. For people who receive regular, weekly paychecks, it typically makes relatively little difference exactly how much they produce in a given week.

Because a **fixed-interval schedule** provides reinforcement for a response only if a fixed time period has elapsed, overall rates of response are relatively low. This is especially true in the period just after reinforcement, when the time before another reinforcement is relatively great. Students' study habits often exemplify this reality. If the periods between exams are relatively long (meaning that the opportunity for reinforcement for good performance is given fairly infrequently), students often study minimally or not at all until the day of the exam draws near. Just before the exam, however, students begin to cram for it, signaling a rapid increase in the rate of their

Fixed-interval schedule A schedule that provides reinforcement for a response only if a fixed time period has elapsed, making overall rates of response relatively low.

studying response. As you might expect, immediately after the exam there is a rapid decline in the rate of responding, with few people opening a book the day after a test. Fixed-interval schedules produce the kind of "scalloping effect" shown in Figure 3.

One way to decrease the delay in responding that occurs just after reinforcement, and to maintain the desired behavior more consistently throughout an interval, is to use a variable-interval schedule. In a **variable-interval schedule,** the time between reinforcements varies around some average rather than being fixed. For example, a professor who gives surprise quizzes that vary from one every three days to one every three weeks, averaging one every two weeks, is using a variable-interval schedule. Compared to the study habits we observed with a fixed-interval schedule, students' study habits under such a variable-interval schedule would most likely be very different. Students would be apt to study more regularly because they would never know when the next surprise quiz was coming. Variable-interval schedules, in general, are more likely to produce relatively steady rates of responding than are fixed-interval schedules, with responses that take longer to extinguish after reinforcement ends.

psych2.0

WWW.MHHE.COM/PSYCHLIFE

Schedules of Reinforcement

» LO5 Shaping: Reinforcing What Doesn't Come Naturally

Consider the difficulty of using operant conditioning to teach people to repair an automobile transmission. If you had to wait until they chanced to fix a transmission perfectly before you provided them with reinforcement, the Model T Ford might be back in style long before they mastered the repair process.

There are many complex behaviors, ranging from auto repair to zoo management, that we would not expect to occur naturally as part of anyone's spontaneous behavior. For such behaviors, for which there might otherwise be no opportunity to provide reinforcement (because the behavior would never occur in the first place), a procedure known as shaping is used. **Shaping** is the process of teaching a complex behavior by rewarding closer and closer approximations of the desired behavior. In shaping, you start by reinforcing any behavior that is at all similar to the behavior you want the person to learn. Later, you reinforce only responses that are closer to the behavior you ultimately want to teach. Finally, you reinforce only the desired response. Each step in shaping, then, moves only slightly beyond the previously learned behavior, permitting the person to link the new step to the behavior learned earlier. Shaping allows even lower animals to learn complex responses that would never occur naturally, ranging from lions jumping through hoops, dolphins rescuing divers lost at sea, or rodents finding hidden land mines.

Variable-interval schedule A schedule by which the time between reinforcements varies around some average rather than being fixed.

Shaping The process of teaching a complex behavior by rewarding closer and closer approximations of the desired behavior.

Comparing Classical and Operant Conditioning

We've considered classical conditioning and operant conditioning as two completely different processes. And, as summarized in Figure 4, there are a number of key distinctions between the two forms of learning. For example, the key concept in classical conditioning is the association between stimuli, whereas in

Concept	Classical Conditioning	Operant Conditioning
Basic principle	Building associations between a conditioned stimulus and conditioned response.	Reinforcement increases the frequency of the behavior preceding it; punishment decreases the frequency of the behavior preceding it.
Nature of behavior	Based on involuntary, natural, innate behavior. Behavior is elicited by the unconditioned or conditioned stimulus.	Organism voluntarily operates on its environment to produce particular consequences. After behavior occurs, the likelihood of the behavior occurring again is increased or decreased by the behavior's consequences.
Order of events	Before conditioning, an unconditioned stimulus leads to an unconditioned response. After conditioning, a conditioned stimulus leads to a conditioned response.	Reinforcement leads to an increase in behavior; punishment leads to a decrease in behavior.
Example	After a physician gives a child a series of painful injections (an unconditioned stimulus) that produce an emotional reaction (an unconditioned response), the child develops an emotional reaction (a conditioned response) whenever he sees the physician (the conditioned stimulus).	A student who, after studying hard for a test, earns an A (the positive reinforcer) is more likely to study hard in the future. A student who, after going out drinking the night before a test, fails the test (punishment) is less likely to go out drinking the night before the next test.

FIGURE 4 Comparing key concepts in classical conditioning and operant conditioning.

operant conditioning it is reinforcement. Furthermore, classical conditioning involves an involuntary, natural, innate behavior, but operant conditioning is based on voluntary responses made by an organism.

becoming an *informed consumer*
OF PSYCHOLOGY

Using Behavior Analysis and Behavior Modification

A couple who had been living together for three years began to fight frequently. The issues of disagreement ranged from who was going to do the dishes to the quality of their love life.

Disturbed, the couple went to a *behavior analyst,* a psychologist who specialized in behavior-modification techniques. He asked them to keep a detailed written record of their interactions over the next two weeks.

When they returned with the data, he carefully reviewed the records with them. In doing so, he noticed a pattern: each of their arguments had occurred just after one or the other had left a household chore undone, such as leaving dirty dishes in the sink or draping clothes on the only chair in the bedroom.

Using the data the couple had collected, the behavior analyst asked them to list all the chores that could possibly arise and assign each one a point value depending on how long it took to complete. Then he had them divide the chores equally and agree in a written contract to fulfill the ones assigned to them. If either failed to carry out one of the assigned chores, he or she would have to place $1 per point in a fund for the other to spend. They also agreed to a program of verbal praise, promising to reward each other verbally for completing a chore.

The couple agreed to try it for a month and to keep careful records of the number of arguments they had during that period. To their surprise, the number declined rapidly.

This case provides an illustration of **behavior modification,** a formalized technique for promoting the frequency of desirable behaviors and decreasing the incidence of unwanted ones. Using the basic principles of learning theory, behavior-modification techniques have proved to be helpful in a variety of situations. People with severe mental retardation have, for the first time in their lives, started dressing and feeding themselves. Behavior modification has also helped people lose weight, give up smoking, and behave more safely (Wadden, Crerand, & Brock, 2005; Delinsky, Latner, & Wilson, 2006; Ntinas, 2007).

> **Behavior modification** A formalized technique for promoting the frequency of desirable behaviors and decreasing the incidence of unwanted ones.

The techniques used by behavior analysts are as varied as the list of processes that modify behavior. They include reinforcement scheduling, shaping, generalization training, discrimination training, and extinction. Participants in a behavior-change program do, however, typically follow a series of similar basic steps that include the following:

- *Identifying goals and target behaviors.* The first step is to define *desired behavior.* Is it an increase in time spent studying? A decrease in weight? A reduction in the amount of aggression displayed by a child? The goals must be stated in observable terms and must lead to specific targets. For instance, a goal might be "to increase study time," whereas the target behavior would be "to study at least two hours per day on weekdays and an hour on Saturdays."

- *Designing a data-recording system and recording preliminary data.* To determine whether behavior has changed, it is necessary to collect data before any changes are made in the situation. This information provides a baseline against which future changes can be measured.

- *Selecting a behavior-change strategy.* The most crucial step is to select an appropriate strategy. Because all the principles of learning can be employed to bring about behavior change, a "package" of treatments is normally used. This might include the systematic use of positive reinforcement for desired behavior (verbal praise or something more tangible, such as food), as well as a program of extinction for undesirable behavior (ignoring a child who throws a tantrum). Selecting the right reinforcers is critical, and it may be necessary to experiment a bit to find out what is important to a particular individual.

- *Implementing the program.* Probably the most important aspect of program implementation is consistency. It is also important to reinforce the intended behavior. For example, suppose a mother wants her daughter to spend more time on her homework, but as soon as the child sits down to study, she asks for a snack. If the mother gets a snack for her, she is likely to be reinforcing her daughter's delaying tactic, not her studying.

- *Keeping careful records after the program is implemented.* Another crucial task is record keeping. If the target behaviors are not monitored, there is no way of knowing whether the program has actually been successful.

- *Evaluating and altering the ongoing program.* Finally, the results of the program should be compared with baseline, preimplementation data to determine its effectiveness. If the program has been successful, the procedures employed can be phased out gradually. For instance, if the program called for reinforcing every instance of picking up one's clothes from the bedroom floor, the reinforcement schedule could be modified to a fixed-ratio schedule in which every third instance was reinforced. However, if the program has not been successful in bringing about the desired behavior change, consideration of other approaches might be advisable.

Behavior-change techniques based on these general principles have enjoyed wide success and have proved to be one of the most powerful means of modifying behavior. Clearly, it is possible to employ the basic notions of learning theory to improve our lives.

RECAP

Define the basics of operant conditioning.

- Operant conditioning is a form of learning in which a voluntary behavior is strengthened or weakened. According to B. F. Skinner, the major mechanism underlying learning is reinforcement, the process by which a stimulus increases the probability that a preceding behavior will be repeated. (p. 170)

- Primary reinforcers are rewards that are naturally effective without prior experience because they satisfy a biological need. Secondary reinforcers begin to act as if they were primary reinforcers through association with a primary reinforcer. (p. 171)

Explain reinforcers and punishment.

- Positive reinforcers are stimuli that are added to the environment and lead to an increase in a preceding response. Negative reinforcers are stimuli that remove something unpleasant from the environment, also leading to an increase in the preceding response. (p. 172)

- Punishment decreases the probability that a prior behavior will occur. Positive punishment weakens a response through the application of an unpleasant stimulus, whereas negative punishment weakens a response by the removal of something positive. In contrast to reinforce-

ment, in which the goal is to increase the incidence of behavior, punishment is meant to decrease or suppress behavior. (p. 172)

Present the pros and cons of punishment.

- Although punishment often presents the quickest route to changing behavior that, if allowed to continue, might be dangerous to an individual, it has disadvantages that make its routine use questionable. For example, punishment is frequently ineffective, particularly if it is not delivered shortly after the undesired behavior. Worse, physical punishment can convey to the recipient the idea that physical aggression is permissible and perhaps even desirable. (p. 173)

- The research findings are clear: reinforcing desired behavior is a more appropriate technique for modifying behavior than using punishment. (p. 174)

Discuss schedules of reinforcement.

- Schedules and patterns of reinforcement affect the strength and duration of learning. Generally, partial reinforcement schedules—in which reinforcers are not delivered on every trial—produce stronger and longer-lasting learning than do continuous reinforcement schedules. (p. 174)

- Among the major categories of reinforcement schedules are fixed- and variable-ratio schedules, which are based on the number of responses made; and fixed- and variable-interval schedules, which are based on the time interval that elapses before reinforcement is provided. (p. 175)

Explain the concept of shaping.

- Shaping is a process for teaching complex behaviors by rewarding closer and closer approximations of the desired final behavior. (p. 177)

EVALUATE

1. _____ conditioning describes learning that occurs as a result of reinforcement.
2. Match the type of operant learning with its definition:
   a. Positive reinforcement
   b. Negative reinforcement
   c. Positive punishment
   d. Negative punishment

   1. An unpleasant stimulus is presented to decrease behavior.
   2. An unpleasant stimulus is removed to increase behavior.
   3. A pleasant stimulus is presented to increase behavior.
   4. A pleasant stimulus is removed to decrease behavior.
3. Sandy had had a rough day, and his son's noisemaking was not helping him relax. Not wanting to resort to scolding, Sandy told his son in a serious manner that he was very tired and would like the boy to play quietly for an hour. This approach worked. For Sandy, the change in his son's behavior was
   a. Positively reinforcing
   b. Negatively reinforcing
4. In a _____ reinforcement schedule, behavior is reinforced some of the time, whereas in a _____ reinforcement schedule, behavior is reinforced all the time.
5. Match the type of reinforcement schedule with its definition:
   a. Fixed-ratio
   b. Variable-interval
   c. Fixed-interval
   d. Variable-ratio

   1. Reinforcement occurs after a set time period.
   2. Reinforcement occurs after a set number of responses.
   3. Reinforcement occurs after a varying time period.
   4. Reinforcement occurs after a varying number of responses.

RETHINK

Using scientific literature as a guide, what would you tell parents who wish to know if the routine use of physical punishment is a necessary and acceptable form of child rearing?

Answers to Evaluate Questions 1. operant; 2. c-1; b-2; a-3; d-4 3. b 4. partial (or intermittent), continuous; 5. c-1, a-2, b-3, d-4

[KEY TERMS]

Cognitive Approaches to Learning

Consider what happens when people learn to drive a car. They don't just get behind the wheel and stumble around until they randomly put the key into the ignition, and later, after many false starts, accidentally manage to get the car to move forward, thereby receiving positive reinforcement. Instead, they already know the basic elements of driving from prior experience as passengers, when they more than likely noticed how the key was inserted into the ignition, the car was put in drive, and the gas pedal was pressed to make the car go forward.

Clearly, not all learning is due to operant and classical conditioning. In fact, activities like learning to drive a car imply that some kinds of learning must involve higher-order processes in which people's thoughts and memories and the way they process information account for their responses. Such situations argue against regarding learning as the unthinking, mechanical, and automatic acquisition of associations between stimuli and responses, as in classical conditioning, or the presentation of reinforcement, as in operant conditioning.

Some psychologists view learning in terms of the thought processes, or cognitions, that underlie it—an approach known as **cognitive learning theory.** Although psychologists working from the cognitive learning perspective do not deny the importance of classical and operant conditioning, they have developed approaches that focus on the unseen mental processes that occur during learning, rather than concentrating solely on external stimuli, responses, and reinforcements.

In its most basic formulation, cognitive learning theory suggests that it is not enough to say that people make responses because there is an assumed link between a stimulus and a response—a link that is the result of a past history of reinforcement for a response. Instead, according to this point of view, people, and even lower animals, develop an *expectation* that they will receive a reinforcer after making a response. Two types of learning in which no obvious prior reinforcement is present are latent learning and observational learning.

LEARNING OUTCOMES

17.1 Explain latent learning and how it works in humans.

17.2 Discuss the influence of observational learning in acquiring skills.

17.3 Describe research findings about observational learning and media violence.

Cognitive learning theory An approach to the study of learning that focuses on the thought processes that underlie learning.

STUDY ALERT

Remember that the cognitive learning approach focuses on the *internal* thoughts and expectations of learners, whereas classical and operant conditioning approaches focus on *external* stimuli, responses, and reinforcement.

» LO1 Latent Learning

Latent learning Learning in which a new behavior is acquired but is not demonstrated until some incentive is provided for displaying it.

Evidence for the importance of cognitive processes comes from a series of animal experiments that revealed a type of cognitive learning called latent learning. In **latent learning,** a new behavior is learned but not demonstrated until some incentive is provided for displaying it (Tolman & Honzik, 1930). In short, latent learning occurs without reinforcement.

In the studies demonstrating latent learning, psychologists examined the behavior of rats in a maze such as the one shown in Figure 1A. In one experiment, a group of rats was allowed to wander around the maze once a day for 17 days without ever receiving a reward. Understandably, those rats made many errors and spent a relatively long time reaching the end of the maze. A second group, however, was always given food at the end of the maze. Not surprisingly,

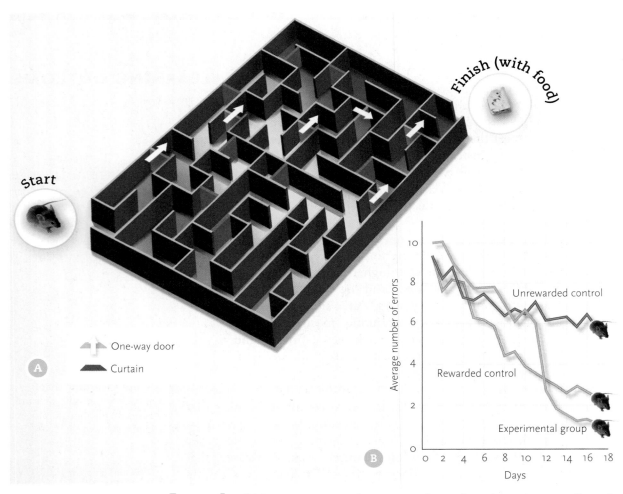

FIGURE 1 (A) In an attempt to demonstrate latent learning, rats were allowed to roam through a maze of this sort once a day for 17 days. (B) The rats that were never rewarded (the nonrewarded control condition) consistently made the most errors, whereas those that received food at the finish every day (the rewarded control condition) consistently made far fewer errors. But the results also showed latent learning: rats that were initially unrewarded but began to be rewarded only after the 10th day (the experimental group) showed an immediate reduction in errors and soon became similar in error rate to the rats that had been rewarded consistently. According to cognitive learning theorists, the reduction in errors indicates that the rats had developed a cognitive map—a mental representation—of the maze. Can you think of other examples of latent learning?

those rats learned to run quickly and directly to the food box, making few errors.

A third group of rats started out in the same situation as the unrewarded rats, but only for the first 10 days. On the 11th day, a critical experimental manipulation was introduced: from that point on, the rats in this group were given food for completing the maze. The results of this manipulation were dramatic, as you can see from the graph in Figure 1B. The previously unrewarded rats, which had earlier seemed to wander about aimlessly, showed such reductions in running time and declines in error rates that their performance almost immediately matched that of the group that had received rewards from the start.

To cognitive theorists, it seemed clear that the unrewarded rats had learned the layout of the maze early in their explorations; they just never displayed their latent learning until the reinforcement was offered. Instead, those rats seemed to develop a *cognitive map* of the maze—a mental representation of spatial locations and directions.

People, too, develop cognitive maps of their surroundings. For example, latent learning may permit you to know the location of a kitchenware store at a local mall you've frequently visited, even though you've never entered the store and don't even like to cook.

> **People, too, develop cognitive maps of their surroundings.**

The possibility that we develop our cognitive maps through latent learning presents something of a problem for strict operant conditioning theorists. If we consider the results of the maze-learning experiment, for instance, it is unclear what reinforcement permitted the rats that initially received no reward to learn the layout of the maze, because there was no obvious reinforcer present. Instead, the results support a cognitive view of learning, in which changes occurred in unobservable mental processes (Beatty, 2002; Voicu & Schmajuk, 2002; Frensch & Rünger, 2003; Stouffer & White, 2006).

» LO2 Observational Learning: Learning Through Imitation

psych2.0
WWW.MHHE.COM/PSYCHLIFE

Observational Learning

Let's return for a moment to the case of a person learning to drive. How can we account for instances in which an individual with no direct experience in carrying out a particular behavior learns the behavior and then performs it? To answer this question, psychologists have focused on another aspect of cognitive learning: observational learning.

According to psychologist Albert Bandura and colleagues, a major part of human learning consists of **observational learning,** which is learning by watching the behavior of another person, or *model*. Because of its reliance on observation of others—a social phenomenon—the perspective taken by Bandura is often referred to as a *social cognitive* approach to learning (Bandura, 2004).

Bandura dramatically demonstrated the ability of models to stimulate learning in a classic experiment. In the study, young children saw a film of an adult wildly hitting a five-foot-tall inflatable punching toy called a Bobo

> **Observational learning** Learning by observing the behavior of another person, or model.

Albert Bandura examined the principles of observational learning.

STUDY ALERT

A key point of observational learning approaches is that the behavior of models who are rewarded for a given behavior is more likely to be imitated than behavior in which the model is punished for the behavior.

doll (Bandura, Ross, & Ross, 1963a, 1963b). Later the children were given the opportunity to play with the Bobo doll themselves, and, sure enough, most displayed the same kind of behavior, in some cases mimicking the aggressive behavior almost identically.

Not only negative behaviors are acquired through observational learning. In one experiment, for example, children who were afraid of dogs were exposed to a model—dubbed the Fearless Peer—playing with a dog (Bandura, Grusec, & Menlove, 1967). After exposure, observers were considerably more likely to approach a strange dog than were children who had not viewed the Fearless Peer.

Observational learning is particularly important in acquiring skills in which the operant conditioning technique of shaping is inappropriate. Piloting an airplane and performing brain surgery, for example, are behaviors that could hardly be learned by using trial-and-error methods without grave cost—literally—to those involved in the learning process.

Observational learning may have a genetic basis. For example, we find observational learning at work with mother animals teaching their young such activities as hunting. In addition, the discovery of *mirror neurons* that fire when we observe another person carrying out a behavior (discussed in the chapter on neuroscience) suggests that the capacity to imitate others may be inborn (see Figure 2; Thornton & McAuliffe, 2006; Lepage & Theoret, 2007; Schulte-Ruther et al., 2007).

Not all behavior that we witness is learned or carried out, of course. One crucial factor that determines whether we later imitate a model is whether the model is rewarded for his or her behavior. If we observe a friend being rewarded for putting more time into her studies by receiving higher grades, we are more likely to imitate her behavior than we would if her behavior resulted only in being stressed and tired. Models who are rewarded for behaving in a particular way are more apt to be mimicked than are models who receive punishment. Observing the punishment of a model, however, does not necessarily stop observers from learning the behavior. Observers can still describe the model's behavior—they are just less apt to perform it (Bandura, 1977, 1986, 1994).

Observational learning is central to a number of important issues relating to the extent to which people learn simply by watching the behavior of others.

This girl is displaying observational learning based on prior observation of her mother. How does observational learning contribute to defining gender roles?

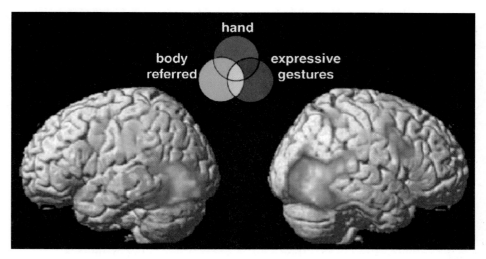

FIGURE 2   This fMRI scan shows the activation of specific regions of the brain related to mirror neuron systems when participants in an experiment observed three different kinds of behavior: hand movements (such as twisting a lid), shown in blue; body-referred movements (such as brushing teeth), shown in green; and expressive gestures (such as threatening gestures), shown in red. The brain activation occurred in perception-related areas in the occipital and temporal lobes of the brain as well as the mirror neuron system in the lateral frontal and superior parietal lobes. *(Source: Lotze et al., 2006, p. 1790.)*

For instance, the degree to which observation of media aggression produces subsequent aggression on the part of viewers is a crucial—and controversial—question, as we discuss next.

» LO3 Violence in Television and Video Games: Does the Media's Message Matter?

In an episode of "The Sopranos" television series, fictional mobster Tony Soprano murdered one of his associates. To make identification of the victim's body difficult, Soprano and one of his henchmen dismembered the body and dumped the body parts.

A few months later, two real-life half brothers in Riverside, California, strangled their mother and then cut her head and hands from her body. Victor Bautista, 20, and Matthew Montejo, 15, were caught by police after a security guard noticed that the bundle they were attempting to throw in a Dumpster had a foot sticking out of it. They told police that the plan to dismember their mother was inspired by "The Sopranos" episode (Martelle, Hanley, & Yoshino, 2003).

Do you think observation of "The Sopranos" television show resulted in an upswing in viewer violence?

Like other "media copycat" killings, the brothers' cold-blooded brutality raises a critical issue: Does observing violent and antisocial acts in the media lead viewers to behave in similar ways? Because research on modeling shows that people frequently learn and imitate the aggression that they observe, this question is among the most important issues being addressed by psychologists.

Certainly, the amount of violence in the mass media is enormous. By the time of elementary school graduation, the average child in the United States will have viewed more than 8,000 murders and more than 800,000 violent acts on network television (Huston et al., 1992; Mifflin, 1998).

Most experts agree that watching high levels of media violence makes viewers more susceptible to acting aggressively, and recent research supports this claim. For example, one survey of serious and violent young male offenders incarcerated in Florida showed that one-fourth of them had attempted to commit a media-inspired copycat crime (Surette, 2002). A significant proportion of those teenage offenders noted that they paid close attention to the media.

Several aspects of media violence may contribute to real-life aggressive behavior (Bushman & Anderson, 2001; Johnson et al., 2002). For one thing, experiencing violent media content seems to lower inhibitions against carrying out aggression—watching television portrayals of violence makes aggression seem a legitimate response to particular situations. Exposure to media violence also may distort our understanding of the meaning of others' behavior, predisposing us to view even nonaggressive acts by others as aggressive. Finally, a continuous diet of aggression may leave us desensitized to violence, and what previously would have repelled us now produces little emotional response. Our sense of the pain and suffering brought about by aggression may be diminished (Bartholow, Bushman, & Sestir, 2006; Weber, Ritterfeld, & Kostygina, 2006; Carnagey, Anderson, & Bushman, 2007).

From the perspective of . . .

A VIDEO GAME DESIGNER   What responsibility would you have regarding how much violence was projected in your design?

EXPLORING diversity

Does Culture Influence How We Learn?

When a member of the Chilcotin Indian tribe teaches her daughter to prepare salmon, at first she only allows the daughter to observe the entire process. A little later, she permits her child to try out some basic parts of the task. Her response to questions is noteworthy. For example, when the

What's Your Receptive Learning Style?

Read each of the following statements and rank them in terms of their usefulness to you as learning approaches. Base your ratings on your personal experiences and preferences, using the following scale:

1 = Not at all useful

2 = Not very useful

3 = Neutral

4 = Somewhat useful

5 = Very useful

	1	2	3	4	5
1. Studying alone	___	___	___	___	___
2. Studying pictures and diagrams to understand complex ideas	___	___	___	___	___
3. Listening to class lectures	___	___	___	___	___
4. Performing a process myself rather than reading or hearing about it	___	___	___	___	___
5. Learning a complex procedure by reading written directions	___	___	___	___	___
6. Watching and listening to film, computer, or video presentations	___	___	___	___	___
7. Listening to a book or lecture on tape	___	___	___	___	___
8. Doing lab work	___	___	___	___	___
9. Studying teachers' handouts and lecture notes	___	___	___	___	___
10. Studying in a quiet room	___	___	___	___	___
11. Taking part in group discussions	___	___	___	___	___
12. Taking part in hands-on classroom demonstrations	___	___	___	___	___
13. Taking notes and studying them later	___	___	___	___	___
14. Creating flash cards and using them as a study and review tool	___	___	___	___	___
15. Memorizing and recalling how words are spelled by spelling them "out loud" in my head	___	___	___	___	___
16. Writing key facts and important points down as a tool for remembering them	___	___	___	___	___
17. Recalling how to spell a word by seeing it in my head	___	___	___	___	___

(continued)

18. Underlining or highlighting important facts or passages in my reading _____ _____ _____ _____ _____

19. Saying things out loud when I'm studying _____ _____ _____ _____ _____

20. Recalling how to spell a word by "writing" it invisibly in the air or on a surface _____ _____ _____ _____ _____

21. Learning new information by reading about it in a textbook _____ _____ _____ _____ _____

22. Using a map to find an unknown place _____ _____ _____ _____ _____

23. Working in a study group _____ _____ _____ _____ _____

24. Finding a place I've been to once by just going there without directions _____ _____ _____ _____ _____

Scoring

The statements cycle through four receptive learning styles:

- **Read/write:** If you have a read/write learning style, you prefer information that is presented visually in a written format. You feel most comfortable reading, and you may recall the spelling of a word by thinking of how the word looks. You probably learn best when you have the opportunity to read about a concept rather than listening to a teacher explain it.

- **Visual/graphic:** Students with a visual/graphic learning style learn most effectively when material is presented visually in a diagram or picture. You might recall the structure of a chemical compound by reviewing a picture in your mind, and you benefit from instructors who make frequent use of visual aids such as videos, maps, and models. Students with visual learning styles find it easier to see things in their mind's eye—to visualize a task or concept—than to be lectured about them.

- **Auditory/verbal:** Have you ever asked a friend to help you put something together by having her read the directions to you while you worked? If you did, you may have an auditory/verbal learning style. People with auditory/verbal learning styles prefer listening to explanations rather than reading them. They love class lectures and discussions, because they can easily take in the information that is being talked about.

- **Tactile/kinesthetic:** Students with a tactile/kinesthetic learning style prefer to learn by doing—touching, manipulating objects, and doing things. For instance, some people enjoy the act of writing because of the feel of a pencil or a computer keyboard—the tactile equivalent of thinking out loud. Or they may find that it helps them to make a three-dimensional model to understand a new idea.

To find your primary learning style, disregard your 1, 2, and 3 ratings. Add up your 4 and 5 ratings for each learning style (i.e., a "4" equals 4 points and a "5" equals 5 points). Use the following chart to link the statements to the learning styles and to write down your summed ratings:

Learning Style	Statements	Total (Sum) of Rating Points
Read/write	1, 5, 9, 13, 17, and 21	_____
Visual/graphic	2, 6, 10, 14, 18, and 22	_____
Auditory/verbal	3, 7, 11, 15, 19, and 23	_____
Tactile/kinesthetic	4, 8, 12, 16, 20, and 24	_____

The total of your rating points for any given style will range from a low of 0 to a high of 30. The highest total indicates your main receptive learning style. Don't be surprised if you have a mixed style, in which two or more styles receive similar ratings.

daughter asks about how to do "the backbone part," the mother's response is to repeat the entire process with another salmon. The reason? The mother feels that one cannot learn the individual parts of the task apart from the context of preparing the whole fish. (Tharp, 1989)

It should not be surprising that children raised in the Chilcotin tradition, which stresses instruction that starts by communicating the entire task, may have difficulty with traditional Western schooling. In the approach to teaching most characteristic of Western culture, tasks are broken down into their component parts. Only after each small step is learned is it thought possible to master the complete task.

Do the differences in teaching approaches between cultures affect how people learn? Some psychologists, taking a cognitive perspective on learning, suggest that people develop particular *learning styles,* characteristic ways of approaching material, based on their cultural background and unique pattern of abilities (Anderson & Adams, 1992; Barmeyer, 2004; Wilkinson & Olliver-Gray, 2006). Learning styles differ along several dimensions. For example, one central dimension relates to our *receptive learning style,* or the way in which we initially receive information from our sense organs and then process that information. As you can see for yourself in the accompanying *Try It!,* you probably have a receptive learning style in which you prefer to have material presented in a particular manner. For example, you may prefer to learn from visual/graphic material, rather than through reading written material.

> *Do the differences in teaching approaches between cultures affect how people learn?*

Another important learning style is relational versus analytical approaches to learning. As illustrated in Figure 3, people with a *relational learning style*

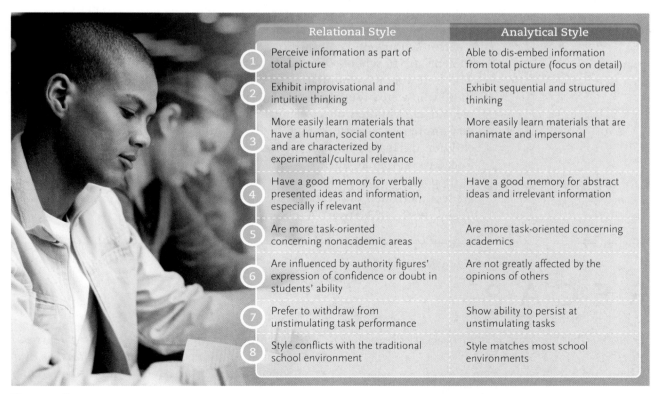

	Relational Style	Analytical Style
1	Perceive information as part of total picture	Able to dis-embed information from total picture (focus on detail)
2	Exhibit improvisational and intuitive thinking	Exhibit sequential and structured thinking
3	More easily learn materials that have a human, social content and are characterized by experimental/cultural relevance	More easily learn materials that are inanimate and impersonal
4	Have a good memory for verbally presented ideas and information, especially if relevant	Have a good memory for abstract ideas and irrelevant information
5	Are more task-oriented concerning nonacademic areas	Are more task-oriented concerning academics
6	Are influenced by authority figures' expression of confidence or doubt in students' ability	Are not greatly affected by the opinions of others
7	Prefer to withdraw from unstimulating task performance	Show ability to persist at unstimulating tasks
8	Style conflicts with the traditional school environment	Style matches most school environments

FIGURE 3   A comparison of analytical versus relational approaches to learning offers one example of how learning styles differ along several dimensions.

Even though these friends have grown up next door to one another and are similar in many ways, they have very different learning styles. What might account for this?

master material best through exposure to a full unit or phenomenon. Parts of the unit are comprehended only when their relationship to the whole is understood.

In contrast, those with an *analytical learning style* do best when they can carry out an initial analysis of the principles and components underlying a phenomenon or situation. By developing an understanding of the fundamental principles and components, they are best able to understand the full picture.

According to James Anderson and Maurianne Adams, particular minority groups in Western societies display characteristic learning styles. For instance, they argue that Caucasian females and African American, Native American, and Hispanic American males and females are more apt to use a relational style of learning than Caucasian and Asian American males, who are more likely to employ an analytical style (Anderson & Adams, 1992; Adams et al., 2000).

The conclusion that members of particular ethnic and gender groups have similar learning styles is controversial. Because there is so much diversity within each particular racial and ethnic group, critics argue that generalizations about learning styles cannot be used to predict the style of any single individual, regardless of group membership.

Still, it is clear that values about learning, which are communicated through a person's family and cultural background, have an impact on how successful students are in school. One theory suggests that members of minority groups who were voluntary immigrants are more apt to be successful in school than those who were brought into a majority culture against their will. For example, Korean children in the United States—the sons and daughters of voluntary immigrants—perform quite well, as a group, in school. In contrast, Korean children in Japan, who were often the sons and daughters of people who were forced to immigrate during World War II, essentially as forced laborers, tend to do poorly in school. Presumably, children in the forced immigration group are less motivated to succeed than those in the voluntary immigration group (Ogbu, 1992, 2003; Foster, 2005).

RECAP

Explain latent learning and how it works in humans.

- Cognitive approaches to learning consider learning in terms of thought processes, or cognition. Phenomena such as latent learning—in which a new behavior is learned but not performed until some incentive is provided for its performance—and the apparent development of cognitive maps support cognitive approaches. (p. 184)

- Learning also occurs from observing the behavior of others. The major factor that determines whether an observed behavior will actually be performed is the nature of the reinforcement or punishment a model receives. (p. 185)

- Observational learning, which may have a genetic basis, is particularly important in acquiring skills in which the operant conditioning technique of shaping is inappropriate. (p. 186)

- Observation of violence is linked to a greater likelihood of subsequently acting aggressively. (p. 188)

- Experiencing violent media content seems to lower inhibitions against carrying out aggression; may distort our understanding of the meaning of others' behavior, predisposing us to view even nonaggressive acts by others as aggressive; and desensitizes us to violence. (p. 188)

EVALUATE

1. Cognitive learning theorists are concerned only with overt behavior, not with its internal causes. True or false?

2. In cognitive learning theory, it is assumed that people develop a(n) _____ about receiving a reinforcer when they behave a certain way.

3. In _____ learning, a new behavior is learned but is not shown until appropriate reinforcement is presented.

4. Bandura's theory of _____ learning states that people learn through watching a(n) _____ —another person displaying the behavior of interest.

RETHINK

The relational style of learning sometimes conflicts with the traditional school environment. Could a school be created that takes advantage of the characteristics of the relational style? How? Are there types of learning for which the analytical style is clearly superior?

Answers to Evaluate Questions 1. false; cognitive learning theorists are primarily concerned with mental processes; 2. expectation; 3. latent; 4. observational, model

[KEY TERMS]

Cognitive learning theory *p. 183*
Latent learning *p. 184*

Observational learning *p. 185*

looking BACK

Psychology on the Web

1. B. F. Skinner had an impact on society and on thought that is only hinted at in our discussion of learning. Find additional information on the Web about Skinner's life and influence. See what you can find out about his ideas for an ideal, utopian society based on the principles of conditioning and behaviorism. Write a summary of your findings.

2. Select a topic discussed in this set of modules that is of interest to you—for example, reinforcement versus punishment, teaching complex behaviors by shaping, violence in video games, relational versus analytical learning styles, behavior modification, and so on. Find at least two sources of information on the Web about your topic and summarize the results of your quest. It may be most helpful to find two different approaches to your topic and compare them.

the case of...

THE MANAGER WHO DOUBLED PRODUCTIVITY

When Cliff Richards took over as the new department manager, he discovered that the existing staff was unusually inefficient and unproductive. Cliff learned that the previous manager often criticized and chided staff members for every little mistake until many of the best people had left, and the rest felt demoralized.

Cliff resolved not to criticize or punish staff members unless it was absolutely necessary. Instead, he frequently complimented them whenever they did a good job. He set daily production goals for them, and every Friday afternoon he bought lunch for all staff members who met their goals every day that week. Moreover, Cliff randomly conducted spot checks on what staff members were doing, and if he found them hard at work, he gave them small rewards such as extra break time.

Within just three months, productivity in Cliff's department nearly doubled. It became the most efficient department in the company.

1. How did Cliff take advantage of principles of operant conditioning to modify his staff's behavior?

2. Why did Cliff's predecessor's strategy of punishing undesirable behavior not work very well? Even if punishment and reinforcement strategies were equally effective at controlling behavior, why would reinforcement remain preferable?

3. How did Cliff make use of partial reinforcement schedules? What kinds of schedules did he use?

4. How could Cliff use his technique to train his staff to complete a complex new task that they had never done before?

5. How might Cliff make use of principles of cognitive learning theory to improve his staff's productivity even further?

full circle

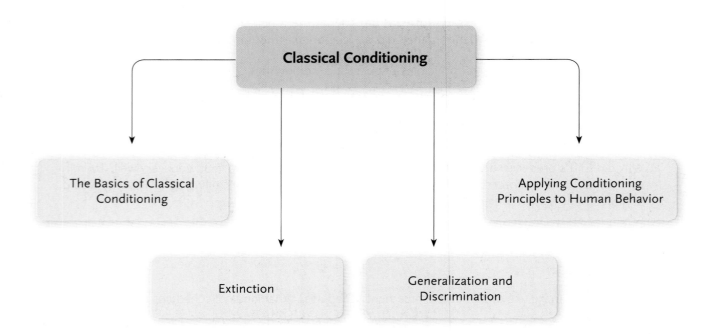

Classical Conditioning

The Basics of Classical Conditioning

Extinction

Generalization and Discrimination

Applying Conditioning Principles to Human Behavior

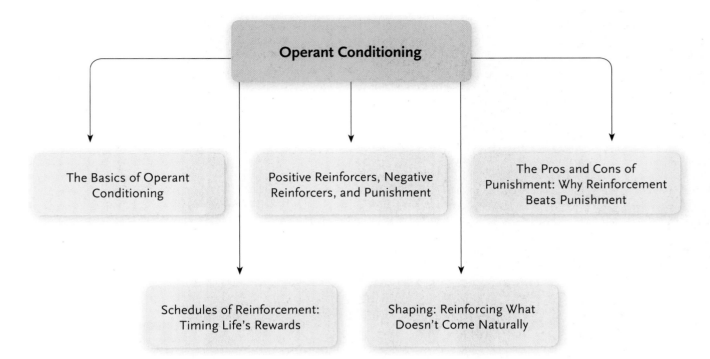

Operant Conditioning

- The Basics of Operant Conditioning
- Positive Reinforcers, Negative Reinforcers, and Punishment
- The Pros and Cons of Punishment: Why Reinforcement Beats Punishment
- Schedules of Reinforcement: Timing Life's Rewards
- Shaping: Reinforcing What Doesn't Come Naturally

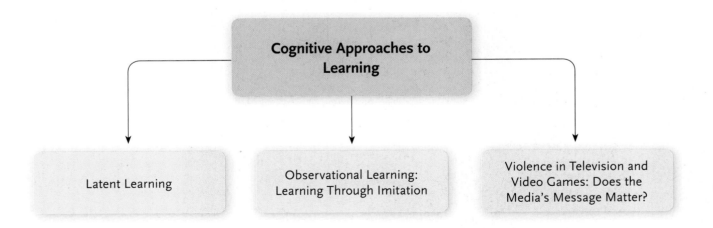

Cognitive Approaches to Learning

- Latent Learning
- Observational Learning: Learning Through Imitation
- Violence in Television and Video Games: Does the Media's Message Matter?

THINKING:
MEMORY,
COGNITION,
AND
LANGUAGE

CHAPTER OUTLINE

Microbe-Busting Bandages

What do jock itch, poison gas, and flesh-eating bacteria have in common? Gregory Schultz, 56, thinks he has the answer. The cancer researcher turned inventor has patented a technique for chemically bonding bacteria-fighting polymers to such fabrics as gauze bandages, cotton T shirts, and men's underpants. It's a technology with an unusually wide variety of uses, from underwear that doesn't stink to hospital dressings that thwart infections.

The bandages, coated with positively charged antimicrobial molecules, dramatically reduce the risk of infection, Schultz says, and as a bonus they can prevent outbreaks of the drug-resistant staph infections that have been racing through U.S. hospitals. "It basically punches holes in the bacteria," he says, "and they pop like balloons." (Morrissey, 2006) ■

Schultz's invention was a long time in coming. Two decades earlier, a student working in a burn unit mentioned that the way in which cells responded to cancer might be harnessed to help burn victims avoid infection. It took 20 years of puzzling over the problem before Schultz invented his antibacterial bandages.

It is clear that Schultz has the elusive quality that marks successful inventors: creativity. Where did his creativity come from? More generally, how do people use information to devise innovative solutions to problems? And how do people think about, understand, and, through language, describe the world?

Answers to these questions come from **cognitive psychology,** the branch of psychology that focuses on the study of higher mental processes, including thinking, language, memory, problem solving, knowing, reasoning, judging, and decision making. Clearly, the realm of cognitive psychology is broad.

> **Cognitive psychology** The branch of psychology that focuses on the study of higher mental processes, including thinking, language, memory, problem solving, knowing, reasoning, judging, and decision making.

Cognitive psychology centers on three major topics: memory, thinking and reasoning, and language. We start this chapter by considering memory and forgetting. Then we examine how people think and reason as well as different strategies for approaching problems. Finally, we discuss how language is developed and acquired, its basic characteristics, and the relationship between language and thought.

looking AHEAD

The Foundations of Memory

LEARNING OUTCOMES

18.1 Define sensory memory.

18.2 Define short-term memory.

18.3 Define long-term memory.

You are playing a game of *Trivial Pursuit,* and winning the game comes down to one question: On what body of water is Bombay located? As you rack your brain for the answer, several fundamental processes relating to memory come into play. You may never, for instance, have been exposed to information regarding Bombay's location. Or if you have been exposed to it, it simply may not have registered in a meaningful way. In other words, the information might not have been recorded properly in your memory. The initial process of recording information in a form usable to memory, a process called *encoding,* is the first stage in remembering something.

Even if you had been exposed to the information and originally knew the name of the body of water, you may still be unable to recall it during the game because of a failure to retain it. Memory specialists speak of *storage,* the maintenance of material saved in memory. If the material is not stored adequately, it cannot be recalled later.

Memory also depends on one last process—*retrieval*: material in memory storage has to be located and brought into awareness to be useful. Your failure to recall Bombay's location, then, may rest on your inability to retrieve information that you learned earlier.

Memory The process by which we encode, store, and retrieve information.

In sum, psychologists consider **memory** to be the process by which we encode, store, and retrieve information (see Figure 1). Each of the three parts of this definition—encoding, storage, and retrieval—represents a different process. You can think of these processes as being analogous to a computer's keyboard (encoding), hard drive (storage), and software that accesses the information for display on the screen (retrieval). Only if all three processes have operated will you experience success and be able to recall the body of water on which Bombay is located: the Arabian Sea.

Recognizing that memory involves encoding, storage, and retrieval gives us a start in understanding the concept. But how does memory actually function? How do we explain what information is initially encoded, what gets stored, and how it is retrieved?

Encoding
(Initial recording
of information)

Storage
(Information saved
for future use)

Retrieval
(Recovery of
stored information)

FIGURE 1   Memory is built on three basic processes—encoding, storage, and retrieval—that are analogous to a computer's keyboard, hard drive, and software to access the information for display on the screen. The analogy is not perfect, however, because human memory is less precise than a computer. How might you modify the analogy to make it more accurate?

According to the *three-system approach to memory* that dominated memory research for several decades, there are different memory storage systems or stages through which information must travel if it is to be remembered (Atkinson & Shiffrin, 1968). Historically, the approach has been extremely influential in the development of our understanding of memory, and—although new theories have augmented it—it still provides a useful framework for understanding how information is recalled

The three-system memory theory proposes the existence of the three separate memory stores shown in Figure 2. **Sensory memory** refers to the initial, momentary storage of information that lasts only an instant. Here an exact replica of the stimulus recorded by a person's sensory system is stored very briefly. In a second stage, **short-term memory** holds information for 15 to 25 seconds

Sensory memory The initial, momentary storage of information, lasting only an instant.

Short-term memory Memory that holds information for 15 to 25 seconds.

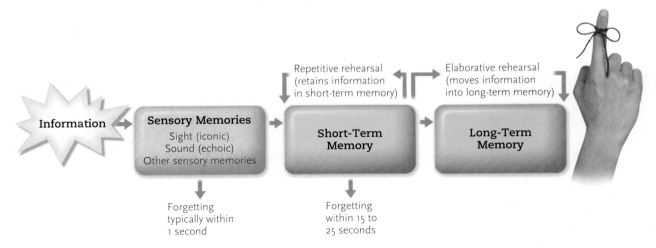

FIGURE 2   In this three-stage model of memory, information initially recorded by the person's sensory system enters sensory memory, which momentarily holds the information. The information then moves to short-term memory, which stores it for 15 to 25 seconds. Finally, the information can move into long-term memory, which is relatively permanent. Whether the information moves from short-term to long-term memory depends on the kind and amount of rehearsal of the material that is carried out. *(Source: Atkinson & Shiffrin, 1968.)*

Long-term memory Memory that stores information on a relatively permanent basis, although it may be difficult to retrieve.

Chunk A meaningful grouping of stimuli that can be stored as a unit in short-term memory.

psych2.0

WWW.MHHE.COM/PSYCHLIFE

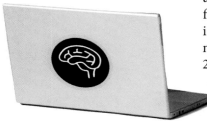

Sensory Memory

A momentary flash of lightning leaves a sensory visual memory, a fleeting but exact replica of the stimulus that fades rapidly.

and stores it according to its meaning rather than as mere sensory stimulation. The third type of storage system is **long-term memory.** Information is stored in long-term memory on a relatively permanent basis, although it may be difficult to retrieve.

» LO1 Sensory Memory

A momentary flash of lightning, the sound of a twig snapping, and the sting of a pinprick all represent stimulation of exceedingly brief duration, but they may nonetheless provide important information that can require a response. Such stimuli are initially—and fleetingly—stored in sensory memory, the first repository of the information the world presents to us.

Sensory memory can store information for only a very short time. If information does not pass into short-term memory, it is lost for good. However, despite the brief duration of sensory memory, its precision is high: sensory memory can store an almost exact replica of each stimulus to which it is exposed (Darwin, Turvey, & Crowder, 1972; Long & Beaton, 1982; Sams et al., 1993; Deouell, Parnes, & Pickard, 2006).

» LO2 Short-Term Memory

Because the information that is stored briefly in sensory memory consists of representations of raw sensory stimuli, it is not meaningful to us. If we are to make sense of it and possibly retain it, the information must be transferred to the next stage of memory: short-term memory. Short-term memory is the memory store in which information first has meaning, although the maximum length of retention there is relatively short (Hamilton & Martin, 2007).

Short-term memory has incomplete representational capabilities: the specific amount of information that can be held in short-term memory has been identified as seven items, or "chunks," of information, with variations up to plus or minus two chunks. A **chunk** is a meaningful grouping of stimuli that can be stored as a unit in short-term memory. According to George Miller (1956), a chunk can be individual letters or numbers, permitting us to hold a seven-digit phone number (like 226-4610) in short-term memory.

But a chunk also may consist of larger categories, such as words or other meaningful units. For example, consider the following list of 21 letters:

P B S F O X C N N A B C C B S M T V N B C

Because the list exceeds seven chunks, it is difficult to recall the letters after one exposure. But suppose they were presented as follows:

PBS FOX CNN ABC CBS MTV NBC

In this case, even though there are still 21 letters, you'd be able to store them in short-term memory, since they represent only seven chunks.

Although it is possible to remember seven or so relatively complicated sets of information entering short-term memory, the information cannot be held there very long. Most psychologists believe that information in short-term memory is lost after 15 to 25 seconds—unless it is transferred to long-term memory.

The transfer of material from short- to long-term memory proceeds largely on the basis of **rehearsal,** the repetition of information that has entered short-term memory. Rehearsal accomplishes two things. First, as long as the information is repeated, it is maintained in short-term memory. More important, however, rehearsal allows us to transfer the information into long-term memory (Kvavilashvili & Fisher, 2007).

Whether the transfer is made from short- to long-term memory seems to depend largely on the kind of rehearsal that is carried out. If the information is simply repeated over

Short-Term Memory

From the perspective of . . .

A MARKETING SPECIALIST   How might ways of enhancing memory be used by advertisers and others to promote their products?

and over again—as we might do with a telephone number while we rush from the phone book to the phone—it is kept current in short-term memory, but it will not necessarily be placed in long-term memory. Instead, as soon as we stop punching in the phone numbers, the number is likely to be replaced by other information and will be completely forgotten.

In contrast, if the information in short-term memory is rehearsed using a process called elaborative rehearsal, it is much more likely to be transferred into long-term memory. *Elaborative rehearsal* occurs when the information is considered and organized in some fashion. The organization might include expanding the information to make it fit into a logical framework, linking it to another memory, turning it into an image, or transforming it in some other way.

Rehearsal The repetition of information that has entered short-term memory.

» LO3 Long-Term Memory

Material that makes its way from short-term memory to long-term memory enters a storehouse of almost unlimited capacity. Like a new file we save on a hard drive, the information in long-term memory is filed and coded so that we can retrieve it when we need it.

Long-Term Memory Modules

Many contemporary researchers now regard long-term memory as having several different components, or *memory modules.* Each of these modules represents a separate memory system in the brain.

The ability to remember specific skills and the order in which they are used is known as procedural memory. If driving involves procedural memory, is it safe to use a cell phone while driving?

One major distinction within long-term memory is that between declarative memory and procedural memory. **Declarative memory** is memory for factual information: names, faces, dates, and facts, such as "a bike has two wheels." In contrast, **procedural memory** (or *nondeclarative memory)* refers to memory for skills and habits, such as how to ride a bike or hit a baseball. Information about *things* is stored in declarative memory; information about *how to do things* is stored in procedural memory (Schacter, Wagner, & Buckner, 2000; Eichenbaum, 2004; Feldhusen, 2006).

Declarative memory can be subdivided into semantic memory and episodic memory. **Semantic memory** is memory for general knowledge and facts about the world, as well as memory for the rules of logic that are used to deduce other facts. Because of semantic memory, we remember that the ZIP code for Beverly Hills is 90210, that Bombay is on the Arabian Sea, and that *memoree* is the incorrect spelling of *memory*. Thus, semantic memory is somewhat like a mental almanac of facts (Nyberg & Tulving, 1996; Tulving, 2002).

Declarative memory Memory for factual information: names, faces, dates, and the like.

Procedural memory Memory for skills and habits, such as riding a bike or hitting a baseball, sometimes referred to as *nondeclarative memory.*

Semantic memory Memory for general knowledge and facts about the world, as well as memory for the rules of logic that are used to deduce other facts.

"The matters about which I'm being questioned, Your Honor, are all things I should have included in my long-term memory but which I mistakenly inserted in my short-term memory."

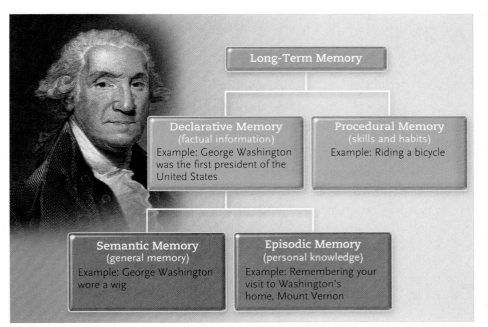

FIGURE 3 Long-term memory can be subdivided into several different types. What type of long-term memory is involved in your recollection of the moment you first arrived on your campus at the start of college? What type of long-term memory is involved in remembering the lyrics to a song, compared with the tune of a song?

STUDY ALERT

Use Figure 3 to help clarify the distinctions between the different types of memory.

In contrast, **episodic memory** is memory for events that occur in a particular time, place, or context. For example, recall of learning to ride a bike, our first kiss, or arranging a surprise 21st birthday party for our brother is based on episodic memories. Episodic memories relate to particular contexts. For example, remembering *when* and *how* we learned that 2 × 2 = 4 would be an episodic memory; the fact itself (that 2 × 2 = 4) is a semantic memory. (Also see Figure 3.)

Episodic memory Memory for events that occur in a particular time, place, or context.

RECAP

Define sensory memory.

- Sensory memory, corresponding to each of the sensory systems, is the first place where information is saved. Sensory memories are very brief, but they are precise, storing a nearly exact replica of a stimulus. (p. 201)

Define short-term memory.

- Roughly seven (plus or minus two) chunks of information can be transferred and held in short-term memory. Information in short-term memory is held from 15 to 25 seconds and, if not transferred to long-term memory, is lost. (p. 202)

Define long-term memory.

- Memories are transferred into long-term storage through rehearsal. If memories are transferred into long-term memory, they become relatively permanent. (p. 203)

- Long-term memory can be viewed in terms of memory modules, each of which is related to separate memory systems in the brain. For instance, we can distinguish between declarative memory and procedural memory. Declarative memory is further divided into semantic memory and episodic memory. (p. 203)

EVALUATE

1. Match the type of memory with its definition:

    1. Long-term memory
    2. Short-term memory
    3. Sensory memory

    a. Holds information 15 to 25 seconds.
    b. Stores information on a relatively permanent basis.
    c. Direct representation of a stimulus.

2. A(n) _____ is a meaningful group of stimuli that can be stored together in short-term memory.

3. There appear to be two types of declarative memory: _____ memory, for knowledge and facts, and _____ memory, for personal experiences.

RETHINK

It is a truism that "you never forget how to ride a bicycle." Why might this be so? In what type of memory is information about bicycle riding stored?

Answers to Evaluate Questions 1. 1-b, 2-a, 3-c; 2. chunk; 3. semantic, episodic

KEY TERMS

Cognitive psychology *p. 199*

Memory *p. 200*

Sensory memory *p. 201*

Short-term memory *p. 201*

Long-term memory *p. 202*

Chunk *p. 202*

Rehearsal *p. 202*

Declarative memory *p. 204*

Procedural memory *p. 204*

Semantic memory *p. 204*

Episodic memory *p. 205*

module 19

Recall and Forgetting

» LO1 Retrieval Cues

Have you ever tried to remember someone's name, convinced that you knew it but unable to recall it no matter how hard you tried? This common occurrence—known as the **tip-of-the-tongue phenomenon**—exemplifies how difficult it can be to retrieve information stored in long-term memory (Schwartz, 2001, 2002; Cleary, 2006).

Perhaps recall of names and other memories is not perfect because there is so much information stored in long-term memory. How do we sort through this vast array of material and retrieve specific information at the appropriate time? One way is through retrieval cues. A *retrieval cue* is a stimulus that allows us to recall more easily information that is in long-term memory. It may be a word, an emotion, or a sound; whatever the specific cue, a memory will suddenly come to mind when the retrieval cue is present. For example, the smell of roasting turkey may evoke memories of Thanksgiving or family gatherings.

Retrieval cues are particularly important when we are making an effort to *recall* information, as opposed to being asked to *recognize* material stored in memory. In **recall,** a specific piece of information must be retrieved—such as that needed to answer a fill-in-the-blank question or to write an essay on a test. In contrast, **recognition** occurs when people are presented with a stimulus and asked whether they have been exposed to it previously, or they are asked to identify it from a list of alternatives. As you might guess, recognition is generally a much easier task than recall (see Figures 1 and 2).

FIGURE 1 Try to recall the names of these characters. Because this is a recall task, it is relatively difficult.

Answer this recognition question:
Which of the following are the names of the seven dwarfs in the Disney movie *Snow White and the Seven Dwarfs*?

Goofy	Bashful
Sleepy	Meanie
Smarty	Doc
Scaredy	Happy
Dopey	Angry
Grumpy	Sneezy
Wheezy	Crazy

(The correct answers are Bashful, Doc, Dopey, Grumpy, Happy, Sleepy, and Sneezy.)

» LO2 Levels of Processing

Tip-of-the-tongue phenomenon The inability to recall information that one realizes one knows—a result of the difficulty of retrieving information from long-term memory.

Recall Memory task in which specific information must be retrieved.

Recognition Memory task in which individuals are presented with a stimulus and asked whether they have been exposed to it in the past or to identify it from a list of alternatives.

Levels-of-processing theory The theory of memory that emphasizes the degree to which new material is mentally analyzed.

One determinant of how well memories are recalled is the way in which material is first perceived, processed, and understood. The **levels-of-processing theory** emphasizes the degree to which new material is mentally analyzed. It suggests that the amount of information processing that occurs when material is initially encountered is central in determining how much of the information is ultimately remembered. According to this approach, the depth of information processing during exposure to material—meaning the degree to which it is analyzed and considered—is critical; the greater the intensity of its initial processing is, the more likely we are to remember it (Craik, 1990; Troyer, Häfliger, & Cadieux, 2006).

Because we do not pay close attention to much of the information to which we are exposed, very little mental processing typically takes place, and we forget new material almost immediately. However, information to which we pay greater attention is processed more thoroughly. Therefore, it enters memory at a deeper level—and is less apt to be forgotten than is information processed at shallower levels.

There are considerable practical implications to the notion that recall depends on the degree to which information is initially processed. For example, the depth of information processing is critical when learning and studying course material. Rote memorization of a list of key terms for a test is unlikely to produce long-term recollection of information, because processing occurs at a shallow level. In contrast, thinking about the meaning of the terms and reflecting on how they relate to information that one currently knows results in far more effective long-term retention (Conway, 2002; Wenzel, Zetocha, & Ferraro, 2007).

» LO3 Explicit and Implicit Memory

psych2.0
WWW.MHHE.COM/PSYCHLIFE

Levels of Processing

Careful studies have found that people who are anesthetized during surgery can sometimes recall snippets of conversations they heard during surgery—even though they have no conscious recollection of the information (Kihlstrom et al., 1990; Sebel, Bonke, & Winograd, 1993). The discovery that people have memories about which they are unaware has been an important one. It has led to speculation that two forms of memory, explicit and implicit, may exist side by side. **Explicit memory** refers to intentional or conscious recollection of information. When we try to remember a name or date we have encountered or learned about previously, we are searching our explicit memory.

In contrast, **implicit memory** refers to memories of which people are not consciously aware, but which can affect subsequent performance and behavior. Skills that operate automatically and without thinking, such as jumping out of the path of an automobile coming toward us as we walk down the side of a road, are stored in implicit memory. Similarly, a feeling of vague dislike for an acquaintance, without knowing why we have that feeling, may be a reflection of implicit memories. Perhaps the person reminds us of someone else in our past whom we didn't like, even though we are not aware of the memory of that other individual (Tulving, 2000; Uttl, Graf, & Consentino, 2003; Coates, Butler, & Berry, 2006).

> *Skills that operate automatically and without thinking, such as jumping out of the path of an automobile coming toward us as we walk down the side of a road, are stored in implicit memory.*

Explicit memory Intentional or conscious recollection of information.

Implicit memory Memories of which people are not consciously aware, but which can affect subsequent performance and behavior.

Flashbulb memories Memories centered on a specific, important, or surprising event that are so vivid it is as if they represented a snapshot of the event.

» LO4 Flashbulb Memories

Where were you on February 1, 2003? You will most likely draw a blank until this piece of information is added: February 1, 2003, was the date the space shuttle *Columbia* broke up in space and fell to Earth.

You probably have little trouble recalling your exact location and a variety of other trivial details that occurred when you heard about the shuttle disaster, even though the incident happened a few years ago. Your ability to remember details about this fatal event illustrates a phenomenon known as flashbulb memory. **Flashbulb memories** are memories related to a specific,

In spite of passing away 30 years apart, both John F. Kennedy and Princess Diana's deaths can be cited as examples of flashbulb memory. Depending on your age and cultural point of view, you are likely to remember where you were when you discovered one of these individuals had died. What is an event in your own life that inspires a flashbulb memory?

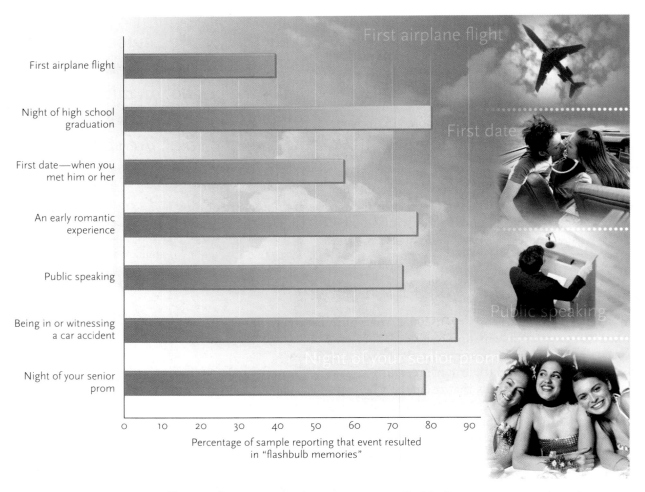

First airplane flight

Night of high school graduation

First date—when you met him or her

An early romantic experience

Public speaking

Being in or witnessing a car accident

Night of your senior prom

0   10   20   30   40   50   60   70   80   90

Percentage of sample reporting that event resulted in "flashbulb memories"

FIGURE 3   These are the most common flashbulb memory events, based on a survey of college students (Rubin, 1985). What are some of your flashbulb memories?

important, or surprising event that are so vivid they represent a virtual snap-shot of the event.

Flashbulb memories illustrate a more general phenomenon about memory: memories that are exceptional are more easily retrieved (although not necessarily accurately) than are those relating to events that are commonplace (see Figure 3). The more distinctive a stimulus is, and the more personal relevance the event has, the more likely we are to recall it later (Berntsen & Thomsen, 2005; Shapiro, 2006).

» LO5 Constructive Processes in Memory: Rebuilding the Past

Constructive processes Processes in which memories are influenced by the meaning we give to events.

As we have seen, although it is clear that we can have detailed recollections of significant and distinctive events, it is difficult to gauge the accuracy of such memories. In fact, it is apparent that our memories reflect, at least in part, **constructive processes,** processes in which memories are influenced by the meaning we give to events. When we retrieve information, then, the memory that is produced is affected not just by the direct prior experience we have had with the stimulus, but also by our guesses and inferences about its meaning.

The notion that memory is based on constructive processes was first put forward by Frederic Bartlett, a British psychologist. He suggested that people tend to remember information in terms of **schemas,** organized bodies of information stored in memory that bias the way new information is interpreted, stored, and recalled (Bartlett, 1932). Our reliance on schemas means that memories often consist of a general reconstruction of previous experience. Bartlett argued that schemas are based not only on the specific material to which people are exposed, but also on their understanding of the situation, their expectations about the situation, and their awareness of the motivations underlying the behavior of others. In short, our expectations and knowledge affect the reliability of our memories (McDonald & Hirt, 1997; Newby-Clark & Ross, 2003).

From the perspective of . . .

A CRIMINAL JUSTICE PROFESSIONAL Given what you know about the constructive nature of memory, why might multiple eyewitnesses to the same event tell different stories about what happened?

Autobiographical Memory: Where Past Meets Present

Your memory of experiences in your own past may well be a fiction—or at least a distortion of what actually occurred. The same constructive processes that make us inaccurately recall the behavior of others also reduce the accuracy of autobiographical memories. **Autobiographical memories** are our recollections of circumstances and episodes from our own lives. Autobiographical memories encompass the episodic memories we hold about ourselves (Rubin, 1999; Sutin & Robins, 2007).

Schemas Organized bodies of information stored in memory that bias the way new information is interpreted, stored, and recalled.

Autobiographical memories Our recollections of circumstances and episodes from our own lives.

For example, we tend to forget information about our past that is incompatible with the way in which we currently see ourselves. One study found that adults who were well adjusted but who had been treated for emotional problems during the early years of their lives tended to forget important but troubling childhood events, such as being in foster care.

Similarly, when a group of 48-year-olds were asked to recall how they had responded on a questionnaire they had completed when they were high school freshman, their accuracy was no better than chance. For example, although 61 percent of the questionnaire respondents said that playing sports and other physical activities was their favorite pastime, only 23 percent of the adults recalled it accurately (Offer et al., 2000).

EXPLORING diversity

Are There Cross-Cultural Differences in Memory?

Travelers who have visited areas of the world in which there is no written language often have returned with tales of people with phenomenal memories. For instance, storytellers in some preliterate cultures can recount long chronicles that recall the names and activities of people over many generations. Those feats led experts to argue initially that people in preliterate societies develop a different, and perhaps better, type of memory than do those in cultures that employ a written language. They suggested that in a society that lacks writing, people are motivated to recall information with accuracy, especially information relating to tribal histories and traditions that would be lost if they were not passed down orally from one generation to another (Daftary & Meri, 2002; Berntsen & Rubin, 2004).

Today, memory researchers dismiss that view. For one thing, preliterate peoples don't have an exclusive claim to amazing memory feats. Some Hebrew scholars memorize thousands of pages of text and can recall the locations of particular words on the page. Similarly, poetry singers in the Balkans can recall thousands of lines of poetry. Even in cultures in which written language exists, then, astounding feats of memory are possible (Strathern & Stewart, 2003; Rubin et al., 2007).

Memory researchers now suggest that there are both similarities and differences in memory across cultures. Basic memory processes such as short-term memory capacity and the structure of long-term memory—the "hardware" of memory—are universal and operate similarly in people in all cultures. In contrast, cultural differences can be seen in the way information is acquired and rehearsed—the "software" of memory. Culture determines how people frame information initially, how much they practice learning and recalling it, and the strategies they use to try to recall it (Mack, 2003; Wang & Conway, 2006). (To get a sense of how you remember information, complete the accompanying Try It!)

try it!

Determine Your Memory Style

What's your dominant memory style? Do you most easily remember sounds, sights, or the way things feel? Read the statements below and circle the response choice that most closely describes your habits.
To help recall lectures, I . . .

V. Read the notes I took during class.

A. Close my eyes and try to hear what the instructor said.

K. Try to place myself back in the lecture room and feel what was going on at the time.

To remember a complex procedure, I . . .

    V. Write down the steps I have to follow.

    A. Listen carefully and repeatedly to the instructions.

    K. Do it over and over again.

To learn sentences in a foreign language, I do best if I . . .

    V. Read them on paper to see how they're written.

    A. Hear them in my head until I can say them aloud.

    K. See someone speaking them and then practice moving my mouth and hands the way the speaker did.

If I have to learn a dance move, I like . . .

    V. To see a diagram of the steps before trying it.

    A. Someone to coach me through it while I try it.

    K. To watch it once and then give it a try.

When I recall a very happy moment, I tend to . . .

    V. Visualize it in my head.

    A. Hear the sounds that I heard when experiencing it.

    K. Feel with my hands and body what I felt at the time.

When I have to remember driving directions, I usually . . .

    V. See a map of the route in my mind.

    A. Repeat the directions aloud to myself.

    K. Feel my hands steering and the car driving along the correct route.

Answer Key

If you chose mostly V's, your main memory style is visual; your preference is to remember things in terms of the way they appear.

If you chose mostly A's, your main memory style is auditory; your preference is to recall material in terms of sound.

If you chose mostly K's, your main memory style is kinesthetic; your preference is to remember using your sense of touch.

Keep in mind that this questionnaire only gives a rough idea of how we usually use our memories. Remember: All of us use all of the memory styles during the course of each day.

Consider these questions: How do you think your memory style affects the way you recall academic information? How does your memory style relate to your learning style? How does it affect the way you learn things initially? How could you make greater use of your less-preferred styles?

» LO6 Forgetting

All of us who have experienced even routine instances of forgetting—such as not remembering an acquaintance's name or a fact on a test—understand the very real consequences of memory failure. Of course, memory failure is also essential to remembering important information. The ability to forget inconsequential details about experiences, people, and objects helps us avoid being burdened and distracted by trivial stores of meaningless data. Forgetting permits us to form general impressions and recollections. For example, the reason our friends consistently look familiar to us is because we're able to forget their clothing, facial blemishes, and other transient features that change from one occasion to the next. Instead, our memories are based on a summary of various critical features—a far more economical use of our memory capabilities.

Forgetting permits us to form general impressions and recollections.

The first attempts to study forgetting were made by German psychologist Hermann Ebbinghaus about a hundred years ago. Using himself as the only participant in his study, Ebbinghaus memorized lists of three-letter nonsense syllables—meaningless sets of two consonants with a vowel in between, such as FIW and BOZ. By measuring how easy it was to relearn a given list of words after varying periods of time had passed since the initial learning, he found that forgetting occurred systematically, as shown in Figure 4. As the figure indicates, the most rapid forgetting occurs in the first nine hours, particularly in the first hour. After nine hours, the rate of forgetting slows and declines little, even after the passage of many days.

Despite his primitive methods, Ebbinghaus's study had an important influence on subsequent research, and his basic conclusions have been upheld. There is almost always a strong initial decline in memory, followed by a more gradual drop over time. Furthermore, relearning of previously mastered material is almost always faster than starting from scratch, whether the material is academic information or a motor skill such as serving a tennis ball (Wixted & Carpenter, 2007).

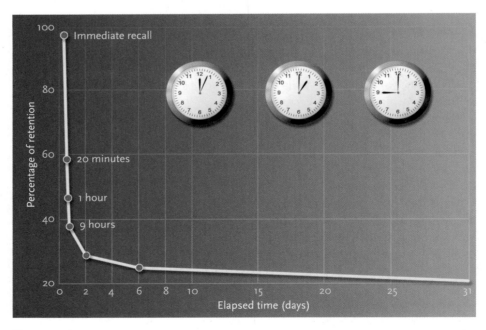

FIGURE 4 In his classic work, Ebbinghaus found that the most rapid forgetting occurs in the first nine hours after exposure to new material. However, the rate of forgetting then slows down and declines very little even after many days have passed (Ebbinghaus, 1885/1913). Check your own memory: What were you doing exactly two hours ago? What were you doing last Tuesday at 5 P.M.? Which information is easier to retrieve?

Why do we forget? One reason is that we may not have paid attention to the material in the first place—a failure of *encoding*. For example, if you live in the United States, you probably have been exposed to thousands of pennies during your life. Despite this experience, you probably don't have a clear sense of the details of the coin. (See this for yourself by looking at Figure 5.) Consequently, the reason for your memory failure is that you probably never encoded the information into long-term memory initially. Obviously, if information was not placed in memory to start with, there is no way the information can be recalled.

But what about material that has been encoded into memory and that can't later be remembered? Several processes account for memory failures, including decay, interference, and cue-dependent forgetting.

Decay is the loss of information through nonuse. This explanation for forgetting assumes that *memory traces,* the physical changes that take place in the brain when new material is learned, simply fade away over time (Grann, 2007).

Although there is evidence that decay does occur, this does not seem to be the complete explanation for forgetting. Often there is no relationship between how long ago a person was exposed to information and how well that information is recalled. Because decay does not fully account for forgetting, memory specialists have proposed an additional mechanism: **interference.** In interference, information in memory disrupts the recall of other information (Naveh-Benjamin, Guez, & Sorek, 2007).

To distinguish between decay and interference, think of the two processes in terms of a row of books on a library shelf. In decay, the old books are constantly crumbling and rotting away, leaving room for new arrivals. Interference processes suggest that new books knock the old ones off the shelf, where they become inaccessible. Finally, forgetting may occur because of **cue-dependent forgetting,** forgetting that occurs when there are insufficient retrieval cues to rekindle information that is in memory (Tulving & Thompson, 1983). For example, you may not be able to remember where you lost a set of keys until you mentally walk through your day, thinking of each place you visited. When you think of the place where you lost the keys—say, the library—the retrieval cue of the library may be sufficient to help you recall that you left them on the desk in the library. Without that retrieval cue, you may be unable to recall the location of the keys.

Most research suggests that interference and cue-dependent forgetting are key processes in forgetting (Mel'nikov, 1993; Bower, Thompson, & Tulving, 1994). We

Decay The loss of information in memory through its nonuse.

Interference The phenomenon by which information in memory disrupts the recall of other information.

Cue-dependent forgetting Forgetting that occurs when there are insufficient retrieval cues to rekindle information that is in memory.

STUDY ALERT

Memory loss through decay comes from nonuse of the memory; memory loss through interference is due to the presence of other information in memory.

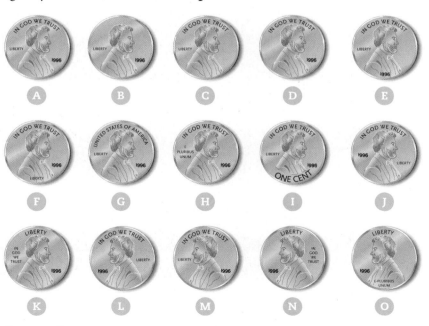

FIGURE 5 One of these pennies is the real thing. Can you find it? Why is this task harder than it seems at first? (*Source: Nickerson & Adams, 1979.*)

If you don't have a penny handy, the correct answer is "A."

forget things mainly because new memories interfere with the retrieval of old ones or because appropriate retrieval cues are unavailable, not because the memory trace has decayed.

» LO8 Proactive and Retroactive Interference: The Before and After of Forgetting

Proactive interference Interference in which information learned earlier disrupts the recall of newer material.

Retroactive interference Interference in which there is difficulty in the recall of information learned earlier because of later exposure to different material.

There are actually two sorts of interference that influence forgetting: proactive and retroactive. In **proactive interference,** information learned earlier disrupts the recall of newer material. For example, suppose you move and get a new telephone number. For the first several months afterward, whenever anyone asks for your telephone number, you can only think of your old number—not your new one (Bunting, 2006).

In contrast, **retroactive interference** refers to difficulty in the recall of information because of later exposure to different material. If, for example, you eventually become unable to recall your old telephone number anymore, retroactive interference is the culprit (see Figure 6). One way to remember the difference between proactive and retroactive interference is to keep in mind that *pro*active interference progresses in time—the past interferes with the present—whereas *retro*active interference retrogresses in time, working backward as the present interferes with the past (Jacoby, Bishara, Hessels, 2007).

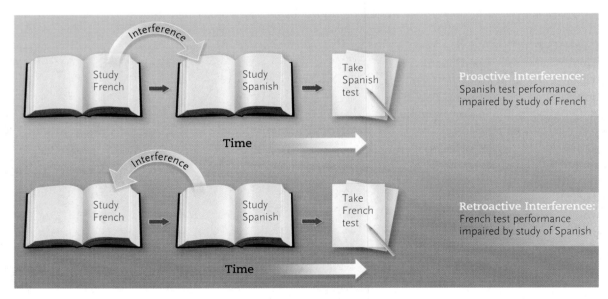

FIGURE 6 Proactive interference occurs when material learned earlier interferes with the recall of newer material. In this example, studying French before studying Spanish interferes with performance on a Spanish test. In contrast, retroactive interference exists when material learned after initial exposure to other material interferes with the recall of the first material. In this case, retroactive interference occurs when recall of French is impaired because of later expqsure to Spanish.

becoming an *informed consumer*
OF PSYCHOLOGY
Improving Your Memory

Apart from the advantages of forgetting, say, a bad date, most of us would like to find ways to improve our memories. Among the effective strategies for studying and remembering course material:

- *The keyword technique.* If you are studying a foreign language, try the *keyword technique* of pairing a foreign word with a common English word that has a similar sound. This English word is known as the *keyword.* For example, to learn the Spanish word for duck (*pato,* pronounced *pot-o*), you might choose the keyword *pot*; for the Spanish word for horse (*caballo,* pronounced *cob-eye-yo*), the keyword might be *eye.* Once you have thought of a keyword, imagine the Spanish word "interacting" with the English keyword. You might envision a duck taking a bath in a pot to remember the word *pato,* or a horse with a large, bulging eye in the center of its head to recall *caballo* (Carney & Levin, 1998; Wyra, Lawon, & Hungi, 2007).

- *Organization cues.* To help recall material you read in textbooks, try organizing the material in memory the first time you read it. Organize your reading on the basis of any advance information you have about the content and about its arrangement. You will then be able to make connections and see relationships among the various facts and process the material at a deeper level, which in turn will later aid recall.

- *Take effective notes.* "Less is more" is perhaps the best advice for taking lecture notes that facilitate recall. Rather than trying to jot down every detail of a lecture, it is better to listen and think about the material, and take down the main points. In effective note taking, thinking about the material when you first hear it is more important than writing it down. This is one reason that borrowing someone else's notes is a bad idea; you will have no framework in memory that you can use to understand them (Feldman, 2009).

- *Practice and rehearse.* Although practice does not necessarily make perfect, it helps. By studying and rehearsing material past initial mastery—a process called *overlearning*—people are able to show better long-term recall than they show if they stop practicing after their initial learning of the material.

- *Don't believe claims about drugs that improve memory.* Advertisements for One-a-Day vitamins with ginkgo biloba or Quanterra Mental Sharpness Product would have you believe that taking a drug can improve your memory. Not so, according to the results of numerous studies. No research has shown that commercial memory enhancers are effective (Gold, Cahill, & Wenk, 2002; McDaniel, Maier, & Einstein, 2002; Burns, Bryan, & Nettelbeck, 2006).

RECAP

Explain retrieval cues.

- The tip-of-the-tongue phenomenon is the temporary inability to remember information that one is certain one knows. Retrieval cues are a major strategy for recalling information successfully. (p. 207)

Discuss levels of processing.

- The levels-of-processing approach to memory suggests that the way in which information is initially perceived and analyzed determines the success with which it is recalled. The deeper the initial processing, the greater the recall. (p. 208)

Compare and contrast implicit and explicit memory.

- Explicit memory refers to intentional or conscious recollection of information. In contrast, implicit memory refers to memories of which people are not consciously aware, but which can affect subsequent performance and behavior. (p. 208)

Define flashbulb memories.

- Flashbulb memories are memories centered on a specific, important event. The more distinctive a memory is, the more easily it can be retrieved. (p. 209)

Describe the constructive process of memory.

- Memory is a constructive process: we relate memories to the meaning, guesses, and expectations we give to events. Specific information is recalled in terms of schemas, organized bodies of information stored in memory that bias the way new information is interpreted, stored, and recalled. (p. 210)

- Autobiographical memory is influenced by constructive processes. (p. 211)

Explain the importance of forgetting.

- Forgetting, or memory failure, plays several important roles. (p. 213)

Explain why we forget information.

- Several processes account for memory failure, including decay, interference (both proactive and retroactive), and cue-dependent forgetting. (p. 215)

- Among the techniques for improving memory are the keyword technique to memorize foreign language vocabulary; using the encoding specificity phenomenon; organizing text material and lecture notes; and practice and rehearsal, leading to overlearning. (p. 217)

Compare and contrast proactive and retroactive interference.

- Proactive interference is interference in which information learned earlier disrupts the recall of newer material. (p. 216)

- Retroactive interference is interference in which there is difficulty in the recall of information learned earlier because of later exposure to different material. (p. 216)

EVALUATE

1. While with a group of friends at a dance, Eva bumps into a man she dated last month, but when she tries to introduce him to her friends, she cannot remember his name. What is the term for this occurrence?

2. _____ is the process of retrieving a specific item from memory.

3. A friend of your mother tells you, "I know exactly where I was and what I was doing when I heard that John Lennon was killed." What is this type of memory phenomenon called?

4. _____ _____ _____ theory states that the more a person analyzes a statement, the more likely he or she is to remember it later.

5. _____ interference occurs when material is difficult to retrieve because of subsequent exposure to other material; _____ interference refers to difficulty in retrieving material as a result of the interference of previously learned material.

R E T H I N K

What study strategies can you think of that would make effective use of the levels-of-processing approach to memory?

Answers to Evaluate Questions 1. tip-of-the-tongue phenomenon; 2. recall; 3. flashbulb memory; 4. levels-of-processing; 5. retroactive, proactive

[K E Y   T E R M S]

Tip-of-the-tongue phenomenon *p. 207*

Recall *p. 207*

Recognition *p. 207*

Levels-of-processing theory *p. 208*

Explicit memory *p. 209*

Implicit memory *p. 209*

Flashbulb memories *p. 209*

Constructive processes *p. 210*

Schemas *p. 211*

Autobiographical memories *p. 211*

Decay *p. 215*

Interference *p. 215*

Cue-dependent forgetting *p. 215*

Proactive interference *p. 216*

Retroactive interference *p. 216*

Thinking, Reasoning, and Problem Solving

LEARNING OUTCOMES

20.1 Explain the concept of mental images.

20.2 Discuss the process of categorizing the world.

20.3 Describe the processes that underlie reasoning and decision making.

20.4 Explain how people approach and solve problems.

> **Thinking** The manipulation of mental representations of information.

Psychologists define **thinking** as the manipulation of mental representations of information. A representation may take the form of a word, a visual image, a sound, or data in any other sensory modality stored in memory. Thinking transforms a particular representation of information into new and different forms, allowing us to answer questions, solve problems, or reach goals.

Although a clear sense of what specifically occurs when we think remains elusive, our understanding of the nature of the fundamental elements involved in thinking is growing. We begin by considering our use of mental images and concepts, the building blocks of thought.

"What do you think I think about what you think I think you've been thinking about?"

» LO1 Mental Images: Examining the Mind's Eye

Think of your best friend. Chances are that you "see" some kind of visual image when asked to think of her or him, or any other person or object, for that matter. To some cognitive psychologists, such mental images constitute a major part of thinking.

Mental images are representations in the mind of an object or event. They are not just visual representations; our ability to "hear" a tune in our heads also relies on a mental image. In fact, every sensory modality may produce corresponding mental images (Kosslyn, 2005; De Beni, Pazzaglia, & Gardini, 2007).

Some experts see the production of mental images as a way to improve various skills. For instance, many athletes use mental imagery in their training. Basketball players may try to produce vivid and detailed images of the court, the basket, the ball, and the noisy crowd. They may visualize themselves taking a foul shot, watching the ball, and hearing the swish as it goes through the net. And it works: the use of mental imagery can lead to improved performance in sports (MacIntyre, Moran, & Jennings, 2002; Mamassis & Doganis, 2004).

Many athletes, such as Tiger Woods, use mental imagery to focus on a task, a process they call "getting in the zone." What are some other occupations that require the use of strong mental imagery?

Mental images Representations in the mind that resemble the object or event being represented.

Concepts Categorizations of objects, events, or people that share common properties.

From the perspective of . . .

A New Supervisor How might you use the research on mental imagery to improve employees' performance?

» LO2 Concepts: Categorizing the World

If someone asks you what is in your kitchen cabinet, you might answer with a detailed list of items ("a jar of peanut butter, three boxes of pasta, six novelty coffee mugs," etc.). More likely, though, you would respond by naming some broader categories, such as "food" and "dishes."

Concepts help us classify newly encountered objects on the basis of our past experience.

Using such categories reflects the operation of concepts. **Concepts** are categorizations of objects, events, or people that share common properties. Concepts enable us to organize complex phenomena into simpler, and therefore more easily usable, cognitive categories (Goldstone & Kersten, 2003; Murphy, 2005; Connolly, 2007).

Concepts help us classify newly encountered objects on the basis of our past experience. For example, we can surmise that someone tapping a handheld screen is probably using some kind of computer or PDA, even if we have never encountered that specific model before. Ultimately, concepts influence behavior; we would assume, for instance, that it might be appropriate to pet an

Ranking of prototype from most to least typical	Concept Category			
	Furniture	**Vehicle**	**Weapon**	**Vegetable**
1—Most typical	Chair	Car	Gun	Peas
2	Sofa	Truck	Knife	Carrots
3	Table	Bus	Sword	String beans
4	Dresser	Motorcycle	Bomb	Spinach
5	Desk	Train	Hand grenade	Broccoli
6	Bed	Trolley car	Spear	Asparagus
7	Bookcase	Bicycle	Cannon	Corn
8	Footstool	Airplane	Bow and arrow	Cauliflower
9	Lamp	Boat	Club	Brussels sprouts
10	Piano	Tractor	Tank	Lettuce
11	Cushion	Cart	Tear gas	Beets
12	Mirror	Wheelchair	Whip	Tomato
13	Rug	Tank	Ice pick	Lima beans
14	Radio	Raft	Fists	Eggplant
15—Least typical	Stove	Sled	Rocket	Onion

FIGURE 1   Prototypes are typical, highly representative examples of a concept. For instance, a highly typical prototype of the concept "furniture" is a chair, whereas a stove is not a good prototype. High agreement exists within a culture about which examples of a concept are prototypes. *(Source: Adapted from Rosch & Mervis, 1975.)*

animal after determining that it is a dog, whereas we would behave differently after classifying the animal as a wolf.

Prototypes Typical, highly representative examples of a concept.

Many real-world concepts are ambiguous and difficult to define. For instance, concepts such as "table" and "bird" have a set of general, relatively loose characteristic features, rather than unique, clearly defined properties that distinguish an example of the concept from a nonexample. When we consider these more ambiguous concepts, we usually think in terms of examples called **prototypes.** Prototypes are typical, highly representative examples of a concept that correspond to our mental image or best example of the concept.

For instance, although a robin and an ostrich are both examples of birds, the robin is an example that comes to most people's minds far more readily. Consequently, robin is a prototype of the concept "bird." Similarly, when we think of the concept of a table, we're likely to think of a coffee table before we think of a drafting table, making a coffee table closer to our prototype of a table.

Relatively high agreement exists among people in a particular culture about which examples of a concept are prototypes, as well as which examples are not. For instance, most people in Western cultures consider cars and trucks good examples of vehicles, whereas elevators and wheelbarrows are not considered very good examples. Consequently, cars and trucks are prototypes of the concept of a vehicle (see Figure 1).

» LO3 Reasoning: Making Up Your Mind

Instructors deciding when students' assignments are due.

An employer determining who to hire out of a pool of job applicants.

The president concluding that it is necessary to send troops to a foreign nation.

What do these three situations have in common? Each of them requires *reasoning*, the process by which information is used to draw conclusions and make decisions.

Algorithms and Heuristics

When faced with making a decision, we often turn to various kinds of cognitive shortcuts, known as algorithms and heuristics, to help us. An **algorithm** is a rule that, if applied appropriately, guarantees a solution to a problem. We can use an algorithm even if we cannot understand why it works. For example, you may know that you can find the length of the third side of a right triangle by using the formula $a^2 + b^2 = c^2$, although you may not have the foggiest notion of the mathematical principles behind the formula.

For many problems and decisions, however, no algorithm is available. In those instances, we may be able to use heuristics to help us. A **heuristic** is a cognitive shortcut that may lead to a solution. Heuristics enhance the likelihood of success in coming to a solution, but, unlike algorithms, they cannot ensure it. For example, when I play tic-tac-toe, I follow the heuristic of placing an X in the center square when I start the game. This tactic doesn't guarantee that I will win, but experience has taught me that it will increase my chances of success. Similarly, some students follow the heuristic of preparing for a test by ignoring the assigned textbook reading and only studying their lecture notes—a strategy that may or may not pay off.

> **Algorithm** A rule that, if applied appropriately, guarantees a solution to a problem.
>
> **Heuristic** A cognitive shortcut that may lead to a solution.

psych2.0
WWW.MHHE.COM/PSYCHLIFE

Heuristics

» LO4 Problem Solving

In the Tower of Hanoi puzzle, three disks are placed on the first of three posts in the order shown in Figure 2. The goal of the puzzle is to move all three disks to the third post, arranged in the same order, by using as few moves as possible. There are two restrictions: only one disk can be moved at a time, and no disk can ever cover a smaller one during a move.

Why are cognitive psychologists interested in the Tower of Hanoi problem? Because the way people go about solving such puzzles helps illuminate how people solve complex, real-life problems. Psychologists have found that

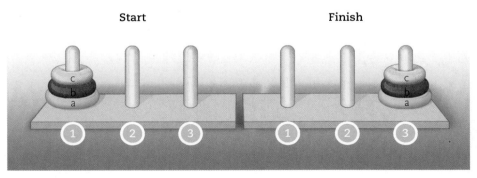

FIGURE 2 The goal of the Tower of Hanoi puzzle is to move all three disks from the first post to the third and still preserve the original order of the disks, using the fewest number of moves possible while following the rules that only one disk at a time can be moved and no disk can cover a smaller one during a move. Try it yourself before you look at the solution, which is listed according to the sequence of moves.

(Solution: Move C to 3, B to 2, C to 2, A to 3, C to 1, B to 3, and C to 3.)

Preparation
Understanding and diagnosing problems

Production
Generating solutions

Judgment
Evaluating solutions

FIGURE 3 Steps in problem solving.

problem solving typically involves the three steps illustrated in Figure 3: preparing to create solutions, producing solutions, and evaluating the solutions that have been generated.

Preparation: Understanding and Diagnosing Problems

When approaching a problem like the Tower of Hanoi, most people begin by trying to understand the problem thoroughly. If the problem is a novel one, they probably will pay particular attention to any restrictions placed on coming up with a solution—such as the rule for moving only one disk at a time in the Tower of Hanoi problem. If, by contrast, the problem is a familiar one, they are apt to spend considerably less time in this preparation stage.

Problems vary from well defined to ill defined (Reitman, 1965; Arlin, 1989; Evans, 2004). In a *well-defined problem*—such as a mathematical equation or the solution to a jigsaw puzzle—both the nature of the problem itself and the information needed to solve it are available and clear. Thus, we can make straightforward judgments about whether a potential solution is appropriate. With an *ill-defined problem*, such as how to increase morale on an assembly line or to bring peace to the Middle East, not only may the specific nature of the problem be unclear, the information required to solve the problem may be even less obvious.

The preparation stage of understanding and diagnosing is critical in problem solving because it allows us to develop our own cognitive representation of the problem and to place it within a personal framework. We may divide the problem into subparts or ignore some information as we try to simplify the task. Winnowing out nonessential information is often a critical step in the preparation stage of problem solving.

Our ability to represent a problem—and the kind of solution we eventually come to—depends on the way a problem is phrased, or framed. Consider, for example, if you were a cancer patient having to choose between surgery and radiation and were given the two sets of treatment

"I don't know about hair care, Rapunzel, but I'm thinking a good cream rinse plus protein conditioner might just solve both our problems."

Problem: Surgery or Radiation?	
Survival Frame	**Mortality Frame**
Surgery: Of 100 people having surgery, 90 live through the postoperative period, 68 are alive at the end of the first year, and 34 are alive at the end of five years	**Surgery:** Of 100 people having surgery, 10 die during surgery, 32 die by the end of the first year, and 66 die by the end of five years
Radiation: Of 100 people having radiation therapy, all live through the treatment, 77 are alive at the end of one year, and 22 are alive at the end of five years	**Radiation:** Of 100 people having radiation therapy, none die during the treatment, 23 die by the end of one year, and 78 die by the end of five years

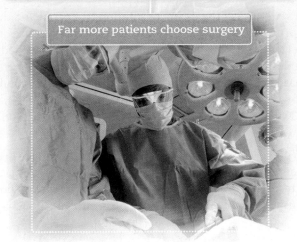

Far more patients choose surgery

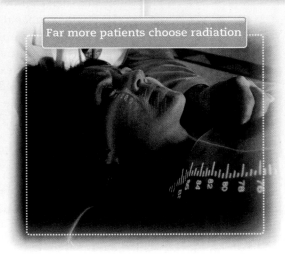

Far more patients choose radiation

FIGURE 4   A decision often is affected by the way a problem is framed. In this case, when mortality is the framework, most would choose radiation over surgery, despite similar results.

options shown in Figure 4 (Tversky & Kahneman, 1987; Chandran & Menon, 2004). When the options are framed in terms of the likelihood of survival, only 18 percent of participants in a study chose radiation over surgery. However, when the choice was framed in terms of the likelihood of dying, 44 percent chose radiation over surgery—even though the outcomes are identical in both sets of framing conditions.

Production: Generating Solutions

After preparation, the next stage in problem solving is the production of possible solutions. If a problem is relatively simple, we may already have a direct solution stored in long-term memory, and all we need to do is retrieve the appropriate information. If we cannot retrieve or do not know the solution, we must generate possible solutions and compare them with information in long- and short-term memory.

Means-ends analysis Repeated testing for differences between the desired outcome and what currently exists.

At the most basic level, we can solve problems through trial and error. The difficulty with this approach, of course, is that some problems are so complicated that it would take a lifetime to try out every possibility. In place of trial and error, complex problem solving often involves the use of heuristics, cognitive shortcuts that can generate solutions. Probably the most frequently applied heuristic in problem solving is a **means-ends analysis,** which involves repeated

Problem Solving

tests for differences between the desired outcome and what currently exists. In a means-end analysis, each step brings the problem solver closer to a resolution. Consider this simple example (Newell & Simon, 1972; Huber, Beckmann, & Herrmann, 2004; Chrysikou, 2006):

> I want to take my son to preschool. What's the difference between what I have and what I want? One of distance. What changes distance? My automobile. My automobile won't work. What is needed to make it work? A new battery. What has new batteries? An auto repair shop . . .

Another heuristic commonly used to generate solutions is to divide a problem into intermediate steps, or *subgoals,* and solve each of those steps. For instance, in our Tower of Hanoi problem, we could choose several obvious subgoals, such as moving the largest disk to the third post.

If solving a subgoal is a step toward the ultimate solution to a problem, identifying subgoals is an appropriate strategy. In some cases, however, forming subgoals is not all that helpful and may actually increase the time needed to find a solution. For example, some problems cannot be subdivided. Others— like some complicated mathematical problems—are so complex that it takes longer to identify the appropriate subdivisions than to solve the problem by other means (Reed, 1996; Kaller et al., 2004; Fishbach, Dhar, & Zhang, 2006).

Judgment: Evaluating the Solutions

The final stage in problem solving is judging the adequacy of a solution. Often this is a simple matter: If the solution is clear—as in the Tower of Hanoi problem—we will know immediately whether we have been successful (Varma, 2007).

> *If the solution is less concrete or if there is no single correct solution, evaluating solutions becomes more difficult.*

If the solution is less concrete or if there is no single correct solution, evaluating solutions becomes more difficult. In such instances, we must decide which alternative solution is best. Unfortunately, we often quite inaccurately estimate the quality of our own ideas. For instance, a team of drug researchers working for a particular company may consider their remedy for an illness to be superior to all others, overestimating the likelihood of their success and downplaying the approaches of competing drug companies (Eizenberg & Zaslavsky, 2004).

Theoretically, if we rely on appropriate heuristics and valid information to make decisions, we can make accurate choices among alternative solutions. However, as we see next, several kinds of obstacles to and biases in problem solving affect the quality of the decisions and judgments we make.

Impediments to Solutions: Why Is Problem Solving Such a Problem?

Consider the following problem-solving test (Duncker, 1945):

> You are given a set of tacks, candles, and matches, each in a small box, and told your goal is to place three candles at eye level on a nearby door, so that wax will not drip on the floor as the candles burn [see Figure 5]. How would you approach this challenge?

If you have difficulty solving the problem, you are not alone. Most people cannot solve it when it is presented in the manner illustrated in the figure, in which the objects are *inside* the boxes. However, if the objects were presented *beside* the boxes, just resting on the table, chances are that you would solve the problem much more readily—which, in case you are wondering, requires tacking the boxes to the door and then placing the candles inside them (see Figure 6 on page 228).

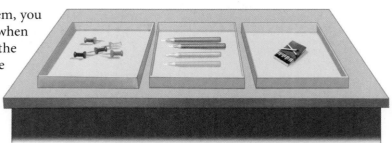

FIGURE 5 The problem here is to place three candles at eye level on a nearby door so that the wax will not drip on the floor as the candles burn—using only materials in the figure. For a solution turn to Figure 6 on p. 228.

The difficulty you probably encountered in solving this problem stems from its presentation, which misled you at the initial preparation stage. Actually, significant obstacles to problem solving can exist at each of the three major stages. Although cognitive approaches to problem solving suggest that thinking proceeds along fairly rational, logical lines as a person confronts a problem and considers various solutions, several factors can hinder the development of creative, appropriate, and accurate solutions.

The difficulty most people experience with the candle problem is caused by **functional fixedness,** the tendency to think of an object only in terms of its typical use. For instance, functional fixedness probably leads you to think of this book as something to read, instead of its potential use as a doorstop or as kindling for a fire. In the candle problem, because the objects are first presented inside the boxes, functional fixedness leads most people to see the boxes simply as containers for the objects they hold rather than as a potential part of the solution. They cannot envision another function for the boxes.

Functional fixedness is an example of a broader phenomenon known as **mental set,** the tendency for old patterns of problem solving to persist. Mental set can affect perceptions, as well as patterns of problem solving. It can prevent you from seeing beyond the apparent constraints of a problem. For example, try to draw four straight lines so that they pass through all nine dots in the grid below—without lifting your pencil from the page.

Functional fixedness The tendency to think of an object only in terms of its typical use.

Mental set The tendency for old patterns of problem solving to persist.

• • •
• • •
• • •

If you had difficulty with the problem, it was probably because you felt compelled to keep your lines within the grid. If you had gone outside the boundaries, however, you would have succeeded by using the solution shown in Figure 7 on page 228. (The phrase "thinking outside the box"—a term commonly used in business today to encourage creativity—stems from research on overcoming the constraining effects of mental set.)

FIGURE 6 A solution to the problem in Figure 5 involves tacking the boxes to the door and placing the candles in the boxes.

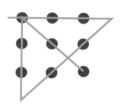

FIGURE 7 A solution to the nine-dot problem requires the use of lines drawn beyond the boundaries of the figure—something that our mental set may prevent us from seeing easily.

RECAP

Explain the concept of mental images.

- Thinking is the manipulation of mental representations of information. Thinking transforms such representations into novel and different forms, permitting people to answer questions, solve problems, and reach goals. (p. 220)

- Mental images are representations in the mind of an object or event. (p. 221)

Discuss the process of categorizing the world.

- Concepts are categorizations of objects, events, or people that share common properties. Prototypes are representative examples of concepts. (p. 221)

Describe the processes that underlie reasoning and decision making.

- Decisions sometimes (but not always) may be improved through the use of algorithms and heuristics. An algorithm is a rule that, if applied appropriately, guarantees a solution; a heuristic is a cognitive shortcut that may lead to a solution but is not guaranteed to do so. (p. 222)

Explain how people approach and solve problems.

- Problem solving typically involves three major stages: preparation, production of solutions, and evaluation of solutions that have been generated. (p. 223)

- A crucial aspect of the preparation stage is the representation and organization of the problem. (p. 224)

- In the production stage, people try to generate solutions. They may find solutions to some problems in long-term memory. Alternatively, they may solve some problems through simple trial and error and use algorithms and heuristics to solve more complex problems. (p. 225)

- Using the heuristic of a means-ends analysis, a person will repeatedly test for differences between the desired outcome and what currently exists, trying each time to come closer to the goal. (p. 225)

- Several factors hinder effective problem solving. Mental set, of which functional fixedness is an example, is the tendency for old patterns of problem solving to persist. Inappropriate use of algorithms and heuristics can also act as an obstacle to the production of solutions. (p. 227)

EVALUATE

1. _____ _____ are representations in the mind of an object or event.
2. _____ are categorizations of objects that share common properties.
3. When you think of the concept "chair," you immediately think of a comfortable easy chair. A chair of this type could be thought of as a _____ of the category "chair."
4. When you ask your friend how best to study for your psychology final, he tells you, "I've always found it best to skim over the notes once, then read the book, then go over the notes again." What decision-making tool might this be an example of?
5. Thinking of an object only in terms of its typical use is known as _____ _____.
   A broader, related tendency for old problem-solving patterns to persist is known as a _____ _____.

RETHINK

Why might people use heuristics, given that they do not assure a solution?

Answers to Evaluate Questions 1. mental images; 2. concepts; 3. prototype; 4. heuristic; 5. functional fixedness, mental set

[KEY TERMS]

Thinking *p. 220*
Mental images *p. 221*
Concepts *p. 221*
Prototypes *p. 222*
Algorithm *p. 223*

Heuristic *p. 223*
Means-ends analysis *p. 225*
Functional fixedness *p. 227*
Mental set *p. 227*

Language

The use of **language**—the communication of information through symbols arranged according to systematic rules—is an important cognitive ability, one that is indispensable for us to communicate with one another. Not only is language central to communication, it is also closely tied to the very way in which we think about and understand the world (Fitch & Sanders, 2005; Stapel & Semin, 2007; Hoff, 2008).

» LO1 Language Development: Developing a Way with Words

Language The communication of information through symbols arranged according to systematic rules.

Babble Meaningless speechlike sounds made by children from around the age of 3 months through 1 year.

To parents, the sounds of their infant babbling and cooing are music to their ears. These sounds also serve an important function. They mark the first step on the road to the development of language.

Babbling

Children **babble**—make speechlike but meaningless sounds—from around the age of 3 months through 1 year. While babbling, they may produce, at one time or another, any of the sounds found in all languages, not just the one to which they are exposed. Even deaf children display their own form of babbling, for infants who are unable to hear yet who are exposed to sign language from birth "babble" with their hands (Pettito, 1993; Locke, 2006).

An infant's babbling increasingly reflects the specific language being spoken in the infant's environment, initially in terms of pitch and tone and eventually in terms of specific sounds. Young infants can distinguish among all the basic units of speech that have been identified across the world's languages. However, after the age of 6 to 8 months, that ability begins to decline. Infants begin to "specialize" in the language to which they are exposed as neurons in their brains reorganize to respond to the particular phonemes infants routinely hear.

Some theorists argue that a *critical period* exists for language development early in life, in which a child is particularly sensitive to language cues and most easily acquires language. In fact, if children are not exposed to language during this critical period, later they will have great difficulty overcoming this deficit (Bates, 2005; Shafer & Garrido-Nag, 2007).

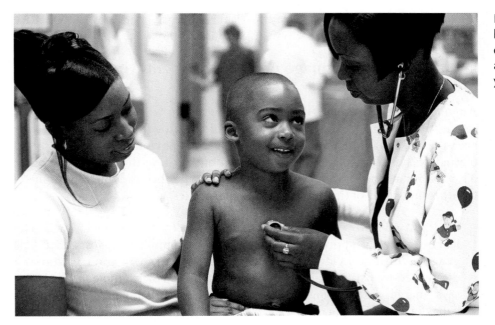

How might a working knowledge of how language develops help this nurse's aide communicate with her young patient?

Production of Language

By the time children are approximately 1 year old, they stop producing sounds that are not in the language to which they have been exposed. It is then a short step to the production of actual words. In English, these are typically short words that start with a consonant sound such as *b, d, m, p,* and *t*—this helps explain why *mama* and *dada* are so often among babies' first words. Of course, even before they produce their first words, children can understand a fair amount of the language they hear. Language comprehension precedes language production.

After the age of 1 year, children begin to learn more complicated forms of language. They produce two-word combinations, the building blocks of sentences, and sharply increase the number of different words they are able to use. By age 2, the average child has a vocabulary of more than 50 words. Just six months later, that vocabulary has grown to several hundred words. At that time, children can produce short sentences, although they use **telegraphic speech**—sentences that sound as if they were part of a telegram, in which words not critical to the message are left out. Rather than saying, "I showed you the book," a child using telegraphic speech may say, "I show book," and "I am drawing a dog" may become "Drawing dog." As children get older, of course, they use less telegraphic speech and produce increasingly complex sentences (Volterra et al., 2003).

By age 3, children learn to make plurals by adding *s* to nouns and to form the past tense by adding *-ed* to verbs. This skill also leads to errors, since children tend to apply rules inflexibly. In such **overgeneralization,** children employ rules even when doing so results in an error. Thus, although it is correct to say "he walked" for the past tense of *walk,* the *-ed* rule doesn't work quite so well when children say "he runned" for the past tense of *run.* By age 5, children have acquired the basic rules of language. However, they do not attain a full vocabulary and the ability

Telegraphic speech Sentences in which words not critical to the message are left out.

Overgeneralization The phenomenon by which children apply language rules even when the application results in an error.

How might these three sisters use language differently?

to comprehend and use subtle grammatical rules until later (Howe, 2002; Rice et al., 2004; Gershkoff-Stowe, Connell, & Smith, 2006).

Understanding Language Acquisition: Identifying the Roots of Language

Anyone who spends even a little time with children will notice the enormous strides that they make in language development throughout childhood. However, the reasons for this rapid growth are far from obvious. Psychologists have offered two major explanations, one based on learning theory and the other based on innate processes. A third approach also has been adopted to reconcile the differing views of the preceding two approaches.

Learning-Theory Approach: Language as a Learned Skill. The **learning-theory approach to language development** suggests that language acquisition follows the principles of reinforcement and conditioning discovered by psychologists who study learning. For example, a child who says "mama" receives hugs and praise from her mother, which reinforce the behavior of saying "mama" and make its repetition more likely. This view suggests that children first learn to speak by being rewarded for making sounds that approximate speech. Ultimately, through a process of shaping, language becomes more and more like adult speech (Skinner, 1957; Ornat & Gallo, 2004).

In support of the learning-theory approach to language acquisition, the more that parents speak to their young children, the more proficient the children become in language use. The learning-theory approach is less successful in explaining how children acquire language rules. Children are reinforced not only when they use language correctly, but also when they use it incorrectly. For example, parents answer a child's "Why the dog won't eat?" as readily as they do the correctly phrased question, "Why won't the dog eat?" Listeners understand both sentences equally well. Learning theory, then, has difficulty fully explaining language acquisition.

Nativist Approach: Language as an Innate Skill. Pointing to such problems with learning-theory approaches to language acquisition, linguist Noam Chomsky (1968, 1978, 1991) provided a groundbreaking alternative. Chomsky argued that humans are born with an innate linguistic capability that emerges primarily as a function of maturation. According to his **nativist approach to language development,** all the world's languages share a common underlying structure called a **universal grammar.** Chomsky suggested that the human brain has a neural system, the **language-acquisition device,** that not only lets us understand the structure language provides but also gives us strategies and techniques for learning the unique characteristics of our native language (McGilvray, 2004; Lidz & Gleitman, 2004; White, 2007).

In support of the nativist approach, scientists have discovered a gene related to the development of language abilities that may have emerged as recently—in evolutionary terms—as 100,000 years ago. Furthermore, it is clear that specific sites exist within the brain that are closely tied to language, and that the shapes of the human mouth and throat are tailored to the production of speech. And there is evidence that features of specific types of languages are tied to particular genes, such as in "tonal" languages in which pitch is used to convey meaning (Hauser, Chomsky, & Fitch, 2002; Chandra, 2007; Dediu & Ladd, 2007).

Learning-theory approach to language development The theory suggesting that language acquisition follows the principles of reinforcement and conditioning.

Nativist approach to language development The theory that a genetically determined, innate mechanism directs language development.

Universal grammar Noam Chomsky's theory that all the world's languages share a common underlying structure.

Language-acquisition device A neural system of the brain hypothesized by Noam Chomsky to permit understanding of language.

Interactionist approach to language development The view that language development is produced through a combination of genetically determined predispositions and environmental circumstances that help teach language.

Linguistic-relativity hypothesis The notion that language shapes and may determine the way people in a particular culture perceive and understand the world.

Interactionist Approach: A Combination. To reconcile the differing views, many theorists take an interactionist approach to language development. The **interactionist approach to language development** suggests that language development is produced through a combination of genetically determined predispositions and environmental circumstances that help teach language.

Specifically, proponents of the interactionist approach suggest that the brain's hardwired language-acquisition device that Chomsky and geneticists point to provides the hardware for our acquisition of language, whereas the exposure to language in our environment that learning theorists observe allows us to develop the appropriate software. But the issue of how language is acquired remains hotly contested (Lana, 2002; Pinker & Jackendoff, 2005; Hoff, 2008).

From the perspective of . . .

A Child-Care Provider How would you encourage children's language abilities at the different stages of development?

LO 2 The Influence of Language on Thinking: Do Eskimos Have More Words for Snow Than Texans?

psych2.0
WWW.MHHE.COM/PSYCHLIFE

Language Development

Do Eskimos living in the frigid Arctic have a more expansive vocabulary for discussing snow than people living in warmer climates?

It makes sense, and arguments that the Eskimo language has many more words for snow than does English have been made since the early 1900s. At that time, linguist Benjamin Lee Whorf contended that because snow is so relevant to Eskimos' lives, their language provides a particularly rich vocabulary to describe it—considerably larger than what we find in other languages, such as English (Martin & Pullum, 1991; Pinker, 1994).

The contention that the Eskimo language is especially abundant in snow-related terms led to the **linguistic-relativity hypothesis,** the notion that language shapes and, in fact, may determine the way people in a specific culture perceive and understand the world. According to this view, language provides us with categories that we use to construct our view of people and events in the world around us. Consequently, language shapes and produces thought (Whorf, 1956; Kay & Regier, 2007; Zhang, He, & Zhang, 2007).

Let's consider another possibility, however. Suppose that instead of language's being the *cause* of certain ways of thinking, thought *produces* language. The only reason to expect that Eskimo language might have more words for snow than English does is that snow is considerably more relevant to Eskimos than it is to people in other cultures.

Noam Chomsky argues that all languages share a universal grammar.

Which view is correct? Most recent research refutes the linguistic-relativity hypothesis and suggests, instead, that thinking produces language. In fact, new analyses of the Eskimo language suggest that Eskimos have no more words for snow than English speakers, for if one examines the English language closely, one sees that it is hardly impoverished when it comes to describing snow (consider, e.g., *sleet, slush, blizzard, dusting,* and *avalanche*).

Although research does not support the linguistic-relativity hypothesis that language *causes* thought, there is evidence that language *influences* how we think. And, of course, it certainly is the case that thought influences language, suggesting that language and thinking interact in complex ways (Kim, 2002; Ross, 2004; Thorkildsen, 2006).

EXPLORING diversity

Teaching with Linguistic Variety: Bilingual Education

In New York City, one in six of the city's 1.1 million students is enrolled in some form of bilingual or English as a Second Language instruction. And New York City is far from the only school district with a significant population of non-native English speakers. From the biggest cities to the most rural areas, the face—and voice—of education in the United States is changing. More and more schoolchildren today have last names like Kim, Valdez, and Karachnicoff. In seven states, including Texas and Colorado, more than one-quarter of the students are not native English speakers. For some 47 million Americans, English is their second language (Holloway, 2000; see Figure 1).

> *How to appropriately and effectively teach the increasing number of children who do not speak English is not always clear.*

How to appropriately and effectively teach the increasing number of children who do not speak English is not always clear. Many educators maintain that *bilingual education* is best. With a bilingual approach, students learn some subjects in their native language while simultaneously learning English. Proponents of bilingualism believe that students must develop a sound footing in basic subject areas and that, initially at least, teaching those subjects in their native language is the only way to provide them with that foundation. During the same period, they learn English, with the eventual goal of shifting all instruction into English.

In contrast, other educators insist that all instruction ought to be in English from the moment students, including those who speak no English at all, enroll in school. In *immersion programs,* students are immediately plunged into English instruction in all subjects. The reasoning—endorsed by voters in California in a referendum designed to end bilingual education—is that teaching students in a language other than English simply hinders non-native English

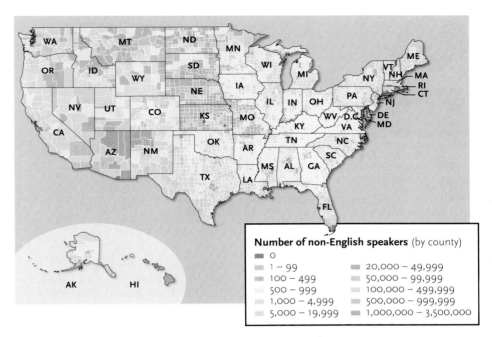

FIGURE 1 The language of diversity. Some 22 percent of the people in the United States speak a language other than English at home. Most of them speak Spanish; the rest speak an astounding variety of different languages. Where are the largest clusters of non-English speakers in the United States, and what do you think explains these concentrations? *(Source: MLA Language Map, 2005, based on 2000 Census).*

speakers' integration into society and ultimately does them a disservice. Proponents of English immersion programs point as evidence to improvements in standardized test scores that followed the end of bilingual education programs (Wildavsky, 2000).

Although the controversial issue of bilingual education versus immersion has strong political undercurrents, evidence shows that the ability to speak two languages provides significant cognitive benefits over speaking only one language. For example, bilingual speakers show more cognitive flexibility and may understand concepts more easily than those who speak only one language. They have more linguistic tools for thinking because of their multiple-language abilities. In turn, this makes them more creative and flexible in solving problems (Heyman & Diesendruck, 2002; Bialystok & Martin, 2004; Kuo, 2007).

Research also suggests that speaking several languages changes the organization of the brain, as does the timing of the acquisition of a second language. For example, one study compared bilingual speakers on linguistic tasks in their native and second languages. The study found that those who had learned their second language as adults showed different areas of brain activation compared with those who had learned their second language in childhood (Kim et al., 1997; see Figure 2).

Related to questions about bilingual education is the matter of *biculturalism,* that is, being a member of two cultures and its psychological impact. Some psychologists argue that society should promote an *alternation model* of bicultural competence. Such a model supports members of a culture in their efforts to maintain their original cultural identity, as well as in their integration into the adopted culture. In this view, a person can belong to two cultures and have two cultural identities without having to choose between them. Whether society will adopt the alternation model remains to be seen (Carter, 2003; Benet-Martínez, Lee, & Leu, 2006; Tadmor, 2007).

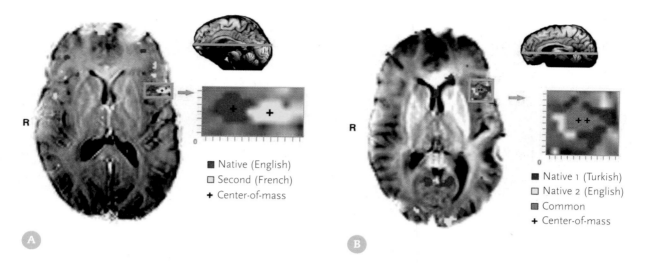

FIGURE 2 Brain functioning in bilingual speakers. When bilingual speakers carried out language tasks in their native and second languages, brain activity differed depending on when in life each speaker learned the second language. For example, the brain scan in (A), which shows two separate areas of the brain activated, is that of a native English speaker who learned French in adulthood. In contrast, the brain scan in (B) is that of a speaker who learned both English and Turkish in infancy. For that person, substantial overlap exists between the areas of the brain that are activated. *(Source: Kim et al., 1997.)*

RECAP

Describe how people use language.

- Language is the communication of information through symbols arranged according to systematic rules. (p. 230)

Explain how language develops.

- Language production develops out of babbling, which then leads to the production of actual words. After 1 year of age, children use two-word combinations, increase their vocabulary, and use telegraphic speech, which drops words not critical to the message. By age 5, acquisition of language rules is relatively complete. (p. 230)

- Learning theorists suggest that language is acquired through reinforcement and conditioning. In contrast, the nativist approach suggests that an innate language-acquisition device guides the development of language. The interactionist approach argues that language development is produced through a combination of genetically determined predispositions and environmental circumstances that help teach language. (p. 232)

- The linguistic-relativity hypothesis suggests that language shapes and may determine the way people think about the world. Most evidence suggests that although language does not determine thought, it does affect the way people store information in memory and how well they can retrieve it. (p. 233)

- People who speak more than one language may have a cognitive advantage over those who speak only one. (p. 234)

EVALUATE

1. _____ _____ refers to the phenomenon in which young children omit nonessential portions of sentences.

2. A child knows that adding -ed to certain words puts them in the past tense. As a result, instead of saying "He came," the child says "He comed." This is an example of _____.

3. _____ theory assumes that language acquisition is based on principles of operant conditioning and shaping.

4. In his theory of language acquisition, Chomsky argues that language acquisition is an innate ability tied to the structure of the brain. True or false?

RETHINK

Do people who use two languages, one at home and one at school, automatically have two cultures? Why might people who speak two languages have cognitive advantages over those who speak only one?

Answers to Evaluate Questions 1. telegraphic speech; 2. overgeneralization; 3. learning; 4. true

[KEY TERMS]

Language *p. 230*

Babble *p. 230*

Telegraphic speech *p. 231*

Overgeneralization *p. 231*

Learning-theory approach to language development *p. 232*

Nativist approach to language development *p. 232*

Universal grammar *p. 232*

Language-acquisition device *p. 232*

Interactionist approach to language development *p. 232*

Linguistic-relativity hypothesis *p. 232*

looking BACK

Psychology on the Web

1. Memory is a topic of serious interest to psychologists, but it is also a source of amusement. Find a Web site that focuses on the amusing side of memory (such as memory games, tests of recall, or lists of mnemonics; hint: there's even a mnemonics generator out there!). Write down the addresses of any interesting sites that you encounter and summarize what you find.

2. Do animals think? What evidence is there on either side of this question? Search the Web for at least one example of research and/or argument on each side of this question. Summarize your findings and use your knowledge of cognitive psychology to state your own position on this question.

the case of . . .
ROB STEERE, THE MAN WHO KNEW TOO MUCH

Rob Steere worked as a document archivist for a large university for almost a decade. His job entailed filing away books, documents, artifacts, multimedia, and other records in a large warehouse—and Rob was very good at it. Despite the complex filing system, Rob saw the logic behind it; and he knew where he could find just about any archived record that was called for.

Realizing that computer tracking eliminated the need to organize the archives topically, the university administrators last year instituted a new computerized filing system that would reorder the archives according to how densely the records could be filed together, thereby saving a great deal of expensive storage space. Since that time, though, Rob has gone from being one of the most efficient archive specialists working at this warehouse to one of the least efficient. He often gets lost and confused when trying to locate records, and he has repeatedly stored materials in the wrong place. Rob just cannot seem to make sense of the new filing system, and he has been looking for a new position elsewhere.

1. Is it reasonable to expect that anyone would be able to make good sense of a filing system such as this new one? Why or why not?

2. How would Rob's knowledge of the earlier filing system and the location of various archived records be organized in his memory?

3. Would the levels-of-processing theory predict that Rob (and other archivists) would have much more trouble with this new filing system than with the old one? Explain.

4. Why might Rob be having so much difficulty finding archived records under the new system? Why might he have developed his problem of filing records in the wrong place?

5. What advice would you give Rob for making the adjustment to this new filing system?

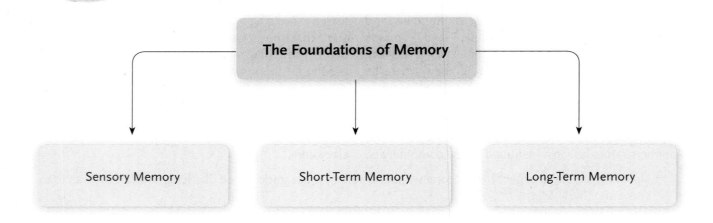

The Foundations of Memory

Sensory Memory

Short-Term Memory

Long-Term Memory

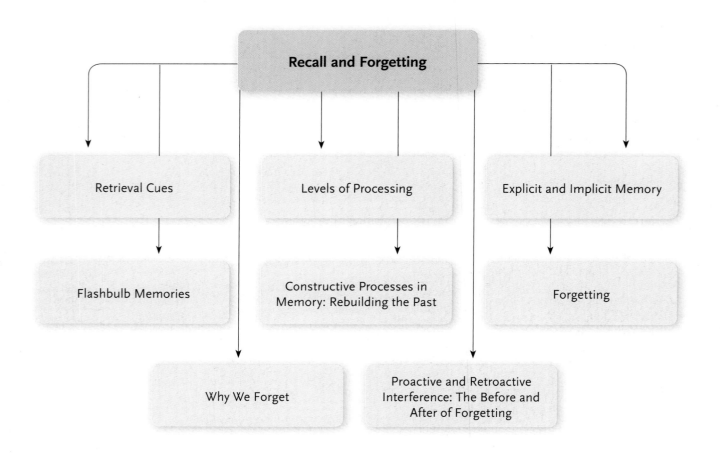

Recall and Forgetting

Retrieval Cues

Levels of Processing

Explicit and Implicit Memory

Flashbulb Memories

Constructive Processes in Memory: Rebuilding the Past

Forgetting

Why We Forget

Proactive and Retroactive Interference: The Before and After of Forgetting

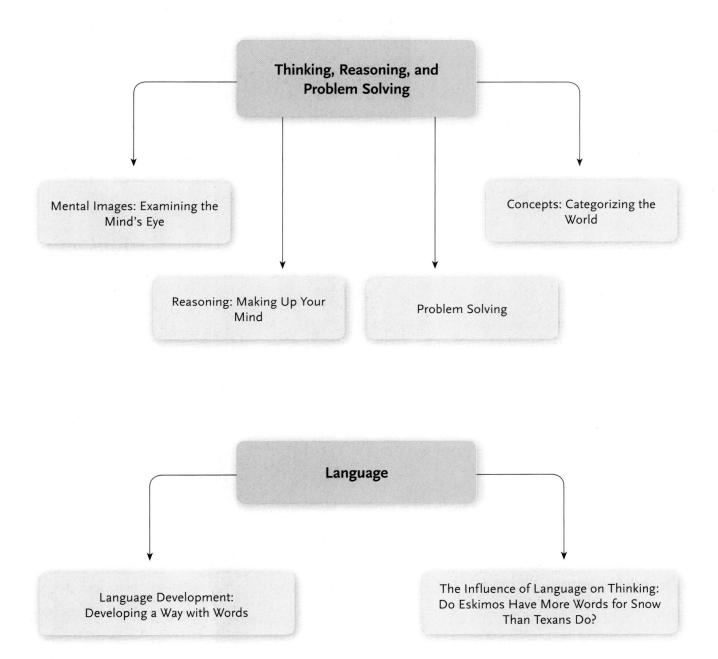

Thinking, Reasoning, and Problem Solving

Mental Images: Examining the Mind's Eye

Reasoning: Making Up Your Mind

Problem Solving

Concepts: Categorizing the World

Language

Language Development: Developing a Way with Words

The Influence of Language on Thinking: Do Eskimos Have More Words for Snow Than Texans Do?

Armed with Bravery

In just a moment, 27-year-old Aron Ralston's life changed. An 800-pound boulder dislodged in a narrow canyon where Ralston was hiking in an isolated Utah canyon, pinning his lower arm to the ground.

For the next five days, Ralston lay in the dense, lonely forest, unable to escape. An experienced climber who had search-and-rescue training, he had ample time to consider his options. He tried unsuccessfully to chip away at the rock, and he rigged up ropes and pulleys around the boulder in a vain effort to move it.

Finally, out of water and nearly dehydrated, Ralston reasoned there was only one option left short of dying. In acts of incredible bravery, Ralston broke two bones in his wrist, applied a tourniquet, and used a dull pen knife to amputate his arm beneath the elbow.

Freed from his entrapment, Ralston climbed down from where he had been pinned, and then hiked five miles to safety (Ralston, 2004; Martin, 2006). ∎

MOTIVATION AND EMOTION

looking AHEAD

Ralston, who now has a prosthetic arm, recovered from his ordeal. He remains an active outdoorsman and hiker.

The topics of motivation and emotion are central in attempting to explain Ralston's extraordinary courage and will to live. Psychologists who study motivation seek to discover the particular desired goals—the motives—that underlie behavior. Behaviors as basic as drinking to satisfy thirst and as inconsequential as taking a stroll to get exercise exemplify motives. Psychologists specializing in the study of motivation assume that such underlying motives steer our choices of activities.

Whereas motivation concerns the forces that direct future behavior, emotion pertains to the feelings we experience throughout our lives. The study of emotions focuses on our internal experiences at any given moment. All of us feel a variety of emotions: happiness at succeeding at a difficult task, sadness over the death of a loved one, anger at being treated unfairly. Because emotions not only play a role in motivating our behavior but also act as a reflection of our underlying motivation, they play an important role in our lives.

We begin this set of modules by focusing on the major conceptions of motivation, discussing how different motives and needs jointly affect behavior. We consider motives that are biologically based and universal in the animal kingdom, such as hunger, as well as motives that are unique to humans, such as the need for achievement.

We then turn to emotions. We consider the roles and functions that emotions play in people's lives and discuss several approaches that explain how people understand their emotions. Finally, we look at how nonverbal behavior communicates emotions.

Explaining Motivation

Motivation The factors that direct and energize the behavior of humans and other organisms.

Instincts Inborn patterns of behavior that are biologically determined rather than learned.

According to instinct approaches to motivation, people and animals are born preprogrammed with sets of behaviors essential to their survival.

What motivation lies behind the resolve of an athlete who might train for years for the remote chance of competing in the Olympics that only occur once every four years? Is it anticipating the emotional thrill of winning a medal? The potential rewards that would follow success? The excitement of participating? The satisfaction of achieving a long-sought goal?

To answer such questions, psychologists employ the concept of **motivation**, the factors that direct and energize the behavior of humans and other organisms. Motivation has biological, cognitive, and social aspects; and the complexity of the concept has led psychologists to develop a variety of approaches. All seek to explain the energy that guides people's behavior in specific directions.

» LO1 Instinct Approaches: Born to Be Motivated

When psychologists first tried to explain motivation, they turned to **instincts,** inborn patterns of behavior that are biologically determined rather than learned. According to instinct approaches to motivation, people and animals are born preprogrammed with sets of behaviors essential to their survival. Those instincts provide the energy that channels behavior in appropriate directions. Hence, sexual behavior may be a response to an instinct to reproduce, and exploratory behavior may be motivated by an instinct to examine one's territory.

This conception presents several difficulties, however. For one thing, psychologists do not agree on what, or even how many, primary instincts exist. Furthermore, explanations based on the concept of instincts do not go very far toward explaining why one specific pattern of behavior, and not others, has appeared in a given species. In addition, although it is clear that much animal behavior is based on instincts, because much of the variety and complexity of human behavior is learned, that behavior cannot be seen as instinctual. As a result of these shortcomings, newer explanations have replaced most conceptions of motivation based on instincts.

» LO2 Drive-Reduction Approaches: Satisfying Our Needs

After rejecting instinct theory, psychologists first proposed simple drive-reduction theories of motivation to take its place (Hull, 1943). **Drive-reduction approaches to motivation** suggest that a lack of some basic biological requirement such as water produces a drive to obtain that requirement (in this case, the thirst drive).

To understand this approach, we begin with the concept of drive. A **drive** is motivational tension, or arousal, that energizes behavior to fulfill a need. Many basic drives, such as hunger, thirst, sleep, and sex, are related to biological needs of the body or of the species as a whole. These are called *primary drives*. Primary drives contrast with secondary drives, in which behavior fulfills no obvious biological need. In *secondary drives*, prior experience and learning bring about needs. For instance, some people have strong needs to achieve academically and professionally. We can say that their achievement need is reflected in a secondary drive that motivates their behavior (McKinley et al., 2004; Seli, 2007).

We usually try to satisfy a primary drive by reducing the need underlying it. For example, we become hungry after not eating for a few hours and may raid the refrigerator, especially if the next scheduled meal is not imminent. If the weather turns cold, we put on extra clothing or raise the setting on the thermostat to keep warm. If our bodies need liquids to function properly, we experience thirst and seek out water.

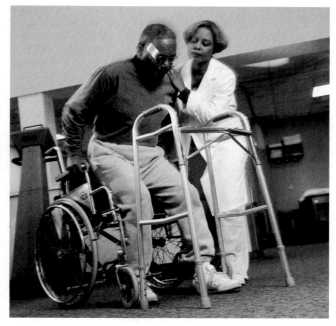

Understanding what motivates people can have a huge impact on how we interact. How would knowing what motivates this man help this physical therapist aid him in his recovery?

Drive-reduction approaches to motivation Theories suggesting that a lack of a basic biological requirement such as water produces a drive to obtain that requirement (in this case, the thirst drive).

Drive Motivational tension, or arousal, that energizes behavior to fulfill a need.

Homeostasis The body's tendency to maintain a steady internal state.

Homeostasis

Homeostasis, the body's tendency to maintain a steady internal state, underlies primary drives. Using feedback loops, homeostasis brings deviations in body functioning back to an optimal state, similar to the way a thermostat and a furnace work in a home heating system to maintain a steady temperature. Receptor cells throughout the body constantly monitor factors such as temperature and nutrient levels. When deviations from the ideal state occur, the body adjusts in an effort to return to an optimal state. Many fundamental needs, including the needs for food, water, stable body temperature, and sleep, operate via homeostasis (Canteras, 2002; Machado, Suchecki, & Tufik, 2005; Black, 2006).

Although drive-reduction theories provide a good explanation of how primary drives motivate behavior, they cannot fully explain a behavior in which the goal is not to reduce a drive, but rather to maintain or even increase the level of excitement or arousal. For instance, some behaviors seem to be motivated by nothing more than curiosity, such as rushing to check e-mail messages. Similarly, many people pursue thrilling activities such as riding a roller coaster or steering a raft down the rapids of a river. Such behaviors certainly don't suggest that people seek to reduce all drives, as drive-reduction approaches would indicate (Begg & Langley, 2001; Rosenbloom & Wolf, 2002).

While some drives are fairly obvious as primary or secondary, others can be more complicated. How would you classify these needs pictured here?

psych2.0
WWW.MHHE.COM/PSYCHLIFE

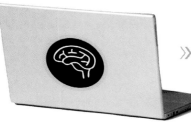

Sensation Seeking

Arousal approaches to motivation The belief that we try to maintain certain levels of stimulation and activity, increasing or reducing them as necessary.

Both curiosity and thrill-seeking behavior, then, shed doubt on drive-reduction approaches as a complete explanation for motivation. In both cases, rather than seeking to reduce an underlying drive, people and animals appear to be motivated to increase their overall level of stimulation and activity. To explain this phenomenon, psychologists have devised an alternative: arousal approaches to motivation.

» LO3 Arousal Approaches: Beyond Drive Reduction

Arousal approaches seek to explain behavior in which the goal is to maintain or increase excitement. According to **arousal approaches to motivation,** each person tries to maintain a certain level of stimulation and activity. People vary widely in the optimal level of arousal they seek out, with some people looking for especially high levels of arousal. For example, people who participate in daredevil sports, high-stakes gamblers, and criminals who pull off high-risk robberies may be exhibiting a particularly high need for arousal (see Figure 1; Zuckerman & Kuhlman, 2000; Zuckerman, 2002; Cavenett & Nixon, 2006). (To get a sense of your own level of stimulation, complete the accompanying Try It!)

» LO4 Incentive Approaches: Motivation's Pull

When a luscious dessert appears on the table after a filling meal, its appeal has little or nothing to do with internal drives or the maintenance of arousal. Rather, if we choose to eat the dessert, such behavior is motivated by the external stimulus of the dessert itself, which acts as an anticipated reward. This reward, in motivational terms, is an *incentive*.

Do You Seek Out Sensation?

How much stimulation do you crave in your everyday life? You will have an idea after you complete the following questionnaire, which lists some items from a scale designed to assess your sensation-seeking tendencies. Circle either A or B in each pair of statements.

1. A   I would like a job that requires a lot of traveling.
   B   I would prefer a job in one location.

2. A   I am invigorated by a brisk, cold day.
   B   I can't wait to get indoors on a cold day.

3. A   I get bored seeing the same old faces.
   B   I like the comfortable familiarity of everyday friends.

4. A   I would prefer living in an ideal society in which everyone was safe, secure, and happy.
   B   I would have preferred living in the unsettled days of our history.

5. A   I sometimes like to do things that are a little frightening.
   B   A sensible person avoids activities that are dangerous.

6. A   I would not like to be hypnotized.
   B   I would like to have the experience of being hypnotized.

7. A   The most important goal of life is to live it to the fullest and to experience as much as possible.
   B   The most important goal of life is to find peace and happiness.

8. A   I would like to try parachute jumping.
   B   I would never want to try jumping out of a plane, with or without a parachute.

9. A   I enter cold water gradually, giving myself time to get used to it.
   B   I like to dive or jump right into the ocean or a cold pool.

10. A   When I go on a vacation, I prefer the comfort of a good room and bed.
    B   When I go on a vacation, I prefer the change of camping out.

11. A   I prefer people who are emotionally expressive, even if they are a bit unstable.
    B   I prefer people who are calm and even-tempered.

12. A   A good painting should shock or jolt the senses.
    B   A good painting should give one a feeling of peace and security.

13. A   People who ride motorcycles must have some kind of unconscious need to hurt themselves.
    B   I would like to drive or ride a motorcycle.

(continued)

try it! —concluded

Incentive approaches to motivation
Theories suggesting that motivation stems from the desire to obtain valued external goals, or incentives.

Cognitive approaches to motivation
Theories suggesting that motivation is a product of people's thoughts, expectations, and goals—their cognitions.

Incentive approaches to motivation suggest that motivation stems from the desire to obtain valued external goals, or incentives. In this view, the desirable properties of external stimuli—whether grades, money, affection, food, or sex—account for a person's motivation.

Although the theory explains why we may succumb to an incentive (such as a mouthwatering dessert) even though we lack internal cues (such as hunger), it does not provide a complete explanation of motivation, because organisms sometimes seek to fulfill needs even when incentives are not apparent. Consequently, many psychologists believe that the internal drives proposed by drive-reduction theory work in tandem with the external incentives of incentive theory to "push" and "pull" behavior, respectively. Thus, at the same time that we seek to satisfy our underlying hunger needs (the push of drive-reduction theory), we are drawn to food that appears very appetizing (the pull of incentive theory). Rather than contradicting each other, then, drives and incentives may work together in motivating behavior (Pinel, Assanand, & Lehman, 2000; Lowery, Fillingim, & Wright, 2003; Berridge, 2004).

> *At the same time that we seek to satisfy our underlying hunger needs (the push of drive-reduction theory), we are drawn to food that appears very appetizing (the pull of incentive theory).*

» LO5 Cognitive Approaches: The Thoughts Behind Motivation

Cognitive approaches to motivation suggest that motivation is a product of people's thoughts, expectations, and goals—their cognitions. For instance, the degree to which people are motivated to study for a test is based on their expectation of how well studying will pay off in terms of a good grade.

Cognitive theories of motivation draw a key distinction between intrinsic and extrinsic motivation. *Intrinsic motivation* causes us to participate in an activity for our own enjoyment rather than for any concrete, tangible reward that it will bring us. In contrast, *extrinsic motivation* causes us to do something for money, a grade, or some other concrete, tangible reward. For example, when a physician works long hours because she loves medicine, intrinsic motivation is prompting her; if she works hard to make a lot of money, extrinsic motivation underlies her efforts (Pedersen, 2002; Lepper, Corpus, & Iyengar, 2005; Shaikholeslami & Khayyer, 2006).

We are more apt to persevere, work harder, and produce work of higher quality when motivation for a task is intrinsic rather than extrinsic. In fact, in some cases providing rewards for desirable behavior (thereby increasing extrinsic motivation) actually may decrease intrinsic motivation (Deci, Koestner, & Ryan, 2001; Henderlong & Lepper, 2002; James, 2005).

» LO6 Maslow's Hierarchy: Ordering Motivational Needs

What do Eleanor Roosevelt, Abraham Lincoln, and Albert Einstein have in common? The common thread, according to a model of motivation devised by psychologist Abraham Maslow, is that each of them fulfilled the highest levels of motivational needs underlying human behavior.

Maslow's model places motivational needs in a hierarchy and suggests that before more sophisticated, higher-order needs can be met, certain primary needs must be satisfied (Maslow, 1987). A pyramid can represent the model, with the more basic needs at the bottom and the higher-level needs at the top (see Figure 1). To activate a specific higher-order need, thereby guiding behavior, a person must first fulfill the more basic needs in the hierarchy.

The basic needs are primary drives: needs for water, food, sleep, sex, and the like. To move up the hierarchy, a person must first meet these basic physiological needs. Safety needs come next in the hierarchy; Maslow suggests that people need a safe, secure environment in order to function effectively. Physiological and safety needs compose the lower-order needs.

Only after meeting the basic lower-order needs can a person consider fulfilling higher-order needs, such as the needs for love and a sense of belonging, esteem, and self-actualization. Love and belongingness needs include the needs to obtain and give affection and to be a contributing member of some group or society. After fulfilling these needs, a person strives for esteem. In Maslow's thinking, esteem relates to the need to develop a sense of self-worth by recognizing that others know and value one's competence.

Once these four sets of needs are fulfilled—no easy task—a person is able to strive for the highest-level need, self-actualization. **Self-actualization** is a state of self-fulfillment in which people realize their highest potentials, each in his or her own unique way. The important thing is that people feel at ease with themselves

Intrinsic and extrinsic motivation are not always separate things. Madonna is well known for her genuine love of music (intrinsic motivation). However, she has always been well compensated for performing (extrinsic motivation). How do you identify your own motivations?

> *Only after meeting the basic lower-order needs can a person consider fulfilling higher-order needs, such as the needs for love and a sense of belonging, esteem, and self-actualization.*

Self-actualization A state of self-fulfillment in which people realize their highest potential, each in his or her own unique way.

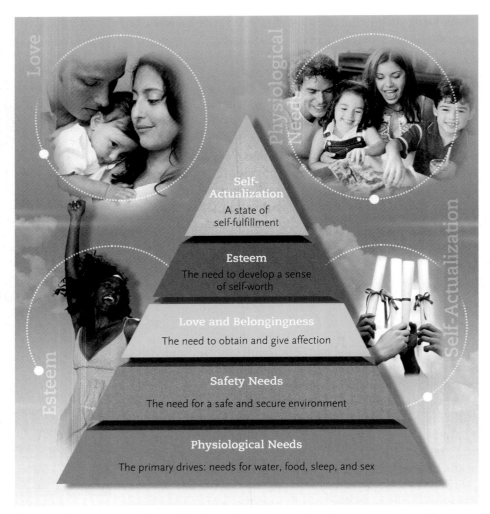

FIGURE 1 Maslow's hierarchy shows how our motivation progresses up the pyramid from the broadest, most fundamental biological needs to higher-order ones. (After Maslow, 1971.) Do you agree that lower-order needs must be satisfied before higher-order needs? Do hermits and monks who attempt to fulfill spiritual needs while denying basic physical needs contradict Maslow's hierarchy?

and satisfied that they are using their talents to the fullest. In a sense, achieving self-actualization reduces the striving and yearning for greater fulfillment that mark most people's lives and instead provides a sense of satisfaction with the current state of affairs (Piechowski, 2003; Reiss & Havercamp, 2005; Laas, 2006).

» LO7 Applying the Different Approaches to Motivation

STUDY ALERT

Review the distinctions between the different explanations for motivation (instinct, drive reduction, arousal, incentive, cognitive, and Maslow's hierarchy of needs).

The various theories of motivation give several different perspectives on motivation. Which provides the fullest account of motivation? Actually, many of the approaches are complementary, rather than contradictory. In fact, employing more than one approach can help us understand motivation in a particular instance.

Consider, for example, Aron Ralston's accident while hiking (described at the beginning of the chapter). His interest in climbing in an isolated and

potentially dangerous area may be explained by arousal approaches to motivation. From the perspective of instinct approaches, we realize that Aron had an overwhelming instinct to preserve his life at all costs. From a cognitive perspective, we see his careful consideration of various strategies to extricate himself from the boulder.

In short, applying multiple approaches to motivation in a given situation provides a broader understanding than we might obtain by employing only a single approach. We'll see this again when we consider specific motives—such as the needs for food, achievement, affiliation, and power—and draw on several of the theories for the fullest account of what motivates our behavior.

From the perspective of . . .

A MARKETING SPECIALIST How might you increase sales of a new snack food by appealing to multiple motivations for its consumption?

RECAP

Explain instinct approaches to motivation.

- Motivation relates to the factors that direct and energize behavior. (p. 244)

Explain drive-reduction approaches to motivation.

- Drive is the motivational tension that energizes behavior to fulfill a need. (p. 245)
- Homeostasis, the maintenance of a steady internal state, often underlies motivational drives. (p. 245)

Explain arousal approaches to motivation.

- Arousal approaches suggest that we try to maintain a particular level of stimulation and activity. (p. 246)

Explain incentive approaches to motivation.

- Incentive approaches focus on the positive aspects of the environment that direct and energize behavior. (p. 246)

Explain cognitive approaches to motivation.

- Cognitive approaches focus on the role of thoughts, expectations, and understanding of the world in producing motivation. (p. 248)

Apply Maslow's hierarchy of needs to motivation.

- Maslow's hierarchy suggests that there are five basic needs: physiological, safety, love and belongingness, esteem, and self-actualization. Only after the more basic needs are fulfilled can a person move toward meeting higher-order needs. (p. 249)

Apply the different approaches to motivation.

- Taken together, the different approaches to motivation provide a broad understanding of behavior. (p. 250)

EVALUATE

1. _____ are forces that guide a person's behavior in a certain direction.

2. Biologically determined, inborn patterns of behavior are known as _____.

3. Your psychology professor tells you, "Explaining behavior is easy! When we lack something, we are motivated to get it." Which approach to motivation does your professor subscribe to?

4. I help an elderly person cross the street because doing a good deed makes me feel good. What type of motivation is at work here? What type of motivation would be at work if I were to help an elderly man across the street because he paid me $20?

5. According to Maslow, a person with no job, no home, and no friends can become self-actualized. True or false?

RETHINK

Which approaches to motivation are more commonly used in the workplace? How might each approach be used to design employment policies that can sustain or increase motivation?

KEY TERMS

Motivation *p. 244*

Instincts *p. 244*

Drive-reduction approaches to motivation *p. 245*

Drive *p. 245*

Homeostasis *p. 245*

Arousal approaches to motivation *p. 246*

Incentive approaches to motivation *p. 248*

Cognitive approaches to motivation *p. 248*

Self-actualization *p. 249*

Human Needs and Motivation

Eat, Drink, and Be Daring

As a sophomore at the University of California, Santa Cruz, Lisa Arndt followed a menu of her own making: For breakfast she ate cereal or fruit, with 10 diet pills and 50 chocolate-flavored laxatives. Lunch was a salad or sandwich; dinner: chicken and rice. But it was the feast that followed that Arndt relished most. Almost every night at about 9 p.m., she would retreat to her room and eat an entire small pizza and a whole batch of cookies. Then she'd wait for the day's laxatives to take effect. "It was extremely painful," says Arndt of those days. . . . "But I was that desperate to make up for my binge-ing. I was terrified of fat the way other people are afraid of lions or guns." (Hubbard, O'Neill, & Cheakalos, 1999, p. 59)

Lisa was 1 of the 10 million women (and 1 million men) who are estimated to suffer from an eating disorder. These disorders, which usually appear during adolescence, can bring about extraordinary weight loss and other forms of physical deterioration. Extremely dangerous, they sometimes result in death.

Why are Lisa and others like her subject to such disordered eating, which revolves around the motivation to avoid weight gain at all costs? And why do so many other people engage in overeating, which leads to obesity?

LEARNING OUTCOMES

23.1 Describe the biological and social factors that underlie hunger.

23.2 Summarize the varieties of sexual behavior.

23.3 Explain how needs related to achievement, affiliation, and power are exhibited.

» LO1 The Motivation Behind Hunger and Eating

Two-thirds of the people in the United States are overweight, and almost a quarter are so heavy that they have **obesity,** body weight that is more than 20 percent above the average weight for a person of a particular height. And the rest of the world is not far behind: a billion people around the globe are overweight or obese. The World Health Organization has said that worldwide obesity has reached epidemic proportions, producing increases in heart disease, diabetes, cancer, and premature deaths (Hill, Catenacci, & Wyatt, 2005; Stephenson & Banet-Weiser, 2007).

Obesity Body weight that is more than 20 percent above the average weight for a person of a particular height.

The most widely used measure of obesity is *body mass index (BMI),* which is based on a ratio of weight to height. People with a BMI greater than 30 are considered obese, whereas those with a BMI between 25 and 30 are overweight. (Use the formulas in Figure 1 to determine your own BMI.)

Biological Factors in the Regulation of Hunger

Although the brain's *hypothalamus* has an important role in regulating food intake, the exact way this organ operates is still unclear. One hypothesis suggests that injury to the hypothalamus affects the **weight set point,** or the particular level of weight that the body strives to maintain, which in turn regulates food intake. Acting as a kind of internal weight thermostat, the hypothalamus calls for either greater or less food intake (Capaldi, 1996; Woods et al., 2000; Berthoud, 2002).

In most cases, the hypothalamus does a good job. Even people who are not deliberately monitoring their weight show only minor weight fluctuations in spite of substantial day-to-day variations in how much they eat and exercise. However, injury to the hypothalamus can alter the weight set point, and a person then struggles to meet the internal goal by increasing or decreasing food consumption. Even temporary exposure to certain drugs can alter the weight set point (Cabanac & Frankham, 2002; Hallschmid et al., 2004).

Genetic factors determine the weight set point, at least in part. People seem destined, through heredity, to have a particular **metabolism,** the rate at which food is converted to energy and expended by the body. People with a high

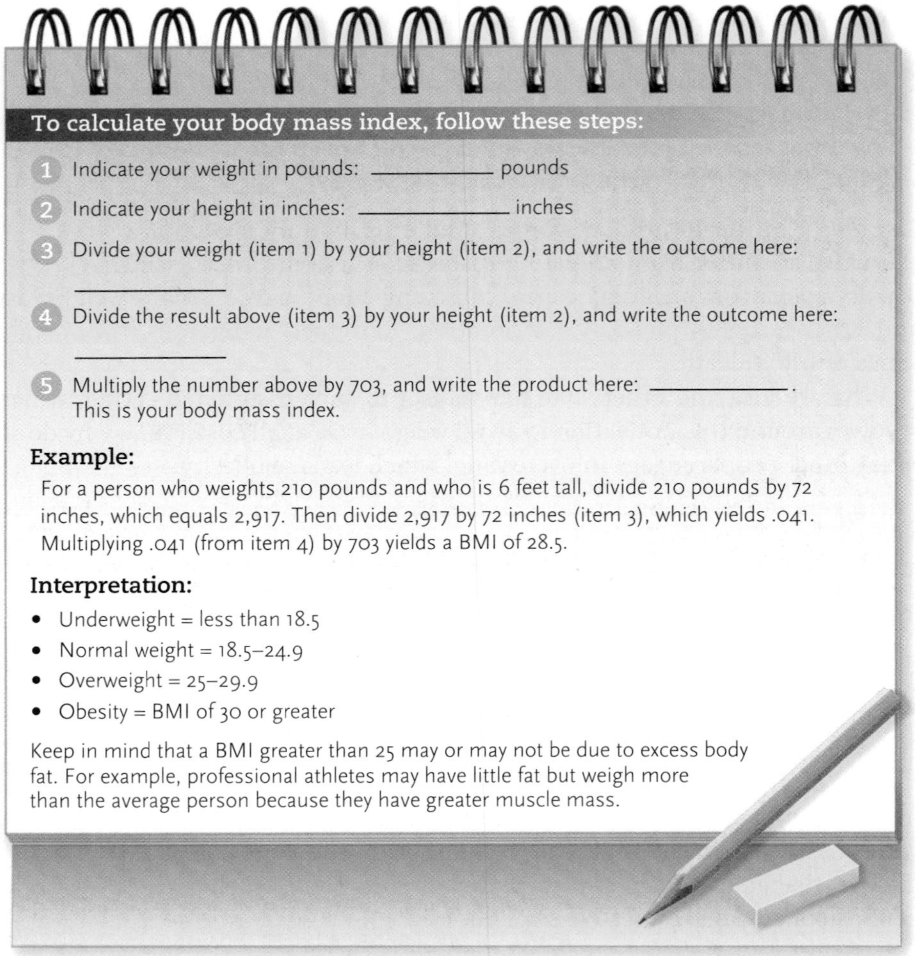

Weight set point The particular level of weight that the body strives to maintain.

Metabolism The rate at which food is converted to energy and expended by the body.

To calculate your body mass index, follow these steps:

1. Indicate your weight in pounds: _____ pounds

2. Indicate your height in inches: _____ inches

3. Divide your weight (item 1) by your height (item 2), and write the outcome here:

   _____

4. Divide the result above (item 3) by your height (item 2), and write the outcome here:

   _____

5. Multiply the number above by 703, and write the product here: _____ . This is your body mass index.

Example:

For a person who weights 210 pounds and who is 6 feet tall, divide 210 pounds by 72 inches, which equals 2,917. Then divide 2,917 by 72 inches (item 3), which yields .041. Multiplying .041 (from item 4) by 703 yields a BMI of 28.5.

Interpretation:

- Underweight = less than 18.5
- Normal weight = 18.5–24.9
- Overweight = 25–29.9
- Obesity = BMI of 30 or greater

Keep in mind that a BMI greater than 25 may or may not be due to excess body fat. For example, professional athletes may have little fat but weigh more than the average person because they have greater muscle mass.

FIGURE 1 Use this procedure to find your body mass index (BMI).

metabolic rate can eat virtually as much as they want without gaining weight, whereas others, with low metabolism, may eat literally half as much yet gain weight readily (Jequier, 2002; Westerterp, 2006).

Social Factors in Eating

You've just finished a full meal and feel completely stuffed. Suddenly your host announces with great fanfare that he will be serving his "house specialty" dessert, bananas flambé, and that he has spent the better part of the afternoon preparing it. Even though you are full and don't even like bananas, you accept a serving of his dessert and eat it all.

Clearly, internal biological factors do not fully explain our eating behavior. External social factors, based on societal rules and on what we have learned about appropriate eating behavior, also play an important role. Take, for example, the simple fact that people customarily eat breakfast, lunch, and dinner at approximately the same times every day. Because we tend to eat on schedule every day, we feel hungry as the usual hour approaches, sometimes quite independently of what our internal cues are telling us.

Similarly, we put roughly the same amount of food on our plates every day, even though the amount of exercise we may have had, and consequently our need for energy replenishment, varies from day to day. We also tend to prefer particular foods over others. Rats and dogs may be a delicacy in certain Asian cultures, but few people in Western cultures find them appealing despite their potentially high nutritional value. Even the amount of food we eat varies according to cultural norms. For instance, people in the United States eat bigger portions than people in France. In sum, cultural influences and our individual habits play important roles in determining when, what, and how much we eat (Miller & Pumariega, 2001; Rozin et al., 2003).

The Roots of Obesity

Given that both biological and social factors influence eating behavior, determining the causes of obesity has proved to be a challenging task. Researchers have followed several paths.

Some psychologists suggest that oversensitivity to external eating cues based on social factors, coupled with insensitivity to internal hunger cues, produces obesity. Others argue that overweight people have higher weight set points than other people do. Because their set points are unusually high, their attempts to lose weight by eating less may make them especially sensitive to external, food-related cues and therefore more apt to overeat, perpetuating their obesity (Tremblay, 2004; West, Harvey-Berino, & Raczynski, 2004).

Another biologically based explanation for obesity relates to fat cells in the body. Starting at birth, the body stores fat either by increasing the number of fat cells or by increasing the size of existing fat cells. Furthermore, any loss of weight past infancy does not decrease the number of fat cells; it only affects their size. Consequently, people are stuck with the number of fat cells they inherit from an early age, and the rate of weight gain during the first four months of life is related to being overweight during later childhood (Stettler et al., 2005).

According to the weight-set-point hypothesis, the presence of too many fat cells from earlier weight gain may result in the set point's becoming

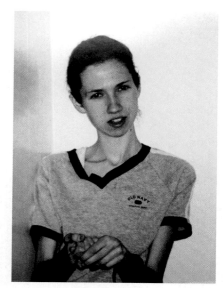

Despite looking skeleton-like to others, people with the weight disorder anorexia nervosa see themselves as overweight.

"stuck" at a higher level than is desirable. In such circumstances, losing weight becomes a difficult proposition, because one is constantly at odds with one's own internal set point when dieting (Freedman, 1995; Leibel, Rosenbaum, & Hirsch, 1995).

Eating Disorders

Eating disorders are among the 10 most frequent causes of disability in young women. One devastating weight-related disorder is **anorexia nervosa.** In this severe eating disorder, people may refuse to eat while denying that their behavior and appearance—which can become skeleton-like—are unusual. Some 10 percent of people with anorexia literally starve themselves to death (Striegel-Moore & Bulik, 2007).

Anorexia nervosa mainly afflicts females between the ages of 12 and 40, although both men and women of any age may develop it. People with the disorder typically come from stable homes, and they are often successful, attractive, and relatively affluent. The disorder often occurs after serious dieting, which somehow gets out of control. Life begins to revolve around food: although people with the disorder eat little, they may cook for others, go shopping for food frequently, or collect cookbooks (Reijonen et al., 2003; Polivy, Herman, & Boivin, 2005; Myers, 2007).

Anorexia nervosa A severe eating disorder in which people may refuse to eat while denying that their behavior and appearance—which can become skeleton-like—are unusual.

Bulimia A disorder in which a person binges on large quantities of food, followed by efforts to purge the food through vomiting or other means.

A related problem, **bulimia,** from which Lisa Arndt (described earlier) suffered, is a disorder in which people binge on large quantities of food. For instance, they may consume an entire gallon of ice cream and a whole pie in a single sitting. After such a binge, sufferers feel guilt and depression and often induce vomiting or take laxatives to rid themselves of the food—behavior known as purging. Constant bingeing-and-purging cycles and the use of drugs to induce vomiting or diarrhea can lead to heart failure. Often, though, the weight of a person with bulimia remains normal (Mora-Giral et al., 2004; Couturier & Lock, 2006).

What are the causes of anorexia nervosa and bulimia? Some researchers suspect a biological cause such as a chemical imbalance in the hypothalamus or pituitary gland, perhaps brought on by genetic factors. Furthermore, scans of the brains of people with eating disorders show that they process information about food differently from healthy individuals (see Polivy & Herman, 2002; Santel et al., 2006).

What are the causes of anorexia nervosa and bulimia?

Others believe that the cause has roots in society's valuation of slenderness and the parallel notion that obesity is undesirable. These researchers maintain that people with anorexia nervosa and bulimia become preoccupied with their weight and take to heart the cliché that one can never be too thin. This may explain why, as countries become more developed and Westernized, and dieting becomes more popular, eating disorders increase. Finally, some psychologists suggest that the disorders result from overly demanding parents or other family problems (Grilo et al., 2003; Couturier & Lock, 2006).

The complete explanations for anorexia nervosa and bulimia remain elusive. These disorders most likely stem from both biological and social causes, and successful treatment probably encompasses several strategies, including therapy and dietary changes (Richard, 2005; O'Brien & LeBow, 2007; Wilson, Grilo, & Vitousek, 2007).

ANOREXIA   HEALTHY

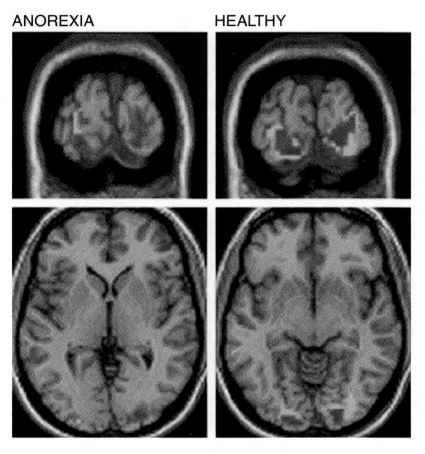

If you or a family member needs advice or help with an eating problem, contact the American Anorexia Bulimia Association at www.aabainc.org or call 212-575-6200. You can get more information at www.nlm.nih.gov/medlineplus/eatingdisorders.html.

becoming an *informed consumer*
OF PSYCHOLOGY

Dieting and Losing Weight Successfully

Although 60 percent of the people in the United States say they want to lose weight, it's a losing battle for most of them. Most people who diet eventually regain the weight they have lost, and so they try again and get caught in a seemingly endless cycle of weight loss and gain (Newport & Carroll, 2002; Parker-Pope, 2003; Cachelin & Regan, 2006).

You should keep several things in mind when trying to lose weight (Gathchel & Oordt, 2003; Heshka et al., 2003):

- *There is no easy route to weight control.* You will have to make permanent changes in your life to lose weight without gaining it back. The most obvious strategy—cutting down on the amount of food you eat—is just the first step toward a lifetime commitment to changing your eating habits.

- *Keep track of what you eat and what you weigh.* Unless you keep careful records, you won't really know how much you are eating and whether any diet is working.

- *Cut out television.* One reason for the epidemic of obesity is the number of hours spent viewing television by people in the United States. Not only does watching television preclude other activities that burn calories (even walking around the house is helpful), people often gorge on junk food while watching (Hu et al., 2003).

- *Exercise.* Exercise at least 30 consecutive minutes three times each week. When you exercise, you use up fat stored in your body as fuel for muscles, which is measured in calories. As you use up this fat, you will probably lose weight. Almost any activity helps burn calories.

- *Decrease the influence of external, social stimuli on your eating behavior.* Serve yourself smaller portions of food, and leave the table before you see what is being served for dessert. Don't even buy snack foods such as nachos and potato chips; if they're not readily available in the kitchen cupboard, you're not apt to eat them. Wrap refrigerated foods in aluminum foil so that you cannot see the contents and be tempted every time you open the refrigerator.

- *Avoid fad diets and diet pills.* No matter how popular they are at a particular time, extreme diets, including liquid diets, usually don't work in the long run and can be dangerous to your health.

- *Set reasonable goals.* Know how much weight you want to lose before you start to diet. Don't try to lose too much weight too quickly or you may doom yourself to failure. Even small changes in behavior—such as walking fifteen minutes a day or eating a few less bites at each meal—can prevent weight gain (Hill et al., 2003).

» LO2 Sexual Motivation

Anyone who has seen two dogs mating knows that sexual behavior has a biological basis. Their sexual behavior appears to occur naturally, without much prompting on the part of others. A number of genetically controlled factors influence the sexual behavior of nonhuman animals. For instance, animal behavior is affected by the presence of certain hormones in the blood. Moreover, female animals are receptive to sexual advances only during certain relatively limited periods of the year.

Human sexual behavior, by comparison, is more complicated, although the underlying biology is not all that different from that of related species. In males, for example, the *testes* begin to secrete **androgens,** male sex hormones, at puberty. (See Figure 3 for the basic anatomy of the male and female **genitals,** or sex organs.) Not only do androgens produce secondary sex characteristics, such as the growth of body hair and a deepening of the voice, they also increase the sex drive. Because the level of androgen production by the testes is fairly constant, men are capable of (and interested in) sexual activities without any regard to biological cycles. Given the proper stimuli leading to arousal, male sexual behavior can occur at any time (Goldstein, 2000).

Women show a different pattern. When they reach maturity at puberty, the two *ovaries* begin to produce **estrogens** and **progesterone,** female sex hormones. However, those hormones are not produced consistently; instead, their production follows a cyclical pattern. The greatest output occurs during **ovulation,** when an egg is released from the ovaries, making the chances of fertilization by a sperm cell highest. Whereas in nonhumans the period

Androgens Male sex hormones secreted by the testes.

Genitals The male and female sex organs.

Estrogens Class of female sex hormones.

Progesterone A female sex hormone secreted by the ovaries.

Ovulation The point at which an egg is released from the ovaries.

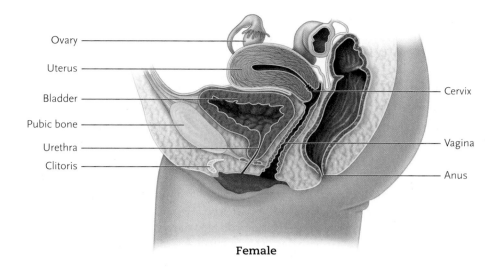

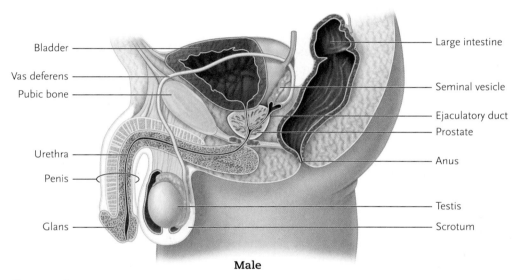

FIGURE 3 Cutaway side views of the female and male sex organs.

around ovulation is the only time the female is receptive to sex, people are different. Although there are variations in reported sex drive, women are receptive to sex throughout their cycles (Lieblum & Chivers, 2007).

In addition, some evidence suggests that males have a stronger sex drive than females, although the difference may be the result of society's discouragement of female sexuality rather than of innate differences between men and women. It is clear that men think about sex more than women: 54 percent of men report thinking about sex every day, but only 19 percent of women report thinking about it on a daily basis (Mendelsohn, 2003; Gangestad et al., 2004; Baumeister & Stillman, 2006).

Though biological factors "prime" people for sex, it takes more than hormones to motivate and produce sexual behavior. In animals the presence of a partner who provides arousing stimuli leads to sexual activity. Humans are considerably more versatile; not only other people but nearly any object, sight, smell, sound, or other stimulus can lead to sexual excitement. Sexual fantasies also play an important role in producing sexual arousal. Not only do people have fantasies of a sexual nature during their everyday activities, but about

60 percent of all people have fantasies during sexual intercourse. In fact, such fantasies often include having sex with someone other than one's partner of the moment (Hicks & Leitenberg, 2001; Trudel, 2002).

Masturbation: Solitary Sex

Masturbation Sexual self-stimulation.

Heterosexuality Sexual attraction and behavior directed to the other sex.

Double standard The view that premarital sex is permissible for males but not for females.

If you listened to physicians 75 years ago, you would have been told that **masturbation,** sexual self-stimulation, often using the hand to rub the genitals, would lead to a wide variety of physical and mental disorders, ranging from hairy palms to insanity. If those physicians had been correct, however, most of us would be wearing gloves to hide the sight of our hair-covered palms—for masturbation is one of the most frequently practiced sexual activities. Some 94 percent of all males and 63 percent of all females have masturbated at least once, and among college students, the frequency ranges from "never" to "several times a day" (Hunt, 1974; Michael et al., 1994; Laqueur, 2003; Polonsky, 2006).

Men and women typically begin to masturbate for the first time at different ages. Furthermore, men masturbate considerably more often than women, although there are differences in frequency according to age. Male masturbation is most common in the early teens and then declines, whereas females both begin and reach a maximum frequency later. There are also some racial differences: African American men and women masturbate less than whites do (Oliver & Hyde, 1993; Pinkerton et al., 2002).

Heterosexuality

People often believe that the first time they have sexual intercourse they have achieved one of life's major milestones. However, **heterosexuality,** sexual attraction and behavior directed to the other sex, consists of far more than male-female intercourse. Kissing, petting, caressing, massaging, and other forms of sex play are all components of heterosexual behavior. Still, the focus of sex researchers has been on the act of intercourse, especially in terms of its first occurrence and its frequency.

Premarital Sex

Until fairly recently, premarital sexual intercourse, at least for women, was considered one of the major taboos in our society. Traditionally, women have been warned by society that "nice girls don't do it"; men have been told that although premarital sex is okay for them, they should make sure they marry virgins. This view that premarital sex is permissible for males but not for females is called the **double standard** (Liang, 2007).

Although as recently as the 1960s the majority of adult Americans believed that premarital sex was always wrong, since that time there has been a dramatic change in public opinion. For example, the percentage of middle-age people who say sex before marriage is "not wrong at all" has increased considerably, and overall 60 percent of Americans say premarital sex is okay. More than half say that living together before marriage is morally acceptable (Thornton & Young-DeMarco, 2001).

Marital Sex

To judge by the number of articles about sex in heterosexual marriages, one would think that sexual behavior was the number one standard by which marital bliss is measured. Married couples are often concerned that they are having too little sex, too much sex, or the wrong kind of sex (Harvey, Wenzel, & Sprecher, 2005).

Although there are many different dimensions along which sex in marriage is measured, one is certainly the frequency of sexual intercourse. What is typical? As with most other types of sexual activities, there is no easy answer to the question, because there are such wide variations in patterns between individuals. We do know that 43 percent of married couples have sexual intercourse a few times a month and 36 percent of couples have it two or three times a week. With increasing age and length of marriage, the frequency of intercourse declines. Still, sex continues into late adulthood, with almost half of people reporting that they engage in sexual activity at least once a month and that its quality is high (Michael et al., 1994; Powell, 2006).

Although early research found **extramarital sex** to be widespread, the current reality appears to be otherwise. According to surveys, 85 percent of married women and more than 75 percent of married men are faithful to their spouses. Furthermore, the median number of sex partners, inside and outside of marriage, since the age of 18 for men was six, and for women two. Accompanying these numbers is a high, consistent degree of disapproval of extramarital sex, with 9 of 10 people saying that it is "always" or "almost always" wrong (Michael et al., 1994; Daines, 2006).

Extramarital sex Sexual activity between a married person and someone who is not his or her spouse.

Homosexuals Persons who are sexually attracted to members of their own sex.

Bisexuals Persons who are sexually attracted to people of the same sex and the other sex.

Homosexuality and Bisexuality

Homosexuals are sexually attracted to members of their own sex, whereas **bisexuals** are sexually attracted to people of the same sex and the other sex. Many male homosexuals prefer the term *gay* and female homosexuals the label *lesbian,* because they refer to a broader array of attitudes and lifestyles than the term *homosexual,* which focuses on the sexual act.

The number of people who choose same-sex sexual partners at one time or another is considerable. Estimates suggest that around 20 to 25 percent of males and about 15 percent of females have had at least one gay or lesbian experience during adulthood. The exact number of people who identify themselves as exclusively homosexual has proved difficult to gauge, with some estimates as low as 1.1 percent and some as high as 10 percent. Most experts suggest that between 5 and 10 percent of both men and women are exclusively gay or lesbian during extended periods of their lives (Hunt, 1974; Sells, 1994; Firestein, 1996).

Although people often view homosexuality and heterosexuality as two completely distinct sexual orientations, the issue is not that simple. Pioneering sex researcher Alfred Kinsey acknowledged this when he considered sexual orientation along a scale or continuum, with "exclusively homosexual" at one end and "exclusively heterosexual" at the other. In the middle were people who showed both homosexual and heterosexual behavior. Kinsey's approach suggests that sexual orientation is dependent on a person's sexual feelings and behaviors and romantic feelings (Weinberg, Williams, & Pryor, 1991).

Extensive research has found that bisexuals and homosexuals enjoy the same overall degree of mental and physical health as heterosexuals.

"Frankly, I've repressed my sexuality so long I've actually forgotten what my orientation is."

What determines whether people become homosexual or heterosexual? Although there are a number of theories, none has proved completely satisfactory.

Some explanations for sexual orientation are biological in nature, suggesting that there are genetic causes. Evidence for a genetic origin of sexual orientation comes from studies of identical twins, which have found that when one twin identified himself or herself as homosexual, the occurrence of homosexuality in the other twin was higher than it was in the general population. Such results occur even for twins who have been separated early in life and who therefore are not necessarily raised in similar social environments (Hamer et al., 1993; Turner, 1995; Kirk, Bailey, & Martin, 2000; Gooren, 2006).

Hormones also may play a role in determining sexual orientation. For example, research shows that women exposed to DES, or diethylstilbestrol, before birth (their mothers took the drug to avoid miscarriage) were more likely to be homosexual or bisexual (Meyer-Bahlburg, 1997).

Some evidence suggests that differences in brain structures may be related to sexual orientation. For instance, the structure of the anterior hypothalamus, an area of the brain that governs sexual behavior, differs in male homosexuals and heterosexuals. Similarly, other research shows that, compared with heterosexual men or women, gay men have a larger anterior commissure, which is a bundle of neurons connecting the right and left hemispheres of the brain (LeVay, 1993; Byne, 1996).

However, research suggesting that biological causes are at the root of homosexuality is not conclusive because most findings are based on only small samples of individuals. Still, the possibility is real that some inherited or biological factor exists that predisposes people toward homosexuality, if certain environmental conditions are met (Veniegas, 2000; Teodorov et al., 2002; Rahman, Kumari, & Wilson, 2003).

Little evidence suggests that sexual orientation is brought about by child-rearing practices or family dynamics. Although proponents of psychoanalytic theories once argued that the nature of the parent-child relationship can produce homosexuality (e.g., Freud, 1922/1959), research evidence does not support such explanations (Isay, 1994; Roughton, 2002).

Because of the difficulty in finding a consistent explanation, we can't answer the question of what determines sexual orientation. It does seem unlikely that that any single factor orients a person toward homosexuality or heterosexuality. Instead, it seems reasonable to assume that a combination of biological and environmental factors is involved (Hyde & Delamater, 2008).

Although we don't know at this point exactly why people develop a certain sexual orientation, one thing is clear: there is no relationship between sexual orientation and psychological adjustment. Gays, lesbians, and bisexuals generally enjoy the same quality of mental and physical health that heterosexuals do, although the discrimination they experience may produce higher rates of some disorders, such as depression (Poteat & Espelage, 2007). Bisexuals and homosexuals also hold equivalent ranges and types of attitudes about themselves, independent of sexual orientation. For such reasons, the American Psychological Association and most other mental health organizations have endorsed efforts to reduce discrimination against gays and

psych2.0

WWW.MHHE.COM/PSYCHLIFE

Attitudes toward Sexuality

lesbians, such as revoking the ban against homosexuals in the military (Cochran, 2000; Perez, DeBord, & Bieschke, 2000; Morris, Waldo, & Rothblum, 2001).

Transsexualism

Transsexuals are people who believe they were born with the body of the other gender. In fundamental ways, transsexualism represents less a sexual concern than a gender issue involving one's sexual identity (Meyerowitz, 2004; Heath, 2006).

Transsexuals sometimes seek sex-change operations in which their existing genitals are surgically removed and the genitals of the desired sex are fashioned. Several steps, including intensive counseling and hormone injections, along with living as a member of the desired sex for several years, precede surgery, which is, not surprisingly, highly complicated. The outcome, though, can be quite positive (O'Keefe & Fox, 2003; Stegerwald & Janson, 2003; Lobato, Koff, & Manenti, 2006).

Transsexualism is part of a broader category known as transgenderism. The term *transgenderism* encompasses not only transsexuals but also people who view themselves as a third gender, transvestites (who dress in the clothes of the other gender), or others who believe that traditional male-female gender classifications inadequately characterize themselves (Prince, 2005; Hyde & Delamater, 2008).

Transsexuals Persons who believe they were born with the body of the other gender.

Need for achievement A stable, learned characteristic in which a person obtains satisfaction by striving for and attaining a level of excellence.

» LO3 The Needs for Achievement, Affiliation, and Power

Although hunger may be one of the more potent primary drives in our day-to-day lives, powerful secondary drives that have no clear biological basis also motivate us. Among the more prominent of these is the need for achievement.

The Need for Achievement: Striving for Excellence

The **need for achievement** is a stable, learned characteristic in which a person obtains satisfaction by striving for and attaining a level of excellence (McClelland et al., 1953). People with a high need for achievement seek out situations in which they can compete against some standard—be it grades, money, or winning at a game—and prove themselves successful. But they are not indiscriminate when it comes to picking their challenges: they tend to avoid situations in which success will come too easily (which would be unchallenging) and situations in which success is unlikely. Instead, people high in achievement motivation generally choose tasks that are of intermediate difficulty (Speirs Neumeister & Finch, 2006).

In contrast, people with low achievement motivation tend to be motivated primarily by a desire to avoid failure. As a result, they seek out easy tasks, being sure to avoid failure, or seek out very difficult tasks for which failure has no negative implications, because almost anyone would fail at them. People with a high fear of failure will stay away from tasks of intermediate difficulty, because they may fail where others have been successful (Martin & Marsh, 2002; Puca, 2005; Morrone & Pintrich, 2006).

A key feature of people with a high need for achievement is that they prefer tasks of *moderate* difficulty.

psych2.0
WWW.MHHE.COM/PSYCHLIFE

Achievement Motivation

Thematic Apperception Test (TAT) A test consisting of a series of pictures about which a person is asked to write a story.

Need for affiliation An interest in establishing and maintaining relationships with other people.

Need for power A tendency to seek impact, control, or influence over others, and to be seen as a powerful individual.

Measuring Achievement Motivation

How can we measure a person's need for achievement? The measuring instrument used most frequently is the **Thematic Apperception Test (TAT).** In the TAT, an examiner shows a series of ambiguous pictures. The examiner tells participants to write a story that describes what is happening, who the people are, what led to the situation, what the people are thinking or wanting, and what will happen next. Researchers then use a standard scoring system to determine the amount of achievement imagery in people's stories. For example, someone who writes a story in which the main character strives to beat an opponent, studies in order to do well at some task, or works hard in order to get a promotion shows clear signs of an achievement orientation. The inclusion of such achievement-related imagery in the participants' stories is assumed to indicate an unusually high degree of concern with—and therefore a relatively strong need for—achievement (Tuerlinckx, De Boeck, & Lens, 2002).

The Need for Affiliation: Striving for Friendship

Few of us choose to lead our lives as hermits. Why?

One main reason is that most people have a **need for affiliation,** an interest in establishing and maintaining relationships with other people. Individuals with a high need for affiliation write TAT stories that emphasize the desire to maintain or reinstate friendships and show concern over being rejected by friends.

People who have higher affiliation needs are particularly sensitive to relationships with others. They desire to be with their friends more of the time, and alone less often, compared with people who are lower in the need for affiliation. However, gender is a greater determinant of how much time is actually spent with friends: regardless of their affiliative orientation, female students spend significantly more time with their friends and less time alone than male students do (Cantwell & Andrews, 2002; Johnson, 2004; Semykina & Linz, 2007).

The Need for Power: Striving for Impact on Others

If your fantasies include becoming president of the United States or running Microsoft, your dreams may reflect a high need for power. The **need for power,** a tendency to seek impact, control, or influence over others and to be seen as a powerful individual, is an additional type of motivation (Lee-Chai & Bargh, 2001; Winter, 2007; Zians, 2007).

As you might expect, people with strong needs for power are more apt to belong to organizations and seek office than are those low in the need for power. They also tend to work

From the perspective of . . .

A NEW SUPERVISOR How might you use characteristics such as need for achievement, need for power, and need for affiliation to select workers for jobs? What additional criteria would you have to consider?

in professions in which their power needs may be fulfilled, such as business management and—you may or may not be surprised—teaching (Jenkins, 1994). In addition, they seek to display the trappings of power. Even in college, they are more likely to collect prestigious possessions, such as electronic equipment and sports cars.

RECAP

Describe the biological and social factors that underlie hunger.

- Eating behavior is subject to homeostasis, as most people's weight stays within a relatively stable range. The hypothalamus in the brain is central to the regulation of food intake. (p. 253)

- Social factors, such as mealtimes, cultural food preferences, and other learned habits, also play a role in the regulation of eating, determining when, what, and how much one eats. An over-sensitivity to social cues and an insensitivity to internal cues may also be related to obesity. In addition, obesity may be caused by an unusu-ally high weight set point—the weight the body attempts to maintain—and genetic factors. (p. 253)

Summarize the varieties of sexual behavior.

- Although biological factors, such as the pres-ence of androgens (male sex hormones) and estrogens and progesterone (female sex hor-mones), prime people for sex, almost any kind of stimulus can produce sexual arousal, depend-ing on a person's prior experience. (p. 258)

- The frequency of masturbation is high, partic-ularly for males. Although increasingly liberal, attitudes toward masturbation have tradition-ally been negative even though no negative consequences have been detected. (p. 260)

- Heterosexuality, or sexual attraction to mem-bers of the other sex, is the most common sexual orientation. (p. 260)

- Homosexuals are sexually attracted to members of their own sex; bisexuals are sexually attracted to people of the same sex and the other sex. No explanation for why people become homosexual has been confirmed; among the possibilities are genetic or biological factors and childhood and family influences. However, no relationship exists between sexual orientation and psycho-logical adjustment. (p. 261)

Explain how needs related to achievement, affiliation, and power are exhibited.

- Need for achievement refers to the stable, learned characteristic in which a person strives to attain a level of excellence. Need for achievement is usually measured through the Thematic Apperception Test (TAT), a series of pictures about which a person writes a story. (p. 263)

- The need for affiliation is a concern with estab-lishing and maintaining relationships with others, whereas the need for power is a tendency to seek to exert an impact on others. (p. 264)

- The need for power is a tendency to seek to exert an impact on others. (p. 264)

EVALUATE

1. The _____ is responsible for regulating food intake.

2. The _____ _____ _____ is the specific level of weight the body strives to maintain.

3. _____ is the rate at which energy is produced and expended by the body.

4. Although the incidence of masturbation among young adults is high, once men and women become involved in intimate relationships, they typically cease masturbating. True or false?

5. The increase in premarital sex in recent years has been greater for women than for men. True or false?

6. Julio is the type of person who constantly strives for excellence. He feels intense satisfaction when he is able to master a new task. Julio most likely has a high need for _____.

7. Debbie's Thematic Apperception Test (TAT) story depicts a young girl who is rejected by one of her peers and seeks to regain her friendship. What major type of motivation is Debbie displaying in her story?
   a. Need for achievement
   b. Need for motivation
   c. Need for affiliation
   d. Need for power

RETHINK

In what ways do societal expectations, expressed by television shows and commercials, contribute to both obesity and excessive concern about weight loss? How could television contribute to better eating habits and attitudes toward weight? Should it be required to do so?

Answers to Evaluate Questions 1. hypothalamus; 2. weight set point; 3. metabolism; 4. false; 5. true; 6. achievement; 7. c.

[KEY TERMS]

Obesity *p. 253*

Weight set point *p. 254*

Metabolism *p. 254*

Anorexia nervosa *p. 256*

Bulimia *p. 256*

Androgens *p. 258*

Genitals *p. 258*

Estrogens *p. 258*

Progesterone *p. 258*

Ovulation *p. 258*

Masturbation *p. 260*

Heterosexuality *p. 260*

Double standard *p. 260*

Extramarital sex *p. 261*

Homosexuals *p. 261*

Bisexuals *p. 261*

Transsexual *p. 263*

Need for achievement *p. 263*

Thematic Apperception Test *p. 264*

Need for affiliation *p. 264*

Need for power *p. 264*

module 24

Understanding Emotional Experiences

At one time or another, all of us have experienced the strong feelings that accompany both very pleasant and very negative experiences. Perhaps we have felt the thrill of getting a sought-after job, the joy of being in love, the sorrow over someone's death, or the anguish of inadvertently hurting someone. Moreover, we experience such reactions on a less intense level throughout our daily lives: the pleasure of a friendship, the enjoyment of a movie, and the embarrassment of breaking a borrowed item.

Despite the varied nature of these feelings, they all represent emotions. Although everyone has an idea of what an emotion is, formally defining the concept has proved to be an elusive task. Here, we'll use a general definition: **emotions** are feelings that generally have both physiological and cognitive elements and that influence behavior.

LEARNING OUTCOMES

24.1 Define the range of emotions.

24.2 Explain the roots of emotions.

Emotions Feelings that generally have both physiological and cognitive elements and that influence behavior.

Emotions are difficult to define or place. Even though it is a happy day, many people cry at weddings. Why do you think that is?

Think, for example, about how it feels to be happy. First, we obviously experience a feeling that we can differentiate from other emotions. It is likely that we also experience some identifiable physical changes in our bodies: perhaps the heart rate increases, or we find ourselves "jumping for joy." Finally, the emotion probably encompasses cognitive elements: our understanding and evaluation of the meaning of what is happening prompts our feelings of happiness.

It is also possible, however, to experience an emotion without the presence of cognitive elements. For instance, we may react with fear to an unusual or novel situation (such as coming into contact with an erratic, unpredictable individual), or we may experience pleasure over sexual excitation without having cognitive awareness or understanding of just what it is about the situation that is exciting.

» LO1 Determining the Range of Emotions: Labeling Our Feelings

If we were to list the words in the English language that have been used to describe emotions, we would end up with at least 500 examples (Averill, 1975). The list would range from such obvious emotions as *happiness* and *fear* to less common ones, such as *adventurousness* and *pensiveness*.

One challenge for psychologists has been to sort through this list to identify the most important, fundamental emotions. Theorists have hotly contested the issue of cataloging emotions and have come up with different lists, depending on how they define the concept of emotion. In fact, some reject the question entirely, saying that *no* set of emotions should be singled out as most basic, and that emotions are best understood by breaking them down into their component parts. Other researchers argue for looking at emotions in terms of a hierarchy, dividing them into positive and negative categories, and then organizing them into increasingly narrower subcategories (see Figure 1; Manstead, Frijda, & Fischer, 2003; Dillard & Shen, 2007).

> One challenge for psychologists has been to sort through this list to identify the most important, fundamental emotions.

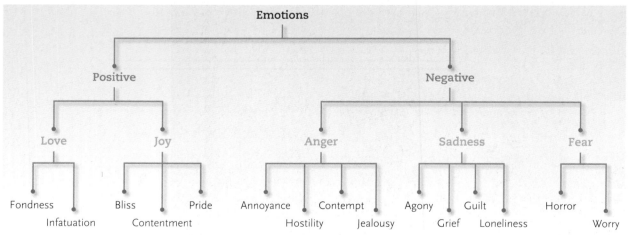

FIGURE 1 One approach to organizing emotions is to use a hierarchy, which divides emotions into increasingly narrow subcategories. (*Source: Adapted from Fischer, Shaver, & Carnochan, 1990.*)

Still, most researchers suggest that a list of basic emotions would include, at a minimum, happiness, anger, fear, sadness, and disgust. Other lists are broader, including emotions such as surprise, contempt, guilt, and joy (Ekman, 1994a; Shweder, 1994; Tracy & Robins, 2004).

» LO2 The Roots of Emotions

Although it is easy to describe the general physical reactions that accompany emotions, defining the specific role that those physiological responses play in the experience of emotions has proved to be a major puzzle for psychologists. As we shall see, some theorists suggest that specific bodily reactions *cause* us to experience a particular emotion—we experience fear, for instance, *because* the heart is pounding and we are breathing deeply. In contrast, other theorists suggest that the physiological reaction results from the experience of an emotion. In this view, we experience fear, and as a result the heart pounds and our breathing deepens.

The James-Lange Theory: Do Gut Reactions Equal Emotions?

To William James and Carl Lange, who were among the first researchers to explore the nature of emotions, emotional experience is, very simply, a reaction to instinctive bodily events that occur as a response to some situation or event in the environment. This view is summarized in James's statement, "we feel sorry because we cry, angry because we strike, afraid because we tremble" (James, 1890).

James and Lange took the view that the instinctive response of crying at a loss leads us to feel sorrow, that striking out at someone who frustrates us results in our feeling anger, that trembling at a menacing threat causes us to feel fear. They suggested that for every major emotion there is an accompanying physiological or "gut" reaction of internal organs—called a *visceral experience*. It is this specific pattern of visceral response that leads us to label the emotional experience.

In sum, James and Lange proposed that we experience emotions as a result of physiological changes that produce specific sensations. The brain interprets these sensations as specific kinds of emotional experiences (see the first part of Figure 2). This view has come to be called the **James-Lange theory of emotion** (Laird & Bresler, 1990; Cobos et al., 2002).

The James-Lange theory has some serious drawbacks, however. For the theory to be valid, visceral changes would have to occur relatively quickly, because we experience some emotions—such as fear upon hearing a stranger rapidly approaching on a dark night—almost instantaneously. Yet emotional experiences frequently occur even before there is time for certain physiological changes to be set into motion. Because of the slowness with which some visceral changes take place, it is hard to see how they could be the source of immediate emotional experience.

The James-Lange theory poses another difficulty: our internal organs produce a relatively limited range of sensations. Although some types of physiological changes are associated with specific emotional experiences, it is difficult to imagine how each of the myriad emotions that people are capable of experiencing could be the result of a unique visceral change. Many emotions actually are associated with relatively similar sorts of visceral changes, a fact that contradicts the James-Lange theory (Davidson et al., 1994; Cameron, 2002).

James-Lange theory of emotion The belief that emotional experience is a reaction to bodily events occurring as a result of an external situation ("I feel sad because I am crying").

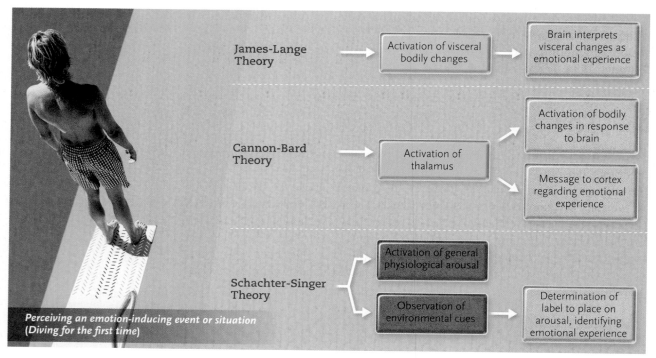

FIGURE 2   A comparison of three models of emotion.

The Cannon-Bard Theory: Physiological Reactions as the Result of Emotions

Cannon-Bard theory of emotion
The belief that both physiological arousal and emotional experience are produced simultaneously by the same nerve stimulus.

In response to the difficulties inherent in the James-Lange theory, Walter Cannon, and later Philip Bard, suggested an alternative view. In what has come to be known as the **Cannon-Bard theory of emotion,** they proposed the model illustrated in the second part of Figure 2 (Cannon, 1929). This theory rejects the view that physiological arousal alone leads to the perception of emotion. Instead, the theory assumes that both physiological arousal *and* the emotional experience are produced simultaneously by the same nerve stimulus, which Cannon and Bard suggested emanates from the thalamus in the brain.

The theory states that after we perceive an emotion-producing stimulus, the thalamus is the initial site of the emotional response. Next, the thalamus sends a signal to the autonomic nervous system, thereby producing a visceral response. At the same time, the thalamus also communicates a message to the cerebral cortex regarding the nature of the emotion being experienced. Hence, it is not necessary for different emotions to have unique physiological patterns associated with them—as long as the message sent to the cerebral cortex differs according to the specific emotion.

The Cannon-Bard theory seems to have been accurate in rejecting the view that physiological arousal alone accounts for emotions. However, more recent research has led to some important modifications of the theory. For one thing, we now understand that the hypothalamus and the limbic system, not the thalamus, play a major role in emotional experience. In addition, the simultaneous occurrence of the physiological and emotional responses, which is a fundamental assumption of the Cannon-Bard theory, has yet to be demonstrated conclusively. This ambiguity has allowed room for yet another theory of emotions: the Schachter-Singer theory.

The Schachter-Singer Theory: Emotions as Labels

According to an explanation that focuses on the role of cognition, the **Schachter-Singer theory of emotion,** we identify the emotion we are experiencing by observing our environment and comparing ourselves with others (Schachter & Singer, 1962). Schachter and Singer's classic experiment found evidence for this hypothesis. In the study, participants were told that they would receive an injection of a vitamin. In reality, they were given epinephrine, a drug that causes an increase in physiological arousal, including higher heart and respiration rates and a reddening of the face, responses that typically occur during strong emotional reactions. The participants were then placed individually in a situation where a confederate of the experimenter acted in one of two ways. In one condition he acted angry and hostile, and in the other condition he behaved as if he were exuberantly happy.

The purpose of the experiment was to determine how the participants would react emotionally to the confederate's behavior. When they were asked to describe their own emotional state at the end of the experiment, the participants exposed to the angry confederate reported that they felt angry, whereas those exposed to the happy confederate reported feeling happy. In sum, the results suggest that participants turned to the environment and the behavior of others for an explanation of the physiological arousal they were experiencing.

The results of the Schachter-Singer experiment, then, supported a cognitive view of emotions, in which emotions are determined jointly by a relatively nonspecific kind of physiological arousal *and* the labeling of that arousal on the basis of cues from the environment (refer to the third part of Figure 2). Later research has found that arousal is not as nonspecific as Schachter and Singer assumed. When the source of physiological arousal is unclear, however, we may look to our surroundings to determine just what we are experiencing.

> **Schachter-Singer theory of emotion** The belief that emotions are determined jointly by a nonspecific kind of physiological arousal and its interpretation, based on environmental cues.

STUDY ALERT

Use Figure 2 to distinguish the three classic theories of emotion (James-Lange, Cannon-Bard, and Schachter-Singer).

From the perspective of . . .

AN ADVERTISING ASSISTANT   How might you use the findings by Schachter and Singer on the labeling of arousal to create interest in a product? Can you think of other examples whereby people's arousal could be manipulated, which would lead to different emotional responses?

Contemporary Perspectives on the Neuroscience of Emotions

When Schachter and Singer carried out their groundbreaking experiment in the early 1960s, the ways in which they could evaluate the physiology that accompanies emotion were relatively limited. However, advances in the measurement of the nervous system and other parts of the body have allowed researchers to examine more closely the biological responses involved in emotion. As a result, contemporary research on emotion points to a revision of earlier views that physiological responses associated with emotions are undifferentiated. Instead, evidence is growing that specific patterns of biological arousal are associated with individual emotions (Vaitl, Schienle, & Stark, 2005; Woodson, 2006).

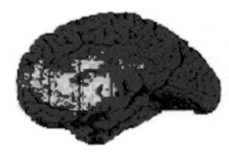

FIGURE 3 Experiencing different emotions activates particular areas of the brain, as these scans illustrate. *(Source: Mark George, NIMH.)*

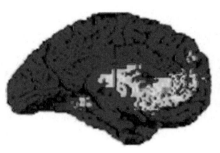

For instance, researchers have found that specific emotions produce activation of very different portions of the brain. In one study, participants undergoing positron emission tomography (PET) brain scans were asked to recall events, such as deaths and funerals, that made them feel sad, or events that made them feel happy, such as weddings and births. They also looked at photos of faces that appeared to be happy or sad. The results of the PET scans were clear: happiness was related to a decrease in activity in certain areas of the cerebral cortex, whereas sadness was associated with increases in activity in particular portions of the cortex (George et al., 1995; Hamann et al., 2002; Prohovnik et al., 2004).

In addition, the *amygdala,* in the brain's temporal lobe, is important in the experience of emotions, for it provides a link between the perception of an emotion-producing stimulus and the recall of that stimulus later. For example, if we've once been attacked by a vicious pit bull, the amygdala processes that information and leads us to react with fear when we see a pit bull later—an example of a classically conditioned fear response (Adolphs, 2002; Miller et al., 2005; Berntson et al., 2007).

Because neural pathways connect the amygdala, the visual cortex, and the *hippocampus* (which plays an important role in the consolidation of memories), some scientists speculate that emotion-related stimuli can be processed and responded to almost instantaneously in specific areas of the brain (see Figure 3). This immediate response occurs so rapidly that higher-order, more rational thinking, which takes more time, seems not to be involved initially. In a slower, but more thoughtful, response to emotion-evoking stimuli, emotion-related sensory information is first evaluated and then sent on to the amygdala. It appears that the quicker system offers an immediate response to emotion-evoking stimuli, whereas the slower system helps confirm a threat and prepare a more thoughtful response (Dolan, 2002).

Making Sense of the Multiple Perspectives on Emotion

As new approaches to emotion continue to develop, it is reasonable to ask why so many theories of emotion exist and, perhaps more important, which one provides the most complete explanation. Actually, we have only scratched the surface. There are almost as many explanatory theories of emotion as there are individual emotions (e.g., DeCoster, 2003; Manstead, Frijda, & Fischer, 2003; Frijda, 2005; Prinz, 2007).

Why are theories of emotion so plentiful? For one thing, emotions are not a simple phenomenon but are intertwined closely with motivation, cognition, neuroscience, and a host of related branches of psychology. For example, evidence from brain-imaging studies shows that even when people come to supposedly rational, nonemotional decisions—such as making moral, philosophical judgments—emotions come into play (Greene et al., 2001).

In short, emotions are such complex phenomena, encompassing both biological and cognitive aspects, that no single theory has been able to explain fully all the facets of emotional experience. Furthermore, contradictory evidence of one sort or another challenges each approach, and therefore no theory has proved invariably accurate in its predictions.

This abundance of perspectives on emotion is not a cause for despair—or unhappiness, fear, or any other negative emotion. It simply reflects the fact that psychology is an evolving, developing science. As we gather more evidence, the specific answers to questions about the nature of emotions will become clearer.

EXPLORING diversity

Do People in All Cultures Express Emotion Similarly?

Consider, for a moment, the six photos displayed in Figure 4. Can you identify the emotions being expressed by the person in each of the photos?

FIGURE 4   These photos demonstrate six of the primary emotions: happiness, anger, sadness, surprise, disgust, and fear.

If you are a good judge of facial expressions, you will conclude that these expressions display six of the basic emotions: happiness, anger, sadness, surprise, disgust, and fear. Hundreds of studies of nonverbal behavior show that these emotions are consistently distinct and identifiable, even by untrained observers (Ekman & O'Sullivan, 1991).

Interestingly, these six emotions are not unique to members of Western cultures; rather, they constitute the basic emotions expressed universally by members of the human race, regardless of where individuals have been raised and what learning experiences they have had. Psychologist Paul Ekman convincingly demonstrated this point when he studied the members of an isolated New Guinea jungle tribe who had had almost no contact with Westerners (Ekman, 1972). The people of the tribe did not speak or understand English, had never seen a movie, and had had very limited experience with Caucasians before Ekman's arrival. Yet their nonverbal responses to emotion-evoking stories, as well as their ability to identify basic emotions, were quite similar to those of Westerners.

Being so isolated, the New Guineans could not have learned from Westerners to recognize or produce similar facial expressions. Instead, their similar abilities and manner of responding emotionally appear to have been present innately. Although one could argue that similar experiences in both cultures led the members of each one to learn similar types of nonverbal behavior, this appears unlikely, because the two cultures are so very different. The expression of basic emotions, then, seems to be universal (Ekman, 1994b; Izard, 1994; Matsumoto, 2002).

Why do people across cultures express emotions similarly? A hypothesis known as the **facial-affect program** gives one explanation. The facial-affect program—which is assumed to be universally present at birth—is analogous to a computer program that is turned on when a particular emotion is experienced. When set in motion, the "program" activates a set of nerve impulses that make the face display an appropriate expression. Each primary emotion produces a unique set of muscular movements, forming the kinds of expressions shown in Figure 4. For example, the emotion of happiness is universally displayed by movement of the zygomatic major, a muscle that raises the corners of the mouth—forming what we would call a smile (Ekman, Davidson, & Friesen, 1990; Ekman, 2003; Kohler et al., 2004; Kim, Kim, & Kim, 2007).

The importance of facial expressions is illustrated by an intriguing notion known as the **facial-feedback hypothesis.** According to this hypothesis, facial expressions not only *reflect* emotional experience, they also help *determine* how people experience and label emotions (Izard, 1990). Basically put, "wearing" an emotional expression provides muscular feedback to the brain that helps produce an emotion congruent with that expression. For instance, the muscles activated when we smile may send a message to the brain indicating the experience of happiness—even if there is nothing in the environment that would produce that

Facial-affect program Activation of a set of nerve impulses that make the face display the appropriate expression.

Facial-feedback hypothesis The hypothesis that facial expressions not only reflect emotional experience but also help determine how people experience and label emotions.

"And just exactly what is that expression intended to convey?"

particular emotion. Some theoreticians have gone further, suggesting that facial expressions are *necessary* for an emotion to be experienced (Rinn, 1984, 1991). According to this view, if no facial expression is present, the emotion cannot be felt.

Support for the facial-feedback hypothesis comes from a classic experiment carried out by Paul Ekman and colleagues (Ekman, Levenson, & Friesen, 1983). In the study, professional actors were asked to follow very explicit instructions regarding the movements of muscles in their faces. You might try this example yourself:

- Raise your brows and pull them together.
- Raise your upper eyelids.
- Now stretch your lips horizontally back toward your ears.

After carrying out these directions—which, as you may have guessed, are meant to produce an expression of fear—the actors' heart rates rose and their body temperatures declined, physiological reactions that characterize fear. Overall, facial expressions representing the primary emotions produced physiological effects similar to those accompanying the genuine emotions in other circumstances (Keillor et al., 2002; Soussignan, 2002).

R E C A P

Define the range of emotions.

- Emotions are broadly defined as feelings that may affect behavior and generally have both a physiological component and a cognitive component. (p. 267)

Explain the roots of emotions.

- Several theories explain emotions. The James-Lange theory suggests that emotional experience is a reaction to bodily, or visceral, changes that occur as a response to an environmental event and are interpreted as an emotional response. (p. 269)

- In contrast, the Cannon-Bard theory contends that both physiological arousal and an emotional experience are produced simultaneously by the same nerve stimulus and that the visceral experience does not necessarily differ among differing emotions. (p. 270)

- The Schachter-Singer theory suggests that emotions are determined jointly by a relatively nonspecific physiological arousal and the

subsequent labeling of that arousal, using cues from the environment to determine how others are behaving in the same situation. (p. 271)

- The most recent approaches to emotions focus on their biological origins. For instance, it now seems that specific patterns of biological arousal are associated with individual emotions. Furthermore, new scanning techniques have identified the specific parts of the brain that are activated during the experience of particular emotions. (p. 271)

- A person's facial expressions can reveal emotions. In fact, members of different cultures understand the emotional expressions of others in similar ways. One explanation for this similarity is that an innate facial-affect program activates a set of muscle movements representing the emotion being experienced. (p. 273)

- The facial-feedback hypothesis suggests that facial expressions not only reflect, but also produce, emotional experiences. (p. 274)

EVALUATE

1. Emotions are always accompanied by a cognitive response. True or false?
2. The _____-_____ theory of emotions states that emotions are a response to instinctive bodily events.
3. According to the _____-_____ theory of emotion, both an emotional response and physiological arousal are produced simultaneously by the same nerve stimulus.
4. Your friend—a psychology major—tells you, "I was at a party last night. During the course of the evening, my general level of arousal increased. Since I was at a party where people were enjoying themselves, I assume I must have felt happy." What theory of emotion does your friend subscribe to?
5. What are the six primary emotions that can be identified from facial expressions?

RETHINK

If researchers learned how to control emotional responses so that targeted emotions could be caused or prevented, what ethical concerns might arise? Under what circumstances, if any, should such techniques be used?

Answers to Evaluate Questions 1. false; emotions may occur without a cognitive response; 2. James-Lange; 3. Cannon-Bard; 4. Schachter-Singer; 5. surprise, sadness, happiness, anger, disgust, and fear.

[KEY TERMS]

Emotions *p. 267*

James-Lange theory of emotion *p. 269*

Cannon-Bard theory of emotion *p. 270*

Schachter-Singer theory of emotion *p. 271*

Facial-affect program *p. 274*

Facial-feedback hypothesis *p. 274*

looking BACK

Psychology on the Web

1. Find two different Web sites that deal with nonverbal behavior. One site should present a fairly "academic" discussion of the topic, and the other should be more informal. (Hint: The terms *nonverbal behavior* and *nonverbal communication* may lead you to more formal discussions of the topic, whereas *body language* may lead you to less formal discussions.) Compare and contrast your findings from the two sites.

2. Use the Web to find instances where politicians have displayed emotions publically. Discuss how attitudes towards emotional displays such as crying by both male and female politicians is interpreted differently.

the case of...
MARIA TOKARSKI, THE HAPPIEST LOSER

Maria Tokarski had been a normal weight for her height throughout much of her life, but after her first child was born she found that she just couldn't lose the extra weight she had gained during her pregnancy. Caring for an infant took a lot of her time and energy, and she wasn't as focused on her health and appearance as she once had been. Rather than returning to her normal weight, Maria slowly gained more until she was almost twice her prepregnancy weight.

Maria's weight gain affected her mood, her social life, and even her marriage. But when her physician delivered the news that it was affecting her health, Maria found the determination to make a change. It took almost two years of regular exercise, careful monitoring of her diet, and regular support group meetings, but Maria eventually returned to her former slim figure. On her son's fifth birthday, Maria pulled out her favorite pair of jeans that had been in storage since just before her maternity days and was overjoyed to find that they finally fit her once again!

1. What may have been some of the motivational and environmental factors contributing to Maria's weight gain after childbirth?

2. If you were Maria's physician, how would you explain to her the weight-set-point hypothesis?

3. Which approaches to motivation might help to explain Maria's unflagging determination to lose all the weight she had gained, and why?

4. If Maria were your friend and she asked your advice on weight-loss strategies, what would you tell her?

5. In what ways do you think emotion was tied in to Maria's weight gain and her subsequent weight loss?

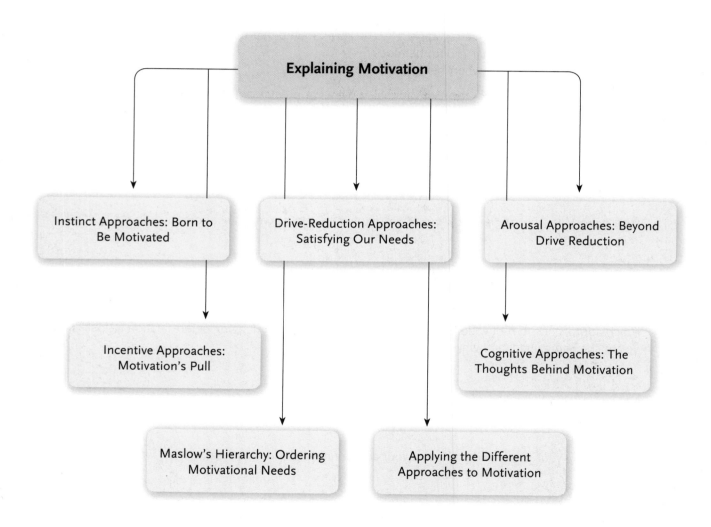

Explaining Motivation

Instinct Approaches: Born to Be Motivated

Incentive Approaches: Motivation's Pull

Drive-Reduction Approaches: Satisfying Our Needs

Maslow's Hierarchy: Ordering Motivational Needs

Applying the Different Approaches to Motivation

Arousal Approaches: Beyond Drive Reduction

Cognitive Approaches: The Thoughts Behind Motivation

Human Needs and Motivation: Eat, Drink, and Be Daring

- The Motivation Behind Hunger and Eating
- Sexual Motivation
- The Needs for Achievement, Affiliation, and Power

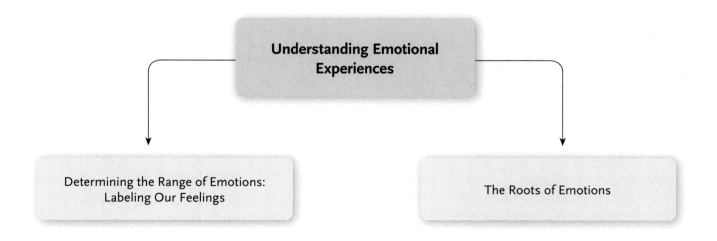

Understanding Emotional Experiences

- Determining the Range of Emotions: Labeling Our Feelings
- The Roots of Emotions

CHAPTER

8

DEVELOPMENT

CHAPTER OUTLINE

They Met in Day Care

Danielle Link and Glen Zilly felt like their first date really didn't go so well. "We didn't think we had any chemistry," says Link. What they didn't know was that they'd actually been on numerous very successful "dates" before as toddlers, under the care of the same Hampton, Virginia, babysitter, Louise Hughes. "I started looking after Glen as a newborn, and I got Danielle when she was about 8 months old," recalls Hughes. "They were together five days a week for years."

Link, 29, and Zilly, 28, who both ended up living in Phoenix and randomly met on an Internet dating site, didn't piece things together until almost six months into their relationship. "I was shocked," says Zilly, whose mother made the connection during a phone chat with Hughes. Adds Link: "I was in love before this happened, but after finding this out, I realized our relationship was meant to be." (*People*, 2007, p. 18) ■

Although it's far from clear that Link's and Zilly's relationship was "meant to be," it does raise questions of whether and how their early experiences affected their relationship decades later. Their story also serves as an introduction to one of the broadest and most important areas of psychology, developmental psychology. *Developmental psychology* is the branch of psychology that studies the patterns of growth and change that occur throughout life. It deals with issues ranging from new ways of conceiving children, to learning how to raise children most sensibly, to understanding the milestones of life that we all face.

Developmental psychologists study the interaction between the unfolding of biologically predetermined patterns of behavior and a constantly changing, dynamic environment. They ask how our genetic background affects our behavior throughout our lives and whether our potential is limited by heredity. Similarly, they seek to understand the way in which the environment works with—or against—our genetic capabilities, how the world we live in affects our development, and how we can be encouraged to reach our full potential.

We begin by examining the approaches developmental psychologists use to study the environmental and genetic factors: the nature–nurture issue. Then we consider the very start of development, beginning with conception and the nine months of life before birth. We look at both genetic and environmental influences on the unborn individual and the way they can affect behavior throughout the remainder of the life cycle.

Next, we examine development that occurs after birth, witnessing the enormous and rapid growth that takes place during the early stages of life, and focusing on physical, social, and cognitive change throughout infancy, toddlerhood, and middle childhood. We then move on to development from adolescence through adulthood. We end with a discussion of the ways in which people prepare themselves for death.

looking **AHEAD**

Nature, Nurture, and Prenatal Development

LEARNING OUTCOMES

25.1 Compare and contrast the influence of nature versus nurture.

25.2 Describe developmental research techniques.

25.3 Discuss prenatal development.

How many bald, six-foot-six, 250-pound volunteer firefighters in New Jersey wear droopy mustaches, aviator-style eyeglasses, and a key ring on the right side of the belt?

The answer is two: Gerald Levey and Mark Newman. They are twins who were separated at birth. Each twin did not even know the other existed until they were reunited—in a fire station—by a fellow firefighter. . .

The lives of the twins, although separate, took remarkably similar paths. Levey went to college, studying forestry; Newman planned to study forestry in college but instead took a job trimming trees. . . .

Both men are unmarried and find the same kind of woman attractive: "tall, slender, long hair." They share similar hobbies, enjoying hunting, fishing, going to the beach, and watching old John Wayne movies and professional wrestling. Both like Chinese food and drink the same brand of beer.

The remarkable range of similarities we see in many pairs of identical twins raises one of the fundamental questions posed by **developmental psychology,** the study of the patterns of growth and change that occur throughout life. The question is this: How can we distinguish between the *environmental* causes of behavior (the influence of parents, siblings, family, friends, schooling, nutrition, and all the other experiences to which a child is exposed) and *hereditary* causes (those based on the genetic makeup of an individual that influence growth and development throughout life)? This question embodies the **nature–nurture issue.** In this context, nature refers to hereditary factors, and nurture to environmental influences.

Although the question was first posed as a nature-*versus*-nurture issue, developmental psychologists today agree that *both* nature

Gerald Levey and Mark Newman

and nurture interact to produce specific developmental patterns and outcomes. Consequently, the question has evolved into *How and to what degree do environment and heredity both produce their effects?* No one grows up free of environmental influences, nor does anyone develop without being affected by his or her inherited *genetic makeup*. However, the debate over the comparative influence of the two factors remains active, with different approaches and different theories of development emphasizing the environment or heredity to a greater or lesser degree (Pinker, 2002; Gottesman & Hanson, 2005; Rutter, 2006).

For example, some developmental theories rely on basic psychological principles of learning and stress the role learning plays in producing changes in behavior in a developing child. Such theories emphasize the role of the environment in development. In contrast, other developmental theories emphasize the influence of one's physiological makeup and functioning on development. Such theories stress the role of heredity and *maturation*—the unfolding of biologically predetermined patterns of behavior—in producing developmental change. Maturation can be seen, for instance, in the development of sex characteristics (such as breasts and body hair) that occurs at the start of adolescence.

Despite their differences over theory, developmental psychologists concur on some points. They agree that genetic factors not only provide the potential for specific behaviors or traits to emerge, but also place limitations on the emergence of such behavior or traits. For instance, heredity defines people's general level of intelligence, setting an upper limit that—regardless of the quality of the environment—people cannot exceed. Heredity also places limits on physical abilities; humans simply cannot run at a speed of 60 miles an hour, nor will they grow as tall as 10 feet, no matter what the quality of their environment (Dodge, 2004; Pinker, 2004).

Figure 1 lists some of the characteristics most affected by heredity. As you consider these items, it is important to keep in mind that these characteristics are not *entirely* determined by heredity, for environmental factors also play a role.

Developmental psychologists also agree that in most instances environmental factors play a critical role in enabling people to reach the potential capabilities that their genetic background makes possible. If Albert Einstein had received no intellectual stimulation as a child and had not been sent to

Developmental psychology The branch of psychology that studies the patterns of growth and change that occur throughout life.

Nature–nurture issue The issue of the degree to which environment and heredity influence behavior.

STUDY ALERT

The nature–nurture issue is a key question that is pervasive throughout the field of psychology, asking how and to what degree environment and heredity produce their joint effects.

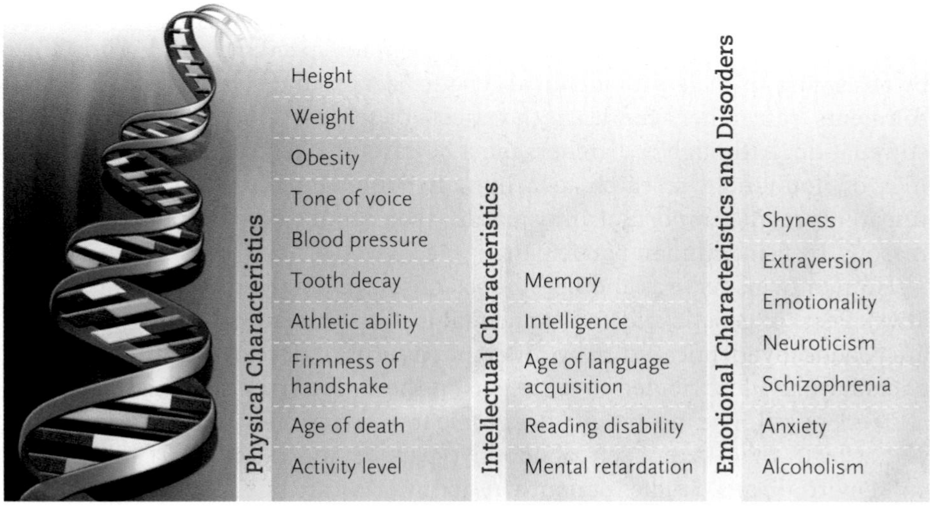

Physical Characteristics
- Height
- Weight
- Obesity
- Tone of voice
- Blood pressure
- Tooth decay
- Athletic ability
- Firmness of handshake
- Age of death
- Activity level

Intellectual Characteristics
- Memory
- Intelligence
- Age of language acquisition
- Reading disability
- Mental retardation

Emotional Characteristics and Disorders
- Shyness
- Extraversion
- Emotionality
- Neuroticism
- Schizophrenia
- Anxiety
- Alcoholism

FIGURE 1 Characteristics influenced significantly by genetic factors. Although these characteristics have strong genetic components, they are also affected by environmental factors.

school, it is unlikely that he would have reached his genetic potential. Similarly, a great athlete such as baseball star Derek Jeter would have been unlikely to display much physical skill if he had not been raised in an environment that nurtured his innate talent and gave him the opportunity to train and perfect his natural abilities.

Clearly, the relationship between heredity and environment is far from simple. As a consequence, developmental psychologists typically take an *interactionist* position on the nature–nurture issue, suggesting that a combination of hereditary and environmental factors influences development. Developmental psychologists face the challenge of identifying the relative strength of each of these influences on the individual, as well as that of identifying the specific changes that occur over the course of development (McGregor & Capone, 2004; Moffitt, Caspi, & Rutter, 2006).

From the perspective of . . .

A CHILD-CARE PROVIDER Consider what factors might determine why a child is not learning to walk at the same pace as his peers. What kinds of environmental influences might be involved? What kinds of genetic influences might be involved? What recommendations might you make to the child's parents about the situation?

» LO1 Determining the Relative Influence of Nature and Nurture

Identical twins Twins who are exactly the same genetically.

Developmental psychologists use several approaches to determine the relative influence of genetic and environmental factors on behavior. In one approach, researchers can experimentally control the genetic makeup of laboratory animals by carefully breeding them for specific traits. For instance, by observing animals with identical genetic backgrounds placed in varied environments, researchers can learn the effects of specific kinds of environmental stimulation. Although researchers must be careful when generalizing the findings of nonhuman research to a human population, findings from animal research provide important information that cannot be obtained, for ethical reasons, by using human participants.

Human twins serve as another important source of information about the relative effects of genetic and environmental factors. If **identical twins** (those who are genetically identical) display different patterns of development, those differences have to be attributed to variations in the environment in which the twins were raised. The most useful data come from identical twins who are adopted at birth by different sets of adoptive parents and raised apart in differing environments. Studies of nontwin siblings who are raised in totally different environments also shed some light on the issue. Because they have relatively similar genetic backgrounds, siblings who show similarities as adults provide strong evidence for the importance of heredity (Gottesman, 1997; Sternberg, 2002a).

psych2.0

WWW.MHHE.COM/PSYCHLIFE

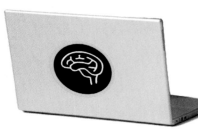

Nature–Nurture

Researchers can also take the opposite tack. Instead of concentrating on people with similar genetic backgrounds who are raised in different environments, they may consider people raised in similar environments who have totally dissimilar genetic backgrounds. If they find, for example, similar courses of development in two adopted children who have different genetic backgrounds and have been raised in the same family, they have evidence for the importance of environmental influences on development.

» LO2 Developmental Research Techniques

Because of the demands of measuring behavioral change across different ages, developmental researchers use several unique methods. The most frequently used, **cross-sectional research,** compares people of different ages at the same point in time. Cross-sectional studies provide information about differences in development between different age groups (Creasey, 2005; Huijie, 2006).

Suppose, for instance, we were interested in the development of intellectual ability in adulthood. To carry out a cross-sectional study, we might compare a sample of 25-, 45-, and 65-year-olds who all take the same IQ test. We then can determine whether average IQ test scores differ in each age group.

Cross-sectional research has limitations, however. For instance, we cannot be sure that the differences in IQ scores we might find in our example are due to age differences alone. Instead, the scores may reflect differences in the educational attainment of the cohorts represented. A *cohort* is a group of people who grow up at similar times, in similar places, and in similar conditions. In the case of IQ differences, any age differences we find in a cross-sectional study may reflect educational differences among the cohorts studied: people in the older age group may belong to a cohort that was less likely to attend college than were the people in the younger groups.

A longitudinal study, the second major research strategy used by developmental psychologists, provides one way around this problem. **Longitudinal research** traces the behavior of one or more participants as the participants

Cross-sectional research A research method that compares people of different ages at the same point in time.

Longitudinal research A research method that investigates behavior as participants age.

Sequential research A research method that combines cross-sectional and longitudinal research by considering a number of different age groups and examining them at several points in time.

Chromosomes Rod-shaped structures that contain all basic hereditary information.

Genes The parts of the chromosomes through which genetic information is transmitted.

age. Longitudinal studies assess *change* in behavior over time, whereas cross-sectional studies assess *differences* among groups of people.

For instance, consider how we might investigate intellectual development during adulthood by using a longitudinal research strategy. First, we might give an IQ test to a group of 25-year-olds. We'd then come back to the same people 20 years later and retest them at age 45. Finally, we'd return to them once more when they were 65 years old and test them again.

By examining changes at several points in time, we can clearly see how individuals develop. Unfortunately, longitudinal research requires an enormous expenditure of time (as the researcher waits for the participants to get older), and participants who begin a study at an early age may drop out, move away, or even die as the research continues. Moreover, participants who take the same test at several points in time may become "test-wise" and perform better each time they take it, having become more familiar with the test.

To make up for the limitations in both cross-sectional and longitudinal research, investigators have devised an alternative strategy. Known as **sequential research,** it combines cross-sectional and longitudinal approaches by taking a number of different age groups and examining them at several points in time. For example, investigators might use a group of 3-, 5-, and 7-year-olds, examining them every six months for a period of several years. This technique allows a developmental psychologist to tease out the specific effects of age changes from other possibly influential factors.

» LO3 Prenatal Development: Conception to Birth

Our increasing understanding of the first stirrings of life spent inside a mother's womb has permitted significant medical advances in prenatal care and childbirth. Yet our increasing knowledge of the biology of *conception*—when a male's sperm cell penetrates a female's egg cell—and its aftermath make the start of life no less of a miracle. Let's consider how an individual is created by looking first at the genetic endowment that a child receives at the moment of conception.

The Basics of Genetics

The one-cell entity established at conception contains 23 pairs of **chromosomes,** rod-shaped structures that contain all basic hereditary information. One member of each pair is from the mother, and the other is from the father.

Each chromosome contains thousands of **genes**—smaller units through which genetic information is transmitted. Either individually or in combination, genes produce the particular characteristics of each person. Composed of sequences of *DNA (deoxyribonucleic acid)* molecules, genes are the biological equivalent of "software" that programs the future development of all parts of the body's hardware. Humans have some 25,000 different genes (see Figure 2).

Some genes control the development of systems common to all members of the human species—the heart, circulatory system, brain, lungs, and so forth; others shape the characteristics that make each human unique, such as facial configuration, height, and eye color. The child's sex is also determined by a particular combination of genes. Specifically, a child inherits an

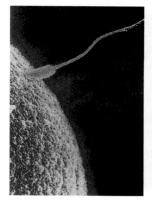

A Conception

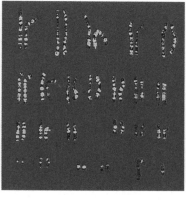

B 23 pairs of chromosomes

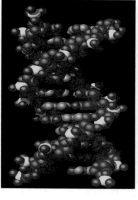

C DNA sequence

D Genes

FIGURE 2   Every individual's characteristics are determined by the individual's specific genetic information. At the moment of conception (A), humans receive 23 pairs of chromosomes (B), half from the mother and half from the father. These chromosomes are made up of coils of DNA (C). Each chromosome contains thousands of genes (D) that "program" the future development of the body.

X chromosome from its mother and either an X or a Y chromosome from its father. When it receives an XX combination, it is a female; with an XY combination, it develops as a male. Male development is triggered by a single gene on the Y chromosome, and without the presence of that specific gene, the individual will develop as a female.

As behavioral geneticists have discovered, genes are also at least partially responsible for a wide variety of personal characteristics, including cognitive abilities, personality traits, and psychological disorders. Of course, few of these characteristics are determined by a single gene. Instead, most traits result from a combination of multiple genes, which operate together with environmental influences (Plomin & McGuffin, 2003; Haberstick et al., 2005; Ramus, 2006).

> As behavioral geneticists have discovered, genes are also at least partially responsible for a wide variety of personal characteristics, including cognitive abilities, personality traits, and psychological disorders.

The Earliest Development

When an egg becomes fertilized by the sperm, the resulting one-celled entity, called a **zygote,** immediately begins to develop. The zygote starts out as a microscopic speck. Three days after fertilization, though, the zygote increases to around 32 cells, and within a week it has grown to 100–150 cells. These first two weeks are known as the *germinal period.*

Two weeks after conception, the developing individual enters the *embryonic period,* which lasts from week 2 through week 8, and he or she is now called an **embryo.** As an embryo develops through an intricate, preprogrammed process of cell division, it grows 10,000 times larger by 4 weeks of age, attaining a length of about one-fifth of an inch. At this point it has developed a rudimentary beating heart, a brain, an intestinal tract, and a number of other organs. Although all these organs are at a primitive stage of development, they are clearly recognizable. Moreover, by week 8, the embryo is about an inch long, and has discernible arms and legs and a face.

From week 8 and continuing until birth, the developing individual enters the *fetal period* and is called a **fetus.** At the start of this period, it begins to be responsive to touch; it bends its fingers when touched on the hand. At 16 to 18 weeks, its movements become strong enough for the mother to sense them. At

Zygote The new cell formed by the union of an egg and sperm.

Embryo A developed zygote that has a heart, a brain, and other organs.

Fetus A developing individual, from eight weeks after conception until birth.

the same time, hair may begin to grow on the fetus's head, and the facial features become similar to those the child will display at birth. The major organs begin functioning, although the fetus could not be kept alive outside the mother. In addition, a lifetime's worth of brain neurons are produced—although it is unclear whether the brain is capable of thinking at this early stage.

By week 24, a fetus has many of the characteristics it will display as a newborn. In fact, when an infant is born prematurely at this age, it can open and close its eyes; suck; cry; look up, down, and around; and even grasp objects placed in its hands, although it is still unable to survive for long outside the mother.

The fetus continues to develop before birth. It begins to grow fatty deposits under the skin, and it gains weight. The fetus reaches the **age of viability,** the point at which it can survive if born prematurely, at about prenatal age 22 weeks, although through advances in medical technology this crucial age is getting earlier. At prenatal age 28 weeks, the fetus weighs less than 3 pounds and is about 16 inches long.

Before birth, a fetus passes through several *sensitive periods* (also referred to as *critical periods*). A sensitive period is the time when organisms are particularly susceptible to certain kinds of stimuli. For example, fetuses are especially affected by their mothers' use of drugs during certain sensitive periods before birth. If they are exposed to a particular drug before or after the sensitive period, it may have relatively little impact, but if exposure comes during a critical period, the impact will be significant (Werker & Tees, 2005; Uylings, 2006).

Sensitive periods can also occur after birth. Some language specialists suggest, for instance, that there is a period in which children are particularly receptive to developing language. If children are not exposed to appropriate linguistic stimuli, their language development may be impaired (Innocenti, 2007; Sohr-Preston & Scaramella, 2006).

In the final weeks of pregnancy, the fetus continues to gain weight and grow. At the end of the normal 38 weeks of pregnancy, a fetus typically weighs around 7 pounds and is about 20 inches in length. However, the story is different for *preterm infants,* who are born before week 38. Because they have not been able to develop fully, they are at higher risk for illness, future problems, and even death. For infants who have been in the womb for more than 30 weeks, the prospects are relatively good. However, for those born before week 30, the story is often less positive. Such newborns, who may weigh as

Age of viability The point at which a fetus can survive if born prematurely.

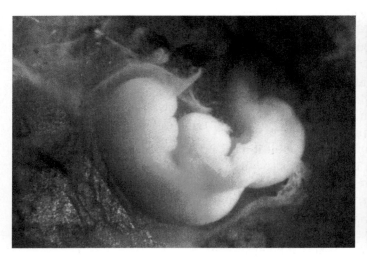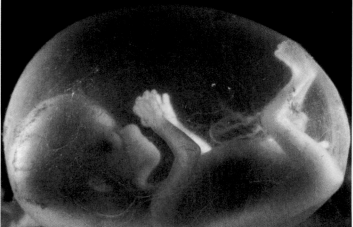

These remarkable photos of live fetuses display the degree of physical development at prenatal ages 4 and 15 weeks.

little as 2 pounds at birth, are in grave danger because they have immature organs; they have less than a 50-50 chance of survival. If they do survive—and it takes extraordinarily heroic (and expensive) medical intervention to assure this—they may later experience significant developmental delays.

Genetic Influences on the Fetus

The process of fetal growth that we have just described reflects normal development, which occurs in 95 to 98 percent of all pregnancies. Some individuals are less fortunate, for in the remaining 2 to 5 percent of cases, children are born with serious birth defects. A major cause of such defects is faulty genes or chromosomes. Here are two of the more common genetic and chromosomal difficulties.

- *Phenylketonuria (PKU).* A child born with the inherited disease phenylketonuria cannot produce an enzyme that is required for normal development. This deficiency results in an accumulation of poisons that eventually cause profound intellectual disabilities. The disease is treatable, however, if it is caught early. Most infants today are routinely tested for PKU, and children with the disorder can be placed on a special diet that allows them to develop normally (Ievers-Landis et al., 2005; Christ, Steiner, & Grange, 2006).

- *Sickle-cell anemia.* About 10 percent of the African American population has the possibility of passing on sickle-cell anemia, a disease that gets its name from the abnormally shaped red blood cells it causes. Children with the disease may have episodes of pain, yellowish eyes, stunted growth, and vision problems (Taras & Potts-Datema, 2005; Selove, 2007).

- *Down syndrome.* Down syndrome, one of the causes of mental retardation, occurs when the zygote receives an extra chromosome at the moment of conception. Down syndrome is often related to the mother's age; mothers over 35 and younger than 18 stand a higher risk than other women of having a child with the syndrome (Roizen & Patterson, 2003).

Prenatal Environmental Influences

Genetic factors are not the only causes of difficulties in fetal development. Environmental influences—the *nurture* part of the nature–nurture equation—also affect the fetus. Some of the more profound consequences are brought about by **teratogens,** environmental agents such as a drug, chemical, virus, or other factor that produce a birth defect. Among the major prenatal environmental influences on the fetus are the following:

Teratogens Environmental agents such as a drug, chemical, virus, or other factor that produce a birth defect.

- *Mother's nutrition.* What a mother eats during her pregnancy can have important implications for the health of her baby. Seriously undernourished mothers cannot provide adequate nutrition to a growing fetus, and they are likely to give birth to underweight babies. Poorly nourished babies are also more susceptible to disease (Zigler, Finn-Stevenson, & Hall, 2002; Najman et al., 2004).

- *Mother's illness.* Several diseases can have devastating consequences for a developing fetus if they are contracted during the early part of a pregnancy. For example, rubella (German measles), syphilis, diabetes, and high blood pressure may each produce a permanent effect on the fetus (Nesheim et al., 2004; Magoni et al., 2005).

- *Alcohol and nicotine use.* Alcohol and nicotine are extremely dangerous to fetal development. For example, 1 out of every 750 infants is born with *fetal alcohol syndrome (FAS)*, a condition resulting in below-average

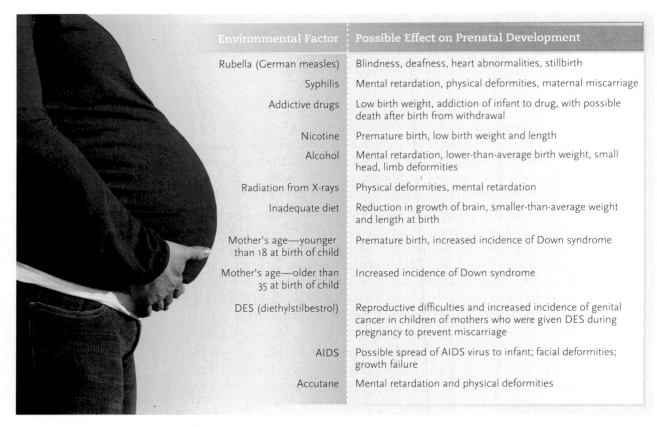

Environmental Factor	Possible Effect on Prenatal Development
Rubella (German measles)	Blindness, deafness, heart abnormalities, stillbirth
Syphilis	Mental retardation, physical deformities, maternal miscarriage
Addictive drugs	Low birth weight, addiction of infant to drug, with possible death after birth from withdrawal
Nicotine	Premature birth, low birth weight and length
Alcohol	Mental retardation, lower-than-average birth weight, small head, limb deformities
Radiation from X-rays	Physical deformities, mental retardation
Inadequate diet	Reduction in growth of brain, smaller-than-average weight and length at birth
Mother's age—younger than 18 at birth of child	Premature birth, increased incidence of Down syndrome
Mother's age—older than 35 at birth of child	Increased incidence of Down syndrome
DES (diethylstilbestrol)	Reproductive difficulties and increased incidence of genital cancer in children of mothers who were given DES during pregnancy to prevent miscarriage
AIDS	Possible spread of AIDS virus to infant; facial deformities; growth failure
Accutane	Mental retardation and physical deformities

FIGURE 3 A variety of environmental factors can play a role in prenatal development.

psych2.0
WWW.MHHE.COM/PSYCHLIFE

Prenatal Development

intelligence, growth delays, and facial deformities. FAS is now the primary preventable cause of mental retardation. Even mothers who use small amounts of alcohol during pregnancy place their child at risk. *Fetal alcohol effects* (*FAE*) is a condition in which children display some, although not all, of the problems of FAS due to their mother's consumption of alcohol during pregnancy. Similarly, pregnant mothers who smoke put their children at considerable risk (Henderson, Kesmodel, & Gray, 2007; Niccols, 2007).

Several other environmental factors have an impact on the child before and during birth (see Figure 3). Keep in mind that although we have been discussing the influences of genetics and environment separately, neither factor works alone. Furthermore, despite the emphasis here on some of the ways in which development can go wrong, the vast majority of births occur without difficulty. And in most instances, subsequent development also proceeds normally.

RECAP

Compare and contrast the influence of nature versus nurture.

- Developmental psychology studies growth and change throughout life. (p. 282)
- One fundamental question is how much developmental change is due to heredity and how much is due to environment—the nature–nurture issue. (p. 282)
- Heredity defines the upper limits of our growth and change, whereas the environment affects the degree to which the upper limits are reached. (p. 283)

Describe developmental research techniques.

- Cross-sectional research compares people of different ages with one another at the same point in time. (p. 285)
- Longitudinal research traces the behavior of one or more participants as the participants become older. (p. 285)
- Sequential research combines the two methods by taking several different age groups and examining them at several points in time. (p. 286)

Discuss prenatal development.

- At the moment of conception, a male's sperm cell and a female's egg cell unite, with each contributing to the new individual's genetic makeup. (p. 286)

- Each chromosome contains genes, through which genetic information is transmitted. (p. 286)
- The union of sperm and egg produces a zygote, which contains 23 pairs of chromosomes—with one member of each pair coming from the father and the other coming from the mother. (p. 287)
- After two weeks the zygote becomes an embryo. By week 8, the embryo is called a fetus and is responsive to touch and other stimulation. At week 22 it reaches the age of viability, which means it may survive if born prematurely. (p. 287)
- A fetus is normally born after 38 weeks of pregnancy, weighing around 7 pounds and measuring about 20 inches. (p. 288)
- Genes affect not only physical attributes but also a wide array of personal characteristics such as cognitive abilities, personality traits, and psychological disorders. (p. 289)
- Genetic abnormalities produce birth defects such as phenylketonuria (PKU) and Down syndrome. (p. 289)
- Among the environmental influences on fetal growth are the mother's nutrition, illnesses, and alcohol and nicotine intake. (p. 289)

EVALUATE

1. Developmental psychologists are interested in the effects of both _____ and _____ on development.

2. Environment and heredity both influence development, with genetic potentials generally establishing limits on environmental influences. True or false?

3. By observing genetically similar animals in differing environments, we can increase our understanding of the influences of hereditary and environmental factors in humans. True or false?

4. _____ research studies the same individuals over a period of time, whereas _____ - _____ research studies people of different ages at the same time.

5. Match each of the following terms with its definition:

    1. Zygote
    2. Gene
    3. Chromosome

    a. Smallest unit through which genetic information is passed
    b. Fertilized egg
    c. Rod-shaped structure containing genetic information

6. Specific kinds of growth must take place during a _____ period if the embryo is to develop normally.

RETHINK

When researchers find similarities in development between very different cultures, what implications might such findings have for the nature–nurture issue?

[KEY TERMS]

Developmental psychology p. 283

Nature–nurture issue p. 283

Identical twins p. 284

Cross-sectional research p. 285

Longitudinal research p. 285

Sequential research p. 286

Chromosomes p. 286

Genes p. 286

Zygote p. 287

Embryo p. 287

Fetus p. 287

Age of viability p. 288

Teratogens p. 289

module 26

Infancy and Childhood

LEARNING OUTCOMES

26.1 Describe the major competencies of newborns.

26.2 Explain the milestones of physical, social, and cognitive development during childhood.

His head was molded into a long melon shape and came to a point at the back . . . He was covered with a thick greasy white material known as "vernix," which made him slippery to hold, and also allowed him to slip easily through the birth canal. In addition to a shock of black hair on his head, his body was covered with dark, fine hair known as "lanugo." His ears, his back, his shoulders, and even his cheeks were furry . . . His skin was wrinkled and quite loose, ready to scale in creased places such as his feet and hands . . . His ears were pressed to his head in unusual positions—one ear was matted firmly forward on his cheek. His nose was flattened and pushed to one side by the squeeze as he came through the pelvis. (Brazelton, 1969, p. 3)

What kind of creature is this? Although the description hardly fits that of the adorable babies seen in advertisements for baby food, we are in fact talking about a normal, completely developed child just after the moment of birth. Called a **neonate,** a newborn arrives in the world in a form that hardly meets the standards of beauty against which we typically measure babies. Yet ask any parents: nothing is more beautiful or exciting than the first glimpse of their newborn.

Neonate A newborn child.

» LO1 The Extraordinary Newborn

Several factors cause a neonate's strange appearance. The trip through the mother's birth canal may have squeezed the incompletely formed bones of the skull together and squashed the nose into the head. The skin secretes *vernix,* a white, greasy covering, for protection before birth, and the baby may have *lanugo,* a soft fuzz, over the entire body for a similar purpose. The infant's eyelids may be puffy with an accumulation of fluids because of the upside-down position during birth.

All these features change during the first two weeks of life as the neonate takes on a more familiar appearance. Even more impressive are the capabilities a neonate begins to display from the moment of birth—capabilities that grow at an astounding rate over the ensuing months.

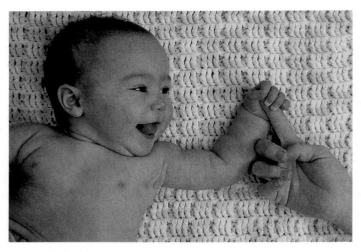

Many of the reflexes that a neonate is born with are critical to survival and unfold naturally as part of an infant's ongoing maturation. Do you think humans have more or fewer reflexes than other animals?

Reflexes

A neonate is born with a number of **reflexes**—unlearned, involuntary responses that occur automatically in the presence of certain stimuli. Critical for survival, many of those reflexes unfold naturally as part of an infant's ongoing maturation. The *rooting reflex,* for instance, causes neonates to turn their heads toward things that touch their cheeks—such as the mother's nipple or a bottle. Similarly, a *sucking reflex* prompts infants to suck at things that touch their lips. Among other reflexes are a *gag reflex* (to clear the throat), the startle reflex (a series of movements in which an infant flings out the arms, fans the fingers, and arches the back in response to a sudden noise), and the *Babinski reflex* (a baby's toes fan out when the outer edge of the sole of the foot is stroked).

Infants lose these primitive reflexes after the first few months of life, replacing them with more complex and organized behaviors. Although at birth a neonate is capable of only jerky, limited voluntary movements, during the first year of life the ability to move independently grows enormously. The typical baby rolls over by the age of about 3 months, sits without support at about 6 months, stands alone at about 11 months, and walks at just over a year old. Not only does the ability to make large-scale movements improve during this time, fine-muscle movements become increasingly sophisticated (see Figure 1).

3.2 months: Rolling over	3.3 months: Grasping rattle	5.9 months: Sitting without support	7.2 months: Standing while holding on	8.2 months: Grasping with thumb and finger
11.5 months: Standing alone well	12.3 months: Walking well	14.8 months: Building tower of two cubes	16.6 months: Walking up steps	23.8 months: Jumping in place

FIGURE 1   Although at birth a neonate can make only jerky, limited voluntary movements, during the first year of life the ability to move independently grows enormously. The ages indicate the time when 50 percent of children are able to perform each skill (Frankenburg et al., 1992). Remember, however, that the time when each skill appears can vary considerably. For example, 25 percent of children are able to walk well at age 11 months, and by 15 months 90 percent of children are walking well.

Development of the Senses: Taking in the World

When proud parents peer into the eyes of their neonate, is the child able to return their gaze? Although it was thought for some time that newborns can see only a hazy blur, most current findings indicate that the capabilities of neonates are far more impressive. Although their eyes have a limited capacity to focus on objects that are not within a seven- to eight-inch distance from the face, neonates can follow objects moving within their field of vision. They also show the rudiments of depth perception, as they react by raising their hands when an object appears to be moving rapidly toward the face (Gelman & Kit-Fong Au, 1996; Maurer et al., 1999).

Neonates can also discriminate facial expressions—and even imitate them. As you can see in Figure 2, newborns who see an adult with a happy, sad, or surprised facial expression can produce a good imitation of the adult's expression. Even very young infants, then, can respond to the emotions and moods that their caregivers' facial expressions reveal. This capability provides the foundation for social interaction skills in children (Meltzoff, 1996; Lavelli & Fogel, 2005; Grossman, Striano, & Friederici, 2007).

In addition to vision, infants display other impressive sensory capabilities. Newborns can distinguish different sounds to the point of being able to recognize their own mothers' voices at the age of 3 days. They can also make the subtle perceptual distinctions that underlie language abilities. For example, at 2 days of age, infants can distinguish between their native tongue and foreign languages, and they can discriminate between such closely related sounds as *ba* and *pa* when they are 4 days old. By 6 months of age, they can discriminate virtually any difference in sound that is relevant to the production of language. Moreover, they can recognize different tastes and smells at a very early age. There even seems to be something of a built-in sweet tooth: neonates prefer liquids that have been sweetened with sugar over their

Reflexes Automatic, involuntary responses to incoming stimuli.

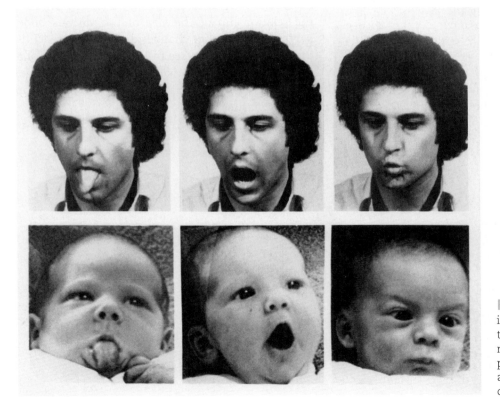

FIGURE 2 This newborn infant is clearly imitating the expressions of the adult model in these amazing photos. How does this ability contribute to social development?

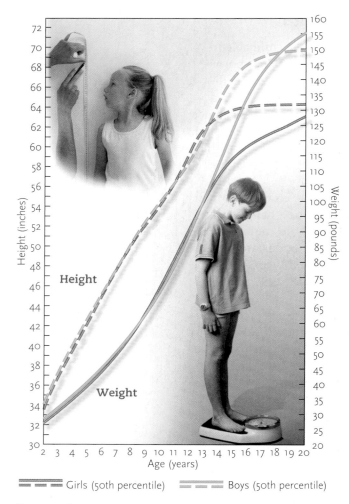

FIGURE 3 The average heights and weights of males and females in the United States from birth through age 20. At what ages are girls typically heavier and taller than boys? *(Source: National Center for Health Statistics, 2000.)*

= = = = = Girls (50th percentile)   = = = = = Boys (50th percentile)

unsweetened counterparts (Cohen & Cashon, 2003; Rivera-Gaxiola et al., 2005).

» LO 2 The Growing Child: Infancy through Middle Childhood

Throughout the remainder of childhood, moving from infancy into middle childhood and the start of adolescence around age 11 or 12, children develop physically, socially, and cognitively in extraordinary ways. In the remainder of this module, we'll consider this development.

Physical Development

Children's physical growth provides the most obvious sign of development. During the first year of life, children typically triple their birth weight, and their height increases by about half. This rapid growth slows down as the child gets older—think how gigantic adults would be if that rate of growth were constant—and from age 3 to the beginning of adolescence at around age 13, growth averages a gain of about 5 pounds and 3 inches a year (see Figure 3).

The physical changes that occur as children develop are not just a matter of increasing growth; the relationship of the size of the various body parts to one another changes dramatically as children age. As you can see in Figure 4, the head of a fetus (and a newborn) is disproportionately large. However, the head soon becomes more proportional in size to the rest of the body as growth occurs mainly in the trunk and legs.

FIGURE 4 As development progresses, the size of the head relative to the rest of the body decreases until the individual reaches adulthood. Why do you think the head starts out so large?

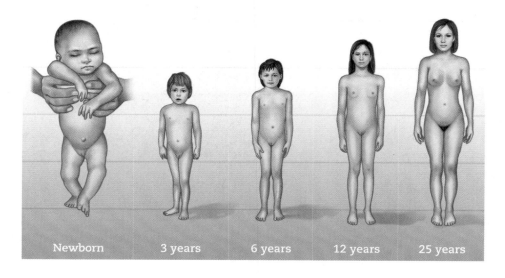

Newborn   3 years   6 years   12 years   25 years

Development of Social Behavior: Forming Social Bonds and Attachment

As anyone who has seen an infant smiling at the sight of his or her mother can guess, at the same time that infants grow physically and hone their perceptual abilities, they also develop socially. The nature of a child's early social development provides the foundation for social relationships that will last a lifetime.

Attachment, the positive emotional bond that develops between a child and a particular individual, is the most important form of social development that occurs during infancy. Our understanding of attachment progressed when psychologist Harry Harlow, in a classic study, gave infant monkeys the choice of cuddling a wire "monkey" that provided milk or a soft, terry-cloth "monkey" that was warm but did not provide milk. Their choice was clear: They spent most of their time clinging to the warm cloth "monkey," although they made occasional forays to the wire monkey to nurse. Obviously, the cloth monkey provided greater comfort to the infants; milk alone was insufficient to create attachment (Harlow & Zimmerman, 1959; Blum, 2002; see Figure 5).

Building on this pioneering work with nonhumans, developmental psychologists have suggested that human attachment grows through the responsiveness of infants' caregivers to the signals the babies provide, such as crying, smiling, reaching, and clinging. The greater the responsiveness of the caregiver to the child's signals, the more likely it is that the child will become securely attached. Full attachment eventually develops as a result of the complex series of interactions between caregiver and child. In the course of these interactions, the infant plays as critical and active a role as the caregiver in the formation of the bond. Infants who respond positively to a caregiver produce more positive behavior on the part of the caregiver, which in turn produces an even stronger degree of attachment in the child.

Assessing Attachment

Developmental psychologists have devised a quick and direct way to measure attachment. Developed by Mary Ainsworth, the *Ainsworth strange situation* consists of a sequence of events involving a child and (typically) his or her mother. Initially, the mother and baby enter an unfamiliar room, and the mother permits the baby to explore while she sits down. An adult stranger then enters the room, after which the mother leaves. The mother returns, and the stranger leaves. The mother once again leaves the baby alone, and the stranger returns. Finally, the stranger leaves, and the mother returns (Ainsworth et al., 1978; Izard & Abe, 2004; Combrink-Graham & McKenna, 2006).

Babies' reactions to the experimental situation vary drastically, depending, according to Ainsworth, on their degree of attachment to the mother. One-year-old children who are *securely attached* employ the mother as a kind of home base, exploring independently but returning

> *The nature of a child's early social development provides the foundation for social relationships that will last a lifetime.*

FIGURE 5 Although the wire "mother" dispensed milk to the hungry infant monkey, the infant preferred the soft, terry-cloth "mother." Do you think human babies would react the same way? What does this experiment tell us about attachment? (*Source: Harry Harlow Primate Laboratory/ University of Wisconsin.*)

to her occasionally. When she leaves, they exhibit distress, and they go to her when she returns. *Avoidant* children do not cry when the mother leaves, and they seem to avoid her when she returns, as if they were indifferent to her. *Ambivalent* children display anxiety before they are separated and are upset when the mother leaves, but they may show ambivalent reactions to her return, such as seeking close contact but simultaneously hitting and kicking her. A fourth reaction is *disorganized-disoriented;* these children show inconsistent, often contradictory behavior.

The Father's Role

Although early developmental research focused largely on the mother-child relationship, more recent research has highlighted the father's role in parenting, and with good reason: the number of fathers who are primary caregivers for their children has grown significantly, and fathers play an increasingly important role in their children's lives. For example, in almost 13 percent of families with children, the father is the parent who stays at home to care for preschoolers (Day & Lamb, 2004; Parke, 2004; Halford, 2006).

When fathers interact with their children, their play often differs from that of mothers. Fathers engage in more physical, rough-and-tumble sorts of activities, whereas mothers play more verbal and traditional games, such as peekaboo. Despite such behavioral differences, the nature of attachment between fathers and children compared with that between mothers and children can be similar. In fact, children can form multiple attachments simultaneously (Paquette, Carbonneau, & Dubeau, 2003; Borisenko, 2007; Pellis & Pellis, 2007).

Social Relationships with Peers

By the time they are 2 years old, children become less dependent on their parents and more self-reliant, increasingly preferring to play with friends. Initially, play is relatively independent: even though they may be sitting side by side, 2-year-olds pay more attention to toys than to one another when playing. Later, however, children actively interact, modifying one another's behavior and later exchanging roles during play (Lindsey & Colwell, 2003; Colwell & Lindsey, 2005).

As children reach school age, their social interactions begin to follow set patterns, as well as becoming more frequent. They may engage in elaborate games involving teams and rigid rules. This play serves purposes other than mere enjoyment. It allows children to become increasingly competent in their social interactions with others. Through play they learn to take the perspective of other people and to infer others' thoughts and feelings, even when those thoughts and feelings are not directly expressed (Royzman, Cassidy, & Baron, 2003).

In short, social interaction helps children interpret the meaning of others' behavior and develop the capacity to respond appropriately. Furthermore, children learn physical and emotional self-control: they learn to avoid hitting a playmate who beats them at a game, be polite, and control their emotional displays and facial expressions (e.g., smiling even when receiving a disappointing gift). Situations that provide children with opportunities for social interaction, then, may enhance their social development (Lengua & Long, 2002; Talukdar & Shastri, 2006).

The Consequences of Child Care Outside the Home

Research on the importance of social interaction is corroborated by work that examines the benefits of child care outside of the home, which is an important part of an increasing number of children's lives. For instance, almost 30 percent of preschool children whose mothers work outside the home spend their days in child-care centers. By the age of 6 months, almost two-thirds of infants are cared for by people other than their mothers for part of the day. Most of these infants begin child care before the age of 4 months and are cared for by people other than their mothers for almost 30 hours per week (NICHD Early Child Care Research Network, 2006; see Figure 6).

Do out-of-the-home child-care arrangements benefit children's development? If the programs are of high quality, they can. According to the results of a large study supported by the U.S. National Institute of Child Health and Development (NICHD), children who attend high-quality child-care centers may not only do as well as children who stay at home with their parents, but in some respects may actually do better. Children in child care are generally more considerate and sociable than other children are, and they interact more positively with teachers. They may also be more compliant and regulate their own behavior more effectively, and their mothers show increased sensitivity to their children (NICHD Early Child Care Research Network, 1999, 2001).

In addition, especially for children from poor or disadvantaged homes, child care in specially enriched environments—those with many toys, books, a variety of children, and high-quality care providers—often proves to be more intellectually stimulating than the home environment. Such child care can lead to increased intellectual achievement, demonstrated in higher IQ scores and better language development. In fact, children in care centers sometimes are found to score higher on tests of cognitive abilities than those who are cared for

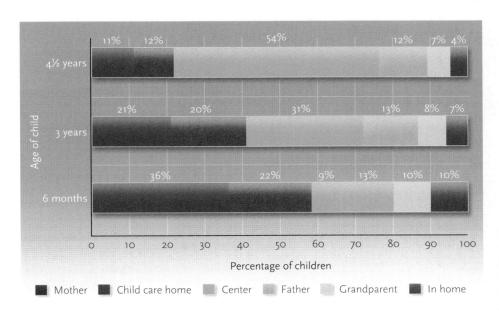

FIGURE 6 As they get older, children are increasingly likely to spend time in some kind of child care outside the home or family (NICHD, 2006).

Authoritarian parents Parents who are rigid and punitive and value unquestioning obedience from their children.

Permissive parents Parents who give their children relaxed or inconsistent direction and, although they are warm, require little of them.

Authoritative parents Parents who are firm, set clear limits, reason with their children, and explain things to them.

by their mothers or by sitters or home day-care providers—effects lasting into adulthood (Wilgoren, 1999; Burchinal, Roberts, & Riggins, 2000).

However, outside-the-home child care does not have universally positive outcomes. Children may feel insecure after placement in low-quality child care or in multiple child-care settings. Furthermore, some research suggests that infants who are involved in outside care more than twenty hours a week in the first year show less secure attachment to their mothers than do those who have not been in outside-the-home child care. Finally, children who spent long hours in child care as infants and preschoolers may have a reduced ability to work independently and to manage their time effectively when they reach elementary school (NICHD Early Child Care Research Network, 1998, 2001; Vandell et al., 2005; Belsky, Burchinal, & McCartney, 2007).

The key to the success of nonparental child care is its quality. High-quality child care produces benefits; low-quality child care provides little or no gain and may even hinder children's development. In short, significant benefits result from the social interaction and intellectual stimulation provided by high-quality child-care centers—especially for children from impoverished environments (NICHD Early Child Care Research Network, 2000, 2002; National Association for the Education of Young Children, 2005; Zaslow, Halle, & Martin, 2006).

Parenting Styles and Social Development

Parents' child-rearing practices are critical in shaping their children's social competence, and—according to classic research by developmental psychologist Diana Baumrind—four main categories describe different parenting styles (Figure 7). Rigid and punitive, **authoritarian parents** value unquestioning obedience from their children. They have strict standards and discourage expressions of disagreement. **Permissive parents** give their children relaxed or inconsistent direction and, although warm, require little of them. In contrast, **authoritative parents** are firm, setting limits for their children. As the

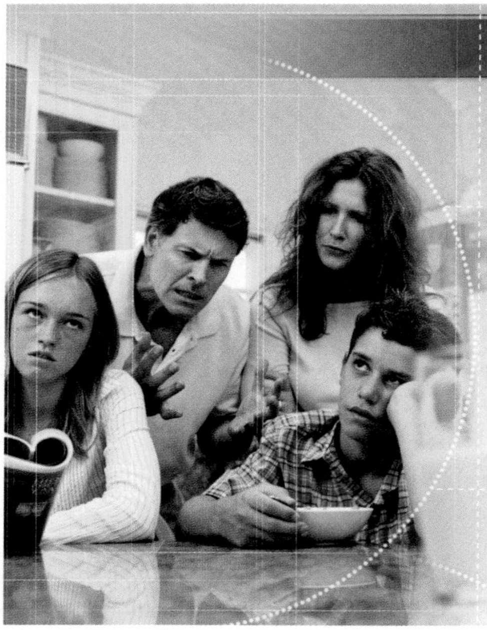

Parenting Style	Parent Behavior	Type of Behavior Produced in Child
Authoritarian	Rigid, punitive, strict standards (example: "If you don't clean your room, I'm going to take away your iPod for good and ground you.")	Unsociable, unfriendly, withdrawn
Permissive	Lax, inconsistent, undemanding (example: "It might be good to clean your room, but I guess it can wait.")	Immature, moody, dependent, low self-control
Authoritative	Firm, sets limits and goals, uses reasoning, encourages independence (example: "You'll need to clean your room before we can go out to the restaurant. As soon as you finish, we'll leave.")	Good social skills, likable, self-reliant, independent
Uninvolved	Detached emotionally, sees role only as providing food, clothing, and shelter (example: "I couldn't care less if your room is a pigsty.")	Indifferent, rejecting behavior

FIGURE 7 According to developmental psychologist Diana Baumrind (1971), four main parenting styles characterize child rearing.

children get older, these parents try to reason and explain things to them. They also set clear goals and encourage their children's independence. Finally, **uninvolved parents** show little interest in their children. Emotionally detached, they view parenting as nothing more than providing food, clothing, and shelter for children. At their most extreme, uninvolved parents are guilty of neglect, a form of child abuse (Baumrind, 2005; Winsler, Madigan, & Aquilino, 2005; Lagacé-Séguin & d'Entremont, 2006).

"Please, Jason. Don't you want to grow up to be an autonomous peson?"

As you might expect, the four kinds of child-rearing styles seem to produce very different kinds of behavior in children (with many exceptions, of course). Children of authoritarian parents tend to be unsociable, unfriendly, and relatively withdrawn. In contrast, permissive parents' children show immaturity, moodiness, dependence, and low self-control. The children of authoritative parents fare best: with high social skills, they are likable, self-reliant, independent, and cooperative. Worst off are the children of uninvolved parents; they feel unloved and emotionally detached, and their physical and cognitive development is impeded. Children with low social skills face peer rejection that can have lasting results (Saarni, 1999; Berk, 2005; Snyder, Cramer, & Afrank, 2005).

Before we congratulate authoritative parents and condemn authoritarian, permissive, and uninvolved ones, it is important to note that in many cases nonauthoritative parents also produce perfectly well-adjusted children. Moreover, children are born with a particular **temperament**—a basic, innate disposition. Some children are naturally easygoing and cheerful, whereas others are irritable and fussy, or pensive and quiet. The kind of temperament a baby is born with may in part bring about specific kinds of parental child-rearing styles (Porter & Hsu, 2003; Lengua & Kovacs, 2005; Majdandzic & van den Boom, 2007).

In sum, a child's upbringing results from the child-rearing philosophy parents hold, the specific practices they use, and the nature of their own and their child's personalities. As is the case with other aspects of development, then, behavior is a function of a complex interaction of environmental and genetic factors.

Erikson's Theory of Psychosocial Development

In tracing the course of social development, some theorists have considered how the challenges of society and culture change as an individual matures. Following this path, psychoanalyst Erik Erikson developed one of the more comprehensive theories of social development. Erikson (1963) viewed the developmental changes occurring throughout life as a series of eight stages of psychosocial development, of which four occur during childhood. **Psychosocial development** involves changes in our interactions and understanding of one another as well as in our knowledge and understanding of ourselves as members of society.

Erikson suggests that passage through each of the stages necessitates the resolution of a crisis or conflict. Accordingly, Erikson represents each stage as a pairing of the most positive and most negative aspects of the crisis of that period. Although each crisis is never resolved entirely—life becomes increasingly complicated as we grow older—it has to be resolved sufficiently to equip us to deal with demands made during the following stage of development.

STUDY ALERT

Know the four major types of child-rearing practices—authoritarian, permissive, authoritative, and uninvolved—and their effects.

Uninvolved parents Parents who show little interest in their children and are emotionally detached.

Temperament The basic, innate disposition that emerges early in life.

Psychosocial development Development of individuals' interactions and understanding of each other and of their knowledge and understanding of themselves as members of society.

STUDY ALERT

Four of Erikson's stages of psychosocial development occur during childhood: trust-versus-mistrust, autonomy-versus-shame-and-doubt, initiative-versus-guilt, and industry-versus-inferiority.

Trust-versus-mistrust stage According to Erikson, the first stage of psychosocial development, occurring from birth to age 1½ years, during which time infants develop feelings of trust or lack of trust.

Autonomy-versus-shame-and-doubt stage The period during which, according to Erikson, toddlers (ages 1½ to 3 years) develop independence and autonomy if exploration and freedom are encouraged, or shame and self-doubt if they are restricted and overprotected.

Initiative-versus-guilt stage According to Erikson, the period during which children ages 3 to 6 years experience conflict between independence of action and the sometimes negative results of that action.

Industry-versus-inferiority stage According to Erikson, the last stage of childhood, during which children ages 6 to 12 years may develop positive social interactions with others or may feel inadequate and become less sociable.

In the first stage of psychosocial development, the **trust-versus-mistrust stage** (ages birth to 1½ years), infants develop feelings of trust if their physical requirements and psychological needs for attachment are consistently met and their interactions with the world are generally positive. In contrast, inconsistent care and unpleasant interactions with others can lead to mistrust and leave an infant unable to meet the challenges required in the next stage of development.

In the second stage, the **autonomy-versus-shame-and-doubt stage** (ages 1½ to 3 years), toddlers develop independence and autonomy if exploration and freedom are encouraged, or they experience shame, self-doubt, and unhappiness if they are overly restricted and protected. According to Erikson, the key to the development of autonomy during this period is that the child's caregivers provide the appropriate amount of control. If parents provide too much control, children cannot assert themselves and develop their own sense of control over their environment; if parents provide too little control, the children become overly demanding and controlling.

Next, children face the crises of the **initiative-versus-guilt stage** (ages 3 to 6). In this stage, children's desire to act independently conflicts with the guilt that comes from the unintended and unexpected consequences of such behavior. Children in this period come to understand that they are persons in their own right, and they begin to make decisions about their behavior. If parents react positively to children's attempts at independence, they will help their children resolve the initiative-versus-guilt crisis positively.

The fourth and last stage of childhood is the **industry-versus-inferiority stage** (ages 6 to 12). During this period, increasing competency in all areas, whether social interactions or academic skills, characterizes successful psychosocial development. In contrast, difficulties in this stage lead to feelings of failure and inadequacy.

Erikson's theory suggests that psychosocial development continues throughout life, and he proposes four more crises that are faced after childhood (described in the next module). Although his theory has been criticized on several grounds—such as the imprecision of the concepts he employs and his greater emphasis on male development than female development—it remains influential and is one of the few theories that encompass the entire life span.

Cognitive Development: Children's Thinking About the World

Suppose you had two drinking glasses of different shapes—one short and broad and one tall and thin. Now imagine that you filled the short, broad one with soda about halfway and then poured the liquid from that glass into the tall one. The soda would appear to fill about three-quarters of the second glass. If someone asked you whether there was more soda in the second glass than there had been in the first, what would you say?

You might think that such a simple question hardly deserves an answer; of course there is no difference in the amount of soda in the two glasses. However, most 4-year-olds would be likely to say that there is more soda in the second glass. If you then poured the soda back into the short glass, they would say there is now less soda than there was in the taller glass.

Why are young children confused by this problem? The reason is not immediately obvious. Anyone who has observed preschoolers must be impressed by how far they have progressed from the early stages of development. They speak with ease, know the alphabet, count, play complex games, use computers, tell stories, and communicate ably. Yet despite this seeming sophistication, there are deep gaps in children's understanding of the world. Some theorists have suggested that children cannot understand certain ideas and concepts until they reach a particular stage of **cognitive development**—the process by which a child's understanding of the world changes as a function of age and experience. In contrast to the theories of physical and social development discussed earlier (such as those of Erikson), theories of cognitive development seek to explain the quantitative and qualitative intellectual advances that occur during development.

Piaget's Theory of Cognitive Development

No theory of cognitive development has had more impact than that of Swiss psychologist Jean Piaget. Piaget (1970) suggested that children around the world proceed through a series of four stages in a fixed order. He maintained that these stages differ not only in the *quantity* of information acquired at each stage but in the *quality* of knowledge and understanding as well. Taking an interactionist point of view, he suggested that movement from one stage to the next occurs when a child reaches an appropriate level of maturation *and* is exposed to relevant types of experiences. Piaget assumed that, without having such experiences, children cannot reach their highest level of cognitive growth.

Piaget proposed four stages: the sensorimotor, preoperational, concrete operational, and formal operational (see Figure 8). Let's examine each of them and the approximate ages that they span.

Sensorimotor Stage: Birth to 2 Years. During the **sensorimotor stage,** children base their understanding of the world primarily on touching, sucking, chewing, shaking, and manipulating objects. In the initial part of the stage, children have relatively little competence in representing the environment by using images, language, or other kinds of symbols. Consequently, infants lack what Piaget calls **object permanence,** the awareness that objects—and people—continue to exist even if they are out of sight.

How can we know that children lack object permanence? Although we cannot ask infants, we can observe their reactions when a toy they are playing with is hidden under a blanket. Until the age of about 9 months, children will

Cognitive development The process by which a child's understanding of the world changes as a function of age and experience.

Sensorimotor stage According to Piaget, the stage from birth to 2 years, during which a child has little competence in representing the environment by using images, language, or other symbols.

Object permanence The awareness that objects—and people—continue to exist even if they are out of sight.

STUDY ALERT

Use Figure 8 to help remember Piaget's stages of cognitive development.

Cognitive Stage	Approximate Age Range	Major Characteristics
Sensorimotor	Birth–2 years	Development of object permanence, development of motor skills, little or no capacity for symbolic representation
Preoperational	2–7 years	Development of language and symbolic thinking, egocentric thinking
Concrete operational mastery	7–12 years	Development of conservation, of concept of reversibility
Formal operational	12 years–adulthood	Development of logical and abstract thinking

FIGURE 8 According to Piaget, all children pass through four stages of cognitive development.

Preoperational stage According to Piaget, the period from 2 to 7 years of age that is characterized by language development.

Egocentric thought A way of thinking in which a child views the world entirely from his or her own perspective.

Principle of conservation The knowledge that quantity is unrelated to the arrangement and physical appearance of objects.

Concrete operational stage According to Piaget, the period from 7 to 12 years of age that is characterized by logical thought and a loss of egocentrism.

Formal operational stage According to Piaget, the period from age 12 to adulthood that is characterized by abstract thought.

make no attempt to locate the hidden toy. However, soon after that age they will begin an active search for the missing object, indicating that they have developed a mental representation of the toy. Object permanence, then, is a critical development during the sensorimotor stage.

Preoperational Stage: 2 to 7 Years. The most important development during the **preoperational stage** is the use of language. Children develop internal representational systems that allow them to describe people, events, and feelings. They even use symbols in play, pretending, for example, that a book pushed across the floor is a car.

Although children use more advanced thinking in this stage than they did in the earlier sensorimotor stage, their thinking is still qualitatively inferior to that of adults. We see this when we observe a preoperational child using **egocentric thought,** a way of thinking in which the child views the world entirely from his or her own perspective. Preoperational children think that everyone shares their perspective and knowledge.

In addition, preoperational children have not yet developed the ability to understand the **principle of conservation,** which is the knowledge that quantity is unrelated to the arrangement and physical appearance of objects. Children who have not mastered this concept do not know that the amount, volume, or length of an object does not change when its shape or configuration changes. The question about the two glasses—one short and broad and the other tall and thin—with which we began our discussion of cognitive development illustrates this point clearly. Children who do not understand the principle of conservation invariably state that the amount of liquid changes as it is poured back and forth. They cannot comprehend that a transformation in appearance does not imply a transformation in amount. Instead, it seems as reasonable to the child that there is a change in quantity as it does to the adult that there is no change.

psych2.0

WWW.MHHE.COM/PSYCHLIFE

Conservation

Concrete Operational Stage: 7 to 12 Years. Mastery of the principle of conservation marks the beginning of the **concrete operational stage.** However, children do not fully understand some aspects of conservation—such as conservation of weight and volume—for a number of years.

During the concrete operational stage, children develop the ability to think in a more logical manner, and they begin to overcome some of the egocentrism characteristic of the preoperational period. However, their thinking still displays one major limitation: they are largely bound to the concrete, physical reality of the world. For the most part, they have difficulty understanding questions of an abstract or hypothetical nature.

Formal Operational Stage: 12 Years to Adulthood. The **formal operational stage** produces a new kind of thinking that is abstract, formal, and logical. Thinking is no longer tied to events that individuals observe in the environment but makes use of logical techniques to resolve problems.

The way in which children approach the "pendulum problem" devised by Piaget (Piaget & Inhelder, 1958) illustrates the emergence of formal operational thinking. The problem solver is asked to figure out what determines how fast a pendulum swings. Is it the length of the string, the weight of the pendulum, or the force with which the pendulum is pushed? (For the record, the answer is the length of the string.)

Children in the concrete operational stage approach the problem haphazardly, without a logical or rational plan of action. For example, they may simultaneously change the length of the string and the weight on the string and the force with which they push the pendulum. Because they are varying all the factors at once, they cannot tell which factor is the critical one. In contrast, people in the formal operational stage approach the problem systematically. Acting as if they were scientists conducting an experiment, they examine the effects of changes in one variable at a time. This ability to rule out competing possibilities characterizes formal operational thought.

Although formal operational thought emerges during the teenage years, some individuals use this type of thinking only infrequently. Moreover, it appears that many individuals never reach this stage at all; most studies show that only 40 to 60 percent of college students and adults fully reach it, with some estimates running as low as 25 percent of the general population. In addition, in certain cultures—particularly those that are less technologically oriented than Western societies—almost no one reaches the formal operational stage (Keating & Clark, 1980; Genovese, 2006).

Information-Processing Approaches: Charting Children's Mental Programs

If cognitive development does not proceed as a series of stages as Piaget suggested, what does underlie the enormous growth in children's cognitive abilities that even the most untutored eye can observe? To many developmental psychologists, changes in **information processing,** the way in which people take in, use, and store information, account for cognitive development (Lacerda, von Hofsten, & Heimann, 2001; Cashon & Cohen, 2004; Munakata, 2006).

Information processing The way in which people take in, use, and store information.

Metacognition An awareness and understanding of one's own cognitive processes.

According to this approach, quantitative changes occur in children's ability to organize and manipulate information. From this perspective, children become increasingly adept at information processing, much as a computer program may become more sophisticated as a programmer modifies it on the basis of experience. Information-processing approaches consider the kinds of "mental programs" that children invoke when approaching problems.

Several significant changes occur in children's information-processing capabilities. For one thing, speed of processing increases with age, as some abilities become more automatic. The speed at which children can scan, recognize, and compare stimuli increases with age. As they grow older, children can pay attention to stimuli longer and discriminate between different stimuli more readily, and they are less easily distracted (Myerson et al., 2003; Van den Wildenberg & Van der Molen, 2004).

Memory also improves dramatically with age. Preschoolers can hold only two or three chunks of information in short-term memory, 5-year-olds can hold four, and 7-year-olds can hold five. (Adults are able to keep seven, plus or minus two, chunks in short-term memory.) The size of chunks also grows with age, as does the sophistication and organization of knowledge stored in memory (see Figure 9). Still, memory capabilities are impressive at a very early age: even before they can speak, infants can remember for months events in which they actively participated (Cowan et al., 2003; Bayliss et al., 2005a, 2005b).

Finally, improvement in information processing relates to advances in **metacognition,** an awareness and understanding of one's own cognitive processes. Metacognition involves the planning, monitoring, and revising of cognitive strategies. Younger children, who lack an awareness of their

Metacognition involves the planning, monitoring, and revising of cognitive strategies.

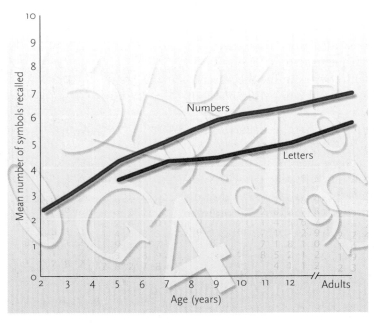

FIGURE 9 Memory span increases with age for both numbers and letters. (*Source: Adapted from Dempster, 1981.*)

own cognitive processes, often do not realize their incapabilities. Thus, when they misunderstand others, they may fail to recognize their own errors. It is only later, when metacognitive abilities become more sophisticated, that children are able to know when they *don't* understand. Such increasing sophistication reflects a change in children's *theory of mind,* their knowledge and beliefs about the way the mind operates (McCormick, 2003; Bernstein, Loftus, & Meltzoff, 2005; Matthews & Funke, 2006).

Vygotsky's View of Cognitive Development: Considering Culture

According to Russian developmental psychologist Lev Vygotsky, the culture in which we are raised significantly affects our cognitive development. In an increasingly influential view, Vygotsky suggests that the focus on individual performance of both Piagetian and information-processing approaches is misplaced. Instead, he holds that we cannot understand cognitive development without taking into account the social aspects of learning (Vygotsky, 1926/1997; Maynard & Martini, 2005; Rieber & Robinson, 2006).

Vygotsky argues that cognitive development occurs as a consequence of social interactions in which children work with others to jointly solve problems. Through such interactions, children's cognitive skills increase, and they gain the ability to function intellectually on their own. More specifically, he suggests that children's cognitive abilities increase when they encounter information that falls within their zone of proximal development. The **zone of proximal development,** or **ZPD,** is the level at which a child can almost, but not fully, comprehend or perform a task on his or her own. When children receive information that falls within the ZPD, they can increase their understanding or master a new task. In contrast, if the information lies outside children's ZPD, they will not be able to master it.

In short, cognitive development occurs when parents, teachers, or skilled peers assist a child by presenting information that is both new and within the ZPD. This type of assistance, called *scaffolding,* provides support for learning and problem solving that encourages independence and growth. Vygotsky claims that scaffolding not only promotes the solution of specific problems, but also aids in the development of overall cognitive abilities (Schaller & Crandall, 2004).

More than other approaches to cognitive development, Vygotsky's theory considers how an individual's specific cultural and social context affects intellectual growth. The way in which children understand the world grows out of interactions with parents, peers, and other members of a specific culture (John-Steiner & Mahn, 2003; Kozulin et al., 2003).

Zone of proximal development (ZPD) According to Lev Vygotsky, the level at which a child can almost, but not fully, comprehend or perform a task on his or her own.

psych2.0

WWW.MHHE.COM/PSYCHLIFE

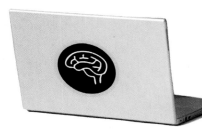

Piaget's Theory, Information-Processing Approaches, and Vygotsky's Theory

RECAP

- Newborns, or neonates, have reflexes, unlearned, involuntary responses that occur automatically in the presence of certain stimuli. (p. 294)

- Sensory abilities also develop rapidly; infants can distinguish color, depth, sound, tastes, and smells relatively soon after birth. (p. 295)

- After birth, physical development is rapid; children typically triple their birth weight in a year. (p. 296)

Explain the milestones of physical, social, and cognitive development during childhood.

- Attachment—the positive emotional bond between a child and a particular individual—marks social development in infancy. (p. 297)

- As children become older, the nature of their social interactions with peers changes. Initially play occurs relatively independently, but it becomes increasingly cooperative. (p. 298)

- The different child-rearing styles include authoritarian, permissive, authoritative, and uninvolved. (p. 300)

- According to Erikson, eight stages of psychosocial development involve people's changing interactions and understanding of themselves and others. During childhood, the four stages are trust-versus-mistrust (birth to 1½ years), autonomy-versus-shame-and-doubt (1½ to 3 years), initiative-versus-guilt (3 to 6 years), and industry-versus-inferiority (6 to 12 years). (p. 301)

- Piaget's theory suggests that cognitive development proceeds through four stages in which qualitative changes occur in thinking: the sensorimotor stage (birth to 2 years), the preoperational stage (2 to 7 years), the concrete operational stage (7 to 12 years), and the formal operational stage (12 years to adulthood). (p. 303)

- Information-processing approaches suggest that quantitative changes occur in children's ability to organize and manipulate information about the world, such as significant increases in speed of processing, attention span, and memory. In addition, children advance in metacognition, the awareness and understanding of one's own cognitive processes. (p. 305)

- Vygotsky argued that children's cognitive development occurs as a consequence of social interactions in which children and others work together to solve problems. (p. 306)

EVALUATE

1. The emotional bond that develops between a child and his or her caregiver is known as _____.

2. Match the parenting style with its definition:
   a. Rigid; highly punitive; demanding obedience
   b. Gives little direction; lax on obedience
   c. Firm but fair; tries to explain parental decisions
   d. Emotionally detached and unloving

   1. Permissive
   2. Authoritative
   3. Authoritarian
   4. Uninvolved

3. Erikson's theory of _____ development involves a series of eight stages, each of which must be resolved for a person to develop optimally.

4. Match the stage of development with the thinking style characteristic of that stage:

a. Sensorimotor   1. Egocentric thought

b. Formal operational   2. Object permanence

c. Preoperational   3. Abstract reasoning

d. Concrete operational   4. Conservation; reversibility

5. _____ - _____ theories of development suggest that the way in which a child handles information is critical to his or her development.

R E T H I N K

Do you think the widespread use of IQ testing in the United States contributes to parents' views that their children's academic success is due largely to the children's innate intelligence? Why? Would it be possible (or desirable) to change this view?

Answers to Evaluate Questions 1. attachment; 2. b-1, c-2, a-3, d-4; 3. psychosocial; 4. c-1, a-2, b-3, d-4; 5. information-processing

[K E Y   T E R M S]

Neonate *p. 293*

Reflexes *p. 295*

Attachment *p. 297*

Authoritarian parents *p. 300*

Permissive parents *p. 300*

Authoritative parents *p. 300*

Uninvolved parents *p. 301*

Temperament *p. 301*

Psychosocial development *p. 301*

Trust-versus-mistrust stage *p. 302*

Autonomy-versus-shame-and-doubt stage *p. 302*

Initiative-versus-guilt stage *p. 302*

Industry-versus-inferiority stage *p. 302*

Cognitive development *p. 303*

Sensorimotor stage *p. 303*

Object permanence *p. 303*

Preoperational stage *p. 304*

Egocentric thought *p. 304*

Principle of conservation *p. 304*

Concrete operational stage *p. 304*

Formal operational stage *p. 304*

Information processing *p. 305*

Metacognition *p. 305*

Zone of proximal development (ZPD) *p. 306*

Adolescence
Becoming an Adult

Trevor Kelson, age 15: "Keep the Hell Out of my Room!" says a sign on Trevor's bedroom wall, just above an unmade bed, a desk littered with dirty T-shirts and candy wrappers, and a floor covered with clothes. Is there a carpet? "Somewhere," he says with a grin. "I think it's gold." (Fields-Meyer, 1999, p. 53)

Like other adolescents, Trevor Kelson has characteristics that are common to adolescence—concerns about friends, parents, appearance, independence, and his future. **Adolescence,** the developmental stage between childhood and adulthood, is a crucial period. It is a time of profound changes and, occasionally, turmoil. Considerable biological change occurs as adolescents attain sexual and physical maturity. At the same time, and rivaling these physiological changes, important social, emotional, and cognitive changes occur as adolescents strive for independence and move toward adulthood.

Because many years of schooling precede most people's entry into the workforce in Western societies, the stage of adolescence is fairly long, beginning just before the teenage years and ending just after them. No longer children but considered by society to be not quite adults, adolescents face a period of rapid physical, cognitive, and social change that affects them for the rest of their lives.

LEARNING OUTCOMES

27.1 Summarize the major physical transitions that characterize adolescence.

27.2 Explain moral and cognitive development in adolescents.

27.3 Discuss social development in adolescents.

> **Adolescence** The developmental stage between childhood and adulthood.

» LO1 Physical Development: The Changing Adolescent

If you think back to the start of your own adolescence, the most dramatic changes you probably remember are physical ones. A spurt in height, the growth of breasts in girls, deepening voices in boys, the development of body hair, and intense sexual feelings cause curiosity, interest, and sometimes embarrassment for individuals entering adolescence.

The physical changes that occur at the start of adolescence result largely from the secretion of various hormones, and they affect virtually every aspect of an adolescent's life. Not since infancy has development been so dramatic. Weight and height increase

> *The physical changes that occur at the start of adolescence result largely from the secretion of various hormones, and they affect virtually every aspect of an adolescent's life.*

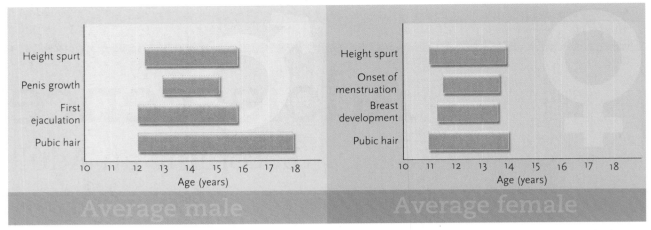

Height spurt
Penis growth
First ejaculation
Pubic hair

Age (years)
10 11 12 13 14 15 16 17 18

Average male

Height spurt
Onset of menstruation
Breast development
Pubic hair

Age (years)
10 11 12 13 14 15 16 17 18

Average female

FIGURE 1   The range of ages during which major sexual changes occur during adolescence is shown by the colored bars. *(Source: Based on Tanner, 1978.)*

Although puberty begins around age 11 or 12 for girls and 13 or 14 for boys, there are wide variations. What are some advantages and disadvantages of early puberty?

Puberty The period at which maturation of the sexual organs occurs, beginning at about age 11 or 12 for girls and 13 or 14 for boys.

rapidly because of a growth spurt that typically begins around age 10 for girls and age 12 for boys. Adolescents may grow as much as five inches in one year.

Puberty, the period at which maturation of the sexual organs occurs, begins at about age 11 or 12 for girls, when menstruation starts. However, there are wide variations (see Figure 1). For example, some girls begin to menstruate as early as age 8 or 9 or as late as age 16. Furthermore, in Western cultures, the average age at which adolescents reach sexual maturity has been steadily decreasing over the last century, most likely as a result of improved nutrition and medical care. Sexual *attraction* to others begins even before the maturation of the sexual organs, at around age 10 (see Figure 1; Tanner, 1990; Finlay, Jones, & Coleman, 2002).

For boys, the onset of puberty is marked by their first ejaculation, known as *spermarche*. Spermarche usually occurs around the age of 13 (see Figure 1). At first, relatively few sperm are produced during an ejaculation, but the amount increases significantly within a few years.

Clearly, the rate at which physical changes occur during adolescence can affect the way in which people are viewed by others and the way they view themselves. Just as important as physical changes, however, are the psychological and social changes that unfold during adolescence.

» LO2 Moral and Cognitive Development: Distinguishing Right from Wrong

In a European country, a woman is near death from a special kind of cancer. The one drug that the doctors think might save her is a medicine that a medical researcher has recently discovered. The drug is expensive to make, and the researcher is charging 10 times the cost, or $5,000, for a small dose. The sick woman's husband, Henry, approaches everyone he knows in hopes of borrowing money, but he can get together only about $2,500. He tells the researcher that his wife is dying and asks him to lower the price of the drug or let him pay later. The researcher says, "No, I discovered the drug, and I'm going to make money from it." Henry is desperate and considers stealing the drug for his wife.

What would you tell Henry to do?

Kohlberg's Theory of Moral Development

In the view of psychologist Lawrence Kohlberg, the advice you give Henry in the preceding scenario reflects your level of moral development. According to Kohlberg, people pass through a series of stages in the evolution of their sense of justice and in the kind of reasoning they use to make moral judgments (Kohlberg, 1984). Largely because of the various cognitive limitations that Piaget described, preadolescent children tend to think either in terms of concrete, unvarying rules ("It is always wrong to steal." or "I'll be punished if I steal.") or in terms of the rules of society ("Good people don't steal." or "What if everyone stole?.").

Adolescents, however, can reason on a higher plane, having typically reached Piaget's formal operational stage of cognitive development. Because they are able to comprehend broad moral principles, they can understand that morality is not always black and white and that conflict can exist between two sets of socially accepted standards.

Kohlberg (1984) suggests that the changes in moral reasoning can be understood best as a three-level sequence (see Figure 2). His theory assumes that people move through the levels in a fixed order, and that they cannot reach the highest level until about age 13—primarily because of limitations in cognitive development before that age. However, many people never reach the highest

Level	Sample Moral Reasoning of Subjects	
	In Favor of Stealing the Drug	Against Stealing the Drug
Level 1 Preconventional morality: At this level, the concrete interests of the individual are considered in terms of rewards and punishments.	"If you let your wife die, you will get in trouble. You'll be blamed for not spending the money to save her, and there'll be an investigation of you and the druggist for your wife's death."	"You shouldn't steal the drug because you'll be caught and sent to jail if you do. If you do get away, your conscience will bother you thinking how the police will catch up with you at any minute."
Level 2 Conventional morality: At this level, people approach moral problems as members of society. They are interested in pleasing others by acting as good members of society.	"If you let your wife die, you'll never be able to look anybody in the face again."	"After you steal the drug, you'll feel bad thinking how you've brought dishonor on your family and yourself; you won't be able to face anyone again."
Level 3 Postconventional morality: At this level, people use moral principles which are seen as broader than those of any particular society.	"If you don't steal the drug, and if you let your wife die, you'll always condemn yourself for it afterward. You won't be blamed and you'll have lived up to the outside rule of the law, but you won't have lived up to your own conscience and standards of honesty."	"If you steal the drug, you won't be blamed by other people, but you'll condemn yourself because you won't have lived up to your own conscience and standards of honesty."

FIGURE 2 Developmental psychologist Lawrence Kohlberg theorized that people move through a three-level sequence of moral reasoning in a fixed order. However, he contended that few people ever reach the highest level of moral reasoning.

STUDY ALERT

The difference between the Kohlberg and the Gilligan approach to moral development is significant, with Kohlberg's theory focusing on stages and Gilligan's resting on gender differences.

psych2.0
WWW.MHHE.COM/PSYCHLIFE

Stages of Moral Development

level of moral reasoning. In fact, Kohlberg found that only a relatively small percentage of adults rise above the second level of his model (Kohlberg & Ryncarz, 1990; Hedgepeth, 2005; Powers, 2006).

Moral Development in Women

One glaring shortcoming of Kohlberg's research is that he primarily used male participants. Furthermore, psychologist Carol Gilligan (1996) argues that because of men's and women's distinctive socialization experiences, a fundamental difference exists in the way each gender views moral behavior. According to Gilligan, men view morality primarily in terms of broad principles, such as justice and fairness. In contrast, women see it in terms of responsibility toward individuals and willingness to make sacrifices to help a specific individual within the context of a particular relationship. Compassion for individuals is a more salient factor in moral behavior for women than it is for men.

Because Kohlberg's model defines moral behavior largely in terms of abstract principles such as justice, Gilligan finds that it inadequately describes the moral development of females. She suggests that women's morality centers on individual well-being and social relationships—a morality of *caring*. In her view, compassionate concern for the welfare of others represents the highest level of morality.

The fact that Gilligan's conception of morality differs greatly from Kohlberg's suggests that gender plays an important role in determining what a person sees as moral. Although the research evidence is not definitive, it seems plausible that their differing conceptions of what constitutes moral behavior may lead men and women to regard the morality of a specific behavior in different ways (Weisz & Black, 2002; Lippa, 2005; Jorgensen, 2006).

» LO3 Social Development: Finding Oneself in a Social World

"Who am I?" "How do I fit into the world?" "What is life all about?"

Questions such as these assume special significance during the teenage years, as adolescents seek to find their place in the broader social world. As we will see, this quest takes adolescents along several routes.

Erikson's Theory of Psychosocial Development: The Search for Identity

Erikson's theory of psychosocial development emphasizes the search for identity during the adolescent years. As was noted earlier, psychosocial development encompasses the way people's understanding of themselves, one another, and the world around them changes during the course of development (Erikson, 1963).

The fifth stage of Erikson's theory (summarized, with the other stages, in Figure 3), the **identity-versus-role-confusion stage,** encompasses adolescence. During this stage, a time of major testing, people try to determine what is unique about themselves. They attempt to discover who they are, what their strengths are, and what kinds of roles they are best suited to play for the rest of their lives—in short, their **identity.** A person confused about the most appropriate role to play in life may lack a stable identity, adopt an unacceptable role such as that of a social deviant, or have difficulty maintaining close personal relationships later in life (Updegraff et al., 2004; Vleioras & Bosma, 2005; Goldstein, 2006).

Identity-versus-role-confusion stage According to Erikson, a time in adolescence of major testing to determine one's unique qualities.

Identity The distinguishing character of the individual: who each of us is, what our roles are, and what we are capable of.

During the identity-versus-role-confusion period, an adolescent feels pressure to identify what to do with his or her life. Because these pressures come at a time of major physical changes as well as important changes in what society expects of them, adolescents can find the period an especially difficult one. The identity-versus-role-confusion stage has another important characteristic: declining reliance on adults for information, with a shift toward using the peer group as a source of social judgments. The peer group becomes increasingly important, enabling adolescents to form close, adult-like relationships and helping them clarify their personal identities. According to Erikson, the identity-versus-role-confusion stage marks a pivotal point in psychosocial development, paving the way for continued growth and the future development of personal relationships.

From the perspective of . . .

A RETAIL MANAGER How might the needs of adolescent employees differ from the needs of adult employees? Would you use different strategies to motivate and reward adolescent and adult workers?

	Stage	Approximate Age	Positive Outcomes	Negative Outcomes
1	Trust-vs.-mistrust	Birth–1½ years	Feelings of trust from environmental support	Fear and concern regarding others
2	Autonomy-vs.-shame-and-doubt	1½–3 years	Self-sufficiency if exploration is encouraged	Doubts about self, lack of independence
3	Initiative-vs.-guilt	3–6 years	Discovery of ways to initiate actions	Guilt from actions and thoughts
4	Industry-vs.-inferiority	6–12 years	Development of sense of competence	Feelings of inferiority, no sense of mastery
5	Identity-vs.-role-confusion	Adolescence	Awareness of uniqueness of self, knowledge of role to be followed	Inability to identify appropriate roles in life
6	Intimacy-vs.-isolation	Early adulthood	Development of loving, sexual relationships and close friendships	Fear of relationships with others
7	Generativity-vs.-stagnation	Middle adulthood	Sense of contribution to continuity of life	Trivialization of one's activities
8	Ego-integrity-vs.-despair	Late adulthood	Sense of unity in life's accomplishments	Regret over lost opportunities of life

FIGURE 3 Erikson's stages of psychosocial development. According to Erikson, people proceed through eight stages of psychosocial development across their lives. He suggested that each stage requires the resolution of a crisis or conflict and may produce both positive and negative outcomes.

THE WORLD'S FIRST GENETICALLY ENGINEERED HUMAN HITS ADOLESCENCE

During early adulthood, people enter the **intimacy-versus-isolation stage.** Spanning the period of early adulthood (from postadolescence to the early thirties), this stage focuses on developing close relationships with others. Difficulties during this stage result in feelings of loneliness and a fear of such relationships, whereas successful resolution of the crises of the stage results in the possibility of forming relationships that are intimate on a physical, intellectual, and emotional level.

Development continues during middle adulthood as people enter the **generativity-versus-stagnation stage.** Generativity is the ability to contribute to one's family, community, work, and society, and to assist the development of the younger generation. Success in this stage results in a person's feeling positive about the continuity of life, whereas difficulties lead a person to feel that his or her activities are trivial or stagnant and have done nothing for upcoming generations. In fact, if a person has not successfully resolved the identity crisis of adolescence, he or she may still be foundering in identifying an appropriate career, for example.

Finally, the last stage of psychosocial development, the **ego-integrity-versus-despair** stage, spans later adulthood and continues until death. Now a sense of accomplishment signifies success in resolving the difficulties presented by this stage of life; failure to resolve the difficulties results in regret over what might have been achieved but was not.

Intimacy-versus-isolation stage According to Erikson, a period during early adulthood that focuses on developing close relationships.

Generativity-versus-stagnation stage According to Erikson, a period in middle adulthood during which we take stock of our contributions to family and society.

Ego-integrity-versus-despair stage According to Erikson, a period from late adulthood until death during which we review life's accomplishments and failures.

Stormy Adolescence: Myth or Reality?

Does puberty invariably foreshadow a stormy, rebellious period of adolescence?

At one time, psychologists thought that most children entering adolescence were beginning a period fraught with stress and unhappiness. However, research now shows that this characterization is largely a myth,

Based on your experiences, do you believe adolescence to be stormy?

that most young people pass through adolescence without appreciable turmoil in their lives, and that parents speak easily—and fairly often—with their children about a variety of topics (van Wel, Linssen, & Abma, 2000; Granic, Hollenstein, & Dishion, 2003).

Not that adolescence is completely calm! In most families with adolescents, the amount of arguing and bickering clearly rises. Most young teenagers, as part of their search for identity, experience tension between their attempts to become independent from their parents and their actual dependence on them. They may experiment with a range of behaviors, flirting with a variety of activities that their parents, and even society as a whole, find objectionable. Happily, though, for most families such tensions stabilize during middle adolescence—around age 15 or 16—and eventually decline around age 18 (Smetana, Daddis, & Chuang, 2003; Smetana, 2005).

Adolescent Suicide

Although the vast majority of teenagers pass through adolescence without major psychological difficulties, some experience unusually severe psychological problems. Sometimes those problems become so extreme that adolescents take their own lives. Suicide is the third-leading cause of death for adolescents (after accidents and homicide) in the United States. More teenagers and young adults die from suicide than from cancer, heart disease, AIDS, birth defects, stroke, pneumonia and influenza, and chronic lung disease combined (Centers for Disease Control [CDC], 2004b).

Male adolescents are five times more likely to commit suicide than are females, although females *attempt* suicide more often than males do. The rate of adolescent suicide is significantly greater among whites than among nonwhites. However, the suicide rate of African American males has increased much more rapidly than has that of white males over the last two decades. Native Americans have the highest suicide rate of any ethnic group in the United States, and Asian Americans have the lowest rate (CDC, 2004b; Gutierrez et al., 2005; Boden, Fergusson, & Horwood, 2007).

Although the question of why adolescent suicide rates are so high remains unanswered, several factors put adolescents at risk. One factor is depression, characterized by unhappiness, extreme fatigue, and—a variable that seems especially important—a profound sense of hopelessness. In other cases, adolescents who commit suicide are perfectionists, inhibited socially and prone to extreme anxiety when they face any social or academic challenge (see Figure 4; CDC, 2004b; Richardson et al., 2005; Caelian, 2006).

Family background and adjustment difficulties are also related to suicide. A long-standing history of conflicts between parents and children may lead to adolescent behavior problems, such as delinquency, dropping out of school, and aggressive tendencies. In addition, teenage alcoholics and abusers of other drugs have a relatively high rate of suicide (Stronski, Ireland, & Michaud, 2000; Winstead & Sanchez, 2005).

These students are mourning the deaths of two classmates who committed suicide. The rate of suicide among teenagers has risen significantly over the last few decades. Can you think of reasons for this phenomenon?

FIGURE 4 According to a review of phone calls to one telephone help line, adolescents who were considering suicide most often mentioned family, peer relationships, and self-esteem problems. *(Source: Boehm & Campbell, 1995.)*

psych2.0

WWW.MHHE.COM/PSYCHLIFE

Suicide Risk Factors

Several warning signs indicate when a teenager's problems may be severe enough to warrant concern about the possibility of a suicide attempt. They include the following:

- School problems, such as missing classes, truancy, and a sudden change in grades
- Frequent incidents of self-destructive behavior, such as careless accidents
- Loss of appetite or excessive eating
- Withdrawal from friends and peers
- Sleeping problems
- Signs of depression, tearfulness, or overt indications of psychological difficulties, such as hallucinations
- A preoccupation with death, an afterlife, or what would happen "if I died"
- Putting affairs in order, such as giving away prized possessions or making arrangements for the care of a pet
- An explicit announcement of thoughts of suicide

For immediate help with a suicide-related problem, call 1-800-273-8255, a national hotline staffed with trained counselors, or visit the Web at www.suicidepreventionlifeline.org.

EXPLORING diversity

Rites of Passage: Coming of Age around the World

It is not easy for male members of the Awa tribe in New Guinea to make the transition from childhood to adulthood. First come whippings with sticks and prickly branches, both for the boys' own past misdeeds and in honor of those tribesmen who were killed in warfare. In the next phase of the ritual, adults jab sharpened sticks into the boys' nostrils. Then they force a five-foot length of vine into the boys' throats, until they gag and vomit. Finally, tribesmen cut the boys' genitals, causing severe bleeding.

Although the rites that mark the coming of age of boys in the Awa tribe sound horrifying to Westerners, they are comparable to those in other cultures. In some, youths must kneel on hot coals without displaying pain. In others, girls must toss wads of burning cotton from hand to hand and allow themselves to be bitten by hundreds of ants (Selsky, 1997).

Other cultures have less fearsome, although no less important, ceremonies that mark the passage from childhood to adulthood. For instance, when a girl first menstruates in traditional Apache tribes, the event is marked by dawn-to-dusk chanting. Western religions, too, have several types of celebrations, including bar and bat mitzvahs at age 13 for Jewish boys and girls and confirmation ceremonies for children in many Christian denominations (Magida, 2006).

In most societies, males, but not females, are the focus of coming-of-age ceremonies. The renowned anthropologist Margaret Mead remarked, only partly in jest, that the preponderance of male ceremonies might reflect the fact that "the worry that boys will not grow up to be men is much more widespread than that girls will not grow up to be women" (1949, p. 195). Said another way, it may be that in most cultures men traditionally have higher status than women, and therefore those cultures regard boys' transition into adulthood as more important.

However, another fact may explain why most cultures place greater emphasis on male rites than on female ones. For females, the transition from childhood is marked by a definite, biological event: menstruation. For males, in contrast, no single event can be used to pinpoint entry into adulthood. Thus, men are forced to rely on culturally determined rituals to acknowledge their arrival into adulthood.

RECAP

Summarize the major physical transitions that characterize adolescence.

- Adolescence, the developmental stage between childhood and adulthood, is marked by the onset of puberty, the point at which sexual maturity occurs. The age at which puberty begins has implications for the way people view themselves and the way others see them. (p. 309)

Explain moral and cognitive development in adolescents.

- Moral judgments during adolescence increase in sophistication, according to Kohlberg's three-level model. Although Kohlberg's levels provide an adequate description of males' moral judgments, Gilligan suggests that women view morality in terms of caring for individuals rather than in terms of broad, general principles of justice. (p. 310)

Describe social development in adolescents.

- According to Erikson's model of psychosocial development, adolescence may be accompanied by an identity crisis. Adolescence is followed by three more stages of psychosocial development that cover the remainder of the life span. (p. 312)
- Suicide is the third-leading cause of death in adolescents. (p. 315)

EVALUATE

1. _____ is the period during which the sexual organs begin to mature.

2. _____ proposed a set of three levels of moral development ranging from reasoning based on rewards and punishments to abstract thinking involving concepts of justice.

3. Gilligan's theory of moral development focuses on the morality of caring, in which concern for others represents the highest level of morality. True or false?

4. Erikson believed that during adolescence, people must search for _____, whereas during the early adulthood, the major task is _____.

RETHINK

What implications does the fact that puberty is starting earlier have for the nature of schooling? In what ways do school cultures help or hurt students who are going through adolescence?

Answers to Evaluate Questions 1. puberty; 2. Kohlberg; 3. True; 4. identity, intimacy

[KEY TERMS]

Adolescence *p. 309*

Puberty *p. 310*

Identity-versus-role-confusion stage *p. 312*

Identity *p. 312*

Intimacy-versus-isolation stage *p. 314*

Generativity-versus-stagnation stage *p. 314*

Ego-integrity-versus-despair stage *p. 314*

module 28

Adulthood

Psychologists generally agree that early adulthood begins around age 20 and lasts until about age 40 to 45, with middle adulthood beginning then and continuing until around age 65. Despite the enormous importance of these periods of life in terms of both the accomplishments that occur in them and their overall length (together they span some 45 years), they have been studied less than has any other stage. For one reason, the physical changes that occur during these periods are less apparent and more gradual than are those at other times during the life span. In addition, the diverse social changes that arise during this period defy simple categorization. However, developmental psychologists have recently begun to focus on the period, particularly on the social changes in the family and women's careers.

» LO1 Physical Development: The Peak of Health

For most people, early adulthood marks the peak of physical health. From about 18 to 25 years of age, people's strength is greatest, their reflexes are quickest, and their chances of dying from disease are quite slim. Moreover, reproductive capabilities are at their highest level.

Around age 25, the body becomes slightly less efficient and more susceptible to disease. Overall, however, ill health remains the exception; most people stay remarkably healthy during early adulthood. (Can you think of any machine other than the body that can operate without pause for so long a period?)

During middle adulthood people gradually become aware of changes in their bodies. People often experience weight gain (although they can avoid such increases through diet and exercise). Furthermore, the sense organs gradually become less sensitive, and reactions to stimuli are slower. But generally, the physical declines that occur during middle adulthood are minor and often unnoticeable (DiGiovanna, 1994; Whitbourne, 2007).

The major biological change that does occur during middle adulthood pertains to reproductive capabilities. On average, during their late forties or early

LEARNING OUTCOMES

28.1 Explain physical development in adulthood.

28.2 Discuss social development in adulthood.

28.3 State the impact of marriage, children, and divorce on families.

28.4 Discuss the later years of adulthood.

28.5 Explain the physical changes that occur in late adulthood.

28.6 Identify the cognitive changes that occur in late adulthood.

28.7 Discuss the social aspects of late adulthood.

28.8 Describe how people can adjust to death.

During middle adulthood people gradually become aware of changes in their bodies.

Women's reactions to menopause vary significantly across cultures, and according to one study, the more a society values old age, the less difficulty its women have during menopause. Why do you think this would be the case?

Menopause The period during which women stop menstruating and are no longer fertile.

fifties, women begin **menopause,** during which they stop menstruating and are no longer fertile. Because menopause is accompanied by a significant reduction in the production of estrogen, a female hormone, women sometimes experience symptoms such as hot flashes, sudden sensations of heat. Many symptoms can be treated through *hormone therapy (HT),* in which menopausal women take the hormones estrogen and progesterone.

However, hormone therapy poses several dangers, such as an increase in the risk of breast cancer, blood clots, and coronary heart disease. These uncertainties make the routine use of HT controversial. Currently, the medical consensus seems to be that younger women with severe menopausal symptoms ought to consider HT on a short-term basis. On the other hand, HT is less appropriate for older women after menopause (Plonczynski & Plonczynski, 2007; Rossouw et al., 2007; Lindh-Åstrand, Brynhildsen, & Hoffmann, 2007).

For men, the aging process during middle adulthood is somewhat subtler. There are no physiological signals of increasing age equivalent to the end of menstruation in women; that is, no male menopause exists. In fact, men remain fertile and are capable of fathering children until well into late adulthood. However, some gradual physical decline occurs: sperm production decreases, and the frequency of orgasm tends to decline. Once again, though, any psychological difficulties associated with these changes are usually brought about not so much by physical deterioration as by the inability of an aging individual to meet the exaggerated standards of youthfulness.

» LO2 Social Development: Working at Life

Whereas physical changes during adulthood reflect development of a quantitative nature, social developmental transitions are qualitative and more profound. During this period, people typically launch themselves into careers, marriage, and families.

The entry into early adulthood is usually marked by leaving one's childhood home and entering the world of work. People envision life goals and make career choices. Their lives often center on their careers, which form an important part of their identity (Vaillant & Vaillant, 1990; Levinson, 1990).

In their early forties, however, people may begin to question their lives as they enter a period called the *midlife transition.* The idea that life will end at some point becomes increasingly influential in their thinking, and they may question their past accomplishments (Gould, 1978). Facing signs of physical aging and feeling dissatisfaction with their lives, some individuals experience what has been popularly labeled a *midlife crisis.*

In most cases, though, the passage into middle age is relatively calm. Most 40-year-olds view their lives and accomplishments positively enough to proceed relatively smoothly through midlife, and the forties and fifties are often a particularly rewarding period. Rather than looking to the future, people concentrate on the present, and their involvement with their families, friends, and other social groups takes on new importance. A major developmental thrust of this period is coming to terms with one's circumstances (Whitbourne, 2000).

Finally, during the last stages of adulthood, people become more accepting of others and of their own lives and are less concerned about issues or problems that once bothered them. People come to accept the fact that death is inevitable, and they try to understand their accomplishments in terms of the broader meaning of life. Although people may begin, for the first time, to label themselves as "old," many also develop a sense of wisdom and feel freer to enjoy life (Baltes & Kunzmann, 2003; Miner-Rubino, Winter, & Stewart, 2004; Ward-Baker, 2007).

» LO3 Marriage, Children, and Divorce: Family Ties

In the typical fairy tale, a dashing young man and a beautiful young woman marry, have children, and live happily ever after. However, that scenario does not match the realities of love and marriage in the twenty-first century. Today, it is just as likely that the man and woman would first live together, then get married and have children, but ultimately get divorced.

The percentage of U.S. households made up of unmarried couples has increased dramatically over the last two decades. At the same time, the average age at which marriage takes place is higher than at any time since the turn of the last century. These changes have been dramatic, and they suggest that the institution of marriage has changed considerably from earlier historical periods.

When people do marry, the probability of divorce is high, especially for younger couples. Even though divorce rates have been declining since they peaked in 1981, about half of all first marriages end in divorce. Before they are 18 years old, two-fifths of children will experience the breakup of their parents' marriages. Moreover, the rise in divorce is not just a U.S. phenomenon: the divorce rate has accelerated over the last several decades in most industrialized countries. In some countries, the increase has been enormous. In South Korea, for example, the divorce rate quadrupled from 11 percent to 47 percent in the 12-year period ending in 2002 (Schaefer, 2000; Lankov, 2004; Olson & DeFrain, 2005).

Changes in marriage and divorce trends have doubled the number of single-parent households in the United States over the last two decades. Almost 25 percent of all family households are now headed by one parent, compared with 13 percent in 1970. If present trends continue, almost three-fourths of American children will spend some portion of their lives in a single-parent family before they turn 18. For children in minority households, the numbers are even higher. Almost 60 percent of all black children and more than a third of Hispanic children live in homes with only one parent. Furthermore, in most single-parent families, it is the mother, rather than the father, with whom the children reside—a phenomenon that is consistent across racial and ethnic groups throughout the industrialized world (U.S. Bureau of the Census, 2000).

Changing Roles of Men and Women: The Time of Their Lives

One of the major changes in family life in the last two decades has been the evolution of men's and women's roles. More women than ever before act simultaneously as wives, mothers, and wage earners—in contrast to women in traditional marriages, in which the husband is the sole wage earner and the wife assumes primary responsibility for care of the home and children.

Close to 75 percent of all married women with school-age children are now employed outside the home, and 55 percent of mothers with children under age 6 are working. In the mid-1960s, only 17 percent of mothers of 1-year-olds worked full-time; now, more than half are in the labor force (U.S. Bureau of the Census, 2000; Halpern, 2005).

From the perspective of . . .

A NEW EMPLOYEE How would an understanding of human development enable you to work more effectively with co-workers who are younger than you? Older than you?

Women's "Second Shift"

The number of hours put in by working mothers can be staggering. One survey, for instance, found that if we add the number of hours worked on the job and in the home, employed mothers of children under 3 years of age put in an average of 90 hours per week! The additional work performed by women is sometimes called the "second shift." National surveys show women who are both employed and mothers put in an extra month of 24-hour days during the course of a year. Researchers see similar patterns in many developing societies throughout the world, with women working at full-time jobs and also having primary responsibilities for child care (Hochschild, 2001; Jacobs & Gerson, 2004; U.S. Bureau of Labor Statistics, 2007).

Consequently, rather than careers being a substitute for what women do at home, they often exist in addition to the role of homemaker. It is not surprising that some wives feel resentment toward husbands who spend less time on child care and housework than the wives had expected before the birth of their children (Stier & Lewin-Epstein, 2000; Kiecolt, 2003; Gerstel, 2005).

» LO4 The Later Years of Life: Growing Old

By focusing on the period of life that starts at around age 65, *gerontologists*, specialists who study aging, are making important contributions to clarifying the capabilities of older adults. Their work is demonstrating that significant developmental processes continue even during old age. And as life expectancy increases, the number of people who reach older adulthood will continue to grow substantially. Consequently, developing an understanding of late adulthood has become a critical priority for psychologists (Birren, 1996; Moody, 2000, Schaie, 2005).

How might an understanding of the physical and mental changes in older adults help you treat an elderly patient, particularly in a high-stress, emergency situation?

» LO5 Physical Changes in Late Adulthood: The Aging Body

psych2.0
WWW.MHHE.COM/PSYCHLIFE

Attitudes toward Aging

Many physical changes are brought about by the aging process. The most obvious are those of appearance—hair thinning and turning gray, skin wrinkling and folding, and sometimes a slight loss of height as the thickness of the disks between vertebrae in the spine decreases—but subtler changes also occur in the body's biological functioning. For example, sensory capabilities decrease as a result of aging: vision, hearing, smell, and taste become less sensitive. Reaction time slows, and physical stamina changes (Stenklev & Laukli, 2004; Schieber, 2006; Madden, 2007).

What are the reasons for these physical declines? **Genetic preprogramming theories of aging** suggest that human cells have a built-in time limit to their reproduction. These theories suggest that after a certain time cells stop dividing or become harmful to the body—as if a kind of automatic self-destruct button had been pushed. In contrast, **wear-and-tear theories of aging** suggest that the mechanical functions of the body simply work less efficiently as people age. Waste by-products of energy production eventually accumulate, and mistakes are made when cells divide. Eventually the body, in effect, wears out, just as an old automobile does (Ly et al., 2000; Miquel, 2006; Hayflick, 2007).

Genetic preprogramming theories of aging Theories that suggest that human cells have a built-in time limit to their reproduction, and that after a certain time they are no longer able to divide.

Wear-and-tear theories of aging Theories that suggest that the mechanical functions of the body simply stop working efficiently.

» LO6 Cognitive Changes: Thinking About—and During—Late Adulthood

STUDY ALERT

Two major theories of aging—the genetic preprogramming and the wear-and-tear views—explain some of the physical changes that take place in older adults.

At one time, many gerontologists would have agreed with the popular view that older adults are forgetful and confused. Today, however, most research indicates that this assessment is far from an accurate one of older people's capabilities. One reason for the change in view is that more sophisticated

Module 28 ADULTHOOD **323**

research techniques exist for studying the cognitive changes that occur in late adulthood.

Still, some declines in intellectual functioning during late adulthood do occur, although the pattern of age differences is not uniform for different types of cognitive abilities (see Figure 1). In general, skills relating to *fluid intelligence* (which involves information-processing skills such as memory, calculations, and analogy solving) show declines in late adulthood. In contrast, skills relating to *crystallized intelligence* (intelligence based on the accumulation of information, skills, and strategies learned through experience) remain steady and in some cases actually improve (Stankov, 2003; Rozencwajg et al., 2005; van Hooren, Valentijn, & Bosma, 2007).

Even when changes in intellectual functioning occur during late adulthood, people often are able to compensate for any decline. They can still learn what they want to; it may just take more time. Furthermore, teaching older adults strategies for dealing with new problems can prevent declines in performance (Saczynski, Willis, & Schaie, 2002; Cavallini, Pagnin, & Vecchi, 2003; Peters et al., 2007).

Memory Changes in Late Adulthood: Are Older Adults Forgetful?

One of the characteristics most frequently attributed to late adulthood is forgetfulness. How accurate is this assumption?

Most evidence suggests that memory change is not an inevitable part of the aging process. Even when people show memory declines during late adulthood, their deficits are limited to certain types of memory. For instance, losses tend to be limited to episodic memories, which relate to specific experiences in people's lives. Other types of memories, such as semantic memories (which refer to general knowledge and facts) and implicit memories (memories of which we are not consciously aware), are largely unaffected by age (Fleischman et al., 2004; Mitchell & Schmitt, 2006; St. Jacques & Levine, 2007).

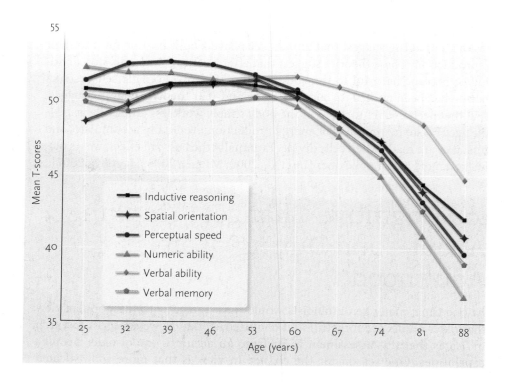

FIGURE 1 Age-related changes in intellectual skills vary according to the specific cognitive ability in question. (*Source: Schaie, 2005.*)

Some cases of memory loss are produced by disease. For instance, **Alzheimer's disease** is a progressive brain disorder that leads to a gradual and irreversible decline in cognitive abilities. Nineteen percent of people age 75 to 84 have Alzheimer's, and almost 50 percent of people over age 85 are affected by the disease. Unless a cure is found, some 14 million people will experience Alzheimer's by 2050—more than three times the current number (Cowley, 2000; Feinberg, 2002; Rogers, 2007).

Alzheimer's occurs when production of the *beta amyloid precursor protein* goes awry, producing large clumps of cells that trigger inflammation and deterioration of nerve cells. The brain shrinks, neurons die, and several areas of the hippocampus and frontal and temporal lobes deteriorate. So far, there is no effective treatment (Blennow & Vanmechelen, 2003; Wolfe, 2006; Medeiros et al., 2007).

In sum, declines in cognitive functioning in late adulthood are, for the most part, not inevitable. The key to maintaining cognitive skills may lie in intellectual stimulation. Like the rest of us, older adults need a stimulating environment in order to hone and maintain their skills (Bosma et al., 2003; Glisky, 2007).

Alzheimer's disease A progressive brain disorder that leads to a gradual and irreversible decline in cognitive abilities.

Disengagement theory of aging A theory that suggests that aging produces a gradual withdrawal from the world on physical, psychological, and social levels.

From the perspective of . . .

A MEDICAL ASSISTANT How would you handle someone who believed that getting older had only negative consequences?

» LO7 The Social World of Late Adulthood: Old but Not Alone

Just as the view that old age predictably means mental decline has proved to be wrong, so has the view that late adulthood inevitably brings loneliness. People in late adulthood most often see themselves as functioning members of society, with only a small number of them reporting that loneliness is a serious problem (Binstock & George, 1996; Jylha, 2004).

Certainly, late adulthood brings significant challenges. People who have spent their adult lives working enter retirement, bringing about a major shift in the role they play. Moreover, many people must face the death of their spouse. Especially if the marriage has been a long and good one, the death of a partner means the loss of a companion, confidante, and lover. It can also bring about changes in economic well-being.

There is no single way to age successfully. According to the **disengagement theory of aging,** aging produces a

Although there are declines in fluid intelligence in late adulthood, skills relating to crystallized intelligence remain steady and may actually improve.

Activity theory of aging A theory that suggests that the elderly who are most successful while aging are those who maintain the interests and activities they had during middle age.

Life review The process by which people examine and evaluate their lives.

gradual withdrawal from the world on physical, psychological, and social levels. However, such disengagement serves an important purpose, providing an opportunity for increased reflectiveness and decreased emotional investment in others at a time of life when social relationships will inevitably be ended by death (Adams, 2004; Wrosch, Bauer, & Scheier, 2005).

The **activity theory of aging** presents an alternative view of aging, holding that the people who age most successfully are those who maintain the interests, activities, and level of social interaction they experienced during middle adulthood. According to activity theory, late adulthood should reflect a continuation, as much as possible, of the activities in which people participated during the earlier part of their lives (Crosnoe & Elder, 2002; Nimrod & Kleiber, 2007).

Regardless of whether people become disengaged or maintain their activities from earlier stages of life, most engage in a process of **life review,** in which they examine and evaluate their lives. Remembering and reconsidering what has occurred in the past, people in late adulthood often come to a better understanding of themselves, sometimes resolving lingering problems and conflicts, and facing their lives with greater wisdom and serenity.

Clearly, people in late adulthood are not just marking time until death. Rather, old age is a time of continued growth and development, as important as any other period of life.

becoming an *informed consumer* **OF PSYCHOLOGY**

Adjusting to Death

At some time in our lives, we all face death—certainly our own, as well as the deaths of friends, loved ones, and even strangers. Although there is nothing more inevitable in life, death remains a frightening, emotion-laden topic. Certainly, little is more stressful than the death of a loved one or the contemplation of our own imminent death, and preparing for death is one of our most crucial developmental tasks (see the Try It! box to assess your own attitudes toward death).

How Do You Feel About Death?

To assess your feelings about death, complete the following questionnaire. For statements 1 through 11, use these scale labels:

   1 = Never; 2 = Rarely; 3 = Sometimes; and 4 = Often

 1. I think about my own death. _____
 2. I think about the death of loved ones. _____
 3. I think about dying young. _____
 4. I think about the possibility of my being killed on a busy road. _____
 5. I have fantasies of my own death. _____
 6. I think about death just before I go to sleep. _____
 7. I think of how I would act if I knew I were to die within a given period of time. _____
 8. I think of how my relatives would act and feel upon my death. _____
 9. When I am sick, I think about death. _____
10. When I am outside during a lightning storm, I think about the possibility of being struck by lightning. _____
11. When I am in a car, I think about the high incidence of traffic fatalities. _____

For statements 12 through 30, use these scale labels:

   1 = I strongly agree; 2 = I somewhat agree; 3 = I somewhat disagree; and 4 = I strongly disagree

12. I think people should first become concerned about death when they are old. _____
13. I am much more concerned about death than those around me. _____
14. Death hardly concerns me. _____
15. My general outlook just doesn't allow for morbid thoughts. _____
16. The prospect of my own death arouses anxiety in me. _____
17. The prospect of my own death depresses me. _____
18. The prospect of the death of my loved ones arouses anxiety in me. _____
19. The knowledge that I will surely die does not in any way affect the conduct of my life. _____
20. I envisage my own death as a painful, nightmarish experience. _____
21. I am afraid of dying. _____
22. I am afraid of being dead. _____
23. Many people become disturbed at the sight of a new grave, but it does not bother me. _____
24. I am disturbed when I think about the shortness of life. _____
25. Thinking about death is a waste of time. _____
26. Death should not be regarded as a tragedy if it occurs after a productive life. _____
27. The inevitable death of humanity poses a serious challenge to the meaningfulness of human existence. _____
28. The death of the individual is ultimately beneficial because it facilitates change in society. _____
29. I have a desire to live on after death. _____

(continued)

30. The question of whether or not there is a future life worries me considerably. _____

Scoring

If you rated any of these items: 13, 16, 17, 18, 20, 21, 22, 24, 27, 29, and 30, as 1, change your score to 4; those you rated as 2, change to 3; those you rated as 3, change to 2; and those you rated as 4, change to 1. Add up your scores.

Average scores on the scale typically range from about 68 to 80. If you scored about 80, death is something that seems to produce some degree of anxiety. On the other hand, scores lower than 68 suggest that you experience little fear of death.

Source: Dickstein, 1972.

A generation ago, talk of death was taboo. The topic was never mentioned to dying people, and gerontologists had little to say about it. That changed, however, with the pioneering work of Elisabeth Kübler-Ross, who brought the subject of death into the open with her observation that those facing impending death tend to move through five broad stages (Kübler-Ross & Kessler, 2005):

- *Denial.* In this stage, people resist the idea that they are dying. Even if told that their chances for survival are small, they refuse to admit that they are facing death.
- *Anger.* After moving beyond the denial stage, dying people become angry—angry at people around them who are in good health, angry at medical professionals for being ineffective, angry at God.
- *Bargaining.* Anger leads to bargaining, in which the dying try to think of ways to postpone death. They may decide to dedicate their lives to religion if God saves them; they may say, "If only I can live to see my son married, I will accept death then."
- *Depression.* When dying people come to feel that bargaining is of no use, they move to the next stage: depression. They realize that their lives really are coming to an end, leading to what Kübler-Ross calls "preparatory grief" for their own deaths.
- *Acceptance.* In this stage, people accept impending death. Usually they are unemotional and uncommunicative; it is as if they have made peace with themselves and are expecting death with no bitterness.

It is important to keep in mind that not everyone experiences each of these stages in the same way. In fact, Kübler-Ross's stages pertain only to people who are fully aware that they are dying and have the time to evaluate their impending death. Furthermore, vast differences occur in the way individuals react to impending death. The specific cause and duration of dying, as well as the person's sex, age, and personality and the type of support received from family and friends, all have an impact on how people respond to death (Carver & Scheier, 2002; Coyle, 2006).

Few of us enjoy the contemplation of death. Yet awareness of its psychological aspects and consequences can make its inevitable arrival less anxiety-producing and perhaps more understandable.

RECAP

Explain physical development in adulthood.

- Early adulthood marks the peak of physical health. Physical changes occur relatively gradually in men and women during adulthood (p. 319)
- One major physical change occurs at the end of middle adulthood for women: they begin menopause, after which they are no longer fertile. (p. 320)

Discuss social development in adulthood.

- During middle adulthood, people typically experience a midlife transition in which the notion that life is not unending becomes more important. In some cases this may lead to a midlife crisis, although the passage into middle age is typically relatively calm. (p. 320)
- As aging continues during middle adulthood, people realize in their fifties that their lives and accomplishments are fairly well set, and they try to come to terms with them. (p. 320)

State the impact of marriage, children, and divorce on families.

- Among the important developmental milestones during adulthood are marriage, family changes, and divorce. Another important determinant of adult development is work. (p. 321)

Discuss the later years of adulthood.

- Gerontologists, specialists who study aging, are making important contributions to clarifying the capabilities of older adults. (p. 322)

Explain the physical changes that occur in late adulthood.

- Old age may bring marked physical declines caused by genetic preprogramming or physical wear and tear. (p. 323)
- Although the activities of people in late adulthood are not all that different from those of younger people, older adults experience declines in reaction time, sensory abilities, and physical stamina. (p. 323)

Identify the cognitive changes that occur in late adulthood.

- Intellectual declines are not an inevitable part of aging. (p. 323)
- Fluid intelligence does decline with age, and long-term memory abilities are sometimes impaired. (p. 324)
- Crystallized intelligence shows slight increases with age, and short-term memory remains at about the same level. (p. 324)

Discuss the social aspects of late adulthood.

- Disengagement theory sees successful aging as a process of gradual withdrawal from the physical, psychological, and social worlds. In contrast, activity theory suggests that the maintenance of interests and activities from earlier years leads to successful aging. (p. 325)

Describe how people can adjust to death.

- According to Kübler-Ross, dying people move through five stages as they face death: denial, anger, bargaining, depression, and acceptance. (p. 328)

EVALUATE

1. Rob recently turned 40 and surveyed his goals and accomplishments to date. Although he has accomplished a lot, he realized that many of his goals will not be met in his lifetime. This stage is called a _____ _____.

2. _____ _____ theories suggest that there is a maximum time span in which cells are able to reproduce. This time limit explains the eventual breakdown of the body during old age.

3. Lower IQ test scores during late adulthood do not necessarily mean a decrease in intelligence. True or false?

4. During old age, a person's _____ intelligence continues to increase, whereas _____ intelligence may decline.

5. In Kübler-Ross's _____ stage, people resist the idea of death. In the _____ stage, they attempt to make deals to avoid death, and in the _____ stage, they passively await death.

RETHINK

Is the possibility that life may be extended for several decades a mixed blessing? What societal consequences might an extended life span bring about?

KEY TERMS

Menopause *p. 320*

Genetic preprogramming theories of aging *p. 323*

Wear-and-tear theories of aging *p. 323*

Alzheimer's disease *p. 325*

Disengagement theory of aging *p. 325*

Activity theory of aging *p. 326*

Life review *p. 326*

looking BACK

Psychology on the Web

1. Find information on the Web about gene therapy. What recent advances in gene therapy have been made by researchers? What developments appear to be on the horizon? What ethical issues have been raised regarding the use of gene therapy to produce children with characteristics specified by their parents?

2. Find different answers to the question "Why do people die?" Search the Web for scientific, philosophical, and spiritual/religious answers. Write a summary in which you compare the different approaches to this question. How does the thinking in any one realm influence the thinking in the others?

the case of ... JEAN SWEETLAND, THE WOMAN WITH TOO MANY HATS

Jean Sweetland never expected that she would one day have so many different hats to wear. But now, in her early forties, when Jean comes home from her full-time job as a nurse and takes off her nurse's cap, it seems as though her day has barely started. With two teenage children living at home, Jean next must put on her mother's hat and enforce household rules, dispense advice, help with homework, or just provide a shoulder to cry on. Before her husband comes home from his own job, Jean has to pop on her chef's hat and get dinner started; the maid's cap will come out later, when Jean does the family's laundry and cleans the bathrooms. As if all this weren't enough, the responsibility has fallen to Jean for looking after her aging mother as well. Two or three evenings a week Jean slips on her daughter's hat and makes the trip across town to her mother's house, where she spends an hour or so paying bills, restocking the cupboards, and helping with other household chores.

Jean loves her family and she tries very hard to be the mother, wife, and daughter that they all need her to be—but the conflicting demands on her time are stressful and often tiresome. In recent months Jean has increasingly found herself wondering what became of her own wants and needs , and she has begun asking herself hard questions about the direction her life is headed.

1. How typical is the Sweetland family structure? In what ways is Jean's situation typical of women her age?

2. What would be your best guess as to Jean Sweetland's parenting style, and why do you think so?

3. Describe the stage of social development that Jean Sweetland's adolescent children are most likely experiencing. In what ways might their own development be influencing Jean's?

4. If you were Jean's physician, how would you explain to her the changes that might be occurring in her aging mother?

5. Describe how Jean might react if her mother were to die? What stages of grief might she pass through?

full circle

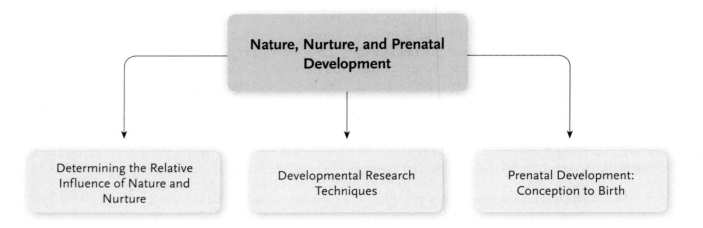

Nature, Nurture, and Prenatal Development

Determining the Relative Influence of Nature and Nurture

Developmental Research Techniques

Prenatal Development: Conception to Birth

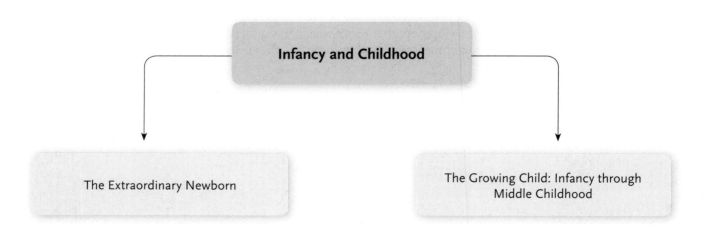

Infancy and Childhood

The Extraordinary Newborn

The Growing Child: Infancy through Middle Childhood

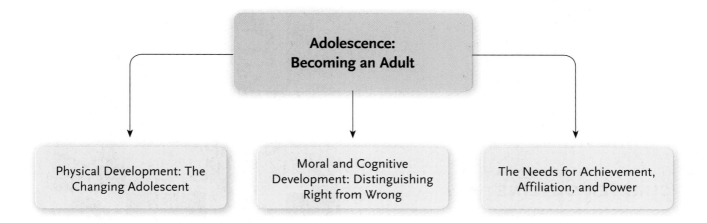

Adolescence: Becoming an Adult

Physical Development: The Changing Adolescent

Moral and Cognitive Development: Distinguishing Right from Wrong

The Needs for Achievement, Affiliation, and Power

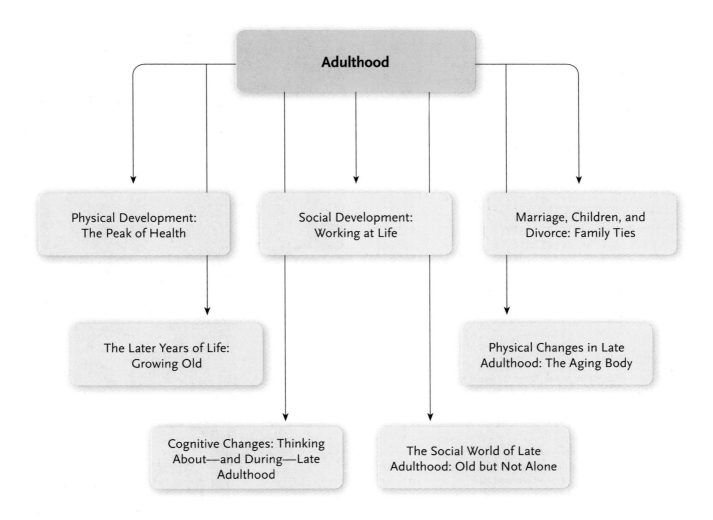

Adulthood

Physical Development: The Peak of Health

Social Development: Working at Life

Marriage, Children, and Divorce: Family Ties

The Later Years of Life: Growing Old

Physical Changes in Late Adulthood: The Aging Body

Cognitive Changes: Thinking About—and During—Late Adulthood

The Social World of Late Adulthood: Old but Not Alone

CHAPTER

9

Wanted: Software engineer.
Must be a messy, extroverted dog owner.

Last summer, Google asked every employee who had been working at the company for at least five months to fill out a 300-question survey.

Some questions were factual: What programming languages are you familiar with? What Internet mailing lists do you subscribe to?

Some looked for behavior: Is your work space messy or neat?

And some looked at personality: Are you an extrovert or an introvert?

And some fell into no traditional category in the human resources world: What magazines do you subscribe to? What pets do you have?

"We wanted to cast a very wide net," said Laszlo Bock, Google's vice president for people operations. "It is not unusual to walk the halls here and bump into dogs. Maybe people who own dogs have some personality trait that is useful." (Hansell, 2007, p. A1) ■

PERSONALITY
AND INDIVIDUAL
DIFFERENCES

looking **AHEAD**

Why is Google concerned about the personal habits and quirks of its thousands of employees? Analysts are seeking to determine if various measures of employees' personality traits and behavior consistently predict who will perform well at a given job. Google executives hope to find enough useful predictors so that they can eventually automate the process of sifting through the hundreds of job applications they receive each week and identify the most promising job candidates.

Although we don't yet know if Google will be successful in identifying the traits that distinguish its most successful employees, it is clear that personality is a central area for psychologists in understanding human behavior. **Personality** is the pattern of enduring characteristics that produce consistency and individuality in a given person. Personality encompasses the behaviors that make each of us unique and that differentiate us from others. It is also personality that leads us to act consistently in different situations and over extended periods of time.

We will consider a number of approaches to personality. We begin with psychodynamic theories of personality, which emphasize the importance of the unconscious. Next, we consider approaches that concentrate on identifying the most fundamental personality traits; theories that view personality as a set of learned behaviors; biological and evolutionary perspectives on personality; and approaches, known as humanistic theories, that highlight the uniquely human aspects of personality. We then focus on how personality is measured and how personality tests can be used before ending our discussion by looking more closely at one central individual difference: intelligence.

> **Personality** The pattern of enduring characteristics that produce consistency and individuality in a given person.

Psychodynamic Approaches to Personality

LEARNING OUTCOMES

29.1 Explain Freud's psychoanalytic theory.

29.2 Discuss Neo-Freudian psychoanalysts.

Psychodynamic approaches to personality Approaches that assume that personality is motivated by inner forces and conflicts about which people have little awareness and over which they have no control.

Psychoanalytic theory Freud's theory that unconscious forces act as determinants of personality.

Unconscious A part of the personality that contains the memories, knowledge, beliefs, feelings, urges, drives, and instincts of which the individual is not aware.

The college student was intent on making a good first impression on an attractive woman he had spotted across a crowded room at a party. As he walked toward her, he mulled over a line he had heard in an old movie the night before: "I don't believe we've been properly introduced yet." To his horror, what came out was a bit different. After threading his way through the crowded room, he finally reached the woman and blurted out, "I don't believe we've been properly seduced yet."

Although this student's error may seem to be merely an embarrassing slip of the tongue, according to some personality theorists such a mistake is not an error at all. Instead, *psychodynamic personality theorists* might argue that the error illustrates one way in which behavior is triggered by inner forces that are beyond our awareness. These hidden drives, shaped by childhood experiences, play an important role in energizing and directing everyday behavior.

Psychodynamic approaches to personality are based on the idea that personality is motivated by inner forces and conflicts about which people have little awareness and over which they have no control. The most important pioneer of the psychodynamic approach was Sigmund Freud. A number of Freud's followers, including Carl Jung, Karen Horney, and Alfred Adler, refined Freud's theory and developed their own psychodynamic approaches.

» LO1 Freud's Psychoanalytic Theory: Mapping the Unconscious Mind

Sigmund Freud, an Austrian physician, developed **psychoanaloytic theory** in the early 1900s. According to Freud's theory, conscious experience is only a small part of our psychological makeup and experience. He argued that much of our behavior is motivated by the **unconscious,** a part of the personality that contains the memories, knowledge, beliefs, feelings urges, drives, and instincts of which the individual is not aware.

Like the unseen mass of a floating iceberg, the contents of the unconscious far surpass in quantity the information in our conscious awareness. Freud maintained that to understand personality, it is necessary to expose what is in the unconscious. But because the unconscious disguises the meaning of the material it holds, the content of the unconscious cannot be observed directly. It is therefore necessary to interpret clues to the unconscious—slips of the tongue, fantasies, and dreams—to understand the unconscious processes that direct behavior. A slip of the tongue such as the one quoted earlier (sometimes termed a *Freudian slip*) may be interpreted as revealing the speaker's unconscious sexual desires.

> *Freud maintained that to understand personality, it is necessary to expose what is in the unconscious.*

To Freud, much of our personality is determined by our unconscious. Some of the unconscious is made up of the *preconscious,* which contains material that is not threatening and is easily brought to mind, such as the knowledge that 2 + 2 = 4. But deeper in the unconscious are instinctual drives—the wishes, desires, demands, and needs that are hidden from conscious awareness because of the conflicts and pain they would cause if they were part of our everyday lives. The unconscious provides a "safe haven" for our recollections of threatening events.

Structuring Personality: Id, Ego, and Superego

To describe the structure of personality, Freud developed a comprehensive theory that held that personality consists of three separate but interacting components: the id, the ego, and the superego. Freud suggested that the three structures can be diagrammed to show how they relate to the conscious and the unconscious (see Figure 1).

Although the three components of personality described by Freud may appear to be actual physical structures in the nervous system, they are not. Instead, they represent abstract conceptions of a general *model* of personality that describes the interaction of forces that motivate behavior.

If personality consisted only of primitive, instinctual cravings and longings, it would have just one component: the id. The **id** is the raw, unorganized, inborn part of personality. From the time of birth, the id attempts to reduce tension created by primitive drives related to hunger, sex, aggression, and irrational impulses. Those drives are fueled by "psychic energy," which we can think of as a limitless energy source constantly putting pressure on the various parts of the personality.

The id operates according to the *pleasure principle,* in which the goal is the immediate reduction of tension and the maximization of satisfaction. However, in most cases reality prevents the fulfillment of the demands of the pleasure principle: we cannot always eat when we are hungry, and we can discharge our sexual drives only when the time and place are appropriate. To account for this fact of life, Freud suggested a second component of personality, which he called the ego.

The **ego,** which begins to develop soon after birth, strives to balance the desires of the id and the realities of the objective, outside world. In contrast to the pleasure-seeking id, the ego operates according to the

Id The raw, unorganized, inborn part of personality whose sole purpose is to reduce tension created by primitive drives related to hunger, sex, aggression, and irrational impulses.

Ego The part of the personality that provides a buffer between the id and the outside world.

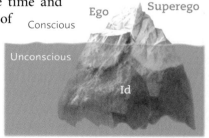

Conscious
Ego
Superego
Unconscious
Id

FIGURE 1 In Freud's model of personality, there are three major components: the id, the ego, and the superego. As the iceberg analogy shows, only a small portion of personality is conscious. Why do you think that only the ego and superego have conscious components?

Freud suggests that the superego, the part of personality that represents the rights and wrongs of society, develops from direct teaching from our parents, teachers, and other significant individuals.

Superego According to Freud, the final personality structure to develop; it represents the rights and wrongs of society as handed down by a person's parents, teachers, and other important figures.

Psychosexual stages Developmental periods that children pass through during which they encounter conflicts between the demands of society and their own sexual urges.

Fixations Conflicts or concerns that persist beyond the developmental period in which they first occur.

Oral stage According to Freud, a stage from birth to age 12 to 18 months, in which an infant's center of pleasure is the mouth.

reality principle, in which instinctual energy is restrained to maintain the safety of the individual and to help integrate the person into society. In a sense, then, the ego is the "executive" of personality: it makes decisions, controls actions, and allows thinking and problem solving of a higher order than the id's capabilities permit.

The **superego,** the final personality structure to develop in childhood, represents the rights and wrongs of society as taught and modeled by a person's parents, teachers, and other significant individuals. The superego includes the *conscience,* which prevents us from behaving in a morally improper way by making us feel guilty if we do wrong. The superego helps us control impulses coming from the id, making our behavior less selfish and more virtuous.

Both the superego and the id are unrealistic in that they do not consider the practical realities imposed by society. The superego, if left to operate without restraint, would create perfectionists unable to make the compromises that life requires. An unrestrained id would create a primitive, pleasure-seeking, thoughtless individual seeking to fulfill every desire without delay. As a result, the ego must mediate between the demands of the superego and the demands of the id.

Developing Personality: Psychosexual Stages

Freud also provided us with a view of how personality develops through a series of five **psychosexual stages,** during which individuals encounter conflicts between the demands of society and their own sexual urges (in which sexuality is more about experiencing pleasure and less about lust). According to Freud, failure to resolve the conflicts at a particular stage can result in **fixations,** conflicts or concerns that persist beyond the developmental period in which they first occur. Such conflicts may be due to having needs ignored or (conversely) being overindulged during the earlier period.

The sequence Freud proposed is noteworthy because it explains how experiences and difficulties during a particular childhood stage may predict specific characteristics in the adult personality. This theory is also unique in associating each stage with a major biological function, which Freud assumed to be the focus of pleasure in a given period.

In the first psychosexual stage of development, called the **oral stage,** the baby's mouth is the focal point of pleasure (see Figure 2 for a summary of the stages). During the first 12 to 18 months of life, children suck, eat, mouth, and bite anything that they can put into their mouths. To Freud, this behavior suggested that the mouth is the primary site of a kind of sexual pleasure, and that weaning (withdrawing the breast or bottle) represents the main conflict during the oral stage. If infants are either overindulged (perhaps by being fed every time they cry) or frustrated in their search for oral gratification, they may become fixated at this stage. For example, fixation might occur if an infant's oral needs were constantly gratified immediately at the first sign of hunger, rather than if the infant learned that feeding takes place on a schedule because eating whenever an infant wants to eat is not always realistic. Fixation

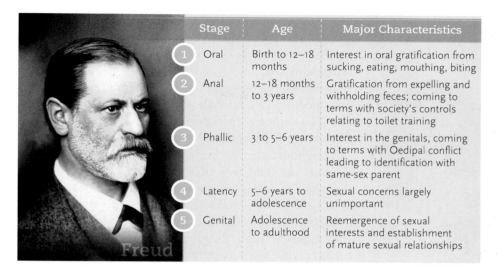

	Stage	Age	Major Characteristics
1	Oral	Birth to 12–18 months	Interest in oral gratification from sucking, eating, mouthing, biting
2	Anal	12–18 months to 3 years	Gratification from expelling and withholding feces; coming to terms with society's controls relating to toilet training
3	Phallic	3 to 5–6 years	Interest in the genitals, coming to terms with Oedipal conflict leading to identification with same-sex parent
4	Latency	5–6 years to adolescence	Sexual concerns largely unimportant
5	Genital	Adolescence to adulthood	Reemergence of sexual interests and establishment of mature sexual relationships

FIGURE 2 Freud's theory of personality development suggests that there are several distinct stages.

at the oral stage might produce an adult who was unusually interested in oral activities—eating, talking, smoking—or who showed symbolic sorts of oral interests: being either "bitingly" sarcastic or very gullible ("swallowing" anything).

From around age 12 to 18 months until 3 years of age—a period when the emphasis in Western cultures is on toilet training—a child enters the **anal stage.** At this point, the major source of pleasure changes from the mouth to the anal region, and children obtain considerable pleasure from both retention and expulsion of feces. If toilet training is particularly demanding, fixation might occur. Fixation during the anal stage might result in unusual rigidity, orderliness, punctuality—or extreme disorderliness or sloppiness—in adulthood.

At about age 3, the **phallic stage** begins. At this point there is another major shift in the primary source of pleasure for the child. Now interest focuses on the genitals and the pleasures derived from fondling them. During this stage the child must also negotiate one of the most important hurdles of personality development: the **Oedipal conflict.** According to Freudian theory, as children focus attention on their genitals, the differences between male and female anatomy become more apparent. Furthermore, according to Freud, at this time the male unconsciously begins to develop a sexual interest in his mother, starts to see his father as a rival, and harbors a wish to kill his father—as Oedipus did in the ancient Greek tragedy. But because he views his father as too powerful, he develops a fear that his father may retaliate drastically by removing the source of the threat: the son's penis. The fear of losing one's penis leads to *castration anxiety,* which ultimately becomes so powerful that the child represses his desires for his mother and identifies with his father. **Identification** is the process of wanting to be like another person as

Anal stage According to Freud, a stage from age 12 to 18 months to 3 years of age, in which a child's pleasure is centered on the anus.

Phallic stage According to Freud, a period beginning around age 3 during which a child's pleasure focuses on the genitals.

Oedipal conflict A child's sexual interest in his or her opposite-sex parent, typically resolved through identification with the same-sex parent.

Identification The process of wanting to be like another person as much as possible, imitating that person's behavior and adopting similar beliefs and values.

According to Freud, a child goes through the anal stage from 12 to 18 months until 3 years of age. Toilet training is a crucial event at this stage, one that psychoanalytical theory claims directly influences the formation of an individual's personality.

Imitating a person's behavior and adopting similar beliefs and values is part of Freud's concept of identification. How can this concept be applied to the definition of gender roles? Is identification similar in all cultures?

much as possible, imitating that person's behavior and adopting similar beliefs and values. By identifying with his father, a son seeks to obtain a woman like his unattainable mother.

For girls, the process is different. Freud reasoned that girls begin to experience sexual arousal toward their fathers and begin to experience penis envy. They wish they had the anatomical part that, at least to Freud, seemed most clearly "missing" in girls. Blaming their mothers for their lack of a penis, girls come to believe that their mothers are responsible for their "castration." (This aspect of Freud's theory later provoked accusations that he considered women to be inferior to men.) Like males, though, they find that they can resolve such unacceptable feelings by identifying with the same-sex parent, behaving like her and adopting her attitudes and values. In this way, a girl's identification with her mother is completed.

At this point, the Oedipal conflict is said to be resolved, and Freudian theory assumes that both males and females move on to the next stage of development. If difficulties arise during this period, however, all sorts of problems are thought to occur, including improper sex-role behavior and the failure to develop a conscience.

After the resolution of the Oedipal conflict, typically at around age 5 or 6, children move into the **latency period,** which lasts until puberty. During this period, sexual interests become dormant, even in the unconscious. Then, during adolescence, sexual feelings reemerge, marking the start of the final period, the **genital stage,** which extends until death. The focus during the genital stage is on mature, adult sexuality, which Freud defined as sexual intercourse.

Defense Mechanisms

Latency period According to Freud, the period between the phallic stage and puberty during which children's sexual concerns are temporarily put aside.

Genital stage According to Freud, the period from puberty until death, marked by mature sexual behavior (i.e., sexual intercourse).

Defense mechanisms In Freudian theory, unconscious strategies that people use to reduce anxiety by concealing the source of the anxiety from themselves and others.

Repression The primary defense mechanism in which unacceptable or unpleasant id impulses are pushed back into the unconscious.

Freud's efforts to describe and theorize about the underlying dynamics of personality and its development were motivated by very practical problems that his patients faced in dealing with *anxiety,* an intense, negative emotional experience. According to Freud, anxiety is a danger signal to the ego. Although anxiety can arise from realistic fears—such as seeing a poisonous snake about to strike—it can also occur in the form of *neurotic anxiety,* in which irrational impulses emanating from the id threaten to burst through and become uncontrollable.

Because anxiety, obviously, is unpleasant, Freud believed that people develop a range of defense mechanisms to deal with it. **Defense mechanisms** are unconscious strategies that people use to reduce anxiety by concealing its source from themselves and others.

The primary defense mechanism is **repression,** in which unacceptable or unpleasant id impulses are pushed back into the unconscious. Repression is the most direct method of dealing with anxiety; instead of handling an anxiety-producing impulse on a conscious level, we simply ignore it. For

Freud's Defence Mechanisms

Defense Mechanism	Explanation	Example
Repression	Unacceptable or unpleasant impulses are pushed back into the unconscious	A woman is unable to recall that she was raped
Regression	People behave as if they were at an earlier stage of development	A boss has a temper tantrum when an employee makes a mistake
Displacement	The expression of an unwanted feeling or thought is redirected from a more threatening powerful person to a weaker one	A brother yells at his younger sister after a teacher gives him a bad grade
Rationalization	People provide self-justifying explanations in place of the actual, but threatening, reason for their behavior	A student who goes out drinking the night before a big test rationalizes his behavior by saying the test isn't all that important
Denial	People refuse to accept or acknowledge an anxiety-producing piece of information	A student refuses to believe that he has flunked a course
Projection	People attribute unwanted impulses and feelings to someone else	A man who is angry at his father acts lovingly to his father but complains that his father is angry with him
Sublimation	People divert unwanted impulses into socially approved thoughts, feelings, or behaviors	A person with strong feelings of aggression becomes a soldier
Reaction formation	Unconscious impulses are expressed as their opposite in consciousness	A mother who unconsciously resents her child acts in an overly loving way toward the child

FIGURE 3   According to Freud, people are able to use a wide range of defense mechanisms to cope with anxieties.

example, a college student who feels hatred for her mother may repress those personally and socially unacceptable feelings. The feelings remain lodged within the unconscious, because acknowledging them would provoke anxiety. Similarly, memories of childhood abuse may be repressed.

If repression is ineffective in keeping anxiety at bay, we might use other defense mechanisms. Freud, and later his daughter Anna Freud (who became a well-known psychoanalyst), formulated an extensive list of potential defense mechanisms. The major defense mechanisms are summarized in Figure 3 (Hentschel et al., 2004; Cramer, 2007).

All of us employ defense mechanisms to some degree, according to Freudian theory, and they can serve a useful purpose by protecting us from unpleasant information. Yet some people fall prey to them to such an extent that they must constantly direct a large amount of psychic energy toward hiding and rechanneling unacceptable impulses. When this occurs, everyday living becomes difficult. In such cases, the result is a mental disorder produced by anxiety—what Freud called "neurosis" (a term rarely used by psychologists today, although it endures in everyday conversation).

Evaluating Freud's Legacy

Freud's theory has had a significant impact on the field of psychology—and even more broadly on Western philosophy and literature. The ideas of the unconscious, defense mechanisms, and childhood roots of adult psychological difficulties have been accepted by many people.

psych2.0
WWW.MHHE.COM/PSYCHLIFE

Defense Mechanisms

However, many contemporary personality psychologists have leveled significant criticisms against psychoanalytic theory. Among the most important is the lack of compelling scientific data to support it. Although individual case studies *seem* supportive, we lack conclusive evidence showing that the personality is structured and operates along the lines Freud laid out. The lack of evidence is due, in part, to the fact that Freud's conception of personality is built on unobservable abstract concepts. Moreover, it is not clear that the stages of personality that Freud laid out provide an accurate description of personality development. We also know now that important changes in personality can occur in adolescence and adulthood—something that Freud did not believe happened. Instead, he argued that personality largely is set by adolescence.

The vague nature of Freud's theory also makes it difficult to predict how certain developmental difficulties will be displayed in an adult. For instance, if a person is fixated at the anal stage, according to Freud, he or she may be unusually messy—or unusually neat. Freud's theory offers no way to predict how the difficulty will be exhibited. Furthermore, Freud can be faulted for seeming to view women as inferior to men, because he argued that women have weaker superegos than men do and in some ways unconsciously yearn to be men (the concept of penis envy).

> *It is not clear that the stages of personality that Freud laid out provide an accurate description of personality development.*

Finally, Freud made his observations and derived his theory from a limited population. His theory was based almost entirely on upper-class Austrian women living in the strict, puritanical era of the early 1900s who had come to him seeking treatment for psychological and physical problems. How far one can generalize beyond this population is a matter of considerable debate.

Still, Freud generated an important method of treating psychological disturbances, called *psychoanalysis*. As we will see when we discuss treatment approaches to psychological disorder, psychoanalysis remains in use today (Messer & McWilliams, 2003; Heller, 2005; Riolo, 2007).

Moreover, Freud's emphasis on the unconscious has been partially supported by current research on dreams and implicit memory. As we first noted when we discussed dreaming, advances in neuroscience are consistent with some of Freud's arguments. Furthermore, cognitive and social psychologists have found evidence that unconscious processes help us think about and evaluate our world, set goals, and choose a course of action (Derryberry, 2006; Litowitz, 2007).

» LO2 The Neo-Freudian Psychoanalysts: Building on Freud

Neo-Freudian psychoanalysts Psychoanalysts who were trained in traditional Freudian theory but who later rejected some of its major points.

Freud laid the foundation for important work done by a series of successors who were trained in traditional Freudian theory but later rejected some of its major points. These theorists are known as **neo-Freudian psychoanalysts.**

The neo-Freudians placed greater emphasis than Freud had on the functions of the ego, suggesting that it has more control than does the id over day-to-day activities. They focused more on the social environment and minimized the importance of sex as a driving force in people's lives. They also paid greater attention to the effects of society and culture on personality development.

Jung's Collective Unconscious

One of the most influential neo-Freudians, Carl Jung (pronounced "yoong"), rejected Freud's view of the primary importance of unconscious sexual urges. Instead, he looked at the primitive urges of the unconscious more positively, arguing that they represented a more general, and positive, life force that encompasses an inborn drive motivating creativity and more positive resolution of conflict (Lothane, 2005; Cassells, 2007).

Jung suggested that we have a universal **collective unconscious,** a common set of ideas, feelings, images, and symbols that we inherit from our relatives, the whole human race, and even nonhuman animal ancestors from the distant past. This collective unconscious is shared by everyone and is displayed in behavior that is common across diverse cultures—such as love of mother, belief in a supreme being, and even behavior as specific as fear of snakes (Oehman & Mineka, 2003; Drob, 2005; Hauke, 2006).

Jung went on to propose that the collective unconscious contains **archetypes,** universal symbolic representations of a particular person, object, or experience. For instance, a mother archetype, which contains reflections of our ancestors' relationships with mother figures, is suggested by the prevalence of mothers in art, religion, literature, and mythology. (Think of the Virgin Mary, Earth Mother, wicked stepmothers in fairy tales, Mother's Day, and so forth!) (Jung, 1961; Bair, 2003; Smetana, 2007).

Collective unconscious According to Jung, a common set of ideas, feelings, images, and symbols that we inherit from our ancestors, the whole human race, and even animal ancestors from the distant past.

Archetypes According to Jung, universal symbolic representations of a particular person, object, or experience (such as good and evil).

From the perspective of . . .

A FASHION DESIGN PROFESSIONAL How might you use Jung's concept of archetypes in designing your products? Which of the archetypes would you use?

To Jung, archetypes play an important role in determining our day-to-day reactions, attitudes, and values. For example, Jung might explain the popularity of the *Star Wars* movies as being due to their use of broad archetypes of good (Luke Skywalker) and evil (Darth Vader).

Although no reliable research evidence confirms the existence of the collective unconscious—and even Jung acknowledged that such evidence would be difficult to produce—Jung's theory has had significant influence in areas beyond psychology. For example, personality types derived from Jung's personality approach form the basis for the Myers-Briggs personality test, which is widely used in business and industry (Gladwell, 2004; Bayne, 2005; Furnham & Crump, 2005).

Horney's Neo-Freudian Perspective

Karen Horney (pronounced "HORN-eye") was one of the earliest psychologists to champion women's issues and is sometimes called the first feminist psychologist. Horney suggested that personality develops in the context of social relationships and depends particularly on the relationship between parents and child and how well the child's needs are met. She rejected Freud's suggestion that women have penis envy, asserting that what women envy most

In the *Star Wars* movies, Darth Vader may represent the archetype of evil. Which character represents the archetype of evil in the *Batman* movies?

Karen Horney was one of the earliest proponents of women's issues.

in men is not their anatomy but the independence, success, and freedom that women often are denied (Horney, 1937; Miletic, 2002; Smith, 2007).

Horney was also one of the first to stress the importance of cultural factors in the determination of personality. For example, she suggested that society's rigid gender roles for women lead them to experience ambivalence about success, fearing that they will lose their friends. Her conceptualizations, developed in the 1930s and 1940s, laid the groundwork for many of the central ideas of feminism that emerged decades later (Eckardt, 2005; Jones, 2006).

Adler's Neo-Freudian Perspective

Alfred Adler, another important neo-Freudian psychoanalyst, also considered Freudian theory's emphasis on sexual needs misplaced. Instead, Adler proposed that the primary human motivation is a striving for superiority, not in terms of superiority over others but in a quest for self-improvement and perfection.

Inferiority complex According to Adler, a problem affecting adults who have not been able to overcome the feelings of inferiority that they developed as children, when they were small and limited in their knowledge about the world.

Adler used the term **inferiority complex** to describe situations in which adults have not been able to overcome the feelings of inferiority they developed as children, when they were small and limited in their knowledge about the world. Early social relationships with parents have an important effect on children's ability to outgrow feelings of personal inferiority and instead to orient themselves toward attaining more socially useful goals, such as improving society.

R E C A P

Explain Freud's psychoanalytic theory.

- Personality is the pattern of enduring characteristics that produce consistency and individuality in a given person. (p. 335)

- According to psychodynamic explanations of personality, much behavior is caused by parts of personality that are found in the unconscious and of which we are unaware. (p. 336)

- Freud's psychoanalytic theory, one of the psychodynamic approaches, suggests that personality is composed of the id, the ego, and the superego. The id is the unorganized, inborn part of personality whose purpose is to immediately reduce tensions relating to hunger, sex, aggression, and other primitive impulses. The ego restrains instinctual energy to maintain the safety of the individual and to help the person be a member of society. The superego represents the rights and wrongs of society and includes the conscience. (p. 336)

- Freud's psychoanalytic theory suggests that personality develops through a series of psychosexual stages (oral, anal, phallic, latency, and genital), each of which is associated with a primary biological function. (p. 338)

- Defense mechanisms, according to Freudian theory, are unconscious strategies with which people reduce anxieties relating to impulses from the id. (p. 340)

- Freud's psychoanalytic theory has provoked a number of criticisms, including a lack of sup-portive scientific data, the theory's inadequacy in making predictions, and its reliance on a highly restricted population . On the other hand, recent neuroscience research has offered some support for the concept of the uncon-scious. (p. 342)

Discuss Neo-Freudian psychoanalysts.

- Neo-Freudian psychoanalytic theorists built on Freud's work, although they placed greater emphasis on the role of the ego and paid more attention to the role of social factors in deter-mining behavior. (p. 342)

EVALUATE

1. _____ approaches state that behavior is motivated primarily by unconscious forces.

2. Match each section of the personality (according to Freud) with its description:

   1. Ego
   2. Id
   3. Superego

   a. Determines right from wrong on the basis of cultural standards.
   b. Operates according to the "reality principle"; energy is redirected to integrate the person into society.
   c. Seeks to reduce tension brought on by primitive drives.

3. Which of the following represents the proper order of personality development, according to Freud?

   a. Oral, phallic, latency, anal, genital
   b. Anal, oral, phallic, genital, latency
   c. Oral, anal, phallic, latency, genital
   d. Latency, phallic, anal, genital, oral

4. _____ _____ is the term Freud used to describe unconscious strategies used to reduce anxiety.

RETHINK

Can you think of ways in which Freud's theories of unconscious motivations are commonly used in popular culture? How accurately do you think such popular uses of Freudian theories reflect Freud's ideas?

Answers to Evaluate Questions 1. psychodynamic; 2. 1-b, 2-c, 3-a; 3. c; 4. defense mechanism

[K E Y T E R M S]

module 30

Trait, Learning, Biological and Evolutionary, and Humanistic Approaches to Personality

"Tell me about Nelson," said Johnetta.

"Oh, he's just terrific. He's the friendliest guy I know—goes out of his way to be nice to everyone. He hardly ever gets mad. He's just so even-tempered, no matter what's happening. And he's really smart, too. About the only thing I don't like is that he's always in such a hurry to get things done. He seems to have boundless energy, much more than I have."

"He sounds great to me, especially in comparison to Rico," replied Johnetta. "He is so self-centered and arrogant that it drives me crazy. I sometimes wonder why I ever started going out with him."

Friendly. Even-tempered. Smart. Energetic. Self-centered. Arrogant.

The preceding exchange is made up of a series of trait characterizations of speakers' friends. In fact, much of our own understanding of others' behavior is based on the premise that people possess certain traits that are consistent across different situations. For example, we generally assume that if someone is outgoing and sociable in one situation, he or she is outgoing and sociable in other situations (Gilbert et al., 1992; Gilbert, Miller, & Ross, 1998; Mischel, 2004).

Dissatisfaction with the emphasis in psychoanalytic theory on unconscious—and difficult to demonstrate—processes in explaining a person's behavior led to the development of alternative approaches to personality, including a number of trait-based approaches. Other theories reflect established psychological perspectives, such as learning theory, biological and evolutionary approaches, and the humanistic approach.

LEARNING OUTCOMES

30.1 Explain trait approaches to personality.

30.2 Explain learning approaches to personality.

30.3 Explain biological and evolutionary approaches to personality.

30.4 Explain humanistic approaches to personality.

30.5 Compare and contrast approaches to personality.

» LO1 Trait Approaches: Placing Labels on Personality

If someone asked you to characterize another person, it is probable that—like Johnetta and her friend—you would come up with a list of that individual's personal qualities, as you see them. But how would you know which of those qualities are most important to an understanding of that person's behavior?

Personality psychologists have asked similar questions. To answer them, they have developed a model of personality known as trait theory. **Trait theory** seeks to explain, in a straightforward way, the consistencies in individuals' behavior. **Traits** are consistent personality characteristics and behaviors displayed in different situations.

Trait theorists do not assume that some people have a trait and others do not; rather, they propose that all people possess certain traits, but that the degree to which a particular trait applies to a specific person varies and can be quantified. For instance, you may be relatively friendly, whereas I may be relatively unfriendly. But we both have a "friendliness" trait, although your degree of "friendliness" is higher than mine. The major challenge for trait theorists taking this approach has been to identify the specific primary traits necessary to describe personality. As we shall see, different theorists have come up with surprisingly different sets of traits.

Eysenck's Approach: The Factors of Personality

Attempts to identify primary personality traits have centered on a statistical technique known as factor analysis. *Factor analysis* is a statistical method of identifying associations among a large number of variables to reveal more general patterns. For example, a personality researcher might administer a questionnaire to many participants, asking them to describe themselves by referring to an extensive list of traits. By statistically combining responses and computing which traits are associated with one another in the same person, a researcher can identify the most fundamental patterns or combinations of traits—called *factors*—that underlie participants' responses.

Psychologist Hans Eysenck (1995) used factor analysis to identify patterns of traits and found that personality could best be described in terms of just three major dimensions: *extraversion, neuroticism,* and *psychoticism.* The extraversion dimension relates to the degree of sociability, whereas the neurotic dimension encompasses emotional stability. Finally,

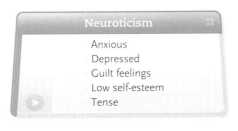

FIGURE 1 According to Eysenck, personality could best be described in terms of just three major dimensions: extraversion, neuroticism, and psychoticism. Eysenck was able to predict behavior accurately in a variety of types of situations by evaluating people along these three dimensions (Eysenck, 1990). How do you think an airline pilot would score on Eysenck's scale?

psychoticism refers to the degree to which reality is distorted. By evaluating people along these three dimensions, Eysenck was able to predict behavior accurately in a variety of situations. Figure 1 lists specific traits associated with each of the dimensions.

The Big Five Personality Traits

For the last two decades, the most influential trait approach contends that five traits or factors—called the "Big Five"—lie at the core of personality. Using modern factor analytic statistical techniques, a host of researchers have identified a similar set of five factors that underlie personality. The five factors, described in Figure 2, are *openness to experience, conscientiousness, extraversion, agreeableness,* and *neuroticism* (emotional stability).

> *For the last two decades, the most influential trait approach contends that five traits or factors—called the "Big Five"—lie at the core of personality.*

The Big Five emerge consistently with different kinds of measures, in different populations of individuals, and across different cultures. In short, a growing consensus exists that the "Big Five" represent the best description of personality traits we have today. Still, the debate over the specific number and kinds of traits—and even the usefulness of trait approaches in general—remains a lively one.

Evaluating Trait Approaches to Personality

Trait approaches have several virtues. They provide a clear, straightforward explanation of people's behavioral consistencies. Furthermore, traits allow

Openness to Experience
Independent—Conforming
Imaginative—Practical
Preference for variety—Preference for routine

Neuroticism (Emotional Stability)
Stable—Tense
Calm—Anxious
Secure—Insecure

The Big Five Personality Factors and Dimensions of Sample Traits

Conscientiousness
Careful—Careless
Disciplined—Impulsive
Organized—Disorganized

Agreeableness
Sympathetic—Fault-finding
Kind—Cold
Appreciative—Unfriendly

Extraversion
Talkative—Quiet
Fun-loving—Sober
Sociable—Retiring

FIGURE 2 Five broad trait factors, referred to as the "Big Five," are considered to be the core of personality. *(Source: Adapted from Pervin, 1990, Chapter 3, and McCrae & Costa, 1986, p. 1002.)*

us to readily compare one person with another. Because of these advantages, trait approaches to personality have had an important influence on the development of several useful personality measures (Funder, 1991; Wiggins, 2003; Larsen & Buss, 2006).

However, trait approaches also have some drawbacks. For example, we have seen that various trait theories describing personality come to very different conclusions about which traits are the most fundamental and descriptive. Moreover, even if we are able to identify a set of primary traits, we are left with little more than a label or description of personality—rather than an explanation of behavior. If we say that someone who donates money to charity has the trait of generosity, we still do not know *why* that person became generous in the first place or the reasons for displaying generosity in a specific situation. In the view of some critics, then, traits do not provide explanations for behavior; they merely describe it.

» LO2 Learning Approaches: We Are What We've Learned

The psychodynamic and trait approaches we've discussed concentrate on the "inner" person—the fury of an unobservable but powerful id or a hypothetical but critical set of traits. In contrast, learning approaches to personality focus on the "outer" person. To a strict learning theorist, personality is simply the sum of learned responses to the external environment. Internal events such as thoughts, feelings, and motivations are ignored. Although the existence of personality is not denied, learning theorists say that it is best understood by looking at features of a person's environment.

Skinner's Behaviorist Approach

According to the most influential learning theorist, B. F. Skinner (who carried out pioneering work on operant conditioning), personality is a collection of learned behavior patterns (Skinner, 1975). Similarities in responses across different situations are caused by similar patterns of reinforcement that have been received in such situations in the past. If I am sociable both at parties and at meetings, it is because I have been reinforced for displaying social behaviors—not because I am fulfilling an unconscious wish based on experiences during my childhood or because I have an internal trait of sociability.

Strict learning theorists such as Skinner are less interested in the consistencies in behavior across situations than in ways of modifying behavior. Their view is that humans are infinitely changeable through the process of learning new behavior patterns. If we are able to control and modify the patterns of reinforcers in a

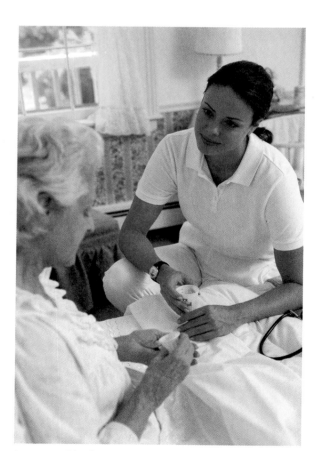

How would a basic understanding of personality help this nurse's assistant deal with a high-maintenance patient?

situation, behavior that other theorists would view as stable and unyielding can be changed and ultimately improved. Learning theorists are optimistic in their attitudes about the potential for resolving personal and societal problems through treatment strategies based on learning theory.

Social Cognitive Approaches to Personality

Not all learning theories of personality take such a strict view in rejecting the importance of what is "inside" a person by focusing solely on the "outside." Unlike other learning approaches to personality, **social cognitive approaches to personality** emphasize the influence of cognition—thoughts, feelings, expectations, and values—as well as observation of others' behavior, on personality. According to Albert Bandura, one of the main proponents of this point of view, people can foresee the possible outcomes of certain behaviors in a specific setting without actually having to carry them out. This understanding comes primarily through *observational learning*—viewing the actions of others and observing the consequences (Bandura, 1986, 1999).

For instance, children who view a model behaving in, say, an aggressive manner tend to copy the behavior if the consequences of the model's behavior are seen to be positive. If, in contrast, the model's aggressive behavior has resulted in no consequences or negative consequences, children are considerably less likely to act aggressively. According to social cognitive approaches, then, personality develops through repeated observation of the behavior of others.

Self-Efficacy. Bandura places particular emphasis on the role played by **self-efficacy,** belief in one's personal capabilities. Self-efficacy underlies people's faith in their ability to carry out a specific behavior or produce a desired outcome. People with high self-efficacy have higher aspirations and greater persistence in working to attain goals and ultimately achieve greater success than do those with lower self-efficacy (Bandura, 2001; Bandura & Locke, 2003; Glickler, 2006).

> **Social cognitive approaches to personality** Theories that emphasize the influence of a person's cognitions—thoughts, feelings, expectations, and values—as well as observation of others' behavior, in determining personality.
>
> **Self-efficacy** Belief in one's personal capabilities. Self-efficacy underlies people's faith in their ability to carry out a particular behavior or produce a desired outcome.

Self-efficacy, the belief in one's own capabilities, leads to higher aspirations and greater persistence. How did self-efficacy factor into your decision to seek further education?

How do we develop self-efficacy? One way is by paying close attention to our prior successes and failures. If we try snowboarding and experience little success, we'll be less likely to try it again. However, if our initial efforts appear promising, we'll be more likely to attempt it again. Direct reinforcement and encouragement from others also play a role in developing self-efficacy (Devonport & Lane, 2006).

Compared with other learning theories of personality, social cognitive approaches are distinctive in their emphasis on the reciprocity between individuals and their environment. Not only is the environment assumed to affect personality, but people's behavior and personalities are also assumed to "feed back" and modify the environment (Bandura, 1999, 2000).

From the perspective of . . .

A HEALTH CARE PROVIDER How might a patient's self-efficacy influence her willingness to engage in health-enhancing behaviors or her ability to follow a prescribed treatment regimen?

Self-esteem The component of personality that encompasses our positive and negative self-evaluations.

Self-Esteem. Our behavior also reflects the view we have of ourselves and the way we value the various parts of our personalities. **Self-esteem** is the component of personality that encompasses our positive and negative self-evaluations. Unlike self-efficacy, which focuses on our views of whether we are able to carry out a task, self-esteem relates to how we feel about ourselves.

Although people have a general level of self-esteem, it is not unidimensional. We may see ourselves positively in one domain but negatively in others. For example, a good student may have high self-esteem in academic domains but lower self-esteem in sports (Crocker & Park, 2004; Swann, Chang-Schneider, & Larsen McClarty, 2007; Salmela-Aro & Nurmi, 2007).

Evaluating Learning Approaches to Personality

Because they ignore the internal processes that are uniquely human, traditional learning theorists such as Skinner have been accused of oversimplifying personality to such an extent that the concept becomes meaningless. In the eyes of their critics, reducing behavior to a series of stimuli and responses, and excluding thoughts and feelings from the realm of personality, leaves behaviorists practicing an unrealistic and inadequate form of science.

Nonetheless, learning approaches have had a major impact on the study of personality. For one thing, they have helped make personality psychology an objective, scientific venture by focusing on observable behaviors and their environment. In addition, they have produced important, successful means of treating a variety of psychological disorders. The degree of success of these treatments is a testimony to the merits of learning theory approaches to personality.

» LO3 Biological and Evolutionary Approaches: Are We Born with Personality?

Approaching the question of what determines personality from a different direction, **biological and evolutionary approaches to personality** suggest that important components of personality are inherited. Building on the work of behavioral geneticists, researchers using biological and evolutionary approaches argue that personality is determined at least in part by our genes, in much the same way that our height is largely a result of genetic contributions from our ancestors (see Figure 3). The evolutionary perspective assumes that personality traits that led to survival and reproductive success of our ancestors are more likely to be preserved and passed on to subsequent generations (Buss, 2001).

It is increasingly clear that the roots of adult personality emerge in the earliest periods of life. Infants are born with a specific **temperament,** an innate disposition. Temperament encompasses several dimensions, including general activity level and mood. For instance, some individuals are quite active, whereas others are relatively calm. Similarly, some are relatively easygoing, but others are irritable, easily upset, and difficult to soothe. Temperament is quite consistent, with significant stability from infancy well into adolescence

> **Biological and evolutionary approaches to personality** Theories that suggest that important components of personality are inherited.
>
> **Temperament** The basic, innate disposition that emerges early in life.

Trait	Percentage	Description
Social potency	61%	Is masterful; a forceful leader who likes to be the center of attention
Traditionalism	60%	Follows rules and authority; endorses high moral standards and strict discipline
Stress reaction	55%	Feels vulnerable and sensitive; is given to worrying and easily upset
Absorption	55%	Has a vivid imagination readily captured by rich experience; relinquishes sense of reality
Alienation	55%	Feels mistreated and used, that "the world is out to get me"
Well-being	54%	Has a cheerful disposition; feels confident and optimistic
Harm avoidance	51%	Shuns the excitement of risk and danger; prefers the safe route even if it is tedious
Aggression	48%	Is physically aggressive and vindictive; has taste for violence; is "out to get the world"
Achievement	46%	Works hard; strives for mastery; puts work and accomplishment ahead of other things
Control	43%	Is cautious and plodding; is rational and sensible; likes carefully planned events
Social closeness	33%	Prefers emotional intimacy and close ties; turns to others for comfort and help

FIGURE 3   The inherited roots of personality. The percentages indicate the degree to which 11 personality characteristics reflect the influence of heredity. *(Source: Tellegen et al., 1988.)*

(Caspi, Harrington, & Milne, 2003; Wachs et al., 2004; Evans & Rothbart, 2007).

Although an increasing number of personality theorists are taking biological and evolutionary factors into account, no comprehensive, unified theory that considers biological and evolutionary factors is widely accepted. Still, it is clear that certain personality traits have substantial genetic components, and that heredity and environment interact to determine personality (Plomin et al., 2003; Ebstein, Benjamin, & Belmaker, 2003; Bouchard, 2004).

Biological and evolutionary approaches to personality seek to explain the consistencies in personality that are found in some families.

Humanistic approaches to personality Theories that emphasize people's innate goodness and desire to achieve higher levels of functioning.

Self-actualization A state of self-fulfillment in which people realize their highest potential, each in a unique way.

psych2.0
WWW.MHHE.COM/PSYCHLIFE

Your Ideal Self

» LO 4 Humanistic Approaches: The Uniqueness of You

Where, in all the approaches to personality that we have discussed, is an explanation for the saintliness of a Mother Teresa, the creativity of a Michelangelo, and the brilliance and perseverance of an Einstein? An understanding of such unique individuals—as well as more ordinary sorts of people who have some of the same attributes—comes from humanistic theory. **Humanistic approaches to personality** emphasize people's inherent goodness and their tendency to move toward higher levels of functioning. It is this conscious, self-motivated ability to change and improve, along with people's unique creative impulses, that humanistic theorists argue make up the core of personality.

Rogers and the Need for Self-Actualization

The major proponent of the humanistic point of view is Carl Rogers (1971). Along with other humanistic theorists, such as Abraham Maslow, Rogers maintains that all people have a fundamental need for **self-actualization,** a state of self-fulfillment in which people realize their highest potential, each in a unique way. He further suggests that people develop a need for positive regard that reflects the desire to be loved and respected. Because others provide this positive regard, we grow dependent on them. We begin to see and judge ourselves through the eyes of other people, relying on their values and being preoccupied with what they think of us.

According to Rogers, one outgrowth of placing importance on the opinions of others is that a conflict may grow between people's experiences and their *self-concepts,* the set of beliefs they hold about what they are like as individuals. If the discrepancies are minor, so are the consequences. But if the discrepancies are great, they will lead to psychological disturbances in daily functioning, such as the experience of frequent anxiety.

Rogers suggests that one way of overcoming the discrepancy between experience and self-concept is through the receipt of unconditional positive

> *We begin to see and judge ourselves through the eyes of other people, relying on their values and being preoccupied with what they think of us.*

regard from another person—a friend, a spouse, or a therapist. **Unconditional positive regard** refers to an attitude of acceptance and respect on the part of an observer, no matter what a person says or does. This acceptance, says Rogers, gives people the opportunity to evolve and grow both cognitively and emotionally and to develop more realistic self-concepts. You may have experienced the power of unconditional positive regard when you confided in someone, revealing embarrassing secrets because you knew the listener would still love and respect you, even after hearing the worst about you (Snyder, 2002; Marshall, 2007).

"So, while extortion, racketeering, and murder may be bad acts, they don't make you a bad person."

In contrast, *conditional positive regard* depends on your behavior. In such cases, others withdraw their love and acceptance if you do something of which they don't approve. The result is a discrepancy between your true self and what others wish you would be, leading to anxiety and frustration.

Evaluating Humanistic Approaches

Although humanistic theories suggest the value of providing unconditional positive regard toward people, unconditional positive regard toward humanistic theories has been less forthcoming. The criticisms have centered on the difficulty of verifying the basic assumptions of the approach, as well as on the question of whether unconditional positive regard does, in fact, lead to greater personality adjustment.

Humanistic approaches have also been criticized for making the assumption that people are basically "good"—a notion that is unverifiable—and, equally important, for using nonscientific values to build supposedly scientific theories. Still, humanistic theories have been important in highlighting the uniqueness of human beings and guiding the development of a significant form of therapy designed to alleviate psychological difficulties (Cain, 2002; Bauman & Kopp, 2006).

> **Unconditional positive regard** An attitude of acceptance and respect on the part of an observer, no matter what a person says or does.

» LO5 Comparing Approaches to Personality

psych2.0
WWW.MHHE.COM/PSYCHLIFE

In light of the multiple approaches we have discussed, you may be wondering which of the theories provides the most accurate description of personality. That is a question that cannot be answered precisely. Each theory is built on different assumptions and focuses on somewhat different aspects of personality (see Figure 4 on page 356). Furthermore, there is no clear way to scientifically test the various approaches and their assumptions against one another. Given the complexity of every individual, it seems reasonable that personality can be viewed from a number of perspectives simultaneously (Pervin, 2003).

Theories of Personality

Theoretical Approach and Major Theorists	Conscious versus Unconscious Determinants of Personality	Nature (Hereditary Factors) versus Nurture (Environmental Factors)	Free Will versus Determinism	Stability versus Modifiability
Psychodynamic (Freud, Jung, Horney, Adler)	Emphasizes the unconscious	Stresses innate, inherited structure of personality while emphasizing importance of childhood experience	Stresses determinism, the view that behavior is directed and caused by factors outside one's control	Emphasizes the stability of characteristics throughout a person's life
Trait (Allport, Cattell, Eysenck)	Disregards both conscious and unconscious	Approaches vary	Stresses determinism, the view that behavior is directed and caused by factors outside one's control	Emphasizes the stability of characteristics throughout a person's life
Learning (Skinner, Bandura)	Disregards both conscious and unconscious	Focuses on the environment	Stresses determinism, the view that behavior is directed and caused by factors outside one's control	Stresses that personality remains flexible and resilient throughout one's life
Biological and evolutionary (Tellegen)	Disregards both conscious and unconscious	Stresses the innate, inherited determinants of personality	Stresses determinism, the view that behavior is directed and caused by factors outside one's control	Emphasizes the stability of characteristics throughout a person's life
Humanistic (Rogers, Maslow)	Stresses the conscious more than unconscious	Stresses the interaction between both nature and nurture	Stresses the freedom of individuals to make their own choices	Stresses that personality remains flexible and resilient throughout one's life

FIGURE 4   The multiple perspectives of personality.

RECAP

Explain trait approaches to personality.

- Trait approaches have been used to identify relatively enduring dimensions along which people differ from one another—dimensions known as traits. (p. 348)

Explain learning approaches to personality.

- Learning approaches to personality concentrate on observable behavior. To a strict learning theorist, personality is the sum of learned responses to the external environment. (p. 350)

- Social cognitive approaches concentrate on the role of cognitions in determining personality. Those approaches pay particular attention to self-efficacy and self-esteem in determining behavior. (p. 351)

Explain biological and evolutionary approaches to personality.

- Biological and evolutionary approaches to personality focus on the way in which personality characteristics are inherited. (p. 353)

Explain humanistic approaches to personality.

- Humanistic approaches emphasize the inherent goodness of people. They consider the core of personality in terms of a person's ability to change and improve. (p. 354)

Compare and contrast approaches to personality.

- The major personality approaches differ substantially from one another; the differences may reflect both their focus on different aspects of personality and the overall complexity of personality (p. 355)

EVALUATE

1. A person who enjoys activities such as parties and hang gliding might be described by Eysenck as high on what trait?

2. Proponents of which approach to personality would be most likely to agree with the statement "Personality can be thought of as learned responses to a person's upbringing and environment"?

    a. Humanistic

    b. Biological and evolutionary

    c. Learning

    d. Trait

3. A person who would make the statement "I know I can't do it" would be rated by Bandura as low on _____ - _____.

4. Which approach to personality emphasizes the innate goodness of people and their desire to grow?

    a. Humanistic

    b. Psychodynamic

    c. Learning

    d. Biological and evolutionary

RETHINK

If personality traits are merely descriptive and not explanatory, of what use are they? Can assigning a trait to a person be harmful—or helpful? Why or why not?

Answers to Evaluate Questions 1. extraversion; 2. c; 3. self-efficacy; 4. a

[KEY TERMS]

Trait theory *p. 348*

Traits *p. 348*

Social cognitive approaches to personality *p. 351*

Self-efficacy *p. 351*

Self-esteem *p. 352*

Biological and evolutionary approaches to personality *p. 353*

Temperament *p. 353*

Humanistic approaches to personality *p. 354*

Self-actualization *p. 354*

Unconditional positive regard *p. 355*

Assessing Personality
Determining What Makes Us Distinctive

Psychological tests Standard measures devised to assess behavior objectively; used by psychologists to help people make decisions about their lives and understand more about themselves.

psych2.0

WWW.MHHE.COM/PSYCHLIFE

Personality Assessment

You have a need for other people to like and admire you.

You have a tendency to be critical of yourself.

You have a great deal of unused potential that you have not turned to your advantage.

Although you have some personality weaknesses, you generally are able to compensate for them.

Although you appear to be disciplined and self-controlled to others, you tend to be anxious and insecure inside.

At times you have serious doubts about whether you have made the right decision or done the right thing.

You do not accept others' statements without satisfactory proof.

You have found it unwise to be too frank in revealing yourself to others.

If you think these statements provide a surprisingly accurate account of your personality, you are not alone: most people think that these descriptions are tailored just to them. In fact, the statements were designed intentionally to be so vague that they apply to just about anyone (Forer, 1949; Russo, 1981).

The ease with which we can agree with such imprecise statements underscores the difficulty in coming up with accurate and meaningful assessments of people's personalities. Psychologists interested in assessing personality must be able to define the most meaningful ways of discriminating between one person's personality and another's. To do this, they use **psychological tests,** standard measures devised to assess behavior objectively. With the results of such tests, psychologists can help people better understand themselves and make decisions about their lives. Psychological tests are also employed by researchers interested in the causes and consequences of personality (Aiken, 2000; Kaplan & Saccuzzo, 2001; Hambleton, 2006).

All psychological tests must have reliability and validity. *Reliability* refers to the measurement consistency of a test. If a test is reliable, it yields the same result each time it is administered to a specific person or group. In contrast, unreliable tests give different results each time they are administered.

For meaningful conclusions to be drawn, tests also must be valid. Tests have *validity* when they actually measure what they are designed to measure. If a test is constructed to measure sociability, for instance, we need to know that it actually measures sociability, not some other trait.

Finally, psychological tests are based on *norms*, standards of test performance that permit the comparison of one person's score on a test with the scores of others who have taken the same test. For example, a norm permits test takers who have received a certain score on a test to know that they have scored in the top 10 percent of all those who have taken the test.

Norms are established by administering a specific test to a large number of people and determining the typical scores. It is then possible to compare a single person's score with the scores of the group, providing a comparative measure of test performance against the performance of others who have taken the test.

The establishment of appropriate norms is not a simple endeavor. For instance, the specific group that is employed to determine norms for a test has a profound effect on the way an individual's performance is evaluated.

> *The establishment of appropriate norms is not a simple endeavor.*

» LO1 Self-Report Measures of Personality

Psychologists use **self-report measures** that ask people about a small sample of their behavior; these are then used to infer the presence of particular personality characteristics. For example, a researcher who was interested in assessing a person's orientation to life might administer the questionnaire shown in the Try It! on page 360. Although the questionnaire consists of only a few questions, the answers can be used to generalize about personality characteristics.

One of the best examples of a self-report measure, and one of the most frequently used personality tests, is the **Minnesota Multiphasic Personality Inventory-2 (MMPI-2).** Although the original purpose of this measure was to identify people with specific sorts of psychological difficulties, it has been found to predict a variety of other behaviors. For instance, MMPI scores have been shown to be good predictors of whether college students will marry within 10 years and will get an advanced degree. Police departments use the test to measure whether police officers are likely to use their weapons (Butcher, 2005; Sellbom & Ben-Porath, 2006).

The test consists of a series of 567 items to which a person responds

Self-report measures A method of gathering data about people by asking them questions about a sample of their behavior.

Minnesota Multiphasic Personality Inventory-2 (MMPI-2) A widely used self-report test that identifies people with psychological difficulties and is employed to predict some everyday behaviors.

By using the Minnesota Multiphasic Personality Inventory-2 (MMPI-2), police departments acknowledge how important personality is to law enforcement. What are some other careers into which personality plays a key role?

The Life Orientation Test

Use the following scale to answer the following items:
0 = Strongly disagree; 1 = Disagree; 2 = Neutral; 3 = Agree; 4 = Strongly agree

1. In uncertain times, I usually expect the best. ____

2. It's easy for me to relax. ____

3. If something can go wrong for me, it will. ____

4. I'm always optimistic about my future. ____

5. I enjoy my friends a lot. ____

6. It's important for me to keep busy. ____

7. I hardly ever expect things to go my way. ____

8. I don't get upset too easily. ____

9. I rarely count on good things happening to me. ____

10. Overall, I expect more good things to happen to me than bad. ____

Scoring

First, reverse your answers to questions 3, 7, and 9. Do this by changing a 0 to a 4, a 1 to a 3, a 3 to a 1, and a 4 to a 0 (answers of 2 stay as 2). Then sum the reversed scores, and add them to the scores you gave to questions 1, 4, and 10. (Ignore questions 2, 5, 6, and 8, which are filler items.)

The total score you get is a measure of a particular orientation to life: your degree of optimism. The higher your scores, the more positive and hopeful you generally are about life. For comparison purposes, the average score for college students is 14.3 (Scheier, Carver, & Bridges, 1994). People with a higher degree of optimism generally deal with stress better than do those with lower scores.

"true," "false," or "cannot say." The questions cover a variety of issues, ranging from mood ("I feel useless at times") to opinions ("People should try to understand their dreams") to physical and psychological health ("I am bothered by an upset stomach several times a week" and "I have strange and peculiar thoughts").

There are no right or wrong answers. Instead, interpretation of the results rests on the pattern of responses. The test yields scores on 10 separate scales, plus 3 scales meant to measure the validity of the respondent's answers. For example, there is a "lie scale" that indicates when people are falsifying their responses in order to present themselves more favorably (through items such as "I can't remember ever having a bad night's sleep") (Butcher, 2005; Stein & Graham, 2005; Bacchiochi, 2006).

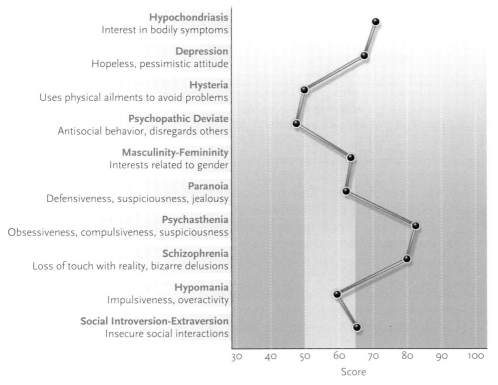

Clinical Scales

Hypochondriasis
Interest in bodily symptoms

Depression
Hopeless, pessimistic attitude

Hysteria
Uses physical ailments to avoid problems

Psychopathic Deviate
Antisocial behavior, disregards others

Masculinity-Femininity
Interests related to gender

Paranoia
Defensiveness, suspiciousness, jealousy

Psychasthenia
Obsessiveness, compulsiveness, suspiciousness

Schizophrenia
Loss of touch with reality, bizarre delusions

Hypomania
Impulsiveness, overactivity

Social Introversion-Extraversion
Insecure social interactions

30 40 50 60 70 80 90 100
Score

FIGURE 1   A profile on the MMPI-2 of a person who suffers from obsessional anxiety, social withdrawal, and delusional thinking. *(Source: Based on data from Halgin & Whitbourne, 1994, p. 72, and Minnesota Multiphasic Personality Inventory-2. Copyright © by the Regents of the University of Minnesota, 1942, 1943 (renewed 1970, 1989).)*

How did the authors of the MMPI determine what specific patterns of responses indicate? The procedure they used is typical of personality test construction—a process known as **test standardization.** To create the test, the test authors asked groups of psychiatric patients with a specific diagnosis, such as depression or schizophrenia, to complete a large number of items. They then determined which items best differentiated members of those groups from a comparison group of normal participants and included those specific items in the final version of the test. By systematically carrying out this procedure on groups with different diagnoses, the test authors were able to devise a number of subscales that identified different forms of abnormal behavior (see Figure 1).

When the MMPI is used for the purpose for which it was devised—identification of personality disorders—it does a good job. However, like other personality tests, it presents an opportunity for abuse. For instance, employers who use it as a screening tool for job applicants may interpret the results improperly, relying too heavily on the results of individual scales instead of taking into account the overall patterns of results, which require skilled interpretation. Although the MMPI remains the most widely used personality test and has been translated into more than 100 different languages, it must be used with caution (Greene & Clopton, 2004; Valsiner, Diriwächter, & Sauck, 2005).

> **Test standardization** A technique used to validate questions in personality tests by studying the responses of people with known diagnoses.

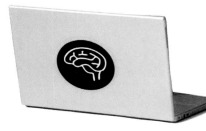

psych2.0
WWW.MHHE.COM/PSYCHLIFE

Rorschach on the Web

» LO 2 Projective Methods

If you were shown the shape presented in Figure 2 and asked what it represented to you, you might not think that your impressions would mean very much. But to a psychodynamic theoretician, your responses to such an ambiguous figure would provide valuable clues to the state of your unconscious, and ultimately to your general personality characteristics.

The shape in the figure is representative of inkblots used in **projective personality tests,** in which a person is shown an ambiguous stimulus and asked to describe it or tell a story about it. The responses are considered to be "projections" of the individual's personality.

The best-known projective test is the **Rorschach test.** Devised by Swiss psychiatrist Hermann Rorschach (1924), the test involves showing a series of symmetrical stimuli, similar to the one in Figure 2, to people who are then asked what the figures represent to them. Their responses are recorded, and through a complex set of clinical judgments on the part of the examiner, people are classified by their personality type. For instance, respondents who see a bear in one inkblot are thought to have a strong degree of emotional control, according to the scoring guidelines developed by Rorschach (Weiner, 2004b; Silverstein, 2007).

The **Thematic Apperception Test (TAT)** is another well-known projective test. The TAT consists of a series of pictures about which a person is asked to write a story. The stories are then used to draw inferences about the writer's personality characteristics (Weiner, 2004b; Langan-Fox & Grant, 2006).

Tests with stimuli as ambiguous as those used in the Rorschach and TAT require particular skill and care in their interpretation—too much, in many critics' estimation. The Rorschach in particular has been criticized for requiring too much inference on the part of the examiner, and attempts to standardize scoring have frequently failed. Furthermore, many critics complain that the Rorschach does not provide much valid information about underlying personality traits. Despite such problems, both the Rorschach and the TAT are widely used, especially in clinical settings, and their proponents suggest that their reliability and validity are great enough to provide useful inferences about personality (Wood et al., 2003; Garb et al., 2005; Society for Personality Assessment, 2005).

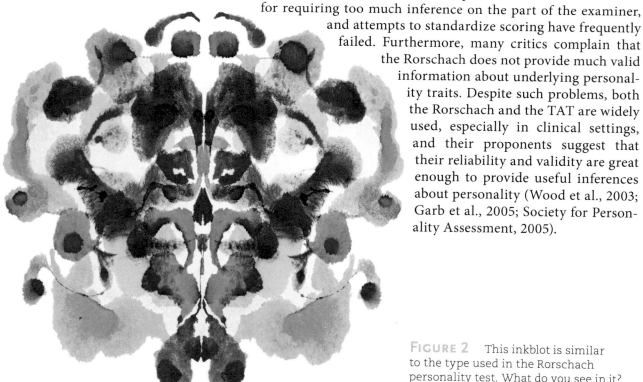

FIGURE 2 This inkblot is similar to the type used in the Rorschach personality test. What do you see in it? (*Source: Alloy, Jacobson, & Acocella, 1999.*)

» LO3 Behavioral Assessment

If you were a psychologist subscribing to a learning approach to personality, you would be likely to object to the indirect nature of projective tests. Instead, you would be more apt to use **behavioral assessment**—direct measures of an individual's behavior designed to describe characteristics indicative of personality. As with observational research, behavioral assessment may be carried out naturalistically by observing people in their own settings: in the workplace, at home, or in school. In other cases, behavioral assessment occurs in the laboratory, under controlled conditions in which a psychologist sets up a situation and observes an individual's behavior (Ramsay, Reynolds, & Kamphaus, 2002; Gladwell, 2004; Miller & Leffard, 2007).

Regardless of the setting in which behavior is observed, an effort is made to ensure that behavioral assessment is carried out objectively, quantifying behavior as much as possible. For example, an observer may record the number of social contacts a person initiates, the number of questions asked, or the number of aggressive acts. Another method is to measure the duration of events: the duration of a temper tantrum in a child, the length of a conversation, the amount of time spent working, or the time spent in cooperative behavior.

Behavioral assessment is particularly appropriate for observing—and eventually remedying—specific behavioral difficulties, such as shyness in children. It provides a means of assessing the specific nature and incidence of a problem and subsequently allows psychologists to determine whether intervention techniques have been successful.

"Rorschach! What's to become of you?"

Used with permission of Sidney Harris. © ScienceCartoonsPlus.com.

Rorschach test A test that involves showing a series of symmetrical visual stimuli to people who then are asked what the figures represent to them.

Thematic Apperception Test (TAT) A test consisting of a series of pictures about which a person is asked to write a story.

Behavioral assessment Direct measures of an individual's behavior used to describe personality characteristics.

From the perspective of . . .

A New Employee How might placing labels on others' personality at your new place of work help or harm your chances of making smart decisions? What aspects of your own personality would you like to showcase at your place of employment?

becoming an *informed consumer*
OF PSYCHOLOGY

Assessing Personality Assessments

Like the personality tests being developed by Google (which we discussed at the beginning of the chapter), assessments of personality are routinely used to help with hiring decisions. However, before relying too heavily on the results of personality testing, keep several points in mind:

- *Understand what the test claims to measure.* Standard personality measures are accompanied by information that discusses how the test was developed, to whom it is most applicable, and how the results should be interpreted. Read any explanations of the test; they will help you understand the results.

- *Base no decision only on the results of any one test.* Test results should be interpreted in the context of other information—academic records, social interests, and home and community activities.

- *Remember that test results are not always accurate.* The results may be in error; the test may be unreliable or invalid. You may, for example, have had a "bad day" when you took the test, or the person scoring and interpreting the test may have made a mistake. You should not place too much significance on the results of a single administration of any test.

In sum, it is important to keep in mind the complexity of human behavior—particularly your own. No single test can provide an understanding of the intricacies of someone's personality without considering a good deal more information than can be provided in a single testing session (Gladwell, 2004; Paul, 2004; Hogan, Davies, & Hogan, 2007).

RECAP

Discuss self-report measures of personality.

- Psychological tests such as the MMPI are standard assessment tools that measure behavior objectively. They must be reliable (measuring what they are trying to measure consistently) and valid (measuring what they are supposed to measure). (p. 359)

- Self-report measures ask people about a sample range of their behaviors. These reports are used to infer the presence of particular personality characteristics. (p. 359)

Define projective methods.

- Projective personality tests (such as the Rorschach and the Thematic Apperception Test) present an ambiguous stimulus; the test administrator infers information about the test taker from his or her responses. (p. 363)

Explain behavioral assessment.

- Behavioral assessment is based on the principles of learning theory. It employs direct measurement of an individual's behavior to determine characteristics related to personality. (p. 363)

EVALUATE

1. _____ is the consistency of a personality test; _____ is the ability of a test to actually measure what it is designed to measure.

2. _____ are standards used to compare scores of different people taking the same test.

3. Tests such as the MMPI-2, in which a small sample of behavior is assessed to determine larger patterns, are examples of
   a. Cross-sectional tests
   b. Projective tests
   c. Achievement tests
   d. Self-report tests

4. A person shown a picture and asked to make up a story about it would be taking a _____ personality test.

RETHINK

Should personality tests be used for personnel decisions? Should they be used for other social purposes, such as identifying individuals at risk for certain types of personality disorders?

[KEY TERMS]

Psychological tests *p. 358*

Self-report measures *p. 359*

Minnesota Multiphasic Personality Inventory-2 (MMPI-2) *p. 359*

Test standardization *p. 361*

Projective personality tests *p. 362*

Rorschach test *p. 363*

Thematic Apperception Test (TAT) *p. 363*

Behavioral assessment *p. 363*

Intelligence

LEARNING OUTCOMES

32.1 Summarize the theories of intelligence.

32.2 Compare and contrast practical and emotional intelligences.

32.3 Explain approaches to assessing intelligence.

32.4 Identify variations in intellectual ability.

Intelligence The capacity to understand the world, think rationally, and use resources effectively when faced with challenges.

***g* or *g*-factor** The single, general factor for mental ability assumed to underlie intelligence in some early theories of intelligence.

Intelligence can take on many different meanings. If, for instance, you lived in a remote part of the Australian outback, the way you would differentiate between more intelligent and less intelligent people might have to do with successfully mastering hunting skills, whereas to someone living in the heart of urban Miami, intelligence might be exemplified by being "street wise" or by achieving success in business.

Each of these conceptions of intelligence is reasonable. Each represents an instance in which more intelligent people are better able to use the resources of their environment than are less intelligent people, a distinction that is presumably basic to any definition of intelligence. Yet it is also clear that these conceptions represent very different views of intelligence.

To psychologists, **intelligence** is the capacity to understand the world, think rationally, and use resources effectively when faced with challenges. This definition does not lay to rest a key question asked by psychologists: Is intelligence a unitary attribute, or are there different kinds of intelligence? We turn now to various theories of intelligence that address the issue.

» LO1 Theories of Intelligence: Are There Different Kinds of Intelligence?

Is intelligence a single, general ability, or is it multifaceted and related to specific abilities?

Perhaps you see yourself as a good writer but as someone who lacks ability in math. Or maybe you view yourself as a "science" person who easily masters physics but has few strengths in interpreting literature. Perhaps you view yourself as generally fairly smart, with intelligence that permits you to excel across domains.

The different ways in which people view their own talents mirrors a question that psychologists have grappled with: Is intelligence a single, general ability, or is it multifaceted and related to specific abilities? Early psychologists interested in intelligence assumed that there was a single, general factor for mental ability, which they called *g*, or the *g*-**factor.** This general intelligence factor was thought to underlie performance in every aspect of intelligence, and it was the *g*-factor that was presumably being measured on tests of intelligence (Spearman, 1927; Gottfredson, 2004; Colom, Jung, & Haier, 2006).

More recent theories see intelligence in a different light. Rather than viewing intelligence as a unitary entity, they consider it to be a multidimensional concept that includes different types of intelligence (Tenopyr, 2002; Stankov, 2003; Sternberg & Pretz, 2005).

Fluid and Crystallized Intelligence

Some psychologists suggest that there are two different kinds of intelligence: fluid intelligence and crystallized intelligence. **Fluid intelligence** reflects information-processing capabilities, reasoning, and memory. If we were asked to solve an analogy, group a series of letters according to some criterion, or remember a set of numbers, we would be using fluid intelligence (Kane & Engle, 2002; Saggino, Perfetti, & Spitoni, 2006).

In contrast, **crystallized intelligence** is the accumulation of information, skills, and strategies that people have learned through experience and that they can apply in problem-solving situations. It reflects our ability to call up information from long-term memory. We would be likely to rely on crystallized intelligence, for instance, if we were asked to participate in a discussion about the solution to the causes of poverty, a task that allows us to draw on our own past experiences and knowledge of the world.

Gardner's Multiple Intelligences: The Many Ways of Showing Intelligence

Psychologist Howard Gardner has taken an approach very different from traditional thinking about intelligence. Gardner argues that rather than asking "How smart are you?" we should be asking a different question: "How are you smart?" In answering the latter question, Gardner has developed a **theory of multiple intelligences** that has become quite influential (Gardner, 2000).

Gardner argues that we have at a minimum eight different forms of intelligence, each relatively independent of the others: musical, bodily kinesthetic, logical-mathematical, linguistic, spatial, interpersonal, intrapersonal, and naturalist. (Figure 1 describes the eight types of intelligence, with some of Gardner's examples of people who excel in each type.) In Gardner's view, each of the multiple intelligences is linked to an independent system in the brain.

Although Gardner illustrates his conception of the specific types of intelligence with descriptions of well-known people, each person has the same eight kinds of intelligence—in different degrees. Moreover, although the eight basic types of intelligence are presented individually, Gardner suggests that these separate intelligences do not operate in isolation. Normally, any activity encompasses several kinds of intelligence working together.

Fluid intelligence Intelligence that reflects information-processing capabilities, reasoning, and memory.

Crystallized intelligence The accumulation of information, skills, and strategies that are learned through experience and can be applied in problem-solving situations.

Theory of multiple intelligences Howard Gardner's theory that proposes that there are eight distinct spheres of intelligence.

In a busy pharmacy, a pharmacy technician will often rely on both fluid and crystallized intelligence. Which do you think will be most important in your chosen career?

Musical Intelligence (skills in tasks involving music). Case example:

When he was 3, Yehudi Menuhin was smuggled into San Francisco Orchestra concerts by his parents. By the time he was 10 years old, Menuhin was an international performer.

Spatial Intelligence (skills involving spatial configurations, such as those used by artists and architects). Case example:

Natives of the Truk Islands navigate at sea without instruments. During the actual trip, the navigator must envision mentally a reference island as it passes under a particular star and from that he computes the number of segments completed, the proportion of the trip remaining, and any corrections in heading.

Bodily Kinesthetic Intelligence (skills in using the whole body or various portions of it in the solution of problems or in the construction of products or displays, exemplified by dancers, athletes, actors, and surgeons). Case example:

Fifteen-year-old Babe Ruth played third base. During one game, his team's pitcher was doing very poorly and Babe loudly criticized him from third base. Brother Matthias, the coach, called out, "Ruth, if you know so much about it, *you* pitch!" Ruth said later that at the very moment he took the pitcher's mound, he *knew* he was supposed to be a pitcher.

Interpersonal Intelligence (skills in interacting with others, such as sensitivity to the moods, temperaments, motivations, and intentions of others). Case example:

When Anne Sullivan began instructing the deaf and blind Helen Keller, her task was one that had eluded others for years. Yet, just two weeks after beginning her work with Keller, Sullivan achieved great success.

Logical-Mathematical Intelligence (skills in problem solving and scientific thinking). Case example:

Barbara McClintock, who won the Nobel Prize in medicine, describes one of her breakthroughs, which came after thinking about a problem for half an hour. . . : "Suddenly I jumped and ran back to the (corn) field. At the top of the field (the others were still at the bottom) I shouted, 'Eureka, I have it!' "

Intrapersonal Intelligence (knowledge of the internal aspects of oneself; access to one's own feelings and emotions). Case example:

In her essay "A Sketch of the Past," Virginia Woolf displays deep insight into her own inner life through these lines, describing her reaction to several specific memories from her childhood that still, in adulthood, shock her: "Though I still have the peculiarity that I receive these sudden shocks, they are now always welcome; after the first surprise, I always feel instantly that they are particularly valuable. And so I go on to suppose that the shock-receiving capacity is what makes me a writer."

Linguistic Intelligence (skills involved in the production and use of language). Case example:

At the age of 10, T. S. Eliot created a magazine called *Fireside*, to which he was the sole contributor.

Naturalist Intelligence (ability to identify and classify patterns in nature). Case example:

During prehistoric times, hunter/gatherers would rely on naturalist intelligence to identify what flora and fauna were edible. People who are adept at distinguishing nuances between large numbers of similar objects may be expressing naturalist intelligence abilities.

FIGURE 1 According to Howard Gardner, there are eight major kinds of intelligences, corresponding to abilities in different domains. In what area does your greatest intelligence reside, and why do you think you have particular strengths in that area? *(Source: Adapted from Gardner, 2000).*

The concept of multiple intelligences has led to the development of intelligence tests that include questions in which more than one answer can be correct; these provide an opportunity for test takers to demonstrate creative thinking. In addition, many educators, embracing the concept of multiple intelligences, have designed classroom curricula that are meant to draw on different aspects of intelligence (Armstrong, 2000, 2003; Kelly & Tangney, 2006).

Is Information Processing Intelligence?

One of the newer contributions to understanding intelligence comes from the work of cognitive psychologists who take an *information-processing approach.* They assert that the way people store material in memory and use that material to solve intellectual tasks provides the most accurate measure of intelligence. Consequently, rather than focusing on the structure of intelligence or its underlying content or dimensions, information-processing approaches examine the *processes* involved in producing intelligent behavior (Hunt, 2005; Neubauer & Fink, 2005; Pressley & Harris, 2006).

For example, research shows that people with high scores on tests of intelligence spend more time on the initial encoding stages of problems, identifying the parts of a problem and retrieving relevant information from long-term memory, than do people with lower scores. This initial emphasis on recalling relevant information pays off in the end; those who use this approach are more successful in finding solutions than are those who spend relatively less time on the initial stages (Sternberg, 1990; Deary & Der, 2005; Hunt, 2005).

Other information-processing approaches examine the sheer speed of processing. For example, research shows that the speed with which people are able to retrieve information from memory is related to verbal intelligence. In general, people with high scores on measures of intelligence react more quickly on a variety of information-processing tasks, ranging from reactions to flashing lights to distinguishing between letters. The speed of information processing, then, may underlie differences in intelligence (Deary & Der, 2005; Jensen, 2005; Gontkovsky & Beatty, 2006).

"To be perfectly frank, I'm not nearly as smart as you seem to think I am."

> **STUDY ALERT**
>
> Remember that Gardner's theory suggests that each individual has every kind of intelligence, but in different degrees.

psych2.0
WWW.MHHE.COM/PSYCHLIFE

Gardner's Multiple Intelligences

» LO2 Practical Intelligence and Emotional Intelligence: Toward a More Intelligent View of Intelligence

Consider the following situation:

> An employee who reports to one of your subordinates has asked to talk with you about waste, poor management practices, and possible violations of both company policy and the law on the part of your subordinate. You have been in your present position only a year, but in that time you have had no indications of trouble about the subordinate in question. Neither you nor your company has an "open door" policy, so it is expected that employees should take their concerns to their immediate supervisors before bringing a matter to the attention of anyone else.

Practical intelligence According to Robert Sternberg, intelligence related to overall success in living.

Emotional intelligence The set of skills that underlie the accurate assessment, evaluation, expression, and regulation of emotions.

The employee who wishes to meet with you has not discussed this matter with her supervisors because of its delicate nature. (Sternberg, 1998, p. 17)

Your response to the preceding situation has a lot to do with your future success in a business career, according to psychologist Robert Sternberg. The question is one of a series designed to help give an indication of your intelligence. However, it is not traditional intelligence that the question is designed to tap, but rather intelligence of a specific kind: practical intelligence. **Practical intelligence** is intelligence related to overall success in living (Sternberg, 2000, 2002b; Sternberg & Hedlund, 2002; Wagner, 2002; Muammar, 2007).

Noting that traditional tests were designed to relate to academic success, Sternberg points to evidence showing that most traditional measures of intelligence do not relate especially well to *career* success (McClelland, 1993). Specifically, although successful business executives usually score at least moderately well on intelligence tests, the rate at which they advance and their ultimate business achievements are only minimally associated with traditional measures of their intelligence.

Whereas academic success is based on knowledge of a specific information base obtained from reading and listening, practical intelligence is learned mainly through observation of others' behavior.

Sternberg argues that career success requires a very different type of intelligence from that required for academic success. Whereas academic success is based on knowledge of a specific information base obtained from reading and listening, practical intelligence is learned mainly through observation of others' behavior. People who are high in practical intelligence are able to learn general norms and principles and apply them appropriately. Consequently, practical intelligence tests, like the one shown in Figure 2, measure the ability to employ broad principles in solving everyday problems (Polk, 1997; Sternberg & Pretz, 2005; Stemler & Sternberg, 2006).

Some psychologists broaden the concept of intelligence even further beyond the intellectual realm to include emotions. **Emotional intelligence** is the set of skills that underlie the accurate assessment, evaluation, expression, and regulation of emotions (Zeidner, Matthews, & Roberts, 2004; Mayer, Salovey, & Caruso, 2004; Humphrey, Curran, & Morris, 2007).

Emotional intelligence underlies the ability to get along well with others. It provides us with an understanding of what other people are feeling and experiencing and permits us to respond appropriately to others' needs. Emotional intelligence is the basis of empathy for others, self-awareness, and social skills.

Abilities in emotional intelligence may help explain why people with only modest scores on traditional intelligence tests can be quite successful, despite their lack of traditional intelligence. High emotional intelligence may enable

As a paralegal, how might high practical intelligence help you in your career? Would high practical intelligence help or hurt you if you suspected unethical work was being done at your firm?

You are given a map of an entertainment park.
You walk from the lemonade stand to the computer games arcade.
Your friend walks from the shooting gallery to the roller coaster.
Which of these are you BOTH most likely to pass?

A the merry-go-round   **B** the music hall
C the pizza stand   **D** the dog show

FIGURE 2   Most standard tests of intelligence primarily measure analytical skills; more comprehensive tests measure creative and practical abilities as well. *(Source: Sternberg, 2000, p. 389).*

an individual to tune into others' feelings, permitting a high degree of responsiveness to others.

The notion of emotional intelligence reminds us that there are many ways to demonstrate intelligent behavior—just as there are multiple views of the nature of intelligence (Fox & Spector, 2000; Barrett & Salovey, 2002). Figure 3 presents a summary of the different approaches used by psychologists.

» LO3 Assessing Intelligence

Given the variety of approaches to the components of intelligence, it is not surprising that measuring intelligence has proved challenging. Psychologists who study intelligence have focused much of their attention on the development of **intelligence tests** and have relied on such tests to quantify a person's level of intelligence. These tests have proved to be of great benefit in identifying students in need of special attention in school, diagnosing cognitive difficulties, and helping people make optimal educational and vocational choices. At the same time, their use has proved controversial, raising important social and educational issues.

Intelligence tests Tests devised to quantify a person's level of intelligence.

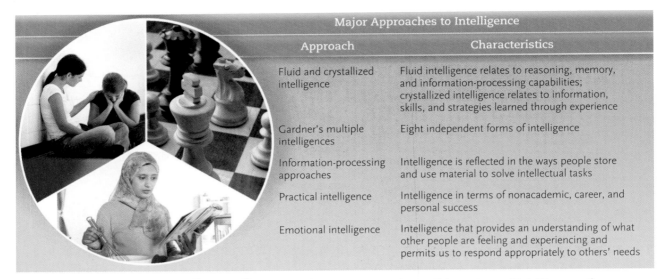

Major Approaches to Intelligence	
Approach	**Characteristics**
Fluid and crystallized intelligence	Fluid intelligence relates to reasoning, memory, and information-processing capabilities; crystallized intelligence relates to information, skills, and strategies learned through experience
Gardner's multiple intelligences	Eight independent forms of intelligence
Information-processing approaches	Intelligence is reflected in the ways people store and use material to solve intellectual tasks
Practical intelligence	Intelligence in terms of nonacademic, career, and personal success
Emotional intelligence	Intelligence that provides an understanding of what other people are feeling and experiencing and permits us to respond appropriately to others' needs

FIGURE 3 Just as there are many views of the nature of intelligence, there are also numerous ways to demonstrate intelligent behavior. This summary provides an overview of the various approaches used by psychologists.

Binet and the Development of IQ Tests

The first real intelligence tests were developed by the French psychologist Alfred Binet (1857–1911). His tests followed from a simple premise: if performance on certain tasks or test items improved with *chronological,* or physical, age, performance could be used to distinguish more intelligent people from less intelligent ones within a particular age group. On the basis of this principle, Binet devised the first formal intelligence test, which was designed to identify the "dullest" students in the Paris school system in order to provide them with remedial aid.

Binet began by presenting tasks to same-age students who had been labeled "bright" or "dull" by their teachers. If a task could be completed by the bright students but not by the dull ones, he retained that task as a proper test item; otherwise it was discarded. In the end he came up with a test that distinguished between the bright and dull groups, and—with further work—one that distinguished among children in different age groups (Binet & Simon, 1916; Sternberg & Jarvin, 2003).

Mental age The average age of individuals who achieve a particular level of performance on a test.

Alfred Binet

On the basis of the Binet test, children were assigned a score relating to their **mental age,** the average age of individuals who achieve a particular level of performance on a test. For example, if the average 8-year-old answered, say, 45 items correctly on a test, anyone who answered 45 items correctly would be assigned a mental age of 8 years. Consequently, whether the person taking the test was 20 years old or 5 years old, he or she would have the same mental age of 8 years (Cornell, 2006).

Assigning a mental age to students provided an indication of their general level of performance. However, it did not allow for adequate comparisons among people of different chronological ages. By using mental age alone, for instance, we might assume that a 20-year-old responding at a 18-year-old's level would be as bright as a 5-year-old answering at a 3-year-old's level, when actually the 5-year-old would be displaying a much greater *relative* degree of slowness.

A solution to the problem came in the form of the **intelligence quotient,** or **IQ,** a score that takes into account an individual's mental *and* chronological ages. Historically, the first IQ scores employed the following formula, in which *MA* stands for mental age and *CA* for chronological age:

$$\text{IQ score} = \frac{MA}{CA} \times 100$$

> **Intelligence quotient (IQ)** A score that takes into account an individual's mental and chronological ages.

Using this formula, we can return to the earlier example of a 20-year-old performing at a mental age of 18 and calculate an IQ score of $(18/20) \times 100 = 90$. In contrast, the 5-year-old performing at a mental age of 3 comes out with a considerably lower IQ score: $(3/5) \times 100 = 60$.

As a bit of trial and error with the formula will show you, anyone who has a mental age equal to his or her chronological age will have an IQ equal to 100. Moreover, people with a mental age that is greater than their chronological age will have IQs that exceed 100.

Although the basic principles behind the calculation of an IQ score still hold, today IQ scores are figured in a different manner and are known as *deviation IQ scores.* First, the average test score for everyone of the same age who takes the test is determined, and that average score is assigned an IQ of 100. Then, with the aid of statistical techniques that calculate the differences (or "deviations") between each score and the average, IQ scores are assigned.

As you can see in Figure 4, when IQ scores from large numbers of people are plotted on a graph, they form a *bell-shaped distribution* (called

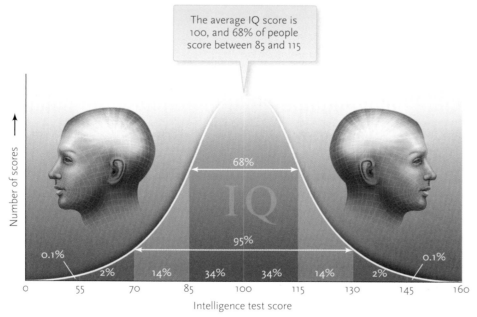

The average IQ score is 100, and 68% of people score between 85 and 115

Number of scores

68%

95%

0.1%   2%   14%   34%   34%   14%   2%   0.1%

0   55   70   85   100   115   130   145   160

Intelligence test score

FIGURE 4 The average and most common IQ score is 100, and 68 percent of all people are within a 30-point range centered on 100. Some 95 percent of the population have scores that are within 30 points above or below 100, and 99.8 percent have scores that are between 55 and 145.

WAIS IV (for adults) Name	Goal of Item	Example
Verbal Scale		
Information	Assess general information	Who wrote *Tom Sawyer?*
Comprehension	Assess understanding and evaluation of social norms and past experience	Why is copper often used for electrical wires?
Arithmetic	Assess math reasoning through verbal problems	Three women divided eighteen golf balls equally among themselves. How many golf balls did each person receive?
Similarities	Test understanding of how objects or concepts are alike, tapping abstract reasoning	In what way are a circle and a triangle alike?
Performance Scale		
Digit symbol	Assess speed of learning	Test taker must learn what symbols correspond to what digits, and then must replace a multidigit number with the appropriate symbols. 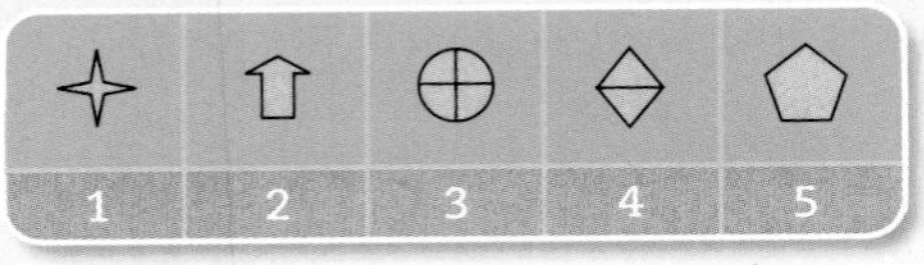
Matrix reasoning	Test spatial reasoning	Test taker must decide which of the five possibilities replaces the question mark and completes the sequence. 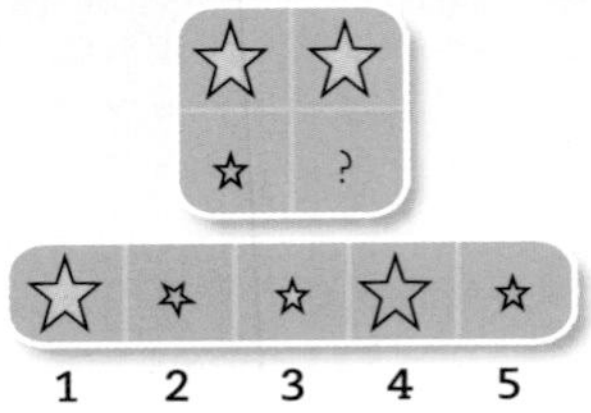
Block design item	Test understanding of relationship of parts to whole	Problems require test takers to reproduce a design in fixed amount of time. 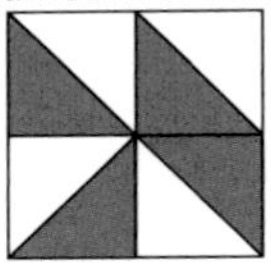

(continues)

FIGURE 5 Typical kinds of items found on the verbal and performance (nonverbal) scales of the Wechsler Adult Intelligence Scale (WAIS-IV) and the Wechsler Intelligence Scale for Children (WISC-IV).

"bell-shaped" because it looks like a bell when plotted). Approximately two-thirds of all individuals fall within 15 IQ points of the average score of 100. As scores increase or fall beyond that range, the percentage of people in a category falls considerably.

Contemporary IQ Tests: Gauging Intelligence

Remnants of Binet's original intelligence test are still with us, although the test has been revised in significant ways. Now in its fifth edition and called the *Stanford-Binet Intelligence Scale,* the test consists of a series of items that vary in nature according to the age of the person being tested (Roid & Pomplun, 2005). For example, young children are asked to copy figures or answer questions about everyday activities. Older people are asked to solve analogies, explain proverbs, and describe similarities that underlie sets of words.

WISC IV (for children) Name	Goal of Item	Example
Verbal Scale		
Information	Assess general information	How many nickels make a dime?
Comprehension	Assess understanding and evaluation of social norms and past experience	What is the advantage of keeping money in the bank?
Arithmetic	Assess math reasoning through verbal problems	If two buttons cost 15 cents, what will be the cost of a dozen buttons?
Similarities	Test understanding of how objects or concepts are alike, tapping abstract reasoning	In what way are an hour and a week alike?
Performance Scale		
Digit symbol	Assess speed of learning	Match symbols to numbers using key.
Picture completion	Visual memory and attention	Identify what is missing.
Object assembly	Test understanding of relationship of parts to wholes	Put pieces together to form a whole.

FIGURE 5 (CONCLUDED)   *(Source: Simulated items similar to those in the Wechsler Intelligence Scale for Children, Fourth Edition. Copyright © 2003 Wechsler Adult Intelligence Scale © 1997 Third Edition by Harcourt Assessment, Inc. Reproduced with permission. All rights reserved.)*

The IQ test most frequently used in the United States was devised by psychologist David Wechsler and is known as the *Wechsler Adult Intelligence Scale–IV,* or, more commonly, the *WAIS-IV.* There is also a children's version, the *Wechsler Intelligence Scale for Children–IV,* or *WISC-IV.* Both the WAIS-IV and the WISC-IV have two major parts: a verbal scale and a performance (or nonverbal) scale. As you can see from the sample questions in Figure 5, the verbal and performance scales include questions of very different types. Verbal tasks consist of more traditional kinds of problems, including vocabulary definition and comprehension of various concepts. In contrast, the performance (nonverbal) part involves the timed assembly of small objects and the arrangement of pictures in a logical order.

Because the Stanford-Binet, WAIS-IV, and WISC-IV all require individualized, one-on-one administration, it is relatively difficult and time-consuming to administer and score them on a large-scale basis. Consequently, there are now a number of IQ tests that allow group administration. Rather than having one examiner ask one person at a time to respond to individual items, group IQ tests are strictly paper-and-pencil tests. The primary advantage of group tests is their ease of administration (Anastasi & Urbina, 1997).

» LO 4 Variations in Intellectual Ability

More than 7 million people in the United States, including around 11 per 1,000 children, have been identified as far enough below average in intelligence that they can be regarded as having a serious deficit. Individuals with low IQs (people with intellectual disabilities) as well as those with unusually high IQs (the intellectually gifted) require special attention if they are to reach their full potential.

Intellectual Disabilities (Mental Retardation)

Although sometimes thought of as a rare phenomenon, intellectual disability occurs in 1 to 3 percent of the population. There is wide variation among those with intellectual disabilities, in large part because of the inclusiveness of the

> There is wide variation among those with intellectual disabilities, in large part because of the inclusiveness of the definition.

definition. **Intellectual disability**—or, as it is also known, **mental retardation**—is characterized by significant limitations in intellectual functioning and in adaptive behavior involving conceptual, social, and practical skills. (Although experts are increasingly using the term "intellectual disability" instead of "mental retardation," the terms are used interchangeably, and we'll use both.)

Although below-average intellectual functioning can be measured in a relatively straightforward manner—using standard IQ tests—it is more difficult to determine how to gauge limitations in adaptive behavior. Ultimately, this imprecision leads to a lack of uniformity in how experts apply the label *intellectual disability*. Furthermore, it has resulted in significant variation in the abilities of people who are categorized as intellectually disabled, ranging from those who can be taught to work and function with little special attention to those who virtually cannot be trained and must receive institutional treatment throughout their lives (Detterman, Gabriel, & Ruthsatz, 2000; Greenspan, 2006).

Most people with intellectual disabilities have relatively minor deficits and are classified as having *mild retardation*. These individuals, who have IQ scores ranging from 55 to 69, constitute some 90 percent of all people with intellectual disabilities. Although their development is typically slower than that of their peers, they can function quite independently by adulthood and are able to hold jobs and have families of their own (Bates et al., 2001; Smith, 2006).

At greater levels of retardation—*moderate retardation* (IQs of 40 to 54), *severe retardation* (IQs of 25 to 39), and *profound retardation* (IQs below 25)—the difficulties are more pronounced. For people with moderate retardation, deficits are obvious early, with language and motor skills lagging behind those of peers. Although these individuals can hold simple jobs, they need to have a moderate degree of supervision throughout their lives. Individuals with severe and profound intellectual disabilities are generally unable to function independently and typically require care for their entire lives (Garwick, 2007).

Intellectual disability Another term for mental retardation.

Mental retardation A condition characterized by significant limitations both in intellectual functioning and in conceptual, social, and practical adaptive skills.

How might an understanding of the causes of mental retardation impact how you deal with patients as a pediatric LPN?

Identifying the Roots of Intellectual Disabilities

What are the causes of intellectual disabilities? In nearly one-third of the cases there is an identifiable biological origin. The most common biological cause is **fetal alcohol syndrome**, caused by a mother's use of alcohol while pregnant. Increasing evidence shows that even small amounts of alcohol intake can produce intellectual deficits (Burd et al., 2003; Coles, Platzman, & Lynch, 2003; West & Blake, 2005).

Down syndrome, the type of intellectual disability experienced by actor Chris Burke, represents another major biological cause of intellectual disabilities. *Down syndrome* results from the presence of an extra chromosome. In other cases of intellectual disabilities, an abnormality occurs in the structure of a chromosome. Birth complications, such as a temporary lack of oxygen, may also cause retardation. In some cases, intellectual disabilities occur after birth, following a head injury, a stroke, or infections such as meningitis (Plomin, & Kovas, 2005; Bittles, Bower, & Hussain, 2007).

However, the majority of cases of intellectual disabilities are classified as **familial retardation,** in which no apparent biological defect exists but there is a history of retardation in the family. Whether the family background of retardation is caused by environmental factors, such as extreme continuous poverty leading to malnutrition, or by some underlying genetic factor is usually impossible to determine (Zigler et al., 2002).

The Intellectually Gifted

Another group of people—the intellectually gifted—differ from those with average intelligence as much as do individuals with intellectual disabilities, although in a different manner. Accounting for 2 to 4 percent of the population, the **intellectually gifted** have IQ scores greater than 130.

Although the stereotype associated with the gifted suggests that they are awkward, shy social misfits who are unable to get along well with peers, most

Fetal alcohol syndrome The most common cause of mental retardation in newborns, occurring when the mother uses alcohol during pregnancy.

Familial retardation Mental retardation in which no apparent biological defect exists, but there is a history of retardation in the family.

Intellectually gifted The 2 to 4 percent of the population who have IQ scores greater than 130.

psych2.0
WWW.MHHE.COM/PSYCHLIFE

Intellectual Disabilities

research indicates that just the opposite is true. The intellectually gifted are most often outgoing, well adjusted, healthy, popular people who are able to do most things better than the average person can (Winner, 2003; Gottfredson & Deary, 2004; Lubinski et al., 2006).

For example, in a famous study by psychologist Lewis Terman that started in the early 1920s, 1,500 children who had IQ scores above 140 were followed for the rest of their lives. From the start, the members of this group were more physically, academically, and socially capable than their nongifted peers. In addition to doing better in school, they also showed better social adjustment than average. All these advantages paid off in terms of career success: as a group, the gifted received more awards and distinctions, earned higher incomes, and made more contributions in art and literature than typical individuals. Perhaps most important, they reported greater satisfaction in life than the nongifted (Hegarty, 2007).

Of course, not every member of the group Terman studied was successful. Furthermore, high intelligence is not a homogeneous quality; a person with a high overall IQ is not necessarily gifted in every academic subject, but may excel in just one or two. A high IQ is not a universal guarantee of success (Shurkin, 1992; Winner, 2003; Clemons, 2006).

E X P L O R I N G diversity

The Relative Influence of Genetics and Environment: Nature, Nurture, and IQ

In an attempt to produce a **culture-fair IQ test,** one that does not discriminate against the members of any minority group, psychologists have tried to devise test items that assess experiences common to all cultures or emphasize questions that do not require language usage. However, test makers have found this difficult to do, because past experiences, attitudes, and values almost always have an impact on respondents' answers.

Culture-fair IQ test A test that does not discriminate against the members of any minority group.

For example, children raised in Western cultures group things on the basis of what they *are* (such as putting *dog* and *fish* into the category of *animal*). In contrast, members of the Kpelle tribe in Africa see intelligence demonstrated by grouping things according to what they *do* (grouping *fish* with *swim*). Similarly, children in the United States asked to memorize the position of objects on a chessboard perform better than do African children living in remote villages if household objects familiar to the U.S. children are used. But if rocks are used instead of household objects, the African children do better. In short, it is difficult to produce a test that is truly culture-fair (Sandoval et al., 1998; Serpell, 2000; Valencia & Suzuki, 2003).

The efforts of psychologists to produce culture-fair measures of intelligence relate to a lingering controversy over differences in intelligence between members of minority and majority groups. In attempting to identify whether there are differences between such groups, psychologists have had to confront the broader issue of determining the relative contribution to intelligence of genetic factors (heredity) and experience (environment)—the nature-nurture issue that is one of the basic issues of psychology.

Richard Herrnstein, a psychologist, and Charles Murray, a sociologist, fanned the flames of the debate with the publication of their book *The Bell Curve* in the mid-1990s (Herrnstein & Murray, 1994). They argued that an analysis of IQ differences between whites and blacks demonstrated that although environmental factors played a role, there were also basic genetic differences between the two races. They based their argument on a number of findings. For instance, on average, whites score 15 points higher than do blacks on traditional IQ tests even when socioeconomic status (SES) is taken into account. According to Herrnstein and Murray, middle- and upper-SES blacks score lower than do middle- and upper-SES whites, just as lower-SES blacks score lower on average than do lower-SES whites. Intelligence differences between blacks and whites, they concluded, could not be attributed to environmental differences alone.

Moreover, intelligence in general shows a high degree of **heritability,** a measure of the degree to which a characteristic can be attributed to genetic, inherited factors (e.g., Plomin, 2003b; Miller & Penke, 2007). As can be seen in Figure 6, the closer the genetic link between two related people, the greater the correspondence of IQ scores. Using data such as these, Herrnstein and Murray argued that differences between races in IQ scores were largely caused by genetically based differences in intelligence.

> **Heritability** A measure of the degree to which a characteristic is related to genetic, inherited factors.

However, many psychologists reacted strongly to the arguments laid out in *The Bell Curve,* refuting several of the book's basic arguments. One criticism is that even when attempts are made to hold socioeconomic conditions constant, wide variations remain among individual households. Furthermore, no one can convincingly assert that the living conditions of blacks and whites are identical even when their socioeconomic status is similar. In addition, there is reason to believe that traditional IQ tests may discriminate against lower-SES urban blacks by asking for information pertaining to experiences they are unlikely to have had (American Psychological Association Task Force on Intelligence, 1996; Hall, 2002; Horn, 2002; Nisbett, 2007).

Moreover, blacks who are raised in economically enriched environments have similar IQ scores to whites in comparable environments. For example, a study by Sandra Scarr and Richard Weinberg (1976) examined black children who had

Relationship	Genetic Overlap	Rearing	Correlation
Monozygotic (identical) twins	100%	Together	.86
Dizygotic (fraternal) twins	50%	Together	.62
Siblings	50%	Together	.41
Siblings	50%	Apart	.24
Parent-child	50%	Together	.35
Parent-child	50%	Apart	.31
Adoptive parent-child	0%	Together	.16
Unrelated children	0%	Together	.25
Spouses	0%	Apart	.29

The difference between these two correlations shows the impact of the environment

The relatively low correlation for unrelated children raised together shows the importance of genetic factors

FIGURE 6 The relationship between IQ and closeness of genetic relationship. In general, the more similar the genetic and environmental background of two people, the greater the correlation. Note, for example, that the correlation for spouses, who are genetically unrelated and have been reared apart, is relatively low, whereas the correlation for identical twins reared together is substantial. *(Source: Adapted from Henderson, 1982.)*

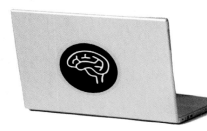

psych2.0

WWW.MHHE.COM/PSYCHLIFE

IQ Issues

been adopted at an early age by white middle-class families of above-average intelligence. The IQ scores of those children averaged 106—about 15 points above the average IQ scores of unadopted black children in the study. Other research shows that the racial gap in IQ narrows considerably after a college education, and cross-cultural data demonstrate that when racial gaps exist in other cultures, it is the economically disadvantaged groups that typically have lower scores. In short, the evidence that genetic factors play the major role in determining racial differences in IQ is not compelling (Winston, 2004; Sternberg, Grigorenko, & Kidd, 2005; Fagan & Holland, 2007).

Furthermore, drawing comparisons between different races on any dimension, including IQ scores, is an imprecise, potentially misleading, and often fruitless venture. By far, the greatest discrepancies in IQ scores occur when comparing *individuals,* not when comparing mean IQ scores of different *groups.* There are blacks who score high on IQ tests and whites who score low, just as there are whites who score high and blacks who score low. For the concept of intelligence to aid in the betterment of society, we must examine how *individuals* perform, not the groups to which they belong (Angoff, 1988; Fagan & Holland, 2002, 2007).

The more critical question to ask is not whether hereditary or environmental factors primarily underlie intelligence, but whether there is anything we can do to maximize the intellectual development of each individual. If we can find ways to do this, we will be able to make changes in the environment—which may take the form of enriched home and school environments—that can lead each person to reach his or her potential.

R E C A P

Summarize the theories of intelligence.

- Because intelligence can take many forms, defining it is challenging. One commonly accepted view is that intelligence is the capacity to understand the world, think rationally, and use resources effectively when faced with challenges. (p. 366)

- The earliest psychologists assumed that there is a general factor for mental ability called *g.* However, later psychologists disputed the view that intelligence is unidimensional. (p. 366)

- Some researchers suggest that intelligence can be broken down into fluid intelligence and crystallized intelligence. Gardner's theory of multiple intelligences proposes that there are eight spheres of intelligence. (p. 367)

- Information-processing approaches examine the processes underlying intelligent behavior rather than focusing on the structure of intelligence. (p. 369)

Compare and contrast practical and emotional intelligences.

- Practical intelligence is intelligence related to overall success in living; emotional intelligence is the set of skills that underlie the accurate assessment, evaluation, expression, and regulation of emotions. (p. 369)

Explain approaches to assessing intelligence.

- Intelligence tests have traditionally compared a person's mental age and chronological age to yield an IQ, or intelligence quotient, score. (p. 370)

- Specific tests of intelligence include the Stanford-Binet test, the Wechsler Adult Intelligence Scale–IV (WAIS-IV), and the Wechsler Intelligence Scale for Children–IV (WISC-IV). (p. 374)

Identify variations in intellectual ability.

- The levels of intellectual disabilities include mild, moderate, severe, and profound retardation. (p. 376)
- About one-third of the cases of retardation have a known biological cause; fetal alcohol syndrome is the most common. Most cases, however, are classified as familial retardation, for which there is no known biological cause. (p. 377)
- The intellectually gifted are people with IQ scores greater than 130. Intellectually gifted people tend to be healthier and more successful than are the nongifted. (p. 377)
- Traditional intelligence tests have frequently been criticized for being biased in favor of the white middle-class population. This controversy has led to attempts to devise culture-fair tests, IQ measures that avoid questions that depend on a particular cultural background. (p. 378)

EVALUATE

1. _____ is a measure of intelligence that takes into account a person's chronological and mental ages.
2. _____ tests predict a person's ability in a specific area; _____ tests determine the specific level of knowledge in an area.
3. _____ _____ _____ is the most common biological cause of intellectual disabilities.
4. People with high intelligence are generally shy and socially withdrawn. True or false?
5. A(n) _____ - _____ test tries to use only questions appropriate to all the people taking the test.

RETHINK

What is the role of emotional intelligence in the classroom? How might emotional intelligence be tested? Should emotional intelligence be a factor in determining academic promotion to the next grade?

Answers to Evaluate Questions 1. IQ; 2. aptitude, achievement; 3. fetal alcohol syndrome; 4. false, the gifted are generally more socially adept than those with lower IQs; 5. culture-fair

[KEY TERMS]

intelligence *p. 366*

g or *g*-factor *p. 366*

fluid intelligence *p. 367*

crystallized intelligence *p. 367*

theory of multiple intelligences *p. 367*

practical intelligence *p. 370*

looking BACK

Psychology on the Web

1. Sigmund Freud is one of the towering figures in psychology. His influence extends far beyond his psychoanalytic work. Find information about Freud on the Web. Pick one aspect of his work or influence (e.g., on therapy, medicine, literature, film, or culture and society) and summarize in writing what you have found, including your attitude toward your findings.

2. Find a Web site that links to personality tests and take one or two tests—remembering to take them with skepticism. For each test, summarize in writing the aspects of personality that were tested, the theoretical approach the test appeared to be based on, and your assessment of the trustworthiness of the results.

the case of ...
MIKE AND MARTY SCANLON, THE UNLIKELY TWINS

People often have difficulty believing that Mike and Marty Scanlon are brothers, let alone twins. The two men bear a resemblance, but the similarity ends there.

Marty Scanlon was always a quiet, well-behaved child. He excelled in all his academic subjects throughout his school years, although he was shy and had few friends. Marty would always be polite to people, but he generally preferred to keep to himself. After college, Marty became a successful network administrator for a large financial company and married his longtime girlfriend. A dedicated family man, Marty spends most of his free time doing home improvement projects and looking after his two children.

Mike Scanlon, on the other hand, could never be described as shy. He was the student that teachers dreaded having in their classroom: boisterous, unruly, and indifferent to authority. Mike had many brushes with the law throughout his high school years, for crimes ranging from vandalism to public drunkenness. Mike dropped out of high school to take a job as an oil-change technician at a local garage; he spends most of his free time and money at local bars—at least the ones that haven't banned him for starting fights. Mike's current legal trouble surrounds two of his ex-girlfriends, who are independently taking him to court for child support. Mike is unfazed, however; he laughs with his friends that they'll never get a dime from him.

1. How would Freud explain the personality differences between Mike and Marty Scanlon?

2. How would you rate Mike and Marty Scanlon on the Big Five personality traits?

3. Given that Mike and Marty Scanlon are twins and share some of their genetic makeup, how would you explain the pronounced differences in their personalities? What role, if any, does temperament seem to be playing?

4. Which of the two brothers seems more likely to be achieving self-actualization, and why do you think so?

5. Do Mike and Marty Scanlon appear to have different levels of intelligence, or do they show intelligence in different ways? Why do you think so?

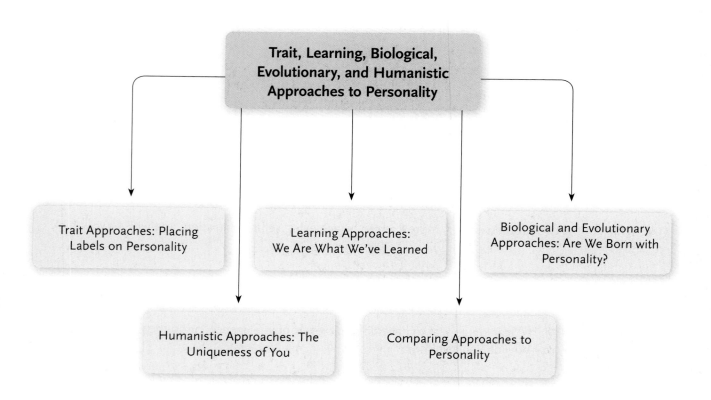

Psychodynamic Approaches to Personality

Freud's Psychoanalytic Theory: Mapping the Unconscious Mind

The Neo-Freudian Psychoanalysts: Building on Freud

Trait, Learning, Biological, Evolutionary, and Humanistic Approaches to Personality

Trait Approaches: Placing Labels on Personality

Learning Approaches: We Are What We've Learned

Biological and Evolutionary Approaches: Are We Born with Personality?

Humanistic Approaches: The Uniqueness of You

Comparing Approaches to Personality

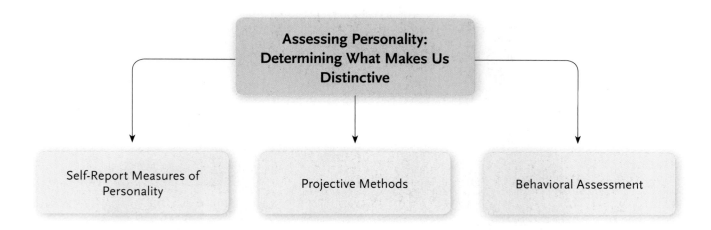

Assessing Personality: Determining What Makes Us Distinctive

- Self-Report Measures of Personality
- Projective Methods
- Behavioral Assessment

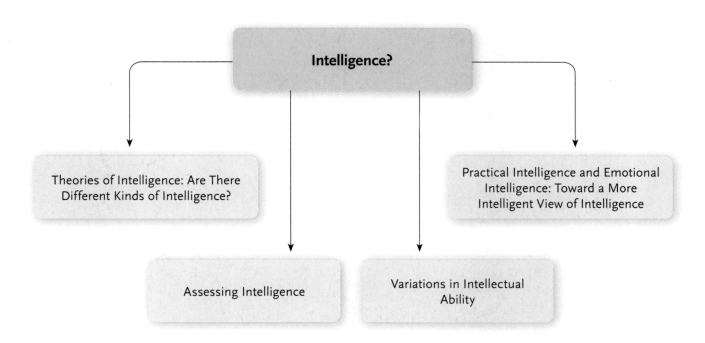

Intelligence?

- Theories of Intelligence: Are There Different Kinds of Intelligence?
- Assessing Intelligence
- Variations in Intellectual Ability
- Practical Intelligence and Emotional Intelligence: Toward a More Intelligent View of Intelligence

PSYCHOLOGICAL

CHAPTER OUTLINE

DISORDERS

Voices of Angels

Angelo, a research scientist working at an American university, was walking home from the laboratory when, all of a sudden, he heard two voices in his head. "It was like hearing thoughts in my mind that were not mine," he explained recently. "They identified themselves as Andrew and Oliver, two angels. In my mind's eye, I could see an image of a bald, middle-aged man dressed in white against a white background. This, I was told, was Oliver." What the angels said, to Angelo's horror, was that in the coming days, he would die of a brain hemorrhage. Terrified, Angelo hurried home and locked himself into his apartment. For three long days he waited out his fate. (Smith, 2007, p. 50) ■

looking AHEAD

Angelo was losing his grip on reality. It turned out that he was suffering from schizophrenia, one of the more severe psychological disorders. Although drug treatments eventually stilled the voices that ran through his head, his experience raises several questions. What caused his disorder? Were genetic factors involved, or were stressors in his life primarily responsible? Were there signs that family and friends should have noticed earlier? Could his schizophrenia have been prevented? And, more generally, how do we distinguish normal from abnormal behavior, and how can Angelo's behavior be categorized and classified in such a way as to pinpoint the specific nature of his problem?

We address the issues raised by Angelo's case in this set of modules. First we discuss the difference between normal and abnormal behavior, which can be surprisingly indistinct. We then examine the most significant kinds of psychological disorders. Finally, we'll consider ways of evaluating behavior—one's own and that of others—to determine whether seeking help from a mental health professional is warranted.

Normal versus Abnormal
Making the Distinction

Universally that person's acumen is esteemed very little perceptive concerning whatsoever matters are being held as most profitable by mortals with sapience endowed to be studied who is ignorant of that which the most in doctrine erudite and certainly by reason of that in them high mind's ornament deserving of veneration constantly maintain when by general consent they affirm that other circumstances being equal by no exterior splendour is the prosperity of a nation . . .

It would be easy to conclude that these words are the musings of a madman. To most people, the passage does not seem to make any sense at all. But literary scholars would disagree. Actually, this passage is from James Joyce's classic *Ulysses,* hailed as one of the major works of twentieth-century literature (Joyce, 1934, p. 377).

As this example illustrates, casually examining a person's writing is insufficient to determine the degree to which that person is "normal." But even when we consider more extensive samples of a person's behavior, we will see that there may be only a fine line between behavior that is considered normal and that which is considered abnormal.

» LO1 Defining Abnormality

Because of the difficulty in distinguishing normal from abnormal behavior, psychologists have struggled to devise a precise, scientific definition of "abnormal behavior." For instance, consider the following definitions, each of which has advantages and disadvantages:

- *Abnormality as deviation from the average.* To employ this statistically based approach, we simply observe what behaviors are rare or occur infrequently in a specific society or culture and label those deviations from the norm "abnormal."

  The difficulty with this definition is that some statistically rare behaviors clearly do not lend themselves to classification as abnormal. Such a concept of abnormality would unreasonably label a person who has an unusually high IQ as abnormal, simply because a high IQ is statistically rare. In short, a definition of abnormality that rests on deviation from the average is insufficient.

- *Abnormality as deviation from the ideal.* An alternative approach considers abnormality in relation to the standard toward which most people are striving—the ideal. This sort of definition considers behavior abnormal if it deviates enough from some kind of ideal or cultural standard. However, society has few standards on which people universally agree. Furthermore, standards that do arise change over time and vary across cultures. Thus, the deviation-from-the-ideal approach is also inadequate.

- *Abnormality as a sense of personal discomfort.* A more useful definition concentrates on the psychological consequences of the behavior for the individual. In this approach, behavior is considered abnormal if it produces a sense of personal distress, anxiety, or guilt in an individual—or if it is harmful to others in some way.

Even a definition that relies on personal discomfort has drawbacks, though, because in some especially severe forms of mental disturbance, people report feeling wonderful, even though their behavior seems bizarre to others. In such cases, a personal state of well-being exists, yet most people would consider the behavior abnormal.

Abnormal behavior Behavior that causes people to experience distress and prevents them from functioning in their daily lives.

- *Abnormality as the inability to function effectively.* Most people are able to feed themselves, hold a job, get along with others, and in general live as productive members of society. Yet there are those who are unable to adjust to the demands of society or function effectively. According to this view of abnormality, people who are unable to function effectively and to adapt to the demands of society are considered abnormal.

- *Abnormality as a legal concept.* To the judicial system, the distinction between normal and abnormal behavior rests on the definition of insanity, which is a legal, but not a psychological, term. The definition of insanity varies from one jurisdiction to another. In some states, insanity simply means that defendants cannot understand the difference between right and wrong at the time they commit a criminal act. Other states consider whether defendants are substantially incapable of understanding the criminality of their behavior or unable to control themselves. And in some jurisdictions pleas of insanity are not allowed at all (Weiner & Wettstein, 1993; Frost & Bonnie, 2001; Sokolove, 2003).

Clearly, none of the previous definitions is broad enough to cover all instances of abnormal behavior. Consequently, the distinction between normal and abnormal behavior often remains ambiguous even to trained professionals. Furthermore, to a large extent, cultural expectations for "normal" behavior in a particular society influence the understanding of "abnormal behavior" (Scheff, 1999; Sanderson, 2007).

Given the difficulties in precisely defining the construct, psychologists typically define **abnormal behavior** broadly, considering it to be behavior that causes people to experience distress and prevents them from functioning in their daily lives (Nolen-Hoeksema, 2007). Because of the imprecision of this definition, it's best to view abnormal behavior and normal behavior as marking two ends of a continuum rather than as absolute states. Behavior should be evaluated in terms of gradations, ranging from fully normal functioning to extremely abnormal behavior. Behavior typically falls somewhere between those extremes.

In a famous case, Andrea Yates was judged sane when she drowned her five children in a bathtub, according to the first jury that heard the case. At a later trial, however, she was found not guilty by reason of insanity.

» LO2 Perspectives on Abnormality: From Superstition to Science

STUDY ALERT

Use Figure 1 to review the six major perspectives on abnormality and consider how they relate to the major perspectives on the field of psychology that we discussed in Chapter 1.

Throughout much of human history, people linked abnormal behavior to superstition and witchcraft. Individuals who displayed abnormal behavior were accused of being possessed by the devil or some sort of demonic god (Howells & Osborn, 1984; Berrios, 1996).

Contemporary approaches take a more enlightened view. Today, six major perspectives are used to understand psychological disorders. These perspectives suggest not only different causes of abnormal behavior but different treatment approaches as well. Furthermore, some perspectives are more applicable to specific disorders than are others. Figure 1 summarizes the perspectives and the ways in which they can be applied to the experience of Angelo, the research scientist described in the opening of the chapter.

Medical Perspective

Medical perspective The perspective that suggests that when an individual displays symptoms of abnormal behavior, the root cause will be found in a physical examination of the individual, which may reveal a hormonal imbalance, a chemical deficiency, or a brain injury.

When people display the symptoms of tuberculosis, medical professionals can generally find tubercular bacteria in their body tissue. Similarly, the **medical perspective** suggests that when an individual displays symptoms of abnormal behavior, the fundamental cause will be found through a physical examination of the individual, which may reveal a hormonal imbalance, a chemical deficiency, or a brain injury.

Because many abnormal behaviors have been linked to biological causes, the medical perspective is a reasonable approach, yet serious criticisms have been leveled against it. For one thing, no biological cause has been identified for many forms of abnormal behavior. Still, recent advances in

FIGURE 1 In considering the case of Angelo, discussed in the chapter opening, we can employ each of the different perspectives on abnormal behavior. Note, however, that because of the nature of his psychological disorder, some of the perspectives are more applicable than others.

Perspectives on Psychological Disorders

Perspective	Description	Possible Application of Perspective to Angelo's Case
Medical perspective	Assumes that physiological causes are at the root of psychological disorders	Examine Angelo for medical problems, such as brain tumor, chemical imbalance in the brain, or disease
Psychoanalytic perspective	Argues that psychological disorders stem from childhood conflicts	Seek out information about Angelo's past, considering possible childhood conflicts
Behavioral perspective	Assumes that abnormal behaviors are learned responses	Concentrate on rewards and punishments for Angelo's behavior, and identify environmental stimuli that reinforce his behavior
Cognitive perspective	Assumes that cognitions (people's thoughts and beliefs) are central to psychological disorders	Focus on Angelo's perceptions of himself and his environment
Humanistic perspective	Emphasizes people's responsibility for their own behavior and the need to self-actualize	Consider Angelo's behavior in terms of his choices and efforts to reach his potential
Sociocultural perspective	Assumes that behavior is shaped by family, society, and culture	Focus on how societal demands contributed to Angelo's disorder

our understanding of the biological bases of behavior underscore the importance of considering physiological factors in abnormal behavior.

Psychoanalytic Perspective

Whereas the medical perspective suggests that biological causes are at the root of abnormal behavior, the **psychoanalytic perspective** holds that abnormal behavior stems from childhood conflicts over opposing wishes regarding sex and aggression. According to Freud, children pass through a series of stages in which sexual and aggressive impulses take different forms and produce conflicts that require resolution. If these childhood conflicts are not dealt with successfully, they remain unresolved in the unconscious and eventually bring about abnormal behavior during adulthood.

To uncover the roots of people's disordered behavior, the psychoanalytic perspective scrutinizes their early life history. However, because there is no conclusive way to link people's childhood experiences with the abnormal behaviors they display as adults, we can never be sure that the causes suggested by psychoanalytic theory are accurate.

On the other hand, the contributions of psychoanalytic theory have been significant. More than any other approach to abnormal behavior, this perspective highlights the fact that people can have a rich, involved inner life and that prior experiences can have a profound effect on current psychological functioning (Elliott, 2002; Bornstein, 2003; Rangell, 2007).

Psychoanalytic perspective The perspective that suggests that abnormal behavior stems from childhood conflicts over opposing wishes regarding sex and aggression.

Behavioral perspective The perspective that looks at the behavior itself as the problem.

Cognitive perspective The perspective that suggests that people's thoughts and beliefs are a central component of abnormal behavior.

Behavioral Perspective

Both the medical and psychoanalytic perspectives look at abnormal behaviors as *symptoms* of an underlying problem. In contrast, the **behavioral perspective** views the behavior itself as the problem. Using the basic principles of learning, behavioral theorists see both normal and abnormal behaviors as responses to various stimuli, responses that have been learned through past experience and that are guided in the present by stimuli in the individual's environment. To explain why abnormal behavior occurs, we must analyze how an individual has learned abnormal behavior and observe the circumstances in which it is displayed.

> *The emphasis on observable behavior represents both the greatest strength and the greatest weakness of the behavioral approach to abnormal behavior.*

The emphasis on observable behavior represents both the greatest strength and the greatest weakness of the behavioral approach to abnormal behavior. This perspective provides the most precise and objective approach for examining behavioral symptoms of specific disorders. At the same time, though, critics charge that the perspective ignores the rich inner world of thoughts, attitudes, and emotions that may contribute to abnormal behavior.

Cognitive Perspective

The medical, psychoanalytic, and behavioral perspectives view people's behavior as the result of factors largely beyond their control. To many critics of these views, however, people's thoughts cannot be ignored.

In response to such concerns, some psychologists employ a **cognitive perspective.** Rather than considering only external behavior, as in traditional behavioral approaches, the cognitive approach assumes that *cognitions* (people's thoughts and beliefs) are central to a person's abnormal behavior. A primary

Abnormal behavior is always of concern. Can you think of how abnormal behavior in a co-worker is of particular concern when your job involves life and death decisions, like for a police officer?

goal of treatment using the cognitive perspective is to explicitly teach new, more adaptive ways of thinking.

The cognitive perspective is not without critics. For example, it is possible that maladaptive cognitions are the symptoms or consequences of disorders, rather than their cause. Furthermore, there are circumstances in which negative beliefs may not be irrational at all, but simply reflect the unpleasant environments in which people live. Still, cognitive theorists would argue that one can find a more adaptive way of framing beliefs even in the most negative circumstances.

Humanistic Perspective

Psychologists who subscribe to the **humanistic perspective** emphasize the responsibility people have for their own behavior, even when their behavior is considered abnormal. The humanistic perspective concentrates on what is uniquely human—that is, a view of people as basically rational, oriented toward a social world, and motivated to seek self-actualization (Rogers, 1995). Rather than assuming that individuals require a "cure," the humanistic perspective suggests that they can, by and large, set their own limits of what is acceptable behavior. As long as they are not hurting others and do not feel personal distress, people should be free to choose the behaviors in which they engage.

Although the humanistic perspective has been criticized for its reliance on unscientific, unverifiable information and its vague, almost philosophical formulations, it offers a distinctive view of abnormal behavior. It stresses the unique aspects of being human and provides a number of important suggestions for helping those with psychological problems.

Humanistic perspective The perspective that emphasizes the responsibility people have for their own behavior, even when such behavior is abnormal.

Sociocultural perspective The perspective that assumes that people's behavior—both normal and abnormal—is shaped by the kind of family group, society, and culture in which they live.

Sociocultural Perspective

The **sociocultural perspective** assumes that people's behavior—both normal and abnormal—is shaped by the kind of family group, society, and culture in which they live. According to this view, the nature of one's relationships with others may support abnormal behaviors and even cause them. Consequently, the kinds of stresses

From the perspective of . . .

A NEW EMPLOYER   Imagine that a well-paid employee was arrested for shoplifting a $15 sweater. What sort of explanation for this behavior would be provided by the proponents of *each* perspective on abnormality: the medical perspective, the psychoanalytic perspective, the behavioral perspective, the cognitive perspective, the humanistic perspective, and the sociocultural perspective? Based on the potential causes of the shoplifting, would you fire the employee? Why or why not?

and conflicts people experience in their daily interactions with others can promote and maintain abnormal behavior.

This perspective finds statistical support for the position that sociocultural factors shape abnormal behavior given the fact that some kinds of abnormal behavior are far more prevalent among certain social classes than they are in others. For instance, proportionally more African American individuals are hospitalized involuntarily for psychological disorders than are whites. Furthermore, poor economic times seem to be linked to general declines in psychological functioning, and social problems such as homelessness are associated with psychological disorders (López & Guarnaccia, 2005; Conger et al., 2002; Nasir & Hand, 2006).

On the other hand, there are many alternative explanations for the association between abnormal behavior and social factors. For example, people from lower socioeconomic levels may be less likely than those from higher levels to seek help, gradually reaching a point where their symptoms become severe and warrant a serious diagnosis (Paniagua, 2000).

"First off, you're not a nut. You're a legume."

» LO3 Classifying Abnormal Behavior: The ABCs of DSM

Providing appropriate and specific names and classifications for abnormal behavior has presented a major challenge to psychologists. It is not hard to understand why, given the difficulties discussed earlier in simply distinguishing normal from abnormal behavior. Yet psychologists and other care providers need to classify abnormal behavior in order to diagnose it and, ultimately, to treat it.

DSM-IV-TR: Determining Diagnostic Distinctions

Over the years, mental health professionals have developed many different classification systems that vary in terms of their utility and the degree to which they

How might an understanding of the *DSM-IV-TR* benefit you when dealing with patients as a medical office manager?

psych2.0

WWW.MHHE.COM/PSYCHLIFE

DSM-IV-TR Classification System

have been accepted. However, one standard system, devised by the American Psychiatric Association, has emerged in the United States. Most professionals today use this classification system, known as the *Diagnostic and Statistical Manual of Mental Disorders, Fourth Edition, Text Revision (DSM-IV-TR)* to diagnose and classify abnormal behavior.

DSM-IV-TR presents comprehensive and relatively precise definitions for more than 200 disorders, divided into 17 major categories. By following the criteria presented in the *DSM-IV-TR* classification system, diagnosticians can identify the specific problem an individual is experiencing. (Figure 2 provides a brief outline of the major diagnostic categories.)

DSM-IV-TR is designed to be primarily descriptive and avoids suggesting an underlying cause for an individual's behavior and problems. Instead, it paints a picture of the behavior that is being displayed. Why should this approach be important? For one thing, it allows communication between mental health professionals of diverse backgrounds and theoretical approaches. In addition, precise classification enables researchers to explore the causes of a problem. Without reliable descriptions of abnormal behavior, researchers would be hard-pressed to find ways to investigate the disorder. Finally, *DSM-IV-TR* provides a kind of conceptual shorthand through which professionals can describe the behaviors that tend to occur together in an individual (Widiger & Clark, 2000; First, Frances, & Pincus, 2002).

Although the *DSM-IV-TR* was developed to provide more accurate and consistent diagnoses of psychological disorders, it has not been entirely successful. For instance, critics charge that it relies too much on the medical perspective. Because it was drawn up by psychiatrists—who are physicians—some condemn

Disorder	Subcategories
Anxiety (problems in which anxiety impedes daily functioning)	Generalized anxiety disorder, panic disorder, phobic disorder, obsessive-compulsive disorder, posttraumatic stress disorder
Somatoform (psychological difficulties displayed through physical problems)	Hypochondriasis, conversion disorder
Dissociative (the splitting apart of crucial parts of personality that are usually integrated)	Dissociative identity disorder (multiple personality), dissociative amnesia, dissociative fugue
Mood (emotions of depression or euphoria that are so strong they intrude on everyday living)	Major depression, bipolar disorder
Schizophrenia (declines in functioning, thought and language disturbances, perception disorders, emotional disturbances, and withdrawal from others)	Disorganized, paranoid, catatonic, undifferentiated, residual
Personality (problems that create little personal distress but that lead to an inability to function as a normal member of society)	Antisocial (sociopathic) personality disorder, narcissistic personality disorder
Sexual (problems related to sexual arousal from unusual objects or problems related to functioning)	Paraphilia, sexual dysfunction
Substance-related (problems related to drug dependence and abuse)	Alcohol, cocaine, hallucinogens, marijuana
Delirium, dementia, amnesia, and other cognitive disorders	

FIGURE 2   This list of disorders represents the major categories from the *DSM-IV-TR*. It is only a partial list of the more than 200 disorders included there.

it for viewing psychological disorders primarily in terms of the symptoms of an underlying physiological disorder. Moreover, critics suggest that the *DSM-IV-TR* compartmentalizes people into inflexible, all-or-none categories, rather than considering the degree to which a person displays psychologically disordered behavior (Schmidt, Kotov, & Joiner, 2004; Samuel & Widiger, 2006).

Still, despite the drawbacks inherent in any labeling system, the *DSM-IV-TR* has had an important influence on the way in which mental health professionals view psychological disorders. It has increased both the reliability and the validity of diagnostic categorization. In addition, it offers a logical way to organize examination of the major types of mental disturbance.

RECAP

Define abnormality.

- Definitions of abnormality include deviation from the average, deviation from the ideal, a sense of personal discomfort, the inability to function effectively, and legal conceptions. (p. 388)

Discuss perspectives on abnormality.

- Although no single definition is adequate, abnormal behavior can be considered to be behavior that causes people to experience distress and prevents them from functioning in their daily lives. Most psychologists believe that abnormal and normal behavior should be considered in terms of a continuum. (p. 390)

- The medical perspective views abnormality as a symptom of an underlying disease. (p. 390)

- Psychoanalytic perspectives suggest that abnormal behavior stems from childhood conflicts in the unconscious. (p. 391)

- Behavioral approaches view abnormal behavior not as a symptom of an underlying problem, but as the problem itself. (p. 391)

- The cognitive approach suggests that abnormal behavior is the result of faulty cognitions (thoughts and beliefs). In this view, abnormal behavior can be remedied by changing one's flawed thoughts and beliefs. (p. 391)

- Humanistic approaches emphasize the responsibility people have for their own behavior, even when such behavior is seen as abnormal. (p. 392)

- Sociocultural approaches view abnormal behavior in terms of difficulties arising from family and other social relationships. (p. 392)

Classify abnormal behavior.

- The most widely used system for classifying psychological disorders is the *DSM-IV-TR—Diagnostic and Statistical Manual of Mental Disorders, Fourth Edition, Text Revision.* (p. 393)

EVALUATE

1. One problem in defining abnormal behavior is that
   a. Statistically rare behavior may not be abnormal.
   b. Not all abnormalities are accompanied by feelings of discomfort.
   c. Cultural standards are too general to use as a measuring tool.
   d. All of the above.

2. If abnormality is defined as behavior that causes personal discomfort or harms others, which of the following people is most likely to need treatment?

   a. An executive is afraid to accept a promotion because it would require moving from his ground-floor office to the top floor of a tall office building.

   b. A woman decides to quit her job and chooses to live on the street in order to live a "simpler life."

   c. A man believes that friendly spacemen visit his house every Thursday.

   d. A photographer lives with 19 cats in a small apartment, lovingly caring for them.

3. Virginia's mother thinks that her daughter's behavior is clearly abnormal because, despite being offered admission to medical school, Virginia decides to become a waitress. What approach is Virginia's mother using to define abnormal behavior?

4. Which of the following is a strong argument against the medical perspective on abnormality?

   a. Physiological abnormalities are almost always impossible to identify.

   b. There is no conclusive way to link past experience and behavior.

   c. The medical perspective rests too heavily on the effects of nutrition.

   d. Assigning behavior to a physical problem takes responsibility away from the individual for changing his or her behavior.

5. Cheryl is painfully shy. According to the behavioral perspective, the best way to deal with her "abnormal" behavior is to

   a. Treat the underlying physical problem.

   b. Use the principles of learning theory to modify her shy behavior.

   c. Express a great deal of caring.

   d. Uncover her negative past experiences through hypnosis.

RETHINK

Do you agree or disagree that *DSM* should be updated every several years? Why? What makes abnormal behavior so variable?

Answers to Evaluate Questions 1. d; 2. a; 3. deviation from the ideal; 4. d; 5. b

[KEY TERMS]

Abnormal behavior *p. 389*

Medical perspective *p. 390*

Psychoanalytic perspective *p. 391*

Behavioral perspective *p. 391*

Cognitive perspective *p. 391*

Humanistic perspective *p. 392*

Sociocultural perspective *p. 392*

Diagnostic and Statistical Manual of Mental Disorders, Fourth Edition, Text Revision p. 394

module 34

The Major Psychological Disorders

LEARNING OUTCOMES

34.1 Discuss anxiety disorders.

34.2 Discuss somatoform disorders.

34.3 Discuss dissociative disorders.

34.4 Discuss mood disorders.

34.5 Explain schizophrenia.

34.6 Discuss personality disorders.

34.7 Discuss childhood disorders.

34.8 List other disorders.

Sally experienced her first panic attack out of the blue, 3 weeks after completing her senior year in college. She had just finished a job interview and was meeting some friends for dinner. In the restaurant, she began to feel dizzy. Within a few seconds, her heart was pounding, and she was feeling breathless, as though she might pass out. Her friends noticed that she did not look well and offered to drive her home. Sally suggested they stop at the hospital emergency room instead. Although she felt better by the time they arrived at the hospital, and tests indicated nothing wrong, Sally experienced a similar episode a week later while at a movie. (Antony, Brown, & Barlow, 1992, p. 79)

Sally suffered from panic disorder, one of the specific psychological disorders we'll consider in this module. Keep in mind that although we'll be discussing these disorders in an objective manner, each represents a very human set of difficulties that influence, and in some cases considerably disrupt, people's lives.

» LO1 Anxiety Disorders

All of us, at one time or another, experience *anxiety,* a feeling of apprehension or tension, in reaction to stressful situations. There is nothing "wrong" with such anxiety. It is a normal reaction to stress that often helps, rather than hinders, our daily functioning. Without some anxiety, for instance, most of us probably would not have much motivation to study hard, undergo physical exams, or spend long hours at our jobs.

> **Anxiety disorder** The occurrence of anxiety without an obvious external cause, affecting daily functioning.

But some people experience anxiety in situations in which there is no external reason or cause for such distress. When anxiety occurs without external justification and begins to affect people's daily functioning, mental health professionals consider it a psychological problem known as **anxiety disorder.** We'll discuss the four major types of anxiety disorders: phobic disorder, panic disorder, generalized anxiety disorder, and obsessive-compulsive disorder. (Before continuing, get a sense of your own level of anxiety by completing the accompanying Try It!)

try it!

How Anxious Are You?

To assess the degree of anxiety you typically experience, complete the following questionnaire by writing T (for true) or F (for false) preceding each of the statements:

_____ 1. I do not tire quickly.

_____ 2. I am troubled by attacks of nausea.

_____ 3. I believe I am no more nervous than most others.

_____ 4. I have very few headaches.

_____ 5. I work under a great deal of tension.

_____ 6. I cannot keep my mind on one thing.

_____ 7. I worry over money and business.

_____ 8. I frequently notice my hands shake when I try to do something.

_____ 9. I blush no more than others.

_____ 10. I have diarrhea once a month or more.

_____ 11. I worry quite a bit about possible misfortunes.

_____ 12. I practically never blush.

_____ 13. I am often afraid that I am going to blush.

_____ 14. I have nightmares every few nights.

_____ 15. My hands and feet are usually warm enough.

_____ 16. I sweat very easily, even on cool days.

_____ 17. Sometimes when I'm embarrassed I break out in a sweat, which annoys me greatly.

_____ 18. I hardly ever notice my heart pounding and I am seldom short of breath.

_____ 19. I feel hungry almost all the time.

_____ 20. I am seldom troubled by constipation.

_____ 21. I have a great deal of stomach trouble.

_____ 22. I have had periods in which I lost sleep over worry.

_____ 23. My sleep is fitful and disturbed.

_____ 24. I dream frequently about things that are best kept to myself.

_____ 25. I am easily embarrassed.

_____ 26. I am more sensitive than most other people.

_____ 27. I frequently find myself worrying about things.

_____ 28. I wish I could be as happy as others seem to be.

_____ 29. I am usually calm and not easily upset.

_____ 30. I cry easily.

_____ 31. I feel anxiety about something or someone almost all the time.

_____ 32. I am happy most of the time.

_____ 33. It makes me nervous to have to wait.

_____ 34. I have periods of such great restlessness that I cannot sit long in a chair.

_____ 35. Sometimes I become so excited that I find it hard to get to sleep.

_____ 36. I have sometimes felt that difficulties were piling up so high that I could not overcome them.

_____ 37. I must admit that I have at times been worried beyond reason over something that really did not matter.

_____ 38. I have very few fears compared to my friends.

_____ 39. I have been afraid of things or people that I know could not hurt me.

_____ 40. I certainly feel useless at times.

_____ 41. I find it hard to keep my mind on a task or job.

_____ 42. I am usually self-conscious.

_____ 43. I am inclined to take things hard.

_____ 44. I am a high-strung person.

_____ 45. Life is a strain for me much of the time.

_____ 46. At times I think I am no good at all.

_____ 47. I am certainly lacking in self-confidence.

_____ 48. I sometimes feel that I am about to go to pieces.

_____ 49. I shrink from facing a crisis or difficulty.

_____ 50. I am entirely self-confident.

Scoring

Give yourself one point for each statement that corresponds to the following key: 1.F; 2.T; 3.F; 4.F; 5.T; 6.T; 7.T; 8.T; 9.F; 10.T; 11.T; 12.F; 13.T; 14.T; 15.F; 16.T; 17.T; 18.F; 19.T; 20.F; 21.T; 22.T; 23.T; 24.T; 25.T; 26.T; 27.T; 28.T; 29.F; 30.T; 31.T; 32.T; 33.T; 34.T; 35.T; 36.T; 37.T; 38.F; 39.T; 40.T; 41.T; 42.T; 43.T; 44.T; 45.T; 46.T; 47.T; 48.T; 49.T; 50.F. The average score for college students is around 14 or 15. A score that is much higher than the average suggests that you experience an unusually high degree of anxiety. Keep in mind that this questionnaire assesses *normal* levels of anxiety, and a high score does not imply that you have an anxiety disorder.

Source: Taylor, 1953.

Phobic Disorder

It's not easy moving through the world when you're terrified of electricity. "Donna," 45, a writer, knows that better than most. Get her in the vicinity of an appliance or a light switch or—all but unthinkable—a thunderstorm, and she is overcome by a terror so blinding she can think of nothing but fleeing. That, of course, is not always possible, so over time, Donna has come up with other answers. When she opens the refrigerator door, rubber-sole shoes are a must. If a light bulb blows, she will tolerate the dark until someone else changes it for her. (Kluger, 2001, p. 51)

Donna suffers from a **phobia,** an intense, irrational fear of a specific object or situation. For example, claustrophobia is a fear of enclosed places, acrophobia is a fear of high places, xenophobia is a fear of strangers, social phobia is the fear of being judged or embarrassed by others, and—as in Donna's case—electrophobia is a fear of electricity.

The objective danger posed by an anxiety-producing stimulus (which can be just about anything, as you can see in Figure 1) is typically small or nonexistent.

> **Phobia** An intense, irrational fear of specific objects or situations.

psych2.0
WWW.MHHE.COM/PSYCHLIFE

Phobia

At first glance it might somehow seem more reasonable to fear heights than flowers, but the reality of phobias is that virtually anything can create paralyzing fear in those suffering from them. What are some coping strategies for phobias?

Unlike phobias, which are stimulated by specific objects or situations, panic disorders do not have any identifiable stimuli.

However, to someone suffering from the phobia, the danger is great, and a full-blown panic attack may follow exposure to the stimulus.

Panic Disorder

In another type of anxiety disorder, **panic disorder,** *panic attacks* occur that last from a few seconds to several hours. Unlike phobias, which are

Phobic Disorder	Description	Example
Agoraphobia	Fear of places where help might not be available in case of emergency	Person becomes housebound because anyplace other than the person's home arouses extreme anxiety symptoms
Specific phobias	Fear of specific objects, places, or situations	
Animal type	Specific animals or insects	Person has extreme fear of dogs, cats, or spiders
Natural environment type	Event or situations in the natural environment	Person has extreme fear of storms, heights, or water
Situational type	Public transportation, tunnels, bridges, elevators, flying, driving	Person becomes extremely claustrophobic in enclosed spaces
Blood-injection-injury type	Blood, injury, injections	Person panics when viewing a child's scraped knee
Social phobia	Fear of being judged or embarrassed by others	Person avoids all social situations and becomes a recluse for fear of encountering others' judgment

FIGURE 1   Phobic disorders differ from generalized anxiety and panic disorders because a specific stimulus can be identified. Listed here are a number of types of phobias and their triggers. *(Adapted from Nolen-Hoeksema, 2007).*

stimulated by specific objects or situations, panic disorders do not have any identifiable stimuli. Instead, during an attack, such as the ones experienced by Sally in the case described earlier, anxiety suddenly—and often without warning—rises to a peak, and an individual feels a sense of impending, unavoidable doom. Although the physical symptoms differ from person to person, they may include heart palpitations, shortness of breath, unusual amounts of sweating, faintness and dizziness, gastric sensations, and sometimes a sense of imminent death. After such an attack, it is no wonder that people tend to feel exhausted (Rachman & deSilva, 2004; Laederach-Hofmann & Messerli-Buergy, 2007).

Panic attacks seemingly come out of nowhere and are unconnected to any specific stimulus. Because they don't know what triggers their feelings of panic, victims of panic attacks may become fearful of going places. In fact, some people with panic disorder develop a complication called *agoraphobia,* the fear of being in a situation in which escape is difficult and in which help for a possible panic attack would not be available. In extreme cases, people with agoraphobia never leave their homes (Marcaurelle, Bélanger, & Marchand, 2003, 2005; Herrán, Carrera, & Sierra-Biddle, 2006).

Generalized Anxiety Disorder

People with **generalized anxiety disorder** experience long-term, persistent anxiety and uncontrollable worry. Sometimes their concerns are about identifiable issues involving family, money, work, or health. In other cases, though, people with the disorder feel that something dreadful is about to happen but can't identify the reason, experiencing "free-floating" anxiety.

Because of persistent anxiety, people with generalized anxiety disorder cannot concentrate or set their worry and fears aside; their lives become centered on their worry. Figure 3 on page 402 shows the most common symptoms of generalized anxiety disorder.

Obsessive-Compulsive Disorder

In **obsessive-compulsive disorder,** people are plagued by unwanted thoughts, called obsessions, or feel that they must carry out actions, termed compulsions, against their will.

An **obsession** is a persistent, unwanted thought or idea that keeps recurring. For example, a man may go on vacation and wonder the whole time whether he locked his house or a woman may hear the same tune running through her head over and over. In each case, the thought or idea is unwanted and difficult to put out of mind. Of course, many people suffer from mild obsessions from time to time, but usually such thoughts persist only for a short period. For people with serious obsessions, however, the thoughts persist for days or months and may consist of bizarre, troubling images (Lee & Kwon, 2003; Lee et al., 2005; Rassin & Muris, 2007).

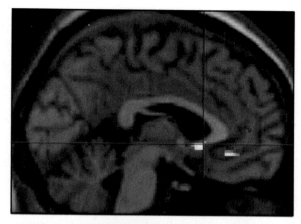
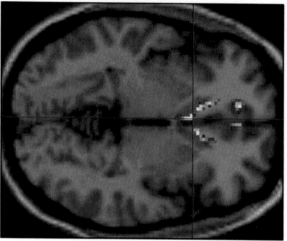

FIGURE 2 Regions of the brain in which there is less activation of the anterior cingulate cortex for patients with panic disorder than for people without the disorder in response to viewing fearful faces. The researchers hypothesize that recurring high levels of emotional arousal experienced by patients with panic disorder desensitizes them to emotional stimuli. *(Source: Pillay et al., 2006, Figure 1.)*

Panic disorder Anxiety disorder that takes the form of panic attacks lasting from a few seconds to as long as several hours.

Generalized anxiety disorder The experience of long-term, persistent anxiety and worry.

Obsessive-compulsive disorder A disorder characterized by obsessions or compulsions.

Obsession A persistent, unwanted thought or idea that keeps recurring.

Symptom

Symptom	Percentage of cases in which symptom occurs

Actual fainting

Feeling of choking

Diarrhea

Nausea

Hands trembling

Difficulty breathing

Fear of dying

Sweating all over

Speech blocked

Wobbly

Heart racing

Hands sweating

Terrified

Weakness all over

Confusion

Unable to control thoughts

Jumpy

Fear of losing control

Frightened

Tense

Difficulty concentrating

Unable to relax

0 10 20 30 40 50 60 70 80 90 100

Percentage of cases in which symptom occurs

FIGURE 3 Frequency of symptoms in cases of generalized anxiety disorder. *(Source: Adapted from Beck & Emery, 1985, pp. 87–88.)*

Compulsion An irresistible urge to repeatedly carry out some act that seems strange and unreasonable.

As part of an obsessive-compulsive disorder, people may also experience **compulsions,** irresistible urges to repeatedly carry out some act that seems strange and unreasonable, even to them. Whatever the compulsive behavior is, people experience extreme anxiety if they cannot carry it out, even if it is something they want to stop. The acts may be relatively trivial, such as repeatedly checking the stove to make sure all the burners are turned off, or more unusual, such as continuously washing oneself (Frost & Steketee, 2002; Clark, 2007). Although such compulsive rituals lead to some immediate reduction of anxiety, in the long term the anxiety returns.

The Causes of Anxiety Disorders

We've considered the four major types of anxiety disorders, but there are others as well. The variety of anxiety disorders means that no single explanation fits all cases. Genetic factors clearly are part of the picture. For example, if one member

Comedian Howie Mandel (pictured on the right) has talked openly about his struggles with OCD. While he has developed coping strategies, he still cannot bring himself to shake hands with contestants on his game show "Deal or No Deal." His alternative is to bump fists.

of a pair of identical twins has panic disorder, there is a 30 percent chance that the other twin will have it also. Furthermore, a person's characteristic level of anxiety is related to a specific gene involved in the production of the neurotransmitter serotonin. This is consistent with findings indicating that certain chemical deficiencies in the brain appear to produce some kinds of anxiety disorder (Rieder, Kaufmann, & Knowles, 1996; Holmes et al., 2003; Beidel & Turner, 2007).

Psychologists who employ the behavioral perspective have taken a different approach that emphasizes environmental factors. They consider anxiety to be a learned response to stress. For instance, suppose a dog bites a young girl. When the girl next sees a dog, she is frightened and runs away—a behavior that relieves her anxiety and thereby reinforces her avoidance behavior. After repeated encounters with dogs in which she is reinforced for her avoidance behavior, she may develop a full-fledged phobia regarding dogs.

Finally, the cognitive perspective suggests that anxiety disorders grow out of inappropriate and inaccurate thoughts and beliefs about circumstances in a person's world. For example, people with anxiety disorders may view a friendly puppy as a ferocious and savage pit bull, or they may see an air disaster looming every moment they are in the vicinity of an airplane. According to the cognitive perspective, people's maladaptive thoughts about the world are at the root of an anxiety disorder (Frost & Steketee, 2002; Wang & Clark, 2002).

» LO2 Somatoform Disorders

Somatoform disorders are psychological difficulties that take on a physical (somatic) form, but for which there is no medical cause. Even though an individual with a somatoform disorder reports physical symptoms, no biological cause exists, or if there is a medical problem, the person's reaction is greatly exaggerated.

Hypochondriasis

One type of somatoform disorder is **hypochondriasis,** in which people have a constant fear of illness and a preoccupation with their health. These individuals

Somatoform disorders Psychological difficulties that take on a physical (somatic) form, but for which there is no medical cause.

Hypochondriasis A disorder in which people have a constant fear of illness and a preoccupation with their health.

Even though an individual with a somatoform disorder reports physical symptoms, no biological cause exists, or if there is a medical problem, the person's reaction is greatly exaggerated.

believe that everyday aches and pains are symptoms of a dread disease. It is not that the "symptoms" are faked; instead, it is the misinterpretation of those sensations as evidence of some serious illness—often in the face of inarguable medical evidence to the contrary—that characterizes hypochondriasis (Noyes et al., 2003; Fallon & Feinstein, 2001; Abramowitz, Olatunji, & Deacon, 2007).

Conversion Disorders

Another somatoform disorder is conversion disorder. Unlike hypochondriasis, in which there is no physical problem, a **conversion disorder** involves an actual physical disturbance, such as the inability to see or hear or to move an arm or leg. The *cause* of such a physical disturbance is purely psychological; there is no biological reason for the problem.

» LO3 Dissociative Disorders

Conversion disorder A major somatoform disorder that involves an actual physical disturbance, such as the inability to use a sensory organ or the complete or partial inability to move an arm or leg.

Dissociative disorders Psychological dysfunctions characterized by the separation of different facets of a person's personality that are normally integrated.

Dissociative identity disorder (DID) A disorder in which a person displays characteristics of two or more distinct personalities; also called *multiple personality disorder.*

Dissociative amnesia A disorder in which a significant, selective memory loss occurs.

The classic movie *The Three Faces of Eve* and the book *Sybil* (about a girl who allegedly had 16 personalities) represent a highly dramatic, rare, and controversial class of disorders: dissociative disorders. **Dissociative disorders** are characterized by the separation (or dissociation) of different facets of a person's personality that are normally integrated and work together. By dissociating key parts of who they are, people are able to keep disturbing memories or perceptions from reaching conscious awareness, thereby reducing their anxiety (Maldonado & Spiegel, 2003; Houghtalen & Talbot, 2007).

Dissociative Identity Disorder

Several dissociative disorders exist, although all of them are rare. A person with a **dissociative identity disorder (DID)** (once called *multiple personality disorder*) displays characteristics of two or more distinct personalities, identities, or personality fragments. Individual personalities often have a unique set of likes and dislikes and their own reactions to situations. Some people with multiple personalities even carry several pairs of glasses because their vision changes with each personality. Moreover, each individual personality can be well adjusted when considered on its own (Ellason & Ross, 2004; Stickley & Nickeas, 2006).

The diagnosis of DID is controversial. It was rarely diagnosed before 1980, when, for the first time, it was added as a category in the third edition of DSM. At that point, the number of cases increased significantly. Some clinicians suggest the increase was due to more precise identification of the disorder, whereas others suggest the increase was due to an overreadiness to use the classification. (Kihlstrom, 2005a; Xiao et al., 2006).

Dissociative Amnesia

Dissociative amnesia is another dissociative disorder in which a significant, selective memory loss occurs. Dissociative amnesia is unlike simple amnesia, which involves an actual loss of information from memory, typically resulting from a physiological cause. In contrast, in cases of dissociative amnesia, the "forgotten" material is still present in memory—it simply cannot be recalled.

The term *repressed memories* is sometimes used to describe the lost memories of people with dissociative amnesia.

In the most severe form of dissociative amnesia, individuals cannot recall their names, are unable to recognize parents and other relatives, and do not know their addresses. In other respects, though, they may appear quite normal. Apart from an inability to remember certain facts about themselves, they may be able to recall skills and abilities that they developed earlier. For instance, even though a chef may not remember where he grew up and received training, he may still be able to prepare gourmet meals.

Dissociative Fugue

A more unusual form of amnesia is a condition known as **dissociative fugue.** In this state, people take sudden, impulsive trips, and sometimes assume a new identity. After a period of time—days, months, or sometimes even years—they suddenly realize that they are in a strange place and completely forget the time they have spent wandering. Their last memories are those from the time just before they entered the fugue state.

Dissociative fugue A form of amnesia in which the individual leaves home and sometimes assumes a new identity.

Mood disorders Disturbances in emotional experience that are strong enough to intrude on everyday living.

Major depression A severe form of depression that interferes with concentration, decision making, and sociability.

» LO4 Mood Disorders

> From the time I woke up in the morning until the time I went to bed at night, I was unbearably miserable and seemingly incapable of any kind of joy or enthusiasm. Everything—every thought, word, movement—was an effort. Everything that once was sparkling now was flat. I seemed to myself to be dull, boring, inadequate, thick brained, unlit, unresponsive, chill skinned, bloodless, and sparrow drab. I doubted, completely, my ability to do anything well. It seemed as though my mind had slowed down and burned out to the point of being virtually useless. (Jamison, 1995a, p. 110)

We all experience mood swings. Sometimes we are happy, perhaps even euphoric; at other times we feel upset, saddened, or depressed. Such changes in mood are a normal part of everyday life. In some people, however, moods are so pronounced and lingering—like the feelings described in the preceding extract by writer (and psychiatrist) Kay Jamison—that they interfere with the ability to function effectively. In extreme cases, a mood may become life-threatening, and in others it may cause the person to lose touch with reality. Situations such as these represent **mood disorders,** disturbances in emotional experience that are strong enough to intrude on everyday living.

Major Depression

President Abraham Lincoln. Queen Victoria. Newscaster Mike Wallace.

The common link among these people? Each suffered from periodic attacks of **major depression,** a severe form of depression that interferes with concentration, decision making, and sociability. Major depression is one of the more common forms of mood disorders. Some 15 million people in the United States suffer from major depression, and at any one time, 6 to 10 percent of the U.S. population is clinically depressed. Almost one in five people in the United States experiences major depression at some point in life, and 15 percent of college students have received a diagnosis of depression. The cost of depression is more than $80 billion a year in lost productivity (Winik, 2006; Scelfo, 2007).

Women are twice as likely to experience major depression as men, with one-fourth of all females apt to encounter it at some point during their lives. Furthermore, although no one is sure why, the rate of depression is going up throughout the world. Results of in-depth interviews conducted in the United States, Puerto Rico, Taiwan, Lebanon, Canada, Italy, Germany, and France indicate that the incidence of depression has increased significantly over previous rates in every area (Staley, Sanacora, & Tamagnan, 2006; Kendler, Gatz, & Gardner, 2006).

When psychologists speak of major depression, they do not mean the sadness that comes from experiencing one of life's disappointments, something that we all have experienced. Some depression is normal after the breakup of a long-term relationship, the death of a loved one, or the loss of a job. It is normal even after less serious problems, such as doing badly on a test or having a romantic partner forget one's birthday.

People who suffer from major depression experience similar sorts of feelings, but the severity tends to be considerably greater. They may feel useless, worthless, and lonely and may think the future is hopeless and that no one can help them. They may lose their appetite and have no energy. Moreover, they may experience such feelings for months or even years. They may cry uncontrollably, have sleep disturbances, and be at risk for suicide. The depth and duration of such behavior are the hallmarks of major depression. (Figure 4 provides a self-assessment of depression.)

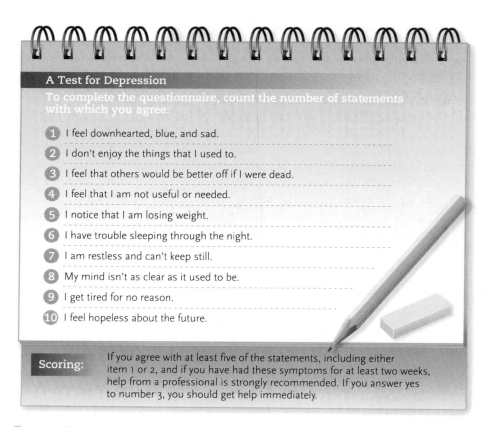

A Test for Depression

To complete the questionnaire, count the number of statements with which you agree:

1. I feel downhearted, blue, and sad.
2. I don't enjoy the things that I used to.
3. I feel that others would be better off if I were dead.
4. I feel that I am not useful or needed.
5. I notice that I am losing weight.
6. I have trouble sleeping through the night.
7. I am restless and can't keep still.
8. My mind isn't as clear as it used to be.
9. I get tired for no reason.
10. I feel hopeless about the future.

Scoring: If you agree with at least five of the statements, including either item 1 or 2, and if you have had these symptoms for at least two weeks, help from a professional is strongly recommended. If you answer yes to number 3, you should get help immediately.

FIGURE 4   This is a version of a test distributed by mental health organizations during the annual National Depression Screening Day, a nationwide event that seeks to identify people who are suffering from depression that is severe enough to warrant psychological intervention. (Source: National Depression Screening Day, 2003.)

Mania and Bipolar Disorder

While depression leads to the depths of despair, mania leads to emotional heights. **Mania** is an extended state of intense, wild elation. People experiencing mania feel intense happiness, power, invulnerability, and energy. They may become involved in wild schemes, believing they will succeed at anything they attempt.

Typically, people sequentially experience periods of mania and depression. This alternation of mania and depression is called **bipolar disorder** (a condition previously known as manic-depressive disorder). The swings between highs and lows may occur a few days apart or may alternate over a period of years. In addition, in bipolar disorder, periods of depression are usually longer than periods of mania.

Causes of Mood Disorders

Because they represent a major mental health problem, mood disorders—and, in particular, depression—have received a good deal of study. Several approaches have been used to explain the disorders.

Some mood disorders clearly have genetic and biochemical roots. In fact, most evidence suggests that bipolar disorders are caused primarily by biological factors. For instance, bipolar disorder (and some forms of major depression) clearly run in some families. Furthermore, researchers have found that several neurotransmitters play a role in depression. For example, alterations in the functioning of serotonin and norepinephrine in the brain are related to the disorder (Plomin & McGuffin, 2003; Kato, 2007).

Other explanations for depression have also included a focus on psychological causes. For instance, proponents of psychoanalytic approaches see depression as the result of feelings of loss (real or potential) or of anger directed at oneself. One psychoanalytic approach, for instance, suggests that depression is produced by the loss or threatened loss of a parent early in life (Vanheule et al., 2006).

Behavioral theories of depression argue that the stresses of life produce a reduction in positive reinforcers. As a result, people begin to withdraw, which only serves to reduce positive reinforcers further. In addition, people receive attention for their depressive behavior, which further reinforces the depression (Lewinsohn & Essau, 2002; Lewinsohn et al., 2003).

Some explanations for mood disorders attribute them to cognitive factors. For example, psychologist Martin Seligman suggests that depression is largely a response to learned helplessness. *Learned helplessness* is a learned expectation that events in one's life are uncontrollable and that one cannot escape from the situation. As a consequence, people simply give up fighting aversive events and submit to them, thereby producing depression. Other theorists go a step further, suggesting that depression results from hopelessness, a combination of learned helplessness and an expectation that negative outcomes in one's life are inevitable (Kwon & Laurenceau, 2002; Maier & Watkins, 2000; Bjornstad, 2006).

Clinical psychologist Aaron Beck has proposed that faulty cognitions underlie people's depressed feelings. Specifically, his cognitive theory of depression suggests that depressed individuals typically view themselves as life's losers, blaming themselves whenever anything goes wrong. By focusing on the negative side of situations, they feel inept and unable to act constructively to change their environment. In sum, their negative cognitions lead to feelings of depression (Newman et al., 2002).

> **Mania** An extended state of intense, wild elation.
>
> **Bipolar disorder** A disorder in which a person alternates between periods of euphoric feelings of mania and periods of depression.

psych2.0
WWW.MHHE.COM/PSYCHLIFE

Bipolar Disorder

> *Learned helplessness is a learned expectation that events in one's life are uncontrollable and that one cannot escape from the situation.*

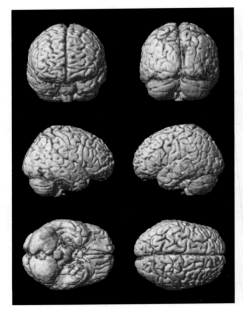
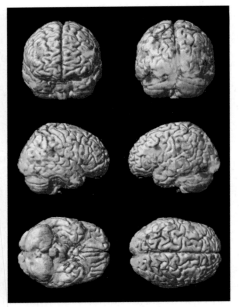

FIGURE 5   The brains of those with depression (left) show significantly less activation in response to photos of sad, angry, and fearful faces than those of people without the disorder (right). *(Source: Ian Gotlib, Stanford Mood and Anxiety Disorders Laboratory, 2005.)*

Brain imaging studies suggest that people with depression experience a general blunting of emotional reactions. For example, one study found that the brains of people with depression showed significantly less activation when they viewed photos of human faces displaying strong emotions than those without the disorder (see Figure 5; Gotlib et al., 2004).

The various theories of depression have not provided a complete answer to an elusive question that has dogged researchers: Why does depression occur in approximately twice as many women as men—a pattern that is similar across a variety of cultures?

One explanation suggests that the stress experienced by women may be greater than that experienced by men at certain points in their lives—such as

How might knowing that almost twice as many women suffer from depression impact how you view yourself and the women in your life?

when a woman must simultaneously earn a living and be the primary caregiver for her children. In addition, women have a higher risk for physical and sexual abuse, typically earn lower wages than men, report greater unhappiness with their marriages, and generally experience chronic negative circumstances. Furthermore, women and men may respond to stress with different coping mechanisms. For instance, men may abuse drugs, whereas women respond with depression (Antonucci et al., 2002; Holden, 2005; Nolen-Hoeksema, 2007).

Biological factors may also explain some women's depression. For example, because the rate of female depression begins to rise during puberty, some psychologists believe that hormones make women more vulnerable to the disorder. In addition, 25 to 50 percent of women who take oral contraceptives report symptoms of depression, and depression that occurs after the birth of a child is linked to hormonal changes. Finally, structural differences in men's and women's brains that we discussed in the neuroscience and behavior chapter may be related to gender differences in depression (Holden, 2005; Graham, Bancroft, & Doll, 2007).

It is clear, ultimately, that researchers have discovered no definitive solutions to the puzzle of depression, and there are many alternative explanations. Most likely, a complex interaction of several factors causes mood disorders.

» LO5 Schizophrenia

I'm a doctor, you know ... I don't have a diploma, but I'm a doctor. I'm glad to be a mental patient, because it taught me how to be humble. I use Cover Girl creamy natural makeup. Oral Roberts has been here to visit me ... This place is where *Mad* magazine is published. The Nixons make Noxon metal polish. When I was a little girl, I used to sit and tell stories to myself. When I was older, I turned off the sound on the TV set and made up dialogue to go with the shows I watched ... I'm a week pregnant. I have schizophrenia—cancer of the nerves. My body is overcrowded with nerves. This is going to win me the Nobel Prize for medicine. I don't consider myself schizophrenic anymore. There's no such thing as schizophrenia, there's only mental telepathy. I once had a friend named Camilla Costello. (Sheehan, 1982, pp. 72–73)

This excerpt illustrates the efforts of a woman with schizophrenia, one of the more severe forms of mental disturbance, to hold a conversation with a clinician. People with schizophrenia account for by far the largest percentage of those hospitalized for mental disorders. They are also in many respects the least likely to recover from their psychological difficulties.

Schizophrenia refers to a class of disorders in which severe distortion of reality occurs. Thinking, perception, and emotion may deteriorate; the individual may withdraw from social interaction; and the person may display bizarre behavior. Although there are several types of schizophrenia (see Figure 6), the distinctions between them are not always clear-cut. Moreover,

Schizophrenia A class of disorders in which severe distortion of reality occurs.

Types of Schizophrenia	
Type	**Symptoms**
Disorganized (hebephrenic) schizophrenia	Inappropriate laughter and giggling, silliness, incoherent speech, infantile behavior; strange and sometimes obscene behavior
Paranoid schizophrenia	Delusions and hallucinations of persecution or of greatness, loss of judgment, erratic and unpredictable behavior
Catatonic schizophrenia	Major disturbances in movement; in some phases, loss of all motion, with patient frozen into a single position, remaining that way for hours and sometimes even days; in other phases, hyperactivity and wild, sometimes violent, movement
Undifferentiated schizophrenia	Variable mixture of major symptoms of schizophrenia; classification used for patients who cannot be typed into any of the more specific categories
Residual schizophrenia	Minor signs of schizophrenia after a more serious episode

FIGURE 6 The distinctions among the different types of schizophrenia are not always clear-cut, and symptoms may vary considerably over time.

the symptoms displayed by persons with schizophrenia may vary considerably over time, and people with schizophrenia show significant differences in the pattern of their symptoms even when they are labeled with the same diagnostic category. Nonetheless, a number of characteristics reliably distinguish schizophrenia from other disorders. They include the following:

- *Decline from a previous level of functioning.* An individual can no longer carry out activities he or she was once able to do.
- *Disturbances of thought and language.* People with schizophrenia use logic and language in a peculiar way. Their thinking often does not make sense, and their information processing is frequently faulty. They also do not follow conventional linguistic rules (Penn et al., 1997). Consider, for example, the following response to the question "Why do you think people believe in God?"

> Uh, let's, I don't know why, let's see, balloon travel. He holds it up for you, the balloon. He don't let you fall out, your little legs sticking down through the clouds. He's down to the smokestack, looking through the smoke trying to get the balloon gassed up you know. Way they're flying on top that way, legs sticking out. I don't know, looking down on the ground, heck, that'd make you so dizzy you just stay and sleep you know, hold down and sleep there. I used to be sleep outdoors, you know, sleep outdoors instead of going home. (Chapman & Chapman, 1973, p. 3)

As this selection illustrates, although the basic grammatical structure may be intact, the substance of thinking characteristic of schizophrenia is often illogical, garbled, and lacking in meaningful content (Holden, 2003; Heinrichs, 2005).

- *Delusions.* People with schizophrenia often have delusions, firmly held, unshakable beliefs with no basis in reality. Among the common delusions experienced by people with schizophrenia are the beliefs that they are being controlled by someone else, they are being persecuted by others, and their thoughts are being broadcast so that others know what they are thinking (Stompe et al., 2003; Coltheart, Langdon, & McKay, 2007).
- *Hallucinations and perceptual disorders.* People with schizophrenia do not perceive the world as most other people do. They also may have *hallucinations,* the experience of perceiving things that do not actually exist. Furthermore, they may see, hear, or smell things differently from others (see Figure 7) and do not even have a sense of their bodies in the way that

FIGURE 7 This unusual art was created by an individual suffering from severe mental disturbance.

others do, having difficulty determining where their bodies stop and the rest of the world begins (Copolov et al., 2003; Botvinick, 2004; Moritz & Laroi, 2008).

■ *Emotional disturbances.* People with schizophrenia sometimes show a lack of emotion in which even the most dramatic events produce little or no emotional response. Conversely, they may display emotion that is inappropriate to a situation. For example, a person with schizophrenia may laugh uproariously at a funeral or react with anger when being helped by someone.

■ *Withdrawal.* People with schizophrenia tend to have little interest in others. They tend not to socialize or hold real conversations with others, although they may talk at another person. In the most extreme cases they do not even acknowledge the presence of other people, appearing to be in their own isolated world.

The symptoms of schizophrenia are classified into two types by *DSM-IV-TR.* Positive-symptom schizophrenia is indicated by the presence of disordered behavior such as hallucinations, delusions, and emotional extremes. In contrast, negative-symptom schizophrenia shows an absence or loss of normal functioning, such as social withdrawal or blunted emotions. Schizophrenia researchers sometimes speak of *Type I schizophrenia,* in which positive symptoms are dominant, and *Type II schizophrenia,* in which negative symptoms are more prominent (Buchanan et al., 2007; Levine & Rabinowitz, 2007).

The distinction between Type I and Type II schizophrenia is important because it suggests that two different processes might trigger schizophrenia, the cause of which remains one of the greatest mysteries facing psychologists who deal with disordered behavior.

Solving the Puzzle of Schizophrenia: Biological Causes

Although schizophrenic behavior clearly departs radically from normal behavior, its causes are less apparent. It does appear, however, that schizophrenia has both biological and environmental origins (Sawa & Snyder, 2002).

Let's first consider the evidence pointing to a biological cause. Because schizophrenia is more common in some families than in others, genetic factors seem to be involved in producing at least a susceptibility to or readiness for developing schizophrenia. For example, the closer the genetic link between a person with schizophrenia and another individual, the greater the likelihood that the other person will experience the disorder (see Figure 8 on page 412; Brzustowicz et al., 2000; Plomin & McGuffin, 2003; Gottesman & Hanson, 2005).

However, if genetics alone were responsible for schizophrenia, the chance of both of two identical twins having schizophrenia would be 100 percent instead of just under 50 percent, because identical twins have the same genetic makeup. Moreover, attempts to find a link between schizophrenia and a particular gene have been only partly successful. Apparently, genetic factors alone do not produce schizophrenia (Franzek & Beckmann, 1996; Lenzenweger & Dworkin, 1998).

One intriguing biological hypothesis to explain schizophrenia is that the brains of people with the disorder may harbor either a biochemical imbalance or a structural abnormality. For example, the *dopamine hypothesis* suggests that schizophrenia occurs when there is excess activity in the areas of the brain that use dopamine as a neurotransmitter. This hypothesis came to light after

psych2.0

WWW.MHHE.COM/PSYCHLIFE

Schizophrenia

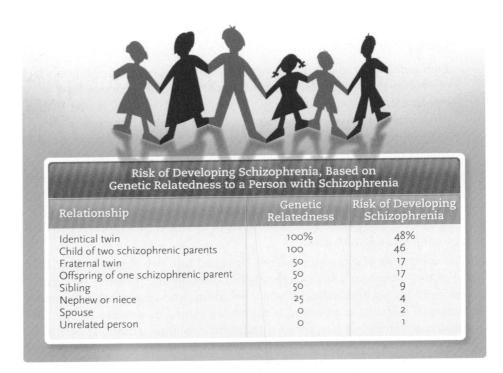

Risk of Developing Schizophrenia, Based on Genetic Relatedness to a Person with Schizophrenia		
Relationship	Genetic Relatedness	Risk of Developing Schizophrenia
Identical twin	100%	48%
Child of two schizophrenic parents	100	46
Fraternal twin	50	17
Offspring of one schizophrenic parent	50	17
Sibling	50	9
Nephew or niece	25	4
Spouse	0	2
Unrelated person	0	1

FIGURE 8   The closer the genetic links between two people, the greater the likelihood that if one experiences schizophrenia, so will the other some time during his or her lifetime. However, genetics is not the full story, because if it were, the risk of identical twins having schizophrenia would be 100 percent, not the 48 percent shown in this figure. *(Source: Gottesman, 1991.)*

the discovery that drugs that block dopamine action in brain pathways can be highly effective in reducing the symptoms of schizophrenia. Other research suggests that glutamate, another neurotransmitter, may be a major contributor to the disorder (Remington, 2003; Baumeister & Francis, 2002; Javitt & Coyle, 2004; Ohara, 2007).

Some biological explanations propose that structural abnormalities exist in the brains of people with schizophrenia, perhaps as a result of exposure to a virus during prenatal development. For example, some research shows abnormalities in the neural circuits of the cortex and limbic systems of individuals with schizophrenia. Consistent with such research, people with schizophrenia and those without the disorder show different brain functioning (see Figure 9; Lenzenweger & Dworkin, 1998; Bartzokis et al., 2003; Reichenberg & Harvey, 2007).

Further evidence for the importance of biological factors shows that when people with schizophrenia hear voices during hallucinations, the parts of the brain responsible for hearing and language processing become active. When they have visual hallucinations, the parts of the brain involved in movement and color are active. At the same time, people with schizophrenia often have unusually low activity in the brain's frontal lobes—the parts of the brain involved with emotional regulation, insight, and the evaluation of sensory stimuli (Stern & Silbersweig, 2001).

Environmental Perspectives on Schizophrenia

Although biological factors provide important pieces of the puzzle of schizophrenia, we still need to consider past and current experiences in the environments of

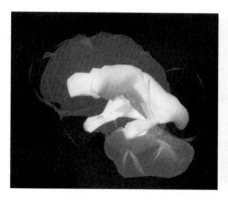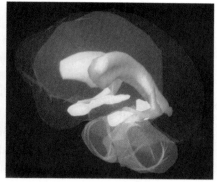

FIGURE 9   Changes in the brain have been found in people with schizophrenia. In the first MRI reconstruction of the brain of a patient with schizophrenia (left), the hippocampus (yellow) is shrunken, and the ventricles (gray) are enlarged and fluid-filled. In contrast, the brain of a person without the disorder (right) appears structurally different. *(Source: N.C. Andreasen, University of Iowa.)*

people who develop the disturbance. For instance, some researchers look toward the emotional and communication patterns of the families of people with schizophrenia, suggesting that the disorder results from high levels of expressed emotion. *Expressed emotion* is an interaction style characterized by criticism, hostility, and emotional intrusiveness by family members. Other researchers suggest that faulty communication patterns lie at the heart of schizophrenia (Miklowitz & Tompson, 2003; Lobban, Barrowclough, & Jones, 2006).

The Multiple Causes of Schizophrenia

The predominant approach used to explain the onset of schizophrenia today, the *predisposition model of schizophrenia,* incorporates a number of biological and environmental factors. This model suggests that individuals may inherit a predisposition or an inborn sensitivity to schizophrenia that makes them particularly vulnerable to stressful factors in the environment, such as social rejection or dysfunctional family communication patterns. The stressors may vary, but if they are strong enough and are coupled with a genetic predisposition, the result will be the onset of schizophrenia. Similarly, a strong genetic predisposition may lead to the onset of schizophrenia even when the environmental stressors are relatively weak.

In short, the models used today associate schizophrenia with several kinds of biological and environmental factors. It is increasingly clear, then, that no single factor, but a combination of interrelated variables, produces schizophrenia (Meltzer, 2000; McDonald & Murray, 2004).

» LO6 Personality Disorders

I had always wanted lots of things; as a child I can remember wanting a bullet that a friend of mine had brought in to show the class. I took it and put it into my school bag and when my friend noticed it was missing, I was the one who stayed after school with him and searched the room, and I was the one who sat with him and bitched about the other kids and how one of them took his bullet. I even went home with him to help him break the news to his uncle, who had brought it home from the war for him. But that was petty compared with the stuff I did later. I wanted a Ph.D. very badly, but I didn't want to work very hard—just enough to get by. I never did the experiments I reported; hell, I was

Personality disorder A disorder characterized by a set of inflexible, maladaptive behavior patterns that keep a person from functioning appropriately in society.

Antisocial personality disorder A disorder in which individuals show no regard for the moral and ethical rules of society or the rights of others.

Borderline personality disorder A disorder in which individuals have difficulty developing a secure sense of who they are.

STUDY ALERT

Unlike most psychological disorders, personality disorders produce little or no personal distress.

smart enough to make up the results. I knew enough about statistics to make anything look plausible. I got my master's degree without even spending one hour in a laboratory. I mean, the professors believed anything. I'd stay out all night drinking and being with my friends, and the next day I'd get in just before them and tell 'em I'd been in the lab all night. They'd actually feel sorry for me. (Duke & Nowicki, 1979, pp. 309–310)

This excerpt provides a graphic first-person account of a person with a personality disorder. A **personality disorder** is characterized by a set of inflexible, maladaptive behavior patterns that keep a person from functioning appropriately in society. Personality disorders differ from the other problems we have discussed because those affected by them often have little sense of personal distress associated with the psychological maladjustment. In fact, people with personality disorders frequently lead seemingly normal lives. However, just below the surface lies a set of inflexible, maladaptive personality traits that do not permit these individuals to function as members of society (Clarkin & Lenzenweger, 2004; Friedman, Oltmanns, & Turkheimer, 2007).

The best-known type of personality disorder, illustrated by the case above, is the **antisocial personality disorder** (sometimes referred to as a *sociopathic personality*). Individuals with this disturbance show no regard for the moral and ethical rules of society or the rights of others. Although they can appear quite intelligent and likable (at least at first), upon closer examination they turn out to be manipulative and deceptive. Moreover, they lack any guilt or anxiety about their wrongdoing. When those with antisocial personality disorder behave in a way that injures someone else, they understand intellectually that they have caused harm but feel no remorse (Lykken, 1995; Goodwin & Hamilton, 2003; Hilarski, 2007).

People with antisocial personality disorder are often impulsive and lack the ability to withstand frustration. They can be extremely manipulative. They also may have excellent social skills; they can be charming, engaging, and highly persuasive. Some of the best con artists have antisocial personalities.

What causes such an unusual constellation of problem behaviors? A variety of factors have been suggested, ranging from an inability to experience emotions appropriately to problems in family relationships. For example, in many cases of antisocial behavior, the individual has come from a home in which a parent has died or left, or one in which there is a lack of affection, a lack of consistency in discipline, or outright rejection. Other explanations concentrate on sociocultural factors, because an unusually high proportion of people with antisocial personalities come from lower socioeconomic groups. Still, no one has been able to pinpoint the specific causes of antisocial personalities, and it is likely that some combination of factors is responsible (Nigg & Goldsmith, 1994; Rosenstein & Horowitz, 1996; Costa & Widiger, 2002).

People with **borderline personality disorder** have difficulty developing a secure sense of who they are. As a consequence, they tend to rely on relationships with others to define their identity. The problem with this strategy is that rejections are devastating. Furthermore, people with this disorder distrust others and have difficulty controlling their anger. Their emotional volatility leads to impulsive

Many experts believe that Scott Peterson, who was convicted of murdering his wife and unborn child, suffered from some sort of personality disorder. This explains how he managed to be both charming and capable of murder.

and self-destructive behavior. Individuals with borderline personality disorder often feel empty and alone. They may form intense, sudden, one-sided relationships, demanding the attention of another person and then feeling angry when they don't receive it. One reason for this behavior is that they may have a background in which others discounted or criticized their emotional reactions, and they may not have learned to regulate their emotions effectively (Linehan, Cochran, & Kehrer, 2001; Trull, Stepp, & Durrett, 2003; Links, Eynan, & Heisel, 2007).

Another example of a personality disturbance is the **narcissistic personality disorder,** which is characterized by an exaggerated sense of self-importance. Those with the disorder expect special treatment from others, while at the same time disregarding others' feelings. In some ways, in fact, the main attribute of the narcissistic personality is an inability to experience empathy for other people.

There are several other categories of personality disorder, ranging in severity from individuals who may simply be regarded by others as eccentric, obnoxious, or difficult, to people who act in a manner that is criminal and dangerous to others. Although they are not out of touch with reality in the way that people with schizophrenia are, people with personality disorders lead lives that put them on the fringes of society (Millon, Davis, & Millon, 2000; Trull & Widiger, 2003).

psych2.0
WWW.MHHE.COM/PSYCHLIFE

Borderline Personality Disorder

Narcissistic personality disorder A personality disturbance characterized by an exaggerated sense of self-importance.

From the perspective of . . .

A MEDICAL ASSISTANT Personality disorders are often not apparent to others, and many people with these problems seem to live basically normal lives and are not a threat to others. Because these people often appear from the outside to function well in society, why should they be considered psychologically disordered? What are the benefits of you having an understanding of the major psychological disorders in your career?

» LO7 Childhood Disorders

We typically view childhood as a time of innocence and relative freedom from stress. In reality, though, almost 20 percent of children and 40 percent of adolescents experience significant emotional or behavioral disorders (Romano et al., 2001; Broidy, Nagan, & Tremblay, 2003; Nolen-Hoeksema, 2007).

For example, although major depression is more prevalent in adults, around 2.5 percent of children and more than 8 percent of adolescents suffer from the disorder. In fact, by the time they reach age 20, between 15 and 20 percent of children and adolescents will experience an episode of major depression (Garber & Horowitz, 2002).

Children do not always display depression in the same way adults do. Rather than showing profound sadness or hopelessness, childhood depression may produce the expression of exaggerated fears, clinginess, or avoidance of everyday activities. In older children, the symptoms may be sulking, school

With the prevalence of ADHD, how would you use your understanding of the disorder when interacting with a child suffering from the disorder?

Attention-deficit hyperactivity disorder (ADHD) A disorder marked by inattention, impulsiveness, a low tolerance for frustration, and a great deal of inappropriate activity.

Autism A severe developmental disability that impairs children's ability to communicate and relate to others.

> *Children with autism have difficulties in both verbal and nonverbal communication, and they may avoid social contact.*

problems, and even acts of delinquency (Wenar, 1994; Seroczynski, Jacquez, & Cole, 2003; Koplewicz, 2002).

A considerably more common childhood disorder is **attention-deficit hyperactivity disorder,** or **ADHD,** a disorder marked by inattention, impulsiveness, a low tolerance for frustration, and generally a great deal of inappropriate activity. Although all children show such behavior some of the time, it is so common in children diagnosed with ADHD that it interferes with their everyday functioning (Barkley, 2005; Swanson, Harris, & Graham, 2003; Smith, Barkley, & Shapiro, 2006).

ADHD is surprisingly widespread, with estimates ranging between 3 and 5 percent of the school-age population—or some 3.5 million children under the age of 18 in the United States. Children diagnosed with the disorder are often exhausting to parents and teachers, and even their peers find them difficult to deal with.

The cause of ADHD is not known, although most experts feel that it is produced by dysfunctions in the nervous system. For example, one theory suggests that unusually low levels of arousal in the central nervous system cause ADHD. To compensate, children with ADHD seek out stimulation to increase arousal. Still, such theories are speculative. Furthermore, because many children occasionally show behaviors characteristic of ADHD, it often is misdiagnosed or, in some cases, overdiagnosed. Only the frequency and persistence of the symptoms of ADHD allow for a correct diagnosis, which can be done only by a trained professional (Hinshaw et al., 1997; Barkley, 2000).

Autism, a severe developmental disability that impairs children's ability to communicate and relate to others, is another childhood disorder that usually appears in the first three years and typically continues throughout life. Children with autism have difficulties in both verbal and nonverbal communication, and they may avoid social contact. About one in 150 children are now thought to have the disorder (Centers for Disease Control and Prevention, 2007).

» LO8 Other Disorders

It's important to keep in mind that the various forms of psychological disorders described in *DSM-IV-TR* cover much more ground than we have been able to discuss in this module. Some relate to topics previously considered in other chapters; there are other disorders that we have not mentioned at all. Moreover, each of the classes we have discussed can be divided into several subcategories (Kopelman & Fleminger, 2002; Pratt et al., 2003; Reijonen et al., 2003).

For example, some common disorders include:

- *Psychoactive substance use disorder*
- *Alcohol use disorder*
- *Eating disorders,* including *anorexia nervosa, bulimia,* and *binge-eating disorder*
- *Sexual disorders,* including *paraphilias* (atypical sexual activities that may include nonhuman objects or nonconsenting partners
- *Organic mental disorders* (such as *Alzheimer's disease*)

RECAP

Discuss anxiety disorders.

- Anxiety disorders are present when a person experiences so much anxiety that it affects daily functioning. Specific types of anxiety disorders include phobic disorder, panic disorder, generalized anxiety disorder, and obsessive-compulsive disorder. (p. 397)

Discuss somatoform disorders.

- Somatoform disorders are psychological difficulties that take on a physical (somatic) form, but for which there is no medical cause. Examples are hypochondriasis and conversion disorders. (p. 403)

Discuss dissociative disorders.

- Dissociative disorders are marked by the separation, or dissociation, of different facets of a person's personality that are usually integrated. Major kinds of dissociative disorders include dissociative identity disorder, dissociative amnesia, and dissociative fugue. (p. 404)

Discuss mood disorders.

- Mood disorders are characterized by emotional states of depression or euphoria so strong that they intrude on everyday living. They include major depression and bipolar disorder. (p. 405)

Explain schizophrenia.

- Schizophrenia is one of the more severe forms of mental illness. Symptoms of schizophrenia include declines in functioning, thought and language disturbances, perceptual disorders, emotional disturbance, and withdrawal from others. (p. 409)
- Strong evidence links schizophrenia to genetic, biochemical, and environmental factors. According to the predisposition model, an interaction among various factors produces the disorder. (p. 411)

Discuss personality disorders.

- People with personality disorders experience little or no personal distress, but they do suffer from an inability to function as normal members of society. These disorders include antisocial personality disorder, borderline personality disorder, and narcissistic personality disorder. (p. 413)

Discuss childhood disorders.

- Childhood disorders include major depression, attention-deficit hyperactivity disorder (ADHD), and autism. (p. 414)

EVALUATE

1. Kathy is terrified of elevators. She could be suffering from a(n)
   a. Obsessive-compulsive disorder.
   b. Phobic disorder.

c. Panic disorder.

d. Generalized anxiety disorder.

2. Carmen described an incident in which her anxiety suddenly rose to a peak and she felt a sense of impending doom. Carmen experienced a(n) _____ _____.

3. Troubling thoughts that persist for weeks or months are known as

a. Obsessions.

b. Compulsions.

c. Rituals.

d. Panic attacks.

4. A. overpowering urge to carry out a strange ritual is called a(n) _____.

5. The separation of the personality, providing escape from stressful situations, is the key factor in _____ disorders.

6. States of extreme euphoria and energy paired with severe depression characterize _____ disorder.

7. The _____ _____ states that schizophrenia may be caused by an excess of certain neurotransmitters in the brain.

RETHINK

What cultural factors might contribute to the rate of anxiety disorders found in a culture? How might the experience of anxiety differ among people of different cultures?

Answers to Evaluate Questions 1. b; 2. panic attack; 3. a; 4. compulsion; 5. dissociative; 6. bipolar; 7. dopamine hypothesis

[KEY TERMS]

Anxiety disorder *p. 397*

Phobia *p. 399*

Panic disorder *p. 401*

Generalized anxiety disorder *p. 401*

Obsessive-compulsive disorder *p. 401*

Obsession *p. 401*

Compulsion *p. 402*

Somatoform disorder *p. 403*

Hypochondriasis *p. 403*

Conversion disorder *p. 404*

Dissociative disorder *p. 404*

Dissociative identity disorder (DID) *p. 404*

Dissociative amnesia *p. 404*

Dissociative fugue *p. 405*

Mood disorder *p. 405*

Major depression *p. 405*

Mania *p. 407*

Bipolar disorder *p. 407*

Schizophrenia *p. 409*

Personality disorder *p. 414*

Antisocial personality disorder *p. 414*

Borderline personality disorder *p. 414*

Narcissistic personality disorder *p. 415*

Attention-deficit hyperactivity disorder (ADHD) *p. 416*

Autism *p. 416*

Psychological Disorders in Perspective

How common are the kinds of psychological disorders we've been discussing? Here's one answer: every second person you meet in the United States is likely to suffer, at some point during his or her life, from a psychological disorder.

LEARNING OUTCOMES

35.1 Discuss the prevalence of psychological disorders.

35.2 Discuss the societal and cultural context for psychological disorders.

» LO1 Prevalence of Psychological Disorders: The Mental State of the Union

The preceding sentence represents the conclusion drawn from a massive study on the prevalence of psychological disorders. In that study, researchers conducted face-to-face interviews with more than 8,000 men and women between the ages of 15 and 54 years. The sample was designed to be representative of the population of the United States. According to results of the study, 48 percent of those interviewed had experienced a disorder at some point in their lives. In addition, 30 percent experienced a disorder in any particular year, and the number of people who experienced simultaneous multiple disorders (known as *comorbidity*) was significant (Welkowitz et al., 2000; Kessler, Berglund, & Demler, 2005; Merikangas et al., 2007).

The most common disorder reported in the study was depression, with 17 percent of those surveyed reporting at least one major episode. Ten percent had suffered from depression during the current year. The next most common disorder was alcohol dependence, which occurred at a lifetime incidence rate of 14 percent. In addition, 7 percent of those interviewed had experienced alcohol dependence in the last year. Other frequently occurring psychological disorders were drug dependence, disorders involving panic (such as an overwhelming fear of talking to strangers and terror of heights), and posttraumatic stress disorder.

STUDY ALERT

Remember that the incidence of various types of psychological disorders in the general population is surprisingly high.

[*Throughout the world, psychological disorders are widespread.*

The significant level of psychological disorders is a problem not only in the United States; according to the World Health Organization, mental health difficulties are also a global concern. Throughout the world, psychological disorders are widespread. Furthermore, there are economic disparities in treatment, such that more affluent people with mild disorders receive more and better treatment than poor people who have more severe disorders. In fact, psychological disorders make up 14 percent of global illness, and 90 percent of people in developing countries receive no care at all for their disorders (see Figure 1; The WHO World Mental Health Survey Consortium, 2004; Wang et al., 2007).

» LO2 The Social and Cultural Context of Psychological Disorders

In considering the nature of the psychological disorders described in *DSM-IV-TR*, it's important to keep in mind that the specific disorders reflect Western cultures at the turn of the twenty-first century. The classification system provides a snapshot of how its authors viewed mental disorder when it was published. In fact, the development of the most recent version of *DSM* was a source of great debate, in part reflecting issues that divide society.

Some disorders caused particular controversy during the revision process. One such category was "premenstrual dysphoric disorder." That disorder is characterized by severe, incapacitating mood changes or depression related to a woman's menstrual cycle. Some critics argued that the classification simply labels normal female behavior as a disorder. Former U.S. surgeon general Antonia Novello suggested that what "in women is called PMS [premenstrual syndrome, a similar classification] in men is called healthy aggression and initiative" (Cotton, 1993, p. 270). Advocates for including the disorder

Developed Countries

Less-Developed Countries

☐ United States ■ Netherlands ■ Spain ☐ Japan
☐ France ■ Belgium ■ Germany ☐ Italy

☐ Lebanon ■ Ukraine ■ Colombia ☐ Nigeria
■ China–Beijing ■ Mexico ☐ China–Shanghai

FIGURE 1 According to a global survey conducted by the World Health Organization, the prevalence of psychological disorders is widespread. These figures show the prevalence of any psychological disorder within the last 12 months. *(Source: The WHO World Mental Health Survey Consortium, 2004, Table 3.)*

prevailed, however, and "premenstrual dysphoric disorder" appears in the appendix of *DSM-IV-TR* (Hartung & Widiger, 1998).

Such controversies underline the fact that our understanding of abnormal behavior reflects the society and culture in which we live. Future revisions of *DSM* may include a different catalog of disorders. Even now, other cultures might include a list of disorders that looks very different from the list that appears in the current *DSM,* as we discuss next.

EXPLORING diversity

DSM and Culture—and the Culture of DSM

In most people's estimation, a person who hears voices of the recently deceased is probably a victim of a psychological disturbance. Yet some Plains Indians routinely hear the voices of the dead calling to them from the afterlife.

This is only one example of the role of culture in labeling behavior as "abnormal." In fact, among all the major adult disorders included in the *DSM* categorization, just four are found across all cultures of the world: schizophrenia, bipolar disorder, major depression, and anxiety disorders. *All* the rest are specific to North America and Western Europe (Kleinman, 1996; Cohen, Slomkowski, & Robins, 1999; López & Guarnaccia, 2000).

Take, for instance, anorexia nervosa, the disorder in which people develop inaccurate views of their body appearance, become obsessed with their weight, and refuse to eat, sometimes starving to death in the process. This disorder occurs only in cultures that hold the societal standard that slender female bodies are the most desirable. In most of the world, where such a standard does not exist, anorexia nervosa does not occur. Interestingly, there is no anorexia nervosa in all of Asia, with two exceptions: the upper and upper-middle classes of Japan and Hong Kong, where Western influence tends to be great. In fact, anorexia nervosa developed fairly recently even in Western cultures. In the 1600s and 1700s it did not occur because the ideal female body in Western cultures at that time was a full-figured one.

Furthermore, even though disorders such as schizophrenia are found throughout the world, cultural factors influence the specific symptoms of the disorder. Hence, catatonic schizophrenia, in which unmoving patients appear to be frozen in the same position, sometimes for days, is rare in North America and Western Europe. In contrast, in India, 80 percent of those with schizophrenia are catatonic.

Other cultures have disorders that do not appear in the West. For example, in Malaysia, a behavior called *amok* is characterized by a wild outburst in which a person, usually quiet

From the perspective of . . .

A HEALTH CARE PROVIDER What indicators might be most important in determining whether a client is experiencing a psychological disorder? How might your responses change if the client were from a different culture (e.g., an African society)?

and withdrawn, kills or severely injures another. *Koro* is a condition found in Southeast Asian males who develop an intense panic that the penis is about to withdraw into the abdomen. Finally, *ataque de nervios* is a disorder found most often among Latinos from the Caribbean. It is characterized by trembling, crying, uncontrollable screams, and verbal or physical aggression (Cohen, Slomkowski, & Robins, 1999; López & Guarnaccia, 2000; Adams & Dzokoto, 2007).

In sum, we should not assume that the *DSM* provides the final word on psychological disorders. The disorders it includes are very much a creation and function of Western cultures at a particular moment in time, and its categories should not be seen as universally applicable (Tseng, 2003).

becoming an *informed consumer*
OF PSYCHOLOGY

Deciding When You Need Help

Keep in mind that from time to time we all experience a wide range of emotions, and it is not unusual to feel deeply unhappy, fantasize about bizarre situations, or feel anxiety about life's circumstances. On the other hand, many people do have problems that merit concern, and in such cases, it is important to consider the possibility that professional help is warranted. The following list of symptoms can serve as a guideline to help you determine whether outside intervention might be useful (Engler & Goleman, 1992):

- Long-term feelings of distress that interfere with your sense of well-being, competence, and ability to function effectively in daily activities
- Occasions in which you experience overwhelmingly high stress, accompanied by feelings of inability to cope with the situation
- Prolonged depression or feelings of hopelessness, especially when they do not have any clear cause (such as the death of someone close)
- Withdrawal from other people
- Thoughts of inflicting harm on oneself or suicide
- A chronic physical problem for which no physical cause can be determined
- A fear or phobia that prevents you from engaging in everyday activities
- Inability to interact effectively with others, preventing the development of friendships and loving relationships

This list offers a rough set of guidelines for determining when the normal problems of everyday living have escalated beyond your ability to deal with them by yourself. In such situations, the *least* reasonable approach would be to pore over the psychological disorders we have discussed in an attempt at self-diagnosis. A more reasonable strategy is to consider seeking professional help.

RECAP

Discuss the prevalence of psychological disorders.

■ About half the people in the United States are likely to experience a psychological disorder at some point in their lives: 30 percent experience a disorder in any specific year. (p. 419)

Discuss the societal and cultural context for psychological disorders.

■ The signals that indicate a need for professional help include long-term feelings of psychological distress, feelings of inability to cope with stress, withdrawal from other people, thoughts of inflicting harm on oneself or suicide, prolonged feelings of hopelessness, chronic physical problems with no apparent causes, phobias and compulsions, paranoia, and an inability to interact with others. (p. 420)

EVALUATE

1. The latest version of *DSM* is considered to be the conclusive guideline on defining psychological disorders. True or false?

2. _____ _____ _____, characterized by severe, incapacitating mood changes or depression related to a woman's menstrual cycle, was eventually added to the appendix of *DSM-IV-TR* despite controversy surrounding its inclusion.

3. Match the disorder with the culture in which it is most common:

   1. amok   a. India
   2. anorexia nervosa   b. Malaysia
   3. catatonic schizophrenia   c. United States

RETHINK

Why is inclusion in the *DSM-IV-TR* of "borderline" disorders such as premenstrual dysphoric disorder so controversial and political? What disadvantages does inclusion bring? Does inclusion bring any benefits?

Answers to Evaluate Questions 1. false; the development of the latest version of *DSM* was a source of great controversy, in part reflecting issues that divide society; 2. premenstrual dysphoric disorder; 3. 1-b, 2-c, 3-a; 4. depression

Psychology on the Web

1. On the Web, research the insanity defense as it is used in U.S. courts of law, consulting at least two sources. Summarize your findings, evaluating them against the perspectives on psychological disorders. Are there differences between legal and psychological interpretations of "sanity"? If so, what are they? Do you think such differences are appropriate?

2. Find information on the Web about the controversy surrounding dissociative (or multiple) personality disorder. Summarize both sides of the controversy. Using your knowledge of psychology, state your opinion on the matter.

the case of . . . . NANCY CHRISTOPHER, THE "CRAZY CAT LADY"

Although none of Nancy Christopher's neighbors knew her, they all knew of her. They usually referred to her as "the crazy cat lady" because of the dozen or more cats she had living on her property and in her home. No one was quite sure what Nancy did for a living, if anything. She lived alone and would only be seen leaving her house on Saturday afternoons, when she would push a shopping cart into town to shop for groceries and supplies. Nancy often appeared disheveled, with uncombed hair, smeared lipstick, and a dirty winter coat that she had owned for years and always wore outdoors, even when the weather was warm.

Nancy was not unfriendly to people—in fact, quite the contrary. On her trips into town, she would talk to almost anybody she encountered, sometimes at great length. Her chatter was always pleasant and it made sense, though people would still feel uncomfortable with her inappropriately intimate disclosures and her habit of talking almost incessantly with frequent and seemingly random changes in topic. All in all, most people considered her harmless and generally left her alone.

1. Do Nancy Christopher's peculiar habits make her abnormal? Why or why not?

2. What more would you need to know about Nancy Christopher to determine whether she likely has a mental disorder or is just eccentric?

3. Imagine that you're Nancy's physician and her daughter has expressed concern that her behavior may indicate the presence of schizophrenia. How would you assure Nancy's daughter that Nancy's behavior may be odd but does not suggest the presence of schizophrenia?

4. Continue to imagine that you're Nancy's physician, and that you suspect Nancy may have an anxiety disorder of some kind. What kinds of symptoms might you check for to confirm your suspicion?

5. If Nancy's behaviors do not fit any *DSM-IV-TR* criteria for diagnosis as a mental disorder, does that mean that she is definitely normal? Why or why not?

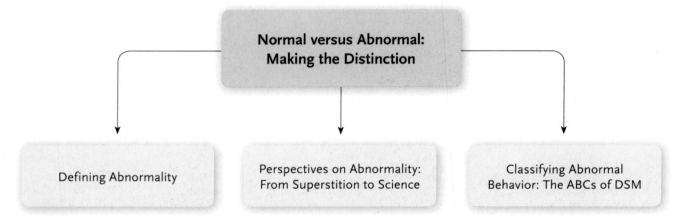

Normal versus Abnormal: Making the Distinction

Defining Abnormality

Perspectives on Abnormality: From Superstition to Science

Classifying Abnormal Behavior: The ABCs of DSM

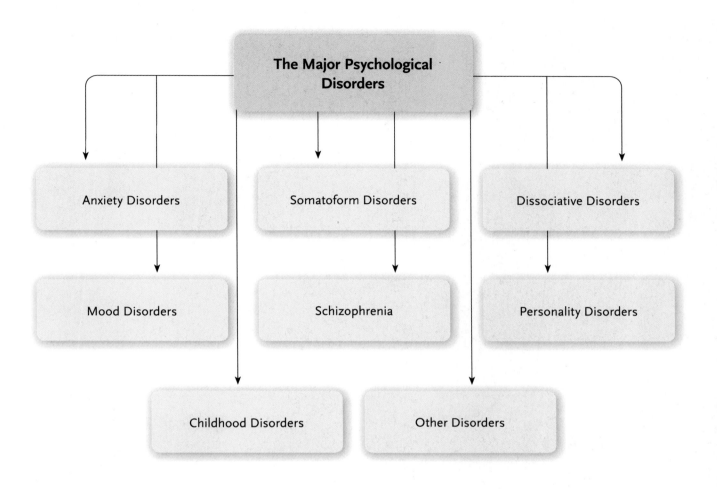

The Major Psychological Disorders

- Anxiety Disorders
- Mood Disorders
- Childhood Disorders
- Somatoform Disorders
- Schizophrenia
- Other Disorders
- Dissociative Disorders
- Personality Disorders

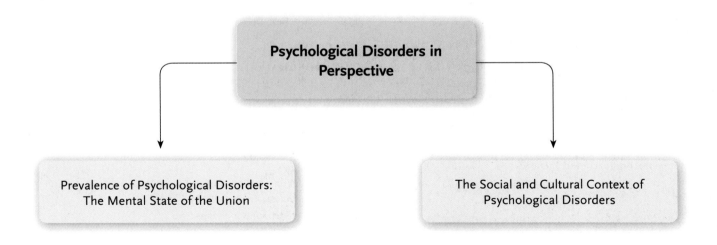

Psychological Disorders in Perspective

- Prevalence of Psychological Disorders: The Mental State of the Union
- The Social and Cultural Context of Psychological Disorders

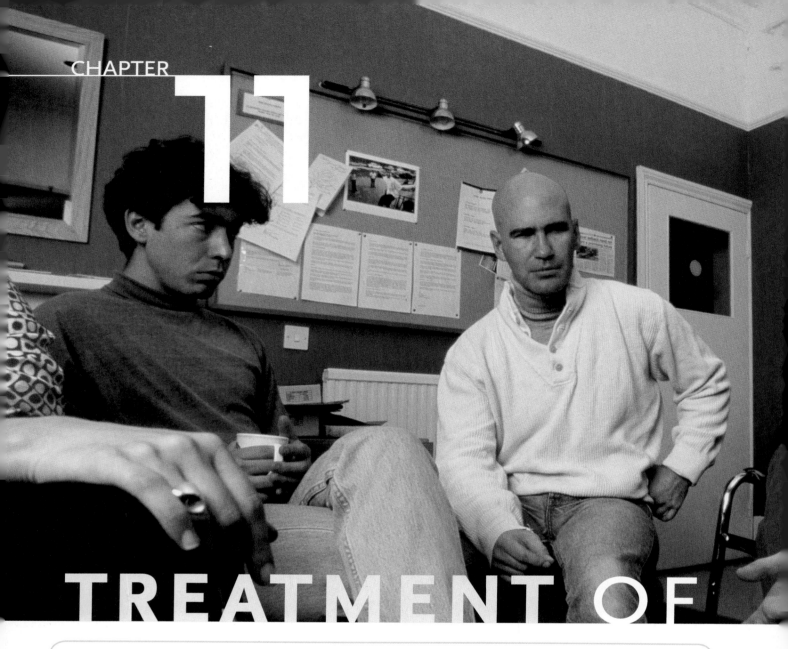

TREATMENT OF

CHAPTER OUTLINE

Facing Their Fears

For most of the 100 or so sleepy-eyed people boarding the U.S. Airways shuttle to Boston from New York on a recent hazy Saturday morning, the 35-minute flight could not have been a bigger non-event. But that was not the case for about 20 passengers clustered nervously near the gate. Many clutched puzzle books and bags of sour candy as though they held talismans. Some made nervous jokes, others sobbed quietly.

"I have pills with me just in case of an emergency," said a teenage girl who planned to distract herself on the flight with celebrity magazines.

Mariasol Flouty, a 44-year-old software developer from White Plains, held fast to her Sudoku book. "I had plane-crash nightmares," she confessed. "I woke up very tense."

No one was more terrified than Beth Brenner, a 45-year-old mother of two teenagers from Somers, N.Y. "I was hysterical last night," she said, "but my son said, 'You're going to be O.K.'" Ms. Brenner was crying quietly on the shoulder of a counselor and staying close to her designated seatmate, Richard Bracken, a retired pilot who had flown for American Airlines for 30 years. "I'm trying to be a father figure here," Mr. Bracken said. (Murphy, 2007, p. F-2). ■

PSYCHOLOGICAL DISORDERS

The procedure that has brought together these very fearful flyers for their first trip on an airplane is just one of many approaches used to treat psychological disorders. Although treatment can take dozens of different approaches, ranging from one-meeting informal counseling sessions to long-term drug therapy to behavioral treatments such as the anxious airline passengers are experiencing, all the approaches have a common objective: the relief of psychological disorders, with the ultimate aim of enabling individuals to achieve richer, more meaningful, and more fulfilling lives.

Despite their diversity, approaches to treating psychological disorders fall into two main categories: psychologically based and biologically based therapies. Psychologically based therapy, or **psychotherapy,** is treatment in which a trained professional—a therapist—uses psychological techniques to help someone overcome psychological difficulties and disorders, resolve problems in living, or bring about personal growth. In psychotherapy, the goal is to produce psychological change in a person (called a "client" or "patient") through discussions and interactions with the therapist. In contrast, **biomedical therapy** relies on drugs and medical procedures to improve psychological functioning.

As we describe the various approaches to therapy, keep in mind that although the distinctions may seem clear-cut, the classifications and procedures overlap a good deal. In fact, many therapists today use a variety of methods with an individual patient, taking an *eclectic approach to therapy.* Assuming that both psychological and biological processes often produce psychological disorders, eclectic therapists may draw from several perspectives simultaneously to address both the psychological and the biological aspects of a person's problems (Goin, 2005; Berman, Jobes, & Silverman, 2006).

looking AHEAD

Psychotherapy
Psychodynamic, Behavioral, and Cognitive Approaches to Treatment

Psychotherapy Treatment in which a trained professional—a therapist—uses psychological techniques to help a person overcome psychological difficulties and disorders, resolve problems in living, or bring about personal growth.

Biomedical therapy Therapy that relies on drugs and other medical procedures to improve psychological functioning.

Psychodynamic therapy Therapy that seeks to bring unresolved past conflicts and unacceptable impulses from the unconscious into the conscious, where patients may deal with the problems more effectively.

Therapists use some 400 different varieties of psychotherapy, approaches to therapy that focus on psychological factors. Although diverse in many respects, all psychological approaches see treatment as a way of solving psychological problems by modifying people's behavior and helping them gain a better understanding of themselves and their past, present, and future.

In light of the variety of psychological approaches, it is not surprising that the people who provide therapy vary considerably in educational background and training (see Figure 1). Regardless of their specific training, almost all psychotherapists employ one of four major approaches to therapy: psychodynamic, behavioral, cognitive, and humanistic treatments. These approaches are based on the models of personality and psychological disorders developed by psychologists. Here we'll consider the psychodynamic, behavioral, and cognitive approaches in turn. In the next module, we'll explore the humanistic approach, as well as interpersonal psychotherapy and group therapy, and evaluate the effectiveness of psychotherapy.

» LO1 Psychodynamic Approaches to Therapy

Psychodynamic therapy seeks to bring unresolved past conflicts and unacceptable impulses from the unconscious into the conscious, where patients may deal with the problems more effectively. Psychodynamic approaches are based on Freud's psychoanalytic approach to personality, which holds that individuals employ *defense mechanisms,* psychological strategies to protect themselves from unacceptable unconscious impulses.

The most common defense mechanism is repression, which pushes threatening conflicts and impulses back into the unconscious. However, since unacceptable conflicts and impulses can never be completely buried, some of the anxiety associated with them can produce abnormal behavior in the form of what Freud called *neurotic symptoms.*

How do we rid ourselves of the anxiety produced by unconscious, unwanted impulses and drives? To Freud, the answer was to confront the

Getting Help from the Right Person

Clinical Psychologists

Psychologists with a Ph.D. or Psy.D. who have also completed a postgraduate internship. They specialize in assessment and treatment of psychological difficulties.

Counseling Psychologists

Psychologists with a Ph.D. or Ed.D. who typically treat day-to-day adjustment problems, often in a university mental health clinic.

Psychiatrists

M.D.s with postgraduate training in abnormal behavior. Because they can prescribe medication, they often treat the most severe disorders.

Psychoanalysts

Either M.D.s or psychologists who specialize in psychoanalysis, the treatment technique first developed by Freud.

Licensed Professional Counselors or Clinical Mental Health Counselors

Professionals with a master's degree who provide therapy to individuals, couples, and families and who hold a national or state certification.

Clinical or Psychiatric Social Workers

Professionals with a master's degree and specialized training who may provide therapy, usually regarding common family and personal problems.

FIGURE 1 A variety of professionals provide therapy and counseling. Each could be expected to give helpful advice and direction. However, the nature of the problem a person is experiencing may make one or another therapy more appropriate. For example, a person who is suffering from a severe disturbance and who has lost touch with reality will typically require some sort of biologically based drug therapy. In that case, a psychiatrist—who is a physician—would be the professional of choice. In contrast, those suffering from milder disorders, such as difficulty adjusting to the death of a family member, have a broader choice that might include any of the professionals listed in the figure. The decision can be made easier by initial consultations with professionals in mental health facilities in communities, colleges, and health organizations, who can provide guidance in selecting an appropriate therapist.

conflicts and impulses by bringing them out of the unconscious part of the mind and into the conscious part. Freud assumed that this technique would reduce anxiety stemming from past conflicts and that the patient could then participate in his or her daily life more effectively.

A psychodynamic therapist, then, faces the challenge of finding a way to assist patients' attempts to explore and understand the unconscious. The technique that has evolved has a number of components, but basically it consists of guiding patients to consider and discuss their past experiences, in explicit detail, from the time of their first memories. This process assumes that patients will eventually stumble upon long-hidden crises, traumas, and conflicts that are producing anxiety in their adult lives. They will then be able to "work through"— understand and rectify—those difficulties.

"Look, call it denial if you like, but I think what goes on in my personal life is none of my own damn business."

Psychoanalysis: Freud's Therapy

Classic Freudian psychodynamic therapy, called psychoanalysis, tends to be a lengthy and expensive affair. **Psychoanalysis** is Freudian psychotherapy in which the goal is to release hidden unconscious thoughts and feelings in order to reduce their power in controlling behavior.

In psychoanalysis, patients may meet with a therapist with considerable frequency, sometimes as much as 50 minutes a day, four to six days a week, for several years. In their sessions, they often use a technique developed by Freud called *free association*. Psychoanalysts using this technique tell patients to say aloud whatever comes to mind, regardless of its apparent irrelevance or senselessness, and the analysts attempt to recognize and label the connections between what a patient says and the patient's unconscious. Therapists also use *dream interpretation,* examining dreams to find clues to unconscious conflicts and problems. Moving beyond the surface description of a dream (called the *manifest content*), therapists seek its underlying meaning (the *latent content*), thereby revealing the true unconscious meaning of the dream (Galatzer-Levy & Cohler, 1997; Auld, Hyman, & Rudzinski, 2005; Bodin, 2006).

The processes of free association and dream interpretation do not always move forward easily. The same unconscious forces that initially produced repression may keep past difficulties out of the conscious mind, producing resistance. *Resistance* is an inability or unwillingness to discuss or reveal particular memories, thoughts, or motivations.

Because of the close, almost intimate interaction between patient and psychoanalyst, the relationship between the two often becomes emotionally charged and takes on a complexity unlike most other relationships. Patients may eventually think of the analyst as a symbol of a significant other in their past, perhaps a parent or a lover, and apply some of their feelings for that person to the analyst—a phenomenon known as transference. **Transference** is the transfer to a psychoanalyst feelings of love or anger that had been originally directed to a patient's parents or other authority figures (Van Beekum, 2005; Evans, 2007).

Psychoanalysis Freudian psychotherapy in which the goal is to release hidden unconscious thoughts and feelings in order to reduce their power in controlling behavior.

Transference The transfer of feelings to a psychoanalyst of love or anger that had been originally directed to a patient's parents or other authority figures.

Freud's psychoanalytic therapy is an intensive, lengthy process that includes techniques such as free association and dream interpretation. What are some advantages and disadvantages of psychoanalysis compared with other approaches?

Contemporary Psychodynamic Approaches

Few people have the time, money, or patience to participate in years of traditional psychoanalysis. Moreover, no conclusive evidence shows that psychoanalysis, as originally conceived by Freud in the nineteenth century, works better than other, more recent forms of psychodynamic therapy.

Today, psychodynamic therapy tends to be of shorter duration, usually lasting no longer than three months or 20 sessions. The therapist takes a more active role than Freud would have liked, controlling the course of therapy and prodding and advising the patient with considerable directness. Finally, the therapist puts less emphasis on a patient's past history and childhood, concentrating instead on an individual's current relationships and specific complaints (Goode, 2003; Charman, 2004; Wolitzky, 2006).

"And when did you first realize you weren't like other precipitation?"

Evaluating Psychodynamic Therapy

Even with its current modifications, psychodynamic therapy has its critics. In its longer versions, it can be time-consuming and expensive, especially in comparison with other forms of psychotherapy, such as behavioral and cognitive approaches. Furthermore, less articulate patients may not do as well as more verbal ones do.

Ultimately, the most important concern about psychodynamic treatment is whether it actually works, and there is no simple answer to this question. Psychodynamic treatment techniques have been controversial since Freud introduced them. Part of the problem is the difficulty in establishing whether patients have improved after psychodynamic therapy. Determining effectiveness depends on reports from the therapist or the patients themselves, reports that are obviously open to bias and subjective interpretation.

Despite the criticism, though, the psychodynamic treatment approach has remained viable. For some people, it provides solutions to difficult psychological issues, provides effective treatment for psychological disturbance, and also permits the potential development of an unusual degree of insight into one's life (Clay, 2000; Ablon & Jones, 2005; Bond, 2006).

» LO2 Behavioral Approaches to Therapy

Perhaps, when you were a child, your parents rewarded you with an ice cream cone when you were especially good . . . or sent you to your room if you misbehaved. Sound principles back up such a child-rearing strategy: Good behavior is maintained by reinforcement, and unwanted behavior can be eliminated by punishment.

These principles represent the basic underpinnings of **behavioral treatment approaches.** Building on the basic processes of learning, behavioral treatment approaches make this fundamental assumption: Both abnormal behavior and normal behavior are *learned*. People who act abnormally either have failed to learn the skills they need to cope with the problems

Behavioral treatment approaches Treatment approaches that build on the basic processes of learning, such as reinforcement and extinction, and assume that normal and abnormal behavior are both learned.

How might understanding aversive conditioning help you help a patient who had a horrible experience with a previous doctor?

of everyday living or have acquired faulty skills and patterns that are being maintained through some form of reinforcement. To modify abnormal behavior, then, proponents of behavioral approaches propose that people must learn new behavior to replace the faulty skills they have developed and unlearn their maladaptive behavior patterns (Bergin & Garfield, 1994; Agras & Berkowitz, 1996; Krijn et al., 2004; Norton & Price, 2007). In this view, then, there is no problem other than the maladaptive behavior itself, and if you can change that behavior, treatment is successful.

Classical Conditioning Treatments

Suppose you bite into your favorite candy bar and find that not only is it infested with ants but you've also swallowed a bunch of them. You immediately become sick to your stomach and throw up. Your long-term reaction? You never eat that kind of candy bar again, and it may be months before you eat any type of candy. You have learned, through the basic process of classical conditioning, to avoid candy so that you will not get sick and throw up.

Aversive conditioning A form of therapy that reduces the frequency of undesired behavior by pairing an aversive, unpleasant stimulus with undesired behavior.

Systematic desensitization A behavioral technique in which gradual exposure to an anxiety-producing stimulus is paired with relaxation to extinguish the response of anxiety.

Aversive Conditioning. This simple example illustrates how a person can be classically conditioned to modify behavior. Behavior therapists use this principle when they employ **aversive conditioning,** a form of therapy that reduces the frequency of undesired behavior by pairing an aversive, unpleasant stimulus with undesired behavior.

Although aversion therapy works reasonably well in inhibiting substance-abuse problems such as alcoholism and certain kinds of sexual disorders, critics question its long-term effectiveness. Clearly, though, aversion therapy offers an important procedure for eliminating maladaptive responses for some period of time—a respite that provides, even if only temporarily, an opportunity to encourage more adaptive behavior patterns (Bordnick et al., 2004; Delgado, Labouliere, & Phelps, 2006).

Systematic Desensitization. Another treatment to grow out of classical conditioning is systematic desensitization. In **systematic desensitization,** gradual exposure to an anxiety-producing stimulus is paired with relaxation to extinguish the response of anxiety (McGlynn, Smitherman, & Gothard, 2004; Pagoto, Kozak, & Spates, 2006; Choy, Fyer, & Lipsitz, 2007).

Suppose, for instance, you were extremely afraid of flying. The very thought of being in an airplane would make you begin to sweat and shake, and you couldn't get yourself near enough to an airport to know how you'd react if you actually had to fly somewhere. Using systematic desensitization to treat your problem, you would first be trained in relaxation techniques by a behavior therapist, learning to relax your body fully—a highly pleasant state, as you might imagine (see Figure 2).

The next step would involve constructing a *hierarchy of fears*—a list, in order of increasing severity, of the things you associate with your fears. For instance, your hierarchy might resemble this one:

1. Watching a plane fly overhead
2. Going to an airport

1. Pick a focus word or short phrase that's firmly rooted in your personal belief system. For example, a nonreligious individual might choose a neutral word like *one* or *peace* or *love*; a Christian person desiring to use a prayer could pick the opening words of Psalm 23, *The Lord is my shepherd*; a Jewish person could choose *Shalom*.

2. Sit quietly in a comfortable position.

3. Close your eyes.

4. Relax your muscles.

5. Breathe slowly and naturally, repeating your focus word or phrase silently as you exhale.

6. Throughout, assume a passive attitude. Don't worry about how well you're doing. When other thoughts come to mind, simply say to yourself, "Oh, well," and gently return to the repetition.

7. Continue for 10 to 20 minutes. You may open your eyes to check the time, but do not use an alarm. When you finish, sit quietly for a minute or so, at first with your eyes closed and later with your eyes open. Then do not stand for one or two minutes.

8. Practice the technique once or twice a day.

FIGURE 2 Following these basic steps will help you achieve a sense of calmness by employing the relaxation response.

3. Buying a ticket
4. Stepping into the plane
5. Seeing the plane door close
6. Having the plane taxi down the runway
7. Taking off
8. Being in the air

Once you had developed this hierarchy and had learned relaxation techniques, you would learn to associate the two sets of responses. To do this, your therapist might ask you to put yourself into a relaxed state and then imagine yourself in the first situation identified in your hierarchy. Once you could consider that first step while remaining relaxed, you would move on to the next situation, eventually moving up the hierarchy in gradual stages until you could imagine yourself being in the air without experiencing anxiety. Ultimately, you would be asked to make a visit to an airport and later to take a flight.

STUDY ALERT

To help remember the concept of hierarchy of fears, think of something that you are afraid of and construct your own hierarchy of fears.

psych2.0
WWW.MHHE.COM/PSYCHLIFE

Systematic Desensitization

From the perspective of . . .

A PARALEGAL How might you use systematic desensitization to help overcome your fear of speaking in public? Meeting new people?

Exposure Treatments. Although systematic desensitization has proven to be a successful treatment, today it is often replaced with a less complicated form of therapy called exposure. **Exposure** is a behavioral treatment for anxiety in which people are confronted, either suddenly or gradually, with a stimulus that they fear. However, unlike systematic desensitization, relaxation training is omitted. Exposure allows the maladaptive response of anxiety or avoidance to extinguish, and research shows that this approach is generally as effective as systematic desensitization (Tryon, 2005; Havermans et al., 2007; Hofmann, 2007).

Exposure A behavioral treatment for anxiety in which people are confronted, either suddenly or gradually, with a stimulus that they fear.

Dialectical behavior therapy A form of treatment in which the focus is on getting people to accept who they are, regardless of whether it matches their ideal.

In most cases, therapists use *graded exposure* in which patients are exposed to a feared stimulus in gradual steps. For example, a patient who is afraid of dogs might first view a video of dogs. Gradually the exposure escalates to seeing a live, leashed dog across the room, and then actually petting and touching the dog (Berle, 2007; Means & Edinger, 2007).

Operant Conditioning Techniques

Some behavioral approaches make use of the operant conditioning principles that we discussed earlier in the book when considering learning. These approaches are based on the notion that we should reward people for carrying out desirable behavior and extinguish undesirable behavior by either ignoring it or punishing it.

One example of the systematic application of operant conditioning principles is the *token system,* which rewards a person for desired behavior with a token such as a poker chip or play money that can later be exchanged for something the person wants. In a variant of the token system, called *contingency contracting,* the therapist and client (or teacher and student, or parent and child) draw up a written agreement. The contract states a series of behavioral goals the client hopes to achieve. It also specifies the positive consequences for the client if the client reaches goals—usually an explicit reward such as money or additional privileges.

Modeling helps when therapists are teaching basic social skills such as maintaining eye contact during conversation and acting assertively.

Behavior therapists also use *observational learning,* the process in which the behavior of other people is modeled, to systematically teach people new skills and ways of handling their fears and anxieties. For example, modeling helps when therapists are teaching basic social skills such as maintaining eye contact during conversation and acting assertively. Similarly, children with dog phobias have been able to overcome their fears by watching another child—called the "Fearless Peer"—repeatedly walk up to a dog, touch it, pet it, and finally play with it. Modeling, then, can play an effective role in resolving some kinds of behavior difficulties, especially if the model receives a reward for his or her behavior (Bandura, Grusec, & Menlove, 1967; Greer, Dudek-Singer, & Gautreaux, 2006).

Dialectical Behavior Therapy

In **dialectical behavior therapy,** the focus is on getting people to accept who they are, regardless of whether it matches their ideal. Even if their childhood has been dysfunctional or they have ruined relationships with others, that's in the past. What matters is who they wish to become (Lynch et al., 2007; Wagner, Rizvi, & Hamed, 2007).

Therapists using dialectical behavior therapy seek to have patients realize that they basically have two choices: Either they remain unhappy, or they change. Once patients agree that they wish to change, it is up to them to modify their behavior. Dialectical behavior therapy teaches behavioral skills that help people behave more effectively and keep their emotions in check. Although it is a relatively new form of therapy, increasing evidence supports its effectiveness, particularly with certain personality disorders (van den Bosch et al., 2005; Clarkin et al., 2007; Swales & Heard, 2007).

Evaluating Behavior Therapy

Behavior therapy works especially well for eliminating anxiety disorders, treating phobias and compulsions, establishing control over impulses, and learning complex social skills to replace maladaptive behavior. More than any of the other therapeutic techniques, it provides methods that nonprofessionals can use to change their own behavior. Moreover, it is efficient, because it focuses on solving carefully defined problems (Richard & Lauterbach, 2006; Barlow, 2007).

This student decided to return to school for her degree, despite academic struggles in the past. How is this decision similar to the concepts behind dialectical behavior therapy?

Critics of behavior therapy believe that because it emphasizes changing external behavior, people do not necessarily gain insight into thoughts and expectations that may be fostering their maladaptive behavior. On the other hand, neuroscientific evidence shows that behavioral treatments can produce actual changes in brain functioning, suggesting that behavioral treatments can produce changes beyond external behavior.

» LO3 Cognitive Approaches to Therapy

If you assumed that illogical thoughts and beliefs lie at the heart of psychological disorders, wouldn't the most direct treatment route be to teach people new, more adaptive modes of thinking? The answer is yes, according to psychologists who take a cognitive approach to treatment.

Cognitive treatment approaches teach people to think in more adaptive ways by changing their dysfunctional cognitions about the world and themselves. Unlike behavior therapists, who focus on modifying external behavior, cognitive therapists attempt to change the way people think as well as their behavior. Because they often use basic principles of learning, the methods they employ are sometimes referred to as the **cognitive-behavioral approach** (Beck & Rector, 2005; Butler et al., 2006; Friedberg, 2006).

Although cognitive treatment approaches take many forms, they all share the assumption that anxiety, depression, and negative emotions develop from

> *Unlike behavior therapists, who focus on modifying external behavior, cognitive therapists attempt to change the way people think as well as their behavior.*

Cognitive treatment approaches Treatment approaches that teach people to think in more adaptive ways by changing their dysfunctional cognitions about the world and themselves.

Cognitive-behavioral approach A treatment approach that incorporates basic principles of learning to change the way people think.

maladaptive thinking. Accordingly, cognitive treatments seek to change the thought patterns that lead to getting "stuck" in dysfunctional ways of thinking. Therapists systematically teach clients to challenge their assumptions and adopt new approaches to old problems.

Cognitive therapy is relatively short term, usually lasting a maximum of 20 sessions. Therapy tends to be highly structured and focused on concrete problems. Therapists often begin by teaching the theory behind the approach and then continue to take an active role throughout the course of therapy, acting as a combination of teacher, coach, and partner.

Rational-Emotive Behavior Therapy

One good example of cognitive treatment, **rational-emotive behavior therapy,** attempts to restructure a person's belief system into a more realistic, rational, and logical set of views. According to psychologist Albert Ellis (2002, 2004), many people lead unhappy lives and suffer from psychological disorders because they harbor irrational, unrealistic ideas such as these:

- We need the love or approval of virtually every significant other person for everything we do.
- We should be thoroughly competent, adequate, and successful in all possible respects in order to consider ourselves worthwhile.
- It is horrible when things don't turn out the way we want them to.

Such irrational beliefs trigger negative emotions, which in turn support the irrational beliefs, leading to a self-defeating cycle.

Rational-emotive behavior therapy aims to help clients eliminate maladaptive thoughts and beliefs and adopt more effective thinking. To accomplish this goal, therapists take an active, directive role during therapy, openly challenging patterns of thought that appear to be dysfunctional. Consider this example:

Martha: The basic problem is that I'm worried about my family. I'm worried about money. And I never seem to be able to relax.

Therapist: Why are you worried about your family? . . . What's to be concerned about? They have certain demands which you don't want to adhere to.

Martha: I was brought up to think that I mustn't be selfish.

Therapist: Oh, we'll have to knock that out of your head! . . .

Martha: I think it's a feeling I was brought up with that you always have to give of yourself. If you think of yourself, you're wrong.

Therapist: That's a belief. Why do you have to keep believing that—at your age? You believed a lot of superstitions when you were younger. Why do you have to retain them? Your parents indoctrinated you with this nonsense, because that's their belief. . . . Who needs that philosophy? All it's gotten you, so far, is guilt. (Ellis, 1974, pp. 223–286)

By poking holes in Martha's reasoning, the therapist is attempting to help her adopt a more realistic view of herself and her circumstances (Dryden, 1999; Ellis, 2002).

Cognitive Therapy

Another influential form of therapy that builds on a cognitive perspective is that of Aaron Beck (Beck, 1995, 2004). Like rational-emotive behavior therapy, Beck's *cognitive therapy* aims to change people's illogical thoughts about themselves and the world.

Rational-emotive behavior therapy A form of therapy that attempts to restructure a person's belief system into a more realistic, rational, and logical set of views by challenging dysfunctional beliefs that maintain irrational behavior.

However, cognitive therapy is considerably less confrontational and challenging than rational-emotive behavior therapy. Instead of the therapist's actively arguing with clients about their dysfunctional cognitions, cognitive therapists more often play the role of teacher. Therapists urge clients to obtain information on their own that will lead them to discard their inaccurate thinking through a process of cognitive appraisal. In *cognitive appraisal,* clients are asked to evaluate situations, themselves, and others in terms of their memories, values, beliefs, thoughts, and expectations. During the course of treatment, therapists help clients discover ways of thinking more appropriately about themselves and others (Rosen, 2000; Beck, Freeman, & Davis, 2004; Moorey, 2007).

Evaluating Cognitive Approaches to Therapy

Cognitive approaches to therapy have proved successful in dealing with a broad range of disorders, including anxiety disorders, depression, substance abuse, and eating disorders. Furthermore, the willingness of cognitive therapists to incorporate additional treatment approaches (e.g., combining cognitive and behavioral techniques in cognitive-behavioral therapy) has made this approach a particularly effective form of treatment (McMullin, 2000; Mitte, 2005; Ishikawa et al., 2007).

At the same time, critics have pointed out that the focus on helping people to think more rationally ignores the fact that life is, in reality, sometimes irrational. Changing one's assumptions to make them more reasonable and logical thus may not always be helpful—even assuming it is possible to bring about true cognitive change. Still, the success of cognitive approaches has made it one of the most frequently employed therapies (Beck, 2007).

psych2.0
WWW.MHHE.COM/PSYCHLIFE

Approaches to Therapy

RECAP

Explain psychodynamic approaches to therapy.

- Psychotherapy (psychologically based therapy) and biomedical therapy (biologically based therapy) share the goal of resolving psychological problems by modifying people's thoughts, feelings, expectations, evaluations, and ultimately behavior. (p. 430)

- Psychoanalytic approaches seek to bring unresolved past conflicts and unacceptable impulses from the unconscious into the conscious, where patients may deal with the problems more effectively. To do this, therapists use techniques such as free association and dream interpretation. (p. 432)

Explain behavioral approaches to therapy.

- Behavioral approaches to treatment view abnormal behavior as the problem, rather than

viewing that behavior as a symptom of some underlying cause. To bring about a "cure," this view suggests that the outward behavior must be changed by using methods such as aversive conditioning, systematic desensitization, observational learning, token systems, contingency contracting, and dialectical behavior therapy. (p. 433)

Explain cognitive approaches to therapy.

- Cognitive approaches to treatment consider the goal of therapy to be to help a person restructure his or her faulty belief system into a more realistic, rational, and logical view of the world. Two examples of cognitive treatments are the rational-emotive behavior therapy and cognitive therapy. (p. 437)

EVALUATE

1. Match the following mental health practitioners with the appropriate description.

   1. Psychiatrist
   2. Clinical psychologist
   3. Counseling psychologist
   4. Psychoanalyst

   a. Ph.D. specializing in the treatment of psychological disorders
   b. Professional specializing in Freudian therapy techniques
   c. M.D. trained in abnormal behavior
   d. Ph.D. specializing in the adjustment of day-to-day problems

2. According to Freud, people use _____ _____ as a means of preventing unwanted impulses from intruding on conscious thought.

3. In dream interpretation, a psychoanalyst must learn to distinguish between the _____ content of a dream, which is what appears on the surface, and the _____ content, its underlying meaning.

4. Which of the following treatments deals with phobias by gradual exposure to the item producing the fear?

   a. Systematic desensitization
   b. Partial reinforcement
   c. Behavioral self-management
   d. Aversion therapy

RETHINK

In what ways are psychoanalysis and cognitive therapy similar, and how do they differ? How would you choose between the two to get treatment for a psychological problem you may be experiencing?

Answers to Evaluate Questions 1. 1-c, 2-a, 3-d, 4-b; 2. defense mechanisms; 3. manifest, latent; 4. a

[KEY TERMS]

Psychotherapy *p. 430*

Biomedical therapy *p. 430*

Psychodynamic therapy *p. 430*

Psychoanalysis *p. 432*

Transference *p. 432*

Behavioral treatment approaches *p. 433*

Aversive conditioning *p. 434*

Systematic desensitization *p. 434*

Exposure *p. 436*

Dialectical behavior therapy *p. 436*

Cognitive treatment approaches *p. 437*

Cognitive-behavioral approach *p. 437*

Rational-emotive behavior therapy *p. 438*

Psychotherapy
Humanistic and Group Approaches to Treatment

» LO 1 Humanistic Therapy

As you know from your own experience, a student cannot master the material covered in a course without some hard work, no matter how good the teacher and the textbook are. *You* must take the time to study, memorize the vocabulary, and learn the concepts. Nobody else can do it for you. If you choose to put in the effort, you'll succeed; if you don't, you'll fail. The responsibility is primarily yours.

Humanistic therapy draws on this philosophical perspective of self-responsibility in developing treatment techniques. The many different types of therapy that fit into this category have a similar rationale: We have control of our own behavior, we can make choices about the kinds of lives we want to live, and it is up to us to solve the difficulties we encounter in our daily lives.

Instead of acting in the more directive manner of some psychodynamic and behavioral approaches, humanistic therapists view themselves as guides or facilitators. Therapists using humanistic techniques seek to help people understand themselves and find ways to come closer to the ideal they hold for themselves. In this view, psychological disorders result from the inability to find meaning in life and from feelings of loneliness and a lack of connection to others (Cain, 2002).

Therapists using humanistic techniques seek to help people understand themselves and find ways to come closer to the ideal they hold for themselves.

Humanistic approaches have produced many therapeutic techniques. Among the most important is person-centered therapy.

Person-Centered Therapy

Person-centered therapy (also called *client-centered therapy*) aims to enable people to reach their potential for self-actualization. By providing a warm and accepting environment, therapists hope to motivate clients to air their problems and feelings. In turn, this enables clients to make realistic and constructive choices and decisions about the things that bother them in their current lives (Bozarth, Zimring, & Tausch, 2002; Kirschenbaum, 2004; Bohart, 2006).

Humanistic therapy Therapy in which the underlying rationale is that people have control of their behavior, can make choices about their lives, and are essentially responsible for solving their own problems.

Person-centered therapy Therapy in which the goal is to reach one's potential for self-actualization.

STUDY ALERT

To better remember the concept of unconditional positive regard, try offering it to a friend during a conversation by showing your support, acceptance, and understanding no matter what thought or attitude is being offered.

Instead of directing the choices clients make, therapists provide what Carl Rogers calls *unconditional positive regard*—expressing acceptance and understanding, regardless of the feelings and attitudes the client expresses. By doing this, therapists hope to create an atmosphere that enables clients to come to decisions that can improve their lives (Kirschenbaum & Jourdan, 2005; Vieira & Freire, 2006).

Furnishing unconditional positive regard does not mean that therapists must approve of everything their clients say or do. Rather, therapists need to communicate that they are caring, nonjudgmental, and *empathetic*—understanding of a client's emotional experiences (Fearing & Clark, 2000).

Evaluating Humanistic Approaches to Therapy

The notion that psychological disorders result from restricted growth potential appeals philosophically to many people. Furthermore, when humanistic therapists acknowledge that the freedom we possess can lead to psychological difficulties, clients find an unusually supportive environment for therapy. In turn, this atmosphere can help clients discover solutions to difficult psychological problems.

However, humanistic treatments lack specificity, a problem that has troubled their critics. Humanistic approaches are not very precise and are probably the least scientifically and theoretically developed type of treatment. Moreover, this form of treatment works best for the same type of highly verbal client who profits most from psychoanalytic treatment.

Interpersonal therapy (IPT) Short-term therapy that focuses on the context of current social relationships.

Group therapy Therapy in which people meet with a therapist to discuss problems with a group.

» LO2 Interpersonal Therapy

Interpersonal therapy (IPT) considers therapy in the context of social relationships. Although its roots stem from psychodynamic approaches, IPT concentrates more on the here and now with the goal of improving a client's current relationships. It typically focuses on interpersonal issues such as conflicts with others, social skills issues, role transitions (such as divorce), or grief (Weissman, Markowitz, & Klerman, 2007).

Interpersonal therapy is more active and directive than traditional psychodynamic approaches, and sessions are more structured. The approach makes no assumptions about the underlying causes of psychological disorders, but focuses on the interpersonal context in which a disorder is developed and maintained. It also tends to be shorter than traditional psychodynamic approaches, typically lasting only 12 to 16 weeks. During those sessions, therapists make concrete suggestions on improving relations with others, offering recommendations and advice.

Because IPT is short and structured, researchers have been able to demonstrate its effectiveness more readily than longer-term types of therapy. Evaluations of the approach have shown that IPT is especially effective in dealing with depression, anxiety, addictions, and eating disorders (De Mello et al., 2005; Salsman, 2006; Grigoriadis & Ravitz, 2007).

» LO3 Group Therapy, Family Therapy, and Self-Help Groups

Although most treatment takes place between a single individual and a therapist, some forms of therapy involve groups of people seeking treatment. In **group therapy**, several unrelated people meet with a therapist to discuss some aspect of their psychological functioning.

People typically discuss with the group their problems, which often center on a common difficulty, such as alcoholism or a lack of social skills. The other members of the group provide emotional support and dispense advice on ways in which they have coped effectively with similar problems (Alonso, Alonso, & Piper, 2003; Scaturo, 2004; Rigby & Waite, 2007).

Groups vary greatly in terms of the particular model they employ; there are psychoanalytic groups, humanistic groups, and groups corresponding to the other therapeutic approaches. Furthermore, groups also differ in regard to the degree of guidance the therapist provides. In some, the therapist is quite directive, whereas in others, the members of the group set their own agenda and determine how the group will proceed (Beck & Lewis, 2000; Stockton, Morran, & Krieger, 2004).

Because in group therapy several people are treated simultaneously, it is a much more economical means of treatment than individual psychotherapy. On the other hand, critics argue that group settings lack the individual attention inherent in one-to-one therapy, and that especially shy and withdrawn individuals may not receive the attention they need in a group setting.

"So, would anyone in the group care to respond to what Clifford has just shared with us?"

Family Therapy

One specialized form of group therapy is family therapy. As the name implies, **family therapy** involves two or more family members, one (or more) of whose problems led to treatment. But rather than focusing simply on the members of the family who present the initial problem, family therapists consider the family as a unit, to which each member contributes. By meeting with the entire family simultaneously, family therapists try to understand how the family members interact with one another (Cooklin, 2000; Strong & Tomm, 2007).

Family therapy An approach that focuses on the family and its dynamics.

Family therapists view the family as a "system," and they assume that individuals in the family cannot improve without understanding the conflicts found in interactions among family members. Thus, the therapist expects each member to contribute to the resolution of the problem being addressed.

Family therapy is often viewed as a good way for families to reopen lines of communication. Is this something you think would work in every family? Why or why not?

Self-Help Therapy

In many cases, group therapy does not involve a professional therapist. Instead, people with similar problems get together to discuss their shared feelings and experiences. For example, people who have recently experienced the death of a spouse might meet in a *bereavement support group,* or college students may get together to discuss their adjustment to college.

One of the best-known self-help groups is Alcoholics Anonymous (AA), designed to help members deal with alcohol-related problems. AA prescribes 12 steps that alcoholics must pass through on their road to recovery, beginning with an admission that they are alcoholics and powerless over alcohol. AA provides more treatment for alcoholics than any other therapy, and it and other 12-step programs (such as Narcotics Anonymous) can be as successful in treating alcohol and other substance-abuse problems (Bogenschutz, Geppert, & George, 2006; Galanter, 2007).

» LO4 Evaluating Psychotherapy: Does Therapy Work?

Spontaneous remission Recovery without treatment.

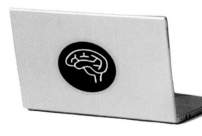

psych2.0
WWW.MHHE.COM/PSYCHLIFE

Effectiveness of Therapy

The question of whether therapy is effective is complex. In fact, identifying the single most appropriate form of treatment is a difficult, and still unresolved, task for psychologists specializing in psychological disorders. In fact, even before considering whether one form of therapy works better than another, we need to determine whether therapy in any form effectively alleviates psychological disturbances.

Most psychologists agree: Therapy does work. Several comprehensive reviews indicate that therapy brings about greater improvement than does no treatment at all, with the rate of **spontaneous remission** (recovery without treatment) being fairly low. In most cases, then, the symptoms of abnormal behavior do not go away by themselves if left untreated—although the issue continues to be hotly debated (Seligman, 1996; Westen, Novotny, & Thompson-Brenner, 2004; Lutz et al., 2006).

Although most psychologists feel confident that psychotherapeutic treatment *in general* is more effective than no treatment at all, the question of whether any specific form of treatment is superior to any other has not been answered definitively (Nathan, Stuart, & Dolan, 2000; Westen et al., 2004; Abboud, 2005).

For instance, one classic study comparing the effectiveness of various approaches found that although success rates vary somewhat by treatment form, most treatments show fairly equal success rates. As Figure 1 indicates, the rates ranged from about 70 to 85 percent greater success for treated compared with untreated individuals. Behavioral and cognitive approaches tended to be slightly more successful, but that result may have been due to differences in the severity of the cases treated (Smith, Glass, & Miller, 1980; Orwin & Condray, 1984).

Other research, relying on *meta-analysis*, in which data from a large number of studies are statistically combined, yields similar general conclusions. Furthermore, a large survey of 186,000 individuals found that respondents felt they had benefited substantially from psychotherapy (see Figure 2). However, there was little difference in "consumer satisfaction" on the basis of the specific type of treatment they had received (Seligman, 1995; Strupp, 1996; Nielsen et al., 2004; Malouff, Thorsteinsson, & Schutte, 2007).

In short, converging evidence allows us to draw several conclusions about the effectiveness of psychotherapy (Strupp & Binder, 1992; Seligman, 1996; Goldfried & Pachankis, 2007):

- *For most people, psychotherapy is effective.* This conclusion holds over different lengths of treatment, specific kinds of psychological disorders, and various types of treatment. Thus, the question "Does psychotherapy work?" appears to have been answered convincingly: It does (Seligman, 1996; Spiegel, 1999; Westen et al., 2004).

- *On the other hand, psychotherapy doesn't work for everyone.* As many as 10 percent of people treated show no improvement or actually deteriorate (Boisvert & Faust, 2003; Pretzer & Beck, 2005; Coffman et al., 2007; Lilienfeld, 2007).

- *No single form of therapy works best for every problem, and certain specific types of treatment are better, although not invariably, for specific types of problems.* For example, cognitive therapy works especially well for panic disorders, and exposure therapy relieves specific phobias effectively. However, there are exceptions to these generalizations, and often the differences in success rates for different types of treatment are not substantial (Miller & Magruder, 1999; Westen et al., 2004).

- *Most therapies share several basic similar elements.* Despite the fact that the specific methods used in different therapies are very different from one another, there are several common themes that lead them to be effective. These elements include the opportunity for a client to develop a positive relationship with a therapist, an explanation or interpretation of a client's symptoms, and confrontation of negative emotions. The fact that these common elements exist in most therapies makes it difficult to compare one treatment against another (Norcross, 2002; Norcross, Beutler, & Levant, 2006).

Consequently, there is no single, definitive answer to the broad question "Which therapy works best?" because of the complexity in sorting out the various factors that enter into successful therapy. Recently, however, clinicians and

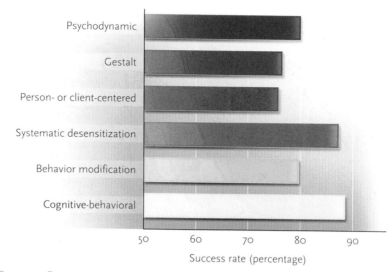

FIGURE 1 Estimates of the effectiveness of different types of treatment, in comparison to control groups of untreated people (adapted from Smith, Glass, & Miller, 1980). The percentile score shows how much more effective a particular type of treatment is for the average patient than is no treatment. For example, people given psychodynamic treatment score, on average, more positively on outcome measures than about three-quarters of untreated people.

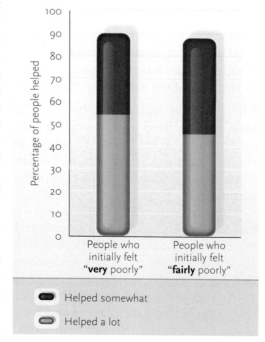

FIGURE 2 A survey of 186,000 individuals found that while the respondents had benefited substantially from psychotherapy, there was little difference in "consumer satisfaction" based on the specific type of treatment they had received. *(Source: "Mental Health: Does Therapy Help?" Consumer Reports, 1995.)*

researchers have reframed the question by focusing on evidence-based psychotherapy practice. *Evidence-based psychotherapy practice* seeks to use the research literature to determine the best practices for treating a specific disorder. To determine best practices, researchers use clinical interviews, client self-reports of improvement in quality of life, reductions in symptoms, observations of behavior, and other outcomes to compare different therapies. By using objective research findings, clinicians are increasingly able to determine the most effective treatment for a specific disorder (APA Presidential Task Force, 2006; Fisher & O'Donohue, 2006; Goodheart, Kazdin, & Sternberg, 2006; Brownlee, 2007).

Because no single type of psychotherapy is invariably effective for every individual, some therapists use an eclectic approach to therapy. In an *eclectic approach to therapy,* therapists use a variety of techniques, integrating several perspectives, to treat a person's problems. By employing more than one approach, therapists can choose the appropriate mix of evidence-based treatments to match the specific needs of the individual. Furthermore, therapists with certain personal characteristics may work better with particular individuals and types of treatments, and—as we consider next—even racial and ethnic factors may be related to the success of treatment (Cheston, 2000; Chambless et al., 2006; Hays, 2008).

E X P L O R I N G diversity

Racial and Ethnic Factors in Treatment: Should Therapists Be Color-Blind?

Consider the following case report, written by a school counselor about Jimmy Jones, a 12-year-old student who was referred to a counselor because of his lack of interest in schoolwork:

> Jimmy does not pay attention, daydreams often, and frequently falls asleep during class. There is a strong possibility that Jimmy is harboring repressed rage that needs to be ventilated and dealt with. His inability to directly express his anger had led him to adopt passive aggressive means of expressing hostility, i.e., inattentiveness, daydreaming, falling asleep. It is recommended that Jimmy be seen for intensive counseling to discover the basis of the anger. (Sue, Sue, & Sue, 1990, p. 44)

The counselor was wrong, however. Rather than suffering from "repressed rage," Jimmy lived in a poverty-stricken and disorganized home. Because of overcrowding at his house, he did not get enough sleep and consequently was tired the next day. Frequently, he was also hungry. In short, the stresses arising from his environment caused his problems, not any deep-seated psychological disturbances.

This incident underscores the importance of taking people's environmental and cultural backgrounds into account during treatment for psychological disorders. In particular, members of racial and ethnic minority groups, especially those who are also poor, may behave in ways that help them deal with a society that discriminates against them. As a consequence, behavior that may signal psychological disorder in middle- and upper-class whites may simply be adaptive in people from other racial and socioeconomic groups. For instance, characteristically suspicious and distrustful people may be displaying a survival strategy to protect themselves from psychological and physical injury, rather than suffering from a psychological disturbance (Paniagua, 2000; Tseng, 2003; Pottick et al., 2007).

In fact, therapists must question some basic assumptions of psychotherapy when dealing with racial, ethnic, and cultural minority-group members. For example, compared with the dominant culture, Asian and Latino cultures typically place much greater emphasis on the group, family, and society. When an Asian or Latino faces a critical decision, the family helps make it—a cultural practice suggesting that family members should also play a role in psychological treatment. Similarly, the traditional Chinese recommendation for dealing with depression or anxiety is to urge people who experience such problems to avoid thinking about whatever is upsetting them. Consider how this advice contrasts with treatment approaches that emphasize the value of insight (Ponterotto, Gretchen, & Chauhan, 2001; McCarthy, 2005; Leitner, 2007).

Clearly, therapists *cannot* be "color-blind." Instead, they must take into account the racial, ethnic, cultural, and social class backgrounds of their clients in determining the nature of a psychological disorder and the course of treatment (Aponte & Wohl, 2000; Pedersen et al., 2002; Hays, 2008).

R E C A P

Discuss the humanistic approaches to therapy.

- Humanistic therapy is based on the premise that people have control of their behavior, that they can make choices about their lives, and that it is up to them to solve their own problems. Humanistic therapies, which take a non-directive approach, include person-centered therapy. (p. 441)

Illustrate interpersonal therapy.

- Interpersonal therapy considers therapy in the context of social relationships. (p. 442)
- It concentrates on improving a client's current relationships. (p. 442)

Explain group therapy, family therapy and self-help groups.

- In group therapy, several unrelated people meet with a therapist to discuss some aspect of

their psychological functioning, often centering on a common problem. (p. 442)

Assess the effectiveness of psychotherapy.

- Most research suggests that, in general, therapy is more effective than no therapy, although how much more effective is not known. (p. 444)
- The more difficult question of which therapy works best is harder to answer, but it is clear particular kinds of therapy are more appropriate for some problems than for others. (p. 445)
- Because no single type of psychotherapy is invariably effective, eclectic approaches, in which a therapist uses a variety of techniques, integrating several perspectives, are sometimes used. (p. 446)

EVALUATE

1. Match each of the following treatment strategies with the statement you might expect to hear from a therapist using that strategy.

   1. Group therapy
   2. Unconditional positive regard
   3. Behavioral therapy
   4. Nondirective counseling

   a. "In other words, you don't get along with your mother because she hates your girlfriend, is that right?"

   b. "I want you all to take turns talking about why you decided to come and what you hope to gain from therapy."

   c. "I can understand why you wanted to wreck your friend's car after she hurt your feelings. Now tell me more about the accident."

   d. "That's not appropriate behavior. Let's work on replacing it with something else."

2. _____ therapies assume that people should take responsibility for their lives and the decisions they make.

3. One of the major criticisms of humanistic therapies is that
   a. They are too imprecise and unstructured.
   b. They treat only the symptom of the problem.
   c. The therapist dominates the patient-therapist interaction.
   d. They work well only on clients of lower socioeconomic status.

4. In a controversial study, Eysenck found that some people go into _____ _____, or recovery without treatment, if they are simply left alone instead of treated.

RETHINK

How can people be successfully treated in group therapy when individuals with the "same" problem are so different? What advantages might group therapy offer over individual therapy?

Answers to Evaluate Questions 1. 1-b, 2-c, 3-d, 4-a; 2. humanistic; 3. a; 4. spontaneous remission

[KEY TERMS]

Humanistic therapy *p. 441*

Person-centered therapy *p. 441*

Interpersonal therapy (IPT) *p. 442*

Group therapy *p. 442*

Family therapy *p. 443*

Spontaneous remission *p. 444*

module 38

Biomedical Therapy
Biological Approaches to Treatment

If you get a kidney infection, your doctor gives you an antibiotic, and with luck, about a week later your kidney should be as good as new. If your appendix becomes inflamed, a surgeon removes it and your body functions normally once more. Could a comparable approach, focusing on the body's physiology, be effective for psychological disturbances?

According to biological approaches to treatment, the answer is yes. Therapists routinely use biomedical therapies. This approach suggests that rather than focusing on a patient's psychological conflicts or past traumas, or on environmental factors that may produce abnormal behavior, focusing treatment directly on brain chemistry and other neurological factors may be more appropriate. To do this, therapists can use drugs, electric shock, or surgery to provide treatment.

LEARNING OUTCOMES

38.1 Discuss options for drug therapy.

38.2 Explain electroconvulsive therapy.

38.3 Offer perspective on biomedical therapies.

38.4 Discuss the community psychology movement.

psych2.0
WWW.MHHE.COM/PSYCHLIFE

Drug Therapy

» LO1 Drug Therapy

Drug therapy, the control of psychological disorders through drugs, works by altering the operation of neurotransmitters and neurons in the brain. Some drugs operate by inhibiting neurotransmitters or receptor neurons, reducing activity at particular synapses, the sites where nerve impulses travel from one neuron to another. Other drugs do just the opposite: They increase the activity of certain neurotransmitters or neurons, allowing particular neurons to fire more frequently (see Figure 1 on page 450).

Antipsychotic Drugs

Probably no greater change has occurred in mental hospitals than the successful introduction in the mid-1950s of **antipsychotic drugs**—drugs used to reduce severe symptoms of disturbance, such as loss of touch with reality and agitation. Previously, the typical mental hospital wasn't very different from the stereotypical nineteenth-century insane asylum, giving mainly custodial care to screaming, moaning, clawing patients who displayed bizarre behaviors.

Drug therapy Control of psychological disorders through the use of drugs.

Antipsychotic drugs Drugs that temporarily reduce psychotic symptoms such as agitation, hallucinations, and delusions.

Drug Treatments			
Class of Drug	**Effects of Drug**	**Primary Action of Drug**	**Examples**
Antipsychotic drugs	Reduction in loss of touch with reality, agitation	Block dopamine receptors	Chlorpromazine (Thorazine®), clozapine (Clozaril®), haloperidol (Haldol®)
Antidepressant drugs			
Tricyclic	Reduction in depression	Permit rise in neuro-transmitters such as norepinepherine	Trazodone (Desyrel), amitriptyline (Elavil), desipramine (Norpramin®)
MAO inhibitors	Reduction in depression	Prevent MAO from breaking down neurotransmitters	Phenelzine (Nardil®), tranylcypromine (Parnate®)
Selective serotonin reuptake inhibitors (SSRIs)	Reduction in depression	Inhibit reuptake of serotonin	Fluoxetine (Prozac®), Luvox, Paxil®, Celexa®, Zoloft®, nefazodone (Serzone)
Mood stabilizers			
Lithium	Mood stabilization	Can alter transmission of impulses within neurons	Lithium (Lithonate), Depakote®, Tegretol®
Antianxiety drugs	Reduction in anxiety	Increase activity of neurotransmitter GABA	Benzodiazepines (Valium®, Xanax®)

FIGURE 1   The major classes of drugs used to treat psychological disorders have different effects on the brain and nervous system.

As a surgical technician or surgical LPN, the need to have patients off their medications prior to surgery can become an issue when withdrawal can trigger psychological symptoms.

Suddenly, in just a matter of days after hospital staff members administered antipsychotic drugs, the wards became considerably calmer environments in which professionals could do more than just try to get patients through the day without causing serious harm to themselves or others.

This dramatic change came about through the introduction of the drug *chlorpromazine*. Along with other similar drugs, chlorpromazine rapidly became the most popular and successful treatment for schizophrenia. Today drug therapy is the preferred treatment for most cases of severely abnormal behavior and, as such, is used for most patients hospitalized with psychological disorders. The newest generation of antipsychotics, referred to as *atypical antipsychotics,* have fewer side effects (Lublin, Eberhard, & Levander, 2005; Savas, Yumru, & Kaya, 2007).

How do antipsychotic drugs work? Most block dopamine receptors at the brain's synapses. Atypical antipsychotics affect both serotonin and dopamine levels in certain parts of the brain, such as those related to planning and goal-directed activity (Sawa & Snyder, 2002; Advokat, 2005).

Despite the effectiveness of antipsychotic drugs, most of the time, when the drug is withdrawn, the symptoms reappear. Furthermore, such drugs can have long-term side effects, such as dryness of the mouth and throat, that may continue after drug treatments are stopped (Voruganti et al., 2007).

Antidepressant Drugs

As their name suggests, **antidepressant drugs** are a class of medications used in cases of severe depression to improve the moods of patients. They are also sometimes used for other disorders, such as anxiety disorders and bulimia (Walsh et al., 2006; Hedges et al., 2007).

Most antidepressant drugs work by changing the concentration of specific neurotransmitters in the brain. For example, *tricyclic drugs* increase the availability of norepinephrine at the synapses of neurons, whereas *MAO inhibitors* prevent the enzyme monoamine oxidase (MAO) from breaking down neurotransmitters. Newer antidepressants—such as Lexapro—are *selective serotonin reuptake inhibitors (SSRIs)*. SSRIs target the neurotransmitter serotonin, permitting it to linger at the synapse. Some antidepressants produce a combination of effects. For instance, nefazodone (Serzone) blocks serotonin at some receptor sites but not others, while bupropion (Wellbutrin and Zyban) affect the norepinephrine and dopamine systems (see Figure 2; Lucki & O'Leary, 2004; Robinson, 2007).

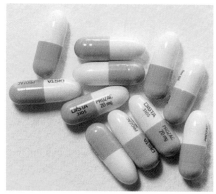

Prozac® is a widely prescribed—but still controversial—antidepressant.

The overall success of antidepressant drugs is good. Unlike antipsychotic drugs, antidepressants can produce lasting, long-term recovery from depression. In many cases, even after patients stop taking the drugs, their depression does not return. On the other hand, antidepressant drugs may produce side effects such as drowsiness and faintness, and there is evidence that SSRI antidepressants can increase the risk of suicide in children and adolescents (Gibbons et al., 2007; Leckman & King, 2007).

Antidepressant drugs Medications that improve a severely depressed patient's mood and feeling of well-being.

Another drug that has received a great deal of publicity is *St. John's wort*, an herb that some have called a "natural" antidepressant. Although it is widely used in Europe for the treatment of depression, the U.S. Food and Drug Administration considers it a dietary supplement, and therefore the substance is available here without a prescription.

Despite the popularity of St. John's wort, some clinical tests have found that the herb is ineffective in the treatment of depression. However, because other research shows that the herb successfully reduces certain symptoms of depression, some proponents argue that using it is reasonable. Clearly, people should not use St. John's wort to medicate themselves without consulting a mental health care professional (Williams et al., 2000; Shelton et al., 2002; Thachil, Mohan, & Bhugra, 2007).

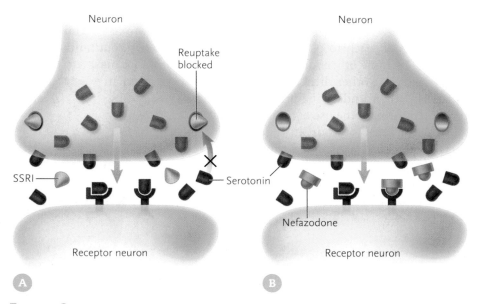

FIGURE 2 In (A), selective serotonin reuptake inhibitors (SSRIs) reduce depression by permitting the neurotransmitter serotonin to remain in the synapse. In (B), a newer antidepressant, Nefazodone (Serzone), operates more selectively to block serotonin at some sites but not others, helping to reduce the side effects of the drug. *(Source: Based on Mischoulon, 2000.)*

Mood Stabilizers

Mood stabilizers are used to treat mood disorders. For example, the drug *lithium,* a form of mineral salts, has been used very successfully in patients with bipolar disorders. Although no one knows definitely why, lithium and other mood stabilizers such as divalproex sodium (Depakote®) and carbamazepine (Tegretol®) effectively reduce manic episodes. However, they do not effectively treat depressive phases of bipolar disorder, so antidepressants are usually prescribed during those phases (Dubovsky, 1999; Fountoulakis et al., 2005; Abraham & Calabrese, 2007).

Lithium and similar drugs have a quality that sets them apart from other drug treatments: They can be a *preventive* treatment, blocking future episodes of manic depression. Often, people who have had episodes of bipolar disorder can take a daily dose of lithium to prevent a recurrence of their symptoms. Most other drugs are useful only when symptoms of psychological disturbance occur.

Antianxiety Drugs

Mood stabilizers Drugs used to treat mood disorders that prevent manic episodes of bipolar disorder.

Antianxiety drugs Drugs that reduce the level of anxiety a person experiences, essentially by reducing excitability and increasing feelings of well-being.

As the name implies, **antianxiety drugs** reduce the level of anxiety a person experiences and increase feelings of well-being. They are prescribed not only to reduce general tension in people who are experiencing temporary difficulties but also to aid in the treatment of more serious anxiety disorders (Zito, 1993).

Antianxiety drugs such as Xanax® are among the medications most frequently prescribed by physicians. In fact, more than half of all U.S. families have someone who has taken such a drug at one time or another.

> *Antianxiety drugs such as Xanax are among the medications most frequently prescribed by physicians.*

Although the popularity of antianxiety drugs suggests that they hold few risks, they can produce a number of potentially serious side effects. For instance, they can cause fatigue, and long-term use can lead to dependence. Moreover, when taken in combination with alcohol, some antianxiety drugs can be lethal. But a more important issue concerns their use to suppress anxiety. Almost every therapeutic approach to psychological disturbance views continuing anxiety as a signal of some other sort of problem. Thus, drugs that mask anxiety may simply be hiding other difficulties. Consequently, rather than confronting their underlying problems, people may be hiding from them through the use of antianxiety drugs.

(To get a sense of your attitudes toward the use of drugs in the treatment of psychological disorders and

From the perspective of . . .

A LEGAL ASSISTANT   Imagine that you're working in a high-stress office and you're having difficulty managing your anxiety. A colleague suggests that you see the staff nurse to get a prescription for an antianxiety drug. Would this action be advisable? Why or why not?

how much control you think patients should have over their treatment, complete the accompanying Try It! questionnaire to explore your feelings about patients' rights.)

What Are Your Attitudes Toward Patient Rights?

Check off whether you Agree or Disagree with each of the following statements:

1. Patients should have the right to refuse psychotropic medications. Agree _____ Disagree _____

2. Staff at mental hospitals should give patients medications, even if the patient doesn't want to take the medication. Agree _____ Disagree _____

3. There are circumstances under which psychologists and other mental health specialists have the right to confine a patient to a mental institution against the patient's will. Agree _____ Disagree _____

4. Patients should be active partners in planning the goals for treatment and choosing particular kinds of treatments. Agree _____ Disagree _____

5. Patients should have the right to stop or refuse psychotherapy. Agree _____ Disagree _____

6. Therapists should have the right to force patients to participate in certain kinds of activities. Agree _____ Disagree _____

7. Therapists should have the right to force hospitalization against an individual's wishes if they pose a threat to themselves or to others. Agree _____ Disagree _____

8. A therapist should be allowed to give information about a patient's mental state to a spouse or other loved one, even if the patient does not wish for that information to be divulged, if the therapist feels it is in the patient's best interests. Agree _____ Disagree _____

9. Patients should be told about the drugs or other treatments that they are being given, even if they do not fully understand what they are being told. Agree _____ Disagree _____

10. There are circumstances under which patients in mental institutions should be prevented from having visitors. Agree _____ Disagree _____

11. Patients should have the right to demand the specific treatment that they want and be allowed to refuse specific treatments. Agree _____ Disagree _____

Scoring

For questions 1, 4, 5, 9, and 11, if you agreed with four or five of these, you tend to believe that patients have the right to participate in decisions regarding their own treatment, and the right to choose the treatments that they believe are best. If you agreed with four or more of questions 2, 3, 6, 7, 8, and 10, you tend to consider health-care providers' opinions to hold more weight than a patient's wishes, and therefore the providers' views should be followed even over a patient's objections.

Keep in mind that you may have a mix of answers, or you may have found some of the questions difficult to answer with a clear yes or no. Doctors, caregivers, and patients struggle with these same questions in the quest to balance the rights of patients with the need to ensure safety.

Source: Adapted from Roe et al., 2002.

» LO2 Electroconvulsive Therapy (ECT)

Electroconvulsive therapy (ECT) A procedure used in the treatment of severe depression in which an electric current of 70 to 150 volts is briefly administered to a patient's head.

Transcranial magnetic stimulation (TMS) A depression treatment in which a precise magnetic pulse is directed to a specific area of the brain.

First introduced in the 1930s, **electroconvulsive therapy (ECT)** is a procedure used in the treatment of severe depression. In the procedure, an electric current of 70 to 150 volts is briefly administered to a patient's head, causing a loss of consciousness and often causing seizures. Typically, health professionals sedate patients and give them muscle relaxants before administering the current, and such preparations help reduce the intensity of muscle contractions produced during ECT. The typical patient receives about 10 such treatments in the course of a month, but some patients continue with maintenance treatments for months afterward (Greenberg & Kellner, 2005; Stevens & Harper, 2007).

ECT is a controversial technique. Apart from the obvious distastefulness of a treatment that evokes images of electrocution, side effects occur frequently. For instance, after treatment patients often experience disorientation, confusion, and sometimes memory loss that may remain for months. Furthermore, ECT often does not produce long-term improvement; one study found that without follow-up medication, depression returned in most patients who had undergone ECT treatments. Finally, even when ECT does work, we do not know why, and some critics believe it may cause permanent brain damage (Valente, 1991; Sackeim et al., 2001; Frank, 2002).

In light of the drawbacks to ECT, why do therapists use it at all? Basically, they use it because, in many severe cases of depression, it offers the only quickly effective treatment. For instance, it may prevent depressed, suicidal individuals from committing suicide, and it can act more quickly than antidepressive medications.

ECT tends to be used only when other treatments have proved ineffective, and researchers continue to search for alternative treatments. One new and promising alternative to ECT is **transcranial magnetic stimulation (TMS).** TMS creates a precise magnetic pulse in a specific area of the brain. By activating particular neurons, TMS has been found to be effective in relieving the symptoms of depression in a number of controlled experiments. However, the therapy can produce side effects, such as seizures and convulsions, and it is still considered experimental by the government (Lefaucheur et al., 2007; Leo & Latif, 2007).

» LO3 Biomedical Therapies in Perspective

In some respects, no greater revolution has occurred in the field of mental health than biological approaches to treatment.

In some respects, no greater revolution has occurred in the field of mental health than biological approaches to treatment. As previously violent, uncontrollable patients have been calmed by the use of drugs, mental hospitals have been able to concentrate more on actually helping patients and less on custodial functions. Similarly, patients whose lives have been disrupted by depression or bipolar episodes have been able to function normally, and other forms of drug therapy have also shown remarkable results.

Furthermore, new forms of biomedical therapy are promising. For example, the newest treatment possibility—which remains experimental at this point—is gene therapy. As we discussed when considering behavioral genetics, specific genes may be introduced to particular regions of the brain. These genes then have the potential to reverse or even prevent biochemical events that give rise to psychological disorders (Lymberis et al., 2004; Sapolsky, 2003; Tuszynski, 2007).

Despite their current usefulness and future promise, biomedical therapies do not represent a cure-all for psychological disorders. For one thing, critics charge that such therapies merely provide relief of the *symptoms* of mental disorder; as soon as the drugs are withdrawn, the symptoms return. Although it is considered a major step in the right direction, biomedical treatment may not solve the underlying problems that led a patient to therapy in the first place. Biomedical therapies also can produce side effects, ranging from minor to serious physical reactions to the development of *new* symptoms of abnormal behavior. Finally, an overreliance on biomedical therapies may lead therapists to overlook alternative forms of treatment that may be helpful.

If you had a loved one suffering with severe depression, how would you feel about him or her undergoing ECT or TMS treatments?

Still, biomedical therapies—sometimes alone and more often in conjunction with psychotherapy—have permitted millions of people to function more effectively. Furthermore, although biomedical therapy and psychotherapy appear distinct, research shows that biomedical therapies ultimately may not be as different from talk therapies as one might imagine, at least in terms of their consequences.

» LO4 Community Psychology: Focus on Prevention

Each of the treatments we have reviewed has a common element: It is a "restorative" treatment, aimed at alleviating psychological difficulties that already exist. However, an approach known as **community psychology** has a different aim: to prevent or minimize the incidence of psychological disorders.

Community psychology came of age in the 1960s, when mental health professionals developed plans for a nationwide network of community mental health centers. The hope was that those centers would provide low-cost mental health services, including short-term therapy and community educational programs. In another development, the population of mental hospitals has plunged as drug treatments made physical restraint of patients unnecessary.

This transfer of former mental patients out of institutions and into the community—a process known as **deinstitutionalization**—was encouraged

Community psychology A branch of psychology that focuses on the prevention and minimization of psychological disorders in the community.

Deinstitutionalization The transfer of former mental patients from institutions to the community.

Although deinstitutionalization has had many successes, it has also contributed to the release of mental patients into the community with little or no support. As a result many have become homeless.

by the growth of the community psychology movement (see Figure 3). Proponents of deinstitutionalization wanted to ensure not only that deinstitutionalized patients received proper treatment but also that their civil rights were maintained (Wolff, 2002; St. Dennis et al., 2006).

Unfortunately, the promise of deinstitutionalization has not been met, largely because insufficient resources are provided to deinstitutionalized patients. What started as a worthy attempt to move people out of mental institutions and into the community ended, in many cases, with former patients being dumped into the community without any real support. Many became homeless—between a third and a half of all homeless adults are thought to have a major psychological disorder—and some became involved in illegal acts caused by their disorders. In short, many people who need treatment do not get it, and in some cases care for people with psychological disorders has simply shifted from one type of treatment site to another (Doyle, 2002; Lamb & Weinberger, 2005; Shinn et al., 2007).

On the other hand, the community psychology movement has had some positive outcomes. Telephone "hotlines" are now common. At any time of the day or night, people experiencing acute stress can call a trained, sympathetic listener who can provide immediate—although obviously limited—treatment (Reese, Conoley, & Brossart, 2002; Paukert, Stagner, & Hope, 2004; Cauce, 2007).

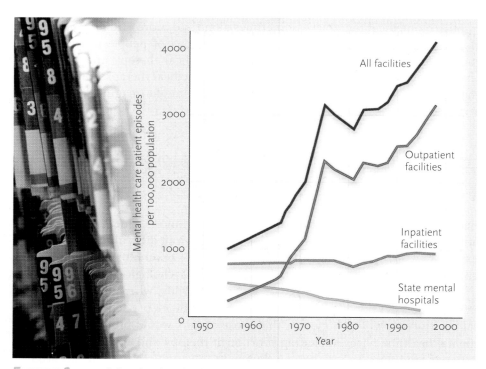

FIGURE 3   As deinstitutionalization has become more prevalent over the last 50 years, the number of patients being treated in state mental hospitals has declined significantly, while the number of outpatient facilities has increased. (*Source: National Mental Health Information Center, U.S. Department of Health and Human Services, reprinted in Scientific American, December, 2002, p. 38.*)

becoming an *informed consumer*
OF PSYCHOLOGY

Choosing the Right Therapist

If you decide to seek therapy, you're faced with a daunting task. Choosing a therapist is not a simple matter. One place to begin the process of identifying a therapist is at the "Help Center" of the American Psychological Association at http://locator.apahelpcenter.org/ or 1-800-964-2000. And, if you start therapy, several general guidelines can help you determine whether you've made the right choice:

- *You and your therapist should agree on the goals for treatment.* They should be clear, specific, and attainable.

- *You should feel comfortable with your therapist.* You should not be intimidated by, or in awe of, a therapist. Instead, you should trust the therapist and feel free to discuss the most personal issues without fearing a negative reaction. In sum, the "personal chemistry" should be right.

- *Therapists should have appropriate training and credentials and should be licensed by appropriate state and local agencies.* Check therapists' membership in national and state professional associations. In addition, the cost of therapy, billing practices, and other business matters should be clear. It is not a breach of etiquette to put these matters on the table during an initial consultation.

- *You should feel that you are making progress after therapy has begun, despite occasional setbacks.* If you have no sense of improvement after repeated visits, you and your therapist should discuss this issue frankly. Although there is no set timetable, the most obvious changes resulting from therapy tend to occur relatively early in the course of treatment. For instance, half of patients in psychotherapy improve by the 8th session, and three-fourths by the 26th session (see Figure 4).

Be aware that you will have to put in a great deal of effort in therapy. Although our culture promises quick cures for any problem, in reality,

> **You and your therapist should agree on the goals for treatment.**

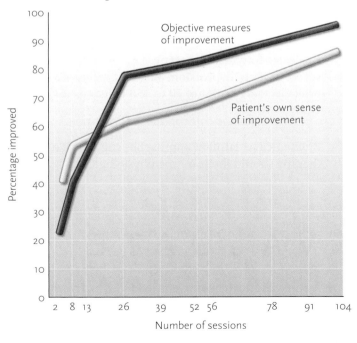

FIGURE 4 For most clients, improvements in psychological functioning occur relatively soon after therapy has begun. *(Source: Howard et al., 1986.)*

"Looking good!"

solving difficult problems is not easy. You must be committed to making therapy work and should know that it is you, not the therapist, who must do most of the work to resolve your problems. The effort has the potential to pay off handsomely—as you experience a more positive, fulfilling, and meaningful life.

RECAP

Discuss options for drug therapy.

- Antipsychotic drugs such as chlorpromazine very effectively reduce psychotic symptoms. Antidepressant drugs such as Prozac reduce depression so successfully that they are used very widely. Antianxiety drugs, or minor tranquilizers, are among the most frequently prescribed medications of any sort. (p. 449)

Explain electroconvulsive therapy.

- In electroconvulsive therapy (ECT), used in severe cases of depression, a patient receives a brief electric current of 70 to 150 volts. (p. 454)

Offer perspective on biomedical therapies.

- Biomedical treatment approaches suggest that therapy should focus on the physiological causes of abnormal behavior, rather than considering psychological factors. Drug therapy, the best example of biomedical treatments, has brought about dramatic reductions in the symptoms of mental disturbance. (p. 454)

Discuss the community psychology movement.

- The community psychology approach encouraged deinstitutionalization, in which previously hospitalized mental patients were released into the community. (p. 455)

EVALUATE

1. Antipsychotic drugs have provided effective, long-term, and complete cures for schizophrenia. True or false?
2. One highly effective biomedical treatment for a psychological disorder, used mainly to arrest and prevent manic-depressive episodes, is
   a. Chlorpromazine
   b. Lithium

c. Librium

d. Valium

3. The trend toward releasing more patients from mental hospitals and into the community is known as

_____ .

RETHINK

One of the main criticisms of biological therapies is that they treat the symptoms of mental disorder without uncovering and treating the underlying problems from which people are suffering. Do you agree with this criticism? Why?

Answers to Evaluate Questions 1. false; schizophrenia can be controlled, but not cured, by medication; 2. b; 3. deinstitutionalization

[KEY TERMS]

Drug therapy *p. 449*

Antipsychotic drugs *p. 449*

Antidepressant drugs *p. 451*

Mood stabilizers *p. 452*

Antianxiety drugs *p. 452*

Electroconvulsive therapy (ECT) *p. 454*

Transcranial magnetic stimulation (TMS) *p. 454*

Community psychology *p. 455*

Deinstitutionalization *p. 455*

looking BACK

Psychology on the Web

1. Investigate computer-assisted psychotherapy on the Web. Locate (a) a computerized therapy program, such as ELIZA, which offers "therapy" over the Internet, and (b) a report on "cybertherapy," in which therapists use the Web to interact with patients. Compare the two approaches, describing how each one works and relating it to the therapeutic approaches you have studied.

2. Find more information on the Web about deinstitutionalization. Try to find pro and con arguments about it and summarize the arguments, including your judgment of the effectiveness and advisability of deinstitutionalization as an approach to dealing with mental illness.

the case of...
TONY SCARPETTA, THE MAN WHO COULDN'T RELAX

Tony Scarpetta worked for over decade as a freelance Web developer. He had a knack for putting his clients at ease and learning exactly what their needs were and delivering creative output to meet those needs. But Tony had a dark secret: Despite acting calm and in control around his clients, Tony often felt as if he were falling to pieces inside. His friendly banter masked a whirlwind of panicky thoughts ranging from "this new advertising director hates my work and I'm going to lose his company's business" to "what if my clients abandon me for a competitor and I can't attract any new business?"

Tony had been dealing with this kind of anxiety for years. Often it was helpful, as when it motivated him to push his creative boundaries and to work hard to please his customers. But in other ways it was a great hindrance, especially when irrational fears would distract him from his work or keep him up at night, leaving him feeling drained the next day. Tony would like to do something to relieve his anxiety, but he's not sure where to begin.

1. If you were Tony's friend, what advice would you give him for seeking out professional help with his anxiety? Where should he begin his search?

2. What kinds of therapies should Tony consider, and why? Are there any kinds of therapy that he should probably not consider?

3. What would be the benefits to Tony of seeing his family physician for a prescription for an antianxiety drug? What might be some disadvantages to taking that approach?

4. What could Tony expect if he visits a psychodynamically oriented therapist about his anxiety? What about if he sees a humanistic therapist?

5. What would a rational-emotive behavior therapist be likely to say to Tony during a therapy session?

Psychotherapy: Psychodynamic, Behavioral, and Cognitive Approaches to Treatment

Psychodynamic Approaches to Therapy

Behavioral Approaches to Therapy

Cognitive Approaches to Therapy

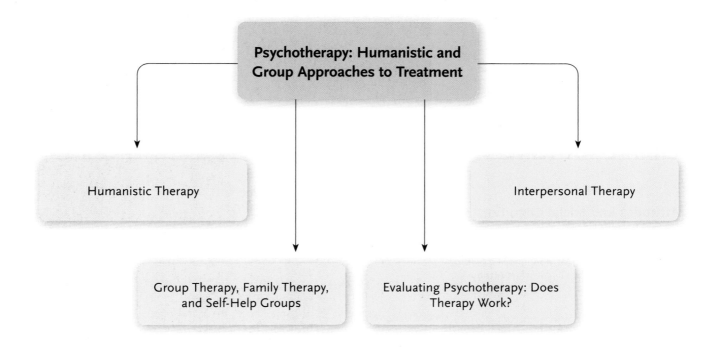

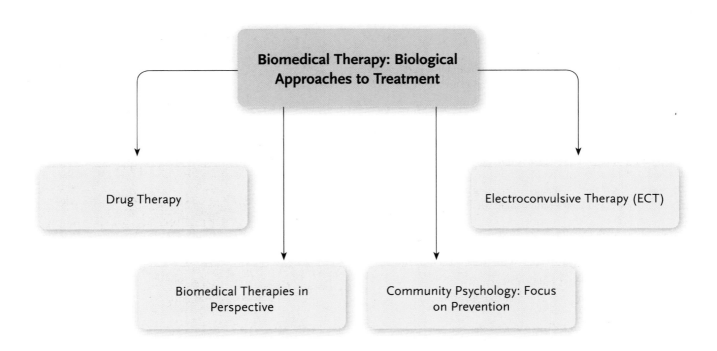

CHAPTER 12

CHAPTER OUTLINE

A Gift of Life

John Kluth approached people outside banks, churches, casinos, libraries, and the federal courthouse. He'd walk up with a look of surprised recognition and greet people as if he knew them.

"You know me!" he'd say. "I'm the guy who drives around the neighborhood in the white truck." Or: "You know my mother. She lives up the hill and walks the dog on your street." Then Kluth would lay out his story, police say. He was driving to Boston on Interstate 95 with hundreds of pounds of lobsters when his truck broke down. He needs several hundred dollars to get it fixed. He has a check, but it hasn't cleared yet. If he doesn't get the cash, the lobsters will die and spoil. He'll pay you back tomorrow at your home. And, to show his appreciation, he'll drop off a few lobsters, too.

Asked for $70, Bob Fricker, a hard-eyed antiques auctioneer, gave Kluth $80. "It was like we'd known each other sometime, someplace. I was just very comfortable with him. It's hard to express. I'd probably do it again tomorrow. He was that good." (Hampson, 2007, p. 2A) ■

SOCIAL PSYCHOLOGY

looking AHEAD

John Kluth's story was just that: a story. Kluth was a successful con artist who made his living duping innocent victims.

What made John Kluth such a successful con artist? Why would anyone at all fall for his ploy, much less the prominent public figures and business leaders he generally targeted? The answer is that Kluth made use of a number of psychological principles: He presented himself in a familiar, likable way that made people feel as if they knew him. He took advantage of biases in the way that people make decisions about others' behavior that led him to be viewed favorably. He used effective compliance tactics to get people to do his bidding willingly. And he capitalized on people's willingness to help out a friend in distress. What made Kluth a successful con artist, then, was his uncanny instinctive knowledge of social psychology.

Social psychology is the scientific study of how people's thoughts, feelings, and actions are affected by others. Social psychologists consider the kinds and causes of the behavior of the individual in social situations. They examine how the nature of situations in which we find ourselves influences our behavior in important ways.

> **Social psychology** The scientific study of how people's thoughts, feelings, and actions are affected by others.

The broad scope of social psychology is conveyed by the kinds of questions social psychologists ask, such as: How can we convince people to change their attitudes or adopt new ideas and values? In what ways do we come to understand what others are like? How are we influenced by what others do and think? Why do some people display so much violence, aggression, and cruelty toward others that people throughout the world live in fear of annihilation at their hands? And why, in comparison, do some people place their own lives at risk to help others?

We begin with a look at how our attitudes shape our behavior and how we form judgments about others. We discuss how we are influenced by others, and we consider prejudice and discrimination, focusing on their roots and the ways in which we can reduce them. After examining what social psychologists have learned about how people form friendships and relationships, we look at the determinants of aggression and helping—two opposing sides of human behavior. Finally, we conclude by addressing stress and the ways that we can cope with it.

$\gg$ $\gg$

Attitudes and Social Cognition

LEARNING OUTCOMES

39.1 Define persuasion.

39.2 Explain social cognition.

What do Tiger Woods, Rachel Ray, and Tom Brady have in common?

Each has appeared in advertisements designed to mold or change our attitudes. Such commercials are part of the barrage of messages we receive each day from sources as varied as politicians, sales staff in stores, and celebrities, all of which are meant to influence us.

» LO1 Persuasion: Changing Attitudes

Attitudes Evaluations of a particular person, behavior, belief, or concept.

Persuasion is the process of changing attitudes, one of the central concepts of social psychology. **Attitudes** are evaluations of a particular person, behavior, belief, or concept. For example, you probably hold attitudes toward the U.S. president (a person), abortion (a behavior), affirmative action (a belief), or architecture (a concept) (Brock & Green, 2005; Hegarty & Massey, 2007).

The ease with which we can change our attitudes depends on a number of factors, including:

- *Message source.* The characteristics of a person who delivers a persuasive message, known as an *attitude communicator,* have a major impact on the

Companies use celebrities such as Queen Latifah to persuade consumers to buy their products. Can celebrities really affect the purchasing habits of consumers? How?

effectiveness of that message. For example, the expertise and trustworthiness of a communicator are related to the impact of a message.

- *Characteristics of the message.* It is not just *who* delivers a message but what the message is like that affects attitudes. Generally, two-sided messages—which include both the communicator's position and the one he or she is arguing against—are more effective than one-sided messages, given the assumption that the arguments for the other side can be effectively refuted and the audience is knowledgeable about the topic.

- *Characteristics of the target.* Once a communicator has delivered a message, characteristics of the *target* of the message may determine whether the message will be accepted. For example, intelligent people are more resistant to persuasion than are those who are less intelligent.

Routes to Persuasion

Recipients' receptiveness to persuasive messages relates to the type of information processing they use. Social psychologists have discovered two primary information-processing routes to persuasion: central route and peripheral route processing. **Central route processing** occurs when the recipient thoughtfully considers the issues and arguments involved in persuasion. In central route processing, people are swayed in their judgments by the logic, merit, and strength of arguments.

> *Social psychologists have discovered two primary information-processing routes to persuasion: central route and peripheral route processing.*

In contrast, **peripheral route processing** occurs when people are persuaded on the basis of factors unrelated to the nature or quality of the content of a persuasive message. Instead, factors that are irrelevant or extraneous to the issue, such as who is providing the message, how long the arguments are, or the emotional appeal of the arguments, influence them (Wegener et al., 2004; Petty et al., 2005; Warden, Wu, & Tsai, 2006).

In general, people who are highly involved and motivated use central route processing to comprehend a message. However, if a person is uninvolved, unmotivated, bored, or distracted, the nature of the message becomes less important, and peripheral factors become more critical (see Figure 1 on page 468). Although both central route and peripheral route processing lead to attitude change, central route processing generally leads to stronger, more lasting attitude change.

STUDY ALERT

<u>C</u>entral route processing involves the <u>c</u>ontent of the message; <u>p</u>eripheral route processing involves how the message is <u>p</u>rovided.

From the perspective of . . .

A GRAPHIC DESIGNER Suppose you were assigned to develop an advertisement for a product for the local newspaper and a store front. How might theories of persuasion guide you to suit the different audiences who will see the ad?

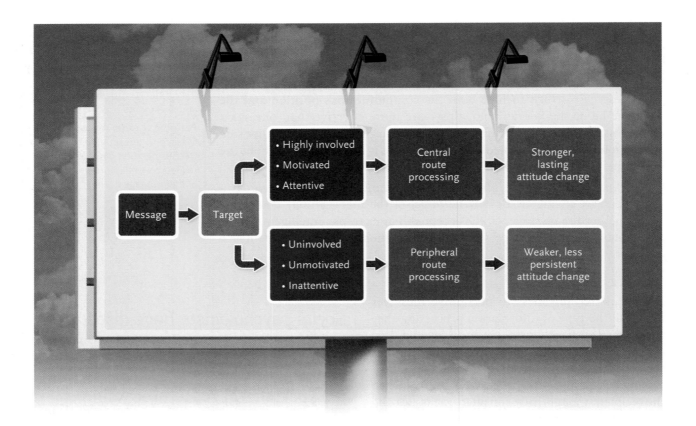

FIGURE 1 Routes to persuasion. Targets who are highly involved, motivated, and attentive use central route processing when they consider a persuasive message, which leads to a more lasting attitude change. In contrast, uninvolved, unmotivated, and inattentive targets are more likely to use peripheral route processing, and attitude change is likely to be less enduring. Can you think of specific advertisements that try to produce central route processing?

The Link Between Attitudes and Behavior

Not surprisingly, attitudes influence behavior. The strength of the link between particular attitudes and behavior varies, of course, but generally people strive for consistency between their attitudes and their behavior. Furthermore, people hold fairly consistent attitudes. For instance, you would probably not hold the attitude that eating meat is immoral and still have a positive attitude toward hamburgers (Conner et al., 2003; Levi, Chan, & Pence, 2006).

Ironically, the consistency that leads attitudes to influence behavior sometimes works the other way around, for in some cases it is our behavior that shapes our attitudes. According to social psychologist Leon Festinger (1957), **cognitive dissonance** is the psychological tension that occurs when a person holds two contradictory attitudes or thoughts (referred to as *cognitions*).

Cognitive dissonance explains many everyday events involving attitudes and behavior. For example, smokers who know that smoking leads to lung cancer hold contradictory cognitions: (1) I smoke, and (2) smoking leads to lung cancer. The theory predicts that these two thoughts will lead to a state of cognitive dissonance. More important, it predicts that—assuming that they don't change their behavior by quitting smoking—smokers will be motivated to reduce their dissonance by one of the following methods: (1) modifying one or both of the cognitions, (2) changing the perceived importance of one

Cognitive dissonance The conflict that occurs when a person holds two contradictory attitudes or thoughts (referred to as *cognitions*).

cognition, (3) adding cognitions, or (4) denying that the two cognitions are related to each other. Hence, a smoker may decide that he really doesn't smoke all that much or that he'll quit soon (modifying the cognition), that the evidence linking smoking to cancer is weak (changing the importance of a cognition), that the amount of exercise he gets compensates for the smoking (adding cognitions), or that there is no evidence linking smoking and cancer (denial). Whichever technique the smoker uses results in reduced dissonance (see Figure 2).

» LO2 Social Cognition: Understanding Others

One of the dominant areas in social psychology during the last few years has focused on learning how we come to understand what others are like and how we explain the reasons underlying others' behavior.

Understanding What Others Are Like

Consider for a moment the enormous amount of information about other people to which we are exposed. How can we decide what is important and what is not and make judgments about the characteristics of others? Social psychologists interested in this question study **social cognition**—the way people understand and make sense of others and themselves. Those psychologists have learned that individuals have highly developed **schemas,** sets of cognitions about people and social experiences. Those schemas organize

> **Social cognition** The cognitive processes by which people understand and make sense of others and themselves.
>
> **Schemas** Sets of cognitions about people and social experiences.

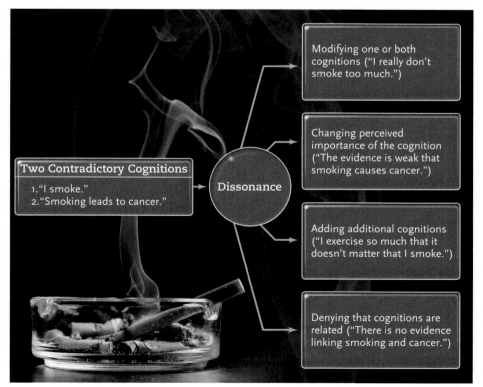

FIGURE 2 Cognitive dissonance. The simultaneous presence of two contradictory cognitions ("I smoke" and "Smoking leads to cancer") produces dissonance, which can be reduced through several methods. What are additional ways in which dissonance can be reduced?

information stored in memory, represent in our minds the way the social world operates, and give us a framework to recognize, categorize, and recall information relating to social stimuli such as people and groups (Brewer & Hewstone, 2003; Moskowitz, 2004; Smith & Semin, 2007).

We typically hold schemas for specific types of people. Our schema for "teacher," for instance, generally consists of a number of characteristics: knowledge of the subject matter he or she is teaching, a desire to impart that knowledge, and an awareness of the student's need to understand what is being said. Or we may hold a schema for "mother" that includes the characteristics of warmth, nurturance, and caring. Regardless of their accuracy, schemas are important because they organize the way in which we recall, recognize, and categorize information about others. Moreover, they help us predict what others are like on the basis of relatively little information (Bargh & Chartrand, 2000; Ruscher, Fiske, & Schnake, 2000).

Impression Formation

How do we decide that Sayreeta is a hard worker, Jacob is obnoxious, or Hector is a really nice guy? The earliest work on social cognition examined *impression formation,* the process by which an individual organizes information about another person to form an overall impression of that person. In a classic study, for instance, students learned that they were about to hear a guest lecturer (Kelley, 1950). Researchers told one group of students that the lecturer was "a rather warm person, industrious, critical, practical, and determined" and told a second group that he was "a rather cold person, industrious, critical, practical, and determined."

The simple substitution of "cold" for "warm" caused drastic differences in the way the students in each group perceived the lecturer, even though he gave the same talk in the same style in each condition. Students who had been told he was "warm" rated him considerably more positively than students who had been told he was "cold."

Central traits The major traits considered in forming impressions of others.

The findings from this experiment led to additional research on impression formation that focused on the way in which people pay particular attention to certain unusually important traits—known as **central traits**—to help them form an overall impression of others. The presence of a central trait alters the meaning of other traits. Hence, the description of the lecturer as "industrious" meant something different when it was associated with the central trait "warm" than it meant when it was associated with "cold" (Widmeyer & Loy, 1988; Glicksohn & Nahari, 2007).

We make impressions about others remarkably quickly. In just a few seconds, using what have been called "thin slices of behavior," we are able to make judgments of people that are accurate and that match those of people who make judgments based on longer snippets of behavior (Choi, Gray, & Ambady, 2004; Pavitt, 2007).

Of course, as we gain more experience with people and see them exhibiting behavior in a variety of situations, our impressions of them become more complex. However, because our knowledge of others usually has gaps, we still tend to fit individuals into personality schemas that represent particular "types" of people. For instance, we may hold a "gregarious person" schema, made up of the traits of friendliness, aggressiveness, and openness. The presence of just one or two of those traits may be sufficient to make us assign a person to a particular schema.

Even when schemas are not entirely accurate, they serve an important function: They allow us to develop expectations about how others will behave. Those expectations permit us to plan our interactions with others more easily and serve to simplify a complex social world.

Attribution Processes: Understanding the Causes of Behavior

When Barbara Washington, a new employee at the Ablex Computer Company, completed a major staffing project two weeks early, her boss, Yolanda, was delighted. At the next staff meeting, she announced how pleased she was with Barbara and explained that *this* was an example of the kind of performance she was looking for in her staff. The other staff members looked on resentfully, trying to figure out why Barbara had worked night and day to finish the project not just on time but two weeks early. She must be an awfully compulsive person, they decided.

At one time or another, most of us have puzzled over the reasons behind someone's behavior. In contrast to theories of social cognition, which describe how people develop an overall impression of others' personality traits, **attribution theory** seeks to explain how we decide, on the basis of samples of an individual's behavior, what the specific causes of that person's behavior are.

In seeking an explanation for behavior, we must answer one central question: Is the cause situational or dispositional? **Situational causes** are those brought about by something in the environment. For instance, someone who knocks over a quart of milk and then cleans it up probably does the cleaning not because he or she is necessarily a neat person but because the *situation* requires it. In contrast, a person who spends hours shining the kitchen floor probably does so because he or she is a neat person—hence, the behavior has a **dispositional cause,** prompted by the person's disposition (his or her internal traits or personality characteristics).

In our example involving Barbara Washington, her fellow employees attributed her behavior to her disposition rather than to the situation. But from a logical standpoint, it is equally plausible that something about the situation caused the behavior. If asked, Barbara might attribute her accomplishment to situational factors, explaining that she had so much other work to do that she just had to get the project out of the way, or that the project was not all that difficult and so it was easy to complete ahead of schedule. To her, then, the reason for her behavior might not be dispositional at all; it could be situational.

Attribution Biases: To Err Is Human

If we always processed information in the rational manner that attribution theory suggests, the world might run a lot more smoothly. Unfortunately, although attribution theory generally makes accurate predictions, people do not always process information about others in as logical a fashion as the theory seems to suggest. In fact, research reveals consistent biases in the ways people make attributions. Typical ones include the following:

- *The halo effect.* Harry is intelligent, kind, and loving. Is he also conscientious? If you were to guess, your most likely response probably would be yes. Your guess reflects the **halo effect,** a phenomenon in which an initial understanding that a person has positive traits is used to infer other uniformly positive characteristics. The opposite would also hold true. Learning that Harry was unsociable and argumentative would probably lead you to assume that he was lazy as well. However, because few people

Attribution theory The theory of personality that seeks to explain how we decide, on the basis of samples of an individual's behavior, what the specific causes of that person's behavior are.

Situational causes (of behavior) Perceived causes of behavior that are based on environmental factors.

Dispositional causes (of behavior) Perceived causes of behavior that are based on internal traits or personality factors.

Halo effect A phenomenon in which an initial understanding that a person has positive traits is used to infer other uniformly positive characteristics.

Assumed-similarity bias The tendency to think of people as being similar to oneself, even when meeting them for the first time.

Self-serving bias The tendency to attribute personal success to personal factors (skill, ability, or effort) and to attribute failure to factors outside oneself.

Fundamental attribution error A tendency to overattribute others' behavior to dispositional causes and the corresponding minimization of the importance of situational causes.

psych2.0

WWW.MHHE.COM/PSYCHLIFE

Fundamental Attribution Error

have either uniformly positive or uniformly negative traits, the halo effect leads to misperceptions of others (Goffin, Jelley, & Wagner, 2003; Dennis, 2007).

- *Assumed-similarity bias.* How similar to you—in terms of attitudes, opinions, and likes and dislikes—are your friends and acquaintances? Most people believe that their friends and acquaintances are fairly similar to themselves. But this feeling goes beyond just people we know to a general tendency—known as the **assumed-similarity bias**—to think of people as being similar to oneself, even when meeting them for the first time. Given the range of people in the world, this assumption often reduces the accuracy of our judgments (Watson, Hubbard, & Wiese, 2000; Lemay, Clark, Feeney, 2007).

- *The self-serving bias.* When their teams win, coaches usually feel that the success is due to their coaching. But when they coach a losing team, coaches may think it's due to the poor skills of their players. Similarly, if you get an A on a test, you may think it's due to your hard work, but if you get a poor grade, it's due to the professor's inadequacies. The reason is the **self-serving bias,** the tendency to attribute success to personal factors (skill, ability, or effort) and attribute failure to factors outside oneself (Spencer et al., 2003; Bergeron, 2006).

- *The fundamental attribution error.* One of the more common attribution biases is the tendency to overattribute others' behavior to dispositional causes and the corresponding failure to recognize the importance of situational causes. Known as the **fundamental attribution error,** this tendency is prevalent in Western cultures. We tend to exaggerate the importance of personality characteristics (dispositional causes) in producing others' behavior, minimizing the influence of the environment (situational factors). For example, we are more likely to jump to the conclusion that someone who is often late to work is too lazy to take an earlier bus (a dispositional cause) than to assume that the lateness is due to situational factors, such as the bus is always running behind schedule.

Despite the importance of the fundamental attribution error in shaping the perceptions of members of Western cultures, it turns out that it's not so fundamental when we look at non-Western cultures, as we discuss next.

EXPLORING diversity

Attributions in a Cultural Context: How Fundamental Is the Fundamental Attribution Error?

Attribution biases do not affect all of us in the same way. The culture in which we are raised clearly plays a role in the way we attribute others' behavior.

Take, for example, the fundamental attribution error, the tendency to overestimate the importance of personal, dispositional factors and underattribute situational factors in determining the causes of others' behavior. The error is pervasive in Western cultures and not in Eastern societies. For instance, adults in India were more likely to use situational attributions than dispositional

472 Chapter 12 SOCIAL PSYCHOLOGY

ones in explaining events. These findings are the opposite of those for the United States, and they contradict the fundamental attribution error (Miller, 1984; Lien et al., 2006).

Cultural differences in attributions may have profound implications. For example, parents in Asia tend to attribute good academic performance to effort and hard work (situational factors). In contrast, parents in Western cultures tend to de-emphasize the role of effort and attribute school success to innate ability (a dispositional factor). As a result, Asian students in general may strive harder to achieve and ultimately outperform U.S. students in school (Stevenson, Lee, & Mu, 2000; Lien et al., 2006).

Students in Asian societies may perform exceptionally well in school because the culture emphasizes academic success and perseverance.

The difference in thinking between people in Asian and Western cultures is a reflection of a broader difference in the way the world is perceived. Asian societies generally have a *collectivistic orientation,* a worldview that promotes the notion of interdependence. People with a collectivistic orientation generally see themselves as parts of a larger, interconnected social network and as responsible to others. In contrast, people in Western cultures are more likely to hold an *individualist orientation,* which emphasizes personal identity and the uniqueness of the individual. They focus more on what sets them apart from others and what makes them special (Markus & Kitayama, 2003; Wang, 2004; Haugen, Lund, & Ommundsen, 2008).

R E C A P

Define persuasion.

- Social psychology is the scientific study of the ways in which people's thoughts, feelings, and actions are affected by others and the nature and causes of individual behavior in social situations. (p. 465)

- Attitudes are evaluations of a particular person, behavior, belief, or concept. (p. 466)

- Cognitive dissonance occurs when an individual simultaneously holds two cognitions—attitudes or thoughts—that contradict each other. To resolve the contradiction, the person may modify one cognition, change its importance, add a cognition, or deny a link between the two cognitions, thereby bringing about a reduction in dissonance. (p. 468)

Explain social cognition.

- Social cognition involves the way people understand and make sense of others and themselves. People develop schemas that organize information about people and social experiences in memory and allow them to interpret and categorize information about others. (p. 469)

- People form impressions of others in part through the use of central traits, personality characteristics that receive unusually heavy emphasis when we form an impression. (p. 470)

- Information-processing approaches have found that we tend to average together sets of traits to form an overall impression. (p. 470)

- Attribution theory tries to explain how we understand the causes of behavior, particularly with respect to situational or dispositional factors. (p. 471)

- Even though logical processes are involved, attribution is prone to error. For instance, people are susceptible to the halo effect, assumed-similarity bias, self-serving bias, and fundamental attribution error (the tendency to overattribute others' behavior to dispositional causes and the corresponding failure to recognize the importance of situational causes). (p. 471)

EVALUATE

1. An evaluation of a particular person, behavior, belief, or concept. is called a(n) _____.

2. One brand of peanut butter advertises its product by describing its taste and nutritional value. It is hoping to persuade customers through _____ route processing. In ads for a competing brand, a popular actor happily eats the product—but does not describe it. This approach hopes to persuade customers through _____ route processing.

3. Cognitive dissonance theory suggests that we commonly change our behavior to keep it consistent with our attitudes. True or false?

4. Sopan was happy to lend his textbook to a fellow student who seemed bright and friendly. He was surprised when his classmate did not return it. His assumption that the bright and friendly student would also be responsible reflects the _____ effect.

RETHINK

Joan sees Annette, a new co-worker, act in a way that seems abrupt and curt. Joan concludes that Annette is unkind and unsociable. The next day Joan sees Annette acting kindly toward another worker. Is Joan likely to change her impression of Annette? Why or why not? Finally, Joan sees several friends of hers laughing and joking with Annette, treating her in a very friendly fashion. Is Joan likely to change her impression of Annette? Why or why not?

Answers to Evaluate Questions 1. attitude; 2. central, peripheral; 3. false; we typically change our behavior, not our attitudes, to reduce cognitive dissonance; 4. halo

[KEY TERMS]

Social psychology *p. 465*

Attitude *p. 466*

Central route processing *p. 467*

Peripheral route processing *p. 467*

Cognitive dissonance *p. 468*

Social cognition *p. 469*

Schema *p. 469*

Central trait *p. 470*

Attribution theory *p. 471*

Situational causes (of behavior) *p. 471*

Dispositional causes (of behavior) *p. 471*

Halo effect *p. 471*

Assumed-similarity bias *p. 472*

Self-serving bias *p. 472*

Fundamental attribution error *p. 472*

Social Influence and Groups

Social influence is the process by which the actions of an individual or group affect the behavior of others. As you undoubtedly know from your own experience, pressures to conform can be painfully strong and can bring about changes in behavior that otherwise never would have occurred.

Why can conformity pressures in groups be so strong? For one reason, groups, and other people generally, play a central role in our lives. Groups develop and hold *norms*, expectations regarding behavior appropriate to the group. Furthermore, we understand that not adhering to group norms can result in retaliation from other group members, ranging from being ignored to being overtly derided or even being rejected or excluded by the group. Thus, people conform to meet the expectations of the group (Baumeister, Twenge, & Nuss, 2002; Jetten, Hornsey, & Adarves-Yorno, 2006).

Groups exert considerable social influence over individuals, ranging from the mundane, such as the decision to wear a certain kind of jeans, to the extreme cases such as the cruelty of guards at the Abu Ghraib prison in Iraq. We'll consider three types of social pressure: conformity, compliance, and obedience.

» LO1 Conformity: Following What Others Do

Conformity is a change in behavior or attitudes brought about by a desire to follow the beliefs or standards of other people. Subtle or even unspoken social pressure results in conformity.

The classic demonstration of pressure to conform comes from a series of studies carried out in the 1950s by Solomon Asch (Asch, 1951). In the experiments, the participants thought they were taking part in a test of perceptual skills with six other people. The experimenter showed the participants one card with three lines of varying length and a second card that had a fourth line that matched one of the first three (see Figure 1 on page 476). The task was seemingly straightforward: Each of the participants had to announce aloud which of the first three lines was identical in length to the "standard" line on the second card. Because the correct answer was always obvious, the task seemed easy to the participants.

LEARNING OUTCOMES

40.1 Define conformity.

40.2 Explain compliance.

40.3 Discuss obedience.

> **Social influence** The process by which the actions of an individual or group affect the behavior of others.
>
> **Conformity** A change in behavior or attitudes brought about by a desire to follow the beliefs or standards of other people.

STUDY ALERT

The distinction between the three types of social pressure—conformity, compliance, and obedience—depends on the nature and strength of the social pressure brought to bear on a person.

Standard line   Comparison lines

FIGURE 1   Which of the three comparison lines is the same length as the "standard" line?

Indeed, because the participants all agreed on the first few trials, the procedure appeared to be simple. But then something odd began to happen. From the perspective of the participant in the group who answered last on each trial, all the answers of the first six participants seemed to be wrong—in fact, unanimously wrong. And this pattern persisted. Over and over again, the first six participants provided answers that contradicted what the last participant believed to be correct. The last participant faced the dilemma of whether to follow his or her own perceptions or follow the group by repeating the answer everyone else was giving.

As you might have guessed, this experiment was more contrived than it appeared. The first six participants were actually confederates (paid employees of the experimenter) who had been instructed to give unanimously erroneous answers in many of the trials. And the study had nothing to do with perceptual skills. Instead, the issue under investigation was conformity.

Asch found that in about one-third of the trials, the participants conformed to the unanimous but erroneous group answer, with about 75 percent of all participants conforming at least once. However, he found strong individual differences. Some participants conformed nearly all the time, whereas others never did. Subsequent research further shows that conformity is considerably higher when people must respond publicly than it is when they can do so privately. Also, having just one person present who shares the minority point of view is sufficient to reduce conformity pressures (Prislin, Brewer, & Wilson, 2002; Goodwin, Costa, & Adonu, 2004; Levine & Moreland, 2006).

Conformity to Social Roles

Conformity also influences behavior through social roles. *Social roles* are the behaviors that are associated with people in a given position, such as a restaurant waiter or a schoolteacher. In some cases, though, social roles influence us so profoundly that we engage in behavior in entirely atypical— and damaging—ways. This fact was brought home in an influential experiment conducted by Philip Zimbardo and colleagues. In the study, the researchers set up a mock prison, complete with cells, solitary confinement cubicles, and a small

In some cases, though, social roles influence us so profoundly that we engage in behavior in entirely atypical—and damaging—ways.

It is easy to think of conformity in the context of teenagers and their desire to fit in. However, conformity is equally as pervasive in adults. Can you think of a time that you conformed to the group norm?

recreation area. The researchers then advertised for participants who were willing to spend 2 weeks in a study of prison life. Once they identified the study participants, a flip of a coin designated who would be a prisoner and who would be a prison guard. Neither prisoners nor guards were told how to fulfill their roles (Zimbardo, 1973; Zimbardo, Maslach, & Haney, 2000; Zimbardo, 2007).

After just a few days in this mock prison, the students assigned to be guards became abusive to the prisoners, waking them at odd hours and subjecting them to arbitrary punishment. They withheld food from the prisoners and forced them into hard labor. On the other hand, the students assigned to the prisoner role soon became docile and submissive to the guards. They became extremely demoralized, and one slipped into a depression so severe he was released after just a few days. In fact, after only 6 days of captivity, the remaining prisoners' reactions became so extreme that the study was ended.

The experiment (which, it's important to note, drew criticism on both methodological and ethical grounds) provided a clear lesson: Conforming to a social role can have a powerful consequence on the behavior of even normal, well-adjusted people, inducing them to change their behavior in sometimes undesirable ways. This phenomenon may explain how the situation in which U.S. Army guards at the Iraq Abu Ghraib prison found themselves could have led to their abusive behavior toward the prisoners (Zimbardo, 2007).

» LO2 Compliance: Submitting to Direct Social Pressure

When we refer to conformity, we usually mean a phenomenon in which the social pressure is subtle or indirect. But in some situations social pressure is much more obvious, with direct, explicit pressure to endorse a particular point of view or behave in a certain way. Social psychologists call the type of behavior that occurs in response to direct social pressure **compliance.**

Compliance Behavior that occurs in response to direct social pressure.

Several specific techniques represent attempts to gain compliance. Those frequently employed include the following:

- *Foot-in-the-door technique.* A volunteer comes to your door and asks you to sign a petition. You agree, thinking you have nothing to lose. A little later comes a request to make a donation, which, because you have already agreed to the first request, you have a hard time turning down.

  The volunteer in this case is using a tried-and-true strategy that social psychologists call the foot-in-the-door technique. In the *foot-in-the-door technique,* you ask a person to agree to a small request and later ask that person to comply with a more important one. It turns out that compliance with the more important request increases significantly when the person first agrees to the smaller favor.

- *Door-in-the-face technique.* A fund-raiser asks for a $500 contribution. You laughingly refuse, telling her that the amount is way out of your league. She then asks for a $10 contribution. What do you do? If you are like most people, you'll probably be a lot more compliant than you would be if she hadn't asked for the huge contribution first. In this tactic, called the *door-in-the-face technique,* someone makes a large request, expecting it to be refused, and follows it with a smaller one. This strategy, which is the opposite of the foot-in-the-door approach, has also proved to be effective (Millar, 2002; Pascual & Guéguen, 2005, 2006).

- *That's-not-all technique.* In this technique, a salesperson offers you a deal at an inflated price. But immediately after the initial offer, the salesperson offers an incentive, discount, or bonus to clinch the deal.

    Although it sounds transparent, this practice can be quite effective. In one study, the experimenters set up a booth and sold cupcakes for 75 cents each. In one condition, the experimenters directly told customers that the price was 75 cents. But in another condition, they told customers that the price was originally $1 but had been reduced to 75 cents. As we might predict, more people bought cupcakes at the "reduced" price—even though it was identical to the price in the other experimental condition (Burger, Reed, & DeCesare, 1999; Pratkanis, 2007).

- *Not-so-free sample.* If you ever receive a free sample, keep in mind that it comes with a psychological cost. Although they may not couch it in these terms, salespeople who provide samples to potential customers do so to instigate the norm of reciprocity. The *norm of reciprocity* is the well-accepted societal standard dictating that we should treat other people as they treat us. Receiving a *not-so-free sample*, then, suggests the need for reciprocation—in the form of a purchase, of course (Spiller & Wymer, 2001; Cialdini, 2006; Park & Antonioni, 2007).

Industrial-organizational (I/O) psychology The branch of psychology focusing on work and job-related issues, including worker motivation, satisfaction, safety, and productivity.

Obedience A change in behavior in response to the commands of others.

Companies seeking to sell their products to consumers often use the techniques identified by social psychologists for promoting compliance. But employers also use them to bring about compliance and raise the productivity of employees in the workplace. In fact, a close cousin to social psychology, **industrial-organizational (I/O) psychology,** considers issues such as worker motivation, satisfaction, safety, and productivity. I/O psychologists also focus on the operation and design of organizations, asking questions such as how decision making can be improved in large organizations and how the fit between workers and their jobs can be maximized.

From the perspective of . . .

A Salesperson Imagine that you have been trained to use the various compliance techniques described in this section. Because these compliance techniques are so powerful, should the use of certain of these techniques be banned? Should consumers be taught defenses against such techniques? Is the use of such techniques ethically and morally defensible? Why?

» LO3 Obedience: Following Direct Orders

Compliance techniques are used to gently lead people toward agreement with a request. In some cases, however, requests aim to produce **obedience,** a change in behavior in response to the commands of others. Although obedience is considerably less common than conformity and compliance, it does occur in several specific kinds of relationships. For example, we may show obedience to our bosses, teachers, or parents merely because of the power they hold to reward or punish us.

To acquire an understanding of obedience, consider for a moment how you might respond if a stranger said to you:

I've devised a new way of improving memory. All I need is for you to teach people a list of words and then give them a test. The test procedure requires only that you give learners a shock each time they make a mistake on the test. To administer the shocks you will use a "shock generator" that gives shocks ranging from 15 to 450 volts. You can see that the switches are labeled from "slight shock" through "danger: severe shock" at the top level, where there are three red X's. But don't worry; although the shocks may be painful, they will cause no permanent damage.

Presented with this situation, you would be likely to think that neither you nor anyone else would go along with the stranger's unusual request. Clearly, it lies outside the bounds of what we consider good sense.

Or does it? Suppose the stranger asking for your help were a psychologist conducting an experiment. Or suppose the request came from your teacher, your employer, or your military commander—all people in authority with a seemingly legitimate reason for the request. If you still believe it's unlikely that you would comply—think again. The situation presented above describes a classic experiment conducted by social psychologist Stanley Milgram in the 1960s. In the study, an experimenter told participants to give increasingly stronger shocks to another person as part of a study on learning (see Figure 2). In reality, the experiment had nothing to do with learning; the real issue under consideration was the degree to which participants would obey the experimenter's requests. In fact, the "learner" supposedly receiving the shocks was a confederate who never really received any punishment (Milgram, 2005).

Most people who hear a description of Milgram's experiment feel that it is unlikely that *any* participant would give the maximum level of shock—or, for that matter, any shock at all. Even a group of psychiatrists to whom the situation was described predicted that fewer than 2 percent of the participants

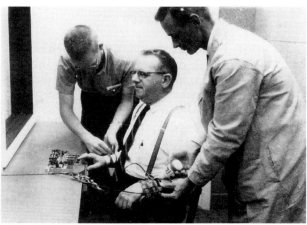

FIGURE 2 This fearsome-looking "shock generator" led participants to believe they were administering electric shocks to another person, who was connected to the generator by electrodes that were attached to the skin. *(Source: Copyright 1965 by Stanley Milgram. From the film Obedience, distributed by the New York University Film Library and Pennsylvania State University, PCR.)*

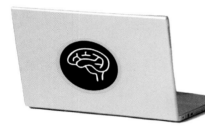

psych2.0

WWW.MHHE.COM/PSYCHLIFE

Milgram Obedience Experiment

would fully comply and administer the strongest shocks. However, the actual results contradicted both experts' and nonexperts' predictions. Some 65 percent of the participants eventually used the highest setting on the shock generator—450 volts—to shock the learner. This obedience occurred even though the learner, who had mentioned at the start of the experiment that he had a heart condition, demanded to be released, screaming, "Let me out of here! Let me out of here! My heart's bothering me. Let me out of here!" Despite the learner's pleas, most participants continued to administer the shocks.

Why did so many individuals comply with the experimenter's demands? The participants, who were extensively interviewed after the experiment, said they obeyed primarily because they believed that the experimenter would be responsible for any potential ill effects that befell the learner. The participants accepted the experimenter's orders, then, because they thought that they personally could not be held accountable for their actions—they could always blame the experimenter (Blass, 1996, 2004).

We need only consider actual instances of obedience to authority to witness some frightening real-life parallels. For instance, after World War II, the major defense that Nazi officers gave to excuse their participation in atrocities during the war was that they were "only following orders." Milgram's experiment, which was motivated in part by his desire to explain the behavior of everyday Germans during World War II, forces us to ask ourselves this question: Would we be able to withstand the intense power of authority?

RECAP

Define conformity.

- Social influence is the area of social psychology concerned with situations in which the actions of an individual or group affect the behavior of others. (p. 475)

- Conformity refers to changes in behavior or attitudes that result from a desire to follow the beliefs or standards of others. (p. 475)

Explain compliance.

- Compliance is behavior that results from direct social pressure. Among the ways of eliciting compliance are the foot-in-the-door, door-in-the-face, that's-not-all, and not-so-free-sample techniques. (p. 477)

Discuss obedience.

- Obedience is a change in behavior in response to the commands of others. (p. 478)

EVALUATE

1. _____ _____, or a person who agrees with the dissenting viewpoint, is likely to reduce conformity.

2. Which of the following techniques asks a person to comply with a small initial request to enhance the likelihood that the person will later comply with a larger request?

   a. Door-in-the-face

   b. Foot-in-the-door

   c. That's-not-all

   d. Not-so-free sample

3. The _____-_____-_____-_____ technique begins with an outrageous request that makes a subsequent, smaller request seem reasonable.

4. _____ is a change in behavior that is due to another person's orders.

RETHINK

Why do you think the Milgram experiment is so controversial? What sorts of effects might the experiment have had on participants? Do you think the experiment would have had similar results if it had been conducted not in a laboratory setting, but among members of a social group (such as a fraternity or sorority) with strong pressures to conform?

Answers to Evaluate Questions 1. social supporter; 2. b; 3. door-in-the-face; 4. obedience

[KEY TERMS]

Social influence *p. 475*

Conformity *p. 475*

Compliance *p. 477*

Industrial-organizational (I/O) psychology *p. 478*

Obedience *p. 478*

Prejudice and Discrimination

LEARNING OUTCOMES

41.1 Identify the foundations of prejudice.

41.2 Distinguish measuring practices for prejudice and discrimination.

41.3 Assess ways to reduce prejudice and discrimination.

Stereotype A set of generalized beliefs and expectations about a particular group and its members.

Prejudice A negative (or positive) evaluation of a particular group and its members.

Discrimination Behavior directed toward individuals on the basis of their membership in a particular group.

What do you think when someone says, "He's African American," "She's Chinese," or "That's a woman driver"?

If you're like most people, you'll probably automatically form some sort of impression of what each person is like. Most likely your impression is based on a **stereotype,** a set of generalized beliefs and expectations about a specific group and its members. Stereotypes, which may be negative or positive, grow out of our tendency to categorize and organize the vast amount of information we encounter in our everyday lives. All stereotypes share the common feature of oversimplifying the world: We view individuals not in terms of their unique, personal characteristics, but in terms of characteristics we attribute to all the members of a particular group.

Stereotypes can lead to **prejudice,** a negative (or positive) evaluation of a group and its members. For instance, racial prejudice occurs when a member of a racial group is evaluated in terms of race and not because of his or her own characteristics or abilities.

Common stereotypes and forms of prejudice involve racial, religious, and ethnic groups. Over the years, various groups have been called "lazy" or "shrewd" or "cruel" with varying degrees of regularity by those who are not members of that group. Even people who on the surface appear to be unprejudiced may harbor hidden prejudice. For example, when white participants in experiments are shown faces on a computer screen so rapidly that they cannot consciously perceive the faces, they react more negatively to black than to white faces—an example of what has been called *modern racism* (Dovidio, Gaertner, & Pearson, 2005; Liu & Mills, 2006; Pearson, Dovidio, & Pratto, 2007).

Although usually backed by little or no evidence, stereotypes can have harmful consequences. Acting on negative stereotypes results in **discrimination**— behavior directed toward individuals on the basis of their membership in a particular group. Discrimination can lead to exclusion from jobs, neighborhoods, and educational opportunities, and it may result in lower salaries and benefits for members of specific groups. Discrimination can also result in more favorable treatment to favored groups, as when an employer hires a job applicant of her own racial group because of the applicant's race.

Stereotyping not only leads to overt discrimination, but also can cause members of stereotyped groups to behave in ways that reflect the stereotype through a phenomenon known as the *self-fulfilling prophecy.* Self-fulfilling prophecies are expectations about the occurrence of a future event or behavior that act to increase the likelihood that the event or behavior will occur. For example, if people think that members of a specific group lack ambition, they may treat them in a way that actually brings about a lack of ambition.

» LO1 The Foundations of Prejudice

No one has ever been born disliking a specific racial, religious, or ethnic group. People learn to hate, in much the same way that they learn the alphabet.

According to *observational learning approaches* to stereotyping and prejudice, the behavior of parents, other adults, and peers shapes children's feelings about members of various groups. For instance, bigoted parents may commend their children for expressing prejudiced attitudes. Likewise, young children learn prejudice by imitating the behavior of adult models. Such learning starts at an early age: children as young as 3 years of age begin to show preferences for members of their own race (Schneider, 2003; Nesdale, Maass, & Durkin, 2005; Dovidio & Gaertner, 2006).

The mass media also provide information about stereotypes, not just for children but for adults as well. Even today, some television shows and movies portray Italians as Mafia-like mobsters, Jews as greedy bankers, and African Americans as promiscuous or lazy. When such inaccurate portrayals are the primary source of information about minority groups, they can lead to the development and maintenance of unfavorable stereotypes (Coltraine & Messineo, 2000; Ward, 2004; Do, 2006).

> *Social identity theory suggests that people tend to be ethnocentric, viewing the world from their own perspective and judging others in terms of their group membership.*

Other explanations of prejudice and discrimination focus on how being a member of a specific group helps to magnify one's sense of self-esteem. According to *social identity theory,* we use group membership as a source of pride and self-worth. Social identity theory suggests that people tend to be *ethnocentric,* viewing the world from their own perspective and judging others in terms of their group membership. Slogans such as "gay pride" and "black is beautiful" illustrate that the groups to which we belong furnish us with a sense of self-respect (Rowley et al., 1998; Tajfel & Turner, 2004; Hogg, 2006).

However, the use of group membership to provide social respect produces an unfortunate outcome. In an effort to maximize our sense of self-esteem, we may come to think that our own group (our *ingroup*) is better than groups to which we don't belong (our *outgroups*). Consequently, we inflate the positive aspects of our ingroup—and, at the same time, devalue outgroups. Ultimately, we come to view members of outgroups as inferior to members of our ingroup (Tajfel & Turner, 2004). The end result is prejudice toward members of groups of which we are not a part.

Neither the observational learning approach nor the social identity approach provides a full

Like father, like son: Social learning approaches to stereotyping and prejudice suggest that attitudes and behaviors toward members of minority groups are learned through the observation of parents and other individuals. How can this cycle be broken?

explanation for stereotyping and prejudice. For instance, some psychologists argue that prejudice results when there is perceived competition for scarce societal resources. Thus, when competition exists for jobs or housing, members of majority groups may believe (however unjustly or inaccurately) that minority group members are hindering their efforts to attain their goals, and this belief can lead to prejudice. In addition, other explanations for prejudice emphasize human cognitive limitations that lead us to categorize people on the basis of visually conspicuous physical features such as race, sex, and ethnic group. Such categorization can lead to the development of stereotypes and, ultimately, to discriminatory behavior (Dovidio, 2001; Fiske, 2002; Mullen & Rice, 2003; Weeks & Lupfer, 2004).

» LO2 Measuring Prejudice and Discrimination: The Implicit Personality Test

psych2.0
WWW.MHHE.COM/PSYCHLIFE

Prejudice

A 34-year-old white woman sat down in her Washington office to take a psychological test. Her office decor attested to her passion for civil rights—as a senior activist at a national gay rights organization, and as a lesbian herself, fighting bias and discrimination is what gets her out of bed every morning. . . .

All [the test] asked her to do was distinguish between a series of black and white faces. When she saw a black face she was to hit a key on the left, when she saw a white face she was to hit a key on the right. Next, she was asked to distinguish between a series of positive and negative words. Words such as "glorious" and "wonderful" required a left key, words such as "nasty" and "awful" required a right key. The test remained simple when two categories were combined: The activist hit the left key if she saw either a white face or a positive word, and hit the right key if she saw either a black face or a negative word.

Then the groupings were reversed. The woman's index fingers hovered over her keyboard. The test now required her to group black faces with positive words, and white faces with negative words. She leaned forward intently. She made no mistakes, but it took her longer to correctly sort the words and images. (Vedantam, 2005, p. W12)

When she found out her results, the activist was shocked: The test showed that she showed bias in favor of whites over blacks.

Could you, like this woman, be prejudiced and not even know it? The answer, according to the researchers who developed the *Implicit Association Test,* is probably yes. People often fool themselves, and they are very careful about revealing their true attitudes about members of various groups, not only to others but to themselves. However, even though they may truly believe that they are unprejudiced, the reality is that they actually routinely differentiate between people on the basis of race, ethnicity, and sexual orientation.

The Implicit Association Test, or IAT, is an ingenious measure of prejudice that permits a more accurate assessment of people's discrimination between members of different groups. It was developed, in part, as a reaction to the difficulty in finding a questionnaire that would reveal prejudice. Direct questions such as, "Would you prefer interacting with a member of Group X rather than Group Y?" typically identify only the most blatant prejudices, because people try to censor their responses (Greenwald, Nosek, & Sriram, 2006; Rudman & Ashmore, 2007).

In contrast, the IAT makes use of the fact that people's automatic reactions often provide the most valid indicator of what they actually believe. Having grown up in a culture that teaches us to think about members of particular groups in specific ways, we tend to absorb associations about those groups that are reflective of the culture (Lane et al., 2007).

The results of the IAT show that almost 90 percent of test takers have a pro-white implicit bias, and more than two-thirds of non-Arab, non-Muslim volunteers display implicit biases against Arab Muslims. Moreover, more than 80 percent of heterosexuals display an implicit bias against gays and lesbians (Wittenbrink & Schwarz, 2007).

Of course, having an implicit bias does not mean that people will overtly discriminate, a criticism that has been made of the test. Yet it does mean that the cultural lessons to which we are exposed have a considerable unconscious influence on us. (Interested in how you would perform on the IAT? Go to this website to take the test: https://implicit.harvard.edu/implicit).

» LO3 Reducing Prejudice and Discrimination

How can we diminish the effects of prejudice and discrimination? Psychologists have developed several strategies that have proved effective, including the following:

- *Increasing contact between the target of stereotyping and the holder of the stereotype.* Research consistently has shown that increasing the amount of interaction between people can reduce negative stereotyping. But only certain kinds of contact are likely to reduce prejudice and discrimination. Situations in which contact is relatively intimate, the individuals are of equal status, or participants must cooperate with one another or are dependent on one another are more likely to reduce stereotyping (Dovidio, Gaertner, & Kawakami, 2003; Tropp & Pettigrew, 2005; Pettigrew & Tropp, 2006).

- *Making values and norms against prejudice more conspicuous.* Sometimes just reminding people about the values they already hold regarding equality and fair treatment of others is enough to reduce discrimination. Similarly, people who hear others making strong, vehement antiracist statements are subsequently more likely to strongly condemn racism (Czopp, Monteith, & Mark, 2006; Tropp & Bianchi, 2006).

From the perspective of . . .

A CRIMINAL JUSTICE WORKER How might overt forms of prejudice and discrimination toward disadvantaged groups (such as African Americans) be reduced in a state or federal prison?

■ *Providing information about the targets of stereotyping.* Probably the most direct means of changing stereotypical and discriminatory attitudes is education: teaching people to be more aware of the positive characteristics of targets of stereotyping. For instance, when the meaning of puzzling behavior is explained to people who hold stereotypes, they may come to appreciate the actual significance of the behavior (Isbell & Tyler, 2003; Banks, 2006; Nagda, Tropp, & Paluck, 2006).

RECAP

Identify the foundations of prejudice.

■ Stereotypes are generalized beliefs and expectations about a specific group and its members. Stereotyping can lead to prejudice and self-fulfilling prophecies. (p. 482)

■ Prejudice is the negative (or positive) evaluation of a particular group and its members. (p. 482)

■ According to observational learning approaches, children learn stereotyping and prejudice by observing the behavior of parents, other adults, and peers. Social identity theory suggests that group membership is used as a source of pride and self-worth, and this may lead people to think of their own group as better than others. (p. 483)

Distinguish measuring practices for prejudice and discrimination.

■ Stereotyping and prejudice can lead to discrimination, behavior directed toward individuals on the basis of their membership in a particular group. (p. 484)

Assess ways to reduce prejudice and discrimination.

■ Among the ways of reducing prejudice and discrimination are increasing contact, demonstrating positive values against prejudice, and education. (p. 485)

EVALUATE

1. Any expectation—positive or negative—about an individual solely on the basis of that person's membership in a group can be a stereotype. True or false?

2. The negative (or positive) evaluation of a group and its members is called

   a. Stereotyping.

   b. Prejudice.

   c. Self-fulfilling prophecy.

   d. Discrimination.

3. Paul is a store manager who does not expect women to succeed in business. He therefore offers important, high-profile responsibilities only to men. If the female employees fail to move up in the company, it could be an example of a _____-_____ prophecy.

RETHINK

Do you think it matters that some people have implicit biases against certain groups if those people never express their biases explicitly? Why or why not?

[KEY TERMS]

Stereotype *p. 482*

Prejudice *p. 482*

Discrimination *p. 482*

Positive and Negative Social Behavior

LEARNING OUTCOMES

42.1 Compare and contrast the concepts of "like" and love.

42.2 Explain aggression and prosocial behavior.

Are people basically good or bad?

Like philosophers and theologians, social psychologists have pondered the basic nature of humanity. Is it represented mainly by the violence and cruelty we see throughout the world, or does something special about human nature permit loving, considerate, unselfish, and even noble behavior as well?

We turn to two routes that social psychologists have followed in seeking answers to these questions. We first consider what they have learned about the sources of our attraction to others, and we end with a look at two opposite sides of human behavior: aggression and helping.

» LO1 Liking and Loving: Interpersonal Attraction and the Development of Relationships

Interpersonal attraction (or close relationship) Positive feelings for others; liking and loving.

Nothing is more important in most people's lives than their feelings for others. Consequently, it is not surprising that liking and loving have become a major focus of interest for social psychologists. Known more formally as the study of **interpersonal attraction** or **close relationships,** this area addresses the factors that lead to positive feelings for others.

How Do I Like Thee? Let Me Count the Ways.

Research has given us a good deal of knowledge about the factors that initially attract two people to each other. The important factors considered by social psychologists are the following:

- *Proximity.* Consider the friends you made when you first moved to a new neighborhood. Chances are that you became friendliest with those who lived geographically closest to you. In fact, this is one of the more firmly established findings in the literature on interpersonal attraction: *Proximity* leads to liking (Burgoon et al., 2002; Smith & Weber, 2005).

- *Mere exposure.* Repeated exposure to a person is often sufficient to produce attraction. Interestingly, repeated exposure to *any* stimulus—a person, picture, compact disc, or virtually anything—usually makes us like the stimulus more. In cases of strongly negative initial interactions, though, repeated exposure may instead intensify our initial dislike (Zajonc, 2001; Butler & Berry, 2004).

- *Similarity.* Discovering that others have similar attitudes, values, or traits makes us like them more. Furthermore, the more similar others are, the more we like them. One reason similarity increases the likelihood of interpersonal attraction is that we assume that people with similar attitudes will evaluate us positively. Because we experience a strong *reciprocity-of-liking effect* (a tendency to like those who like us), knowing that someone evaluates us positively promotes our attraction to that person (Bates, 2002; Umphress, Smith-Crowe, & Brief, 2007).

- *Physical attractiveness.* For most people, the equation *beautiful = good* is literally true. As a result, physically attractive people are more popular than are physically unattractive ones, if all other factors are equal. This finding, which contradicts the values that most people say they hold, is apparent even in childhood—with nursery-school-age children rating their peers' popularity on the basis of attractiveness—and continues into adulthood (Zebrowitz & Montepare, 2005; Little, Burt, & Perrett, 2006).

"I'm attracted to you, but then I'm attracted to me, too."

How Do I Love Thee? Let Me Count the Ways

As a first step to investigating love, researchers tried to identify the characteristics that distinguish between mere liking and full-blown love. They discovered that love is not simply a greater quantity of liking, but a qualitatively different psychological state. For instance, at least in its early stages, love includes relatively intense physiological arousal, an all-encompassing interest in another individual, fantasizing about the other, and relatively rapid swings of emotion. Similarly, love, unlike liking, includes elements of passion, closeness, fascination, exclusiveness, sexual desire, and intense caring. We idealize partners by exaggerating their good qualities and minimizing their imperfections (Garza-Guerrero, 2000; Murray, Holmes, & Griffin, 2004).

Other researchers have theorized that there are two main types of love: passionate love and companionate love. **Passionate (or romantic) love** represents a state of intense absorption in someone. It includes intense physiological arousal, psychological interest, and caring for the needs of another. In contrast, **companionate love** is the strong affection we have for those with whom our lives are deeply involved. The love we feel for our parents, other family members, and even some close friends falls into the category of companionate love (Hendrick & Hendrick, 2003; Masuda, 2003; Regan, 2006).

Psychologist Robert Sternberg makes an even finer differentiation between types of love. He proposes that love consists of three parts:

- *Decision/commitment,* the initial thoughts that one loves someone and the longer-term feelings of commitment to maintain love.

psych2.0
WWW.MHHE.COM/PSYCHLIFE

First Impressions and Attraction

Passionate (or romantic) love A state of intense absorption in someone that includes intense physiological arousal, psychological interest, and caring for the needs of another.

Companionate love The strong affection we have for those with whom our lives are deeply involved.

- *Intimacy component,* feelings of closeness and connectedness.

  - *Passion component,* the motivational drives relating to sex, physical closeness, and romance.

According to Sternberg, these three components combine to produce the different types of love (see Figure 1). He suggests that different combinations of the three components vary over the course of relationships. For example, in strong, loving relationships the level of commitment peaks and then remains stable. Passion, on the other hand, peaks quickly, and then declines and levels off relatively early in most relationships. In addition, relationships are happiest in which the strength of the various components are similar between the two partners (Sternberg, Hojjat, & Barnes, 2001; Sternberg, 2004, 2006).

Is love a necessary ingredient in a good marriage? Yes, if you live in the United States. But it's considerably less important in other cultures. Although mutual attraction and love are the two most important characteristics desired in a mate by men and women in the United States, men in China rated good health as most important, and women there rated emotional stability and maturity as most important. Among the Zulu in South Africa, men rated emotional stability first and women rated dependable character first (Buss, Abbott, & Angleitner, 1990; see Figure 2). (To consider how you approach relationships, complete the Try It! on page 492.)

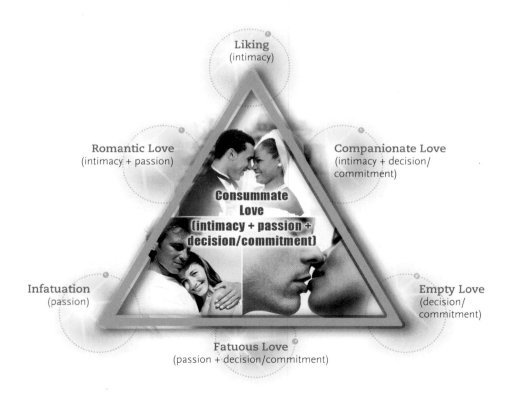

FIGURE 1 According to Sternberg, love has three main components: intimacy, passion, and decision/commitment. Different combinations of these components can create other types of love. Nonlove contains none of the three components.

Rank Ordering of Desired Characteristics in a Mate							
	United States		China		South Africa Zulu	
	Females	Males	Females	Males	Females	Males
Mutual attraction—love	1	1	8	4	5	10
Emotional stability and maturity	2	2	1	5	2	1
Dependable character	3	3	7	6	1	3
Pleasing disposition	4	4	16	13	3	4
Education and intelligence	5	5	4	8	6	6
Good health	9	6	3	1	4	5
Good looks	13	7	15	11	16	14
Sociability	8	8	9	12	8	11
Desire for home and children	7	9	2	2	9	9
Refinement, neatness	12	10	10	7	10	7
Ambition and industriousness	6	11	5	10	7	8
Similar education	10	12	12	15	12	12
Good cook and houskeeper	16	13	11	9	15	2
Favorable social status or rating	14	14	13	14	14	17
Similar religious background	15	15	18	18	11	16
Good financial prospect	11	16	14	16	13	18
Chastity (no prior sexual intercourse)	18	17	6	3	18	13
Similar political background	17	18	17	17	17	15

FIGURE 2   Although love may be an important factor in choosing a marriage partner if you live in the United States, other cultures place less importance on it. (Source: Buss et al., 1990.)

Liking and loving clearly show a positive side of human social behavior. Now we turn to behaviors that are just as much a part of social behavior: aggression and helping behavior.

» LO2 Aggression and Prosocial Behavior: Hurting and Helping Others

Drive-by shootings, carjackings, and abductions are just a few examples of the violence that seems all too common today. But also common are the simple kindnesses of life: lending a valued compact disc, stopping to help a child who has fallen off her bicycle, or merely sharing a candy bar with a friend. Such instances of helping are no less characteristic of human behavior than are the distasteful examples of aggression.

Hurting Others: Aggression

We need look no further than the daily paper or the nightly news to be bombarded with examples of **aggression,** the intentional injury of or harm to another person, both on a societal level (war, invasion, assassination) and on an individual level (crime, child abuse, and the many petty cruelties humans are capable of inflicting on one another). Is such aggression an inevitable part

Aggression The intentional injury of, or harm to, another person.

Understand Your Relationship Style

Each of us has a general manner in which we approach close relationships with others. Read the three statements below, and determine which best describes you:

1. I find it relatively easy to get close to others and am comfortable depending on them and having them depend on me. I don't often worry about being abandoned or about someone getting too close to me.

2. I am somewhat uncomfortable being close to others; I find it difficult to trust them completely and to allow myself to depend on them. I am nervous when anyone gets too close, and often love partners want me to be more intimate than I feel comfortable being.

3. I find that others are reluctant to get as close as I would like. I often worry that my partner doesn't really love me or won't want to stay with me. I want to merge completely with another person, and this desire sometimes scares people away.

The choice you make suggests the general style of emotional bonds that you develop with others.

If you thought the first statement described you best, it is probably easy for you to develop close ties with others. Around 55 percent of people describe themselves in this way.

If statement 2 describes you best, you probably have a more difficult time getting close to others, and you may have to work harder to develop close ties with other people. About 25 percent of people place themselves in this category.

Finally, if statement 3 describes you best, you, along with the 20 percent of people who describe themselves in this way, aggressively seek out close relationships. However, they probably present a source of concern to you.

Keep in mind that this is an inexact assessment and presents only a very rough estimate of your general approach to close relationships. But your response can be helpful in answering these questions: Are you generally satisfied with your relationships? Would you like to change them in some way?

of the human condition? Or is aggression primarily a product of particular circumstances that, if changed, could lead to its reduction?

Instinct Approaches: Aggression as a Release. Instinct theories, noting the prevalence of aggression not only in humans but in animals as well, propose that aggression is primarily the outcome of innate—or inborn—urges.

Sigmund Freud was one of the first to suggest, as part of his theory of personality, that aggression is a primary instinctual drive. Konrad Lorenz, an ethologist (a scientist who studies animal behavior), expanded on Freud's notions by arguing that humans, along with members of other species, have a fighting instinct, which in earlier times ensured protection of food supplies and weeded out the weaker of the species (Lorenz, 1966, 1974). Lorenz's instinct approach led to the controversial notion that aggressive energy constantly builds up within an individual until the person finally discharges it in a process called **catharsis.** The longer the energy builds up, says Lorenz, the greater will be the amount of the aggression displayed when it is discharged.

Catharsis The process of discharging built-up aggressive energy.

Probably the most controversial idea to come out of instinct theories of aggression is Lorenz's proposal that society should provide acceptable ways of permitting catharsis. For example, he suggested that participation in aggressive sports and games would prevent the discharge of aggression in less socially desirable ways. However, little research has found evidence for the existence of a pent-up reservoir of aggression that needs to be released. In fact, some studies flatly contradict the notion of catharsis, leading psychologists to look for other explanations for aggression (Bushman & Anderson, 2002; Bushman, Wang, & Anderson, 2005; Scheele & DuBois, 2006).

Frustration-Aggression Approaches: Aggression as a Reaction to Frustration. Frustration-aggression theory suggests that *frustration* (the reaction to the thwarting or blocking of goals) produces anger, leading to a readiness to act aggressively. Whether actual aggression occurs depends on the presence of *aggressive cues,* stimuli that have been associated in the past with actual aggression or violence and that will trigger aggression again (Berkowitz, 2001).

What kinds of stimuli act as aggressive cues? They can range from the most explicit, such as the presence of weapons, to more subtle cues, such as the mere mention of the name of an individual who behaved violently in the past (Berkowitz, 2001; Marcus-Newhall, Pederson, & Carlson, 2000).

Is road rage a result of frustration? According to frustration-aggression approaches, frustration is a likely cause.

Observational Learning Approaches: Learning to Hurt Others. Do we learn to be aggressive? The observational learning (sometimes called social learning) approach to aggression says that we do. Taking an almost opposite view from instinct theories, which focus on innate explanations of aggression, observational learning theory emphasizes that social and environmental conditions can teach individuals to be aggressive. The theory sees aggression not as inevitable, but rather as a learned response that can be understood in terms of rewards and punishments.

Observational learning theory pays particular attention not only to direct rewards and punishments that individuals themselves receive, but also to the rewards and punishments that models— individuals who provide a guide to appropriate behavior—receive for their aggressive behavior. According to observational learning theory, people observe the behavior of models and the subsequent consequences of that behavior. If the consequences are positive, the behavior is likely to be imitated when observers find themselves in a similar situation.

Suppose, for instance, a girl hits her younger brother when he damages one of her new toys. Whereas instinct theory would suggest that the aggression had been pent up and was now being discharged and frustration-aggression theory would examine the girl's frustration at no longer being able to use her new toy, observational learning theory would look to previous situations in which the girl had viewed others being rewarded for their aggression.

> *What kinds of stimuli act as aggressive cues? They can range from the most explicit, such as the presence of weapons, to more subtle cues, such as the mere mention of the name of an individual who behaved violently in the past.*

STUDY ALERT

Understand the distinction between the instinctual, frustration-aggression, and observational learning approaches to aggression.

For example, perhaps she had watched a friend get to play with a toy after he painfully twisted it out of the hand of another child.

Observational learning theory has received wide research support. For example, nursery-school-age children who have watched an adult model behave aggressively and then receive reinforcement for it later display similar behavior themselves if they have been angered, insulted, or frustrated after exposure. Furthermore, a significant amount of research links watching television shows containing violence with subsequent viewer aggression (Coyne & Archer, 2005; Winerman, 2005; Greer, Dudek-Singer, & Gautreaux, 2006).

Prosocial behavior Helping behavior.

Diffusion of responsibility The tendency for people to feel that responsibility for acting is shared, or diffused, among those present.

From the perspective of . . .

A CRIMINAL JUSTICE WORKER How would the aggression of Eric Rudolph, who was convicted of exploding a bomb during the 1996 Summer Olympics in Atlanta and later attacking several women's clinics, be interpreted by proponents of the three main approaches to the study of aggression: instinct approaches, frustration-aggression approaches, and observational learning approaches? Do you think any of these approaches fits the Rudolph case more closely than the others?

Helping Others: The Brighter Side of Human Nature

Turning away from aggression, we move now to the opposite—and brighter—side of human nature: helping behavior. Helping behavior, or **prosocial behavior** as it is more formally known, has been considered under many different conditions. However, the question that psychologists have looked at most closely relates to bystander intervention in emergency situations. What are the factors that lead someone to help a person in need?

One critical factor is the number of others present. When more than one person witnesses an emergency situation, a sense of **diffusion of responsibility** can arise among the bystanders. Diffusion of responsibility is the tendency for people to feel that responsibility for acting is shared, or diffused, among those present. The more people who are present in an emergency, the less personally responsible each individual feels—and therefore the less help

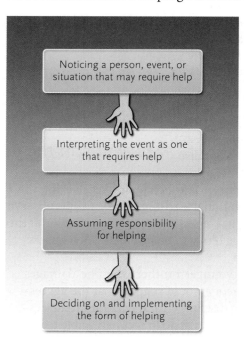

FIGURE 3 The basic steps of helping. (Source: Based on Latané & Darley, 1970).

Noticing a person, event, or situation that may require help

Interpreting the event as one that requires help

Assuming responsibility for helping

Deciding on and implementing the form of helping

he or she provides (Blair, Thompson, & Wuensch, 2005; Barron & Yechiam, 2002; Gray, 2006).

Although most research on helping behavior supports the diffusion-of-responsibility explanation, other factors are clearly involved in helping behavior. According to a model of the helping process, the decision to give aid involves four basic steps (Latané & Darley, 1970; Garcia et al., 2002; see Figure 3):

- *Noticing a person, event, or situation that may require help.*

- *Interpreting the event as one that requires help.* Even if we notice an event, it may be sufficiently ambiguous for us to interpret it as a non-emergency situation. It is here that the presence of others first affects helping behavior. The presence of inactive others may indicate to us that a situation does not require help—a judgment we do not necessarily make if we are alone.

- *Assuming responsibility for helping.* It is at this point that diffusion of responsibility is likely to occur if others are present.

- *Deciding on and implementing the form of helping.* After we assume responsibility for helping, we must decide how to provide assistance. Helping can range from very indirect forms of intervention, such as calling the police, to more direct forms, such as giving first aid or taking the victim to a hospital. After determining the nature of the assistance needed, the actual help must be implemented. A rewards-costs analysis suggests that we are most likely to use the least costly form of implementation. However, this is not always the case: In some situations, people behave altruistically. **Altruism** is helping behavior that is beneficial to others but clearly requires self-sacrifice. For example, people who helped strangers escape from the burning World Trade Center towers during the 9/11 terrorist attack, putting themselves at mortal risk, would be considered altruistic (Krueger, Hicks, & McGue, 2001; Batson & Powell, 2003; Manor & Gailliot, 2007).

Altruism Helping behavior that is beneficial to others but clearly requires self-sacrifice.

Altruism is often the only bright side of a natural disaster.

RECAP

Compare and contrast the concepts of "like" and love.

- The primary determinants of liking include proximity, exposure, similarity, and physical attractiveness. (p. 488)

- Loving is distinguished from liking by the presence of intense physiological arousal, an all-encompassing interest in another, fantasies about the other, rapid swings of emotion, fascination, sexual desire, exclusiveness, and strong feelings of caring. (p. 489)

- Love can be categorized as passionate or companionate. In addition, love has several components: intimacy, passion, and decision/commitment. (p. 489)

Explain aggression and prosocial behavior.

- Aggression is intentional injury of or harm to another person. (p. 491)

- Explanations of aggression include instinct approaches, frustration-aggression theory, and observational learning. (p. 492)

- Helping behavior in emergencies is determined in part by the phenomenon of diffusion of responsibility, which results in a lower likelihood of helping when more people are present. (p. 494)

- Deciding to help is the outcome of a four-stage process consisting of noticing a possible need for help, interpreting the situation as requiring aid, assuming responsibility for taking action, and deciding on and implementing a form of assistance. (p. 495)

EVALUATE

1. We tend to like people who are similar to us. True or false?

2. Which of the following sets are the three components of love proposed by Sternberg?
   a. Passion, closeness, sexuality
   b. Attraction, desire, complementarity
   c. Passion, intimacy, decision/commitment
   d. Commitment, caring, sexuality

3. Based on research evidence, which of the following might be the best way to reduce the amount of fighting a young boy does?
   a. Take him to the gym and let him work out on the boxing equipment.
   b. Make him repeatedly watch violent scenes from the film *The Matrix Reloaded* in the hope that it will provide catharsis.
   c. Reward him if he doesn't fight during a certain period.
   d. Ignore it and let it die out naturally.

4. If a person in a crowd does not help in an apparent emergency situation because many other people are present, that person is falling victim to the phenomenon of _____ _____ _____.

RETHINK

Can love be studied scientifically? Is there an elusive quality to love that makes it at least partially unknowable? How would you define "falling in love"? How would you study it?

Answers to Evaluate Questions 1. true; 2. c; 3. c; 4. diffusion of responsibility

[KEY TERMS]

Stress and Coping

43.1 Define stress and discuss how it affects us.

43.2 Explain the nature of stressors.

43.3 Describe how we people cope with stress.

Anthony Lepre started feeling awful almost as soon as [U.S. Homeland Security Secretary] Tom Ridge put the nation on high alert for a terrorist attack . . . He awoke in the middle of the night short of breath, his heart pounding. And the sound of his telephone seemed a sure sign of bad news. By midweek, he was rushing off to Costco to stock up on fruit juice, bottled water, peanut butter, canned tuna "and extra food for my cats Monster, Monkey and Spike." He also picked up a first-aid kit, six rolls of duct tape and a bulk package of plastic wrap to seal his windows. "The biggest problem was that I felt helpless," he says, "completely powerless over the situation." (Cowley, 2003, pp. 43–44.)

» LO1 Stress: Reacting to Threat and Challenge

Stress A person's response to events that are threatening or challenging.

Most of us need little introduction to the phenomenon of **stress,** people's response to events that threaten or challenge them. Whether it is a family problem or even the ongoing threat of a terrorist attack, life is full of circumstances and events, known as *stressors,* that produce threats to our well-being. Even pleasant events—such as planning a party or beginning a sought-after job—can produce stress, although negative events result in greater detrimental consequences than do positive ones.

All of us face stress in our lives. Some psychologists believe that daily life actually involves a series of repeated sequences of perceiving a threat, considering ways to cope with it, and ultimately adapting to the threat, with greater or lesser success. Although adaptation is often minor and occurs without our awareness, adaptation requires a major effort when stress is more severe or longer lasting. Ultimately, our attempts to overcome stress may produce biological and psychological responses that result in health problems (Boyce & Ellis, 2005; Dolbier, Smith, & Steinhardt, 2007).

Remember the distinction between stressors and stress, which can be tricky: stressors (like an exam) *cause* stress (the physiological and psychological reaction that comes from the exam).

» LO2 The Nature of Stressors: My Stress Is Your Pleasure

Stress is a very personal thing. Although certain kinds of events, such as the death of a loved one or participation in military combat, are universally stressful, other situations may or may not be stressful to a specific person.

Consider, for instance, bungee jumping. Some people would find jumping off a bridge while attached to a slender rubber tether extremely stressful. However, there are individuals who see such an activity as challenging and fun-filled. Whether bungee jumping is stressful depends in part, then, on a person's perception of the activity.

For people to consider an event stressful, they must perceive it as threatening or challenging and must lack all the resources to deal with it effectively. Consequently, the same event may at some times be stressful and at other times provoke no stressful reaction at all. A young man may experience stress when he is turned down for a date—if he attributes the refusal to his unattractiveness or unworthiness. But if he attributes it to some factor unrelated to his self-esteem, such as a previous commitment by the woman he asked, the experience of being refused may create no stress at all. Hence, a person's interpretation of events plays an important role in the determination of what is stressful (Folkman & Moskowitz, 2000; Giacobbi et al., 2004; MacKinnon & Luecken, 2008).

Categorizing Stressors

What kinds of events tend to be seen as stressful? There are three general types of stressors: cataclysmic events, personal stressors, and background stressors.

Cataclysmic events are strong stressors that occur suddenly and typically affect many people simultaneously. Disasters such as tornadoes and plane crashes, as well as terrorist attacks, are examples of cataclysmic events that can affect hundreds or thousands of people simultaneously.

Although it might seem that cataclysmic events would produce potent, lingering stress, in many cases they do not. In fact, cataclysmic events involving natural disasters may produce less stress in the long run than do events that initially are not as devastating. One reason is that natural disasters have a clear resolution. Once they are over, people can look to the future knowing that the worst is behind them. Moreover, the stress induced by cataclysmic events is shared by others who also experienced the disaster. Such sharing permits people to offer one another social support and a firsthand understanding of the difficulties others are going through (Hobfoll et al., 1996; Benight, 2004; Yesilyaprak, Kisac, & Sanlier, 2007).

The second major category of stressor is the personal stressor. **Personal stressors** include major life events such as the death of a parent or spouse, the loss of one's job, a major personal failure, or even something positive such as getting married. Typically, personal stressors produce an immediate major reaction that soon tapers off. For example, stress arising from the death of a loved one tends to be greatest just after the time of death, but people begin to feel less stress and are better able to cope with the loss after the passage of time.

Some victims of major catastrophes and severe personal stressors experience **posttraumatic stress disorder,** or **PTSD,** in which a person has experienced a significantly stressful event that has long-lasting effects that may include reexperiencing the event in vivid flashbacks or dreams.

psych2.0
WWW.MHHE.COM/PSYCHLIFE

Stress

Cataclysmic events Strong stressors that occur suddenly, affecting many people at once (e.g., natural disasters).

Personal stressors Major life events, such as the death of a family member, that have immediate negative consequences that generally fade with time.

Posttraumatic stress disorder (PTSD) A phenomenon in which victims of major catastrophes or strong personal stressors feel long-lasting effects that may include reexperiencing them even in vivid flashbacks or dreams.

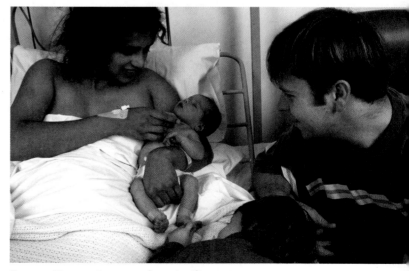

Even positive events can produce significant stress.

An episode of PTSD may be triggered by an otherwise innocent stimulus, such as the sound of a honking horn that leads someone to reexperience a past event that produced considerable stress.

Symptoms of posttraumatic stress disorder also include emotional numbing, sleep difficulties, interpersonal problems, alcohol and drug abuse, and—in some cases—suicide. For instance, the suicide rate for veterans of the Iraq war is considerably higher than it is for the general population (Dohrenwend et al., 2006; Pole, 2007).

Background stressors, or more informally, *daily hassles,* are the third major category of stressors. Exemplified by standing in a long line at a bank and getting stuck in a traffic jam, daily hassles are the minor irritations of life that we all face time and time again. Another type of background stressor is a long-term, chronic problem, such as experiencing dissatisfaction with school or a job, being in an unhappy relationship, or living in crowded quarters without privacy (Lazarus, 2000; Weinstein et al., 2004).

> *Exemplified by standing in a long line at a bank and getting stuck in a traffic jam, daily hassles are the minor irritations of life that we all face time and time again.*

By themselves, daily hassles do not require much coping or even a response on the part of the individual, although they certainly produce unpleasant emotions and moods. Yet daily hassles add up—and ultimately they may take as great a toll as a single, more stressful incident does. In fact, the *number* of daily hassles people face is associated with psychological symptoms and health problems such as flu, sore throat, and backaches.

The flip side of hassles is *uplifts,* the minor positive events that make us feel good—even if only temporarily. As indicated in Figure 1, uplifts range from relating well to a companion to finding one's surroundings pleasing. What is especially intriguing about uplifts is that they are associated with people's psychological health in just the opposite way that hassles are: The greater the number of uplifts we experience, the fewer the psychological symptoms we report later (Chamberlain & Zika, 1990; Ravindran et al., 2002; Jain, Mills, & Von Känel, 2007).

Everyone confronts daily hassles, or background stressors, at some point. At what point do daily hassles become more than mere irritants?

The High Cost of Stress

Stress can produce both biological and psychological consequences. Often the most immediate reaction to stress is a biological one. Exposure to stressors generates a rise in hormone secretions by the adrenal glands, an increase in heart rate and blood pressure, and changes in how well the skin conducts electrical impulses. On a short-term basis, these responses may be adaptive because they produce an "emergency reaction" in which the body prepares to defend itself through activation of the sympathetic nervous system. Those responses may allow more effective coping with the stressful situation (Akil & Morano, 1996; McEwen, 1998).

However, continued exposure to stress results in a decline in the body's overall level of biological functioning because of the constant secretion of stress-related hormones. Over time, stressful reactions can promote deterioration of body tissues such as blood vessels and the heart. Ultimately, we become more susceptible to disease as our ability to fight off infection is lowered (Kemeny, 2003; Brydon et al., 2004; Dean-Borenstein, 2007).

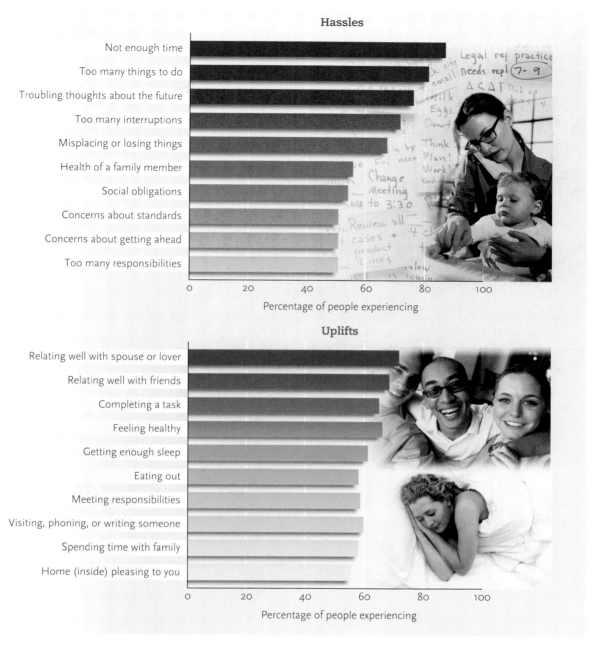

Hassles

- Not enough time
- Too many things to do
- Troubling thoughts about the future
- Too many interruptions
- Misplacing or losing things
- Health of a family member
- Social obligations
- Concerns about standards
- Concerns about getting ahead
- Too many responsibilities

Percentage of people experiencing (0, 20, 40, 60, 80, 100)

Uplifts

- Relating well with spouse or lover
- Relating well with friends
- Completing a task
- Feeling healthy
- Getting enough sleep
- Eating out
- Meeting responsibilities
- Visiting, phoning, or writing someone
- Spending time with family
- Home (inside) pleasing to you

Percentage of people experiencing (0, 20, 40, 60, 80, 100)

FIGURE 1   The most common everyday hassles and uplifts (hassles: Chamberlain & Zika, 1990; uplifts: Kanner et al., 1981). How many of these are part of your life, and how do you cope with them?

Furthermore, an entire class of physical problems known as **psychophysiological disorders** often result from or are worsened by stress. Once referred to as *psychosomatic disorders* (a term dropped because people assumed that the disorders were somehow unreal), psychophysiological disorders are actual medical problems that are influenced by an interaction of psychological, emotional, and physical difficulties. The more common psychophysiological disorders range from major problems such as high blood pressure to usually less serious conditions, such as headaches, backaches, skin rashes, indigestion, fatigue, and constipation. Stress has even been linked to the common cold (Cohen et al., 2003; Andrasik, 2006).

Psychophysiological disorders Medical problems influenced by an interaction of psychological, emotional, and physical difficulties.

In short, stress affects us in multiple ways. It may increase the risk that we will become ill, it may directly cause illness, it may make us less able to recover from a disease, and it may reduce our ability to cope with future stress. (See Figure 2 to get a measure of your own level of stress.)

Q How Stressful Is Your Life?

Test your level of stress by answering these questions, and adding the score from each box. Questions apply to the last month only. A key below will help you determine the extent of your stress.

1 How often have you been upset because of something that happened unexpectedly?

☐ 0 = never, 1 = almost never, 2 = sometimes, 3 = fairly often, 4 = very often

2 How often have you felt that you were unable to control the important things in your life?

☐ 0 = never, 1 = almost never, 2 = sometimes, 3 = fairly often, 4 = very often

3 How often have you felt nervous and "stressed"?

☐ 0 = never, 1 = almost never, 2 = sometimes, 3 = fairly often, 4 = very often

4 How often have you felt confident about your ability to handle your personal problems?

☐ 4 = never, 3 = almost never, 2 = sometimes, 1 = fairly often, 0 = very often

5 How often have you felt that things were going your way?

☐ 4 = never, 3 = almost never, 2 = sometimes, 1 = fairly often, 0 = very often

6 How often have you been able to control irritations in your life?

☐ 4 = never, 3 = almost never, 2 = sometimes, 1 = fairly often, 0 = very often

7 How often have you found that you could not cope with all the things that you had to do?

☐ 0 = never, 1 = almost never, 2 = sometimes, 3 = fairly often, 4 = very often

8 How often have you felt that you were on top of things?

☐ 4 = never, 3 = almost never, 2 = sometimes, 1 = fairly often, 0 = very often

9 How often have you been angered because of things that were outside your control?

☐ 0 = never, 1 = almost never, 2 = sometimes, 3 = fairly often, 4 = very often

10 How often have you felt difficulties were piling up so high that you could not overcome them?

☐ 0 = never, 1 = almost never, 2 = sometimes, 3 = fairly often, 4 = very often

How You Measure Up

Stress levels vary among individuals—compare your total score to the averages below:

AGE		GENDER	
18–29	14.2	Men	12.1
30–44	13.0	Women	13.7
45–54	12.6		
55–64	11.9		
65 & over	12.0		

MARITAL STATUS

Widowed	12.6
Married or living with a partner	12.4
Single or never wed	14.1
Divorced	14.7
Separated	16.6

FIGURE 2 To get a sense of the level of stress in your life, complete this questionnaire. (*Source: Cohen, 1999.*)

FIGURE 3   The general adaptation syndrome (GAS) suggests that there are three major stages to stress responses. *(Source: Selye, 1976.)*

The General Adaptation Syndrome Model: The Course of Stress

The effects of long-term stress are illustrated in a series of stages proposed by Hans Selye (pronounced "sell-yay"), a pioneering stress theorist (Selye, 1976, 1993). This model, the **general adaptation syndrome (GAS),** suggests that the physiological response to stress follows the same set pattern regardless of the cause of stress.

As shown in Figure 3, the GAS has three phases. The first stage—*alarm and mobilization*—occurs when people become aware of the presence of a stressor. On a biological level, the sympathetic nervous system becomes energized, helping a person cope initially with the stressor.

However, if the stressor persists, people move into the second response stage: *resistance*. During this stage, the body prepares to fight the stressor. During resistance, people use a variety of means to cope with the stressor—sometimes successfully but at a cost of some degree of physical or psychological well-being. For example, a worker who faces the stress of impending layoffs might spend long hours working overtime, seeking to cope with the stress.

psych2.0
WWW.MHHE.COM/PSYCHLIFE

The Various Sources of Stress

> **General adaptation syndrome (GAS)** A theory developed by Hans Selye that suggests that a person's response to a stressor consists of three stages: alarm and mobilization, resistance, and exhaustion.

From the perspective of . . .

A Supervisor   How would you help people deal with and avoid stress in their everyday lives? How might you encourage people to create social support networks?

Direct Physiological Effects
- Elevated blood pressure
- Decrease in immune system functioning
- Increased hormonal activity
- Psychophysiological conditions

Harmful Behaviors
- Increased smoking, alcohol use
- Decreased nutrition
- Decreased sleep
- Increased drug use

Indirect Health-Related Behaviors
- Decreased compliance with medical advice
- Increase in delays in seeking medical advice
- Decrease in likelihood of seeking medical advice

Stress

FIGURE 4   Three major types of consequences result from stress: direct physiological effects, harmful behaviors, and indirect health-related behaviors. *(Source: Adapted from Baum, 1994.)*

If resistance is inadequate, people enter the last stage of the GAS: *exhaustion.* During the exhaustion stage, a person's ability to adapt to the stressor declines to the point where negative consequences of stress appear: physical illness and psychological symptoms in the form of an inability to concentrate, heightened irritability, or, in severe cases, disorientation and a loss of touch with reality. In a sense, people wear out, and their physical reserves are used up.

How do people move out of the third stage after they have entered it? In some cases, exhaustion allows people to avoid a stressor. For example, people who become ill from overwork may be excused from their duties for a time, giving them a temporary respite from their responsibilities. At least for a time, then, the immediate stress is reduced.

Psychoneuroimmunology and Stress

Psychologists specializing in **psychoneuroimmunology,** or **PNI,** the study of the relationship among psychological factors, the immune system, and the brain, have taken a broader approach to stress. Focusing on the outcomes of stress, they have identified three main consequences (see Figure 4).

First, stress has direct physiological results, including an increase in blood pressure, an increase in hormonal activity, and an overall decline in the functioning of the immune system. Second, stress leads people to engage in behaviors that are harmful to their health, including increased nicotine, drug, and alcohol use; poor eating habits; and decreased sleep. Finally, stress produces indirect consequences that result in declines in health: a reduction in the likelihood of obtaining health care and decreased compliance with medical advice when it is sought (Sapolsky, 2003; Broman, 2005; Lindblad, Lindahl, & Theorell, 2006).

Psychoneuroimmunology (PNI) The study of the relationship among psychological factors, the immune system, and the brain.

Coping The efforts to control, reduce, or learn to tolerate the threats that lead to stress.

» LO3   Coping with Stress

Stress is a normal part of life—and not necessarily a completely bad part. For example, without stress, we might not be sufficiently motivated to complete the activities we need to accomplish. However, it is also clear that too much stress can take a toll on physical and psychological health. How do people deal with stress? Is there a way to reduce its negative effects?

Efforts to control, reduce, or learn to tolerate the threats that lead to stress are known as **coping.** We habitually use certain coping responses to deal with stress. Most of the time, we're not aware of these responses—just as we may be unaware of the minor stressors of life until they build up to harmful levels (Wrzesniewski & Chylinska, 2007).

We also have other, more direct, and potentially more positive ways of coping with stress, which fall into two main categories (Folkman & Moskowitz, 2000, 2004):

The ability to fight off disease is related to psychological factors. Here a cell from the body's immune system engulfs and destroys disease-producing bacteria.

- *Emotion-focused coping.* In emotion-focused coping, people try to manage their emotions in the face of stress, seeking to change the way they feel about or perceive a problem. Examples of emotion-focused coping include strategies such as accepting sympathy from others and looking at the bright side of a situation.

- *Problem-focused coping.* Problem-focused coping attempts to modify the stressful problem or source of stress. Problem-focused strategies lead to changes in behavior or to the development of a plan of action to deal with stress. Getting your resume ready when impending layoffs are announced is an example of problem-focused coping.

People often employ several types of coping strategies simultaneously. Furthermore, they use emotion-focused strategies more frequently when they perceive circumstances as being unchangeable and problem-focused approaches more often in situations they see as relatively modifiable (Penley, Tomaka, & Wiebe, 2002).

Some forms of coping are less successful. One of the least effective forms of coping is avoidant coping. In *avoidant coping,* a person may use wishful thinking to reduce stress or use more direct escape routes, such as drug use, alcohol use, and overeating. Avoidant coping usually results in a postponement of dealing with a stressful situation, and this often makes the problem even worse (Hutchinson, Baldwin, & Oh, 2006).

Learned Helplessness

Have you ever faced an intolerable situation that you just couldn't resolve, and you finally simply gave up and accepted things the way they were? This example illustrates one of the possible consequences of being in an environment in which control over a situation is not possible—a state that produces learned helplessness. **Learned helplessness** occurs when people conclude that unpleasant or aversive stimuli cannot be controlled—a view of the world that becomes so ingrained that they cease trying to remedy the aversive circumstances, even if they actually can exert some influence on the situation (Seligman, 1975, 2007; Aujoulat, Luminet, & Deccache, 2007).

Victims of learned helplessness have concluded that there is no link between the responses they make and the outcomes that occur. People experience more physical symptoms and depression when they perceive that they have little or no control than they do when they feel a sense of control over a situation (Chou, 2005; Bjornstad, 2006).

Learned helplessness A state in which people conclude that unpleasant or aversive stimuli cannot be controlled—a view of the world that becomes so ingrained that they cease trying to remedy the aversive circumstances, even if they actually can exert some influence.

Social support A mutual network of caring, interested others.

Social Support: Turning to Others

Our relationships with others also help us cope with stress. Researchers have found that **social support,** the knowledge that we are part of a mutual network of caring, interested others, enables us to experience lower levels of stress and be better able to

cope with the stress we do undergo (Cohen, 2004; Martin & Brantley, 2004; Bolger & Amarel, 2007).

The social and emotional support people provide each other helps in dealing with stress in several ways. For instance, such support demonstrates that a person is an important and valued member of a social network. Similarly, other people can provide information and advice about appropriate ways of dealing with stress (Day & Livingstone, 2003; Lindorff, 2005). Finally, people who are part of a social support network can provide actual goods and services to help others in stressful situations. For instance, they can supply temporary living quarters to a person whose house has burned down, or they can offer babysitting to a parent who is experiencing stress because of the serious illness of a spouse (Natvig, Albrektsen, & Ovarnstrom, 2003; Takizawa, Kondo, & Sakihara, 2007).

becoming an *informed consumer* OF PSYCHOLOGY

Effective Coping Strategies

How can we deal with the stress in our lives? Although there is no universal solution, because effective coping depends on the nature of the stressor and the degree to which it can be controlled, here are some general guidelines (Aspinwall & Taylor, 1997; Folkman & Moskowitz, 2000):

- *Turn a threat into a challenge.* When a stressful situation might be controllable, the best coping strategy is to treat the situation as a challenge, focusing on ways to control it. For instance, if you experience stress because your car is always breaking down, you might take a course in auto mechanics and learn to deal directly with the car's problems.

- *Make a threatening situation less threatening.* When a stressful situation seems to be uncontrollable, you need to take a different approach. It is possible to change your appraisal of the situation, view it in a different light, and modify your attitude toward it. The old truism "Look for the silver lining in every cloud" is supported by research (Smith & Lazarus, 2001; Cheng & Cheung, 2005).

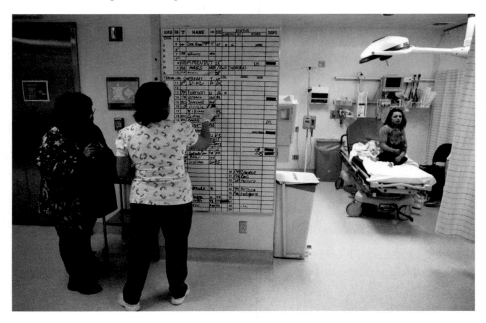

Most jobs are stressful. How would good stress coping techniques help you in this situation?

- *Change your goals.* If you are faced with an uncontrollable situation, a reasonable strategy is to adopt new goals that are practical in view of the particular situation. For example, a dancer who has been in an automobile accident and has lost full use of her legs may no longer aspire to a career in dance but might modify her goals and try to become a choreographer.

- *Take physical action.* Exercise can be effective in reducing stress.

- *Prepare for stress before it happens.* A final strategy for coping with stress is *proactive coping,* anticipating and preparing for stress *before* it is encountered (Aspinwall & Taylor, 1997; Bode et al., 2007).

RECAP

Define stress and discuss how it affects us.

- Stress is a response to threatening or challenging environmental conditions. People encounter stressors—the circumstances that produce stress—of both a positive and a negative nature. (p. 498)

Explain the nature of stressors.

- The way an environmental circumstance is interpreted affects whether it will be considered stressful. Still, there are general classes of events that provoke stress: cataclysmic events, personal stressors, and background stressors (daily hassles). (p. 499)

- Stress produces immediate physiological reactions. In the short term those reactions may be adaptive, but in the long term they may

have negative consequences, including the development of psychophysiological disorders. (p. 500)

- The consequences of stress can be explained in part by Selye's general adaptation syndrome (GAS), which suggests that there are three stages in stress responses: alarm and mobilization, resistance, and exhaustion. (p. 503)

Describe how we people cope with stress.

- Stress can be reduced by developing a sense of control over one's circumstances. In some cases, however, people develop a state of learned helplessness. (p. 505)

- Coping with stress can take a number of forms, including the use of emotion-focused or problem-focused coping strategies. (p. 505)

EVALUATE

1. _____ is defined as a response to challenging or threatening events.

2. Match each portion of the GAS with its definition

   1. Alarm and mobilization   a. Ability to adapt to stress diminishes; symptoms appear.
   2. Exhaustion   b. Activation of sympathetic nervous system.
   3. Resistance   c. Various strategies are used to cope with a stressor.

3. Stressors that affect a single person and produce an immediate major reaction are known as
   a. Personal stressors.
   b. Psychic stressors.
   c. Cataclysmic stressors.
   d. Daily stressors.

RETHINK

Why are cataclysmic stressors less stressful in the long run than are other types of stressors? Does the reason relate to the coping phenomenon known as social support? How?

[KEY TERMS]

Stress *p. 498*

Cataclysmic events *p. 499*

Personal stressors *p. 499*

Posttraumatic stress disorder (PTSD) *p. 499*

Background stressors (daily hassles) *p. 500*

Psychophysiological disorders *p. 501*

General adaptation syndrome (GAS) *p. 503*

Psychoneuroimmunology (PNI) *p. 504*

Coping *p. 504*

Learned helplessness *p. 505*

Social support *p. 505*

looking BACK

Psychology on the Web

1. Find examples on the Web of advertisements or other persuasive messages that use central route processing and peripheral route processing. What type of persuasion appears to be more prevalent on the Web? For what type of persuasion does the Web appear to be better suited? Is there a difference between Web-based advertising and other forms of advertising?

2. Is "hate crimes legislation" a good idea? Use the Web to find at least two discussions of hate crimes legislation—one in favor and one opposed—and summarize in writing the main issues and arguments presented. Using your knowledge of prejudice and aggression, evaluate the arguments for and against hate crimes legislation. State your opinion about whether this type of legislation is advisable.

the case of...
JOHN BUCKINGHAM, THE NEW GUY ON THE JOB

When John Buckingham moved across the country to take a new job, he didn't expect to run into much difficulty. He would be doing the same kind of work he was used to doing, just for a new company. But when he arrived on his first day, he realized there was more for him to adjust to than he had realized.

Clearly, John had moved to a region where the culture was much more laid back and casual than he was used to. He showed up for his first day in his usual business suit only to find that almost all the other employees wore jeans, Western shirts, and cowboy boots. Many of them merely stared awkwardly when they first saw John, and then hurriedly tried to look busy while avoiding eye contact.

John got the message. On his second day at work John also wore jeans and a casual shirt, although he didn't yet own a pair of cowboy boots. He found that people seemed more relaxed around him, but that they continued to treat him warily. It would be several weeks—after he'd gone out and bought boots and started wearing them to work—before certain people warmed up to John enough to even talk to him.

1. What does the behavior of John's co-workers toward John suggest about their attributions for his initial manner of dress?

2. Describe the kinds of biases that might have affected John's co-workers as they formed impressions of him on his first day. Could they have been using a faulty schema to understand him? Is there evidence of the halo effect?

3. Explain why John changed his manner of dress so soon after starting his new job. What processes were likely involved in his decision to do so?

4. John's co-workers seemed very hesitant to "warm up" to John. How would you explain to John their initial reluctance to like him very much?

5. If you were the human resources director for this company, what strategies could you employ to prevent experiences like John's? How would you justify the implementation of these strategies to the company president?

full circle

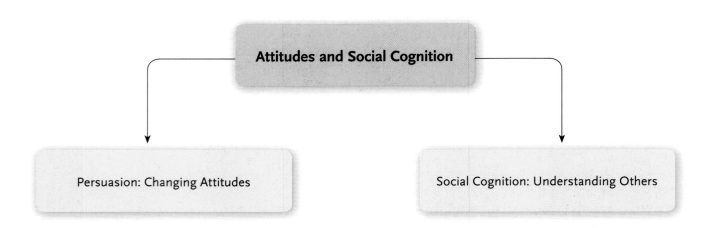

Attitudes and Social Cognition

Persuasion: Changing Attitudes

Social Cognition: Understanding Others

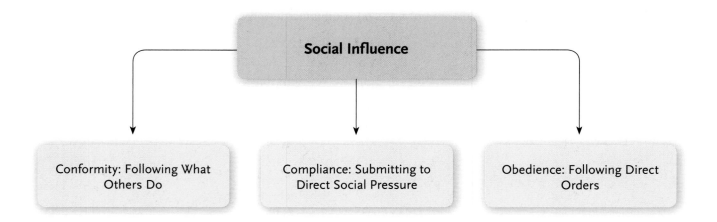

Social Influence

Conformity: Following What Others Do

Compliance: Submitting to Direct Social Pressure

Obedience: Following Direct Orders

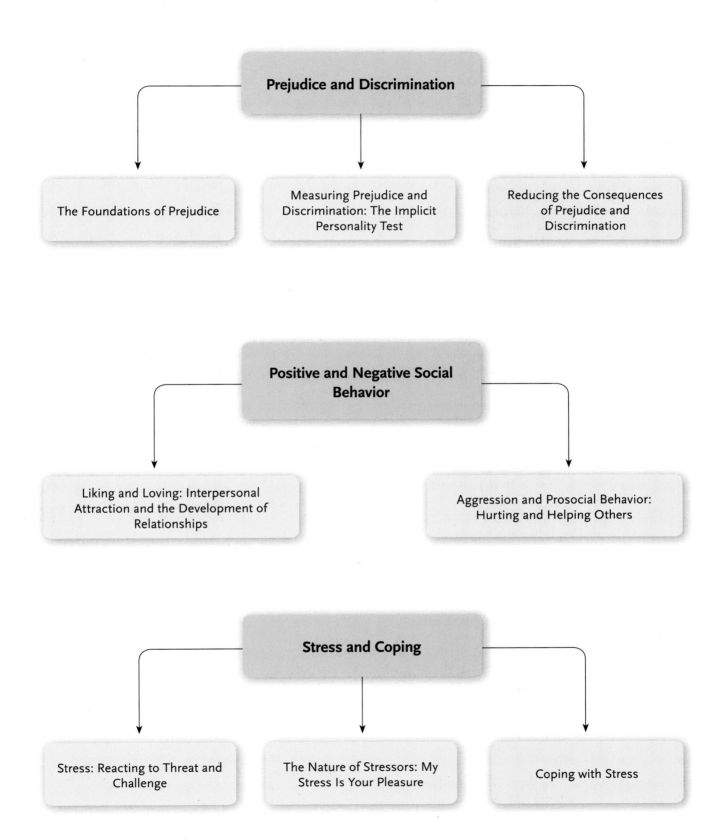

Prejudice and Discrimination

- The Foundations of Prejudice
- Measuring Prejudice and Discrimination: The Implicit Personality Test
- Reducing the Consequences of Prejudice and Discrimination

Positive and Negative Social Behavior

- Liking and Loving: Interpersonal Attraction and the Development of Relationships
- Aggression and Prosocial Behavior: Hurting and Helping Others

Stress and Coping

- Stress: Reacting to Threat and Challenge
- The Nature of Stressors: My Stress Is Your Pleasure
- Coping with Stress

GLOSSARY

abnormal behavior Behavior that causes people to experience distress (hardship) and prevents them from functioning in their daily lives (Module 33)

absolute threshold The smallest intensity (force) of a stimulus (*see glossary definition*) that must be present for the stimulus to be detected (Module 8)

action potential An electric nerve impulse (stimulation) that travels through a neuron (nerve cell) when it is set off by a "trigger," changing the neuron's charge from negative to positive (Module 5)

activation-synthesis theory J. Allan Hobson's theory that the brain produces random (no pattern) electrical energy during REM (rapid eye movement) sleep that stimulates memories lodged in various portions of the brain (Module 12)

activity theory of aging A theory (proposition or idea) that suggests that the elderly who are more successful while aging are those who maintain the interests and activities they had during middle age (Module 28)

adaptation An adjustment in sensory capacity (space or room) after prolonged exposure to unchanging stimuli (stimulus) (Module 8)

addictive drugs Drugs that produce a biological or psychological dependence (reliance) in the user so that withdrawal from them leads to a craving for the drug that, in some cases, may be nearly irresistible (Module 14)

adolescence The developmental (growth) stage between childhood and adulthood (Module 27)

age of viability The point at which a fetus (developing human—*see glossary definition*) can survive if born prematurely (early) (Module 25)

aggression The intentional (on purpose) injury of, or harm to, another person (Module 42)

algorithm A rule that, if applied appropriately (properly), guarantees a solution to a problem (Module 20)

all-or-none law The rule that neurons (nerve cells) are either on or off (Module 5)

altruism Helping behavior that is beneficial to others but clearly requires self-sacrifice (Module 42)

Alzheimer's disease A progressive (advancing) brain disorder that leads to a gradual and irreversible (not reversible) decline in cognitive (thinking) abilities (Module 28)

anal stage According to Sigmund Freud, a stage from age 12 to 18 months to 3 years of age, in which a child's pleasure is centered on the anus (Module 29)

androgens Male sex hormones secreted by the testes (testicles) (Module 23)

anorexia nervosa A severe eating disorder in which people may refuse to eat while denying that their behavior and appearance—which can become skeleton-like—are unusual (Module 23)

antianxiety drugs Drugs that reduce the level of anxiety (unease, nervousness) a person experiences, essentially (basically) by reducing excitability (easily stimulated) and increasing feelings of well-being (Module 38)

antidepressant drugs Medications that improve a severely depressed patient's mood and feeling of well-being (Module 38)

antipsychotic drugs Drugs that temporarily reduce psychotic (loss of reality) symptoms such as agitation, hallucinations (false perception), and delusions (false belief) (Module 38)

antisocial personality disorder A disorder (illness) in which individuals show no regard for the moral and ethical rules of society or the rights of others (Module 34)

anxiety disorder The occurrence (happening) of anxiety (unease, nervousness) without an obvious external cause, affecting daily functioning (Module 34)

archetypes According to Carl Jung, universal symbolic representations (images) of a particular person, object, or experience (such as good and evil) (Module 29)

archival research Research in which existing data (information), such as census documents, college records, and newspaper clippings, are examined to test a hypothesis (Module 3)

arousal approaches to motivation The belief that we try to maintain certain levels of stimulation and activity, increasing or reducing them as necessary (Module 22)

association areas One of the major regions of the cerebral cortex (*see glossary definition*); the site of the higher mental processes, such as thought, language, memory, and speech (Module 7)

assumed-similarity bias The tendency to think of people as being similar to oneself, even when meeting them for the first time (Module 39)

attachment The positive emotional bond that develops between a child and a particular individual (Module 26)

attention-deficit hyperactivity disorder (ADHD) A disorder (illness) marked by inattention, impulsiveness (acting on urges), a low tolerance for frustration, and a great deal of inappropriate (improper) activity (Module 34)

attitudes Evaluations of a particular person, behavior, belief, or concept (Module 39)

attribution theory The theory of personality (*see glossary definition*) that seeks to explain how we decide, on the basis of samples of an individual's behavior, what the specific causes of that person's behavior are (Module 39)

authoritarian parents Parents who are rigid and punitive (disciplinary) and value unquestioning obedience from their children (Module 26)

authoritative parents Parents who are firm, set clear limits, reason with their children, and explain things to them (Module 26)

autism A severe developmental disability that impairs children's ability to communicate and relate to others (Module 34)

autobiographical memories Our recollections of circumstances and episodes (events) from our own lives (Module 19)

autonomic division The part of the peripheral nervous system (*see glossary definition*) that controls involuntary movement of the heart, glands, lungs, and other organs (Module 6)

autonomy-versus-shame-and-doubt stage The period which, according to Erik Erikson, toddlers (ages 1½ to 3 years) develop independence and autonomy (self-rule) if exploration and freedom are encouraged, or shame and self-doubt if they are restricted and overprotected (Module 26)

aversive conditioning A form of therapy that reduces the frequency of undesired behavior by pairing an aversive (disliked), unpleasant stimulus (*see glossary definition*) with undesired behavior (Module 36)

axon The part of the neuron (nerve cell) that carries messages destined for other neurons (Module 5)

babble Meaningless speechlike sounds made by children from around the age of 3 months through 1 year (Module 21)

background stressors ("daily hassles") Everyday annoyances, such as being stuck in traffic, that cause minor irritations and may have long-term ill effects if they continue or are compounded by other stressful events (Module 43)

basilar membrane A vibrating structure that runs through the center of the cochlea (*see glossary definition*), dividing it into an upper chamber and a lower chamber and containing sense receptors (receivers) for sound (Module 10)

behavior modification A formalized (formal) technique for promoting the frequency (occurrence) of desirable behaviors and decreasing the incidence (rate) of unwanted ones (Module 16)

behavioral assessment Direct measures of an individual's behavior used to describe personality (*see glossary definition*) characteristics (Module 31)

behavioral genetics The study of the effects of heredity (inherited) on behavior (Module 6)

behavioral neuroscientists (or biopsychologists) Psychologists who specialize in considering the ways in which the biological structures and functions of the body affect behavior (Module 5)

behavioral perspective The approach that suggests that observable, measurable behavior should be the focus of study (Module 2)

behavioral perspective on psychological disorders The perspective (view) that looks at the behavior itself as the problem (Module 33)

behavioral treatment approaches Treatment approaches that build on the basic processes of learning, such as reinforcement and extinction (*see glossary definitions*), and assume that normal and abnormal (unusual) behavior are both learned (Module 36)

biofeedback A procedure in which a person learns to control through conscious thought internal physiological processes such as blood pressure, heart and respiration rate, skin temperature, sweating, and the constriction (tightening) of particular muscles (Module 7)

biological and evolutionary approaches to personality Theories that suggest that important components (parts) of personality (*see glossary definition*) are inherited (Module 30)

biomedical therapy Therapy that relies on drugs and other medical procedures to improve psychological functioning (Module 36)

biopsychologists *See* behavioral neuroscientists (Module 5)

bipolar disorder A disorder (illness) in which a person alternates between periods of euphoric (elated, joyous) feelings of mania (excited, intense) and periods of depression (Module 34)

bisexuals Persons who are sexually attracted to people of the same sex and the other sex (Module 23)

borderline personality disorder A disorder (illness) in which individuals have difficulty developing a secure sense of who they are (Module 34)

bottom-up processing Perception that consists of the progression of recognizing and processing information from individual components (parts) of a stimuli (stimulus) and moving to the perception (*see glossary definition*) of the whole (Module 11)

bulimia An eating disorder (illness) in which a person binges (gorges) on large quantities of food, followed by efforts to purge the food through vomiting or other means (Module 23)

Cannon-Bard theory of emotion The belief that both physiological arousal and emotional experience are produced simultaneously (at the same time) by the same nerve stimulus (*see glossary definition*) (Module 24)

case study An in-depth, intensive investigation of an individual or small group of people (Module 3)

cataclysmic events Strong stressors that occur suddenly, affecting many people at once (e.g., natural disasters) (Module 43)

catharsis The process of discharging built-up aggressive (hostile) energy (Module 42)

central core The "old brain," which controls basic functions such as eating and sleeping and is common to all vertebrates (Module 7)

central nervous system (CNS) The part of the nervous system that includes the brain and spinal cord (Module 6)

central route processing Message interpretation characterized by thoughtful consideration of the issues and arguments used to persuade (Module 39)

central traits The major traits considered in forming impressions of others (Module 39)

cerebellum (ser uh BELL um) The part of the brain that controls bodily balance (Module 7)

cerebral cortex The "new brain," responsible for the most sophisticated information processing in the brain; contains four lobes (Module 7)

chromosomes Rod-shaped structures that contain all basic hereditary (inherited) information (Module 25)

chunk A meaningful grouping of stimuli (stimulus) that can be stored as a unit in short-term memory (Module 18)

circadian rhythms Biological processes that occur regularly on approximately a 24-hour cycle (Module 12)

classical conditioning A type of learning in which a neutral stimulus (*see glossary definition*) comes to bring about a response after it is paired with a stimulus that naturally brings about that response (Module 15)

cochlea (KOKE lee uh) A coiled tube in the ear filled with fluid that vibrates in response to sound (Module 10)

cognitive approaches to motivation Theories suggesting that motivation is a product of people's thoughts, expectations, and goals—their cognitions (Module 22)

cognitive-behavioral approach A treatment approach that incorporates basic principles of learning to change the way people think (Module 36)

cognitive development The process by which a child's understanding of the world changes as a function (role) of age and experience (Module 26)

cognitive dissonance The conflict that occurs when a person holds two contradictory (different) attitudes or thoughts (referred to as *cognitions*) (Module 39)

cognitive learning theory An approach to the study of learning that focuses on the thought processes that underlie learning (Module 17)

cognitive perspective The approach that focuses on how people think, understand, and know about the world (Module 2)

cognitive perspective on psychological disorders The perspective (view) that suggests that people's thoughts and beliefs are a central component (part) of abnormal (irregular) behavior (Module 33)

cognitive psychology The branch of psychology that focuses on the study of higher mental processes, including thinking, language, memory, problem solving, knowing, reasoning, judging, and decision making (Module 18)

cognitive treatment approaches Treatment approaches that teach people to think in more adaptive (different) ways by changing their dysfunctional (improper) cognitions (thoughts) about the world and themselves (Module 36)

collective unconscious According to Carl Jung, a common set of ideas, feelings, images, and symbols that we inherit from our ancestors, the whole human race, and even nonhuman ancestors from the distant past (Module 29)

community psychology A branch of psychology that focuses on the prevention and minimization (making smaller) of psychological disorders (illnesses) in the community (Module 38)

companionate love The strong affection we have for those with whom our lives are deeply involved (Module 42)

compliance Behavior that occurs in response to direct social pressure (Module 40)

compulsion An irresistible urge to carry out some act that seems strange or unreasonable (Module 34)

concepts Categorizations (organization) of objects, events, or people that share common properties (Module 20)

concrete operational stage According to Jean Piaget, the period from 7 to 12 years of age that is characterized by logical (rational) thought and a loss of egocentrism (selfishness) (Module 26)

conditioned response (CR) A response (reaction) that, after conditioning, follows a previously (before) neutral stimulus (*see glossary definition*) (e.g., salivation at the ringing of a bell) (Module 15)

conditioned stimulus (CS) A once-neutral stimulus (*see glossary definition*) that has been paired with an unconditioned stimulus to bring about a response formerly caused only by the unconditioned stimulus (Module 15)

cones Cone-shaped, light-sensitive receptor (receiving) cells in the retina (*see glossary definition*) that are responsible for sharp focus and color perception (*see glossary definition*), particularly in bright light (Module 9)

conformity A change in behavior or attitudes brought about by a desire to follow the beliefs or standards of other people (Module 40)

consciousness The awareness of sensations, thoughts, and feelings being experienced at a given moment (Module 12)

constructive processes Processes in which memories are influenced by the meaning we give to events (Module 19)

continuous reinforcement schedule Reinforcing (*see glossary definition*) of a behavior every time it occurs (Module 16)

control group A group participating in an experiment that receives no treatment (Module 3)

conversion disorder A major somatoform disorder (*see glossary definition*) that involves an actual physical disturbance (trouble), such as the inability to use a sensory (sense) organ or the complete or partial inability to move an arm or a leg (Module 34)

coping The efforts to control, reduce, or learn to tolerate (handle) the threats that lead to stress (Module 43)

correlational research Research in which the relationship between two sets of variables is examined to determine whether they are associated, or "correlated" (Module 3)

cross-sectional research A research method that compares people of different ages at the same point in time (Module 25)

crystallized intelligence The accumulation (gathering) of information, skills, and strategies that are learned through experience and can be applied in problem-solving situations (Module 32)

cue-dependent forgetting Forgetting that occurs when there are insufficient (not enough) retrieval cues to rekindle information that is in memory (Module 19)

culture-fair IQ test A test that does not discriminate (show favoritism) against the members of any minority group (Module 32)

daily hassles *See* background stressors (Module 43)

decay The loss of information in memory through its nonuse (Module 19)

declarative memory Memory for factual information: names, faces, dates, and the like (Module 18)

defense mechanisms In Freudian theory, unconscious (*see glossary definition*) strategies (plans or ideas) that people use to reduce anxiety (unease, nervousness) by concealing (hide or mask) the source of the anxiety from themselves and others (Module 29)

deinstitutionalization The transfer of former mental patients from institutions (place of care, hospital) to the community (Module 38)

dendrites A cluster of fibers at one end of a neuron (nerve cell) that receive messages from other neurons (Module 5)

dependent variable The variable (*see glossary definition*) that is measured and is expected to change as a result of changes caused by the experimenter's manipulation (handling) of the independent variable (Module 3)

depressants Drugs that slow down the nervous system (Module 14)

depth perception The ability to view the world in three dimensions (lifelike aspects) and to perceive distance (Module 11)

descriptive research An approach to research designed to systematically (scientifically) investigate a person, group, or patterns of behavior (Module 3)

determinism The idea that people's behavior is produced primarily (mostly) by factors outside of their willful control (Module 2)

developmental psychology The branch of psychology that studies the patterns of growth and change that occur throughout life (Module 25)

Diagnostic and Statistical Manual of Mental Disorders®, Fourth Edition, Text Revision **(DSM-IV-TR)** A system, devised (created) by the American Psychiatric Association, used by most professionals to diagnose and classify abnormal (unusual) behavior (Module 33)

dialectical behavior therapy A form of treatment in which the focus is on getting people to accept who they are, regardless of whether it matches their ideal (Module 36)

difference threshold (just noticeable difference) The smallest level of added or reduced stimulation required to sense that a change in stimulation has occurred (Module 8)

diffusion of responsibility The tendency for people to feel that responsibility for acting is shared, or diffused (spread), among those present (Module 42)

discrimination Behavior directed toward individuals on the basis of their membership in a particular group (Module 41)

disengagement theory of aging A theory that suggests that aging produces a gradual withdrawal from the world on physical, psychological, and social levels (Module 28)

dispositional causes (of behavior) Perceived (seeming) causes of behavior that are based on internal traits or personality (*see glossary definition*) factors (Module 39)

dissociative amnesia A disorder (illness) in which a significant (major), selective memory loss occurs (Module 34)

dissociative disorders Psychological dysfunctions (disturbance) characterized by the separation of different facets of a person's personality that are normally integrated (combined) (Module 34)

dissociative fugue A form of amnesia in which the individual leaves home and sometimes assumes a new identity (Module 34)

dissociative identity disorder (DID) A disorder (illness) in which a person displays (shows) characteristics (features) of two or more distinct (separate) personalities; also called *multiple personality disorder* (Module 34)

double standard The view that premarital sex is permissible (acceptable) for males but not for females (Module 23)

dreams-for-survival theory The theory suggesting that dreams permit information that is critical for our daily survival to be reconsidered and reprocessed (rethought) during sleep (Module 12)

drive Motivational tension, or arousal, that energizes (makes active) behavior to fulfill a need (Module 22)

drive-reduction approaches to motivation Theories suggesting that a lack of a basic biological requirement such as water produces a drive to obtain that requirement (in this case, the thirst drive) (Module 22)

drug therapy Control of psychological disorders (illness) through the use of drugs (Module 38)

eardrum The part of the ear that vibrates when sound hits it (Module 10)

ego The part of the personality (*see glossary definition*) that provides a buffer (cushion) between the id and the outside world (Module 29)

egocentric thought A way of thinking in which a child views the world entirely from his or her own perspective (point of view) (Module 26)

ego-integrity-versus-despair stage According to Erik Erikson, a period from late adulthood until death during which we review life's accomplishments and failures (Module 27)

electroconvulsive therapy (ECT) A procedure used in the treatment of severe depression in which an electric current of 70 to 150 volts is briefly administered (applied) to a patient's head (Module 38)

embryo A developed zygote (*see glossary definition*) that has a heart, a brain, and other organs (Module 25)

emotional intelligence The set of skills that underlie the accurate assessment, evaluation, expression, and regulation of emotions (Module 32)

emotions Feelings that generally have both physiological (physical) and cognitive (thinking, processing) elements and that influence behavior (Module 24)

endocrine system A chemical communication network that sends messages throughout the body via the bloodstream (Module 6)

episodic memory Memory for events that occur in a particular time, place, or context (Module 18)

estrogens Class of female sex hormones (Module 23)

evolutionary psychology The branch of psychology that seeks to identify behavior patterns that are a result of our genetic inheritance from our ancestors (Module 6)

excitatory messages Chemical messages that make it more likely that a receiving neuron (nerve cell) will fire and an action potential will travel down its axon (*see glossary definition*) (Module 5)

experiment The investigation of the relationship between two (or more) variables (*see glossary definition*) by deliberately (on purpose) producing a change in one variable in a situation and observing the effects of that change on other aspects of the situation (Module 3)

experimental bias Factors that distort (alter) how the independent variable affects the dependent variable in an experiment (Module 4)

experimental group Any group participating in an experiment (*see glossary definition*) that receives a treatment (Module 3)

experimental manipulation The change that an experimenter deliberately (on purpose) produces in a situation (Module 3)

explicit memory Intentional or conscious recollection (remembering) of information (Module 19)

exposure A behavioral treatment for anxiety (unease, nervousness) in which people are confronted, either suddenly or gradually, with a stimulus (*see glossary definition*) that they fear (Module 36)

extinction A basic phenomenon (event, incident) of learning that occurs when a previously conditioned response (*see glossary definition*) decreases in frequency and eventually disappears (Module 15)

extramarital sex Sexual activity between a married person and someone who is not his or her spouse (Module 23)

facial-affect program Activation of a set of nerve impulses that make the face display the appropriate expression (Module 24)

facial-feedback hypothesis The hypothesis that facial expressions not only reflect emotional experience but also help determine how people experience and label emotions (Module 24)

familial retardation Mental retardation in which no apparent biological defect exists, but there is a history of retardation in the family (Module 32)

family therapy An approach that focuses on the family and its dynamics (relationships) (Module 37)

feature detection The activation (turning on) of neurons (nerve cells) in the cortex by visual stimuli (stimulus) of specific shapes or patterns (Module 9)

fetal alcohol syndrome The most common cause of mental retardation in newborns, occurring (happening) when the mother uses alcohol during pregnancy (Module 32)

fetus A developing individual, from eight weeks after conception until birth (Module 25)

fixations Conflicts or concerns that persist (continue) beyond the developmental period in which they first occur (Module 29)

fixed-interval schedule A schedule that provides reinforcement (*see glossary definition*) for a response only if a fixed time period has elapsed, making overall rates of response relatively low (Module 16)

fixed-ratio schedule A schedule by which reinforcement (*see glossary definition*) is given only after a specific number of responses are made (Module 16)

flashbulb memories Memories centered on a specific, important, or surprising event that are so vivid it is as if they represented a snapshot of the event (Module 19)

fluid intelligence Intelligence that reflects information-processing capabilities, reasoning, and memory (Module 32)

formal operational stage According to Jean Piaget, the period from age 12 to adulthood that is characterized by abstract thought (Module 26)

free will The idea that behavior is caused primarily (mainly) by choices that are made freely by the individual (Module 2)

functional fixedness The tendency (trend) to think of an object only in terms of its typical use (Module 20)

functionalism An early approach to psychology that concentrated on what the mind does—the functions of mental activity—and the role of behavior in allowing people to adapt (adjust) to their environments (Module 2)

fundamental attribution error A tendency to overattribute others' behavior to dispositional (personality, system) causes and the corresponding minimization of the importance of situational causes (Module 39)

g or g-factor The single, general factor for mental ability assumed to underlie intelligence in some early theories of intelligence (Module 32)

gate-control theory of pain The theory that particular nerve receptors (receivers) lead to specific areas of the brain related to pain (Module 10)

general adaptation syndrome (GAS) A theory developed by Hans Selye that suggests that a person's response to a stressor (something that causes stress) consists of three stages: alarm and mobilization, resistance, and exhaustion (Module 43)

generalized anxiety disorder The experience of long-term, persistent (continuing) anxiety (unease, nervousness) and worry (Module 34)

generativity-versus-stagnation stage According to Erik Erikson, a period in middle adulthood during which we take stock of our contributions to family and society (Module 27)

genes The parts of the chromosomes (*see glossary definition*) through which genetic information is transmitted (Module 25)

genetic preprogramming theories of aging Theories that suggest that human cells have a built-in time limit to their reproduction, and that after a certain time they are no longer able to divide (Module 28)

genital stage According to Sigmund Freud, the period from puberty until death, marked by mature sexual behavior (i.e., sexual intercourse) (Module 29)

genitals The male and female sex organs (Module 23)

gestalt (geh SHTALLT) laws of organization A series of principles that describe how we organize bits and pieces of information into meaningful wholes (Module 11)

gestalt psychology An approach to psychology that focuses on the organization of perception (*see glossary definition*) and thinking in a "whole" sense rather than on the individual elements of perception (Module 2)

group therapy Therapy in which people meet with a therapist to discuss problems with a group (Module 37)

habituation The decrease in response to a stimulus (*see glossary definition*) that occurs after repeated presentations of the same stimulus (Module 15)

hair cells Tiny cells covering the basilar membrane (part of the inner ear) that, when bent by vibrations entering the cochlea (*see glossary definition*), transmit neural messages to the brain (Module 10)

hallucinogen A drug that is capable of producing hallucinations, or changes in the perceptual process (Module 14)

halo effect A phenomenon (event) in which an initial understanding that a person has positive traits is used to infer other uniformly positive characteristics (Module 39)

hemispheres Symmetrical (balanced, proportioned) left and right halves of the brain that control the side of the body opposite to their location (Module 7)

heritability A measure of the degree to which a characteristic (defined feature) is related to genetic, inherited factors (Module 32)

heterosexuality Sexual attraction and behavior directed to the other sex (Module 23)

heuristic A cognitive (thought process) shortcut that may lead to a solution (Module 20)

homeostasis The body's tendency to maintain a steady internal state (Module 22)

homosexuals Persons who are sexually attracted to members of their own sex (Module 23)

hormones Chemicals that circulate through the blood and regulate the functioning or growth of the body (Module 6)

humanistic approaches to personality Theories that emphasize people's innate goodness and desire to achieve higher levels of functioning (performance) (Module 30)

humanistic perspective The approach that suggests that all individuals naturally strive to grow, develop, and be in control of their lives and behavior (Module 2)

humanistic perspective on psychological disorders The perspective (view) that emphasizes the responsibility people have for their own behavior, even when such behavior is abnormal (unusual) (Module 33)

humanistic therapy Therapy in which the underlying rationale (foundation) is that people have control of their behavior, can make choices about their lives, and are essentially (basically) responsible for solving their own problems (Module 37)

hypnosis A trancelike state of heightened susceptibility (openness) to the suggestions of others (Module 13)

hypochondriasis A disorder (illness) in which people have a constant fear of illness and a preoccupation (concern) with their health (Module 34)

hypothalamus A tiny part of the brain, located below the thalamus (*see glossary definition*), that maintains homeostasis (balance) and produces and regulates vital (essential) behavior, such as eating, drinking, and sexual behavior (Module 7)

hypothesis A prediction, stemming from a theory (supposition), stated in way that allows it to be tested (Module 3)

id The raw, unorganized, inborn part of personality (*see glossary definition*) whose sole purpose is to reduce tension created by primitive (ancient) drives related to hunger, sex, aggression, and irrational (unreasonable) impulses (Module 29)

identical twins Twins who are exactly the same genetically (inherited) (Module 25)

identification The process of wanting to be like another person as much as possible, imitating that person's behavior and adopting (take on) similar beliefs and values (Module 29)

identity The distinguishing (unique) character of the individual: who each of us is, what our roles are, and what we are capable of (Module 27)

identity-versus-role-confusion stage According to Erik Erikson, a time in adolescence of major testing to determine one's unique qualities (Module 27)

implicit memory Memories of which people are not consciously aware, but which can affect subsequent (following) performance and behavior (Module 19)

incentive approaches to motivation Theories suggesting that motivation (*see glossary definition*) stems (comes) from the desire to obtain valued external goals, or incentives (Module 22)

independent variable The variable that is manipulated (controlled) by an experimenter (Module 3)

industrial-organizational (I/O) psychology The branch of psychology focusing on work and job-related issues, including worker motivation, satisfaction, safety, and productivity (Module 40)

industry-versus-inferiority stage According to Erik Erikson, the last stage of childhood, during which children age 6 to 12 years may develop positive social interactions (exchanges) with others or may feel inadequate (not good enough, lacking) and become less sociable (friendly) (Module 26)

inferiority complex According to Alfred Adler, a problem affecting (influencing) adults who have not been able to overcome the feelings of inferiority (not good enough) that they developed as children, when they were small and limited in their knowledge about the world (Module 29)

information processing The way in which people take in, use, and store information (Module 26)

informed consent A document signed by participants affirming (confirming) that they have been told the basic outlines of the study and are aware of what their participation will involve (Module 4)

inhibitory messages Chemical messages that prevent or decrease the likelihood that a receiving neuron (nerve cell) will fire (Module 5)

initiative-versus-guilt stage According to Erik Erikson, the period during which children ages 3 to 6 years experience conflict between independence (self-rule) of action and the sometimes negative results of that action (Module 26)

instincts Inborn patterns of behavior that are biologically (naturally) determined (fixed, inborn) rather than learned (Module 22)

intellectual disability Another term for mental retardation (Module 32)

intellectually gifted The 2 to 4 percent of the population who have IQ scores greater than 130 (Module 32)

intelligence The capacity to understand the world, think rationally, and use resources effectively when faced with challenges (Module 32)

intelligence quotient (IQ) A score that takes into account an individual's mental and chronological (in order, physical age) ages (Module 32)

intelligence tests Tests devised to quantify (measure) a person's level of intelligence (Module 32)

interactionist approach to language development The view that language development is produced through a combination of genetically determined predispositions and environmental circumstances that help teach language (Module 21)

interference The phenomenon (event) by which information in memory disrupts the recall of other information (Module 19)

interneurons Neurons (nerve cells) that connect sensory (sensations) and motor neurons, carrying messages between the two (Module 6)

interpersonal attraction (or close relationship) Positive feelings for others; liking and loving (Module 42)

interpersonal therapy (IPT) Short-term therapy that focuses on the context (situation) of current social relationships (Module 37)

intimacy-versus-isolation stage According to Erik Erikson, a period during early adulthood that focuses on developing close relationships (Module 27)

introspection A procedure used to study the structure of the mind in which subjects are asked to describe in detail what they are experiencing when they are exposed to a stimulus (*see glossary definition*) (Module 2)

James-Lange theory of emotion The belief that emotional experience is a reaction to bodily events occurring as a result of an external situation ("I feel sad because I am crying") (Module 24)

just noticeable difference *See* difference threshold (Module 8)

language The communication of information through symbols arranged according to systematic rules (Module 21)

language-acquisition device A neural (nerve) system of the brain hypothesized (*see* hypothesis) by Noam Chomsky to permit understanding of language (Module 21)

latency period According to Sigmund Freud, the period between the phallic stage and puberty during which children's sexual concerns are temporarily put aside (Module 29)

latent content of dreams According to Sigmund Freud, the "disguised" meaning of dreams, hidden by more obvious subjects (Module 12)

latent learning Learning in which a new behavior is acquired (obtained) but is not demonstrated until some incentive (motivation) is provided for displaying it (Module 17)

lateralization The dominance (control) of one hemisphere (side—*see* hemispheres) of the brain in specific functions, such as language (Module 7)

learned helplessness A state in which people conclude that unpleasant or aversive stimuli (stimulus) cannot be controlled—a view of the world that becomes so ingrained (fixed) that they cease trying to remedy the aversive (unpleasant) circumstances, even if they actually can exert some influence (Module 43)

learning A relatively permanent change in behavior brought about by experience (Module 15)

learning-theory approach to language development The theory suggesting that language acquisition (gaining) follows the principles of reinforcement (*see glossary definitions*) and conditioning (Module 21)

levels-of-processing theory The theory of memory that emphasizes (stresses) the degree to which new material is mentally analyzed (Module 19)

life review The process by which people examine and evaluate their lives (Module 28)

limbic system The part of the brain that controls eating, aggression (hostility), and reproduction (Module 7)

linguistic-relativity hypothesis The notion that language shapes and may determine the way people in a particular culture perceive (see) and understand the world (Module 21)

lobes The four major sections of the cerebral cortex (*see glossary definition*): frontal, parietal, temporal, and occipital (Module 7)

longitudinal research A research method that investigates behavior as participants age (Module 25)

long-term memory Memory that stores information on a relatively permanent basis, although it may be difficult to retrieve (Module 18)

major depression A severe form of depression that interferes with concentration (focus), decision making, and sociability (interaction with others) (Module 34)

mania An extended state of intense (strong), wild elation (Module 34)

manifest content of dreams According to Sigmund Freud, the apparent story line of dreams (Module 12)

masturbation Sexual self-stimulation (Module 23)

means-ends analysis Repeated testing for differences between the desired outcome and what currently exists (Module 20)

medical perspective on psychological disorders The perspective (view) that suggests that when an individual displays symptoms of abnormal (unusual) behavior, the root cause will be found in a physical examination of the individual, which may reveal a hormonal imbalance, a chemical deficiency (lacking), or a brain injury (Module 33)

meditation A learned technique for refocusing attention that brings about an altered state of consciousness (Module 13)

memory The process by which we encode (program), store, and retrieve (call back) information (Module 18)

menopause The period during which women stop menstruating and are no longer fertile (Module 28)

mental age The average age of individuals who achieve a particular level of performance on a test (Module 32)

mental images Representations (visual pictures) in the mind that resemble the object or event being represented (Module 20)

mental retardation A condition characterized by significant limitations both in intellectual functioning and in conceptual (*see* concept), social, and practical adaptive (adjustable) skills (Module 32)

mental set The tendency for old patterns of problem solving to persist (keep on) (Module 20)

metabolism The rate at which food is converted (changed) to energy and expended (used) by the body (Module 23)

metacognition An awareness and understanding of one's own cognitive (thinking) processes (Module 26)

Minnesota Multiphasic Personality Inventory-2 (MMPI-2) A widely used self-report test that identifies people with psychological difficulties and is employed to predict some everyday behaviors (Module 31)

mirror neurons Neurons (nerve cells) that fire when a person enacts a particular behavior and also when a person views others' behavior (Module 5)

mood disorders Disturbances (illness) in emotional experience that are strong enough to intrude (interrupt) on everyday living (Module 34)

mood stabilizers Drugs used to treat mood disorders that prevent manic episodes of bipolar disorder (Module 38)

motivation The factors that direct and energize the behavior of humans and other organisms (Module 22)

motor area The part of the cortex that is largely responsible for the body's voluntary movement (Module 7)

motor (efferent) neurons Neurons (nerve cells) that communicate information from the nervous system to muscles and glands (Module 6)

multiple personality disorder *See* dissociative identity disorder (Module 34)

myelin sheath A protective coat of fat and protein that wraps around the neuron (nerve cell) (Module 5)

narcissistic personality disorder A personality (*see glossary definition*) disturbance characterized by an exaggerated (inflated) sense of self-importance (Module 34)

narcotics Drugs that increase relaxation and relieve pain and anxiety (unease, nervousness) (Module 14)

nativist approach to language development The theory that a genetically determined, innate mechanism directs language development (Module 21)

naturalistic observation Research in which an investigator simply observes some naturally occurring (happening) behavior and does not make a change in the situation (Module 3)

nature-nurture issue The issue of the degree to which environment (surroundings) and heredity (inherited) influence behavior (Module 25)

need for achievement A stable, learned characteristic in which a person obtains satisfaction by striving for and attaining (reaching) a level of excellence (Module 23)

need for affiliation An interest in establishing and maintaining relationships with other people (Module 23)

need for power A tendency to seek impact, control, or influence over others, and to be seen as a powerful individual (Module 23)

negative reinforcer An unpleasant stimulus (*see glossary definition*) whose *removal* leads to an increase in the probability that a preceding response will be repeated in the future (Module 16)

neo-Freudian psychoanalysts Psychoanalysts who were trained in traditional Freudian theory but who later rejected some of its major points (Module 29)

neonate A newborn child (Module 26)

neurons Nerve cells, the basic elements of the nervous system (Module 5)

neuroplasticity Changes in the brain that occur throughout the life span relating to the addition of new neurons (nerve cell), new interconnections (relationships) between neurons, and the reorganization of information-processing areas (Module 7)

neuroscience perspective The approach that views behavior from the perspective (view) of the brain, the nervous system, and other biological functions (Module 2)

neurotransmitters Chemicals that carry messages across the synapse (*see glossary definition*) to the dendrite (and sometimes the cell body) of a receiver neuron (nerve cell) (Module 5)

neutral stimulus A stimulus (*see glossary definition*) that, before conditioning, does not naturally bring about the response of interest (Module 15)

obedience A change in behavior in response to the commands of others (Module 40)

obesity Body weight that is more than 20 percent above the average weight for a person of a particular height (Module 23)

object permanence The awareness that objects—and people—continue to exist even if they are out of sight (Module 26)

observational learning Learning by observing the behavior of another person, or model (Module 17)

obsession A persistent (constant), unwanted thought or idea that keeps recurring (returning) (Module 34)

obsessive-compulsive disorder A disorder (illness) characterized by obsessions (fascination) or compulsions (compelling) (Module 34)

Oedipal conflict A child's sexual interest in his or her opposite-sex parent, typically resolved through identification with the same-sex parent (Module 29)

operant conditioning Learning in which a voluntary response is strengthened or weakened, depending on its favorable or unfavorable consequences (result) (Module 16)

operational definition The translation of a hypothesis (*see glossary definition*) into specific, testable procedures that can be measured and observed (Module 3)

opponent-process theory of color vision The theory that receptor (receiving) cells for color are linked in pairs, working in opposition (opposite) to each other (Module 9)

optic nerve A bundle of ganglion axons (*see glossary definition*) that carry visual information to the brain (Module 9)

oral stage According to Sigmund Freud, a stage from birth to age 12 to 18 months, in which an infant's center of pleasure is the mouth (Module 29)

overgeneralization The phenomenon (event, process) by which children apply language rules even when the application results in an error (Module 21)

ovulation The point at which an egg is released from the ovaries (Module 23)

panic disorder Anxiety (unease, nervousness) disorder (illness) that takes the form of panic attacks lasting from a few seconds to as long as several hours (Module 34)

parasympathetic division The part of the autonomic (automatic) division of the nervous system that acts to calm the body after an emergency or a stressful situation has ended (Module 6)

partial (or intermittent) reinforcement schedule Reinforcing of a behavior some but not all of the time (Module 16)

passionate (or romantic) love A state of intense absorption (interest) in someone that includes intense physiological (body's processes) arousal, psychological interest, and caring for the needs of another (Module 42)

perception The sorting out, interpretation, analysis, and integration (combining) of stimuli by the sense organs and brain (Module 8)

peripheral nervous system The part of the nervous system that includes the autonomic (automatic) and somatic (bodily) subdivisions; made up of neurons with long axons and dendrites (*see glossary definitions*), it branches out from the spinal cord and brain and reaches the extremities (outer parts) of the body (Module 6)

peripheral route processing Message interpretation characterized by consideration of the source and related general information rather than of the message itself (Module 39)

permissive parents Parents who give their children relaxed or inconsistent direction and, although they are warm, require little of them (Module 26)

personal stressors Major life events, such as the death of a family member, that have immediate consequences (results) that generally fade with time (Module 43)

personality The pattern of enduring (lasting) characteristics (traits, distinctive) that produce consistency and individuality in a given person (Module 29)

personality disorder A disorder (illness) characterized by a set of inflexible, maladaptive (not adapting) behavior patterns that keep a person from functioning appropriately (properly) in society (Module 34)

person-centered therapy Therapy in which the goal is to reach one's potential for self-actualization (*see glossary definition*) (Module 37)

phallic stage According to Sigmund Freud, a period beginning around age 3 during which a child's pleasure focuses on the genitals (Module 29)

phobia An intense, irrational (unfounded) fear of specific objects or situations (Module 34)

pituitary gland The major component of the endocrine system (*see glossary definition*), or "master gland," which secretes hormones that control growth and other parts of the endocrine system (Module 6)

placebo A false treatment, such as a pill, "drug," or other substance, without any significant (major) chemical properties or active ingredient (Module 4)

positive reinforcer A stimulus (*see glossary definition*) added to the environment (surroundings) that brings about an increase in a preceding response (Module 16)

posttraumatic stress disorder (PTSD) A phenomenon (event) in which victims of major catastrophes (disaster) or strong personal stressors feel long-lasting effects that may include reexperiencing the event in vivid flashbacks or dreams (Module 43)

practical intelligence According to Robert Sternberg, intelligence related to overall success in living (Module 32)

prejudice A negative (or positive) evaluation of a particular group and its members (Module 41)

preoperational stage According to Jean Piaget, the period from 2 to 7 years of age that is characterized by language development (Module 26)

principle of conservation The knowledge that quantity is unrelated to the arrangement and physical appearance of objects (Module 26)

proactive interference Interference (intrusion) in which information learned earlier disrupts the recall of newer material (Module 19)

procedural memory Memory for skills and habits, such as riding a bike or hitting a baseball, sometimes referred to as *nondeclarative memory* (Module 18)

progesterone A female sex hormone secreted by the ovaries (Module 23)

projective personality tests Tests in which a person is shown an ambiguous (unclear) stimulus (*see glossary definition*) and asked to describe it or tell a story about it (Module 31)

prosocial behavior Helping behavior (Module 42)

prototypes Typical, highly representative samples of a concept (*see glossary definition*) (Module 20)

psychoactive drugs Drugs that influence a person's emotions, perceptions (*see glossary definition*), and behavior (Module 14)

psychoanalysis Freudian psychotherapy in which the goal is to release hidden unconscious (*see glossary definition*) thoughts and feelings in order to reduce their power in controlling behavior (Module 36)

psychoanalytic perspective on psychological disorders The perspective (view) that suggests that abnormal (unusual) behavior stems from childhood conflicts over opposing wishes regarding sex and aggression (Module 33)

psychoanalytic theory Sigmund Freud's theory that unconscious (*see glossary definition*) forces act as determinants (cause, source) of personality (*see glossary definition*) (Module 29)

psychodynamic approaches to personality Approaches that assume that personality (*see glossary definition*) is motivated by inner forces and conflicts about which people have little awareness and over which they have no control (Module 29)

psychodynamic perspective The approach based on the view that behavior is motivated by unconscious (*see glossary definition*) inner forces over which the individual has little control (Module 2)

psychodynamic therapy Therapy that seeks to bring unresolved past conflicts and unacceptable impulses from the unconscious (*see glossary definition*) into the conscious, where patients may deal with the problems more effectively (Module 36)

psychological tests Standard measures devised to assess (evaluate) behavior objectively; used by psychologists to help people make decisions about their lives and understand more about themselves (Module 31)

psychology The scientific study of behavior and mental processes (Module 1)

psychoneuroimmunology (PNI) The study of the relationship among psychological factors, the immune system, and the brain (Module 43)

psychophysics The study of the relationship between the physical aspects of stimuli (stimulus) and our psychological experience of them (Module 8)

psychophysiological disorders Medical problems influenced by an interaction of psychological, emotional, and physical difficulties (Module 43)

psychosexual stages Developmental (growth) periods that children pass through during which they encounter conflicts between the demands of society and their own sexual urges (Module 29)

psychosocial development Development of individuals' interactions and understanding of each other and of their knowledge and understanding of themselves as members of society (Module 26)

psychotherapy Treatment in which a trained professional—a therapist—uses psychological techniques to help a person overcome psychological difficulties and disorders (illness), resolve problems in living, or bring about personal growth (Module 36)

puberty The period at which maturation (maturity) of the sexual organs occurs, beginning at about age 11 or 12 for girls and 13 or 14 for boys (Module 27)

punishment A stimulus (*see glossary definition*) that decreases the probability that a previous behavior will occur again (Module 16)

random assignment to condition A procedure in which participants are assigned to different experimental groups or "conditions" on the basis of chance and chance alone (Module 3)

rapid eye movement (REM) sleep Sleep occupying 20 percent of an adult's sleeping time, characterized by increased heart rate, blood pressure, and breathing rate; erections (in males); eye movements; and the experience of dreaming (Module 12)

rational-emotive behavior therapy A form of therapy that attempts to restructure (reorganize) a person's belief system into a more realistic, rational (balanced), and logical set of views by challenging dysfunctional (not functioning) beliefs that maintain irrational behavior (Module 36)

recall Memory task in which specific information must be retrieved (Module 19)

recognition Memory task in which individuals are presented with a stimulus (*see glossary definition*) and asked whether they have been exposed to it in the past or to identify it from a list of alternatives (Module 19)

reflex An automatic, involuntary response to an incoming stimulus (Modules 6, 26)

rehearsal The repetition of information that has entered short-term memory (Module 18)

reinforcement The process by which a stimulus (*see glossary definition*) increases the probability (chance) that a preceding behavior will be repeated (Module 16)

reinforcer Any stimulus (*see glossary definition*) that increases the probability (chance) that a preceding behavior will occur again (Module 16)

replication The repetition of research, sometimes using other procedures, settings, and groups of participants, to increase confidence in prior findings (Module 3)

repression The primary (main) defense mechanism (device, tool) in which unacceptable or unpleasant id (*see glossary definition*) impulses are pushed back into the unconscious (*see glossary definition*) (Module 29)

resting state The state in which there is a negative electrical charge of about -70 millivolts within a neuron (nerve cell) (Module 5)

reticular formation The part of the brain extending from the medulla through the pons and made up of groups of nerve cells that can immediately activate other parts of the brain to produce general bodily arousal (stimulation) (Module 7)

retina The part of the eye that converts the electromagnetic energy of light to electrical impulses for transmission to the brain (Module 9)

retroactive interference Interference (hinderance) in which there is difficulty in the recall of information learned earlier because of later exposure to different material (Module 19)

reuptake The reabsorption of neurotransmitters (*see glossary definition*) by a terminal button (*see glossary definition*) (Module 5)

rods Thin, cylindrical receptor (receiving) cells in the retina that are highly sensitive to light (Module 9)

Rorschach test A test that involves showing a series of symmetrical (balanced, proportional) visual stimuli (stimulus) to people who then are asked what the figures represent to them (Module 31)

Schachter-Singer theory of emotion The belief that emotions are determined jointly by a nonspecific kind of physiological (bodily function) arousal and its interpretation, based on environmental (natural surroundings) cues (Module 24)

schedules of reinforcement Different patterns of frequency (occurrences) and timing of reinforcement (*see glossary definition*) following desired behavior (Module 16)

schemas Organized bodies of information stored in memory that bias (prejudice) the way new information is interpreted, stored, and recalled; sets of cognitions (thoughts) about people and social experiences (Modules 19, 39)

schizophrenia A class of disorders (illness) in which severe distortion (twisting) of reality occurs (Module 34)

scientific method The approach (view) through which psychologists systematically (scientifically) acquire knowledge and understanding about behavior and other phenomena (happenings) of interest (Module 3)

self-actualization A state of self-fulfillment in which people realize their highest potential, each in his or her own unique way (Modules 22, 30)

self-efficacy Belief in one's personal capabilities (abilities). Self-efficacy underlies people's faith in their ability to carry out a particular behavior or produce a desired outcome (Module 30)

self-esteem The component of personality (*see glossary definition*) that encompasses our positive and negative self-evaluations (Module 30)

self-report measures A method of gathering data about people by asking them questions about a sample of their behavior (Module 31)

self-serving bias The tendency (leaning) to attribute (attach) personal success to personal factors (skill, ability, or effort) and to attribute failure to factors outside oneself (Module 39)

semantic memory Memory for general knowledge and facts about the world, as well as memory for the rules of logic that are used to deduce (figure out) other facts (Module 18)

semicircular canals Three tubelike structures of the inner ear containing fluid that sloshes through them when the head moves, signaling rotational (turning) or angular movement to the brain (Module 10)

sensation The activation of the sense organs by a source of physical energy (Module 8)

sensorimotor stage According to Jean Piaget, the stage from birth to 2 years, during which a child has little competence in representing the environment by using images, language, or other symbols (Module 26)

sensory area The site in the brain of the tissue that corresponds to each of the senses, with the degree of sensitivity related to the amount of the tissue allocated (set aside) to that sense (Module 7)

sensory memory The initial (primary), momentary storage of information, lasting only an instant (Module 18)

sensory (afferent) neurons Neurons (nerve cells) that transmit information from the perimeter (outer part) of the body to the central nervous system (*see glossary definition*) (Module 6)

sequential research A research method that combines cross-sectional (representative sample) and longitudinal (long-term) research by considering a number of different age groups and examining them at several points in time (Module 25)

shaping The process of teaching a complex behavior by rewarding closer and closer approximations (similarities) of the desired behavior (Module 16)

short-term memory Memory that holds information for 15 to 25 seconds (Module 18)

situational causes (of behavior) Perceived (apparent) causes of behavior that are based on environmental (surrounding world) factors (Module 39)

skin senses The senses of touch, pressure, temperature, and pain (Module 10)

social cognition The cognitive (thinking) processes by which people understand and make sense of others and themselves (Module 39)

social cognitive approaches to personality Theories that emphasize the influence of a person's cognitions—thoughts, feelings, expectations, and values—as well as observation of others' behavior, in determining personality (*see glossary definition*) (Module 30)

social influence The process by which the actions of an individual or group affect (influence) the behavior of others (Module 40)

social psychology The scientific study of how people's thoughts, feelings, and actions are affected (influenced) by others (Module 39)

social support A mutual network of caring, interested others (Module 43)

sociocultural perspective on psychological disorders The perspective (view) that assumes that people's behavior—both normal and abnormal—is shaped by the kind of family group, society, and culture in which they live (Module 33)

somatic division The part of the peripheral nervous system (*see glossary definition*) that specializes in the control of

voluntary (controlled) movements and the communication of information to and from the sense organs (Module 6)

somatoform disorders Psychological difficulties that take on a physical (somatic) form, but for which there is no medical cause (Module 34)

sound The movement of air molecules brought about by a source of vibration (Module 10)

spinal cord A bundle of neurons (nerve cells) that leaves the brain and runs down the length of the back and is the main means for transmitting messages between the brain and the body (Module 6)

spontaneous recovery The reemergence (reoccurrence) of an extinguished conditioned response (*see glossary definition*) after a period of rest and with no further conditioning (Module 15)

spontaneous remission Recovery without treatment (Module 37)

stage 1 sleep The state of transition between wakefulness and sleep, characterized by relatively rapid, low-amplitude (volume, size) brain waves (Module 12)

stage 2 sleep A sleep deeper than that of stage 1, characterized by a slower, more regular wave pattern, along with momentary interruptions of sleep spindles (Module 12)

stage 3 sleep A sleep characterized by slow brain waves, with greater peaks and valleys in the wave pattern than in stage 2 sleep (Module 12)

stage 4 sleep The deepest stage of sleep, during which we are least responsive to outside stimulation (Module 12)

stereotype A set of generalized (general) beliefs and expectations about a particular group and its members (Module 41)

stimulants Drugs that have an arousal (stimulating) effect on the central nervous system (*see glossary definition*), causing a rise in heart rate, blood pressure, and muscular tension (Module 14)

stimulus Energy that produces a response in a sense organ (Module 8)

stimulus discrimination The process that occurs if two stimuli (stimulus) are sufficiently distinct (different) from each other that one evokes (brings up) a conditioned response (*see glossary definition*) but the other does not; the ability to differentiate (tell the difference) between stimuli (Module 15)

stimulus generalization Occurs when a conditioned response (*see glossary definition*) follows a stimulus (*see glossary definition*) that is similar to the original conditioned stimulus; the more similar the two stimuli are, the more likely generalization is to occur (Module 15)

stress A person's response to events that are threatening or challenging (Module 43)

structuralism Wilhelm Wundt's approach, which focuses on uncovering the fundamental mental components (parts) of consciousness, thinking, and other kinds of mental states and activities (Module 2)

superego According to Sigmund Freud, the final personality (*see glossary definition*) structure to develop; it represents the rights and wrongs of society as handed down by a person's parents, teachers, and other important figures (Module 29)

survey research Research in which people chosen to represent a larger population are asked a series of questions about their behavior, thoughts, or attitudes (Module 3)

sympathetic division The part of the autonomic division (*see glossary definition*) of the nervous system that acts to prepare the body for action in stressful situations, engaging all the organism's (living thing) resources to respond to a threat (Module 6)

synapse The space between two neurons (nerve cells) where the axon (*see glossary definition*) of a sending neuron communicates with the dendrites (*see glossary definition*) of a receiving neuron by using chemical messages (Module 5)

systematic desensitization A behavioral (way of behaving) technique in which gradual exposure to an anxiety-producing (unease, nervousness) stimulus is paired with relaxation to extinguish the response of anxiety (Module 36)

telegraphic speech Sentences in which words not critical to the message are left out (Module 21)

temperament The basic, innate (inborn) disposition (tendency) that emerges early in life (Modules 26, 30)

teratogens Environmental agents such as a drug, chemical, virus, or other factor that produce a birth defect (Module 25)

terminal buttons Small bulges at the end of axons (*see glossary definition*) that send messages to other neurons (nerve cells) (Module 5)

test standardization A technique used to validate (confirm) questions in personality (*see glossary definition*) tests by studying the responses of people with known diagnoses (identify an illness) (Module 31)

thalamus The part of the brain located in the middle of the central core that acts primarily to relay information about the senses (Module 7)

Thematic Apperception Test (TAT) A test consisting of a series of pictures about which a person is asked to write a story (Module 31)

theories Broad explanations and predictions concerning phenomena (happenings) of interest (Module 3)

theory of multiple intelligences Howard Gardner's theory that proposes that there are eight distinct spheres (areas) of intelligence (Module 32)

thinking The manipulation (handling, controlling) of mental representations of information (Module 20)

tip-of-the-tongue phenomenon The inability to recall information that one realizes one knows—a result of the difficulty of retrieving information from long-term memory (Module 19)

top-down processing Perception (*see glossary definition*) that is guided by higher-level knowledge, experience, expectations, and motivations (Module 11)

trait theory A model of personality (*see glossary definition*) that seeks to identify the basic traits necessary to describe personality (Module 30)

traits Consistent personality (*see glossary definition*) characteristics and behaviors displayed in different situations (Module 30)

transcranial magnetic stimulation (TMS) A depression treatment in which a precise magnetic pulse is directed to a specific area of the brain (Module 38)

transference The transfer of feelings to a psychoanalyst of love or anger that had been originally directed to a patient's parents or other authority figures (Module 36)

transsexuals Persons who believe they were born with the body of the other gender (Module 23)

treatment The manipulation (handling, controlling) implemented (carried out) by the experimenter (Module 3)

trichromatic theory of color vision The theory that there are three kinds of cones in the retina, each of which responds primarily to a specific range of wavelengths (Module 9)

trust-versus-mistrust stage According to Erik Erikson, the first stage of psychosocial development, occurring from birth to age 1½ years, during which time infants develop feelings of trust or lack of trust (Module 26)

unconditional positive regard An attitude of acceptance and respect on the part of an observer, no matter what a person says or does (Module 30)

unconditioned response (UCR) A response that is natural and needs no training (e.g., salivation at the smell of food) (Module 15)

unconditioned stimulus (UCS) A stimulus (*see glossary definition*) that naturally brings about a particular response without having been learned (Module 15)

unconscious A part of the personality (*see glossary definition*) that contains the memories, knowledge, beliefs, feelings, urges, drives, and instincts of which the individual is not aware (Module 29)

unconscious wish fulfillment theory Sigmund Freud's theory that dreams represent unconscious (*see glossary definition*) wishes that dreamers desire to see fulfilled (Module 12)

uninvolved parents Parents who show little interest in their children and are emotionally detached (Module 26)

universal grammar Noam Chomsky's theory that all the world's languages share a common underlying structure (Module 21)

variable-interval schedule A schedule by which the time between reinforcements (*see glossary definition*) varies around some average rather than being fixed (Module 16)

variable-ratio schedule A schedule by which reinforcement (*see glossary definition*) occurs after a varying number of responses rather than a fixed number (Module 16)

variables Behaviors, events, or other characteristics that can change, or vary, in some way (Module 3)

visual illusions Physical stimuli (stimulus) that consistently produce errors in perception (*see glossary definition*) (Module 11)

wear-and-tear theories of aging Theories that suggest that the mechanical functions of the body simply stop working efficiently (Module 28)

Weber's law A basic law of psychophysics (*see glossary definition*) stating that a just noticeable difference is in constant proportion to the intensity of an initial stimulus (Module 8)

weight set point The particular level of weight that the body strives to maintain (Module 23)

zone of proximal development (ZPD) According to Lev Vygotsky, the level at which a child can almost, but not fully, comprehend (understand) or perform a task on his or her own (Module 26)

zygote The new cell formed by the union of an egg and sperm (Module 25)

REFERENCES

Aazh, H., & Moore, B. C. J. (2007). Dead regions in the cochlea at 4 kHz in elderly adults: Relation to absolute threshold, steepness of audiogram, and pure-tone average. *Journal of the American Academy of Audiology, 18,* 97–106.

Abboud, L. (2005, July 27). The next phase in psychiatry. *The Wall Street Journal,* pp. D1, D5.

Ablon, J. S., & Jones, E. E. (2005). On analytic process. *Journal of the American Psychoanalytic Association, 53,* 541–568.

Abraham, P. F., & Calabrese, J. R. (2007). Review of: Lithium treatment of mood disorders: A practical guide, 6th revised edition. *Bipolar Disorders, 9,* 548.

Abramowitz, J. S., Olatunji, B. O., & Deacon, B. J. (2007). Health anxiety, hypochondriasis, and the anxiety disorders. *Behavior Therapy, 38,* 86–94.

Adams, G., & Dzokoto, V. A. (2007). Genital-shrinking panic in Ghana: A cultural psychological analysis. *Culture & Psychology, 13,* 83–104.

Adams, K. B. (2004). Changing investment in activities and interests in elders' lives: Theory and measurement. *International Journal of Aging and Human Development, 58,* 87–108.

Adams, M., Zuniga, X., Hackman, H. W., Castaneda, C. R., & Blumenfeld, W. J. (2000). *Readings for diversity and social justice: An anthology on racism, sexism, anti-Semitism, heterosexism, classism, and ableism.* New York: Routledge.

Addus, A. A., Chen, D., & Khan, A. S. (2007). Academic performance and advisement of university students: A case study. *College Student Journal, 41,* 316–326.

Adolphs, R. (2002). Neural systems for recognizing emotion. *Current Opinion in Neurobiology, 12,* 169–177.

Advokat, C. (2005). Differential effects of clozapine versus other antipsychotics on clinical outcome and dopamine release in the brain. *Essential Psychopharmacology, 6,* 73–90.

Aftanas, L., & Golosheykin, S. (2005). Impact of regular meditation practice on EEG activity at rest and during evoked negative emotions. *International Journal of Neuroscience, 115,* 893–909.

Aghajanian, G. K. (1994). Serotonin and the action of LSD in the brain. *Psychiatric Annals, 24,* 137–141.

Agras, W. S., & Berkowitz, R. I. (1996). Behavior therapy. In R. E. Hales & S. C. Yudofsky (Eds.), *The American Psychiatric Press synopsis of psychiatry.* Washington, DC: American Psychiatric Press.

Aiken, L. R. (2000). *Personality: Theories, assessment, research, and applications.* Springfield, IL: Charles C Thomas.

Ainsworth, M. D. S., Blehar, M. C., Waters, E., & Wall, S. (1978). *Patterns of attachment: A psychological study of the strange situation.* Hillsdale, NJ: Erlbaum.

Akil, H., & Morano, M. I. (1996). The biology of stress: From periphery to brain. In S. J. Watson (Ed.), *Biology of schizophrenia and affective disease.* Washington, DC: American Psychiatric Press.

Alloy, L. B., Jacobson, N. S., & Acocella, J. (1999). *Abnormal psychology* (8th ed.). New York: McGraw-Hill.

Aloia, M. S., Smith, K., & Arnedt, J. T. (2007). Brief behavioral therapies reduce early positive airway pressure discontinuation rates in sleep apnea syndrome: Preliminary findings. *Behavioral Sleep Medicine, 5,* 89–104.

Alonso, A., Alonso, S., & Piper, W. (2003). Group psychotherapy. In G. Stricker & T. A. Widiger, et al. (Eds.), *Handbook of psychology: Clinical psychology* (Vol. 8). New York: Wiley.

Amato, L., Davoili, M., Perucci, C. A., Ferri, M., Faggiano, F., & Mattick R. P. (2005). An overview of systematic reviews of the effectiveness of opiate maintenance therapies: Available evidence to inform clinical practice and research. *Journal of Substance Abuse Treatment, 28,* 321–329.

American Insomnia Association (2005). Causes of insomnia. In L. VandeCreek (Ed.), *Innovations in clinical practice: Focus on adults.* Sarasota, FL: Professional Resource Press/ Professional Resource Exchange.

American Psychological Association (APA). (2002, August 21). *APA Ethics Code, 2002.* Washington, DC: American Psychological Association.

American Psychological Association Task Force on Intelligence. (1996). *Intelligence: Knowns and unknowns.* Washington, DC: American Psychological Association.

Anand, G., & Burton, T. M. (2003, April 11). Drug debate: New antipsychotics pose a quandary for FDA, doctors. *The Wall Street Journal,* pp. A1, A8.

Anastasi, A., & Urbina, S. (1997). *Psychological testing* (7th ed.).Englewood Cliffs, NJ: Prentice Hall.

Anderson, J. A., & Adams, M. (1992). Acknowledging the learning styles of diverse student populations: Implications for instructional design. *New Directions for Teaching and Learning, 49,* 19–33.

Andrasik, F. (2006). Psychophysiological disorders: Headache as a case in point. In F. Andrasik, *Comprehensive handbook of personality and psychopathology: Vol. 2: Adult psychopathology.* Hoboken, NJ: Wiley.

Andrasik, F. (2007). What does the evidence show? Efficacy of behavioural treatments for recurrent headaches in adults. *Neurological Science, 28, Supplement,* S70–S77.

Andreasen, N. C. (2005). *Research advances in genetics and genomics: Implications for psychiatry.* Washington, DC: American Psychiatric Publishing.

Anderson, C., & Home, J. A. (2006). Sleepiness enhances distraction during a monotonous task. *Sleep: Journal of Sleep and Sleep Disorders Research, 29,* 573–576.

Angoff, W. H. (1988). The nature-nurture debate, aptitudes, and group differences. *American Psychologist, 43,* 713–720.

Ansaldo, A. I., Arguin, M., & RochLocours, L. A. (2002). The contribution of the right cerebral hemisphere to the recovery from aphasia: A single longitudinal case study. *Brain Languages, 82,* 206–222.

Antonucci, T.C., Lansford, J.E., Akiyama, H., Smith, J., Baltes, M.M., Takahashi, K., et al. (2002). Differences between men and women in social relations, resource deficits, and depressive symptomatology during later life in four nations. *Journal of Social Issues, 58*(4), 767–783.

Antony, M. M., Brown, T. A., & Barlow, D. H. (1992). Current perspectives on panic and panic disorder. *Current Directions in Psychological Science, 1,* 79–82.

APA Presidential Task Force on Evidence-Based Practice. (2006). Evidence-based practice in psychology, *61,* 271–285.

Apkarian, A. V., Bushnell, M. C., Treede, R. D., & Zubeita, J. K. (2005). Human brain mechanisms of pain perception and regulation in health and disease. *European Journal of Pain, 9,* 463–484.

Aponte, J. F., & Wohl, J. (2000). *Psychological intervention and cultural diversity*. Needham Heights, MA: Allyn & Bacon.

Arambula, P., Peper, E., Kawakami, M., & Gibney, K. H. (2001). The physiological correlates of Kundalini yoga meditation: A study of a yoga master. *Applied Psychophysiology & Biofeedback, 26*, 147–153.

Arangure, J., Jr. (2005, August 2). Orioles star denied use before Congress. *The Washington Post*, p. A01.

Archambault, D. L. (1992). Adolescence: A physiological, cultural, and psychological no man's land. In G. W. Lawson & A. W. Lawson (Eds.), *Adolescent substance abuse: Etiology, treatment, and prevention*. Gaithersburg, MD: Aspen.

Arlin, P. K. (1989). The problem of the problem. In J. D. Sinnott (Ed.), *Everyday problem solving: Theory and applications*. New York: Praeger.

Armstrong, T. (2000). *Multiple intelligences in the classroom* (2nd ed.). Washington, DC: Association for Supervision & Curriculum Development.

Armstrong, T. (2003). *The multiple intelligences of reading and writing: Making the words come alive* (2nd ed.). Washington, DC: Association for Supervision & Curriculum Development.

Asch, S. E. (1951). Effects of group pressure upon the modification and distortion of judgments. In H. Guetzkow (Ed.), *Groups, leadership, and men*. Pittsburgh: Carnegie Press.

Aspinwall, L. G., & Taylor, S. E. (1997). A stitch in time: Self-regulation and proactive coping. *Psychological Bulletin, 121*, 417–436.

Atkinson, R. C., & Shiffrin, R. M. (1968). Human memory: A proposed system and its control processes. In K. W. Spence & J. T. Spence (Eds.), *The psychology of learning and motivation: Advances in research and theory* (Vol. 2, pp. 80–195). New York: Academic Press.

Auer, J. A., Goodship, A., Arnoczky, S., Pearce, S., Price, J., Claes, L., von Rechenberg, B., Hofmann-Amtenbrinck, M., Schneider, E., Muller-Terpitz, R., Thiele, F., Rippe, K. P., & Grainger, D. W. (2007). Refining animal models in fracture research: Seeking consensus for changing the agenda in optimising both animal welfare and scientific validity for appropriate biomedical use. *BMC Musculoskelet Disorders, 8*, 72.

Aujoulat, I., Luminet, O., & Deccache, A. (2007). The perspective of patients on their experience of powerlessness. *Quality Health Research, 17*, 772–785.

Auld, F., Hyman, M., & Rudzinski, D. (2005). Theory and strategy of dream interpretation. In F. Auld & M. Hyman (Eds.), *Resolution of inner conflict: An introduction to psychoanalytic therapy* (2nd ed.). Washington, DC: American Psychological Association.

Averill, J. R. (1975). A semantic atlas of emotional concepts. *Catalog of Selected Documents in Psychology, 5*, 330.

Bacchiochi, J. R. (2006). Development and validation of the Malingering Discriminant Function Index (M-DFI) for the Minnesota Multiphasic Personality Inventory - 2 (MMPI-2). *Dissertation Abstracts International: Section B: The Sciences and Engineering, 66*(10-B), 5673.

Bains, O. S. (2006). Insomnia: Difficulty falling and staying asleep. In N. F. Watson, & B. V. Bradley, *Clinician's guide to sleep disorders*. Philadelphia: Taylor & Francis.

Bair, D. (2003). *Jung: A biography*. New York: Little, Brown.

Baltes, P. B., & Kunzmann, U. (2003). Wisdom. *Psychologist, 16*, 131–133.

Bandura, A. (1977). *Social learning theory*. Englewood Cliffs, NJ: Prentice Hall.

Bandura, A. (1986). *Social foundations of thought and action: A social cognitive theory*. Englewood Cliffs, NJ: Prentice Hall.

Bandura, A. (1994). Social cognitive theory of mass communication. In J. Bryant & D. Zillmann (Eds.), *Media effects: Advances in theory and research: LEA's communication series*. Hillsdale, NJ: Erlbaum.

Bandura, A. (1999). Social cognitive theory of personality. In D. Cervone & Y. Shod (Eds.), *The coherence of personality*. New York: Guilford.

Bandura, A. (2000). Self-efficacy: The foundation of agency. In W. J. Perrig & A. Grob (Eds.), *Control of human behavior, mental processes, and consciousness: Essays in honor of the 60th birthday of August Flammer*. Mahwah, NJ: Erlbaum.

Bandura, A. (2001). Social cognitive theory: An agentic perspective. *Annual Review of Psychology, 52*, 1–26.

Bandura, A. (2004). Swimming against the mainstream: The early years from chilly tributary to transformative mainstream. *Behaviour Research and Therapy, 42*, 613–630.

Bandura, A., & Locke, E. A. (2003). Negative self-efficacy and goal effects revisited. *Journal of Applied Psychology, 88*, 87–99.

Bandura, A., Grusec, J. E., & Menlove, F. L. (1967). Vicarious extinction of avoidance behavior. *Journal of Personality and Social Psychology, 5*, 16–23.

Bandura, A., Ross, D., & Ross, S. (1963a). Imitation of film-mediated aggressive models. *Journal of Abnormal and Social Psychology, 66*, 3–11.

Bandura, A., Ross, D., & Ross, S. (1963b). Vicarious reinforcement and imitative learning. *Journal of Abnormal and Social Psychology, 67*, 601–607.

Banich, T., & Heller, W. (1998). Evolving perspectives on lateralization of function. *Current Directions in Psychological Science, 7*, 1–2.

Banks, J. A. (2006). Improving race relations in schools: From theory and research to practice. *Journal of Social Issues, 62*, 607–614.

Baraas, R. C., Foster, D. H. & Amano, K. (2006). Anomalous trichromats' judgments of surface color in natural scenes under different daylights. *Neuroscience, 23*, 629–635.

Bargh, J. A., & Chartrand, T. L. (2000). The mind in the middle: A practical guide to priming and automaticity research. In H. T. Reis & C. M. Judd (Eds.), *Handbook of research methods in social and personality psychology*. New York: Cambridge University Press.

Barkley, R. (2000). *Taking charge of ADHD* (rev. ed.). New York: Guilford Press.

Barkley, R. (2005). *ADHD and the nature of self-control*. New York: Guildford Press.

Barlow, D. H. (2007). *Clinical handbook of psychological disorders: A step-by-step treatment manual* (4th ed.). New York: Guilford Press.

Barmeyer, C. I. (2004). Learning styles and their impact on cross-cultural training: An international comparison in France, Germany and Quebec. *International Journal of Intercultural Relations, 28*, 577–594.

Barnes, V. A., Davis, H. C., Murzynowski, J., & Treiber, F. A. (2004). Impact of meditation on resting and ambulatory blood pressure and heart rate in youth. *Medicine, 66*, 909–914.

Barnett, J. E., Wise, E. H., & Johnson-Greene, D. (2007). Informed consent: Too much of a good thing or not enough? *Professional Psychology: Research and Practice, 38*, 179–186.

Barrett, L. F., & Salovey, P. (Eds). (2002). *The wisdom in feeling: Psychological processes in emotional intelligence*. New York: Guilford Press.

Barron, G., & Yechiam, E. (2002). Private e-mail requests and the diffusion of responsibility. *Computers in Human Behavior, 18*, 507–520.

Bartholow, B. D., Bushman, B. J., & Sestir, M. A. (2006). Chronic violent video game exposure and desensitization to violence: Behavioral and event-related brain potential data. *Journal of Experimental Social Psychology, 42*, 532–539.

Bartlett, F. (1932). *Remembering: A study in experimental and social psychology*. Cambridge, England: Cambridge University Press.

Bartocci, G. (2004). Transcendence techniques and psychobiological mechanisms underlying religious experience. *Mental Health, Religion and Culture, 7*, 171–181.

Bartoshuk, L. (2000, July/August). The bitter with the sweet. *APS Observer, 11*, 33.

Bartoshuk, L., & Lucchina, L. (1997, January 13). Are you a supertaster? *U.S. News & World Report*, pp. 58–59.

Bartzokis, G., Nuechterlein, K. H., Lu, P. H., Gitlin, M., Rogers, S., & Mintz, J. (2003). Dysregulated brain development in adult men with schizophrenia: A magnetic resonance imaging study. *Biological Psychiatry, 53,* 412–421.

Bates, E. (2005). Plasticity, localization, and language development. In S. T. Parker and J. Langer (Eds.), *Biology and knowledge revisited: From neurogenesis to psychogenesis.* Mahwah, NJ: Erlbaum.

Bates, P. E., Cuvo, T., Miner, C. A., & Korabek, C. A. (2001). Simulated and community-based instruction involving persons with mild and moderate mental retardation. *Research in Developmental Disabilities, 22,* 95–115.

Bates, R. (2002). Liking and similarity as predictors of multi-source ratings. *Personnel Review, 31,* 540–552.

Batson, C. D., & Powell, A. A. (2003). Altruism and prosocial behavior. In T. Millon & M. J. Lerner (Eds.), *Handbook of psychology: Personality and social psychology* (Vol. 5). New York: Wiley.

Baum, A. (1994). Behavioral, biological, and environmental interactions in disease processes. In S. Blumenthal, K. Matthews, & S. Weiss (Eds.), *New research frontiers in behavioral medicine: Proceedings of the National Conference.* Washington, DC: NIH Publications.

Bauman, S., & Kopp, T. G. (2006). Integrating a humanistic approach in outpatient sex offender groups. *Journal for Specialists in Group Work, 31,* 247–261.

Baumeister, A. A., & Francis, J. L. (2002). Historical development of the dopamine hypothesis of schizophrenia. *Journal of the History of the Neurosciences, 11,* 265–277.

Baumeister, R. F., & Stillman, T. (2006). Erotic plasticity: Nature, culture, gender, and sexuality. In R. D. McAnulty, & M. M. Burnette, *Sex and sexuality, Vol 1: Sexuality today: Trends and controversies.* Westport, CT: Praeger Publishers/Greenwood Publishing.

Baumeister, R. F., Twenge, J. M., & Nuss, C. K. (2002). Effects of social exclusion on cognitive processes: Anticipated aloneness reduces intelligent thought. *Journal of Personality and Social Psychology, 83,* 817–827.

Baumrind, D. (1971). Current patterns of parental authority. *Developmental Psychology Monographs, 4* (1, pt. 2).

Baumrind, D. (2005). Patterns of parental authority ad adolescent autonomy. *New Directions for Child and Adolescent Development, 108,* 61–69.

Baumrind, D., Larzelere, R. E., & Cowan, P. A. (2002). Ordinary physical punishment: Is it harmful? Comment on Gershoff (2002). *Psychological Bulletin, 32,* 42–51.

Bayliss, D. M., Jarrold, C., Baddeley, A. D., & Gunn, D. M. (2005a). The relationship between short-term memory and working memory: Complex span made simple? *Memory, 13,* 414–421.

Bayliss, D. M., Jarrold, C., Baddeley, A. D., Gunn, D. M., & Leigh, E. (2005b). Mapping the developmental constraints on working memory span performance. *Developmental Psychology, 41,* 579–597.

Bayne, R. (2005). *Ideas and evidence: Critical reflections on MBTI® theory and practice.* Gainesville, FL: Center for Applications of Psychological Type, CAPT.

Beatty, J. (2000). *The human brain: Essentials of behavioral neuroscience.* Thousand Oaks, CA: Sage.

Beatty, W. W. (2002). Sex difference in geographical knowledge: Driving experience is not essential. *Journal of the International Neuropsychological Society, 8,* 804–810.

Beck, A. P., & Lewis, C. M. (Eds.). (2000). *The process of group psychotherapy: Systems for analyzing change.* Washington, DC: American Psychological Association.

Beck, A. T. (1995). Cognitive therapy: Past, present, and future. In M. J. Mahoney (Ed.), *Cognitive and constructive psychotherapies: Theory, research, and practice.* New York: Springer.

Beck, A. T. (2004). Cognitive therapy, behavior therapy, psychoanalysis, and pharmacotherapy: A cognitive continuum. In A. Freeman, M. J. Mahoney, P. Devito, & D. Martin (Eds.), *Cognition and psychotherapy* (2nd ed.). New York: Springer.

Beck, A.T. (2007). *Cognitive therapy in clinical practice.* (J. Scott., J. Williams., G. Mark. & A.T. Beck (Eds.). New York: Taylor & Francis.

Beck, A. T., & Emery, G., with Greenberg, R. L. (1985). *Anxiety disorders and phobias: A cognitive perspective.* New York: Basic Books.

Beck, A. T., & Rector, N. A. (2005). Cognitive approaches to schizophrenia: Theory and therapy. *Annual Review of Clinical Psychology, 1,* 577–606.

Beck, A. T., Freeman, A., & Davis, D. D. (2004). *Cognitive therapy of personality disorders* (2nd ed.). New York: Guilford Press.

Bedard, W. W., & Persinger, M. A. (1995). Prednisolone blocks extreme intermale social aggression in seizure-induced, brain-damaged rats: Implications for the amygdaloid central nucleus, corticotrophin-releasing factor, and electrical seizures. *Psychological Reports, 77,* 3–9.

Beersma, D. G. M., & Gordijn, M. C. M. (2007). Circadian control of the sleep-wake cycle. *Physiology & Behavior, 90,* 190–195.

Begg, D., & Langley, J. (2001). Changes in risky driving behavior from age 21 to 26 years. *Journal of Safety Research, 32,* 491–499.

Beidel, D. C., & Turner, S. M. (2007). Etiology of social anxiety disorder. In D. C. Beidel, & S. M. Turner, *Shy children, phobic adults: Nature and treatment of social anxiety disorders* (2nd ed.). Washington, DC: American Psychological Association.

Belsky, J., Burchinal, M., & McCartney, K. (2007). Are there long-term effects of early child care? *NICHD Early Child Care Research Network; Child Development, 78,* 681–701.

Benca, R. M. (2005). Diagnosis and treatment of chronic insomnia: A review. *Psychiatric Services, 56,* 332–343.

Benet-Martínez, V., Lee, F., & Leu, J. (2006). Biculturalism and cognitive complexity: Expertise in cultural representations. *Journal of Cross-Cultural Psychology, 37,* 386–407.

Benham, G., Woody, E. Z., & Wilson, K. S. (2006). Expect the unexpected: Ability, attitude, and responsiveness to hypnosis. *Journal of Personality and Social Psychology, 91,* 342–350.

Benight, C. C. (2004). Collective efficacy following a series of natural disasters. *Stress and Coping: An International Journal, 17,* 401–420.

Benson, H., Kornhaber, A., Kornhaber, C., LeChanu, M. N., et al. (1994). Increases in positive psychological characteristics with a new relaxation-response curriculum in high school students. *Journal of Research and Development in Education, 27,* 226–231.

Bergeron, J. M. (2006). Self-serving bias: A possible contributor of construct-irrelevant variance in high-stakes testing. *Dissertation Abstracts International Section A: Humanities and Social Sciences, 67*(1-A), 88.

Bergin, A. E., & Garfield, S. L. (Eds.). (1994). *Handbook of psychotherapy and behavior change* (4th ed.). New York: Wiley.

Berk, L. E. (2005). Why parenting matters. In S. Olfman (Ed.), *Childhood lost: How American culture is failing our kids* (pp. 19–53). Westport, CT: Praeger Publishers/Greenwood Publishing Group.

Berkowitz, L. (2001). On the formation and regulation of anger and aggression: A cognitive-neoassociationistic analysis. In W. G. Parrott (Ed.), *Emotions in social psychology: Essential readings.* New York: Psychology Press.

Berle, D. (2007). Graded exposure therapy for long-standing disgust-related cockroach avoidance in an older male. *Clinical Case Studies, 6,* 339–347.

Berman, A. L., Jobes, D. A., & Silverman, M. M. (2006). An integrative-eclectic approach to treatment. In A. L. Berman, D. A. Jobes, & M. M. Silverman, *Adolescent suicide: Assessment and intervention* (2nd ed.). Washington, DC: American Psychological Association.

Bernstein, D. M., Loftus, G. R., & Meltzoff, A. N. (2005). Object identification in preschool children and adults. *Developmental Science, 8,* 151–161.

Berntsen, D., & Rubin, D. C. (2004). Cultural life scripts structure recall from autobiographical memory. *Memory and Cognition, 32,* 427–442.

Berntsen, D., & Thomsen, D. K. (2005). Personal memories for remote historical events: Accuracy and clarity of flashbulb memories related to World War II. *Journal of Experimental Psychology: General, 134,* 242–257.

Berntson, G., Bechara, A., & Damasio, H., Tranel, D., & Cacioppo, J. (2007). Amygdala contribution to selective dimensions of emotion. *Social Cognitive and Affective Neuroscience, 2,* 123–129.

Berridge, K. C. (2004). Motivation concepts in behavioral neuroscience. *Physiology and Behavior, 81,* 179–209.

Berrios, G. E. (1996). *The history of mental symptoms: Descriptive psychopathology since the nineteenth century.* Cambridge, England: Cambridge University Press.

Berthoud, H. R. (2002). Multiple neural systems controlling food intake and body weight. *Neuroscience and Biobehavioral Reviews, 26,* 393–428.

Bhardwaj, R. D., Curtis, M. A., Spalding, K. L., Buchholz, B. A., Fink, D., Bjork-Eriksson, T., Nordborg, C., Gage, F. H., Druid, H., Eriksson, P. S., & Frisen, J. (2006). Neocortical neurogenesis in humans is restricted to development. *Proceedings of the National Academy of Sciences, 103,* 12564–12568.

Bialystok, E., & Martin, M. M. (2004). Attention and inhibition in bilingual children: Evidence from the dimensional change card sort task. *Developmental Science, 7,* 325–339.

Binet, A., & Simon, T. (1916). *The development of intelligence in children (The Binet-Simon Scale).* Baltimore: Williams & Wilkins.

Binstock, R., & George, L. K. (Eds.). (1996). *Handbook of aging and the social sciences* (4th ed.). San Diego, CA: Academic Press.

Birren, J. E. (Ed.). (1996). *Encyclopedia of gerontology: Age, aging and the aged.* San Diego, CA: Academic Press.

Bitterman, M. E. (2006). Classical conditioning since Pavlov. *Review of General Psychology, 10,* 365–376.

Bittles, A. H., Bower, C., & Hussain, R. (2007). The four ages of Down syndrome. *European Journal of Public Health, 17,* 121–225.

Bjornstad, R. (2006). Learned helplessness, discouraged workers, and multiple unemployment equilibria. *The Journal of Socio-Economics, 35,* 458–475.

Black, P. (2006). Thrust to wholeness: The nature of self-protection. *Review of General Psychology, 10,* 191–209.

Blair, C. A., Thompson, L. F., & Wuensch, K. L. (2005). Electronic helping behavior: The virtual presence of others makes a difference. *Basic and Applied Social Psychology, 27,* 171–178.

Blakeslee, S. (1991, August 7). Levels of caffeine in various foods. *The New York Times.*

Blakeslee, S. (1992, August 11). Finding a new messenger for the brain's signals to the body. *The New York Times,* p. C3.

Blass, T. (1996). Attribution of responsibility and trust in the Milgram obedience experiment. *Journal of Applied Social Psychology, 26,* 1529–1535.

Blass, T. (2004). *The man who shocked the world: The life and legacy of Stanley Milgram.* New York: Basic Books.

Blatter, K., & Cajochen, C., (2007). Circadian rhythms in cognitive performance: Methodological constraints, protocols, theoretical underpinnings. *Physiology & Behavior, 90,* 196–208.

Blennow, K., & Vanmechelen, E. (2003). CSF markers for pathogenic processes in Alzheimer's disease: Diagnostic implications and use in clinical neurochemistry. *Brain Research Bulletin, 61*(3), 235–242.

Block, R. I., O'Leary, D. S., Ehrhardt, J. C., Augustinack, J. C., Ghoneim, M. M., Arndt, S., & Hall, J. A. (2000). Effects of frequent marijuana use on brain tissue volume and composition. *Neuroreport, 11,* 491–496.

Blum, D. (2002). *Love at Goon Park: Harry Harlow and the science of affection.* Cambridge, MA: Perseus.

Boahen, K. (2005, May). Neuromorphic microchips. *Scientific American,* pp. 56–64.

Bode, C., de Ridder, D. T., Kuijer, R. G., & Bensing, J. M. (2007). Effects of an intervention promoting proactive coping competencies in middle and late adulthood. *Gerontologist, 47,* 42–51.

Boden, J. M., Fergusson, D. M., & Horwood, L. J. (2007). Anxiety disorders and suicidal behaviours in adolescence and young adulthood: Findings from a longitudinal study. *Psychological Medicine, 37,* 431–440.

Bodin, G. (2006). Review of harvesting free association. *Psychoanalytic Quarterly, 75,* 629–632.

Boehm, K. E., & Campbell, N. B. (1995). Suicide: A review of calls to an adolescent peer listening phone service. *Child Psychiatry and Human Development, 26,* 61–66.

Bogart, R. K., McDaniel, R. J., Dunn, W. J., Hunter, C., Peterson, A. L., & Write, E. E. (2007). Efficacy of group cognitive behavior therapy for the treatment of masticatory myofascial pain. *Military Medicine, 172,* 169–174.

Bogenschutz, M. P., Geppert, C. M., & George, J. (2006). The role of twelve-step approaches in dual diagnosis treatment and recovery. *American Journal of Addiction, 15,* 50–60.

Bohart, A. C. (2006). Understanding person-centered therapy: A review of Paul Wilkins' person-centered therapy in focus. *Person-Centered and Experiential Psychotherapies, 5,* 138–143.

Boisvert, C.M., & Faust, D. (2003). Leading researchers' consensus on psychotherapy research findings: Implications for the teaching and conduct of psychotherapy. *Professional Psychology: Research and Practice, 34,* 508–513.

Boles, D. B. (2005). A large-sample study of sex differences in functional cerebral lateralization. *Journal of Clinical and Experimental Neuropsychology, 27,* 759–768.

Bolger, N., & Amarel, D. (2007). Effects of social support visibility on adjustment to stress: Experimental evidence. *Journal of Personality and Social Psychology, 92,* 458–475.

Bolonna, A. A., & Kerwin, R. W. (2005). Partial agonism and schizophrenia. *British Journal of Psychiatry, 186,* 7–10.

Bond, M. (2006). Psychodynamic psychotherapy in the treatment of mood disorders. *Current Opinion in Psychiatry, 19*(1), 40–43.

Bonnardel, V. (2006). Color naming and categorization in inherited color vision deficiencies. *Visual Neuroscience, 23,* 637–643.

Borbely, A. (1986). *Secrets of sleep* (p. 43, graph). New York: Basic Books.

Bordnick, P. S., Elkins, R. L., Orr, T. E., Walters, P., & Thyer, B. A. (2004). Evaluating the relative effectiveness of three aversion therapies designed to reduce craving among cocaine abusers. *Behavioral Interventions, 19,* 1–24.

Borisenko, J. (2007). Fatherhood as a personality development factor in men. *The Spanish Journal of Psychology, 10,* 82–90.

Bornstein, R. F. (2003). Psychodynamic models of personality. In T. Millon & M. J. Lerner (Eds.), *Handbook of psychology: Personality and social psychology* (Vol. 5). New York: Wiley.

Bosma, H., van Boxtel, M. P. J., Ponds, R. W. H. M., Houx, P. J. H., Burdorf, A., & Jolles, J. (2002). Mental work demands protect against cognitive impairment: MAAS prospective cohort study. *Experimental Aging Research, 29,* 33–45.

Botvinick, M. (2004, August 6). Probing the neural basis of body ownership. *Science, 305,* 782–783.

Bouchard, T. J., Jr. (2004). Genetic influence on human psychological traits: A survey. *Current Directions in Psychological Science, 13,* 148–151.

Bower, G. H., Thompson, S. S., & Tulving, E. (1994). Reducing retroactive interference: An interference analysis. *Journal of Experimental Psychology Learning, Memory, and Cognition, 20,* 51–66.

Boyce, W. T., & Ellis, B. J. (2005). Biological sensitivity to context: An evolutionary-developmental theory of the origins and functions of stress reactivity. *Development and Psychopathology, 17,* 271–301.

Bozarth, J. D., Zimring, F. M., & Tausch, R. (2002). Client-centered therapy: The evolution of a revolution. In D. J. Cain (Ed.), *Humanistic psychotherapies: Handbook of research and practice* (pp. 147–188). Washington, DC: American Psychological Association.

Brazelton, T. B. (1969). *Infants and mothers: Differences in development.* New York: Dell.

Brecht, M., Huang, D., Evans, E., & Hser, Y. (2008). Polydrug use and implications for longitudinal research: Ten-year trajectories for heroin, cocaine, and methamphetamine users. *Drug and Alcohol Dependence, 96*(3), 193–201.

Brewer, M. B., & Hewstone, M. (Eds.). (2003). *Social cognition.* Malden, MA: Blackwell Publishers.

Brock, T. C., & Green, M. C. (Eds). (2005). *Persuasion: Psychological insights and perspectives* (2nd ed.). Thousand Oaks, CA: Sage.

Broidy, L. M., Nagin, D. S., & Tremblay, R. E. (2003). Developmental trajectories of childhood disruptive behaviors and adolescent delinquency: A six-site, cross-national study. *Developmental Psychology, 39,* 222–245.

Broman, C. L. (2005). Stress, race and substance use in college. *College Student Journal, 39,* 340–352.

Brooker, R. J., Widmaier, E. P., Graham, L., & Stilling, P. (2008). *Biology* (pp. 943, 956, 1062). New York: McGraw-Hill.

Brown, P. K., & Wald, G. (1964). Visual pigments in single rod and cones of the human retina. *Science, 144,* 45–52.

Brown, S., & Martinez, M. J. (2007). Activation of premotor vocal areas during musical discrimination. *Brain and Cognition, 63,* 9–69.

Brownlee, K. (2007). What works for whom? A critical review of psychotherapy research. (2nd ed.). *Psychiatric Rehabilitation Journal, 30,* 239–240.

Bruce, V., Green, P. R., & Georgeson, M. (1997). *Visual perception: Physiology, psychology and ecology* (3rd ed.). Mahwah, NJ: Erlbaum.

Bruggeman, H., Yonas, A., & Konczak, J. (2007). The processing of linear perspective and binocular information for action and perception. *Neuropsychologia, 45,* 1420–1426.

Bryant, R. M., Coker, A. D., Durodoye, B. A., McCollum, V. J., Pack-Brown, S. P., Constantine, M. G., & O'Bryant, B. J. (2005). Having our say: African American women, diversity, and counseling. *Journal of Counseling and Development, 83,* 313–319.

Brydon, L., Edwards, S., Mohamed-Ali, V., & Steptoe, A. (2004). Socioeconomic status and stress-induced increases in interleukin-6. *Brain, Behavior, and Immunity, 18,* 281–290.

Brzustowicz, L. M., Hodgkinson, K. A., Chow, E. W. C., Honer, W. G., & Bassett, A. S. (2000, April 28). Location of major susceptibility locus for familial schizophrenia on chromosome 1q21-q22. *Science, 288,* 678–682.

Buchanan, R. W., Javitt, D. C., Marder, S. R., Schooler, N. R., Gold, J. M., McMahon, R. P., Heresco-Levy, U., & Carpenter, W. T. (2007). The Cognitive and Negative Symptoms in Schizophrenia Trial (CONSIST): The efficacy of glutamatergic agents for negative symptoms and cognitive impairments. *American Journal of Psychiatry, 164,* 1593–1602.

Buchert, R., Thomasius, R., Wilke, F., Petersen, K., Nebeling, B., Obrocki, J., Schulze, O., Schmidt, U., & Clausen, M. (2004). A voxel-based PET investigation of the long-term effects of "ecstasy" consumption on brain serotonin transporters. *American Journal of Psychiatry, 161,* 1181–1189.

Buckley, C. (2007, January 3). A man down, a train arriving, and a stranger makes a choice. *The New York Times,* p. 1.

Bunting, M. (2006). Proactive interference and item similarity in working memory. *Journal of Experimental Psychology: Learning, Memory, and Cognition, 32,* 183–196.

Burchinal, M. R., Roberts, J. E., & Riggins, R., Jr. (2000). Relating quality of center-based child care to early cognitive and language development longitudinally. *Child Development, 71,* 338–357.

Burd, L., Cotsonas-Hassler, T. M., Martsolf, J. T., & Kerbeshian, J. (2003). Recognition and management of fetal alcohol syndrome. *Neurotoxicological Teratology, 25,* 681–688.

Burger, J. M., Reed, M., & DeCesare, K. (1999). The effects of initial request size on compliance: More about the that's-not-all technique. *Basic and Applied Social Psychology, 21,* 243–249.

Burgoon, J. K., Bonito, J. A., Ramirez, A. J. R., Dunbar, N. E., Kam, K., & Fischer, J. (2002). Testing the interactivity principle: Effects of mediation, propinquity, and verbal and nonverbal modalities in interpersonal interaction [Special issue: Research on the relationship between verbal and nonverbal communication: Emerging integrations]. *Journal of Communication, 52,* 657–677.

Burns, N. R., Bryan, J., & Nettlebeck, T. (2006). Ginkgo biloba: No robust effect on cognitive abilities or mood in healthy young or older adults. *Human Psychopharmacology: Clinical and Experimental, 21,* 27–37.

Buschman, T. J., & Miller, E. K. (2007, March 30). Top-down versus bottom-up control of attention in the prefrontal and posterior parietal cortices. *Science, 315,* 1860–1862.

Busey, T. A., & Loftus, G. R. (2007). Cognitive science and the law. *Trends in Cognitive Science, 11,* 111–117.

Bushman, B. J., & Anderson, C. A. (2001). Media violence and the American public: Scientific facts versus media misinformation. *American Psychologist, 56,* 477–489.

Bushman, B. J., & Anderson, C. A. (2002). Violent video games and hostile expectations: A test of the general aggression model. *Personality and Social Psychology Bulletin, 28,* 1679–1686.

Bushman, B. J., Wang, M. C., & Anderson, C. A. (2005). Is the curve relating temperature to aggression linear or curvilinear? Assaults and temperature in Minneapolis reexamined. *Journal of Personality and Social Psychology, 89,* 62–66.

Buss, D. M. (2001). Human nature and culture: An evolutionary psychological perspective. *Journal of Personality, 69,* 955–978.

Buss, D. M. (2003). *Evolutionary psychology.* Boston: Allyn & Bacon.

Buss, D. M., Abbott, M., & Angleitner, A. (1990). International preferences in selecting mates: A study of 37 cultures. *Journal of Cross-Cultural Psychology, 21,* 5–47.

Butcher, J. N. (2005). *A beginner's guide to the MMPI-2* (2nd ed.). Washington, DC: American Psychological Association.

Butler, A. C., Chapman, J. E., Forman, E. M., & Beck, A. T. (2006). The empirical status of cognitive-behavioral therapy: A review of meta-analyses. *Clinical Psychology Review, 26,* 17–31.

Butler, L. T., & Berry, D. C. (2004). Understanding the relationship between repetition priming and mere exposure. *British Journal of Psychology, 95,* 467–487.

Byne, W. (1996). Biology and homosexuality: Implications of neuroendocrino-logical and neuroanatomical studies. In R. P. Cabaj & T. S. Stein (Eds.), *Textbook of homosexuality and mental health.* Washington, DC: American Psychiatric Press.

Cabanac, M., & Frankham, P. (2002). Evidence that transient nicotine lowers the body weight set point. *Physiology & Behavior, 76,* 539–542.

Cachelin, F. M., & Regan, P. C. (2006). Prevalence and correlates of chronic dieting in a multi-ethnic U.S. community sample. *Eating and Weight Disorders, 11,* 91–99.

Caelian, C. F. (2006). The role of perfectionism and stress in the suicidal behaviour of depressed adolescents. *Dissertation Abstracts International: Section B: The Sciences and Engineering, 66* (12-B), 6915.

Cahill, L. (2005, May). His brain, her brain. *Scientific American,* pp. 40–47.

Cain, D. J. (Ed.). (2002). *Humanistic psychotherapies: Handbook of research and practice.* Washington, DC: American Psychological Association.

Calin-Jageman, R. J., & Fischer, T. M. (2007) Behavioral adaptation of the aplysia aiphon-withdrawal response is accompanied by sensory adaptation. *Behavioral Neuroscience, 121,* 200–211.

Cameron, O. G. (2002). *Visceral sensory neuroscience: Interoception.* London: Oxford University Press.

Cannon, W. B. (1929). Organization for physiological homeostatics. *Physiological Review, 9,* 280–289.

Canteras, N. S. (2002). The medial hypothalamic defensive system: Hodological organization and functional implications [Special issue: Functional role of specific systems within the extended amygdala and hypothalamus]. *Pharmacology, Biochemistry and Behavior, 71,* 481–491.

Cantwell, R. H., & Andrews, B. (2002). Cognitive and psychological factors underlying secondary school students' feelings towards group work. *Educational Psychology, 22,* 75–91.

Capaldi, E. D. (Ed.). (1996). *Why we eat what we eat: The psychology of eating.* Washington, DC: American Psychological Association.

Carhart-Harris, R., (2007). Speed > Ecstasy > Ritalin: The science of amphetamines. *Journal of Psychopharmacology, 21,* 225.

Carnagey, N. L., Anderson, C. A., & Bushman, B. J. (2007). The effect of video game violence on physiological desensitization to real-life violence. *Journal of Experimental Social Psychology, 43,* 489–496.

Carney, R. N., & Levin, J. R. (1998). Coming to terms with the keyword method in introductory psychology: A "neuromnemonic" example. *Teaching of Psychology, 25,* 132–135.

Carpenter, S. (2001). Sleep deprivation may be undermining teen health. *APA Monitor, 32,* 42–45.

Carpenter, S. (2002, April). What can resolve the paradox of mental health disparities? *APA Monitor, 33,* 18.

Carter, R. T. (2003). Becoming racially and culturally competent: The racial-cultural counseling laboratory. *Journal of Multicultural Counseling and Development, 31,* 20–30.

Cartwright, R. (2006). A neuroscientist looks at how the brain makes up our minds. *PsycCRITQUES, 51,* 35–41.

Cartwright, R., Agargum, M. Y., & Kirkby, J. (2006). Relation of dreams to waking concerns. *Psychiatry Research, 141,* 261–270.

Carver, C., & Scheier, M. (2002). Coping processes and adjustment to chronic illness. In A. Christensen and M. Antoni (Eds.), *Chronic physical disorders: Behavioral medicine's perspective.* Malden: Blackwell Publishers.

Cary, P. (2007). A brief history of the concept of free will: Issues that are and are not germane to legal reasoning [Special issue: Free will]. *Behavioral Sciences & the Law, 25,* 165–181.

Casey, S. D., Cooper-Brown, L. J., & Wacher, D. P. (2006). The use of descriptive analysis to identify and manipulate schedules of reinforcement in the treatment of food refusal. *Journal of Behavioral Education, 15,* 41–52.

Cashon, C. H., & Cohen, L. B. (2004). Beyond U-shaped development in infants' processing of faces: An information-processing account. *Journal of Cognition and Development, 5,* 59–80.

Caspi, A., Harrington, H., & Milne, B. (2003). Children's behavioral styles at age 3 are linked to their adult personality traits at age 26. *Journal of Personality, 71,* 495–513.

Cassells, J. V. S. (2007). The virtuous roles of truth and justice in integral dialogue: Research, theory, and model practice of the evolution of collective consciousness. *Dissertation Abstracts International Section A: Humanities and Social Sciences, 67* (10-A), 4005.

Cauce, A. M. (2007). Bringing community psychology home: The leadership, community and values initiative. *American Journal of Community Psychology, 39,* 1–11.

Cavallini, E., Pagnin, A., and Vecchi, T. (2003). Aging and everyday memory: The beneficial effect of memory training. *Archives of Gerontology & Geriatrics, 37,* 241–257.

Cavenett, T., & Nixon, R. D. V. (2006). The effect of arousal on memory for emotionally-relevant information: A study of skydivers. *Behaviour Research and Therapy, 44,* 1461–1469.

Centers for Disease Control (CDC). (2004b, June 11). Suicide and attempted suicide. *MMWR, 53,* 471.

Centers for Disease Control and Prevention. (2007). Physical activity and good nutrition: Essential elements to prevent chronic diseases and obesity, 2007. www.cdc.gov/nccdphp/publications/aag/pdf/dnpa.pdf.

Centers for Disease Control and Prevention. (2007, February 9). Prevalence of Autism Spectrum Disorders—Autism and Developmental Disabilities Monitoring Network, 14 Sites.United States.2002.

Chamberlain, K., & Zika, S. (1990). The minor events approach to stress: Support for the use of daily hassles. *British Journal of Psychology, 81,* 469–481.

Chambless, D. L., Crits-Christoph, P., Wampold, B. E., Norcross, J. C., Lambert, M. J., Bohart, A. C., Beutler, L. E., & Johannsen, B. E. (2006). What should be validated? In J. C. Norcross, L. E. Beutler, & R. F. Levant, (Eds.), *Evidence-based practices in mental health: Debate and dialogue on the fundamental questions.* Washington, DC: American Psychological Assocation.

Chandra, P. (2007). Review of language, mind, and brain: Some psychological and neurological constraints on theories of grammar. *Cognitive Systems Research, 8,* 53–56.

Chandran, S., & Menon, G. (2004). When a day means more than a year: Effects of temporal framing on judgments of health risk. *Journal of Consumer Research, 31,* 375–389.

Chapman, L. J., & Chapman, J. P. (1973). *Disordered thought in schizophrenia.* New York: Appleton-Century-Crofts.

Charman, D. P. (2004). *Core processes in brief psychodynamic psychotherapy: Advancing effective practice.* Mahwah, NJ: Erlbaum.

Chen, A., Zhou, Y., & Gong, H. (2004). Firing rates and dynamic correlated activities of ganglion cells both contribute to retinal information processing. *Brain Research, 1017,* 13–20.

Cheng, C., & Cheung, M. L. (2005). Cognitive processes underlying coping flexibility: Differentiation and integration. *Journal of Personality, 73,* 859–886.

Cheston, S. E. (2002). A new paradigm for teaching counseling theory and practice. *Counselor Education & Supervision, 39,* 254–269.

Child care and mother-child interaction in the first three years of life. (1999). *Developmental Psychology, 35,* 1399–1413.

Cho, A. (2000, June 16). What's shakin' in the ear? *Science, 288,* 1954–1955.

Cho, S. H., Shin, H. K., Kwon, Y. H., Lee, M. Y., Lee, Y. H., Lee, C. H., Yang, D. S., & Jang, S. H. (2007). Cortical activation changes induced by visual biofeedback tracking training in chronic stroke patients. *Neurorehabilitation and Neural Repair, 22,* 77–84.

Choi, Y. S. , Gray, H. , & Ambady, N. (2004). Glimpses of others: Unintended communication and unintended perception. In J. Bargh, J. Uleman, & R. Hassin (Eds.), *Unintended thought* (2nd. ed.). New York: Oxford University Press.

Chomsky, N. (1968). *Language and mind.* New York: Harcourt Brace Jovanovich.

Chomsky, N. (1978). On the biological basis of language capacities. In G. A. Miller & E. Lenneberg (Eds.), *Psychology and biology of language and thought.* New York: Academic Press.

Chomsky, N. (1991). Linguistics and cognitive science: Problems and mysteries. In A. Kasher (Ed.), *The Chomskyan turn.* Cambridge, MA: Blackwell.

Chou, K. (2005). Everyday competence and depressive symptoms: Social support and sense of control as mediators or moderators? *Aging and Mental Health, 9,* 177–183.

Choy, Y., Fyer, A.J., & Lipsitz, J.D. (2007). Treatment of specific phobia in adults. *Clinical Psychology Review, 27*(3), 266–286.

Christ, S. E., Steiner, R. D., & Grange, D. K. (2006). Inhibitory control in children with phenylketonuria. *Developmental Neuropsychology, 30,* 845–864.

Chrysikou, E. G. (2006). When a shoe becomes a hammer: Problem solving as goal-derived, ad hoc categorization. *Dissertation Abstracts International: Section B: The Sciences and Engineering, 67* (1-B), 569.

Cialdini, R. B. (2006). *Influence: The psychology of persuasion.* New York: Collins.

Clark, D. A. (2007). Obsessions and compulsions. In N. Kazantzis, & L. L'Abate, *Handbook of homework assignments in psychotherapy: Research, practice, prevention.* New York: Springer Science + Business Media.

Clarkin, J. F., & Lenzenweger, M. F. (Eds.) (2004). *Major theories of personality disorders* (2nd ed.). New York: Guilford.

Clarkin, J. F., Levy, K. N., Lenzenweger, M. F., & Kernberg, O. F. (2007). Evaluating three treatments for borderline personality disorder: A multiwave study. *American Journal of Psychiatry, 164*, 922–928.

Clay D. L. (2000). Commentary: Rethinking our interventions in pediatric chronic pain and treatment research. *Journal of Pediatric Psychology, 25*, 53–55.

Claydon, L.S., Chesterton, L.S., Barlas, P. & Sim, J. (2008). Effects of simultaneous dual-site TENS stimulation on experimental pain. *European Journal of Pain, 12*(6), 696–704.

Cleary, A. M. (2006). Relating familiarity-based recognition and the tip-of-the-tongue phenomenon: Detecting a word's recency in the absence of access to the word. *Memory & Cognition, 34*, 804–816.

Clements, A., M., Rimrodt, S. L., & Abel, J. R. (2006). Sex differences in cerebral laterality of language and visuospatial processing. *Brain and Language, 98*, 150–158.

Clemons, T. L. (2006). Underachieving gifted students: A social cognitive model. *Dissertation Abstracts International Section A: Humanities and Social Sciences, 66*(9-A), 3208.

Cloud, J. (2000, June 5). The lure of ecstasy. *Time*, pp. 60–68.

Coates, S. L., Butler, L. T., & Berry, D. C. (2006). Implicit memory and consumer choice: The mediating role of brand familiarity. *Applied Cognitive Psychology, 20*, 1101–1116.

Cobos, P., Sanchez, M., Garcia, C., Vera, M. N., & Vila, J. (2002). Revisiting the James versus Cannon debate on emotion: Startle and autonomic modulation in patients with spinal cord injuries. *Biological Psychology, 61*, 251–269.

Cochran, S. D. (2000). Emerging issues in research on lesbians' and gay men's mental health: Does sexual orientation really matter? *American Psychologist, 56*, 33–41.

Coffman, S. J., Martell, C. R., Dimidjian, S., Gallop, R., & Holon, S. D. (2007). Extreme nonresponse in cognitive therapy: Can behavioral activation succeed where cognitive therapy fails? *Journal of Consulting Clinical Psychology, 75*, 531–545.

Cohen, L., & Cashon, C. (2003). Infant perception and cognition. In R. Lerner & M. Easterbrooks (Eds.), *Handbook of psychology: Developmental psychology* (Vol. 6). New York: Wiley.

Cohen, P., Slomkowski, C., & Robins, L. N. (Eds.). (1999). *Historical and geographical influences on psychopathology.* Mahwah, NJ: Erlbaum.

Cohen, S. (2004, November). Social relationships and health. *American Psychologist*, 676–684.

Cohen, S., Doyle, W. J., Turner, R., Alper, C. M., & Skoner, D. P. (2003). Sociability and susceptibility to the common cold. *Psychological Science, 14*, 389–395.

Coles, C. D., Platzman, K. A., & Lynch, M. E. (2003). Auditory and visual sustained attention in adolescents parentally exposed to alcohol. *Clinical and Experimental Research, 26*, 263–271.

Collins, S. L., & Izenwasser, S. (2004). Chronic nicotine differentially alters cocaine-induced locomotor activity in adolescent vs. adult male and female rats. *Neuropharmacology, 46*, 349–362.

Colom, R., Jung, R. E., & Haier, R. J. (2006). Finding the g-factor in brain structure using the method of correlated vectors. *Intelligence, 34*, 561–570.

Coltheart, M., Langdon, R., & McKay, R. (2007). Schizophrenia and monothematic delusions. *Schizophrenia Bulletin, 33*, 642–647.

Coltraine, S., & Messineo, M. (2000). The perpetuation of subtle prejudice: Race and gender imagery in 1990s television advertising. *Sex Roles, 42*, 363–389.

Colwell, M. J., & Lindsey, E. W. (2005). Preschool children's pretend and physical play and sex of play partner: Connections to peer competence. *Sex Roles, 52*, 497–509.

Combrink-Graham, L., & McKenna, S. B. (2006). Families with children with disrupted attachments. In L. Combrink-Graham, *Children in family contexts: Perspectives on treatment.* New York: Guilford Press.

Compagni, A., & Manderscheid, R. W. (2006). A neuroscientist-consumer alliance to transform mental health care. *Journal of Behavioral Health Services & Research, 33*, 265–274.

Conduit, R., Crewther, S. G., & Coleman, G. (2004). Spontaneous eyelid movements (ELMS) during sleep are related to dream recall on awakening. *Journal of Sleep Research, 13*, 137–144.

Conger, R. D., Wallace, L. E., Sun, Y., Simons, R. L., McLoyd, V. C., & Brody, G. H. (2002). Economic pressure in African American families: A replication and extension of the family stress model. *Developmental Psychology, 38*, 179–193.

Conner, M., Povey, R., Sparks, P., James, R., & Shepherd, R. (2003). Moderating role of attitudinal ambivalence within the theory of planned behaviour. *British Journal of Social Psychology, 42*, 75–94.

Connolly, A. C. (2007). Concepts and their features: Can cognitive science make good on the promises of concept empiricism? *Dissertation Abstracts International: Section B: The Sciences and Engineering, 67*(7-B), 4125.

Consumer Reports (CR). (1995, November). Mental health: Does therapy help? pp. 734–739.

Conway, M. A. (Ed) (2002). *Levels of processing 30 years on special issue of memory.* Hove, UK: Psychology Press.

Cooke, J. R., & Ancoli-Israel, S. (2006). Sleep and its disorders in older adults. *Psychiatric Clinics of North America, 29*, 1077–1093.

Cooklin, A. (2000). Therapy, the family and others. In H. Maxwell (Ed.), *Clinical psychotherapy for health professionals.* Philadelphia: Whurr Publishers, Ltd.

Copolov, D. L., Seal, M. L., Maruff, P., Ulusoy, R., Wong, M. T. H., TochonDanguy, H. J., & Egan, G. F. (2003). Cortical activation associated with the human experience of auditory hallucinations and perception of human speech in schizophrenia: A PET correlation study. *Psychiatry Research: Neuroimaging, 123*, 139–152.

Coren, S. (1992). The moon illusion: A different view through the legs. *Perceptual and Motor Skills, 75*, 827–831.

Coren, S., & Ward, L. M. (1989). *Sensation and perception* (3rd ed.). San Diego, CA: Harcourt Brace Jovanovich.

Cornelius, M. D., Taylor, P. M., Geva, D., & Day, N. L. (1995). Prenatal tobacco and marijuana use among adolescents: Effects on offspring gestational age, growth, and morphology. *Pediatrics, 95*, 57–68.

Cornell, C. B. (2006). A graduated scale for determining mental age. *Dissertation Abstracts International: Section B: The Sciences and Engineering, 66* (9-B), 5121.

Costa, P. T., Jr., & Widiger, T. A. (Eds.). (2002). *Personality disorders and the five-factor model of personality* (2nd ed.). Washington, DC: American Psychological Association.

Cotton, P. (1993, July 7). Psychiatrists set to approve DSM-IV. *Journal of the American Medical Association, 270*, 13–15.

Couturier, J., & Lock, J. (2006). Eating disorders: Anorexia nervosa, bulimia nervosa, and binge eating disorder. In T. G. Plante, *Mental disorders of the new millennium: Biology and function* (Vol 3). Westport, CT: Praeger Publishers/Greenwood Publishing.

Cowan, N., Towse, J. N., Hamilton, Z., Saults, J. S., Elliott, E. M., Lacey, J. F., Moreno, M. V., & Hitch, G. J. (2003). Children's working-memory processes: A response-timing analysis. *Journal of Experimental Psychology: General, 132*, 113–132.

Cowley, G. (2000, January 31). Alzheimer's: Unlocking the mystery. *Time*, pp. 46–54.

Cowley, G. (2003, February 24). Our bodies, our fears. *Newsweek*, 43–44.

Coyle, N. (2006). The hard work of living in the face of death. *Journal of Pain and Symptom Management, 32*, 266–274.

Coyne, S. M., & Archer, J. (2005). The relationship between indirect and physical aggression on television and in real life. *Social Development, 14*, 324–338.

Craik, F. I. M. (1990). Levels of processing. In M. E. Eysenck (Ed.), *The Blackwell dictionary of cognitive psychology.* London: Blackwell.

Cramer, P. (2007). Longitudinal study of defense mechanisms: Late childhood to late adolescence. *Journal of Personality, 75*, 1–23.

Crawford, N. (2002). Science-based program curbs violence in kids. *APA Monitor, 33,* 38–39.

Creasey, G. L. (2005). *Research methods in lifespan development* (6th ed.). Boston: Allyn & Bacon.

Crocker, J., & Park, L. E. (2004). The costly pursuit of self-esteem. *Psychological Bulletin, 130,* 392–414.

Crosnoe, R., & Elder, G. H., Jr. (2002). Successful adaptation in the later years: A life course approach to aging. *Social Psychology Quarterly, 65,* 309–328.

Crum, A. J., & Langer, E. J. (2007). Mind-set matters: Exercise and the placebo effect. *Psychological Science, 18,* 165–171.

Cullinane, C.A., Chu, D.Z.J. & Mamelak, A.N. (2002). Current surgical options in the control of cancer pain. *Cancer Practice, 10* (Suppl.1), s21–s26.

Cynkar, A. (2007). The changing gender composition of psychology. *Monitor on Psychology, 38,* 46–48.

Czopp, A.M., Monteith, M.J. & Mark, A.Y. (2006). Standing up for a change: Reducing bias through interpersonal confrontation. *Journal of Personality and Social Psychology, 90*(5), 784–803.

Daftary, F., & Meri, J. W. (2002). *Culture and memory in medieval Islam.* London: I. B. Tauris.

Daines, B. (2006). Violations of agreed and implicit sexual and emotional boundaries in couple relationships—some thoughts arising from Levine's "A clinical perspective on couple infidelity." *Sexual and Relationship Therapy, 21,* 45–53.

Dale, A. (2006). Quality issues with survey research [Special issue: Quality in social research]. *International Journal of Social Research Methodology: Theory & Practice, 9,* 143–158.

Damasio, A. (1999). *The feeling of what happens: Body and emotion in the making of consciousness.* New York: Harcourt Brace.

Damasio, A. (2003, May 15). Mental self: The person within. *Nature, 423,* 227.

Darwin, C. J., Turvey, M. T., & Crowder, R. G. (1972). An auditory analogue of the Sperling partial-report procedure: Evidence for brief auditory storage. *Cognitive Psychology, 3,* 255–267.

Davidson, R. J., Gray, J. A., LeDoux, J. E., Levenson, R. W., Panksepp, J., & Ekman, P. (1994). Is there emotion-specific physiology? In P. Ekman & R. J. Davidson (Eds.), *The nature of emotion.* New York: Oxford University Press.

Day, A. L., & Livingstone, H. A. (2003). Gender differences in perceptions of stressors and utilization of social support among university students. *Canadian Journal of Behavioural Science, 35,* 73–83.

Day, R. D., & Lamb, M. E. (2004). *Conceptualizing and measuring father involvement.* Mahwah, NJ: Erlbaum.

De Beni, R., Pazzaglia, F., & Gardini, S. (2007). The generation and maintenance of visual mental images: Evidence from image type and aging. *Brain and Cognition, 63,* 271–278.

De Mello, M. F., De Jesus Mari, J., Bacaltchuk, J., Verdeli, H., & Neugebauer, R. (2005). A systematic review of research findings on the efficacy of interpersonal therapy for depressive disorders. *European Archives of Psychiatry and Clinical Neuroscience, 255,* 75–82.

Dean, C., & Dresbach, T. (2006). Neuroligins and neurexins: Linking cell adhesion, synapse formation and cognitive function. *International Journal of Psychiatry in Clinical Practice, 10*(Suppl.), 5–11.

Dean-Borenstein, M. T. (2007). The long-term psychosocial effects of trauma on survivors of human-caused extreme stress situations. *Dissertation Abstracts International: Section B: The Sciences and Engineering, 67* (11-B), 6733.

Deary, I. J., & Der, G. (2005). Reaction time, age, and cognitive ability: Longitudinal findings from age 16 to 63 years in representative population samples. *Aging, Neuropsychology, & Cognition, 12,* 187–215.

Deci, E. L., Koestner, R., & Ryan, R. M. (2001). Extrinsic rewards and intrinsic motivation in education: Reconsidered once again. *Review of Educational Research, 71,* 1–27.

DeCoster, V. A. (2003). Predicting emotions in everyday social interactions: A test and comparison of affect control and social interactional theories. *Journal of Human Behavior in the Social Environment, 6,* 53–73.

Dediu, D., & Ladd, D. R. (2007). From the cover: Linguistic tone is related to the population frequency of the adaptive haplogroups of two brain size genes, ASPM and Microcephalin. *Proceedings of the National Academy of Sciences, 104,* 10944–10949.

Delgado, M. R., Labouliere, C. D., & Phelps, E. A. (2006). Fear of losing money? Aversive conditioning with secondary reinforcers [Special issue: Genetic, comparative and cognitive studies of social behavior]. *Social Cognitive and Affective Neuroscience, 1,* 250–259.

Delinsky, S. S., Latner, J. D., & Wilson, G. T. (2006). Binge eating and weight loss in a self-help behavior modification program. *Obesity, 14,* 1244–1249.

Dempster, F. N. (1981). Memory span: Sources for individual and developmental differences. *Psychological Bulletin, 89,* 63–100.

Denmark, G. L., & Fernandez, L. C. (1993). Historical development of the psychology of women. In F. L. Denmark & M. A. Paludi (Eds.), *A handbook of issues and theories.* Westport, CT: Greenwood Press.

Dennett, D. C. (2003). *Freedom evolves.* New York: Viking.

Dennis, I. (2007). Halo effects in grading student projects. *Journal of Applied Psychology, 92,* 1169–1176.

Deouell, L. Y., Parnes, A., & Pickard, N. (2006). Spatial location is accurately tracked by human auditory sensory memory: Evidence from the mismatch negativity. *European Journal of Neuroscience, 24,* 1488–1494.

Deregowski, J. B. (1973). Illusion and culture. In R. L. Gregory & G. H. Combrich (Eds.), *Illusion in nature and art* (pp. 161–192). New York: Scribner.

Derryberry, W. P. (2006). Review of social motivation: Conscious and unconscious processes. *Journal of Moral Education, 35,* 276–278.

Detterman, D. K., Gabriel, L. T., & Ruthsatz, J. M. (2000). Intelligence and mental retardation. In R. J. Sternberg et al. (Eds.), *Handbook of intelligence.* New York: Cambridge University Press.

Devonport, J. J., & Lane, A. M. (2006). Relationships between self-efficacy, coping and student retention. *Social Behavior and Personality, 34,* 127–138.

DiCano, P., & Everitt, B. J. (2002). Reinstatement and spontaneous recovery of cocaine-seeking following extinction and different durations of withdrawal. *Behavioural Pharmacology, 13,* 397–406.

Dickstein, L.S. (1972). Death concern: Measurement and correlates. *Psychological Reports, 30*(2), 563–571.

DiGiovanna, A. G. (1994). *Human aging: Biological perspectives.* New York: McGraw-Hill.

Dillard, J. P., & Shen, L. (2007). Self-report measures of discrete emotions. In R. A. Reynolds, R. Woods, & J. D. Baker, *Handbook of research on electronic surveys and measurements.* Hershey, PA: Idea Group Reference/IGI Global.

DiLorenzo, P. M., & Yougentob, S. L. (2003). Olfaction and taste. In M. Gallagher & R. J. Nelson, *Handbook of psychology: Biological psychology* (Vol. 3). New York: Wiley.

Dinges, D. F., Pack, F., Wiliams, K., Gillen, K. A., Powell, J. W., Ott, G. E., Aptowicz, C., & Pack, A. I. (1997). Cumulative sleepiness, mood disturbance, and psychomotor vigilance performance decrements during a week of sleep restricted to 4–5 hours per night. *Sleep, 20,* 267–273.

Do, V. T. (2006). Asian American men and the media: The relationship between ethnic identity, self-esteem, and the endorsement of stereotypes. *Dissertation Abstracts International: Section B: The Sciences and Engineering, 67* (6-B), 3446.

Dobbins, A. C., Jeo, R. M., Fiser, J., & Allman, J. M. (1998, July 24). Distance modulation of neural activity in the visual cortex. *Science, 281,* 552–555.

Dodge, K. A. (2004). The nature-nurture debate and public policy. *Merrill-Palmer Quarterly, 50,* 418–427.

Dohrenwend, B. P., Turner, J. B., Turse, N. A., Adams, B. G., Koenen, K. C., & Marshall, R. (2006, August 18). The psychological risks of Vietnam for U.S. veterans: A revisit with new data and methods. *Science, 313,* 979–982.

Dolan, R. J. (2002, November 8). Emotion, cognition, and behavior. *Science, 298,* 1191–1194.

Dolbier, C. L., Smith, S. E., & Steinhardt, M. A. (2007). Relationships of protective factors to stress and symptoms of illness. *American Journal of Health Behavior, 31,* 423–433.

Domhoff, G. W. (1996). *Finding meaning in dreams: A quantitative approach.* New York: Plenum Press.

Domhoff, G. W., & Schneider, A. (1999). Much ado about very little: The small effect sizes when home and laboratory collected dreams are compared. *Dreaming, 9,* 139–151.

Dortch, S. (1996, October). Our aching heads. *American Demographics,* pp. 4–8.

Doty, R. L., Green, P. A., Ram, C., & Yankell, S. L. (1982). Communication of gender from human breath odors: Relationship to perceived intensity and pleasantness. *Hormones and Behavior, 16,* 13–22.

Dovidio, J. F. (2001). On the nature of contemporary prejudice: The third wave. *Journal of Social Issues, 57,* 829–849.

Dovidio, J. F., & Gaertner, S. L. (2006). A multilevel perspective on prejudice: Crossing disciplinary boundaries. In P. A. M. Van Lange, *Bridging social psychology: Benefits of transdisciplinary approaches.* Mahwah, NJ: Erlbaum.

Dovidio, J. F., Gaertner, S. L., & Kawakami, K. (2003). Intergroup contact: The past, present, and the future. *Group Processes and Intergroup Relations, 6,* 5–20.

Dovidio, J. F., Gaertner, S. L., & Pearson, A. R. (2005). On the nature of prejudice: The psychological foundations of hate. In R. J. Sternberg (Ed.), *Psychology of hate.* Washington, DC: American Psychological Association.

Doyle, K. A. (2002). Rational Emotive Behavior Therapy and its application to women's groups. In W. Dryden, & M. Neenan (Eds.), *Rational emotive behaviour group therapy.* London: Whurr Publishers.

Drob, S. (2005). The mystical symbol: Some comments on Ankor, Giegerich, Scholem, and Jung. *Journal of Jungian Theory & Practice, 7,* 25–29.

Dryden, W. (1999). *Rational emotive behavior therapy: A training manual.* New York: Springer.

Dubovsky, S. (1999, February 25). Tuning in to manic depression. *HealthNews, 5,* p. 8.

Duke, M., & Nowicki, S., Jr. (1979). *Abnormal psychology: Perspectives on being different.* Monterey, CA: Brooks/ Cole.

Duncker, K. (1945). On problem solving. *Psychological Monographs, 58* (5, whole no. 270).

Ebbinghaus, H. (1885/1913). *Memory: A contribution to experimental psychology* (H. A. Roger & C. E. Bussenius, Trans.). New York: Columbia University Press.

Ebstein, R. P., Benjamin, J., & Belmaker, R. H. (2003). Behavioral genetics, genomics, and personality. In R. Plomin & J. C. DeFries (Eds.), *Behavioral genetics in the postgenomic era* (pp. 365–388). Washington, DC: American Psychological Association.

Eckardt, M. H. (2005). Karen Horney: A portrait: The 120th aniversay, Karen Horney, September 16, 1885. *American Journal of Psychoanalysis, 65,* 95–101.

Edinger, J. D., Wohlgemuth, W. K., Radtke, R. A., Marsh, G. R., & Quillian, R. E. (2001). Cognitive behavioral therapy for treatment of chronic primary insomnia: A randomized controlled trial. *Journal of the American Medical Association, 285,* 1856–1864.

Edwards, R. R., & Fillingim, R. B. (2007). Self-reported pain sensitivity: Lack of correlation with pain threshold and tolerance. *European Journal of Pain, 11,* 594–598.

Eichenbaum, H. (2004). Toward an information processing framework for memory representation by the hippocampus. In M. S. Gazzaniga (Ed.), *Cognitive neurosciences* (3rd ed., pp. 679–690). Cambridge, MA: MIT.

Eizenberg, M. M., & Zaslavsky, O. (2004). Students' verification strategies for combinatorial problems. *Mathematical Thinking and Learning, 6,* 15–36.

Ekman, P. (1972). Universals and cultural differences in facial expressions of emotion. In J. Cole (Ed.), *Darwin and facial expression: A century of research in review* (pp. 169–222). New York: Academic Press.

Ekman, P. (1994a). All emotions are basic. In P. Ekman & R.J. Davidson (Eds.), *The nature of emotion: Fundamental questions.* New York: Oxford University Press.

Ekman, P. (1994b). Strong evidence for universals in facial expressions: A reply to Russell's mistaken critique. *Psychological Bulletin, 115,* 268–287.

Ekman, P. (2003). *Emotions revealed: Recognizing faces and feelings to improve communication and emotional life.* New York: Times Books.

Ekman, P., Davidson, R. J., & Friesen, W. V. (1990). Emotional expression and brain physiology: II. The Duchenne smile. *Journal of Personality and Social Psychology, 58,* 342–353.

Ekman, P., Levenson, R. W., & Friesen, W. V. (1983, September 16). Autonomic nervous system activity distinguishes among emotions. *Science, 223,* 1208–1210.

Ekman, P., & O'Sullivan, M. (1991). Facial expression: Methods, means, and moues. In R. S. Feldman & B. Rimé (Eds.), *Fundamentals of nonverbal behavior.* Cambridge, England: Cambridge University Press.

Ellason, J. W., & Ross, C. A. (2004). SCL-90-R norms for dissociative identity disorder. *Journal of Trauma and Dissociation, 5,* 85–91.

Elliott, A. (2002). *Psychoanalytic theory: An introduction* (2nd ed.). Durham, NC: Duke University Press.

Ellis, A. (1974). *Growth through reason.* Hollywood, CA: Wilshire Books.

Ellis, A. (2002). *Overcoming resistance: A rational emotive behavior therapy integrated approach* (2nd ed.). New York: Springer.

Ellis, A. (2004). Expanding the ABCs of rational emotive behavior therapy. In A. Freeman, M. J. Mahoney, P. Devito, & D. Martin (Eds.), *Cognition and psychotherapy* (2nd ed.). New York: Springer.

El-Mallakh, R. S., & Abraham, H. D. (2007). MDMA (Ecstasy). *Annals of Clinical Psychiatry, 19,* 45–52.

Engler, J., & Goleman, D. (1992). *The consumer's guide to psychotherapy.* New York: Simon & Schuster.

Erikson, E. H. (1963). *Childhood and society* (2nd ed.). New York: Norton.

Ervik, S., Abdelnoor, M., & Heier, M. S. (2006). Health-related quality of life in narcolepsy. *Acta Neurologica Scandinavica, 114,* 198–204.

Evans, A. M. (2007). Transference in the nurse-patient relationship. *Journal of Psychiatric and Mental Health Nursing, 14,* 189–195.

Evans, D. E., & Rothbart, M. K. (2007). Developing a model for adult temperament. *Journal of Research in Personality, 41,* 868–888.

Evans, J. B. T. (2004). Informal reasoning: Theory and method. *Canadian Journal of Experimental Psychology, 58,* 69–74.

Evcik, D., Kavuncu, V., Cakir, T., Subasi, V., & Yaman, M. (2007). Laser therapy in the treatment of carpal tunnel syndrome: A randomized controlled trial. *Photomedical Laser Surgery, 25,* 34–39.

Eysenck, H. J. (1990). Biological dimensions of personality. In L. A. Pervin (Ed.), *Handbook of personality: Theory and research* (p. 246). New York: Guilford Press.

Eysenck, H. J. (1995). *Eysenck on extraversion.* New York: Wiley.

Fagan, J. F., & Holland, C. R. (2002). Equal opportunity and racial differences in IQ. *Intelligence, 30,* 361–387.

Fagan, J. F., & Holland, C. R. (2007). Racial equality in intelligence: Predictions from a theory of intelligence as processing. *Intelligence, 35,* 319–334.

Fallon, A. (2006). Informed consent in the practice of group psychotherapy. *International Journal of Group Psychotherapy, 56,* 431–453.

Fallon, B. A., & Feinstein, S. (2001). Hypochondriasis. In K. A. Phillips (Ed.), *Somatoform and factitious disorders*. Washington, DC: American Psychiatric Association.

Fanselow, M. S., & Poulos, A. M. (2005). The neuroscience of mammalian associative learning. *Annual Review of Psychology, 56*, 207–234.

Fearing, V. G., & Clark, J. (Eds.). (2000). *Individuals in context: A practical guide to client-centered practice*. Chicago: Slack Publishing.

Feinberg, A. W. (2002, April). Homo-cysteine may raise Alzheimer's risk: A physician's perspective. *HealthNews*, p. 4.

Feldhusen, J. F., (2006). The role of the knowledge base in creative thinking. In J. C. Kaufman, & J. Baer, *Creativity and reason in cognitive development*. New York: Cambridge University Press.

Feldman, R. S. (2009). *P.O.W.E.R. Learning* (4th ed.). New York: McGraw-Hill.

Festinger, L. (1957). *A theory of cognitive dissonance*. Stanford, CA: Stanford University Press.

Fields-Meyer, T. (1999, October 25). The whiz kids. *People*, pp. 59–63.

Fine, L. (1994). Personal communication.

Fingelkurts, A., Fingelkurts, A. A., Kallio, S. & Revonsuo, A. (2007). Hypnosis induces a changed composition of brain oscillations in EEG: A case study. *Contemporary Hypnosis, 24*, 3–18.

Finkler, K. (2004). Traditional healers in Mexico: The effectiveness of spiritual practices. In U. P. Gielen, J. M. Fish, & J. G. Draguns (Eds.), *Handbook of culture, therapy, and healing*. Mahwah, NJ: Erlbaum.

Finlay, F. O., Jones, R., & Coleman, J. (2002). Is puberty getting earlier? The views of doctors and teachers. *Child: Care, Health and Development, 28*, 205–209.

Finley, C. L., & Cowley, B. J. (2005). The effects of a consistent sleep schedule on time taken to achieve sleep. *Clinical Case Studies, 4*, 304–311.

Firestein, B. A. (Ed.). (1996). *Bisexuality: The psychology and politics of an invisible minority*. Thousand Oaks, CA: Sage.

First, M. B., Frances, A., & Pincus, H. A. (2002). *DSM-IV-TR handbook of differential diagnosis*. Washington, DC: American Psychiatric Publishing.

Fischer, K. W., Shaver, P. R., & Carnochan, P. (1990). How emotions develop and how they organize development. *Cognition and Emotion, 4*, 81–127.

Fishbach, A., Dhar, R., & Zhang, Y. (2006). Subgoals as substitutes or complements: The role of goal accessibility. *Journal of Personality and Social Psychology, 91*, 232–242.

Fisher, C. B. (2003). *Decoding the ethics code: A practical guide for psychologists*. Thousand Oaks, CA: Sage.

Fisher, C. B., Hoagwood, K., Boyce, C., Duster, T., Frank, D. A., Grisso, T., Levine, R. J., Macklin, R., Spencer, M. B., Takanishi, R., Trimble, J. E., & Zayas, L. H. (2002). Research ethics for mental health science involving ethnic minority children and youths. *American Psychologist, 57*, 1024–1040.

Fisher, J. E., & O'Donohue, W. T. (2006). *Practitioner's guide to evidence-based psychotherapy*. New York: Springer Science + Business Media.

Fiske, S. T. (2002). What we know now about bias and intergroup conflict, the problem of the century. *Current Directions in Psychological Science, 11*, 123–128.

Fitch, K. L., & Sanders, R. E. (2005). *Handbook of language and social interaction*. Mahwah, NJ: Erlbaum.

Flam, F. (1991, June 14). Queasy riders. *Science, 252*, 1488.

Flavell, S. W., Cowan, C. W., Kim, T., Greer, P. L., Lin, Y., Paradis, S., Griffith, E. C., Hu, L. S., Chen, C., & Greenberg, M. E. (2006, February 17). Activity-dependent regulation of MEF2 transcription factors suppresses excitatory synapse number. *Science, 311*, 1008–1010.

Fleischman, D. A., Wilson, R. S., Gabrieli, J. D. E., Bienias, J. L., & Bennett, D. A. (2004). A longitudinal study of implicit and explicit memory in old persons. *Psychology and Aging, 19*, 617–625.

Folkman, S., & Moskowitz, J. T. (2000). Stress, positive emotion, and coping. *Current Directions in Psychological Science, 9*, 115–118.

Folkman, S., & Moskowitz, J. T. (2004). Coping: Pitfalls and promise. *Annual Review of Psychology, 55*, 745–774.

Forer, B. (1949). The fallacy of personal validation: A classroom demonstration of gullibility. *Journal of Abnormal and Social Psychology, 44*, 118–123.

Forlenza, M. J., & Baum, A. (2004). Psychoneuroimmunology. In T. J. Boll & R. G. Frank (Eds.),. *Handbook of clinical health psychology: Volume 3. Models and perspectives in health psychology*. Washington, DC: American Psychological Association.

Foster, K. M. (2005). Introduction: John Uzo Ogbu (1939–2003): How do you ensure the fair consideration of a complex ancestor? Multiple approaches to assessing the work and legacy of John Uzo Ogbu. *International Journal of Qualitative Studies in Education, 18*, 559–564.

Fountoulakis, K. N., Vieta, E., Sanchez-Moreno, J., Kaprinis, S. G., Goikolea, J. M., & Kaprinis, G. S. (2005). Treatment guidelines for bipolar disorder: A critical review. *Journal of Affective Disorders, 86*, 1–10.

Fox, S., & Spector, P. E. (2000). Relations of emotional intelligence, practical intelligence, general intelligence, and trait affectivity with interview outcomes: It's not all just "G." *Journal of Organizational Behavior, 21*, 203–220.

Frank, L. R. (2002). Electroshock: A crime against the spirit. *Ethical Human Sciences and Services, 4*, 63–71.

Frankenburg, W. K., et al., (1992). *Denver II training manual*. Denver: Denver Developmental Materials.

Franks, D. D., & Smith, T. S. (1999) (Eds.). *Mind, brain, and society: Toward a neuro-sociology of emotion*. Stamford, CT: JAI Press.

Franzek, E., & Beckmann, H. (1996). Gene-environment interaction in schizophrenia: Season-of-birth effect reveals etiologically different subgroups. *Psychopathology, 29*, 14–26.

Freedman, D. S. (1995). The importance of body fat distribution in early life. *American Journal of the Medical Sciences, 310*, S72–S76.

Frensch, P. A., & Rünger, D. (2003). Implicit learning. *Current Directions in Psychological Science, 12*, 13–17.

Freud, S. (1900). *The interpretation of dreams*. New York: Basic Books.

Freud, S. (1922/1959). *Group psychology and the analysis of the ego*. London: Hogarth.

Friedberg, R. D. (2006). A cognitive-behavioral approach to family therapy. *Journal of Contemporary Psychotherapy, 36*, 159–165.

Friedman, J. N. W., Oltmanns, T. F., & Turkheimer, E. (2007). Interpersonal perception and personality disorders: Utilization of a thin slice approach. *Journal of Research in Personality, 41*, 667–688.

Frijda, N. H. (2005). Emotion experience. *Cognition and Emotion, 19*, 473–497.

Frincke, J. L., & Pate, W. E, II. (2004, March). *Yesterday, today, and tomorrow. Careers in Psychology 2004, what students need to know*. Paper presented at the Annual Convention of the Southeastern Psychological Association, Atlanta, GA.

Frings, L., Wagner, K., Unterrainer, J., Spreer, J., Halsband, U., & Schulze-Bonhage, A. (2006). Gender-related differences in lateralization of hippocampal activation and cognitive strategy. *Neuroreport, 17*, 417–421.

Frost, L. E., & Bonnie, R. J. (Eds.). (2001). *The evolution of mental health law*. Washington, DC: American Psychological Association.

Frost, R. O., & Steketee, G. (Eds.). (2002). *Cognitive approaches to obsessions and compulsions: Theory, assessment, and treatment*. New York: Pergamon Press.

Funder, D. C. (1991). Global traits: A neoAllportian approach to personality. *Psychological Science, 2*, 31–39.

Furnham, A., & Crump, J. (2005). Personality traits, types, and disorders: An examination of the relationship between three self-report measures. *European Journal of Personality, 19*, 167–184.

Furumoto, L., & Scarborough, E. (2002). Placing women in the history of psychology: The first American women psychologists. In W. E. Pickren (Ed.), *Evolving perspectives on the history of psychology* (pp. 527–543). Washington, DC: American Psychological Association.

Galanter, E. (1962). Contemporary psychophysics. In R. Brown, E. Galanter, E. Hess, & G. Maroler (Eds.), *New directions in psychology* (pp. 87–157). New York: Holt.

Galanter, M. (2007). Spirituality and recovery in 12-step programs: An empirical model. *Journal of Substance Abuse Treatment, 33,* 265–272.

Galatzer-Levy, R. M., & Cohler, B. J. (1997). *Essential psychoanalysis: A contemporary introduction.* New York: Basic Books.

Gami, A. S., Howard, D. E., Olson, E. J., Somers, V. K. (2005). Day-night pattern of sudden death in obstructive sleep apnea. *New England Journal of Medicine, 353,* 1206–1214.

Gangestad, S. W., Simpson, J. A., Cousins, A. J., Garver-Apgar, C. E., & Christensen, P. N. (2004). Women's preferences for male behavioral displays change across the menstrual cycle. *Psychological Science, 15,* 203–207.

Garb, H. N., Wood, J. M., Lilenfeld, S. O., & Nezworski, M. T. (2005). Roots of the Rorschach controversy. *Clinical Psychology Review, 25,* 97–118.

Garber, J., & Horowitz, J. L. (2002). Depression in children. In I. H. Gotlib & C. L. Hammen (Eds.), *Handbook of depression.* New York: Guilford Press.

Garcia, S. M., Weaver, K., Moskowitz, G. B., & Darley, J. M. (2002). Crowded minds: The implicit bystander effect. *Journal of Personality and Social Psychology, 83,* 843–853.

Gardner, E. P., & Kandel, E. R. (2000). Touch. In E. R. Kandel, J. H. Schwartz, & T. M. Jessell (Eds.), *Principles of neural science* (4th ed.). New York: McGraw-Hill.

Gardner, H. (2000). *Intelligence reframed: Multiple intelligences for the 21st century.* New York: Basic Books.

Gardner, H. (2005). Scientific psychology: Should we bury it or praise it? In R. J. Sternberg (Ed.), *Unity in psychology: Possibility or pipe dream?* (pp. 77–90). Washington, DC: American Psychological Association.

Garwick, G. B. (2007). Intelligence-related terms in mental retardation, learning disability, and gifted/talented professional usage, 1983–2001: The 1992 mental retardation redefinition as natural experiment. *Dissertation Abstracts International Section A: Humanities and Social Sciences, 67*(9-A), 3296.

Garza-Guerrero, C. (2000). Idealization and mourning in love relationships: Normal and pathological spectra. *Psychoanalytic Quarterly, 69,* 121–150.

Gass, C. S., Luis, C. A., Meyers, T. L., & Kuljis, R. O. (2000). Familial Creutzfeldt-Jakob disease: A neuro-psychological case study. *Archives of Clinical Neuropsychology, 15,* 165–175.

Gatchel, R. J., & Weisberg, J. N. (2000). *Personality characteristics of patients with pain.* Washington, DC: APA Books.

Gatchel, R. J., & Oordt, M. S. (2003). Obesity. In R. J. Gatchel & M. S. Oordt, *Clinical health psychology and primary care: Practical advice and clinical guidance for successful collaboration* (pp. 149–167). Washington, DC: American Psychological Association.

Gazzaniga, M. S. (1998, July). The split brain revisited. *Scientific American,* 50–55.

Gazzaniga, M. S., Ivry, R. B., & Mangun, G. R. (2002). *Cognitive neuroscience: The biology of the mind* (2nd ed.). New York: W. W. Norton.

Gegenfurtner, K. R. (2003). Color vision. *Annual Review of Neuroscience, 26,* 181–206.

Gelman, R., & Kit-Fong Au, T. (Eds.). (1996). *Perceptual and cognitive development.* New York: Academic Press.

Genovese, J. E. C. (2006). Piaget, pedagogy, and evolutionary psychology. *Evolutionary Psychology, 4,* 2127–2137.

George, M. S., Wassermann, E. M., Williams, W. A., Callahan, A., et al. (1995). Daily repetitive transcranial magnetic stimulations (rTMS) improves mood in depression. *Neuroreport: An International Journal for the Rapid Communication of Research in Neuroscience, 6,* 1853–1856.

George, S., & Moselhy, H. (2005). Cocaine-induced trichotillomania. *Addiction, 100,* 255–256.

Gershkoff-Stowe, L., Connell, B., & Smith, L. (2006). Priming overgeneralizations in two- and four-year-old children. *Journal of Child Language, 33,* 461–486.

Gerstel, N. (2005, April 8). In search of time. *Science, 308,* 204–205.

Giacobbi, P. R., Jr., Lynn, T. K. Wetherington, J. M., Jenkins, J., Bodendorf, M., & Langley, B. (2004). Stress and coping during the transition to university for first-year female athletes. *Sports Psychologist, 18,* 1–20.

Gibbons, R. D., Brown, C. H., Hur, K., Marcus, S. M., Bhaumik, D. K., Erkens, J. A., Herrings, R. M. C., & Mann, J. J. (2007). Early evidence on the effects of regulators' suicidality warnings on SSRI prescriptions and suicide in children and adolescents. *American Journal of Psychiatry, 164,* 1356–1363.

Gilbert, D. T., McNulty, S. E., Guiliano, T. A., & Benson, J. E. (1992). Blurry words and fuzzy deeds: The attribution of obscure behavior. *Journal of Personality and Social Psychology, 62,* 18–25.

Gilbert, D. T., Miller, A. G., & Ross, L. (1998). Speeding with Ned: A personal view of the correspondence bias. In J. M. Darley & J. Cooper (Eds.), *Attribution and social interaction: The legacy of Edward E. Jones.* Washington, DC: American Psychological Association.

Gilligan, C. (1996). The centrality of relationships in psychological development: A puzzle, some evidence, and a theory. In G. G. Noam & K. W. Fischer (Eds.), *Development and vulnerability in close relationships.* Hillsdale, NJ: Erlbaum.

Gladwell, M. (2004, September 20). Annals of psychology: Personality, plus how corporations figure out who you are. *The New Yorker,* 42–45.

Glickler, J. (2006). Advancing in advancement: A self-efficacy study of development practitioners in higher education. *Dissertation Abstracts International: Section B: The Sciences and Engineering, 67* (2-B), 1190.

Glicksohn, J., & Nahari, G. (2007). Interacting personality traits? Smoking as a test case. *European Journal of Personality, 21,* 225–234.

Glisky, E. L. (2007). Changes in cognitive function in human aging. In D. R. Riddle, *Brain aging: Models, methods, and mechanisms.* Boca Raton, FL: CRC Press.

Goffin, R. D., Jelley, R. B., & Wagner, S. H. (2003). Is halo helpful? Effects of inducing halo on performance rating accuracy. *Social Behavior and Personality, 31,* 625–636.

Goin, M. K. (2005). A current perspective on the psychotherapies. *Psychiatric Services, 56,* 255–257.

Gold, P. E., Cahill, L., & Wenk, G. L. (2002). Ginkgo biloba: A cognitive enhancer? *Psychological Science in the Public Interest, 3,* 2–7.

Goldfried, M. R., & Pachankis, J. E. (2007). On the next generation of process research. *Clinical Psychological Review, 27,* 760–768.

Goldstein, I. (2000). Female sexual arousal disorder: new insights. *International Journal of Impotence Research, 12*(Suppl. 4), S152–S157.

Goldstein, S. N. (2006). The exploration of spirituality and identity status in adolescence. *Dissertation Abstracts International: Section B: The Sciences and Engineering, 67*(6-B), 3481.

Goldstone, R. L., & Kersten, A. (2003). Concepts and categorization. In A. F. Healy & R. W. Proctor (Eds.), *Handbook of psychology: Experimental psychology* (Vol. 4, pp. 599–621). New York: Wiley.

Gontkovsky, S. T. (2005). Neurobiological bases and neuropsychological correlates of aggression and violence. In J. P. Morgan (Ed.), *Psychology of aggression.* Hauppauge, NY: Nova Science Publishers.

Gontkovsky, S. T., & Beatty, W. W. (2006). Practical methods for the clinical assessment of information processing speed. *International Journal of Neuroscience, 116,* 1317–1325.

Goode, E. (1999, April 13). If things taste bad, "phantoms" may be at work. *The New York Times,* pp. D1–D2.

Goode, E. (2003, January 28). Even in the age of Prozac, some still prefer the couch. *The New York Times,* Section F, p. 1.

Goodheart, C. D., Kazdin, A. E., & Sternberg, R. J. (Eds). (2006). *Evidence-based psychotherapy: Where practice and research meet.* Washington, DC: American Psychological Association.

Goodwin, R. D., & Hamilton, S. P. (2003). Lifetime comorbidity of antisocial personality disorder and anxiety disorders among adults in the community. *Psychiatry Research, 117,* 159–166.

Goodwin, R., Costa, P., & Adonu, J. (2004). Social support and its consequences: "Positive" and "deficiency" values and their implications for support and self-esteem. *British Journal of Social Psychology, 43,* 465–474.

Gooren, L. (2006). The biology of human psychosexual differentiation. *Hormones and Behavior, 50,* 589–601.

Gotlib, I. H., Krasnoperova, E., Yue, D. N., & Joorman, J. (2004). Attentional biases for negative interpersonal stimuli in clinical depression. *Journal of Abnormal Psychology, 113,* 127–135.

Gottesman, I. I. (1991). *Schizophrenia genesis: The origins of madness.* New York: Freeman.

Gottesman, I. I. (1997, June 6). Twin: En route to QTLs for cognition. *Science, 276,* 1522–1523.

Gottesman, I. I., & Hanson, D. R. (2005). Human development: Biological and genetic processes. *Annual Review of Psychology, 56,* 263–286.

Gottfredson, L. S. (2004). Schools and the *g* factor. *Wilson Quarterly,* pp. 35–45.

Gottfredson, L. S., & Deary, I. J. (2004). Intelligence predicts health and longevity, but why? *Current Directions in Psychological Science, 13,* 1–4.

Gottlieb, D. A. (2004). Acquisition with partial and continuous reinforcement in pigeon autoshaping. *Learning and Behavior, 32,* 321–334.

Gottlieb, D. A. (2006). Effects of partial reinforcement and time between reinforced trials on terminal response rate in pigeon autoshaping. *Behavioural Processes, 72,* 6–13.

Gould, R. L. (1978). *Transformations.* New York: Simon & Schuster.

Grady, D., & Kolata, G. (2003, August, 29). Gene therapy used to treat patient with Parkinson's. *The New York Times,* pp. A1, A18.

Graham, C. A., Bancroft, J., & Doll, H. A. (2007). Does oral contraceptive-induced reduction in free testosterone adversely affect the sexuality or mood of women? *Psychoneuroendocrinology, 32,* 246–255.

Graham, S. (1992). "Most of the subjects were white and middle class": Trends in published research on African Americans in selected APA journals, 1970–1989. *American Psychologist, 47,* 629–639.

Granic, I., Hollenstein, T., & Dishion, T. (2003). Longitudinal analysis of flexibility and reorganization in early adolescence: A dynamic systems study of family interactions. *Developmental Psychology, 39,* 606–617.

Grann, J. D. (2007). Confidence in knowledge past: An empirical basis for a differential decay theory of very long-term memory monitoring. *Dissertation Abstracts International Section A: Humanities and Social Sciences, 67,* 2462.

Gray, G. C. (2006). The regulation of corporate violations: Punishment, compliance, and the blurring of responsibility. *British Journal of Criminology, 46,* 875–892.

Greenberg, R. M., & Kellner, C. H. (2005). Electroconvulsive therapy: A selected review. *American Journal of Geriatric Psychiatry, 13,* 268–281.

Greene, J. D., Sommerville, R. B., Nystrom, L. E., Darley, J. M., & Cohen, J. D. (2001, September 14). An fMRI investigation of emotional engagement in moral judgment. *Science, 293,* 2105–2108.

Greene, R. L., & Clopton, J. R. (2004). Minnesota Multiphasic Personality Inventory-2 (MMPI-2). In M. E. Maruish (Ed.), *Use of psychological testing for treatment planning and outcomes assessment: Instruments for adults* (Vol. 3, 3rd ed.). Mahwah, NJ: Erlbaum.

Greenspan, S. (2006). Functional concepts in mental retardation: Finding the natural essence of an artificial category. *Exceptionality, 14,* 205–224.

Greenwald, A. G., Nosek, B. A., & Sriram, N. (2006). Consequential validity of the implicit association test: Comment on Blanton and Jaccard. *American Psychologist, 61,* 56–61.

Greer, R. D., Dudek-Singer, J., & Gautreaux, G. (2006). Observational learning. *International Journal of Psychology, 41,* 486–499.

Gregory, R. L. (1978). *The psychology of seeing* (3rd ed.). New York: McGraw-Hill.

Grigoriadis, S., & Ravitz, P. (2007). An approach to interpersonal psychotherapy for postpartum depression: Focusing on interpersonal changes. *Canadian Family Physician, 53,* 1469–1475.

Grilo, C. M., Sanislow, C. A., Skodol, A. E., Gunderson, J. G., Stout, R. L., Shea, M. T., Zanarini, M. C., Bencer, D. S., Morey, L. C., Dyck, I. R., & McGlashan, T. H. (2003). Do eating disorders co-occur with personality disorders? Comparison groups matter. *International Journal of Eating Disorders, 33,* 155–164.

Grossmann, T., Striano, T., & Friederici, A. D. (2007). Developmental changes in infants' processing of happy and angry facial expressions: A neurobehavioral study. *Brain and Cognition, 64,* 30–41.

Groves, R.M., Fowler, F.J., Couper, M.P., Lepkowski, J.M., Singer, E., & Tourangeau, R. (2004). *Survey methodology.* New York: Wiley.

Guilleminault, C., Kirisoglu, C., Bao, G., Arias, V., Chan, A., & Li, K. K. (2005). Adult chronic sleepwalking and its treatment based on polysomnography. *Brain, 128*(Pt. 5), 1062–1069.

Guthrie, R. V. (1998). *Even the rat was white: A historical view of psychology* (2nd ed.). Needham Heights, MA: Allyn & Bacon.

Gutierrez, P. M., Muehlenkamp, J. L., Konick, L. C., & Osman, A. (2005). What role does race play in adolescent suicidal ideation? *Archives of Suicide Research, 9,* 177–192.

Gwynn, M. I., & Spanos, N. P. (1996). Hypnotic responsiveness, nonhypnotic suggestibility, and responsiveness to social influence. In R. G. Kunzendorf, N. P. Spahos, & B. Wallace (Eds.), *Hypnosis and imagination.* Amityville, NY: Baywood.

Haberstick, B. C., Schmitz, S., Young, S. E., & Hewitt, J. K. (2005). Contributions of genes and environments to stability and change in externalizing and internalizing problems during elementary and middle school. *Behavior Genetics, 35,* 381–396.

Haberstick, B. C., Timberlake, D., & Ehringer, M. A. (2007). Genes, time to first cigarette and nicotine dependence in a general population sample of young adults. *Addiction, 102,* 655–665.

Hadjistavropoulos, T., Craig, K. D., & Fuchs-Lacelle, S. (2004). *Social influences and the communication of pain.* Mahwah, NJ: Erlbaum.

Halford, S. (2006). Collapsing the boundaries? Fatherhood, organization and home-working. *Gender, Work & Organization, 13,* 383–402.

Halgin, R. P., & Whitbourne, S.K. (1994). *Abnormal psychology.* Fort Worth, TX: Harcourt Brace.

Hall, R. E. (2002). *The Bell Curve:* Implications for the performance of black/white athletes. *Social Science Journal, 39,* 113–118.

Hallschmid, M., Benedict, C., Born, J., Fehm, H., & Kern, W. (2004). Manipulating central nervous mechanisms of food intake and body weight regulation by intranasal administration of neuropeptides in man. *Physiology and Behavior, 83,* 55–64.

Halpern, D. F. (2005). Psychology at the intersection of work and family: Recommendations for employers, working families, and policymakers. *American Psychologist, 60,* 397–409.

Hamann, S. B., Ely, T. D., Hoffman, J. M., & Kilts, C. D. (2002). Ecstasy and agony: Activation of human amygdala in positive and negative emotion. *Psychological Science, 13,* 135–141.

Hambleton, R. K. (2006). Psychometric models, test designs and item types for the next generation of educational and psychological tests. In D. Bartram & R. K. Hambleton, *Computer-based testing and the Internet: Issues and advances.* New York: Wiley.

Hamer, D. H., Hu, S., Magnuson, V. L., Hu, N., & Pattatucci, A. M. L. (1993, July 16). A linkage between DNA markers on the X chromosome and male sexual orientation. *Science, 261,* 321–327.

Hamilton, A. C., & Martin, R. C. (2007). Semantic short-term memory deficits and resolution of interference: A case for inhibition? In D. S. Gorfein & C. M. MacLeod, *Inhibition in cognition.* Washington, DC: American Psychological Association.

Hampson, R. (2007, October 8). Dozens feel pinched by R.I. lobsterman's tale; victims say alleged con artist knew their names, soft spots. *USA Today,* p. 2A.

Hansell, S. (2007, January 3). Google answer to filling jobs is an algorithm. *The New York Times,* p. A1.

Harlaar, N., Spinath, F. M., Dale, P. S., & Plomin, R. (2005). Genetic influences on early word recognition abilities and disabilities: A study of 7-year-old twins. *Journal of Child Psychology and Psychiatry, 46,* 373–384.

Harlow, H. F., & Zimmerman, R. R. (1959). Affectional responses in the infant monkey. *Science, 130,* 421–432.

Harlow, J. M. (1869). Recovery from the passage of an iron bar through the head. *Massachusetts Medical Society Publication, 2,* 329–347.

Hartmann, E. (1967). *The biology of dreaming.* Springfield, IL: Charles C Thomas.

Hartung, C. M., & Widiger, T. A. (1998). Gender differences in the diagnosis of mental disorders: Conclusions and controversies of the DSM-IV. *Psychological Bulletin, 123,* 260–278.

Harvey, J.H., Wenzel, A. & Sprecher, S. (Eds.). (2005) *Handbook of sexuality in close relationships.* Mahwah, NJ: Erlbaum.

Haugen, R., Lund, T. & Ommundsen, Y. (2008). Personality dispositions, expectancy and context in attributional thinking. *Scandinavian Journal of Educational Research. 52*(2), 171–185.

Hauke, C. (2006). The unconscious: Personal and collective. In R. K. Papadopoulos, *The handbook of Jungian psychology: Theory, practice and applications.* New York: Routledge.

Hauser, M. D., Chomsky, N., & Fitch, W. T. (2002, November, 22). The faculty for language: What is it, who has it, and how did it evolve? *Science, 298,* 1569–1579.

Havermans, R. C., Mulkens, S., Nederkoorn, C., & Jansen, A. (2007). The efficacy of cue exposure with response prevention in extinguishing drug and alcohol cue reactivity. *Behavioral Interventions, 22,* 121–135.

Haviland-Jones, J., & Chen, D. (1999, April 17). *Human olfactory perception.* Paper presented at the Association for Chemoreception Sciences, Sarasota, Florida.

Hayflick, L. (2007). Biological aging is no longer an unsolved problem. *Annals of the New York Academy of Sciences, 1100,* 1–13.

Hays, P. A. (2008). *Addressing cultural complexities in practice: Assessment, diagnosis, and therapy* (2nd ed.). Washington, DC: American Psychological Association.

Heath, R. A. (2006). *The Praeger handbook of transsexuality: Changing gender to match mindset.* Westport, CT: Praeger Publishers/Greenwood Publishing.

Hedgepeth, E. (2005). Different lenses, different vision. *School Administrator, 62,* 36–39.

Hedges, D. W., Brown, B. L., Shwalk, D. A., Godfrey, K., & Larcher, A. M. (2007). The efficacy of selective serotonin reuptake inhibitors in adult social anxiety disorder: A meta-analysis of double-blind, placebo-controlled trials. *Journal of Psychopharmacology, 21,* 102–111.

Hegarty, P. (2007). From genius inverts to gendered intelligence: Lewis Terman and the power of the norm [Special issue: Power matters: Knowledge politics in the history of psychology]. *History of Psychology, 10,* 132–155.

Hegarty, P., & Massey, S. (2007). Anti-homosexual prejudice . . . as opposed to what? Queer theory and the social psychology of anti-homosexual attitudes. *Journal of Homosexuality, 52,* 47–71.

Heinrichs, R. W. (2005). The primacy of cognition in schizophrenia. *American Psychologist, 60,* 229–242.

Heller, S. (2005). *Freud A to Z.* New York: Wiley.

Helmuth, L. (2000, August 25). Synapses shout to overcome distance. *Science, 289,* 1273.

Henderlong, J., & Lepper, M. R. (2002). The effects of praise on children's intrinsic motivation: A review and synthesis. *Psychological Bulletin, 128,* 774–795.

Henderson, J., Kesmodel, U., & Gray, R. (2007). Systematic review of the fetal effects of prenatal binge-drinking. *Journal of Epidemiology Community Health, 61,* 1069–1073.

Henderson, N. D. (1982). Correlations in IQ for pairs of people with varying degrees of genetic relatedness and shared environment. *Annual Review of Psychology, 33,* 219–243.

Hendrick, C., & Hendrick, S. S. (2003). Romantic love: Measuring Cupid's arrow. In S. J. Lopez & C. R. Snyder (Eds.), *Positive psychological assessment: A handbook of models and measures.* Washington, DC: American Psychological Association.

Hentschel, U., Smith, G., Draguns, J. G., & Elhers, W. (2004). *Defense mechanisms: Theoretical, research and clinical perspectives.* Oxford, England: Elsevier Science Ltd.

Herrán, A., Carrera, M., & Sierra-Biddle, D. (2006). Panic disorder and the onset of agoraphobia. *Psychiatry and Clinical Neurosciences, 60,* 395–396.

Herrnstein, R. J., & Murray, D. (1994). *The bell curve.* New York: Free Press.

Herz, R.S. & Engen, T. (1996). Odor memory: Review and analysis. *Psychonomic Bulletin & Review, 3*(3), 300–313.

Heshka, S., Anderson, J. W., Atkinson, R. L., Greenway, F. L., Hill, J. O., Phinney, S. D., Kolotkin, R. L., Miller-Kovach, K., & Pi-Sunyer, F. X. (2003). Weight loss with self-help compared with a structured commercial program: A randomized trial. *Journal of the American Medical Association, 289,* 1792–1798.

Hess, D. W., Kolakowsky-Hayner, S. A., Cifu, D. X., & Huang, M. E. (2000). A comparative study of outcomes and expenses following tetraplegia and paraplegia. *Journal of Spinal Cord Medicine, 23,* 228–233.

Heyman, G. D., & Diesendruck, G. (2002). The Spanish *ser/estar* distinction in bilingual children's reasoning about human psychological characteristics. *Developmental Psychology, 38,* 407–417.

Hiby, E. F., Rooney, N. J., & Bradshaw, J. W. S. (2004). Dog training methods: Their use, effectiveness and interaction with behaviour and welfare. *Animal Welfare, 13,* 63–69.

Hicks, T. V., & Leitenberg, H. (2001). Sexual fantasies about one's partner versus someone else: Gender differences in incidence and frequency. *Journal of Sex Research, 38,* 43–50.

Hilarski, C. (2007). Antisocial personality disorder. In B. A. Thyer, & J. S. Wodarski, *Social work in mental health: An evidence-based approach.* Hoboken, NJ: Wiley.

Hilgard, E. (1992). Dissassociation and theories of hypnosis. In E. Fromm & M. E. Nash (Eds.), *Contemporary hypnosis research.* New York: Guilford Press.

Hill, J. O., Catenacci, V., & Wyatt, H. R. (2005). Obesity: Overview of an epidemic. *Psychiatric Clinics of North America, 28,* 1–23.

Hill, J. O., Wyatt, H. R., Reed, G. W., & Peters, J. C. (2003, February 7). Obesity and the environment: Where do we go from here? *Science, 299,* 853–855.

Hines, M. (2004) *Brain gender.* New York: Oxford University Press.

Hinshaw, S. P., Zupan, B. A., Simmel, C., Nigg, J. T., & Melnick, S. (1997). Peer status in boys with and without attention-deficit hyperactivity disorder: Predictions from overt and covert antisocial behavior, social isolation, and authoritative parenting beliefs. *Child Development, 68,* 880–896.

Hirschler, B. (2007, May 1). Doctors test gene therapy to treat blindness. *Reuters,* p. 9.

Hobfoll, S. E., Freedy, J. R., Green B. L., & Solomon, S. D. (1996). Coping in reaction to extreme stress: The roles of resource loss and resource availability. In M. Zeidner & N. S. Endler (Eds.), *Handbook of coping: Theory, research, applications.* New York: Wiley.

Hobson, J. A. (1988). *The dreaming brain.* New York: Basic Books.

Hobson, J. A. (2005). In bed with Mark Solms? What a nightmare! A reply to Domhoff (2005). *Dreaming, 15,* 21–29.

Hobson, J. (2007). States of consciousness: Normal and abnormal variation. In P. D. Zelazo, M. Moscovitch & E. Thompson (Eds.), *The Cambridge handbook of consciousness* (pp. 435–444). New York, NY: Cambridge University Press.

Hochschild, A. (2001, February). A generation without public passion. *Atlantic Monthly,* pp. 33–42.

Hock, H. S., & Ploeger, A. (2006). Linking dynamical perceptual decisions at different levels of description in motion pattern formation: Psychophysics. *Perception & Psychophysics, 68,* 505–514.

Hoff, E. (2008). *Language development.* New York: Wadsworth.

Hofmann, S. G. (2007). Enhancing exposure-based therapy from a translational research perspective. *Behaviour Research and Therapy, 45,* 1987–2001.

Hogan, J., Davies, S., & Hogan, R. (2007). Generalizing personality-based validity evidence. In S. M. McPhail, *Alternative validation strategies: Developing new and leveraging existing validity evidence.* Hoboken, NJ: Wiley.

Hogg, M. A. (2006). Social identity theory. In P. J. Burke, *Contemporary social psychological theories.* Stanford, CA: Stanford University Press.

Holden, C. (2003, January 17). Deconstructing schizophrenia. *Science, 299,* 333–335.

Holden, C. (2005, June 10). Sex and the suffering brain. *Science, 308,* 1574–1577.

Hollingworth, H. L. (1943/1990). *Leta Stetter Hollingworth: A biography.* Boston: Anker.

Holloway, L. (2000, December 16). Chief of New York City schools plans to revamp bilingual study. *The New York Times,* p. A1.

Holmes, A., Yang, R. J., Lesch, K. P., Crawley, J. N., & Murphy, D. L. (2003). Mice lacking the Serotonin Transporter Exhibit 5-HT-sub(1A) receptor-mediated abnormalities in tests for anxiety-like behavior. *Neuropsychopharmacology, 28,* 2077–2088.

Holowka, S., & Pettito, L. A. (2002, August 30). Left hemisphere cerebral specialization for babies while babbling. *Science, 297,* 1515.

Holt, M., & Jahn, R. (2004, March, 26). Synaptic vesicles in the fast lane. *Science, 303,* 1986–1987.

Hongchun, W., & Ming, L. (2006). About the research on suggestibility and false memory. *Psychological Science (China), 29,* 905–908.

Horn, J. L. (2002). Selections of evidence, misleading assumptions, and over-simplifications: The political message of *The Bell Curve.* In J. M. Fish (Ed.), *Race and intelligence: Separating science from myth* (pp. 297–325). Mahwah, NJ: Erlbaum.

Horney, K. (1937). *Neurotic personality of our times.* New York: Norton.

Houghtalen, R. P., & Talbot, N. (2007). Dissociative disorders and cognitive disorders. In O. J. Z. Sahler, & J. E. Carr, *The behavioral sciences and health care* (2nd rev. and updated ed.). Ashland, OH: Hogrefe & Huber Publishers.

Howard, A., Pion, G.M., Gottfredson, G.D., Flattau, P.E., Oskamp, S., Pfaffin, S.M., et al. (1986). The changing face of American psychology: A report from the Committee on Employment and Human Resources. *American Psychologist. 41*(12), 1311–1327.

Howe, C. J. (2002). The countering of overgeneralization. *Journal of Child Language, 29,* 875–895.

Howells, J. G., & Osborn, M. L. (1984). *A reference companion to the history of abnormal psychology.* Westport, CT: Greenwood Press.

Hu, F. B., Li, T. Y., Colditz, G. A., Willett, W. C., & Manson, J. E. (2003). Television watching and other sedentary behaviors in relation to risk of obesity and type 2 diabetes mellitus in women. *Journal of the American Medical Association, 289,* 1785–1791.

Hubbard, K., O'Neill, A., & Cheakalos, C. (1999, April 12). Out of control. *People,* pp. 52–72.

Hubel, D. H., & Wiesel, T. N. (2004). *Brain and visual perception: The story of a 25-year collaboration.* New York: Oxford University Press.

Huber, F., Beckmann, S. C., & Herrmann, A. (2004). Means-end analysis: Does the affective state influence information processing style? *Psychology and Marketing, 21,* 715–737.

Hudson, W. (1960). Pictorial depth perception in subcultural groups in Africa. *Journal of Social Psychology, 52,* 183–208.

Hudspeth, A. J. (2000). Hearing. In E. R. Kandel, J. H. Schwartz, & T. M. Jessell (Eds.), *Principles of neural science* (4th ed.). New York: McGraw-Hill.

Huijie, T. (2006). The measurement and assessment of mental health: A longitudinal and cross-sectional research on undergraduates, adults and patients. *Psychological Science (China), 29,* 419–422.

Hull, C. L. (1943). *Principles of behavior.* New York: Appleton-Century-Crofts.

Humphrey, N., Curran, A., & Morris, E. (2007). Emotional intelligence and education: A critical review. *Educational Psychology, 27,* 235–254.

Humphreys, G. W., & Müller, H. (2000). A search asymmetry reversed by figure-ground assignment. *Psychological Science, 11,* 196–200.

Hunt, E. (2005). Information processing and intelligence: Where we are and where we are going. In R. J. Sternberg & J. E. Pretz, *Cognition and intelligence: Identifying the mechanisms of the mind.* New York: Cambridge University Press.

Hunt, M. (1974). *Sexual behaviors in the 1970s.* New York: Dell.

Huston, A. C., Donnerstein, E., Fairchild, H. H., Feshback, N. D., Katz, P., Murray, J. P., Rubinstein, E. A., Wilcox, B. L., & Zuckerman, D. (1992). *Big world, small screen: The role of television in American society.* Omaha, NE: University of Nebraska Press.

Hutchinson, S. L., Baldwin, C. K., & Oh, S-S. (2006). Adolescent coping: Exploring adolescents' leisure-based responses to stress. *Leisure Sciences, 28,* 115–131.

Hyde, J. & DeLamater, J. (2008). *Understanding human sexuality (*10th ed.) New York: McGraw-Hill.

Ievers-Landis, C. E., Hoff, A. L., Brez, C., Cancilliere, M. K., McConnell, J., & Kerr, D. (2005). Situational analysis of dietary challenges of the treatment regimen for children and adolescents with phenylketonuria and their primary caregivers. *Journal of Developmental and Behavioral Pediatrics, 26,* 186–193.

Igo, S. E. (2006). Review of A telescope on society: Survey research and social science at the University of Michigan and beyond. *Journal of the History of the Behavioral Sciences, 42,* 95–96.

Ilies, R., Arvey, R. D., & Bouchard, T. J., Jr. (2006). Darwinism, behavioral genetics, and organizational behavior: A review and agenda for future research [Special issue: Darwinian perspectives on behavior in organizations]. *Journal of Organizational Behavior, 27,* 121–141.

Imamura, M., & Nakamizo, S. (2006). An empirical test of formal equivalence between Emmert's Law and the size-distance invariance hypothesis. *The Spanish Journal of Psychology, 9*(2), 295–299.

Innocenti, G. M. (2007). Subcortical regulation of cortical development: Some effects of early, selective deprivations. *Progressive Brain Research, 164,* 23–37.

Irwin, R. R. (2006). Spiritual development in adulthood: Key concepts and models. In C. Hoare, *Handbook of adult development and learning.* New York: Oxford University Press.

Isay, R. A. (1994). *Being homosexual: Gay men and their development.* Lanham, MD: Jason Aronson.

Isbell, L. M., & Tyler, J. M. (2003). Teaching students about in-group favoritism and the minimal groups paradigm. *Teaching of Psychology, 30,* 127–130.

Ishikawa, S., Okajima, I., Matsuoka, H., & Sakano, Y. (2007). Cognitive behavioural therapy for anxiety disorders in children and adolescents: A meta-analysis. *Child and Adolescent Mental Health, 12*(4), 164–172.

Iversen, L. L. (2000). *The science of marijuana.* Oxford, England: Oxford University Press.

Iversen, L. (2004). How cannabis works in the brain. In D. Castle & R. Murray (Eds.), *Marijuana and madness: Psychiatry and neurobiology.* (pp. 19–40). New York: Cambridge University Press.

Iverson, S. D, & Iversen, L. L. (2007). Dopamine: 50 years in perspective. *Trends in Neurosciences, 30,* 188–191.

Izard, C. E. (1990). Facial expressions and the regulation of emotions. *Journal of Personality and Social Psychology, 58,* 487–498.

Izard, C. E. (1994). Innate and universal facial expressions: Evidence from developmental and cross-cultural research. *Psychological Bulletin, 115,* 288–299.

Izard, C. E., & Abe, J. A. (2004). Developmental changes in facial expressions of emotions in the strange situation during the second year of life. *Emotion, 4,* 251–265.

Jacobs, J. A., & Gerson, K. (2004). *The time divide: Work, family, and gender inequality.* Cambridge, MA: Harvard University Press.

Jacoby, L. L., Bishara, A. J., & Hessels, S. (2007). Probabilistic retroactive interference: The role of accessibility bias in interference effects. *Journal of Experimental Psychology: General, 136,* 200–216.

Jaffé, A., Prasad, S. A., & Larcher, V. (2006). Gene therapy for children with cystic fibrosis—who has the right to choose? *Journal of Medical Ethics, 32,* 361–364.

Jain, S., Mills, P. J., & Von Känel, R. (2007). Effects of perceived stress and uplifts on inflammation and coagulability. *Psychophysiology, 44,* 154–160.

James, H. S., Jr. (2005). Why did you do that? An economic examination of the effect of extrinsic compensation on intrinsic motivation and performance. *Journal of Economic Psychology, 26,* 549–566.

James, R. C. (1966). Photo of dog. In J. Thurston & R. G. Carraher. *Optical illusions and the visual arts.* New York: Von Nostrand Reinhold.

James, W. (1890). *The principles of psychology.* New York: Holt.

Jamieson, G. A. (2007). *Hypnosis and conscious states: The cognitive neuroscience perspective.* New York: Oxford University Press.

Jamison, K. R. (1995a). *An unquiet mind: A memoir of moods and madness.* New York: Knopf.

Jang, S. J., You, S. H., & Ahn, S. H. (2007). Neurorehabilitation-induced cortical reorganization in brain injury: A 14-month longitudinal follow-up study. *NeuroRehabilitation, 22,* 117–122.

Jarlais, D. C. D., Arasteh, K., & Perlis, T. (2007). The transition from injection to non-injection drug use: Long-term outcomes among heroin and cocaine users in New York City. *Addiction, 102,* 778–785.

Javitt, D. C., & Coyle, J. T. (January 2004). Decoding schizophrenia. *Scientific American,* pp. 46–55.

Jenkins, S. R. (1994). Need for power and women's careers over 14 years: Structural power, job satisfaction, and motive change. *Journal of Personality and Social Psychology, 66,* 155–165.

Jensen, A. R. (2005). Psychometric g and mental chronometry. *Cortex, 41,* 230–231.

Jequier, E. (2002). Pathways to obesity. *International Journal of Obesity and Related Metabolic Disorders, 26,* S12–S17.

Jetten, J., Hornsey, M. J., & Adarves-Yorno, I. (2006). When group members admit to being conformist: The role of relative intragroup status in conformity self-reports. *Personality and Social Psychology Bulletin, 32,* 162–173.

Joe, G. W., Flynn, P. M., & Broome, K. M. (2007). Patterns of drug use and expectations in methadone patients. *Addictive Behaviors, 32,* 1640–1656.

Johnson, G. B. (2000). *The living world* (p. 600). Boston: McGraw-Hill.

Johnson, H. D. (2004). Gender, grade and relationship differences in emotional closeness within adolescent friendships. *Adolescence, 39,* 243–255.

Johnson, J. G., Cohen, P., Smailes, E. M., Kasen, S., & Brook, J. S. (2002, March 29). Television viewing and aggressive behavior during adolescence and adulthood. *Science, 295,* 2468–2471.

John-Steiner, V., & Mahn, H. (2003). Sociocultural contexts for teaching and learning. In W. M. Reynolds & G. E. Miller (Eds.), *Handbook of psychology: Educational psychology* (Vol. 7, pp. 125–151). New York: Wiley.

Jones, A. L. (2006). The contemporary psychoanalyst: Karen Horney's theory applied in today's culture. *PsycCRITIQUES, 51,* 127–134.

Johnston, L. D., O'Malley, P. M., Bachman, J. G., & Schulenberg, J. E. (2007). *Monitoring the Future national results on adolescent drug use: Overview of key findings, 2006.* (NIH Publication No. 07-6202). Bethesda, MD: National Institute on Drug Abuse.

Jorgensen, G. (2006). Kohlberg and Gilligan: Duet or duel? *Journal of Moral Education, 35,* 179–196.

Joyce, J. (1934). *Ulysses.* New York: Random House.

Juliano, L. M., & Griffiths, R. R. (2004). A critical review of caffeine withdrawal: Empirical validation of symptoms and signs, incidence, severity, and associated features. *Psychopharmacology, 176,* 1–29.

Julien, R. M (2001). *A primer of drug action* (9th ed.). New York: Freeman.

Jung, C. G. (1961). *Freud and psychoanalysis.* New York: Pantheon.

Jung, J. (2002). *Psychology of alcohol and other drugs: A research perspective.* Thousand Oaks, CA: Sage.

Jylha, M. (2004). Old age and loneliness: Cross-sectional and longitudinal analyses in the Tampere longitudinal study on aging. *Canadian Journal on Aging/La Revue canadienne du vieillissement, 23,* 157–168.

Kaasinen, V., & Rinne, J. O. (2002). Functional imaging studies of dopa-mine system and cognition in normal aging and Parkinson's disease. *Neuroscience & Biobehavioral Reviews, 26,* 785–793.

Kaller, C. P., Unterrainer, J. M., Rahm, B., & Halsband, U. (2004). The impact of problem structure on planning: Insights from the Tower of London task. *Cognitive Brain Research, 20,* 462–472.

Kallio, S., & Revonsuo, A. (2003). Hypnotic phenomena and altered states of consciousness: A multilevel framework of description and explanation. *Contemporary Hypnosis, 20,* 111–164.

Kandell, E. R., Schwartz, J. H., & Jessell, T. M. (Eds.) (2000). *Principles of neural science* (4th ed.). New York: McGraw-Hill.

Kane, M. J., & Engle, R. W. (2002). The role of prefrontal cortex in working-memory capacity, executive attention, and general fluid intelligence: An individual-differences perspective. *Psychonomic Bulletin and Review, 9,* 637–671.

Kanner, A. D., Coyne, J. C., Schaefer, C., & Lazarus, R. (1981). Comparison of two modes of stress measurement: Daily hassles and uplifts versus major life events. *Journal of Behavioral Medicine, 4,* 14.

Kantrowitz, B. (2006, April 24). The quest for rest. *Newsweek,* p. 51.

Kaplan, J. R., & Manuck, S. B. (1989). The effect of propranolol on behavioral interactions among adult male cynomolgus monkeys (Macaca fascicularis) housed in disrupted social groupings. *Psychosomatic Medicine, 51,* 449–462.

Kaplan, R. M., & Saccuzzo, D. P. (2001). *Psychological testing: Principles, applications, and issues* (5th ed.). Belmont, CA: Wadsworth/Thomson Learning.

Kassin, S., M. (2005). On the psychology of confessions: Does innocence put innocents at risk? *American Psychologist, 60,* 215–228.

Kato, T. (2007). Molecular genetics of bipolar disorder and depression. *Psychiatry and Clinical Neurosciences, 61,* 3–19.

Kaufman, J. C., & Baer, J. (2006). Creativity and reason in cognitive development. New York: Cambridge University Press.

Kay, P., & Regier, T. (2007). Color naming universals: The case of Berinmo. *Cognition, 102,* 289–298.

Keating, D. P., & Clark, L. V. (1980). Development of physical and social reasoning in adolescence. *Developmental Psychology, 16,* 23–30.

Keillor, J. M., Barrett, A. M., Crucian, G. P., Kortenkamp, S., & Heilman, K. M. (2002). Emotional experience and perception in the absence of facial feedback. *Journal of the International Neuropsychological Society, 8,* 130–135.

Kelley, H. (1950). The warm-cold variable in first impressions of persons. *Journal of Personality and Social Psychology, 18,* 431–439.

Kelly, D. & Tangney, B. (2006). Adapting to intelligence profile in an adaptive educational system. *Interacting with Computers, 18*(3), 385–409.

Kemeny, M. E. (2003). The psychobiology of stress. *Current Directions in Psychological Science, 12,* 124–129.

Kendler, K. S., Gatz, M., & Gardner, C. O. (2006). Personality and major depression. *Archives of General Psychiatry, 63,* 1113–1120.

Kendler, K. S., Myers, J., & Gardner, C. O. (2006). Caffeine intake, toxicity and dependence and lifetime risk for psychiatric and substance use disorders: An epidemiologic and co-twin control analysis. *Psychological Medicine, 36,* 1717–1725.

Kenneally, C. (2006, July 3). The deepest cut. *The New Yorker,* pp. 36–38.

Kenshalo, D. R. (1968). *The skin senses.* Springfield, IL: Charles C Thomas.

Kenway, L., & Wilson, M. A. (2001). Temporally structured replay of awake hippocampal ensemble activity during rapid eye movement sleep. *Neuron, 29,* 145–156.

Kessler, R. C., Berglund, P., & Demler, O. (2005). Lifetime prevalence and age-of-onset distributions of DSM-IV disorders in the National Comorbidity Survey replication. *Archives of General Psychiatry, 62,* 593–602.

Kiecolt, J. K. (2003). Satisfaction with work and family life: No evidence of a cultural reversal. *Journal of Marriage and Family, 65,* 23–35.

Kihlstrom, J. F. (2005a). Dissociative disorders. *Annual Review of Clinical Psychology, 1,* 227–253.

Kihlstrom, J. F. (2005b). Is hypnosis an altered state of consciousness or what? Comment. *Contemporary Hypnosis, 22,* 34–38.

Kihlstrom, J. F., Schacter, D. L., Cork, R. C., Hurt, C. A., & Behr, S. E. (1990). Implicit and explicit memory following surgical anesthesia. *Psychological Science, 1,* 303–306.

Kim, H. S. (2002). We talk, therefore we think? A cultural analysis of the effect of talking on thinking. *Journal of Personality and Social Psychology, 83,* 828–842.

Kim, K. H., Relkin, N. R., Lee, K. M., & Hirsch, J. (1997, July 10). Distinct cortical areas associated with native and second languages. *Nature, 388,* 171–174.

Kim, S-E., Kim, J-W, & Kim, J-J. (2007). The neural mechanism of imagining facial affective expression. *Brain Research, 1145,* 128-137.

Kirk, K. M., Bailey, J. M., & Martin, N. G. (2000). Etiology of male sexual orientation in an Australian twin sample. *Psychology, Evolution & Gender, 2,* 301–311.

Kirsch, I., & Braffman, W. (2001). Imaginative suggestibility and hypnotizability. *Current Directions in Psychological Science, 10,* 57–61.

Kirschenbaum, H. (2004). Carl Rogers's life and work: An assessment on the 100th anniversary of his birth. *Journal of Counseling and Development, 82,* 116–124.

Kirschenbaum, H., & Jourdan, A. (2005). The current status of Carl Rogers and the person-centered approach. *Psychotherapy: Theory, Research, Practice, Training, 42,* 37–51.

Kleinman, A. (1996). How is culture important for DSM-IV? In J. E Mezzich, A. Kleinman, H. Fabrega, Jr., & D. L. Parron (Eds.), *Culture and psychiatric diagnosis: A DSM-IV perspective.* Washington, DC: American Psychiatric Press.

Klötz, F., Garle, M., & Granath, F. (2006). Criminality among individuals testing positive for the presence of anabolic androgenic steroids. *Archives of General Psychiatry, 63,* 1274–1279.

Kluger, J. (2001, April 2). Fear not! *Time,* pp. 51–62.

Knoblich, G., & Sebanz, N. (2006). The social nature of perception and action. *Current Directions in Psychological Science, 15,* 99–111.

Kohlberg, L. (1984). *The psychology of moral development: Essays on moral development* (Vol. 2). San Francisco: Harper & Row.

Kohlberg, L., & Ryncarz, R. A. (1990). Beyond justice reasoning: Moral development and consideration of a seventh stage. In C. N. Alexander & E. J. Langer (Eds.), *Higher stages of human development: Perspectives on adult growth.* New York: Oxford University Press.

Kohler, C. G., Turner, T., Stolar, N. M., Bilker, W. B., Brensinger, C. M., Gur, R. E., & Gur, R. C. (2004). Differences in facial expressions of four universal emotions. *Psychiatry Research, 128,* 235–244.

Kolata, G. (2002, December 2). With no answers on risks, steroid users still say "yes." *The New York Times,* p. 1A.

Konijn, E., Bijvank, M. N., & Bushman, B. J. (2007). I wish I were a warrior: The role of wishful identification in the effects of violent video games on aggression in adolescent boys. *Developmental Psychology, 43,* 1038–1044.

Koocher, G. P., Norcross, J. C., & Hill, S. S. (2005). *Psychologists' Desk Reference* (2nd ed.). New York: Oxford University Press.

Kopelman, M. D., & Fleminger, S. (2002). Experience and perspectives on the classification of organic mental disorders. *Psychopathology, 35,* 76–81.

Koplewicz, H. (2002). *More than moody: Recognizing and treating adolescent depression.* New York: Putnam.

Kosslyn, S. M. (2005). Mental images and the brain. *Cognitive Neuropsychology, 22,* 333–347.

Kosslyn, S. M., Cacioppo, J. T., Davidson, R. J., Hugdahl, K., Lovallo, W. R., Spiegel, D., & Rose, R. (2002). Bridging psychology and biology. *American Psychologist, 57,* 341–351.

Kozulin, A., Gindis, B., Ageyev, V. S., & Miller, S. M. (2003). *Vygotsky's educational theory in cultural context.* New York: Cambridge University Press.

Krijn, M., Emmelkamp, P. M. G., Olafsson, R. P., & Biemond, R. (2004). Virtual reality exposure therapy of anxiety disorders: A review. *Clinical Psychology Review, 24,* 259–281.

Krueger, R. G., Hicks, B. M., & McGue, M. (2001). Altruism and antisocial behavior: Independent tendencies, unique personality correlates, distinct etiologies. *Psychological Science, 12,* 397–402.

Kübler-Ross, E. & Kessler, D. (2005). *On Grief and Grieving.* Simon & Schuster.

Kuo, L-J. (2007). Effects of bilingualism on development of facets of phonological competence (China). *Dissertation Abstracts International Section A: Humanities and Social Sciences, 67* (11-A), 4095.

Kuriyama, K., Stickgold, R., & Walker, M. P. (2004). Sleep-dependent learning and motor-skill complexity. *Learning and Memory, 11,* 705–713.

Kvavilashvili, L., & Fisher, L. (2007). Is time-based prospective remembering mediated by self-initiated rehearsals? Role of incidental cues, ongoing activity, age, and motivation. *Journal of Experimental Psychology: General, 136,* 112–132.

Kwon, P., & Laurenceau, J. P. (2002). A longitudinal study of the hopelessness theory of depression: Testing the diathesis-stress model within a differential reactivity and exposure framework [Special issue: Reprioritizing the role of science in a realistic version of the scientist-practitioner model]. *Journal of Clinical Psychology, 50,* 1305–1321.

Laas, I. (2006). Self-actualization and society: A new application for an old theory. *Journal of Humanistic Psychology, 46,* 77–91.

Lacerda, F., von Hofsten, C., & Heimann, M. (2001). *Emerging cognitive abilities in early infancy.* Mahwah, NJ: Erlbaum.

Laederach-Hofmann, K., & Messerli-Buergy, N. (2007). Chest pain, angina pectoris, panic disorder, and Syndrome X. In J. Jordan, B. Barde, & A. M. Zeiher (Eds.), *Contributions toward evidence-based psychocardiology: A systematic review of the literature.* Washington, DC: American Psychological Association.

Lagacé-Séguin, D. G., & d'Entremont, M. L. (2006). The role of child negative affect in the relations between parenting styles and play. *Early Child Development and Care, 176,* 461–477.

Lai, Y., Chen, S. & Chien, N. (2007). Video-assisted thoracoscopic neurectomy of intercostal nerves in a patient with intractable cancer pain. *American Journal of Hospice & Palliative Medicine, 23*(6), 475–478.

Laird, J. D., & Bressler, C. (1990). William James and the mechanisms of emotional experience. *Personality and Social Psychology Bulletin, 16,* 636–651.

Lal, S. (2002). Giving children security: Mamie Phipps Clark and the racialization of child psychology. *American Psychologist, 57,* 20–28.

Lamal, P. A. (1979). College students' common beliefs about psychology. *Teaching of Psychology, 6,* 155–158.

Lamb, H. R., & Weinberger, L. E. (2005). One-year follow-up of persons discharged from a locked intermediate care facility. *Psychiatric Services, 56,* 198–201.

Lana, R. E. (2002). The cognitive approach to language and thought [Special issue: Choice and chance in the formation of society: Behavior and cognition in social theory]. *Journal of Mind and Behavior, 23,* 51–57.

Lane, K. A., Banaji, M. R., Nosek, B. A., & Greenwald, A. G. (Eds.). (2007). Understanding and using the implicit association test: iv: What we know (so far) about the method. In B. Wittenbrink, & N. Schwarz, *Implicit measures of attitudes.* New York: Guilford Press.

Lane, S. D., Cherek, D. R., & Tcheremissine, O. V. (2007). Response perseveration and adaptation in heavy marijuana-smoking adolescents. *Addictive Behaviors, 32,* 977–990.

Lang, A. J., Sorrell, J. T., & Rodgers, C. S. (2006). Anxiety sensitivity as a predictor of labor pain. *European Journal of Pain, 10,* 263–270.

Langan-Fox, J., & Grant, S. (2006). The Thematic Apperception Test: Toward a standard measure of the big three motives. *Journal of Personality Assessment, 87,* 277–291.

Lankov, A. (2004). The dawn of modern Korea: Changes for better or worse. *The Korea Times,* p. A1.

Laqueur, T. W. (2003). *Solitary sex: A cultural history of masturbation.* New York: Zone.

Larsen, R. J., & Buss, D. M. (2006). *Personality psychology: Domains of knowledge about human nature with PowerWeb* (2nd ed.). New York: McGraw-Hill.

Latané, B., & Darley, J. M. (1970). *The unresponsive bystander: Why doesn't he help?* New York: Appleton-Century-Crofts.

Lavelli, M., & Fogel, A. (2005). Developmental changes in the relationship between the infant's attention and emotion during early face-to-face communication. *Developmental Psychology, 41,* 265–280.

Lazarus, R. S. (2000). Toward better research on stress and coping. *American Psychologist, 55,* 665–673.

Leckman, J. F., & King, R. A. (2007). A developmental perspective on the controversy surrounding the use of SSRIs to treat pediatric depression. *American Journal of Psychiatry, 164,* 1304–1306.

Lee, H. J., & Kwon, S. M. (2003). Two different types of obsession: Autogenous obsessions and reactive obsessions. *Behaviour Research & Therapy, 41,* 11–29.

Lee, H. J., Kwon, S. M., Kwon, J. S., & Telch, M. J. (2005). Testing the auto-genous-reactive model of obsessions. *Depression and Anxiety, 21,* 118–129.

Lee, S. H., Ahn, S. C., & Lee, Y. J. (2007). Effectiveness of a meditation-based stress management program as an adjunct to pharmacotherapy in patients with anxiety disorder. *Journal of Psychosomatic Research, 62,* 189–195.

Lee-Chai, A. Y., Bargh, J. A. (Eds.). (2001). *The use and abuse of power: Multiple perspectives on the causes of corruption.* Philadelphia, PA: Psychology Press.

Lee-Chiong, T. Part VI: Parasomnias. (2006). In T. L. Lee-Chiong, *Sleep: A comprehensive handbook.* New York: Wiley-Liss.

Lefaucheur, J. P., Brugieres, P., Menard-Lefaucheur, I., Wendling, S., Pommier, M., & Bellivier, F. (2007). The value of navigation-guided rTMS for the treatment of depression: An illustrative case. *Neurophysiologic Clinics, 37,* 265–271.

Lehar, S. (2003). *The world in your head: A gestalt view of the mechanism of conscious experience.* Mahwah, NJ: Erlbaum.

Leibel, R. L., Rosenbaum, M., & Hirsch, J. (1995, March 9). Changes in energy expenditure resulting from altered body. *New England Journal of Medicine, 332,* 621–628.

Leitner, L. M. (2007). Diversity issues, postmodernism, and psychodynamic therapy. *PsycCRITIQUES, 52,* No pagination specified.

Lemay, E. P., Jr., Clark, M. S., & Feeney, B. C. (2007). Projection of responsiveness to needs and the construction of satisfying communal relationships. *Journal of Personality and Social Psychology, 92,* 834–853.

Lemonick, M. D. (2000, December 11). Downey's downfall. *Time,* p. 97.

Lengua, L. J., & Kovacs, E. A. (2005). Bidirectional associations between temperament and parenting and the prediction of adjustment problems in middle childhood. *Journal of Applied Developmental Psychology, 26,* 21–38.

Lengua, L. J., & Long, A. C. (2002). The role of emotionality and self-regulation in the appraisal-coping process: Tests of direct and moderating effects. *Journal of Applied Developmental Psychology, 23,* 471–493.

Lenzenweger, M. F., & Dworkin, R. H. (Eds.). (1998). *The origins and development of schizophrenia: Advances in experimental psychopathology.* Washington, DC: American Psychological Association.

Leo, R. J., & Latif, T. (2007). Repetitive transcranial magnetic stimulation (rTMS) in experimentally induced and chronic neuropathic pain: A review. *The Journal of Pain, 8,* 453–459.

Lepage, J. F., & Theoret, H. (2007). The mirror neuron system: Grasping others' actions from birth? *Developmental Science, 10,* 513–523.

Lepper, M. R., Corpus, J. H., & Iyengar, S. S. (2005). Intrinsic and extrinsic motivational orientations in the classroom: Age differences and academic correlates. *Journal of Educational Psychology, 97,* 184–196.

LeVay, S. (1993). *The sexual brain.* Cambridge, MA: MIT.

Levenson, R. W. (1994). The search for autonomic specificity. In P. Ekman & R. J. Davidson (Eds.), *The nature of emotion: Fundamental questons.* New York: Oxford University Press.

Levi, A., Chan, K. K., & Pence, D. (2006). Real men do not read labels: The effects of masculinity and involvement on college students' food decisions. *Journal of American College Health, 55,* 91–98.

Levine, J. M., & Moreland, R. L. (2006). Small groups: An overview. In J. M. Levine & R. L. Moreland, *Small groups.* New York: Psychology Press.

Levine, S. Z., & Rabinowitz, J. (2007). Revisiting the 5 dimensions of the Positive and Negative Syndrome Scale. *Journal of Clinical Psychopharmacology, 27,* 431–436.

Levinson, D. J. (1990). A theory of life structure development in adulthood. In C. N. Alexander & E. J. Langer (Eds.), *Higher stages of human development: Perspectives on adult growth.* New York: Oxford University Press.

Lewinsohn, P. M., & Essau, C. A. (2002). Depression in adolescents. In I. H. Gotlib & C. L. Hammen (Eds.), *Handbook of depression* (pp. 541–559). New York: Guilford Press.

Lewinsohn, P. M., Petit, J. W., Joiner, T. E., Jr., & Seeley, J. R. (2003). The symptomatic expression of major depressive disorder in adolescents and young adults. *Journal of Abnormal Psychology, 112,* 244–252.

Li, T-K., Volkow, N. D., & Baler, R. D. (2007). The biological bases of nicotine and alcohol co-addiction. *Biological Psychiatry, 61,* 1–3.

Liang, K. A. (2007). Acculturation, ambivalent sexism, and attitudes toward women who engage in premarital sex among Chinese American young adults. *Dissertation Abstracts International: Section B: The Sciences and Engineering, 67* (10-B), 6065.

Lidz, J., & Gleitman, L. R. (2004). Argument structure and the child's contribution to language learning. *Trends in Cognitive Sciences, 8,* 157–161.

Lieblum, S. R., & Chivers, M. L. (2007). Normal and persistent genital arousal in women: New perspectives. *Journal of Sex & Marital Therapy, 33,* 357–373.

Lien, Y-W., Chu, R-L., Jen, C-H., & Wu, C-H. (2006). Do Chinese commit neither fundamental attribution error nor ultimate attribution error? *Chinese Journal of Psychology, 48,* 163–181.

Lilienfeld, S. O. (2007). Psychological treatments that cause harm. *Perspectives on Psychological Science, 2,* 53–58.

Lindblad, F., Lindahl, M., & Theorell, T. (2006). Physiological stress reactions in 6th and 9th graders during test performance. *Stress and Health: Journal of the International Society for the Investigation of Stress, 22,* 189–195.

Lindh-Åstrand, L., Brynhildsen, J., & Hoffmann, M. (2007). Attitudes towards the menopause and hormone therapy over the turn of the century. *Maturitas, 56,* 12–20.

Lindley, L. D. (2006). The paradox of self-efficacy: Research with diverse populations. *Journal of Career Assessment, 14,* 143–160.

Lindorff, M. (2005). Determinants of received social support: Who gives what to managers? *Journal of Social and Personal Relationships, 22,* 323–337.

Lindsey, E., & Colwell, M. (2003). Preschoolers' emotional competence: Links to pretend and physical play. *Child Study Journal, 33,* 39–52.

Linehan, M. M., Cochran, B. N., & Kehrer, C. A. (2001). Dialectical behavior therapy for borderline personality disorder. In D. H. Barlow (Ed.), *Clinical handbook of psychological disorders: A step-by-step treatment manual* (3rd ed., pp. 470–522). New York: Guilford Press.

Links, P. S., Eynan, R., & Heisel, M. J. (2007). Affective instability and suicidal ideation and behavior in patients with borderline personality disorder. *Journal of Personality Disorders, 21,* 72–86.

Lippa, R. A. (2005). *Gender, nature, and nurture* (2nd ed.). Mahwah, NJ: Erlbaum.

Litowitz, B. E. (2007). Unconscious fantasy: A once and future concept. *Journal of the American Psychoanalytic Association, 55,* 199–228.

Little, A., Burt, D. M., & Perrett, D. I. (2006). What is good is beautiful: Face preference reflects desired personality. *Personality and Individual Differences, 41,* 1107–1118.

Liu, J. H., & Mills, D. (2006). Modern racism and neo-liberal globalization: The discourses of plausible deniability and their multiple functions. *Journal of Community & Applied Social Psychology, 16,* 83–99.

Lobato, M. I., Koff, W. J., & Manenti, C. (2006). Follow-up of sex reassignment surgery in transsexuals: A Brazilian cohort. *Archives of Sexual Behavior, 35,* 711–715.

Lobban, F., Barrowclough, C., & Jones, S. (2006). Does expressed emotion need to be understood within a more systemic framework? An examination of discrepancies in appraisals between patients diagnosed with schizophrenia and their relatives. *Social Psychiatry and Psychiatric Epidemiology, 41,* 50–55.

Locke, J. L. (2006). Parental selection of vocal behavior: Crying, cooking, babbling, and the evolution of language. *Human Nature, 17,* 155–168.

Long, G. M., & Beaton, R. J. (1982). The case for peripheral persistence: Effects of target and background luminance on a partial-report task. *Journal of Experimental Psychology: Human Perception and Performance, 8,* 383–391.

López, S. R., & Guarnaccia, P. J. (2000). Cultural psychopathology: Uncovering the social world of mental illness. *Annual Review of Psychology, 51,* 571–598.

López, S. R., & Guarnaccia, P. J. (2005). Cultural dimensions of psychopathology: The social world's impact on mental illness. In J. E. Maddux & B. A. Winstead (Eds.), *Foundations for a contemporary understanding.* Mahwah, NJ: Erlbaum.

Lorenz, K. (1966). *On aggression.* New York: Harcourt Brace Jovanovich.

Lorenz, K. (1974). *Civilized man's eight deadly sins.* New York: Harcourt Brace Jovanovich.

Lothane, Z. (2005). Jung, A biography. *Journal of the American Psychoanalytic Association, 53,* 317–324.

Lotze, M., Heymans, U., Birbaumer, N., Veit, R., Erb, M., Flor, H., & Halsband, U. (2006). Differential cerebral activation during observation of expressive gestures and motor acts. *Neuropsychologia, 44,* 1787–1795.

Lowe, P., Humphreys, C., & Williams, S. J. (2007). Night terrors: Women's experiences of (not) sleeping where there is domestic violence. *Violence Against Women, 13,* 549–561.

Lowery, D., Fillingim, R. B., & Wright, R. A. (2003). Sex differences and incentive effects on perceptual and cardiovascular responses to cold pressor pain. *Psychosomatic Medicine, 65,* 284–291.

Lu, J., Sherman, D., Devor, M. & Saper, C.B. (2006). A putative flip-flop switch for control of REM sleep. *Nature, 441*(7093), 589–594.

Lubinski, D., Benbow, C. P., Webb, R. M., & Bleske-Rechek, A. (2006). Tracking exceptional human capital over two decades. *Psychological Science, 17,* 194–199.

Lublin, H., Eberhard, J., & Levander, S. (2005). Current therapy issues and unmet clinical needs in the treatment of schizophrenia: A review of the new generation antipsychotics. *International Clinical Psychopharmacology, 20,* 183–198.

Lucki, I., & O'Leary, O. F. (2004). Distinguishing roles for norepinephrine and serotonin in the behavioral effects of antidepressant drugs. *Journal of Clinical Psychiatry, 65,* 11–24.

Luders, E., Narr, K. L., Zaidel, E., Thompson, P. M., & Toga, A. W. (2006). Gender effects on callosal thickness in scaled and unscaled space. *Neuroreport, 17,* 1103–1106.

Lutz, C.K. & Novak, M. A. (2005). Environmental enrichment for nonhuman primates: Theory and application. *ILAR Journal, 46,* 178–191.

Lutz, W., Lambert, M. J., Harmon, S. C., Tschitsaz, A., Schurch, E., & Stulz, N. (2006). The probability of treatment success, failure and duration—what can be learned from empirical data to support decision making in clinical practice? *Clinical Psychology & Psychotherapy, 13,* 223–232.

Ly, D. H., Lockhart, D. J., Lerner, R. A., & Schultz, P. G. (2000, March 31). Mitotic misregulation and human aging. *Science, 287,* 2486–2492.

Lykken, D. T. (1995). *The antisocial personalities.* Mahwah, NJ: Erlbaum.

Lymberis, S. C., Parhar, P. K., Katsoulakis, E., & Formenti, S. C. (2004). Pharmacogenomics and breast cancer. *Pharmacogenomics, 5,* 31–55.

Lynch, T. R., Trost, W. T, Salsman, N., & Linehan, M. M. (2007). Dialectical behavior therapy for borderline personality disorder. *Annual Review of Clinical Psychology, 3,* 181–205.

Lynn, S. J., Fassler, O., & Knox, J. (2005). Hypnosis and the altered state debate: Something more or nothing more? Comment. *Contemporary Hypnosis, 22,* 39–45.

Lynn, S. J., Kirsch, I., Barabasz, A., Cardena, E., & Patterson, D. (2000). Hypnosis as an empirically supported clinical intervention: The state of the evidence and a look to the future. *International Journal of Clinical and Experimental Hypnosis, 48,* 23–259.

Lynn, S. J., Lock, T., Loftus, E. F., Krackow, E., & Lilienfeld, S. O. (2003). The remembrance of things past: Problematic memory recovery techniques in psychotherapy. In S. O. Lilienfeld, S. J. Lynn, & J. M. Lohr (Eds.), *Science and pseudoscience in clinical psychology.* New York: Guilford Press.

Machado, R. B., Suchecki, D., & Tufik, S. (2005). Sleep homeostasis in rats assessed by a long-term intermittent paradoxical sleep deprivation protocol. *Behavioural Brain Research, 160,* 356–364.

MacIntyre, T., Moran, A., & Jennings, D. J. (2002). Is controllability of imagery related to canoe-slalom performance? *Perceptual & Motor Skills, 94,* 1245–1250.

Mack, J. (2003). *The museum of the mind.* London: British Museum Publications.

MacKinnon, D.P. & Luecken, L.J. (2008). How and for whom? Mediation and moderation in health psychology. *Health Psychology, 27*(Suppl.2), S99–S100.

Madden, D. J. (2007). Aging and visual attention. *Current Directions in Psychological Science, 16,* 70–74.

Mader, S. S. (2000). *Biology.* Boston: McGraw-Hill.

Magida, A. J. (2006). *Opening the doors of wonder: Reflections on religious rites of passage.* Berkeley, CA: University of California Press.

Magoni, M., Bassani, L., Okong, P., Kituuka, P., Germinario, E. P., Giuliano, M., & Vella, S. (2005). Mode of infant feeding and HIV infection in children in a program for prevention of mother-to-child transmission in Uganda. *AIDS, 19,* 433–437.

Mahmood, M., & Black, J. (2005). Narcolepsy-cataplexy: How does recent understanding help in evaluation and treatment. *Current Treatment Options in Neurology, 7,* 363–371.

Maier, S. F., & Watkins, L. R. (2000). Learned helplessness. In A. E. Kazdin, *Encyclopedia of psychology* (Vol. 4). Washington, DC: American Psychological Association.

Majdandzic, M., & van den Boom, D. C. (2007). Multimethod longitudinal assessment of temperament in early childhood. *Journal of Personality, 75,* 121–167.

Maldonado, J. R., & Spiegel, D. (2003). Dissociative disorders. In R. E. Hales & S. C. Yudofsky, *The American Psychiatric Publishing textbook of clinical psychiatry* (4th ed.). Washington, DC: American Psychiatric Publishing.

Malouff, J. M., Thorsteinsson, E. B., & Schutte, N. S. (2007). The efficacy of problem solving therapy in reducing mental and physical health problems: A meta-analysis. *Clinical Psychology Review, 27,* 46–57.

Mamassis, G., & Doganis, G. (2004). The effects of a mental training program on juniors pre-competitive anxiety, self-confidence, and tennis performance. *Journal of Applied Sport Psychology, 16,* 118–137.

Mancinelli, R., Binetti, R., & Ceccanti, M. (2007). Woman, alcohol and environment: Emerging risks for health. *Neuroscience & Biobehavioral Reviews, 31,* 246–253.

Mann, K., Ackermann, K., Croissant, B., Mundle, G., Nakovics, H., & Diehl, A. (2005). Neuroimaging of gender differences in alcohol dependence: Are women more vulnerable? *Alcoholism: Clinical & Experimental Research, 29,* 896–901.

Manor, J. K., & Gailliot, M. T. (2007). Altruism and egoism: Prosocial motivations for helping depend on relationship context. *European Journal of Social Psychology, 37,* 347–358.

Manstead, A. S. R., Frijda, N., & Fischer, A. H. (Eds.) (2003). *Feelings and emotions: The Amsterdam Symposium.* Cambridge, England: Cambridge University Press.

Marcaurelle, R., Bélanger, C., & Marchand, A. (2003). Marital relationship and the treatment of panic disorder with agoraphobia: A critical review. *Clinical Psychology Review, 23,* 247–276.

Marcaurelle, R., Bélanger, C., & Marchand, A. (2005). Marital predictors of symptom severity in panic disorder with agoraphobia. *Journal of Anxiety Disorders, 19,* 211–232.

Marcus-Newhall, A., Pedersen, W. C., & Carlson, M. (2000). Displaced aggression is alive and well: A meta-analytic review. *Journal of Personality and Social Psychology, 78,* 670–689.

Markus, H. R., & Kitayama, S. (2003). Models of agency: Sociocultural diversity in the construction of action. In V. Murphy-Berman & J. J. Berman (Eds.), *Cross-cultural differences in perspectives on the self.* Lincoln, NE: University of Nebraska Press.

Markus, H. R., Uchida, Y., Omoregie, H., Townsend, S. S., & Kitayama, S. (2006). Going for the gold: Models of agency in Japanese and American contexts. *Psychological Science, 17,* 103–112.

Marshall, K., Laing, D. G., & Jinks, A. L. (2006). The capacity of humans to identify components in complex odor-taste mixtures. *Chemical Senses, 31,* 539–545.

Marshall, M. K. (2007). The critical factors of coaching practice leading to successful coaching outcomes. *Dissertation Abstracts International: Section B: The Sciences and Engineering, 67* (7-B), 4092.

Martelle, S., Hanley, C., & Yoshino K. (2003, January 28). "Sopranos" scenario in slaying? *Los Angeles Times,* p. B1.

Martin, A. J., & Marsh, H. W. (2002). Fear of failure: Friend or foe? *Australian Psychologist, 38,* 31–38.

Martin, H. (2006, July 3). New heights. *Los Angeles Times.* P. 1, Part E.

Martin, L., & Pullum, G. K. (1991). *The great Eskimo vocabulary hoax.* Chicago: University of Chicago Press.

Martin, P. D., & Brantley, P. J. (2004). Stress, coping, and social support in health and behavior. In J. M. Raczynski & L. C. Leviton (Eds.), *Handbook of clinical health psychology: Vol. 2. Disorders of behavior and health.* Washington, DC: American Psychological Association.

Martin, R. C., & Hull, R. (2007). The case study perspective on psychological research. In R. Sternberg, R. Roediger, & D. Halpern (Eds.), *Critical thinking in psychology.* New York: Cambridge University Press.

Martindale, C. (1981). *Cognition and consciousness.* Homewood, IL: Dorsey.

Maslow, A.H. (1971). *The Farther Reaches of Human Nature.* New York: Viking Press.

Maslow, A. H. (1987). *Motivation and personality* (3rd ed.). New York: Harper & Row.

Masuda, M. (2003). Meta-analyses of love scales: Do various love scales measure the same psychological constructs? *Japanese Psychological Research, 45,* 25–37.

Matsumoto, D. (2002). Methodological requirements to test a possible in-group advantage in judging emotions across cultures: Comment on Elfenbein and Ambady (2002) and evidence. *Psychological Bulletin, 128,* 236–242.

Matthews, G., & Funke, G. J. (2006). Worry and information-processing. In G. C. L. Davey & A. Wells, *Worry and its psychological disorders: Theory, assessment and treatment.* Hoboken, NJ: Wiley.

Maurer, D., Lewis, T. L., Brent, H. P., & Levin, A. V. (1999, October 1). Rapid improvement in the acuity of infants after visual input. *Science, 286,* 108–110.

Mayer, J. D., Salovey, P., & Caruso, D. R. (2004). Emotional intelligence: Theory, findings, and implications. *Psychological Inquiry, 15,* 197–215.

Maynard, A. E., & Martini, M. I. (2005). *Learning in cultural context: Family, peers, and school.* New York: Kluwer Academic/Plenum Publishers.

McCarthy, J. (2005). Individualism and collectivism: What do they have to do with counseling? *Journal of Multicultural Counseling and Development, 33,* 108–117.

McClelland, D. C. (1993). Intelligence is not the best predictor of job performance. *Current Directions in Psychological Research, 2,* 5–8.

McClelland, D. C., Atkinson, J. W., Clark, R. A., & Lowell, E. L. (1953). *The achievement motive.* New York: Appleton-Century-Crofts.

McClelland, L. E., & Pilcher, J. J. (2007). Assessing subjective sleepiness during a night of sleep deprivation: Examining the internal state and behavioral dimensions of sleepiness. *Behavioral Medicine, 33,* 17–26.

McCormick, C. G. (2003). Metacognition and learning. In W. M. Reynolds & G. E. Miller (Eds.), *Handbook of psychology: Educational psychology* (Vol. 7. pp. 79–102). New York: Wiley.

McCrae, R. R., & Costa, P. T., Jr. (1986). A five-factor theory of personality. In L. A. Pervin & O. P. John (Eds.), *Handbook of personality: Theory and research* (2nd ed.). New York: Guilford.

McDaniel, M. A., Maier, S. F., & Einstein, G. O. (2002). "Brain specific" nutrients: A memory cure? *Psychological Science in the Public Interest, 3,* 12–18.

McDonald, C., & Murray, R. M. (2004). Can structural magnetic resonance imaging provide an alternative phenotype for genetic studies of schizophrenia? In M. S. Keshavan, J. L. Kennedy, & R. M. Murray (Eds.), *Neurodevelopment and schizophrenia.* New York: Cambridge University Press.

McDonald, H. E., & Hirt, E. R. (1997). When expectancy meets desire: Motivational effects in reconstructive memory. *Journal of Personality and Social Psychology, 72,* 5–23.

McEwen, B. S. (1998, January 15). Protective and damaging effects of stress mediators [Review article]. *New England Journal of Medicine, 338,* 171–179.

McGilvray, J. (Ed.). (2004). *The Cambridge companion to Chomsky.* Oxford, England: Cambridge University Press.

McGlynn, F. D., Smitherman, T. A., & Gothard, K. D. (2004). Comment on the status of systematic desensitization. *Behavior Modification, 28,* 194–205.

McGregor, K. K., & Capone, N. C. (2004). Genetic and environmental interactions in determining the early lexicon: Evidence from a set of tri-zygotic quadruplets. *Journal of Child Language, 31,* 311–337.

McGuire, W. J. (1997). Creative hypothesis generating in psychology: Some useful heuristics. *Annual Review of Psychology, 48,* 1–30.

McKenzie-McLean, J. (2006, August 3). On the scent of a new detector. *The Press* (Christchurch, New Zealand), p. 7.

McKinley, M. J., Cairns, M. J., Denton, D. A., Egan, G., Mathai, M. L., Uschakov, A., Wade, J. D., Weisinger, R. S., & Oldfield, B. J. (2004). Physiological and pathophysiological influences on thirst. *Physiology and Behavior, 81,* 795–803.

McManus, C. (2004). *Right hand, left hand: The origins of asymmetry in brains, bodies, atoms and cultures.* Cambridge, MA: Harvard University Press.

McMullin, R. E. (2000). *The new handbook of cognitive therapy techniques.* New York: Norton.

McNamara, P. (2004). *An evolutionary psychology of sleep and dreams.* Westport, CT: Praeger Publishers/Greenwood Publishing Group.

Mead, M. (1949). *Male and female.* New York: Morrow.

Means, M. K., & Edinger, J. D. (2007). Graded exposure therapy for addressing claustrophobic reactions to continuous positive airway pressure: A case series report. *Behavioral Sleep Medicine, 5,* 105–116.

Medeiros, R., Prediger, R.D.S., Passos, G.F., Pandolfo, P., Duarte, F.S., Franco, J.L., et al. (2007). Connecting TNF-α signaling pathways to iNOS expression in a mouse model of Alzheimer's disease: Relevance for the behavioral and synaptic deficits induced by amyloid β protein. *Journal of Neuroscience, 27*(20), 5394–5404.

Mel, B. W. (2002, March 8). What the synapse tells the neuron. *Science, 295,* 1845–1846.

Mel'nikov, K. S. (1993, October–December). On some aspects of the mechanistic approach to the study of processes of forgetting. *Vestnik Moskovskogo Universiteta Seriya 14 Psikhologiya,* pp. 64–67.

Meltzer, H. Y. (2000). Genetics and etiology of schizophrenia and bipolar disorder. *Biological Psychiatry, 47,* 171–173.

Meltzoff, A. N. (1996). The human infant as imitative generalist: A 20-year progress report on infant imitation with implications for comparative psychology. In C. M. Heyes & B. G. Galef, Jr. (Eds.), *Social learning in animals: The roots of culture.* San Diego, CA: Academic Press.

Melzack, R., & Katz, J. (2004). *The gate control theory: Reaching for the brain.* Mahwah, NJ: Erlbaum.

Mendelsohn, J. (2003, November 7–9). What we know about sex. *USA Weekend,* pp. 6–9.

Merikangas, K. R., Ames, M., Cui, L., Stang, P. E., Ustun, T. B., VonKorff, M., & Kessler, R. C. (2007). The impact of comorbidity of mental and physical conditions on role disability in the US adult household population. *Archives of General Psychiatry, 64,* 1180–1188.

Messer, S. B., & McWilliams, N. (2003). The impact of Sigmund Freud and *The Interpretation of Dreams.* In R. J. Sternberg (Ed.), *The anatomy of impact: What makes the great works of psychology great* (pp. 71–88). Washington, DC: American Psychological Association.

Meyer-Bahlburg, H. (1997). The role of prenatal estrogens in sexual orientation. In L. Ellis & L. Ebertz (Eds.), *Sexual orientation: Toward biological understanding.* Westport, CT: Praeger.

Meyerowitz, J. (2004). *How sex changed: A history of transsexuality in the United States.* Cambridge, MA: Harvard University Press.

Michael, R. T., Gagnon, J. H., Laumann, E. O., & Kolata, G. (1994). *Sex in America: A definitive survey.* Boston: Little, Brown.

Midanik, L. T., Tam, T. W., & Weisner, C. (2007). Concurrent and simultaneous drug and alcohol use: Results of the 2000 national alcohol survey. *Drug and Alcohol Dependence, 90,* 72–80.

Middlebrooks, J. C., Furukawa, S., Stecker, G. C., & Mickey, B. J. (2005). Distributed representation of sound-source location in the auditory cortex. In R. König, P. Heil, E. Budinger, & H. Scheich (Eds.), *Auditory cortex: A synthesis of human and animal research.* Mahwah, NJ: Erlbaum.

Mifflin, L. (1998, January 14). Study finds a decline in TV network violence. *The New York Times,* p. A14.

Miklowitz, D. J., & Tompson, M. C. (2003). Family variables and interventions in schizophrenia. In G. Sholevar & G. Pirooz (Eds.), *Textbook of family and couples therapy: Clinical applications* (pp. 585–617). Washington, DC: American Psychiatric Publishing.

Miletic, M. P. (2002). The introduction of a feminine psychology to psychoanalysis: Karen Horney's legacy [Special issue: Interpersonal psychoanalysis and feminism]. *Contemporary Psychoanalysis, 38,* 287–299.

Milgram, S. (2005). *Obedience to authority.* Pinter & Martin: New York.

Millar, M. (2002). Effects of guilt induction and guilt reduction on door-in-the-face. *Communication Research, 29,* 666–680.

Miller, G. A. (1956). The magical number seven, plus or minus two: Some limits on our capacity for processing information. *Psychology Review, 63,* 81–97.

Miller, G. F., & Penke, L. (2007). The evolution of human intelligence and the coefficient of additive genetic variance in human brain size. *Intelligence, 35,* 97–114.

Miller, J. A., & Leffard, S. A. (2007). Behavioral assessment. In S. R. Smith & L. Handler, *The clinical assessment of children and adolescents: A practitioner's handbook.* Mahwah, NJ: Erlbaum.

Miller, J. G. (1984). Culture and the development of everyday social explanation. *Journal of Personality and Social Psychology, 46,* 961–978.

Miller, L. A., Taber, K. H., Gabbard, G. O., & Hurley, R. A. (2005). Neural underpinnings of fear and its modulation: Implications for anxiety disorders. *Journal of Neuropsychiatry and Clinical Neurosciences, 17,* 1–6.

Miller, M. N., & Pumariega, A. J. (2001). Culture and eating disorders: A historical and cross-cultural review. *Psychiatry: Interpersonal and Biological Processes, 64,* 93–110.

Miller, N. E., & Magruder, K. M. (Eds.). (1999). *Cost-effectiveness of psychotherapy: A guide for practitioners, researchers, and policymakers.* New York: Oxford University Press.

Millon, T., & Davis, R. O. (1996). *Disorders of personality: DSM-IV and beyond* (2nd ed.). New York: Wiley.

Millon, T., Davis, R., & Millon, C. (2000). *Personality disorders in modern life.* New York: Wiley.

Miner-Rubino, K., Winter, D. G., & Stewart, A. J. (2004). Gender, social class, and the subjective experience of aging: Self-perceived personality change from early adulthood to late midlife. *Personality and Social Psychology Bulletin, 30,* 1599–1610.

Miquel, J., (2006). Integración de teorías del envejecimiento (parte I). [Integration of theories of ageing.] *Revista Espanola de Geriatria y Gerontologia, 41,* 55–63.

Mischel, W. (2004). Toward an integrative science of the person. *Annual Review of Psychology, 55,* 1–22.

Mischoulon, D. (2000, June). Anti-depressants: Choices and controversy. *HealthNews,* p. 4.

Mitte, K. (2005). Meta-analysis of cognitive-behavioral treatments for generalized anxiety disorder: A comparison with pharmacotherapy. *Psychological Bulletin, 131,* 785–795.

MLA (2005). MLA Language Map; all languages other than English combined. Retrieved from http://www. mla.org/ census_map&source=county (based on 2000 U.S. Census Bureau figures).

Moffitt, T. E., & Caspi, A. (2007). Evidence from behavioral genetics for environmental contributions to antisocial conduct. In J. E. Grusec, & P. D. Hastings, *Handbook of socialization: Theory and research*. New York: Guilford Press.

Moffitt, T. E., Caspi, A., & Rutter, M. (2006). Measured gene-environment interactions in psychopathology: Concepts, research strategies, and implications for research, intervention, and public understanding of genetics. *Perspectives on Psychological Science, 1*, 5–27.

Mohapel, P., Leanza, G., Kokaia, M., & Lindvall, O. (2005). Forebrain acetylcholine regulates adult hippo-campal neurogenesis and learning. *Neurobiology of Aging, 26*, 939–946.

Montgomery, C., Fisk, J. E., Newcombe, R., Wareing, M., & Murphy, P. N. (2005). Syllogistic reasoning performance in MDMA (Ecstasy) users. *Experimental and Clinical Psychopharmacology, 13*, 137–145.

Moody, H. R. (2000). *Aging: Concepts and controversies*. Thousand Oaks, CA: Sage.

Moorey, S. (2007) Cognitive therapy. In W. Dryden, *Dryden's handbook of individual therapy* (5th ed.). Thousand Oaks, CA: Sage.

Mora-Giral, M., Raich-Escursell, R. M., Segues, C. V., Torras-Clarasó, J., & Huon, G. (2004). Bulimia symptoms and risk factors in university students. *Eating and Weight Disorders, 9*, 163–169.

Moritz, S., & Laroi, F. (2008). Differences and similarities in the sensory and cognitive signatures of voice-hearing, intrusions and thoughts. *Schizophrenia Research, 102*,(1-3), 96–107.

Morone, N. E., & Greco, C. M. (2007). Mind-body interventions for chronic pain in older adults: a structured review. *Pain Medicine, 8*, 359–375.

Morris, J. F., Waldo, C. R., & Rothblum, E. D. (2001). A model of predictors and outcomes of outness among lesbian and bisexual women. *American Journal of Orthopsychiatry, 71*, 61–71.

Morrissey, S. (2006, March 12). Microbe-busting bandages. *Time*.

Morrone, A. S., & Pintrich, P. R. (2006). Achievement motivation. In G. G. Bear & K. M. Minke, (Eds.), *Children's needs III: Development, prevention, and intervention*. Washington, DC: National Association of School Psychologists.

Morrow, J., & Wolff, R. (1991, May). Wired for a miracle. *Health*, pp. 64–84.

Morton, B. E. (2003). Asymmetry questionnaire outcomes correlate with several hemisphericity measures. *Brain and Cognition, 51*, 372–374.

Mosher, C. J., & Akins, S. (2007). *Drugs and drug policy: The control of consciousness alteration*. Thousand Oaks, CA: Sage.

Moskowitz, G. B. (2004). *Social cognition: Understanding self and others*. New York: Guilford Press.

Motley, M. T. (1987, February). What I meant to say. *Psychology Today*, pp. 25–28.

Muammar, O. M. (2007). An integration of two competing models to explain practical intelligence. *Dissertation Abstracts International: Section B: The Sciences and Engineering, 67*(7-B), 4128.

Mullen, B., & Rice, D. R. (2003). Ethnophaulisms and exclusion: The behavioral consequences of cognitive representation of ethnic immigrant groups. *Personality and Social Psychology Bulletin, 29*, 1056–1067.

Munakata, Y. (2006). Information processing approaches to development. In D. Kuhn, R. S. Siegler, W. Damon, & R. M. Lerner, *Handbook of child psychology: Vol. 2, Cognition, perception, and language* (6th ed.). Hoboken, NJ: Wiley.

Murphy, G. J., Glickfield, L. L., Balsen, Z., & Isaacson, J. S. (2004). Sensory neuron signaling to the brain: Properties of transmitter release from olfactory nerve terminals. *Journal of Neuroscience, 24*, 3023–3030.

Murphy, G. L. (2005). The study of concepts inside and outside the laboratory: Medin versus Medin. In W. Ahn, R. L. Goldstone, B. C. Love, A. B. Markman, & P. Wolff (Eds.), *Categorization inside and outside the laboratory: Essays in honor of Douglas L. Medin*. Washington, DC: American Psychological Association.

Murphy, S., Monahan, JL., & Miller, L.C.. (1998). Interference under the influence. *Personality and Social Psychology Bulletin, 24*, 517–528.

Murphy, T. (2007, July 24). For fear of flying, therapy takes to the skies. *The New York Times*, Section F, p. 6.

Murray, S. L., Holmes, J. G., & Griffin, D. W. (2004). The benefits of positive illusions: Idealization and the construction of satisfaction in close relationships. In H. T. Reis & C. E. Rusbult (Eds.), *Close relationships: Key readings*. Philadelphia, PA: Taylor & Francis.

Myers, L. L. (2007). Anorexia nervosa, bulimia nervosa, and binge eating disorder. In B. A. Thyer, & J. S. Wodarski, (Eds.), *Social work in mental health: An evidence-based approach*. Hoboken, NJ: Wiley.

Myerson, J., Adams, D. R., Hale, S., & Jenkins, L. (2003). Analysis of group differences in processing speed: Brinley plots, Q-Q plots, and other conspiracies. *Psychonomic Bulletin and Review, 10*, 224–237.

Nagai, Y., Goldstein, L. H., Fenwick, P. B. C., & Trimble, M. R. (2004). Clinical efficacy of galvanic skin response biofeedback training in reducing seizures in adult epilepsy: A preliminary randomized controlled study. *Epilepsy and Behavior, 5*, 216–223.

Nagda, B. A., Tropp, L. R., & Paluck, E. L. (2006). Looking back as we look ahead: Integrating research, theory, and practice on intergroup relations. *Journal of Social Research, 62*, 439–451.

Najman, J. M., Aird, R., Bor, W., O'Callaghan, M., Williams, G. M., & Shuttlewood, G. J. (2004). The generational transmission of socioeconomic inequalities in child cognitive development and emotional health. *Social Science and Medicine, 58*, 1147–1158.

Nakamura, M., Kyo, S., Kanaya, T., Yatabe, N., Maida, Y., Tanaka, M., Ishida, Y., Fujii, C., Kondo, T., Inoue, M., & Mukaida, N. (2004). hTERT-promoter-based tumor-specific expression of MCP-1 effectively sensitizes cervical cancer cells to a low dose of cisplatin. *Cancer Gene Therapy, 2*, 1–7.

Nakamura, Y., Ando, S., Nagahara, A., Sano, T., Ochiya, S., Maeda, T., Kawaji, M., Ogawa, A., Hirata, H., Terazaki, K., Haraoka, H., Tanihara, M., Ueda, M., Uchino, M., & Yamamura, K. (2004). Targeted conversion of the transthyretin gene *in vitro* and *in vivo*. *Gene Therapy, 11*, 838–846

Nasir, N. S., & Hand, V. M. (2006). Exploring sociocultural perspectives on race, culture, and learning. *Review of Educational Research, 76*, 449-475.

Nathan, P. E., Stuart, S. P., & Dolan, S. L. (2000). Research on psychotherapy efficacy and effectiveness: Between Scylla and Charybdis? *Psychological Bulletin, 126*, 964–981.

National Academy of Sciences (1999). *Marijuana and medicine: Assessing the science base*. Washington, DC: National Academy Press.

National Association for the Education of Young Children. (2005). *Position statements of the NAEYC*. www.naeyc.org/about/positions.asp#where.

National Center for Health Statistics. (2000). 2000 CDC Growth Charts: United States. 28 pp. (PHS) 2000-1250. Washington, DC.

National Depression Screening Day. (2003, March 26). Questionnaire on Web site. Retrieved from www.mentalhealthscreening.org/dep/depsample.htm#sampletest.

National Institute of Child Health and Human Development (NICHD). (2002). Child-care structure—process—outcome: Direct and indirect effects of child-care quality on young children's development. *Psychological Science, 13*, 199–206.

National Institute on Drug Abuse. (2000). *Principles of drug addiction treatment: A research-based guide*. Washington, DC: National Institute on Drug Abuse.

National Mental Health Information Center, U.S. Department of Health and Human Services. Reprinted in *Scientific American*, December 2002, p. 38.

Natvig, G. K., Albrektsen, G., & Ovarnstrom, U. (2003). Methods of teaching and class participation in relation to perceived social support and stress: Modifiable factors for improving health and well-being among students. *Educational Psychology, 23*, 261–274.

Naveh-Benjamin, M., Guez, J., & Sorek, S. (2007). The effects of divided attention on encoding processes in memory: Mapping the locus of interference. *Canadian Journal of Experimental Psychology, 61,* 1–12.

Neitz, J., Neitz, M., & Kainz, P. M. (1996, November 1). Visual pigment gene structure and the severity of color vision defects. *Science, 274,* 801–804.

Neron, S., & Stephenson, R. (2007). Effectiveness of hypnotherapy with cancer patients' trajectory: Emesis, acute pain, and analgesia and anxiolysis in procedures. *International Journal of Clinical Experimental Hypnosis, 55,* 336–354.

Nesdale, D., Maass, A., & Durkin, K. (2005). Group norms, threat, and children's racial prejudice. *Child Development, 76,* 652–663.

Nesheim, S., Henderson, S., Lindsay, M., Zuberi, J., Grimes, V., Buehler, J., Lindegren, M. L., & Bulterys, M. (2004). *Prenatal HIV testing and antiretroviral prophylaxis at an urban hospital—Atlanta, Georgia, 1997–2000.* Atlanta, GA: Centers for Disease Control.

Nestler, E. J. (2001, June 22). Total recall—the memory of addiction. *Science, 292,* 2266–2267.

Neubauer, A. C., & Fink, A. (2005). Basic information processing and the psychophysiology of intelligence. In R. J. Sternberg & J. E. Pretz (Eds.), *Cognition and intelligence: Identifying the mechanisms of the mind.* New York: Cambridge University Press, 2005.

Newby-Clark, I. R., & Ross, M. (2003). Conceiving the past and future. *Personality and Social Psychology Bulletin, 29,* 807–818.

Newell, A., & Simon, H. (1972). *Human problem solving.* Englewood Cliffs, NJ: Prentice Hall.

Newman, C. F., Leahy, R. L., Beck, A. T., Reilly-Harrington, N. A., & Gyulai, L. (2002). *Bipolar disorder: A cognitive therapy approach.* Washington, DC: American Psychological Association.

Newport, F., & Carroll, J. (2002, November 27). Battle of the bulge: Majority of Americans want to lose weight. *Gallup News Service,* pp. 1–9.

Niccols, A. (2007). Fetal alcohol syndrome and the developing socio-emotional brain. *Brain Cognition, 65,* 135–142.

NICHD Early Child Care Research Network. (1998). Early child care and self-control, compliance, and problem behavior at twenty-four and thirty-six months. *Child Development, 69,* 1145–1170.

NICHD Early Child Care Research Network. (2000). Characteristics and quality of child care for toddlers and preschoolers. *Applied Developmental Science, 4,* 116–135.

NICHD Early Child Care Research Network (2001). Child-care and family predictors of preschool attachment and stability from infancy. Preview. *Developmental Psychology, Vol 37,* 847–862.

NICHD Early Child Care Research Network (2006a). Infant-mother attachment classification: Risk and protection in relation to changing maternal caregiving quality. Preview. *Developmental Psychology, 42.* 38–58.

NICHD Early Child Care Research Network. (2006b). Child-care effect sizes for the NICHD study of early child care and youth development. *American Psychologist, 61,* 99–116.

Nickerson, R. S., & Adams, M. J. (1979). *Cognitive Psychology, 11,* 297.

Nielsen, S. L., Smart, D. W., Isakson, R. L., Worthen, V. E., Gregersen, A. T., & Lambert, M. J. (2004). The *Consumer Reports* effectiveness score: What did consumers report? *Journal of Counseling Psychology, 51,* 25–37.

Nigg, J. T., & Goldsmith, H. H. (1994). Genetics of personality disorders: Perspectives from personality and psychopathology research. *Psychological Bulletin, 115,* 346–380.

Nikles, C. D., II, Brecht, D. L., Klinger, E., & Bursell, A. L. (1998). The effects of current concern- and nonconcern-related waking suggestions on nocturnal dream content. *Journal of Personality and Social Psychology, 75,* 242–255.

Nimrod, G., & Kleiber, D. A. (2007). Reconsidering change and continuity in later life: Toward an innovation theory of successful aging. *International Journal of Human Development, 65,* 1–22.

Nisbett, R.E. (2007, December 9). All brains are the same color. *The New York Times,* p. E11.

Nittrouer, S., Lowenstein, J. H. (2007). Children's weighting strategies for word-final stop voicing are not explained by auditory sensitivies. *Journal of Speech, Language, and Hearing Research, 50,* 58–73.

Nolen-Hoeksema, S. (2007). *Abnormal Psychology.* New York: McGraw-Hill.

Norcross, J. C. (2002). Empirically supported therapy relationships. In J. C. Norcross (Ed.), *Psychotherapy relationships that work: Therapist contributions and responsiveness to patients.* New York: Oxford University Press.

Norcross, J. C., Beutler, L. E., & Levant, R. F. (2006). *Evidence-based practices in mental health: Debate and dialogue on the fundamental questions.* Washington, DC: American Psychological Association.

Norton, P. J., & Price, E. C. (2007). A meta-analytic review of adult cognitive-behavioral treatment outcome across the anxiety disorders. *Journal of Nervous and Mental Disease, 195,* 521–531.

Noyes, R., Jr., Stuart, S. P., Langbehn, D. R., Happel, R. L., Longley, S. L., Muller, B. A., & Yagla, S. J. (2003). Test of an interpersonal model of hypochondriasis. *Psychosomatic Medicine, 65,* 292–300.

Ntinas, K. M. (2007). Behavior modification and the principle of normalization: Clash or synthesis? *Behavioral Interventions, 22,* 165–177.

Nurnberger, J. I., Jr., & Bierut, L. J. (2007, April). Seeking the connections: Alcoholism and our genes. *Scientific American,* 46–53.

Nyberg, L., & Tulving, E. (1996). Classifying human long-term memory: Evidence from converging dissociations. *European Journal of Cognitive Psychology, 8,* 163–183.

O'Brien, K. M., & LeBow, M. D. (2007). Reducing maladaptive weight management practices: Developing a psychoeducational intervention program. *Eating Behaviors, 8,* 195–210.

O'Keefe, T., & Fox, K. (Eds.). (2003). *Finding the real me: True tales of sex and gender diversity.* San Francisco: Jossey-Bass.

Oberman, L. M., Pineda, J. A., & Ramachandran, V. S. (2007). The human mirror neuron system: A link between action observation and social skills. *Social Cognitive and Affective Neuroscience, 2,* 62–66.

Oehman, A., & Mineka, S. (2003). The malicious serpent: Snakes as a prototypical stimulus for an evolved module of fear. *Current Directions in Psychological Science, 12,* 5–9.

Offer, D., Kaiz, M., Howard, K. I., & Bennett, E. S. (2000). The altering of reported experiences. *Journal of the American Academy of Child & Adolescent Psychiatry, 39,* 735–742.

Ogbu, J. (1992). Understanding cultural diversity and learning. *Educational Researcher, 21,* 5–14.

Ogbu, J.U. (2003). *Black American students in an affluent suburb.* Mahwah, NJ: Erlbaum.

Ohara, K. (2007). The n-3 polyunsaturated fatty acid/dopamine hypothesis of schizophrenia. *Progress in Neuro-Psychopharmacology & Biological Psychiatry, 31,* 469–474.

Olijslagers, J. E., Werkman, T. R., & McCreary, A. C. (2006). Modulation of midbrain dopamine neurotransmission by serotonin, a versatile interaction between neurotransmitters and significance for antipsychotic drug action. *Current Neuropharmacology, 4,* 59–68.

Oliver, M. B., & Hyde, J. S. (1993). Gender differences in sexuality: A meta-analysis. *Psychological Bulletin, 114,* 29–51.

Olson, D. H., & DeFrain, J. (2005). *Marriages and families: Intimacy, diversity, and strengths with PowerWeb.* New York: McGraw-Hill.

Ornat, S. L., & Gallo, P. (2004). Acquisition, learning, or development of language? Skinner's "Verbal behavior" revisited. *Spanish Journal of Psychology, 7,* 161–170.

Orwin, R. G., & Condray, D. S. (1984). Smith and Glass' psychotherapy conclusions need further probing: On Landman and Dawes' re-analysis. *American Psychologist, 39,* 71–72.

Pagonis, T. A., Angelopoulos, N., & Koukoulis, G. N. (2006). Psychiatric side effects induced by supraphysiological doses of combinations of anabolic steroids correlate to the severity of abuse. *European Psychiatry, 21*, 551–562.

Pagoto, S. L., Kozak, A. T., & Spates, C. R (2006). Systematic desensitization for an older woman with a severe specific phobia: An application of evidenced-based practice. *Clinical Gerontologist, 30*, 89–98.

Paniagua, F. A. (2000). *Diagnosis in a multicultural context: A casebook for mental health professionals.* Thousand Oaks, CA: Sage.

Paquette, D., Carbonneau, R., & Dubeau, D. (2003). Prevalence of father-child rough-and-tumble play and physical aggression in preschool children. *European Journal of Psychology of Education, 18*, 171–189.

Paquier, P. F., & Mariën, P. (2005). A synthesis of the role of the cerebellum in cognition. *Aphasiology, 19*, 3–19.

Park H., & Antonioni, D. (2007). Personality, reciprocity, and strength of conflict resolution strategy. *Journal of Research in Personality, 41*, 110–125.

Parke, R. D. (2004). Development in the family. *Annual Review of Psychology, 55*, 365–399.

Parker-Pope, T. (2003, April 22). The diet that works. *The Wall Street Journal*, pp. R1, R5.

Parrott, A. C. (2002). Recreational ecstasy/ MDMA, the serotonin syndrome, and serotonergic neurotoxicity [Special issue: Serotonin]. *Pharmacology, Biochemistry & Behavior, 71*, 837–844.

Pascual, A., & Guéguen, N. (2005). Foot-in-the-door and door-in-the-face: A comparative meta-analytic study. *Psychological Reports, 96*, 122–128.

Pascual, A., & Guéguen, N. (2006). Door-in-the-face technique and monetary solicitation: An evaluation in a field setting. *Perceptual and Motor Skills, 103*, 974–978.

Pascual, M. A., & Rodríguez, M. A. (2006). Learning by operant conditioning as a nonlinear self-organized process. *Nonlinear Dynamics, Psychology, and Life Sciences, 10*, 341–364.

Passer, M. W., & Smith, R. E. (2001). *Psychology.* New York: McGraw-Hill.

Patterson, D. R. (2004). Treating pain with hypnosis. *Current Directions in Psychological Science, 13*, 252–255.

Paukert, A., Stagner, B., & Hope, K. (2004). The assessment of active listening skills in helpline volunteers. *Stress, Trauma, and Crisis: An International Journal, 7*, 61–76.

Paul, A. M. (2004). *Cult of personality: How personality tests are leading us to miseducate our children, mismanage our companies and misunderstand ourselves.* New York: Free Press.

Paulozzi, L. J. (2006). Opioid analgesic involvement in drug abuse deaths in American metropolitan areas. *American Journal of Public Health, 96*, 1755–1757.

Pavitt, C. (2007). Impression formation. In B. B. Whaley & W. Samter, *Explaining communication: Contemporary theories and exemplars.* Mahwah, NJ: Erlbaum.

Pavlov, I. P. (1927). *Conditioned reflexes.* London: Oxford University Press.

Pearson, A. R., Dovidio, J. F., & Pratto, F. (2007). Racial prejudice, intergroup hate, and blatant and subtle bias of whites toward blacks in legal decision making in the United States. *International Journal of Psychology & Psychological Therapy, 7*, 125–134.

Pedersen, D. M. (2002). Intrinsic-extrinsic factors in sport motivation. *Perceptual & Motor Skills, 95*, 459–476.

Pedersen, P. B., Draguns, J. G., Lonner, W. J., & Trimble, J. E. (Eds.). (2002). *Counseling across cultures* (5th ed.). Thousand Oaks, CA: Sage.

Pellegrini, S., Muzio, R. N., Mustaca, A. E., & Papini, M. R. (2004). Successive negative contrast after partial reinforcement in the consummatory behavior of rats. *Learning and Motivation, 35*, 303–321.

Pelli, D. G., Burns, C. W., & Farell, B. (2006). Feature detection and letter identification. *Vision Research, 46*, 4646–4674.

Pellis, S. M., & Pellis, V. C. (2007). Rough-and-tumble play and the development of the social brain. *Current Directions in Psychological Science, 16*, 95–97.

Penley, J. A., Tomaka, J., & Wiebe, J. S. (2002). The association of coping to physical and psychological health outcomes: A meta-analytic review. *Journal of Behavioral Medicine, 25*, 551–603.

Penn, D. L., Corrigan, P. W., Bentall, R. P., Racenstein, J. M., & Newman, L. (1997). Social cognition in schizophrenia. *Psychological Bulletin, 121*, 114–132.

Penney, J. B., Jr. (2000). Neurochemistry. In B. S. Fogel, R. B. Schiffer, et al. (Eds.), *Synopsis of neuropsychiatry.* New York: Lippincott Williams & Wilkins.

People. (2007, July 13). Love Stories You'll Never Forget. p. 18.

Perez, R. M., DeBord, K. A., & Bieschke, K. J. (Eds). (2000). *Handbook of counseling and psychotherapy with lesbian, gay, and bisexual clients.* Washington, DC: American Psychological Association.

Pervin, L. A. (2003). *The science of personality* (2nd ed.). London: Oxford University Press.

Pesmen, C. (2006, March). Don't let pain get in your way. *Money*, 48.

Peters, E., Hess, T. M., Västfjäll, D., & Auman, C. (2007). Adult age differences in dual information processes. *Perspectives on Psychological Science, 2*, 1–23.

Peterson, R. A., & Brown, S. P. (2005). On the use of beta coefficients in meta-analysis. *Journal of Applied Psychology, 90*, 175–181.

Petersson, K. M., Silva, C., Castro-Caldas, A., Ingvar, M., & Reis, A. (2007). Literacy: A cultural influence on functional left-right differences in the inferior parietal cortex. *European Journal of Neuroscience, 26*, 791–799.

Pettigrew, T. F., & Tropp, L. R. (2006). A meta-analytic test of intergroup contact theory. *Journal of Personality and Social Psychology, 90*, 751–783.

Pettito, L. A. (1993). On the ontogenetic requirements for early language acquisition. In B. de Boysson-Bardies, S. de Schonen, P. W. Jusczyk, P. McNeilage, & J. Morton (Eds.), *Developmental neurocognition: Speech and face processing in the first year of life. NATO ASI series D: Behavioural and social sciences* (Vol. 69). Dordrecht, Netherlands: Kluwer Academic.

Petty, R. E., Cacioppo, J. T., Strathman, A. J., & Priester, J. R. (2005). To think or not to think: Exploring two routes to persuasion. In T. C. Brock & M. C. Green (Eds.), *Persuasion: Psychological insights and perspectives* (2nd ed.). Thousand Oaks, CA: Sage.

Philip, P., Sagaspe, P., Moore, N., Taillard, J., Charles, A., Guilleminault, C., & Bioulac, B. (2005). Fatigue, sleep restriction and driving performance. *Accident Analysis and Prevention, 37*, 473–478.

Piaget, J. (1970). Piaget's theory. In P. H. Mussen (Ed.), *Carmichael's manual of child psychology* (3rd ed., Vol. I). New York: Wiley.

Piaget, J., & Inhelder, B. (1958). *The growth of logical thinking from childhood to adolescence* (A. Parsons & S. Seagrin, Trans.). New York: Basic Books.

Picchioni, D., Goeltzenleucher, B., Green, D. N., Convento, M. J., Crittenden, R., Hallgren, M., & Hick, R. A. (2002). Nightmares as a coping mechanism for stress. *Dreaming: Journal of the Association for the Study of Dreams, 12*, 155–169.

Pickering, G. J., & Gordon, R. (2006). Perception of mouthfeel sensations elicited by red wine are associated with sensitivity to 6-N-propylthiouracil. *Journal of Sensory Studies, 21*, 249–265.

Piechowski, M. M. (2003). From William James to Maslow and Dabrowski: Excitability of character and self-actualization. In D. Ambrose, L. M. Cohen, et al. (Eds.), *Creative intelligence: Toward theoretic integration: Perspectives on creativity* (pp. 283–322). Cresskill, NJ: Hampton Press.

Pillay, S. S., Gruber, S. A., Rogowska, J., Simpson, N., & Yurgelun-Todd, D. A. (2006). fMRI of fearful facial affect recognition in panic disorder: The cingulate gyrus-amygdala connection. *Journal of Affective Disorders, 94*(1-3) 173–181.

Pincus, T., & Morley, S. (2001). Cognitive-processing bias in chronic pain: A review and integration. *Psychological Bulletin, 127*, 599–617.

Pinel, J. P. J., Assanand, S., & Lehman, D. R. (2000). Hunger, eating and ill health. *American Psychologist, 55*, 1105–1116.

Pinker, S. (1994). *The language instinct.* New York: William Morrow.

Pinker, S. (2002). *The blank slate: The modern denial of human nature.* New York: Viking.

Pinker, S. (2004). *How the mind works.* New York: Gardner Books.

Pinker, S., & Jackendoff, R. (2005). The faculty of language: What's special about it? *Cognition, 96,* 201–236.

Pinkerton, S. D., Bogart, L. M., Cecil, H., & Abramson, P. R. (2002). Factors associated with masturbation in a collegiate sample. *Journal of Psychology and Human Sexuality, 14,* 103–121.

Plomin, R. (2003a). 50 years of DNA: What it has meant to psychological science. *American Psychological Society, 16,* 7–8.

Plomin, R. (2003b). General cognitive ability. In R. Plomin, J. C. DeFries, et al. (Eds.), *Behavioral genetics in the postgenomic era.* Washington, DC: American Psychological Association.

Plomin, R., DeFries, J.C., McClearn, G.E., McGuffin, P. (2008). *Behavioral Genetics* (5th ed.) New York: Worth.

Plomin, R., & Kovas, Y. (2005). Generalist genes and learning disabilities. *Psychological Bulletin, 131,* 592–617.

Plomin, R., & McGuffin, P. (2003). Psychopathology in the postgenomic era. *Annual Review of Psychology, 54,* 205–228.

Plomin, R., DeFries, J. C., Craig, I. W., & McGuffin, P. (2003). *Behavioral genetics in the postgenomic era.* Washington, DC: American Psychological Association.

Plonczynski, D. J., & Plonczynski, K. J. (2007). Hormone therapy in perimenopausal and postmenopausal women: Examining the evidence on cardiovascular disease risks. *Journal of Gerontological Nursing, 33,* 48–55.

Plowright, C. M. S., Simonds, V. M., & Butler, M. A. (2006). How bumblebees first find flowers: Habituation of visual pattern preferences, spontaneous recovery, and dishabituation. *Learning and Motivation, 37,* 66–78.

Pole, N. (2007).The psychophysiology of posttraumatic stress disorder: A meta-analysis. *Psychological Bulletin, 133,* 34–45.

Polivy, J., & Herman, C. P. (2002). Causes of eating disorders. *Annual Review of Psychology, 53,* 187–213.

Polivy, J., Herman, C. P., & Boivin, M. (2005). Eating disorders. In J. E. Maddux and B. A. Winstead, *Psychopathology: Foundations for a contemporary understanding* (pp. 229–254). Mahwah, NJ: Erlbaum.

Polk, N. (1997, March 30). The trouble with school testing systems. *The New York Times,* p. CN3.

Polonsky, D. C. (2006). Review of the big book of masturbation: From angst to zeal. *Journal of Sex & Marital Therapy, 32,* 75–78.

Ponterotto, J. G., Gretchen, D., & Chauhan, R. V. (2001). Cultural identity and multicultural assessment: Quantitative and qualitative tools for the clinician. In L. A. Suzuki, & J. G. Ponterotto (Eds.), *Handbook of multicultural assessment: Clinical, psychological, and educational applications* (2nd ed.). San Francisco: Jossey-Bass/Pfeiffer.

Poo, C., & Isaacson, J. S. (2007). An early critical period for long-term plasticity and structural modification of sensory synapses in olfactory cortex. *Journal of Neuroscience, 27,* 7553–7558.

Porkka-Heiskanen, T., Strecker, R. E., Thakkar, M., Bjorkum, A. A., Greene, R. W., & McCarley, R. W. (1997, May 23). Adensosine: A mediator of the sleep-inducing effects of prolonged wakefulness. *Science, 276,* 1265–1268.

Porte, H. S., & Hobson, J. A. (1996). Physical motion in dreams: One measure of three theories. *Journal of Abnormal Psychology, 105,* 329–335.

Porter, C. L., & Hsu, H. C. (2003). First-time mothers' perceptions of efficacy during the transition to motherhood: Links to infant temperament. *Journal of Family Psychology, 17,* 54–64.

Posner, M. I., & DiGirolamo, G. J. (2000). Cognitive neuroscience: Origins and promise. *Psychological Bulletin, 126,* 873–889.

Poteat, V. P., & Espelage, D. L. (2007). Predicting psychosocial consequences of homophobic victimization in middle school students. *Journal of Early Adolescence, 27,* 175–191.

Pottick, K. J., Kirk, S. A., Hsieh, D. K., & Tian, X. (2007). Judging mental disorder in youths: Effects of client, clinician, and contextual differences. *Journal of Consulting Clinical Psychology, 75,* 1–8.

Powell, L. H. (2006). Review of marital and sexual lifestyles in the United States: attitudes, behaviors, and relationships in social context. *Family Relations, 55,* 149.

Powers, K. D. (2006). An analysis of Kohlbergian moral development in relationship to biblical factors of morality in seminary students (Lawrence Kohlberg). *Dissertation Abstracts International: Section B: The Sciences and Engineering, 67* (6-B), 3485.

Pratkanis, A. R. (2007). Social influence analysis: An index of tactics. In A. R. Pratkanis, *The science of social influence: Advances and future progress.* New York: Psychology Press.

Pratt, H. D., Phillips, E. L., Greydanus, D. E., & Patel, D. R. (2003). Eating disorders in the adolescent population: Future directions [Special issue: Eating disorders in adolescents]. *Journal of Adolescent Research, 18,* 297–317.

Pressley, M. P., & Harris., K. R. (2006). Cognitive strategies instruction: From basic research to classroom instruction. In P. A. Alexander, & P. H. Winne, *Handbook of educational psychology.* Mahwah, NJ: Erlbaum.

Pretzer, J. L., & Beck, A. T. (2005). A cognitive theory of personality disorders. In M. F. Lenzenweger & J. F. Clarkin (Eds.), *Major theories of personality disorder* (2nd ed.). New York: Guilford Press.

Prince, C.V. (2005). Homosexuality, transvestism and transsexuality: Reflections on their etymology and differentiation. *International Journal of Transgenderism, 8,* 15–18.

Prinz, J. J. (2007). Emotion: Competing theories and philosophical issues. In P. Thagard, *Philosophy of psychology and cognitive science.* Amsterdam, Netherlands: North Holland/Elsevier.

Prislin, R., Brewer, M., & Wilson, D. J. (2002). Changing majority and minority positions within a group versus an aggregate. *Personality and Social Psychology Bulletin, 28,* 650–647.

Proffitt, D. R. (2006). Distance perception. *Current Directions in Psychological Science, 15,* 131–139.

Prohovnik, I., Skudlarski, P., Fulbright, R. K., Gore, J. C., & Wexler, B. E. (2004). Functional MRI changes before and after onset of reported emotions. *Psychiatry Research: Neuroimaging, 132,* 239–250.

Puca, R. M. (2005). The influence of the achievement motive on probability estimates in pre- and post-decisional action phases. *Journal of Research in Personality, 39,* 245–262.

Puhl, R., & Latner, J. (2007). Stigma, obesity, and the health of the nation's children. *Psychological Bulletin, 133,* 557–580.

Rabin, J. (2004). Quantification of color vision with cone contrast sensitivity. *Visual Neuroscience, 21,* 483–485.

Rachman, S., & deSilva, P. (2004). *Panic disorders: The facts.* Oxford, England: Oxford University Press.

Rahman, Q., Kumari, V., & Wilson, G. D. (2003). Sexual orientation-related differences in prepulse inhibition of the human startle response. *Behavioral Neuroscience, 117,* 1096–1102.

Rajagopal, S. (2006). The placebo effect. *Psychiatric Bulletin, 30,* 185–188.

Ralston, A. (2004). *Between a rock and a hard place.* New York: Simon & Schuster.

Rambaud, C., & Guilleminault, C. (2004). "Back to sleep" and unexplained death in infants. *Journal of Sleep and Sleep Disorders, 27,* 1359–1366.

Ramsay, M. C., Reynolds, C. R., & Kamphaus, R. W. (2002). *Essentials of behavioral assessment.* New York: Wiley.

Ramus, F. (2006). Genes, brain, and cognition: A roadmap for the cognitive scientist. *Cognition, 101,* 247–269.

Rangell, L. (2007). *The road to unity in psychoanalytic theory.* Lanham, MD: Jason Aronson.

Rassin, E., & Muris, P. (2007). Abnormal and normal obsessions: A reconsideration. *Behaviour Research and Therapy, 45,* 1065–1070.

Rastad, C., Ulfberg, J., & Lindberg, P. (2008). Light room therapy effective in mild forms of seasonal affective disorder—A randomised controlled study. *Journal of Affective Disorders, 108*(3) 291–296.

Rattazzi, M. C., LaFuci, G., & Brown, W. T. (2004). Prospects for gene therapy in the Fragile X Syndrome. *Mental Retardation and Developmental Disabilities Research Reviews, 10,* 75–81.

Ravindran, A. V., Matheson, K., Griffiths, J., Merali, Z., & Anisman, H. (2002). Stress, coping, uplifts, and quality of life in subtypes of depression: A conceptual framework and emerging data. *Journal of Affective Disorders, 71,* 121–130.

Raz, A. (2007). Suggestibility and hypnotizability: Mind the gap. *American Journal of Clinical Hypnosis, 49,* 205–210.

Redding, G. M. (2002). A test of size-scaling and relative-size hypotheses for the moon illusion. *Perception and Psychophysics, 64,* 1281–1289.

Redding, G. M., & Hawley, E. (1993). Length illusion in fractional Müller-Lyer stimuli: An object-perception approach. *Perception, 22,* 819–828.

Redish, A. D. (2004). Addiction as a computational process gone awry. *Science, 306,* 1944–1947.

Reed, S. K. (1996). *Cognition: Theory and applications* (4th ed.). Pacific Grove, CA: Brooks/Cole.

Reese, R. J., Conoley, C. W., & Brossart, D. F. (2002). Effectiveness of telephone counseling: A field-based investigation. *Journal of Counseling Psychology, 49,* 233–242.

Regan, P. C. (2006). Love. In R. D. McAnulty, & M. M. Burnette, *Sex and sexuality, Vol 2: Sexual function and dysfunction.* Westport, CT: Praeger Publishers/Greenwood Publishing.

Reichenberg, A., & Harvey, P. D. (2007). Neuropsychological impairments in schizophrenia: Integration of performance-based and brain imaging findings. *Psychological Bulletin, 133,* 212–223.

Reif, A., & Lesch, K. P. (2003). Toward a molecular architecture of personality. *Behavioural Brain Research, 139,* 1–20.

Reijonen, J. H., Pratt, H. D., Patel, D. R., & Greydanus, D. E. (2003). Eating disorders in the adolescent population: An overview [Special issue: Eating disorders in adolescents]. *Journal of Adolescent Research, 18,* 209–222.

Reiss, S., & Havercamp, S. M. (2005). Motivation in developmental context: A new method for studying self-actualization. *Journal of Humanistic Psychology, 45,* 41–53.

Reitman, J. S. (1965). *Cognition and thought.* New York: Wiley.

Remington, G. (2003). Understanding antipsychotic "atypicality": A clinical and pharmacological moving target. *Journal of Psychiatry & Neuroscience, 28,* 275–284.

Rende, R. (2007). Thinking inside and outside the (black) box: Behavioral genetics and human development. *Human Development, 49,* 343–346.

Repp, B. H., & Knoblich, G. (2007). Action can affect auditory perception. *Psychological Science, 18,* 6–7.

Rice, M. L., Tomblin, J. B., Hoffman, L., Richman, W. A., & Marquis, J. (2004). Grammatical tense deficits in children with SLI and nonspecific language impairment: Relationships with non-verbal IQ over time. *Journal of Speech, Language, and Hearing Research, 47,* 816–834.

Richard, D. C. S., & Lauterbach, D. (Eds). (2006). *Handbook of exposure therapies.* New York: Academic Press.

Richard, M. (2005). Effective treatment of eating disorders in Europe: Treatment outcome and its predictors. *European Eating Disorders Review, 13,* 169–179.

Richardson, A. S., Bergen, H. A., Martin, G., Roeger, L., & Allison, S. (2005). Perceived academic performance as an indicator of risk of attempted suicide in young adolescents. *Archives of Suicide Research, 9,* 163–176.

Rieber, R. W., & Robinson, D. K. (2006). Review of the essential Vygotsky. *Journal of the History of the Behavioral Sciences, 42,* 178–180.

Rieder, R. O., Kaufmann, C. A., & Knowles, J. A. (1996). Genetics. In R. E. Hales & S. C. Yudofsky (Eds.), *The American Psychiatric Press synopsis of psychiatry.* Washington, DC: American Psychiatric Press.

Rigby, L., & Waite, S. (2007). Group therapy for self-esteem, using creative approaches and metaphor as clinical tools. *Behavioural and Cognitive Psychotherapy, 35,* 361–364.

Rinn, W. E. (1984). The neuropsychology of facial expression: A review of neurological and psychological mechanisms for producing facial expressions. *Psychological Bulletin, 95,* 52–77.

Rinn, W. E. (1991). Neuropsychology of facial expression. In R. S. Feldman & B. Rimé (Eds.), *Fundamentals of nonverbal behavior.* Cambridge, England: Cambridge University Press.

Riolo, F. (2007). Ricordare, ripetere e rielaborare: Un lascito di Freud alia psicoanalisi futura. [Remembering, repeating, and working through: Freud's legacy to the psychoanalysis of the future.] *Rivista di Psicoanalisi, 53,* 439–446.

Rivera-Gaxiola, M., Klarman, L., Garcia-Sierra, A., & Kuhl, P. K. (2005). Neural patterns to speech and vocabulary growth in American infants. *Neuroreport: For Rapid Communication of Neuroscience Research, 16,* 495–498.

Robinson, D. N. (2007). Theoretical psychology: What is it and who needs it? *Theory & Psychology, 17,* 187–198.

Robinson, D. S. (2007). Antidepressant drugs: Early onset of therapeutic effect. *Primary Psychiatry, 14,* 23–24.

Rodd, Z. A., Bell, R. L., Sable, H. J. K., Murphy, J. M., & McBride, W. J. (2004). Recent advances in animal models of alcohol craving and relapse. *Pharmacology, Biochemistry and Behavior, 79,* 439–450.

Roe, D., Weishut, D.J.N., Jaglom, M. & Rabinowitz, J. (2002). Patients' and staff members' attitudes about the rights of hospitalized psychiatric patients. *Psychiatric Services, 53*(1), 87–91.

Rogers, C. R. (1971). A theory of personality. In S. Maddi (Ed.), *Perspectives on personality.* Boston: Little, Brown.

Rogers, C. R. (1995). *A way of being.* Boston: Houghton Mifflin.

Rogers, S. (2007). The underlying mechanisms of semantic memory loss in Alzheimer's disease and semantic dementia. *Dissertation Abstracts International: Section B: The Sciences and Engineering, 67* (10-B), 5591.

Roid, G.H. & Pomplun, M. (2005). Interpreting the Stanford-Binet Intelligence Scales (5th ed.). In D.P. Flanagan & P.L. Harrison (Eds.), *Contemporary intellectual assessment: Theories, tests, and issues* (pp. 325–343). New York: Guilford Press

Roizen, N. J., & Patterson, D. (2003). Down's syndrome. *Lancet, 361,* 1281–1289.

Rollman, G. B. (2004). *Ethnocultural variations in the experience of pain.* Mahwah, NJ: Erlbaum.

Romano, E., Tremblay, R. E, Vitaro, E., Zoccolillo, M., & Pagani, L. (2001.) Prevalence of psychiatric diagnoses and the role of perceived impairment: Findings from an adolescent community sample. *Journal of Child Psychology and Psychiatry and Allied Disciplines, 42,* 451–461.

Rorschach, H. (1924). *Psychodiagnosis: A diagnostic test based on perception.* New York: Grune & Stratton.

Rosch, E., & Mervis, C. B. (1975). Family resemblances: Studies in the internal structure of categories. *Cognitive-Psychology, 7,* 573–605.

Rosen, H. (2000). The creative evolution of the theoretical foundations for cognitive therapy [Special issue: Creativity in the context of cognitive therapy]. *Journal of Cognitive Psychotherapy, 14,* 123–134.

Rosenbloom, T., & Wolf, Y. (2002). Sensation seeking and detection of risky road signals: A developmental perspective. *Accident Analysis and Prevention, 34,* 569–580.

Rosenstein, D. S., & Horowitz, H. A. (1996). Adolescent attachment and psychopathology. *Journal of Consulting and Clinical Psychology, 64,* 244–253.

Rosenthal, R. (2002). Covert communication in classrooms, clinics, courtrooms and cubicles. *American Psychologist, 57,* 838–849.

Rosenthal, R. (2003). Covert communication in laboratories, classrooms, and the truly real world. *Current Directions in Psychological Science, 12,* 151–154.

Ross, H. E. (2000). Sensation and perception. In D. S. Gupta, S. Deepa, & R. M. Gupta, et al. (Eds.), *Psychology for psychiatrists* (pp. 20–40). London: Whurr Publishers.

Ross, H. E., & Plug, C. (2002). *The mystery of the moon illusion: Exploring size perception.* Oxford: University Press.

Ross, J. (2006). Sleep on a problem. . . . It works like a dream. *The Psychologist, 19,* 738-740.

Ross, P. E. (2004, April). Draining the language out of color. *Scientific American,* pp. 46–51.

Rossell, S. L., Bullmore, E. T., Williams, S. C. R., & David, A. S. (2002). Sex differences in functional brain activation during a lexical visual field task. *Brain and Language, 80,* 97–105.

Rossouw, J. E., Prentice, R. L., Manson, J. E., Wu, L., Barad, D., Barnabei, V. M., Ko, M., LaCroix, A. Z., Margolis, K. L., & Stefanick, M. L. (2007). Postmenopausal hormone therapy and risk of cardiovascular disease by age and years since menopause. *Journal of the American Medical Association, 297,* 1465–1477.

Roughton, R. E. (2002). Rethinking homosexuality: What it teaches us about psychoanalysis. *Journal of the American Psychoanalytic Association, 50,* 733–763.

Rowe, J. B., Toni, I., Josephs, O., Frackowiak, R. S. J., & Passingham, R. E. (2000, June 2). The prefrontal cortex: Response selection or maintenance within working memory? *Science, 288,* 1656–1660.

Rowley, S. J., Sellers, R. M., Chavous, T. M., & Smith, M. A. (1998). The relationship between racial identity and self-esteem in African American college and high school students. *Journal of Personality and Social Psychology, 74,* 715–724.

Royzman, E. B., Cassidy, K. W., & Baron, J. (2003). "I know, you know": Epistemic egocentrism in children and adults. *Review of General Psychology, 7,* 38–65.

Rozencwajg, P., Cherfi, M., Ferrandez, A. M., Lautrey, J., Lemoine, C., & Loarer, E. (2005). Age-related differences in the strategies used by middle aged adults to solve a block design task. *International Journal of Aging and Human Development, 60,* 159–182.

Rozin, P., Kabnick, K., Pete, E., Fischler, C., & Shields, C. (2003). The ecology of eating: Smaller portion sizes in France than in the United States help explain the French paradox. *Psychological Science, 14,* 450–454.

Rubichi, S., Ricci, F., Padovani, R., & Scaglietti, L. (2005). Hypnotic susceptibility, baseline attentional functioning, and the Stroop task. *Consciousness and Cognition: An International Journal, 14,* 296–303.

Rubin, D. C. (1985, September). The subtle deceiver: Recalling our past. *Psychology Today,* pp. 39–46.

Rubin, D. C. (1999). *Remembering our past: Studies in autobiographical memory.* New York: Cambridge University Press.

Rubin, D. C., Schrauf, R. W., Gulgoz, S., & Naka, M. (2007). Cross-cultural variability of component processes in autobiographical remembering: Japan, Turkey, and the USA. *Memory, 15,* 536-547.

Rudman, L. A., & Ashmore, R. D. (2007). Discrimination and the Implicit Association Test. *Group Processes & Intergroup Relations, 10,* 359–372.

Rusche, B. (2003). The 3Rs and animal welfare—conflict or the way forward? *ALTEX, 20* (Suppl 1), 63–76.

Ruscher, J. B., Fiske, S. T., & Schnake, S. B. (2000). The motivated tactician's juggling act: Compatible vs. incompatible impression goals. *British Journal of Social Psychology, 39,* 241–256.

Rushton, J. P., & Jensen, A. R. (2006). The totality of available evidence shows the race IQ gap still remains. *Psychological Science, 17,* 921–922.Russo, N. (1981).Women in psychology. In L. T. Benjamin, Jr., & K. D. Lowman (Eds.), *Activities handbook for the teaching of psychology.* Washington, DC: American Psychological Association.

Rusting, M. (2006). Infant observation research: What have we learned so far? *Infant Observation, 9,* 35–52.

Rutter, M. (2006). *Genes and behavior: Nature-nurture interplay explained.* Malden, MA: Blackwell Publishing.

Saarni, C. (1999). *Developing emotional competence.* New York: Guilford Press.

Sackeim, H. A., Haskett, R. F., Mulsant, B. H., Thase, M. E., Mann, J. J., Pettinati, H. M., Greenberg, R. M., Crowe, R. R., Cooper, T. B., & Prudic, J. (2001). Continuation pharmacotherapy in the prevention of relapse following electroconvulsive therapy: A randomized controlled trial. *Journal of the American Medical Association, 285,* 1299–1307.

Saczynski, J., Willis, S., and Schaie, K. (2002). Strategy use in reasoning training with older adults. *Aging, Neuropsychology, & Cognition, 9,* 48–60.

Saggino, A., Perfetti, B., & Spitoni, G. (2006). Fluid intelligence and executive functions: New perspectives. In L. V. Wesley, *Intelligence: New research.* Hauppauge, NY: Nova Science Publishers.

Salmela-Aro, K., & Nurmi, J-E. (2007). Self-esteem during university studies predicts career characteristics 10 years later. *Journal of Vocational Behavior, 70,* 463–477.

Salsman, N. L. (2006). Interpersonal change as an outcome of Time-Limited Interpersonal Therapy. *Dissertation Abstracts International: Section B: The Sciences and Engineering, 66* (9-B), 5103.

Sams, M., Hari, R., Rif, J., & Knuutila, J. (1993). The human auditory memory trace persists about 10 sec: Neuromagnetic evidence. *Journal of Cognitive Neuroscience, 5,* 363–370.

Samuel, D. B., & Widiger, T. A. (2006). Differentiating normal and abnormal personality from the perspective of the DSM. In S. Strack, *Differentiating normal and abnormal personality* (2nd ed.). New York: Springer Publishing.

Sanderson, M. (2007). Assessment of manic symptoms in different cultures. *British Journal of Psychiatry, 190,* 178.

Sandoval, J., Frisby, C. L., Geisinger, K. F., Scheuneman, J. D., & Grenier, J. R. (Eds.). (1998). *Test interpretation and diversity: Achieving equity in assessment.* Washington, DC: American Psychological Association.

Santel, S., Baving, L., Krauel, K., Munte, T.F., & Rotte, M. (2006). Hunger and satiety in anorexia nervosa: fMRI during cognitive processing of food pictures. *Brain Research, 1114,* 138–148.

Saper, C. B., Lu, J., Chou, T. C., & Gooley, J. (2005). The hypothalamic integrator for circadian rhythms. *Trends in Neuroscience, 28,* 152–157.

Sapolsky, R. M. (2003). Gene therapy for psychiatric disorders. *American Journal of Psychiatry, 160,* 208–220.

Satel, S. (2006). Is caffeine addictive?—A review of the literature. *American Journal of Drug and Alcohol Abuse, 32,* 493–502.

Savas, H. A., Yumru, M., & Kaya, M. C. (2007). Atypical antipsychotics as "mood stabilizers": A retrospective chart review. *Progress in Neuro-Psychopharmacology & Biological Psychiatry, 31,* 1064–1067.

Savazzi, S., Fabri, M., Rubboli, G., Paggi, A., Tassinari, C. A., & Marzi, C. A. (2007). Interhemispheric transfer following callosotomy in humans: Role of the superior colliculus, *Neuropsychologia, 45,* 2417–2427.

Sawa, A., & Snyder, S. H. (2002, April 26). Schizophrenia: Diverse approaches to a complex disease. *Science, 296,* 692–695.

Sayette, M. A. (1993). An appraisal disruption model of alcohol's effects on stress responses in social drinkers. *Psychological Bulletin, 114,* 459–476.

Scarr, S., & Weinberg, R. A. (1976). I.Q. test performance of black children adopted by white families. *American Psychologist, 31,* 726–739.

Scaturo, D. J. (2004). Fundamental clinical dilemmas in contemporary group psychotherapy. *Group Analysis, 37,* 201–217.

Scelfo, J. (2007, February 26). Men & depression: Facing darkness. *Newsweek,* 43–50.

Schachter, S., & Singer, J. E. (1962). Cognitive, social, and physiological determinants of emotional state. *Psychological Review, 69,* 379–399.

Schacter, D. L., Wagner, A. D., & Buckner, R. L. (2000). Memory systems of 1999. In E. Tulving, F. I. Craik, I. M. Fergus, et al. (Eds.), *The Oxford handbook of memory.* New York: Oxford University Press.

Schaefer, R. T. (2000). *Sociology: A brief introduction* (3rd ed.). Boston: McGraw-Hill.

Schaie, K. W. (2005) *Developmental influences on adult intelligence: The Seattle Longitudinal Study.* New York: Oxford University Press.

Schaller, M., & Crandall, C. S. (Eds.) (2004). *The psychological foundations of culture.* Mahwah, NJ: Erlbaum.

Scheele, B., & DuBois, F. (2006). Catharsis as a moral form of entertainment. In J. Bryant, & P. Vorderer, *Psychology of entertainment.* Mahwah, NJ: Erlbaum.

Scheff, T. J. (1999). *Being mentally ill: A sociological theory* (3rd ed.). Hawthorne, NY: Aldine de Gruyter.

Scheier, M. F., Carver, C. S., & Bridges, M. W. (1994). Distinguishing optimism from neuroticism (and trait anxiety, self-mastery, and self-esteem): A revision of the Life Orientation Test. *Journal of Personality and Social Psychology, 67,* 1063–1078.

Schieber, F. (2006). Vision and aging. In J. E. Birren, & K. W. Schaire, *Handbook of the psychology of aging* (6th ed.). Amsterdam, Netherlands: Elsevier.

Schmidt, J. P. (2006). The discovery of neurotransmitters: A fascinating story and a scientific object lesson. *PsycCRITIQUES, 61,* 101–115.

Schmidt, N. B., Kotov, R., & Joiner, T. E., Jr. (2004). *Taxometrics: Toward a new diagnostic scheme for psychopathology.* Washington, DC: American Psychological Association.

Schneider, D. J. (2003). *The psychology of stereotyping.* New York: Guilford Press.

Schredl, M., & Piel, E. (2005). Gender differences in dreaming: Are they stable over time? *Personality and Individual Differences, 39,* 309–316.

Schulte-Ruther, M., Markowitsch, J. J., Fink, G. R., & Piefke, M. (2007). Mirror neuron and theory of mind mechanisms involved in face-to-face interactions: A functional magnetic resonance imaging approach to empathy. *Journal of Cognitive Neuroscience, 19,* 1354–1372.

Schutt, R. K. (2001). *Investigating the social world: The process and practice of research.* Thousand Oaks, CA: Sage.

Schwartz, B. L. (2001). The relation of tip-of-the-tongue states and retrieval time. *Memory & Cognition, 29,* 117–126.

Schwartz, B. L. (2002). The phenomenology of naturally-occurring tip of-the-tongue states: A diary study. In S. P. Shohov (Ed.), *Advances in psychology research* (Vol. 8, pp. 73–84). Huntington, NY: Nova.

Seamon, M. J., Fass, J. A., Maniscalco-Feichtl, M., & Abu-Shraie, N. A. (2007). Medical marijuana and the developing role of the pharmacist. *American Journal of Health System Pharmacy, 64,* 1037–1044.

Sebel, P. S., Bonke, B., & Winograd, E. (Eds.). (1993). *Memory and awareness in anesthesia.* Englewood Cliffs, NJ: Prentice Hall.

Seeley, R., Stephens, T., & Tate, P. (2000). *Anatomy & Physiology* (5th ed., p. 384). Boston: McGraw-Hill.

Sefcek, J. A., Brumbach, B. H., & Vasquez, G. (2007). The evolutionary psychology of human mate choice: How ecology, genes, fertility, and fashion influence mating strategies. *Journal of Psychology & Human Sexuality,18,* 125–182.

Segall, M. H., Campbell, D. T., & Herskovits, M. J. (1966). *The influence of culture on visual perception.* New York: Bobbs-Merrill.

Seli, H. (2007). "Self" in self-worth protection: The relationship of possible selves to achievement motives and self-worth protective strategies. *Dissertation Abstracts International Section A: Humanities and Social Sciences, 67* (9-A), 3302.

Seligman, M. E. (2007). *What you can change . . . and what you can't: The complete guide to successful self-improvement.* New York: Vintage.

Seligman, M. E. P. (1975). *Helplessness: On depression, development, and death.* San Francisco: Freeman.

Seligman, M. E. P. (1995, December). The effectiveness of psychotherapy: The *Consumer Reports* study. *American Psychologist, 50,* 965–974.

Seligman, M. E. P. (1996, October). Science as an ally of practice. *American Psychologist, 51,* 1072–1079.

Sellbom, M., & Ben-Porath, Y. S. (2006). The Minnesota Multiphasic Personality Inventory-2. In R. P. Archer, *Forensic uses of clinical assessment instruments.* Mahwah, NJ: Erlbaum.

Sells, R. (1994, August). *Homosexuality study.* Paper presented at the annual meeting of the American Statistical Assocation, Toronto.

Selove, R. (2007). The glass is half full: Current knowledge about pediatric cancer and sickle cell anemia. *PsycCRITIQUES, 52,* 88–99.

Selsky, A. (1997, February 16). African males face circumcision rite. *The Boston Globe,* p. C7.

Selye, H. (1976). *The stress of life.* New York: McGraw-Hill.

Selye, H. (1993). History of the stress concept. In L. Goldberger & S. Breznitz (Eds.), *Handbook of stress: Theoretical and clinical aspects* (2nd ed.). New York: Free Press.

Semykina, A., & Linz, S. J. (2007). Gender differences in personality and earnings: Evidence from Russia. *Journal of Economic Psychology, 28,* 387–410.

Seroczynski, A. D., Jacquez, F. M., & Cole, D. A. (2003). Depression and suicide during adolescence. In G. R. Adams & M. D. Berzonsky (Eds.), *Blackwell handbook of adolescence.* Malden, MA: Blackwell Publishers.

Serpell, R. (2000). Intelligence and culture. In R. Sternberg (Ed.), *Handbook of intelligence.* Cambridge, England: Cambridge University Press.

Shafer, V. L., & Garrido-Nag, K. (2007). The neurodevelopmental bases of language. In E. Hoff & M. Shatz, *Blackwell handbook of language development* (pp. 21–45). Malden, MA: Blackwell Publishing.

Shaikholeslami, R., & Khayyer, M. (2006). Intrinsic motivation, extrinsic motivation, and learning English as a foreign language. *Psychological Reports, 99,* 813–818.

Shapiro, L. R. (2006). Remembering September 11th: The role of retention interval and rehearsal on flashbulb and event memory. *Memory, 14,* 129–147.

Sheehan, S. (1982). *Is there no place on earth for me?* Boston: Houghton Mifflin.

Shelton, R. C., Keller, M. B., Gelenberg, A., Dunner, D. L., Hirschfeld, R. M. A., Thase, M. E., Russell, J., Lydiard, R. B., Crits-Cristoph, P., Gallop, R., Todd, L., Hellerstein, D., Goodnick, P., Keitner, G., Stahl, S. M., & Halbreich, R. U. (2002). The effectiveness of St. John's wort in major depression: A multi-center, randomized placebo-controlled trial. *Journal of the American Medical Association, 285,* 1978–1986.

Shier, D., Butler, J., & Lewis, R. (2000). *Hole's essentials of human anatomy and physiology* (7th ed., p. 283). Boston: McGraw-Hill.

Shimono, K., & Wade N. J. (2002). Monocular alignment in different depth planes. *Vision Research, 42,* 1127–1135.

Shinn, M., Gottlieb, J., Wett, J. L., Bahl, A., Cohen, A., & Baron, E. D. (2007). Predictors of homelessness among older adults in New York City: Disability, economic, human and social capital and stressful events. *Journal of Health Psychology, 12,* 696–708.

Shurkin, J. N. (1992). *Terman's kids: The groundbreaking study of how the gifted grow up.* Boston: Little, Brown.

Shweder, R. A. (1994). "You're not sick, you're just in love": Emotion as an interpretive system. In P. Ekman & R. J. Davidson (Eds.), *The nature of emotion: Fundamental questions.* New York: Oxford.

Sidman, M. (2006). The distinction between positive and negative reinforcement: Some additional considerations. *Behavior Analyst, 29,* 135–139.

Siegel, B. (1989). *Peace, love, and healing.* New York: Harper Perennial.

Siegel, J. M. (2003, November). Why we sleep. *Scientific American,* pp. 92–97.

Silverstein, M. L. (2007). Rorschach test findings at the beginning of treatment and 2 years later, with a 30-year follow-up. *Journal of Personality Assessment, 88,* 131–143.

Sininger, Y. S., & Cone-Wesson, B. (2004, September 10). Asymmetric cochlear processing mimics hemispheric specialization. *Science, 305,* 1581.

Sininger, Y. S., & Cone-Wesson, B. (2006). Lateral asymmetry in the ABR of neonates: Evidence and mechanisms. *Hearing Research, 212,* 203–211.

Skinner, B. F. (1957). *Verbal behavior.* New York: Appleton-Century-Crofts.

Skinner, B. F. (1975). The steep and thorny road to a science of behavior. *American Psychologist, 30,* 42–49.

Sloan, E. P., Hauri, P., Bootzin, R., Morin, C., et al. (1993). The nuts and bolts of behavioral therapy for insomnia. *Journal of Psychosomatic Research, 37* (Suppl.), 19–37.

Smetana, J. B. (2007). Strategies for understanding archetypes and the collective unconscious of an organization. *Dissertation Abstracts International Section A: Humanities and Social Sciences, 67* (12-A), 4714.

Smetana, J. G. (2005). Adolescent-parent conflict: Resistance and subversion as developmental process. In L. Nucci (Ed.), *Conflict, contradiction, and contrarian elements in moral development and education.* (pp. 69–91). Mahwah, NJ: Erlbaum.

Smetana, J., Daddis, C., and Chuang, S. (2003). "Clean your room!" A longitudinal investigation of adolescent-parent conflict and conflict resolution in middle-class African American families. *Journal of Adolescent Research, 18,* 631–650.

Smith, B. H., Barkley, R. A., & Shapiro, C. J. (2006). Attention-deficit/hyperactivity disorder. In E. J. Mash & R. A. Barkley, *Treatment of childhood disorders* (3rd ed.). New York: Guilford Press.

Smith, C. (2006). Symposium V—Sleep and learning: New developments [Special issue: Methods and learning in functional MRI.] *Brain and Cognition, 60,* 331–332.

Smith, C. A., & Lazarus, R. S. (2001). Appraisal components, core relational themes, and the emotions. In W. G. Parrott (Ed.), *Emotions in social psychology: Essential readings* (pp. 94–114). Philadelphia: Psychology Press.

Smith, C. D., Chebrolu, J., Wekstein, D. R., Schmitt, F. A., & Markesbery, W. R. (2007). Age and gender effects on human brain anatomy: A voxel-based morphometric study in healthy elderly. *Neurobiology of Aging, 28,* 1057–1087.

Smith, D. (October 2001). Can't get your 40 winks? Here's what the sleep experts advise. *Monitor on Psychology, 37.*

Smith, D.B. (2007). Can you live with the voices in your head? *The New York Times Magazine.* P. 50.

Smith, E. R., & Semin, G. R. (2007). Situated social cognition. *Current Directions in Psychological Science, 16,* 132–135.

Smith, J. D. (2006). Speaking of mild mental retardation: It's no box of chocolates, or is it? *Exceptionality, 14,* 191–204.

Smith, M. B. (2003). Moral foundations in research with human participants. In A. E. Kazdin (Ed.), *Methodological issues & strategies in clinical research* (3rd ed.). Washington, DC: American Psychological Association.

Smith, M. L., Glass, G. V., & Miller, T. J. (1980). *The benefits of psychotherapy.* Baltimore: Johns Hopkins University Press.

Smith, R. A., & Weber, A. L. (2005). Applying social psychology in everyday life. In F. W. Schneider, J. A. Gruman, & L. M. Coutts, *Applied social psychology: Understanding and addressing social and practical problems.* Thousand Oaks, CA: Sage.

Smith, W. B. (2007). Karen Horney and psychotherapy in the 21st century. *Clinical Social Work Journal, 35,* 57–66.

Snyder, D. J., Fast, K., & Bartoshuk, L. M. (2004). Valid comparisons of suprathreshold sensations. *Journal of Consciousness Studies, 11,* 96–112.

Snyder, J., Cramer, A., & Afrank, J. (2005). The contributions of ineffective discipline and parental hostile attributions of child misbehavior to the development of conduct problems at home and school. *Developmental Psychology, 41,* 30–41.

Snyder, M. (2002). Applications of Carl Rogers' theory and practice to couple and family therapy: A response to Harlene Anderson and David Bott. *Journal of Family Therapy, 24,* 317–325.

Society for Personality Assessment. (2005). The status of Rorschach in clinical and forensic practice: An official statement by the board of trustees of the Society for Personality Assessment. *Journal of Personality Assessment, 85,* 219–237.

Sohr-Preston, S.L. & Scaramella, L.V. (2006). Implications of timing of maternal depressive symptoms for early cognitive and language development. *Clinical Child and Family Psychology Review, 9*(1), 65–83.

Sokolove, M. (2003, November 16). Should John Hinckley go free? *The New York Times Magazine,* pp. 52–54, 92.

Sommer, R., & Sommer, B. (2001). *A practical guide to behavioral research: Tools and techniques* (5th ed.). New York: Oxford University Press.

Sorbring, E., Deater-Deckard, K., & Palmerus, K. (2006). Girls' and boys' perception of mothers' intentions of using physical punishment and reasoning as discipline methods. *European Journal of Developmental Psychology, 3,* 142-162.

Soussignan, R. (2002). Duchenne smile, emotional experience, and automatic reactivity: A test of the facial feedback hypothesis. *Emotion, 2,* 52–74.

Spanos, N.P., Barber, T.X. & Lang, G. (2005). Cognition and self-control: Cognitive control of painful sensory input. *Integrative Physiological & Behavioral Science, 40*(3), 119–128.

Spearman, C. (1927). *The abilities of man.* London: Macmillan.

Speirs Neumeister, K. L., & Finch, H. (2006). Perfectionism in high-ability students: Relational precursors and influences on achievement motivation. *Gifted Child Quarterly, 50,* 238–251.

Spencer, S. J., Fein, S., Zanna, M. P., & Olson, J. M. (Eds.) (2003). *Motivated social perception: The Ontario Symposium* (Vol. 9). Mahwah, NJ: Erlbaum.

Sperry, R. (1982). Some effects of disconnecting the cerebral hemispheres. *Science, 217,* 1223–1226.

Spiegel, D. (Ed.). (1999). *Efficacy and cost-effectiveness of psychotherapy.* New York: American Psychiatric Press.

Spiller, L. D., & Wymer, W. W., Jr. (2001). Physicians' perceptions and use of commercial drug information sources: An examination of pharmaceutical marketing to physicians. *Health Marketing Quarterly, 19,* 91–106.

Springen, K. (2004, August 9). Sweet, elusive sleep. *Newsweek,* p. 47.

St. Dennis, C., Hendryx, M., Henriksen, A. L., Setter, S. M., & Singer, B. (2006). Postdischarge treatment costs following closure of a state geropsychiatric ward: Comparison of 2 levels of community care. *Primary Care Companion Journal of Clinical Psychiatry, 8,* 279–284.

St. Jacques, P. L., & Levine, B. (2007). Ageing and autobiographical memory for emotional and neutral events. *Memory, 15,* 129–144.

Staddon, J. E. R., & Cerutti, D. T. (2003). Operant conditioning. *Annual Review of Psychology, 54,* 115–144.

Staley, J. K., & Sanacora, G., & Tamagnan, G. (2006). Sex differences in diencephalon serotonin transporter availability in major depression. *Biological Psychiatry, 59,* 40–47.

Stankov, L. (2003). Complexity in human intelligence. In R. J. Sternberg, J. Lautrey, et al. (Eds.), *Models of intelligence: International perspectives* (pp. 27–42). Washington, DC: American Psychological Association.

Stapel, D. A., & Semin, G. R. (2007). The magic spell of language: Linguistic categories and their perceptual consequences. *Journal of Personality and Social Psychology, 93,* 23–33.

Steele, C. M., & Josephs, R. A. (1990). Alcohol myopia: Its prized and dangerous effects. *American Psychologist, 45,* 921–933.

Stegerwald, F., & Janson, G. R. (2003). Conversion therapy: Ethical considerations in family counseling. *Family Journal—Counseling and Therapy for Couples and Families, 11,* 55–59.

Steiger, A. (2007). Neurochemical regulation of sleep. *Journal of Psychiatric Research, 41,* 537–552.

Stein, L. A. R., & Graham, J. R. (2005). Ability of substance abusers to escape detection on the Minnesota Multiphasic Personality Inventory-Adolescent (MMPI-A) in a juvenile correctional facility. *Assessment, 12,* 28–39.

Steiner, B., Wolf, S., & Kempermann, G. (2006). Adult neurogenesis and neurodegenerative disease. *Regenerative Medicine, 1,* 15–28.

Stemler, S. E., & Sternberg, R. J. (2006). Using situational judgment tests to measure practical intelligence. In J. A. Weekley & R. E. Ployhart (Eds.), *Situational judgment tests: Theory, measurement, and application.* Mahwah, NJ: Erlbaum.

Stenbacka, L., & Vanni, S. (2007). fMRI of peripheral visual field representation. *Clinical Neurophysiology, 108,* 1303–1314.

Stenklev, N. C., & Laukli, E. (2004). Cortical cognitive potentials in elderly persons. *Journal of the American Academy of Audiology, 15,* 401–413.

Stephenson, R. H., & Banet-Weiser, S. (2007). Super-sized kids: Obesity, children, moral panic, and the media. In J. A. Bryant, *The children's television community.* Mahwah, NJ: Erlbaum.

Stern, E., & Silbersweig, D. A. (2001). Advances in functional neuroimaging methodology for the study of brain systems underlying human neuropsychological function and dysfunction. In D.A. Silbersweig & E. Stern (Eds.), *Neuropsychology and functional neuro-imaging: Convergence, advances and new directions.* Amsterdam, Netherlands: Swets and Zeitlinger.

Stern, R. M., & Koch, K. L. (1996). Motion sickness and differential susceptibility. *Current Directions in Psychological Science, 5,* 115–120.

Sternberg, R. J. (1990). *Metaphors of mind: Conceptions of the nature of intelligence.* New York: Cambridge University Press.

Sternberg, R. J. (1998). *Successful intelligence: How practical and creative intelligence determine success in life.* New York: Plume.

Sternberg, R. J. (2000). Intelligence and wisdom. In R. J. Sternberg et al. (Eds.), *Handbook of intelligence.* New York: Cambridge University Press.

Sternberg, R. J. (2002a). Individual differences in cognitive development. In U. Goswami (Ed.), *Blackwell handbook of childhood cognitive development. Blackwell handbooks of developmental psychology* (pp. 600–619). Malden, MA: Blackwell.

Sternberg, R. J. (Ed.). (2002b). *Why smart people can be so stupid.* New Haven, CT: Yale University Press.

Sternberg, R. J. (2004). A triangular theory of love. In H. T. Reis & C. E. Rusbult (Eds.), *Close relationships: Key readings.* Philadelphia, PA: Taylor & Francis.

Sternberg, R. J. (2006). A duplex theory of love. In R. J. Sternberg, (Ed.), *The new psychology of love.* New Haven, CT: Yale University Press.

Sternberg, R. J., & Beall, A. E. (1991). How can we know what love is? An epistemological analysis. In G. J. O. Fletcher & F. D. Fincham (Eds.), *Cognition in close relationships.* Hillsdale, NJ: Erlbaum.

Sternberg, R. J., & Hedlund, J. (2002). Practical intelligence, "g," and work psychology. *Human Performance, 15,* 143–160.

Sternberg, R. J., & Jarvin, L. (2003). Alfred Binet's contributions as a paradigm for impact in psychology. In R. J. Sternberg (Ed.), *The anatomy of impact: What makes the great works of psychology great*

(pp. 89–107). Washington, DC: American Psychological Association.

Sternberg, R. J., & Pretz, J. E. (2005). *Cognition and intelligence: Identifying the mechanisms of the mind.* New York: Cambridge University Press, 2005.

Sternberg, R. J., Grigorenko, E. L., & Kidd, K. K. (2005). Intelligence, race, and genetics. *American Psychologist, 60,* 46-59.

Sternberg, R. J., Hojjat, M., & Barnes, M. L. (2001). Empirical aspects of a theory of love as a story. *European Journal of Personality, 15,* 1–20.

Stettler, N., Stallings, V. A., Troxel, A. B., Zhao, J., Z., Schinnar, R., Nelson, S. E., Ziegler, E. E., & Strom, B. L. (2005). Weight gain in the first week of life and overweight in adulthood. *Circulation, 111,* 1897–1903.

Stevens, G., & Gardner, S. (1982). *The women of psychology: Pioneers and innovators* (Vol. 1). Cambridge, MA: Schenkman.

Stevens, P. & Harper, D. J. (2007). Professional accounts of electroconvulsive therapy: A discourse analysis. *Social Science & Medicine, 64,* 1475–1486.

Stevenson, H. W., Lee, S., & Mu, X. (2000). Successful achievement in mathematics: China and the United States. In C. F. M. van Lieshout & P. G. Heymans (Eds.), *Developing talent across the life span.* New York: Psychology Press.

Stevenson, R. J., & Case, T. I. (2005). Olfactory imagery: A review. *Psychonomic Bulletin and Review, 12,* 244–264.

Stewart, W.F., Ricci, J.A., Chee, E., Morganstein, D. & Lipton, R. (2003). Lost Productive Time and Cost Due to Common Pain Conditions in the US Workforce. *Journal of the American Medical Association, 290,* 2443–2454.

Stickgold, R. A., Winkelman, J. W., & Wehrwein, P. (2004, January 19). You will start to feel very sleepy . . . . *Newsweek,* pp. 58–60.

Stickgold, R., Hobson, J. A., Fosse, R., & Fosse, M. (2001, November 2). Sleep, learning, and dreams: Off-line memory reprocessing. *Science, 294,* 1052–1057.

Stickley, T., & Nickeas, R. (2006). Becoming one person: Living with dissociative identity disorder. *Journal of Psychiatric and Mental Health Nursing, 13,* 180–187.

Stier, H., & Lewin-Epstein, N. (2000). Women's part-time employment and gender inequality in the family. *Journal of Family Issues, 21,* 390–410.

Stockton, R., Morran, D. K., & Krieger, K. M. (2004). An overview of current research and best practices for training beginning group leaders. In D. A. Gerrity, C. R. Kalodner, & M. T. Riva (Eds.), *Handbook of group counseling and psychotherapy.* Thousand Oaks, CA: Sage.

Stompe, T., Ortwein-Swoboda, G., Ritter, K., & Schanda, H. (2003). Old wine in new bottles? Stability and plasticity of the contents of schizophrenic delusions. *Psychopathology, 36,* 6–12.

Stouffer, E. M., & White, N. M. (2006). Neural circuits mediating latent learning and conditioning for salt in the rat. *Neurobiology of Learning and Memory, 86,* 91–99.

Strathern, A., & Stewart, P. J. (2003). *Landscape, memory and history: Anthropological perspectives.* London: Pluto Press.

Strauss, E. (1998, May 8). Writing, speech separated in split brain. *Science, 280,* 287.

Strayer, D. L., Drews, F. A., Crouch, D. J., & Johnston, W. A. (2005). Why do cell phone conversations interfere with driving? In W. R. Walker & D. Herrmann (Eds.) *Cognitive technology: Transforming thought and society.* Jefferson, NC: McFarland & Company.

Striegel-Moore, R., & Bulik, C. M. (2007). Risk factors for eating disorders. *American Psychologist, 62,* 181–198.

Strong, T., & Tomm, K. (2007). Family therapy as re-coordinating and moving on together. *Journal of Systemic Therapies, 26,* 42–54.

Stronski, S. M., Ireland, M., & Michaud, P. (2000). Protective correlates of stages in adolescent substance use: A Swiss national study. *Journal of Adolescent Health, 26,* 420–427.

Strupp, H. H. (1996, October). The tripartite model and the *Consumer Reports* study. *American Psychologist, 51,* 1017–1024.

Strupp, H. H., & Binder, J. L. (1992). Current developments in psychotherapy. *The Independent Practitioner, 12,* 119–124.

Sue, D. W., Sue, D., & Sue, S. (1990). *Understanding abnormal behavior* (3rd ed.). Boston: Houghton-Mifflin.

Sun, T., Patoine, C., Abu-Khalil, A., Visvader, J., Sum, E., Cherry, T. J., Orkink, S. H., Geschwind, D. H., & Walsh, C. A. (2005, June 17). Early asymmetry of gene transcriptions in embryonic human left and right cerebral cortex. *Science, 308,* 1794–1796.

Surette, R. (2002). Self-reported copycat crime among a population of serious and violent juvenile offenders. *Crime & Delinquency, 48,* 46–69.

Sutin, A. R., & Robins, R. W. (2007). Phenomenology of autobiographical memories: The Memory Experiences Questionnaire. *Memory, 15,* 390–411.

Svartdal, F. (2003). Extinction after partial reinforcement: Predicted vs. judged persistence. *Scandinavian Journal of Psychology, 44,* 55–64.

Swales, M. A., & Heard, H. L. (2007). The therapy relationship in dialectical behaviour therapy. In P. Gilbert & R. L. Leahy (Eds.), *The therapeutic relationship in the cognitive behavioral psychotherapies.* New York: Routledge/Taylor & Francis.

Swann, W. B., Jr., Chang-Schneider, C., & Larsen McClarty, K. (2007). Do people's self-views matter? Self-concept and self-esteem in everyday life. *American Psychologist, 62,* 84–94.

Swanson, H. L., Harris, K. R., & Graham, S. (Eds.). (2003). *Handbook of learning disabilities*. New York: Guilford Press.

Tadmor, C., T. (2007). Biculturalism: The plus side of leaving home? The effects of second-culture exposure on integrative complexity and its consequences for overseas performance. *Dissertation Abstracts International Section A: Humanities and Social Sciences, 67* (8-A), 3068.

Taggi, F., Crenca, A., Cedri, C., Giustini, M., Dosi, G., & Marturano, P. (2007). Road safety and the tsunami of cell phones. *Anali di igiene: Medicina preventiva e di comunità 19,* 269–274.

Tajfel, H., & Turner, J. C. (2004). The social identity theory of intergroup behavior. In J. T. Jost & J. Sidanius (Eds.), *Political psychology: Key readings.* New York: Psychology Press.

Takizawa, T., Kondo, T., & Sakihara, S. (2007). "Stress buffering effects of social support on depressive symptoms in middle age: Reciprocity and community mental health": Corrigendum. *Psychiatry and Clinical Neurosciences, 61,* 336–337.

Talukdar, S., & Shastri, J. (2006). Contributory and adverse factors in social development of young children. *Psychological Studies, 51,* 294–303.

Tanner, J. M. (1978). *Education and physical growth* (2nd ed.). New York: International Universities Press.

Tanner, J. M. (1990). *Foetus into man: Physical growth from conception to maturity* (Rev. ed.). Cambridge, MA: Harvard University Press.

Taras, H., & Potts-Datema, W. (2005). Chronic health conditions and student performance at school. *Journal of School Health, 75,* 255–266.

Taylor, F., & Bryant, R. A. (2007). The tendency to suppress, inhibiting thoughts, and dream rebound. *Behaviour Research and Therapy, 45,* 163–168.

Taylor, J. A. (1953). A personality scale of manifest anxiety. *The Journal of Abnormal and Social Psychology, 48*(2), 285–290.

Tellegen, A., Lykken, D. T., Bouchard, T. J., Jr., Wilcox, K. J., Segal, N. L., & Rich, S. (1988). Personality similarity in twins reared apart and together. *Journal of Personality and Social Psychology, 54,* 1031–1039.

Tenenbaum, H. R., & Ruck, M. D. (2007). Are teachers' expectations different for racial minority than for European American students? A meta-analysis. *Journal of Educational Psychology, 99,* 253–273.

Tenopyr, M. L. (2002). Theory versus reality: Evaluation of 'g' in the workplace. *Human Performance, 15,* 107–122.

Teodorov, E., Salzgerber, S. A., Felicio, L. F., Varolli, F. M. F., & Bernardi, M. M. (2002). Effects of perinatal picrotoxin and sexual experience on heterosexual and homosexual behavior in male rats. *Neurotoxicology and Teratology, 24,* 235–245.

Tervaniemi, M., Jacobsen, T., & Röttger, S. (2006). Selective tuning of cortical sound-feature processing by language experience. *European Journal of Neuroscience, 23,* 2538–2541.

Tesoriero, H. (July 5, 2007). Mysteries of the "faceblind" could illuminate the brain. *The Wall Street Journal,* p. A1.

Thachil, A. F., Mohan, R., & Bhugra, D. (2007). The evidence base of complementary and alternative therapies in depression. *Journal of Affective Disorders, 97,* 23–35.

Tharp, R. G. (1989). Psychocultural variables and constants: Effects on teaching and learning in schools [Special issue: Children and their development: Knowledge base, research agenda, and social policy application]. *American Psychologist, 44,* 349–359.

Thatcher, D. L., & Clark, D. B. (2006). Adolescent alcohol abuse and dependence: Development, diagnosis, treatment and outcomes. *Current Psychiatry Reviews, 2,* 159–177.

Thompson, P. M., Hayaski, K. M., Simon, S. L., Geaga, J. A., Hong, M. S., Sui, Y., Lee, J. Y., Toga, A. W., Ling, W., & London, E. D. (2004, June 30). Structural abnormalities in the brains of human subjects who use methamphetamine. *The Journal of Neuroscience, 24,* 6028–6036.

Thorkildsen, T. A. (2006). An empirical exploration of language and thought. *PsycCRITIQUES, 51,* No pagination specified.

Thornton, A., & McAuliffe, K. (2006, July 14). Teaching in wild meerkats. *Science, 313,* 227–229.

Thornton, A., & Young-DeMarco, L. (2001). Four decades of trends in attitudes toward family issues in the United States: The 1960s through the 1990s. *Journal of Marriage and the Family, 63,* 1009–1017.

Titone, D. A. (2002). Memories bound: The neuroscience of dreams. *Trends in Cognitive Science, 6,* 4–5.

Tolman, E. C., & Honzik, C. H. (1930). Introduction and removal of reward and maze performance in rats. *University of California Publications in Psychology, 4,* 257–275.

Tracy, J. L., & Robins, R. W. (2004). Show your pride: Evidence for a discrete emotion expression. *Psychological Science, 15,* 194–197.

Travis, F. (2006). From I to I: Concepts of self on a object-referral/self-referral continuum. In A. P. Prescott, *The concept of self in psychology.* Hauppauge, NY: Nova Science Publishers.

Tremblay, A. (2004). Dietary fat and body weight set point. *Nutrition Review, 62* (7 Pt 2), S75–S77.

Triesch, J., Jasso, H., & Deák, G. O. (2007). Emergence of mirror neurons in a model of gaze following. *Adaptive Behavior, 15,* 149–165.

Tropp, L. R., & Bianchi, R. A. (2006). Valuing diversity and interest in intergroup contact. *Journal of Social Issues, 62,* 533–551.

Tropp, L. R., & Pettigrew, T. F. (2005). Differential relationships between intergroup contact and affective and cognitive dimensions of prejudice. *Personality and Social Psychology Bulletin, 31,* 1145–1158.

Troyer, A. K., Häfliger, A., & Cadieux, M. J. (2006). Name and face learning in older adults: Effects of level of processing, self-generation, and intention to learn. *Journals of Gerontology: Series B: Psychological Sciences and Social Sciences, 61,* P67–P74.

Trudel, G. (2002). Sexuality and marital life: Results of a survey. *Journal of Sex and Marital Therapy, 28,* 229–249.

Trull, T. J., & Widiger, T. A. (2003). Personality disorders. In G. Stricker, T. A. Widiger, et al. (Eds.), *Handbook of psychology: Clinical psychology* (Vol. 8, pp. 149–172). New York: Wiley.

Trull, T. J., Stepp, S. D., & Durrett, C. A. (2003). Research on borderline personality disorder: An update. *Current Opinion in Psychiatry, 16,* 77–82.

Tryon, W. W. (2005). Possible mechanisms for why desensitization and exposure therapy work. *Clinical Psychology Review, 25,* 67–95.

Tsai, K. J., Tsai, Y. C., & Shen, C. K. (2007). G-CSF rescues the memory impairment of animal models of Alzheimer's disease. *Journal of Experimental Medicine, 11,* 1273–1289.

Tseng, W. S. (2003). *Clinician's guide to cultural psychiatry.* San Diego, CA: Elsevier Publishing.

Tuerlinckx, F., De Boeck, P., & Lens, W. (2002). Measuring needs with the Thematic Apperception Test: A psychometric study. *Journal of Personality and Social Psychology, 82,* 448–461.

Tugay, N., Akbayrak, T., Demirturk, F., Karakaya, I. C., Kocaacar, O., Tugay, U., Karakay, M. G., & Demirturk, F. (2007). Effectiveness of transcutaneous electrical nerve stimulation and interferential current in primary dysmenorrhea. *Pain Medicine, 8,* 295–300.

Tulving, E. (2000). Concepts of memory. In E. Tulving, F. I. M. Craik, et al. (Eds.). *The Oxford handbook of memory.* New York: Oxford University Press.

Tulving, E. (2002). Episodic memory and common sense: How far apart? In A. Baddeley & J. P. Aggleton (Eds.), *Episodic memory: New directions in research* (pp. 269–287). London: Oxford University Press.

Tulving, E., & Thompson, D. M. (1983). Encoding specificity and retrieval processes in episodic memory. *Psychological Review, 80,* 352–373.

Turk, D. C. (1994). Perspectives on chronic pain: The role of psychological factors. *Current Directions in Psychological Science, 3,* 45–49.

Turkewitz, G. (1993). The origins of differential hemispheric strategies for information processing in the relationships between voice and face perception. In B. de Boysson-Bardies, S. de Schonen, P. W. Jusczyk, P. McNeilage, & J. Morton (Eds.), *Developmental neurocognition: Speech and face processing in the first year of life. NATO ASI Series D: Behavioural and social sciences* (Vol. 69). Dordrecht, Netherlands: Kluwer Academic.

Turner, W. J. (1995). Homosexuality, Type 1: An Xq28 phenomenon. *Archives of Sexual Behavior, 24,* 109–134.

Tuszynski, M. H. (2007). Nerve growth factor gene therapy in Alzheimer's disease. *Alzheimer's Disease and Associated Disorders, 21,* 179–1898.

Tversky, A., & Kahneman, D. (1987). Rational choice and the framing of decisions. In R. Hogarth & M. Reder (Eds.), *Rational choice: The contrast between economics and psychology.* Chicago: University of Chicago Press.

Ubell, E. (1993, January 10). Could you use more sleep? *Parade,* pp. 16–18.

Umphress, E. E., Smith-Crowe, K., & Brief, A. P. (2007). When birds of a feather flock together and when they do not: Status composition, social dominance orientation, and organizational attractiveness. *Journal of Applied Psychology, 92,* 396–409.

Underwood, A. (2005, October 3). The Good Heart. *Newsweek,* p. 49.

Updegraff, K. A., Helms, H. M., McHale, S. M., Crouter, A. C., Thayer, S. M., & Sales, L. H. (2004). Who's the boss? Patterns of perceived control in adolescents' friendships. *Journal of Youth & Adolescence, 33,* 403–420.

U.S. Bureau of the Census. (2000). *Census 2000.* Retrieved from American Fact Finder http://factfinder.census.gov/servlet/BasicFactsServlet.

U.S. Bureau of Labor Statistics. (2007). *American time use survey.* Washington, DC: Bureau of Labor Statistics.

Uttl, B., Graf, P., & Consentino, S. (2003). Implicit memory for new associations: Types of conceptual representations. In J. S. Bowers & C. J. Marsolek (Eds.), *Rethinking implicit memory* (pp. 302–323). London: Oxford University Press.

Uylings, H. B. M. (2006). Development of the human cortex and the concept of 'critical' or 'sensitive' periods. *Language Learning, 56,* 59–90.

Vaillant, G. E., & Vaillant, C. O. (1990). Natural history of male psychological health: XII. A 46-year study of predictors of successful aging at age 65. *American Journal of Psychiatry, 147,* 31–37.

Vaitl, D., Schienle, A., & Stark, R. (2005). Neurobiology of fear and disgust. *International Journal of Psychophysiology, 57,* 1–4.

Valencia, R. R., & Suzuki, L. A. (2003). *Intelligence testing and minority students: Foundations, performance factors, and assessment issues.* Thousand Oaks, CA: Sage.

Valente, S. M. (1991). Electroconvulsive therapy. *Archives of Psychiatric Nursing, 5,* 223–228.

Valsiner, J., Diriwächter, R., & Sauck, C. (2005). Diversity in unity: Standard questions and nonstandard interpretations. In *Science and medicine in dialogue: Thinking through particulars and universals* (pp. 289–307). Westport, CT: Praeger Publishers/Greenwood Publishing Group.

Van Beekum, S. (2005). The therapist as a new object. *Transactional Analysis Journal, 35,* 187–191.

Van De Graaff, K. (2000). *Human anatomy* (5th ed.). Boston: McGraw-Hill.

van den Bosch, L. M., Koeter, M. W., Stijnen, T., Verheul, R., & van den Brink, W. (2005). Sustained efficacy of dialectical behaviour therapy for borderline personality disorder. *Behavioral Research Therapy, 43,* 1231–1241.

Van den Wildenberg, W. P. M., & Van der Molen, M. W. (2004). Developmental trends in simple and selective inhibition of compatible and incompatible responses. *Journal of Experimental Child Psychology, 87,* 201–220.

van der Helm, P. A. (2006). Review of perceptual dynamics: Theoretical foundations and philosophical implications of gestalt psychology. *Philosophical Psychology, 19,* 274–279.

van Hooren, S. A. H., Valentijn, A. M., & Bosma, H. (2007). Cognitive functioning in healthy older adults aged 64–81: A cohort study into the effects of age, sex, and education. *Aging, Neuropsychology, and Cognition, 14,* 40–54.

van Wel, F., Linssen, H., & Abma, R. (2000). The parental bond and the well-being of adolescents and young adults. *Journal of Youth & Adolescence, 29,* 307–318.

Vandell, D. L., Burchinal, M. R., Belsky, J., Owen, M. T., Friedman, S. L., Clarke-Stewart, A., McCartney, K., & Weinraub, M. (2005). *Early child care and children's development in the primary grades: Follow-up results from the NICHD Study of Early Child Care.* Paper presented at the biennial meeting of the Society for Research in Child Development, Atlanta, GA.

Vandervert, L. R., Schimpf, P. H., & Liu, H. (2007). How working memory and the cerebellum collaborate to produce creativity and innovation. *Creativity Research Journal, 19,* 1–18.

Vanheule, S., Desmet, M., Rosseel, Y., & Meganck, R. (2006). Core transference themes in depression. *Journal of Affective Disorders, 91,* 71–75

Varma, S., (2007). A computational model of Tower of Hanoi problem solving. *Dissertation Abstracts International: Section B: The Sciences and Engineering, 67* (8-B), 4736.

Veasey, S., Rosen, R., Barzansky, B., Rosen, I., & Owens, J. (2002). Sleep loss and fatigue in residency training: A reappraisal. *Journal of the American Medical Association, 288,* 1116–1124.

Vedantam, S. (2005, January 23). See no bias. *The Washington Post,* p. W12.

Veniegas, R. C. (2000). Biological research on women's sexual orientations: Evaluating the scientific evidence. *Journal of Social Issues, 56,* 267–282.

Verdejo, A., Toribio, I., & Orozco, C. (2005). Neuropsychological functioning in methadone maintenance patients versus abstinent heroin abusers. *Drug and Alcohol Dependence, 78,* 283–288.

Viding, E., Blair, R. J., Moffitt, T. E., & Plomin, R. (2005). Evidence for substantial genetic risk for psychopathy in 7-year-olds. *Journal of Child Psychology and Psychiatry, 46,* 592–597.

Vieira, E. M., & Freire, J. C. (2006). Alteridade e Psicologia Humanista: Uma leitura ética da abordagem centrada na pessoa. [Alterity and humanistic psychology: An ethical reading of the Person-Centered Approach.] *Estudos de Psicologia, 23,* 425–432.

Vitiello, A. L., Bonello, R. P., & Pollard, H. P. (2007). The effectiveness of ENAR(R) for the treatment of chronic neck pain in Australian adults: A preliminary single-blind, randomised controlled trial. *Chiropractic Osteopathology, 9,* 9.

Vleioras, G., & Bosma, H. A. (2005). Are identity styles important for psychological well-being? *Journal of Adolescence, 28,* 397–409.

Voicu, H., & Schmajuk, N. (2002). Latent learning, shortcuts and detours: A computational model. *Behavioural Processes, 59,* 67–86.

Volterra, V., Caselli, M. C., Capirci, O., Tonucci, F., & Vicari, S. (2003). Early linguistic abilities of Italian children with Williams syndrome [Special issue: Williams syndrome]. *Developmental Neuropsychology, 23,* 33–58.

Voruganti, L. P., Awad, A. G., Parker, B., Forrest, C., Usmani, Y., Fernando, M. L. D., & Senthilal, S. (2007). Cognition, functioning and quality of life in schizophrenia treatment: Results of a one-year randomized controlled trial of olanzapine and quetiapine. *Schizophrenia Research, 96,* 146–155.

Vygotsky, L. S. (1926/1997). *Educational psychology.* Delray Beach, FL: St. Lucie Press.

Wachs, T. D., Pollitt, E., Cueto, S., & Jacoby, E. (2004). Structure and cross-contextual stability of neonatal temperament. *Infant Behavior and Development, 27,* 382–396.

Wadden, T. A., Crerand, C. E., & Brock, J. (2005). Behavioral treatment of obesity. *Psychiatric Clinics of North America, 28,* 151–170.

Wagner, A. W., Rizvi, S. L., & Harned, M. S. (2007). Applications of dialectical behavior therapy to the treatment of complex trauma-related problems: When one case formulation does not fit all. *Journal of Trauma Stress, 20,* 391–400.

Wagner, H. J., Bollard, C. M., Vigouroux, S., Huls, M. H., Anderson, R., Prentice, H. G., Brenner, M. K., Heslop, H. E., & Rooney, C. M. (2004). A strategy for treatment of Epstein Barr virus-positive Hodgkin's disease by targeting interleukin 12 to the tumor environment using tumor antigen-specific T cells. *Cancer Gene Therapy, 2,* 81–91.

Wagner, R. K. (2002). Smart people doing dumb things: The case of managerial incompetence. In R. J. Sternberg (Ed.), *Why smart people can be so stupid* (pp. 42–63). New Haven, CT: Yale University Press.

Walsh, B. T., Kaplan, A. S., Attia, E., Olmstead, M., Parides, M., Carter, J. C., Pike, K. M., Devlin, M. J., Woodside, B., Robert, C. A., & Rockert, W. (2006). Fluoxetine after weight restoration in anorexia nervosa: A randomized controlled trial. *Journal of the American Medical Association, 295,* 2605–2612.

Walsh, R., & Shapiro, S. L. (2006). The meeting of meditative disciplines and western psychology. *American Psychologist, 61,* 227–239.

Wang, A., & Clark, D. A. (2002). Haunting thoughts: The problem of obsessive mental intrusions [Special issue: Intrusions in cognitive behavioral therapy]. *Journal of Cognitive Psychotherapy, 16,* 193–208.

Wang, P. S., Aguilar-Gaxiola, S., Alonso, J., Angermeyer, M. C., Borges, G., Bromet, E. J., Bruffaerts, R., deGirolamo, G., deGraaf, R., Gureje, O., Haro, J. M., Karam, E. G., Kessler, R. C., Kovess, V., Lane, M. C., Lee, S., Levinson, D., Ono, Y., Petukhova, M., Posada-Villa, J., Seedat, S., & Wells, J. E. (2007, September 8). Use of mental health services for anxiety, mood, and substance disorders in 17 countries in the WHO world mental health surveys. *Lancet, 370,* 841–850.

Wang, Q. (2004). The emergence of cultural self-constructs: Autobiographical memory and self-description in European American and Chinese children. *Developmental Psychology, 40,* 3–15.

Wang, Q., & Conway, M. A. (2006). Autobiographical memory, self, and culture. In L-G. Nilsson & N. Ohta (Eds.), *Memory and society: Psychological perspectives.* New York: Psychology Press.

Wang, X., Lu, T., Snider, R. K., & Liang, L. (2005). Sustained firing in auditory cortex evoked by preferred stimuli. *Nature, 435,* 341–346.

Ward, L. M. (2004). Wading through the stereotypes: Positive and negative associations between media use and black adolescents' conceptions of self. *Developmental Psychology, 40,* 284–294.

Ward-Baker, P. D. (2007). The remarkable oldest old: A new vision of aging. *Dissertation Abstracts International Section A: Humanities and Social Sciences, 67* (8-A), 3115.

Warden, C. A., Wu, W-Y., & Tsai, D. (2006). Online shopping interface components: Relative importance as peripheral and central cues. *CyberPsychology & Behavior, 9,* 285–296.

Watson, D., Hubbard, B., & Wiese, D. (2000). Self-other agreement in personality and affectivity: The role of acquaintanceship, trait visibility, and assumed similarity. *Journal of Personality and Social Psychology, 78,* 546–558.

Watson, J. B., & Rayner, R. (1920). Conditioned emotional reactions. *Journal of Experimental Psychology, 3,* 1–14.

Weber, R., Ritterfeld, U., & Kostygina, A. (2006). Aggression and violence as effects of playing violent video games? In P. Vorderer & J. Bryant, *Playing video games: Motives, responses, and consequences.* Mahwah, NJ: Erlbaum.

Wechsler, D. (1997). Wechsler Adult Intelligence Scale—3rd Ed. (WAIS—III). New York: Harcourt Assessment, Inc.

Wechsler, D. (2003). Wechsler Intelligence Scale for Children—4th Ed. (WISC-IV; Wechsler, 2003) New York: Harcourt Assessment, Inc.

Wechsler, H., Lee, J. E., Nelson, T. F., & Kuo, M. (2002). Underage college students' drinking behavior, access to alcohol, and the influence of deterrence policies. *Journal of American College Health, 50,* 223–236.

Weeks, M., & Lupfer, M. B. (2004). Complicating race: The relationship between prejudice, race, and social class categorizations. *Personality and Social Psychology Bulletin, 30,* 972–984.

Wegener, D. T., Petty, R. E., Smoak, N. D., & Fabrigar, L. R. (2004). Multiple routes to resisting attitude change. In E. S. Knowles & J. A. Linn (Eds.), *Resistance and persuasion.* Mahwah, NJ: Erlbaum.

Weinberg, M. S., Williams, C. J., & Pryor, D. W. (1991, February 27). Personal communication. Indiana University, Bloomington.

Weiner, B. A., & Wettstein, R. (1993). *Legal issues in mental health care.* New York: Plenum Press.

Weiner, I. B. (2004). Rorschach inkblot method. In M. E. Maruish (Ed.), *Use of psychological testing for treatment planning and outcomes assessment: Vol. 3: Instruments for adults* (3rd ed.). Mahwah, NJ: Erlbaum.

Weinstein, M., Glei, D. A., Yamazaki, A., & Ming-Cheng, C. (2004). The role of intergenerational relations in the association between life stressors and depressive symptoms. *Research on Aging, 26,* 511–530.

Weissman, M., Markowitz, J., & Klerman, G. L. (2007). *Clinician's quick guide to interpersonal psychotherapy.* New York: Oxford University Press.

Weisz, A., & Black, B. (2002). Gender and moral reasoning: African American youth respond to dating dilemmas. *Journal of Human Behavior in the Social Environment, 5,* 35–52.

Welkowitz, L. A., Struening, E. L., Pittman, J., Guardino, M., & Welkowitz, J. (2000). Obsessive-compulsive disorder and comorbid anxiety problems in a national anxiety screening sample. *Journal of Anxiety Disorders, 14,* 471–482.

Wenar, C. (1994). *Developmental psychopathology: From infancy through adolescence* (3rd ed.). New York: McGraw-Hill.

Wenzel, A., Zetocha, K., & Ferraro, R. F. (2007). Depth of processing and recall of threat material in fearful and nonfearful individuals. *Anxiety, Stress & Coping: An International Journal, 20,* 223–237.

Werblin, F., & Roska, B. (2007, April). The movies in our eyes. *Scientific American,* 73–77.

Werker, J. F., & Tees, R. C. (2005). Speech perception as a window for understanding plasticity and commitment in language systems of the brain. *Developmental Psychobiology, 46,* 233–234.

Werner, J. S., Pinna, B., & Spillmann, L. (2007, March). Illusory color and the brain. *Scientific American,* 90–96.

Wertheimer, M. (1923). Untersuchungen zur Lehre von der Gestalt. II. *Psychol. Forsch., 5,* 301–350. In R. Beardsley and M. Wertheimer (Eds.). (1958), *Readings in perception.* New York: Van Nostrand.

West, D. S., Harvey-Berino, J., & Raczynski, J. M. (2004). Behavioral aspects of obesity, dietary intake, and chronic disease. In J. M. Raczynski and L. C. Leviton (Eds.), *Handbook of clinical health psychology: Vol. 2. Disorders of behavior and health.* (pp. 9–41). Washington, DC: American Psychological Association.

West, J. R., & Blake, C. A. (2005). Fetal alcohol syndrome: An assessment of the field. *Experimental Biological Medicine, 6,* 354–356.

Westen, D., Novotny, C. M., & Thompson-Brenner, H. (2004). The empirical status of empirically supported psychotherapies: Assumptions, findings, and reporting in controlled clinical trials. *Psychological Bulletin, 130,* 631–663.

Westerterp, K. R. (2006). Perception, passive overfeeding and energy metabolism. *Physiology & Behavior, 89,* 62–65.

Whitbourne, S. K. (2000). The normal aging process. In S. K. Whitbourne & S. Krauss (Eds.), *Psychopathology in later adulthood*. New York: Wiley.

Whitbourne, S. (2007). *Adult Development and Aging. Biopsychosocial Perspectives*. New York: Wiley.

White, L. (2007). Linguistic theory, universal grammar, and second language acquisition. In B. Van Patten, & J. Williams (Eds.), *Theories in second language acquisition: An introduction*. Mahwah, NJ: Erlbaum.

Whitfield, J. B., Zhu, G., Madden, P. A., Neale, M. C., Heath, A. C., & Martin, N. G. (2004). The genetics of alcohol intake and of alcohol dependence. *Alcoholism: Clinical and Experimental Research, 28*, 1153–1160.

WHO World Mental Health Survey Consortium. (2004). Prevalence, severity, and unmet need for treatment of mental disorders in the World Health Organization World Mental Health Surveys. *Journal of the American Medical Association, 291*, 2581–2590.

Whorf, B. L. (1956). *Language, thought, and reality*. New York: Wiley.

Wickelgren, E. A. (2004). Perspective distortion of trajectory forms and perceptual constancy in visual event identification. *Perception and Psychophysics, 66*, 629–641.

Widiger, T. A., & Clark, L. A. (2000). Toward *DSM-V* and the classification of psychopathology. *Psychological Bulletin, 126*, 946–963.

Widmeyer, W. N., & Loy, J. W. (1988). When you're hot, you're hot! Warm-cold effects in first impressions of persons and teaching effectiveness. *Journal of Educational Psychology, 80*, 118–121.

Wiggins, J. S. (2003). *Paradigms of personality assessment*. New York: Guilford Press.

Wildavsky, B. (2000, September 4). A blow to bilingual education. *U.S. News & World Report*, pp. 22–28.

Wilgoren, J. (1999, October 22). Quality day care, early, is tied to achievements as an adult. *The New York Times*, p. A16.

Wilkinson, L., & Olliver-Gray, Y. (2006). The significance of silence: Differences in meaning, learning styles, and teaching strategies in cross-cultural settings. *Psychologia: An International Journal of Psychology in the Orient, 49, Special issue: Child language*, 74–88.

Willander, J., & Larsson, M. (2006). Smell your way back to childhood: Autobiographical odor memory. *Psychonomic Bulletin & Review, 13*, 240–244.

Williams, J. W., Mulrow, C. D., Chiquette, E., Noel, P. H., Aguilar, C., & Cornell, J. (2000). A systematic review of newer pharmacotherapies for depression in adults: Evidence report summary. *Annals of Internal Medicine, 132*, 743–756.

Willis, G. L. (2005). The therapeutic effects of dopamine replacement therapy and its psychiatric side effects are mediated by pineal function. *Behavioural Brain Research, 160*, 148–160.

Wilson, T. G., Grilo, C. M., & Vitousek, K. M. (2007). Psychological treatment of eating disorders [Special issue: Eating disorders]. *American Psychologist, 62*, 199–216.

Winerman, L. (2005, June). ACTing up. *Monitor on Psychology*, pp. 44–45.

Winik, L. W. (2006, October 1). The true cost of depression. *Parade, 7*.

Winner, E. (2003). Creativity and talent. In M. H. Bornstein & L. Davidson (Eds.), *Well-being: Positive development across the life course* (pp. 371–380). Mahwah, NJ: Erlbaum.

Winsler, A., Madigan, A. L., & Aquilino, S. A. (2005). Correspondence between maternal and paternal parenting styles in early childhood. *Early Childhood Research Quarterly, 20*, 1–12.

Winson, J. (1990, November). The meaning of dreams. *Scientific American*, pp. 86–96.

Winstead, B. A., & Sanchez, A. (2005). Gender and psychopathology. In J. E. Maddux & B. A. Winstead, *Psychopathology: Foundations for a contemporary understanding*. Mahwah, NJ: Erlbaum.

Winston, A. S. (2004). *Defining difference: Race and racism in the history of psychology*. Washington, DC: American Psychological Association.

Winston, J. S., O'Doherty, J., & Kilner, J. M. (2007). Brain systems for assessing facial attractiveness. *Neuropsychologia, 45*, 195–206.

Winter, D. G. (2007). The role of motivation, responsibility, and integrative complexity in crisis escalation: Comparative studies of war and peace crises. *Journal of Personality and Social Psychology, 92*, 920–937.

Wittenbrink, B., & Schwarz, N. (2007). *Implicit measures of attitudes*. New York: Guilford Press.

Wixted, J. T., & Carpenter, S. K. (2007). The Wickelgren Power Law and the Ebbinghaus Savings Function. *Psychological Science, 18*, 133–134.

Wolfe, M.S. (2006). Shutting down Alzheimer's. *Scientific American, 294*(5) 72–79.

Wolff, N. (2002). Risk, response, and mental health policy: Learning from the experience of the United Kingdom. *Journal of Health Politic and Policy Law, 27*, 801–802.

Wolitzky, D. L. (2006). Psychodynamic theories. In J. C. Thomas, D. L. Segal, & M. Hersen, *comprehensive handbook of personality and psychopathology, Vol. 1: Personality and everyday functioning*. Hoboken, NJ: Wiley.

Wood, J. M., Nezworski, M. T., Lilienfeld, S. O., & Garb, H. N. (2003). *What's wrong with the Rorschach? Science confronts the controversial inkblot test*. New York: Wiley.

Woods, S. C., Schwartz, M. W., Baskin, D. G., & Seeley, R. J. (2000). Food intake and the regulation of body weight. *Annual Review of Psychology, 51*, 255–277.

Woodson, S. R. J. (2006). Relationships between sleepiness and emotion experience: An experimental investigation of the role of subjective sleepiness in the generation of positive and negative emotions. *Dissertation Abstracts International: Section B: The Sciences and Engineering, 67* (5-B), 2849.

Wrosch, C., Bauer, I., & Scheier, M.F. (2005). Regret and quality of life across the adult life span: The influence of disengagement and available future goals. *Psychology and Aging, 20*(4), 657–670.

Wrzesniewski, K., & Chylinska, J. (2007). Assessment of coping styles and strategies with school-related stress. *School Psychology International, 28*, 179–194.

Wu, L-T., Schlenger, W. E., & Galvin, D. M. (2006). Concurrent use of methamphetamine, MDMA, LSD, ketamine, GHB, and flunitrazepam among American youths. *Drug and Alcohol Dependence, 84*, 102–113.

Wuethrich, B. (2001, March 16). Does alcohol damage female brains more? *Science, 291*, 2077–2079.

Wurtz, R. H., & Kandel, E. R. (2000). Central visual pathways. In E. R. Kandel, J. H. Schwartz, & T. M. Jessell (Eds.), *Principles of neural science* (4th ed.). New York: McGraw-Hill.

Wyra, M., Lawson, M.J., & Hungi, N. (2007). The mnemonic keyword method: The effects of bidirectional retrieval training and of ability to image on foreign language vocabulary recall. *Learning and Instruction, 17*(3) 360–371.

Xiao, Z., Yan, H., Wang, Z., Zou, Z., Xu, Y., Chen, J., Zhang, H., Ross, C. A., & Keyes, B. B. (2006). Trauma and dissociation in China. *American Journal of Psychiatry, 163*, 1388–1391.

Yeomans, M. R., Tepper, B. J., & Reitzschel, J. (2007). Human hedonic responses to sweetness: Role of taste genetics and anatomy. *Physiology & Behavior, 91*, 264–273.

Yesilyaprak, B., Kisac, I., & Sanlier, N. (2007). Stress symptoms and nutritional status among survivors of the Marmara region earthquakes in Turkey. *Journal of Loss & Trauma, 12*, 1–8.

Young, M. W. (2000, March). The tick-tock of the biological clock. *Scientific American*, pp. 64–71.

Zajonc, R. B. (2001). Mere exposure: A gateway to the subliminal. *Current Directions in Psychological Science, 10*, 224–228.

Zaslow, M., Halle, T., & Martin, L. (2006). Child outcome measures in the study of child care quality. *Evaluation Review, 30,* 577–610.

Zebrowitz, L. A., & Montepare, J. M. (2005, June 10). Appearance DOES matter. *Science, 308,* 1565–1566.

Zeidner, M., Matthews, G., & Roberts, R. D. (2004). Emotional intelligence in the workplace: A critical review. *Applied Psychology: An International Review, 53,* 371–399.

Zeigler, D. W., Wang, C. C., Yoast, R. A., Dickinson, B. D., McCaffree, M. A., Robinowitz, C. B., & Sterling, M. L. (2005). The neurocognitive effects of alcohol on adolescents and college students. *Preventive Medicine: An International Journal Devoted to Practice and Theory, 40,* 23–32.

Zhang, Q., He, X., & Zhang, J. (2007). A comparative study on the classification of basic color terms by undergraduates from Yi nationality, Bai nationality and Naxi nationality. *Acta Psychologica Sinica, 39,* 18–26.

Zhou, Z., Liu, Q., & Davis, R. L. (2005). Complex regulation of spiral ganglion neuron firing patterns by neurotrophin-3. *Journal of Neuroscience, 25,* 7558–7566.

Zians, J. (2007). A comparison of trait anger and depression on several variables: Attribution style, dominance, submissiveness, 'need for power', efficacy and dependency. *Dissertation Abstracts International: Section B: The Sciences and Engineering, 67* (7-B), 4124.

Zigler, E. F., Finn-Stevenson, M., & Hall, N. W. (2002). *The first three years and beyond: Brain development and social policy.* In E. F. Zigler, M. Finn-Stevenson, & N. W. Hall (Eds.), *Current perspectives in psychology.* New Haven, CT: Yale University Press.

Zigler, E., Bennett-Gates, D., Hodapp, R., & Henrich, C. (2002). Assessing personality traits of individuals with mental retardation. *American Journal on Mental Retardation, 107,* 181–193.

Zimbardo, P. G. (1973). On the ethics of intervention in human psychological research: With special reference to the Stanford Prison Experiment. *Cognition, 2,* 243–256.

Zimbardo, P. G. (2007). *The Lucifer effect: Understanding how good people turn evil.* New York: Random House.

Zimbardo, P.G., Maslach, C., & Haney, C. (2000). Reflections on the Stanford Prison Experiment: Genesis, transformations, consequences. In T. Blass (Ed.), *Obedience to authority: Current perspectives on the Milgram paradigm.* Mahwya, NJ: Erlbaum.

Zimmerman, U. S., Blomeyer, D., & Laucht, M. (2007). How gene-stress-behavior interactions can promote adolescent alcohol use: The roles of predrinking allostatic load and childhood behavior disorders [Special issue: Adolescents, drug abuse and mental disorders.] *Pharmacology, Biochemistry and Behavior, 86,* 246–262.

Zito, J. M. (1993). *Psychotherapeutic drug manual* (3rd ed., rev.). New York: Wiley.

Zou, Z., & Buck, L. B. (2006, March 10). Combinatorial effects of odorant mixes in olfactory cortex. *Science,* 1477–1481.

Zuckerman, M. (1978). The search for high sensation. *Psychology Today,* pp. 30–46.

Zuckerman, M. (2002). Genetics of sensation seeking. In J. Benjamin, R. P. Ebstein, et al. (Eds.), *Molecular genetics and the human personality,* pp. 193–210. Washington, DC: American Psychiatric Publishing.

Zuckerman, M., & Kuhlman, D. M. (2000). Personality and risk-taking: Common biosocial factors [Special issue: Personality processes and problem behavior]. *Journal of Personality, 68,* 999–1029.

CREDITS

Text Credits

CHAPTER 1 **Prologue:** From C. Buckley, "A Man Down, A Train Arriving, and A Stranger Makes a Choice," *The New York Times,* January 3, 2007. Reprinted with permission of PARS International Corp. **Module 1: Cut 1A:** Copyright © The New Yorker Collection 1998 Roz Chast from cartoonbank.com. All Rights Reserved. **Cut 1B:** Copyright © The New Yorker Collection 1993 J.B. Handelsman from cartoonbank.com. All Rights Reserved. **Cut 1C:** Copyright © The New Yorker Collection 2004 Mike Twohy from cartoonbank.com. All Rights Reserved. **Cut 1D:** Copyright © The New Yorker Collection 1993 Donald Reilly from cartoonbank.com. All Rights Reserved. **CHAPTER 2** **Module 5: Figure 1:** From K. Van De Graaff, *Human Anatomy* 5/e, 2000. Copyright © 2000 The McGraw-Hill Companies. Reprinted with permission. **Figure 2:** Stevens, 1979. **Figure 3:** From S.S. Mader, *Biology,* 2000. Copyright © 2000 The McGraw-Hill Companies. Reprinted with permission. **Module 6: Figure 3:** From Michael Passer and Ronald Smith, *Psychology: Frontiers and Applications,* 2001. Copyright © 2001 The McGraw-Hill Companies. Reprinted with permission. **Figure 4:** From Robert Brooker, Eric Widmaier, Linda Graham and Peter Stiling, *Biology* 1E, 2008. Copyright © 2008 The McGraw-Hill Companies. Reprinted with permission. **Module 7: Figure 2:** From Rod Seeley, Trent Stephens and Philip Tate, *Anatomy & Physiology* 5E, 2000. Copyright © 2000 The McGraw-Hill Companies. Reprinted with permission. **Figure 3:** From George Johnson and Thomas Emmel, *The Living World* 2E, 2000. Copyright © 2000 The McGraw-Hill Companies. Reprinted with permission. **Figure 7:** From Robert Brooker, Eric Widmaier, Linda Graham and Peter Stiling, *Biology* 1E, 2008. Copyright © 2008 The McGraw-Hill Companies. Reprinted with permission. **CHAPTER 3** **Module 8: Figure 1:** From E. Galanter, 1962, "Contemporary Psychophysics" in R. Brown, E. Galanter, E. Hess, and G. Maroler (eds.) *New Directions in Psychology,* pp. 87–157, Holt. **Module 9: Figure 3:** From David Shier, Jackie Butler and Ricki Lewis, *Human Anatomy and Physiology* 7E, 2000. Copyright © 2000 The McGraw-Hill Companies. Reprinted with permission. **Figure 5:** From Sylvia Mader, *Biology* 7E, 2001. Copyright © 2001 The McGraw-Hill Companies. Reprinted with permission.

Module 10: Figure 1: From Robert Brooker, Eric Widmaier, Linda Graham and Peter Stiling, *Biology* 1E, 2008. Copyright © 2008 The McGraw-Hill Companies. Reprinted with permission. **Figure 2:** From D.R. Kenshalo, *The Skin Senses,* 1968, p. 201. Courtesy of Charles C. Thomas Publisher, Ltd., Springfield, Illinois. **Cut 3A:** Copyright © The New Yorker Collection 2006 Paul North from cartoonbank.com. All Rights Reserved. **Module 11: Figure 3:** James, 1966. **Figure 4:** From S. Coren, L.M. Ward, 1989, *Sensation and Perception* 3e, John Wiley & Sons, Inc. Reprinted with permission of John Wiley & Sons, Inc. **Figure 5:** From S. Coren, L.M. Ward, 1989, *Sensation and Perception* 3e, John Wiley & Sons, Inc. Reprinted with permission of John Wiley & Sons, Inc. **CHAPTER 4** **Module 12: Figure 2:** From *Dreaming Brain* by Allan Hobson. Copyright © 1988. Reprinted by permission of Basic Books, a member of Perseus Books Group. **Figure 3:** From E. Hartman, *The Biology of Dreaming,* 1967. Courtesy of Charles C. Thomas Publisher, Ltd., Springfield, Illinois. **Figure 4:** From *Secrets of Sleep* by Alexander Borbely. Copyright © 1986. Reprinted by permission of Basic Books, a member of Perseus Books Group. **Figure 8:** Text adapted from *Search,* Spring 1998. **Module 13: Cut 4B:** Copyright © The New Yorker Collection 1993 Mischa Richter from cartoonbank.com. All Rights Reserved. **Figure 1:** Brefczynski-Lewis, Luz, Schaefer, Levinson, & Davidson (2007, July 3), p. 11484, "Neural correlates of attentional expertise in long-term meditation practitioners," *PNAS,* vol. 104. **Module 14: Figure 3:** *The New York Times,* 1991 **Figure 5:** From "Underage College Students' Drinking Behavior, Access to Alcohol, and the Influence of Deterrence Policies," by H. Wechsler, J.E. Lee, T.F. Nelson and M. Kuo, *Journal of American College Health,* Vol. 50, pp. 223–236, March 2002. Reprinted with permission of Helen Dwight Reid Educational Foundation. Published by Heldref Publications, 1319 Eighteenth St., N.W., Washington, DC 20036-1802. Copyright © 2002. **Figure 7:** L.D. Johnston, P.M. O'Malley, J.G. Bachman, J.E. Schulenberg, "Monitoring the Future National Results on Adolescent Drug Use: Overview of Key Findings, 2006, National Institute on Drug Abuse, NIH Publication No. 07-6202. **CHAPTER 5** **Module 16: Cut 5A:** Copyright © The New Yorker Collection 2001 Christopher Weyant

from cartoonbank.com. All Rights Reserved. **Module 17: Cut 5B:** Copyright © The New Yorker Collection 1995 Gahan Wilson from cartoonbank.com. All Rights Reserved. **Figure 2:** Reprinted from *Neuropsychologia,* Volume 44, No. 10, 2006 "Differential Cerebral Activation During Observation of Expressive Gestures and Motor Acts," by M. Lotze, U. Heymans, N. Birbaumer, R. Veit, M. Erb, H. Flor and U. Halsband. Copyright © 2006 with permission from Elsevier. **CHAPTER 6** **Module 18: Figure 2:** R.C. Atkinson, R.M. Schiffrin, 1968, "Human Memory: A Proposed System and its Control Processes," in K.W. Spence and J.T. Spence (eds.) *The Psychology of Learning and Motivation: Advances in Research and Theory,* Vol. 2, pp. 80–195, Academic Press. **Cut 6A:** Copyright © The New Yorker Collection 1994 Roz Chast from cartoonbank.com. All Rights Reserved. **Cut 6B:** Copyright © The New Yorker Collection 1983 Ed Fisher from cartoonbank.com. All Rights Reserved. **Module 19: Figure 3:** D.C. Rubin, "The Subtle Deceiver: Recalling Our Past," *Psychology Today,* September 1985, pp. 39–46. **Figure 4:** From *Memory: A Contribution to Experimental Psychology* by Hermann Ebbinghaus; translated by Henry A. Ruger and Clara E. Bussenius, 1987. Reprinted with permission of Dover Publications, Inc. **Figure 5:** Reprinted from *Cognitive Psychology,* July 1979, "Long-Term Memory for a Common Object," by Raymond S. Nickerson and Marilyn Jager Adams. Copyright © 1979 with permission from Elsevier. **Module 20: Cut 6C:** Copyright © The New Yorker Collection 1995 Michael Maslin from cartoonbank.com. All Rights Reserved. **Figure 1:** Reprinted from *Cognitive Psychology,* October 1975, "Family Resemblances: Studies in the Internal Structure of Categories," by Eleanor Rosch and Carolyn B. Mervis. Copyright © 1975 with permission from Elsevier. **Cut 6D:** Copyright © The New Yorker Collection 2000 Michael Maslin from cartoonbank.com. All Rights Reserved. **Module 21: Figure 1:** MLA Language Map, 2005, based on 2000 Census. **Figure 2:** Reprinted by permission from Macmillan Publishers Ltd: Karl H. Kim, Norman R. Relkin, Kyoung-Min Lee, and Joy Hirsch, "Distinct Cortical Areas Associated with Native and Second Languages," *Nature,* July 10, 1997, Vol. 388, pp. 171–174. **CHAPTER 7** **Module 22: Try It:** M. Zuckerman, "The Search for High Sensation," *Psychology Today,*

1978, pp. 30–46. **Module 23: Cut 7A:** Copyright © The New Yorker Collection 1997 Robert Mankoff from cartoonbank.com. All Rights Reserved. **Module 24: Figure 3:** R.J. Dolan, "Emotion, Cognition, & Behavior," *Science,* November 8, 2002, Vol. 298, pp. 1191–1194. **Cut 7B:** Copyright © The New Yorker Collection 2000 Gahan Wilson from cartoonbank.com. All Rights Reserved. **CHAPTER 8 Module 26: Figure 5:** Reprinted with permission of Harlow Primate Laboratory, Madison, Wisconsin. **Figure 7:** From Diana Baumrind, "Current Patterns of Parental Authority," *Developmental Psychology Monographs,* 1971, Vol. 41, (1,pt2). Reprinted with permission of the author. **Cut 8A:** Copyright © The New Yorker Collection 1985 Lee Lorenz from cartoonbank.com. All Rights Reserved. **Module 27: Cut 8B:** Copyright © The New Yorker Collection 1993 Roz Chast from cartoonbank.com. All Rights Reserved. **Figure 4:** Reprinted with kind permission from Springer Science/Business Media: *Child Psychiatry and Human Development,* Volume 26, 1995, pp. 61–66, Kathryn E. Boehm, et al., "Suicide: A Review of Calls to an Adolescent Peer Listening Phone Service." **Module 28: Figure 1:** K.W. Schaie, 2005, *Developmental Influences on Adult Intelligence: The Seattle Longitudinal Study,* Oxford University Press. **Cut 8C:** Copyright © The New Yorker Collection 1993 Roz Chast from cartoonbank.com. All Rights Reserved. **Try It:** From L.S. Dickstein, "Death Concern: Measurement and Correlates," *Psychological Reports,* Vol. 30. Copyright 1972 by Ammons Scientific, Ltd. Reproduced with permission of Ammons Scientific, Ltd. via Copyright Clearance Center. **CHAPTER 9 Module 30: Figure 1:** From H.J. Eysenck, 1990, *Biological Dimensions of Personality* in L.A. Pervin (ed), *Handbook of Personality: Theory and Research,* p. 246. Reprinted with permission of Guilford Press. **Figure 3:** From A. Tellegen, D.T. Lykken, T.J. Bouchard, Jr., K. J. Wilcox, N.L. Segal, and S. Rich, "Personality Similarity in Twins Reared Apart and Together," *Journal of Personality and Social Psychology,* 1988, Vol. 54, pp. 1031–1039. **Cut 9A:** Copyright © The New Yorker Collection 1991 Robert Mankoff from cartoonbank.com. All Rights Reserved. **Module 31: Figure 1:** Based on data from Halgin & Whitbourne, 1994, p. 72, and Minnesota Multiphasic Personality Inventory-2. **Figure 2:** From Lauren Alloy, Neil Jacobson and Joan Acocella, *Abnormal Psychology: Current Perspectives 8E,* 1999. Copyright © 1999 The McGraw-Hill Companies. Reprinted with permission. **Cut 9B:** Reprinted with permission of Sidney Harris, www.ScienceCartoonsPlus.com. **Module 32: Cut 9C:** Copyright © The New Yorker Collection 1983 W.B. Park from cartoonbank.com. All Rights Reserved. **Figure 1:** From *Intelligence Reframed* by Howard Gardner. Copyright © 2000. Reprinted by permission of Basic Books, a member of Perseus Books Group. **Figure 2:** From Robert J. Sternberg,

Handbook of Intelligence, Copyright © 2000, p. 389. Reprinted with permission of Cambridge University Press. **Figure 5:** Simulated items similar to those in the Wechsler Adult Intelligence Scale-Third Edition and the Wechsler Intelligence Scale for Children-Fourth Edition. Copyright © 1997 and 2003 by NCS Pearson, Inc. Reproduced with permission. All rights reserved. **CHAPTER 10 Module 33: Cut 10A:** Copyright © The New Yorker Collection 2000 Arnie Levin from cartoonbank.com. All Rights Reserved. **Module 34: Try It:** From J. A. Taylor, 1953, "A Personality Scale of Manifest Anxiety," *Journal of Abnormal Psychology,* Vol. 48, pp. 285–290. **Figure 2:** Reprinted from *Journal of Affective Disorders,* Volume 94, August 2006, "fMRI of Fearful Facial Affect Recognition in Panic Disorder: The Cingulate Gyrus-Amygdala Connection," by Srinivasan S. Pillay, Staci A. Gruber, Jadwiga Rogowska, Norah Simpson and Deborah A. Yurgelun-Todd. Copyright © 2006 with permission from Elsevier. **Figure 3:** From *Anxiety Disorders and Phobias* by Aaron Beck. Copyright © 1985. Reprinted by permission of Basic Books, a member of Perseus Books Group. **Figure 5:** Ian Gotlib, *Stanford Mood and Anxiety Disorders Laboratory,* Stanford University, 2005. Reprinted courtesy of Ian Gotlib. **Figure 8:** From *Schizophrenia Genesis: The Origin of Madness* by Irving I. Gottesman. Copyright © 1991 by Irving I. Gottesman. Used with permission of Worth Publishers. **Figure: 9:** N.C. Andreasen, University of Iowa. **Module 35: Figure 1:** From World Health Organization, World Mental Health Survey Consortium, 2004, Table 3. Reprinted with permission. **CHAPTER 11 Module 36: Cut 11A:** Copyright © The New Yorker Collection 2000 Robert Mankoff from cartoonbank.com. All Rights Reserved. **Cut 11B:** Copyright © The New Yorker Collection 2007 Michael Maslin from cartoonbank.com. All Rights Reserved. **Module 37: Cut 11C:** Copyright © The New Yorker Collection 2005 Tom Cheney from cartoonbank.com. All Rights Reserved. **Figure 1:** M.L. Smith, G.V. Glass, T.J. Miller, 1980, *The Benefits of* Psychotherapy, Johns Hopkins University Press. **Figure 2:** Copyright © 1995 by Consumers Union of U.S., Inc. Yonkers NY 10703-1057, a nonprofit organization. Reprinted with permission from the November 1995 issue of *Consumer Reports* ® for educational purposes only. No commercial use or reproduction permitted. www.ConsumerReports.org. **Figure 1:** From *Scientific American,* December 2002, p. 38. Reprinted with permission of Rodger Doyle. **Figure 4:** K.I. Howard, S.M. Kopta, M.S. Krause, and D.E. Orlinsky, 1986, "The Dose-Effect Relationship in Psychotherapy," *American Psychologist,* Vol. 41, pp. 159–164, figure 1. **Cut 11D:** Copyright © The New Yorker Collection 1994 Gahan Wilson from cartoonbank.com. All Rights Reserved. **CHAPTER 12 Module 42: Cut 12A:** Copyright © The New Yorker Collection 1999

Richard Cline from cartoonbank.com. All Rights Reserved. **Figure 2:** From D.M. Buss, et al., "International Preferences in Soliciting Mates: A Study of 37 Cultures," *Journal of Cross-Cultural Psychology,* Vol. 21, pp. 5–47. Copyright © 1990 by Sage Publications Inc, Journals. Reproduced with permission of Sage Publication Inc. via Copyright Clearance Center. **Module 43: Figure 1 (uplifts):** From K. Chamberlain and S. Zika, 1990, "The Minor Events Approach to Stress: Support for the Use of Daily Hassles, *British Journal of Psychology,* Vol. 81, pp. 469–481. Reproduced with permission from the *British Journal of Psychology,* © The British Psychological Society; **(hassles):** Reprinted with kind permission from Springer Science/Business Media: *Journal of Behavioral Medicine,* Volume 4, 1981, pp. 1–39, Allen D. Kanner, et al., "Comparisons of Two Modes of Stress Measurements: Daily Hassles & Uplifts Versus Major Life Events," p. 14. **Figure 2:** From Patricia Cohen, et al., *Historical and Geographical Influences on Psychopathology.* Copyright © 1999 by Taylor & Francis Group LLD–Books. Reproduced with permission of Taylor & Frances Group LLC via Copyright Clearance Center. **Figure 3:** From Hans Selye, *The Stress of Life,* 1976. Copyright © 1976 The McGraw-Hill Companies. Reprinted with permission.

Figure Photo Credits

CHAPTER 1 Module 1: Figure 1: (top to bottom) Bruce Ayres/Getty Images, (DNA) Lawrence Lawry/Getty Images, David Buffington/Getty Images, Manchan/Getty Images (Scrabble tile background) Jeffrey Coolidge/Getty Images. **Module 2: Figure 1:** left page, (top left): ©Corbis Images; (top right): Courtesy Wellesley College Archives. Photographed by Notman; (center left): ©Photo Researchers; (center): ©The Granger Collection; (center right): ©Bettmann/Corbis Images; right page, (top left): ©Culver Pictures; (top right, center): ©The Granger Collection; (center right): Courtesy, Elizabeth Loftus. **Figure 2:** (from second to fourth image, left to right) David Sanger/Getty Images, Camille Tokerud/Getty Images, White Packert/Getty Images. **Figure 3:** (second to fourth image, left to right) David Sanger/Getty Images, Camille Tokerud/Getty Images, White Packert/Getty Images. **Module 3: Figure 1:** Creativ Studio Heinemann/Getty Images. **Figure 4:** (top to bottom) Romilly Lockyer/Getty Images, Hans Neleman/Getty Images, Asia Images Group/Getty Images. **CHAPTER 2 Module 5: Figure 1,** ©Dennis Kunket/Visuals Unlimited. **Figure 4:** ©Moonrunner Design Ltd. **Module 6: Figure 2:** Larry Williams/Getty Images. **Module 7: Figure 3:** Dana Neely/Getty Images. **Figure 5:** Ron Krisel/Getty Images. **CHAPTER 3 Module 10: Figure 1:** Alan Frank/Getty Images. **Figure 2:** Chase Jarvis/Getty Images. **Module 11: Figure 3:** James, R.C. (1966). Photo of dog. In J. Thurston & R.G. Carraher.

Optical Illusions and the Visual Arts. NY: Von Nostrand Reinhold. **Figure 5:** ©John G. Ross/ Photo Researchers. **Chapter 4 Module 12: Figure 3:** Dominic Burke/Getty Images. **Figure 4:** Brad Wilson/Getty Images. **Figure 5:** (counter clockwise) BananaStock/ PunchStock, Image Source/PunchStock, George Doyle/Getty Images, Cocoon/Getty Images, Digital Vision/Getty Images, John Knill/Getty Images. **Figure 6:** Stockbyte/ Getty Images. **Figure 8:** Medioimages/ Photodisc/Getty Images. **Module 14: Figure 1:** (top) Ingram Publishing/AGE Fotostock, (bottom) BananaStock/PunchStock, (cigarette background) Brand X Pictures/Punchstock;. **Figure 3:** Ingram Publishing/SuperStock. **Figure 4:** (left to right) Seth Resnick/Getty Images, Stockbyte/PunchStock, Jonnie Miles/Getty Images, Per-Anders Pettersson/Getty Images. **Figure 5:** C Squared Studios/Getty Images. **Chapter 5 Module 16: Figure 2:** (top left) ©PhotoDisc/Getty Images; (top right) ©Corbis Images; (bottom left) ©Banana Stock/Alamy; (bottom right) ©Amy Etra/PhotoEdit. **Figure 4:** (left) Bruce Ayres/Getty Images, (right) Veer. **Module 17: Figure 3:** Stockbyte/Getty Images. **Chapter 6 Module 18: Figure 2:** C Squared Studios/Getty Images. **Figure 3:** English School/Getty Images. **Module 19: Figure 3:** (top to bottom) Medioimages/ Superstock, Ryuichi Sato/Getty Images, Nick Daly/Getty Images, Tony Anderson/Getty Images. **Module 20: Figure 4:** (left and right) David Joel/Getty Images, Brownie Harris/ CORBIS/Corbis. **Module 21: Figure 2:** From Kim, K. H., Relkin, N. R., Lee, K. M., Hirsch, J. Distinct cortical areas associated with native and second languages. *Nature 388*, p. 171; Figs. 1, 5 (1997). **Chapter 7 Module 22: Figure 1:** (clockwise from top left) Trinette Reed/Brand X Pictures/Jupiterimages, BananaStock/age fotosota, Stockbyte, Supernova/Getty Images. **Module 24: Figure 2:** Stuart McClymont/Getty Images. **Figure 3:** George, M. S., et al. "Brain activity during transient sadness and happiness in healthy women." *American Journal of Psychiatry*, 152:341–351, 1995. ©1995, The American Psychiatric Association. Reprinted by permission. **Chapter 8 Module 25: Figure 3:** Dougal Waters/Getty Images; **Module 26: Figure 3:** (top) Image Source/Alamy, (bottom) Kay Blaschke/Getty Images. **Figure 7:** BananaStock/PunchStock. **Figure 8:** (clockwise from top right) JGI/Getty Images, RubberBall, Wides & Holl/Getty Images, Gary Buss/Getty Images. **Module 27: Figure 2:** Purestock/Getty Images. **Figure 3:** ©Olive Pierce/Black Star. **Figure 4:** Judith Haeusler/Getty Images. **Chapter 9 Module 29: Figure 2:** ©Bettmann/Corbis Images. **Module 30: Figure 3:** (top to bottom) Jetta Productions/Getty Images, fStop, Purestock/ PunchStock, Stockbyte/Getty Images. **Module 32: Figure 1:** (1) ©Getty Images; (2) ©Bettmann/Corbis Images; (3) ©Cold Spring Harbor Laboratory; (4) ©Bettmann/Corbis Images; (5) ©David Hiser/Photographers/ Aspen/Network Aspen; (6) ©Bettmann/

Corbis Images; (7) ©George C. Beresford/ Getty Images; (8) ©PhotoDisc/Getty Images. **Figure 3:** (clockwise from top left) ThinkStock/Corbis, Photodisc/DAL, Insy Shah/Getty Images. **Chapter 10 Module 34: Figure 1:** (top) Felipe Dupouy/Getty Images, (bottom) Lena Granefelt/Getty Images. **Figure 3:** (top) Stockbyte/Getty Images, (bottom) Paul Thomas/Getty Images. **Figure 7:** ©Victoria and Albert Museum. **Chapter 11 Module 36: Figure 2:** Alex Mares-Manton/Getty Images. **Module 38: Figure 1:** Stockdisc/PunchStock. **Figure 3:** Steven Peters/Getty Images. **Chapter 12 Module 39: Figure 2:** PhotoAlto/PictureQuest. **Module 42: Figure 1:** (clockwise from top) Brand X Pictures/ PunchStock, Digital Vision/Getty Images, BananaStock/age footstock. **Module 43: Figure 1:** (top to bottom) Purestock/PunchStock, Purestock/PunchStock, Royalty-Free/CORBIS, (Stick paper background) Gary S Chapman/ Getty Images. **Figure 4:** Russell Monk Photography/Getty Images.

Photo Credits

Preface p. xxiii: Comstock/CORBIS. **p. xxix:** Tetra Images/Getty Images. **p. xxxiii:** Comstock Images/Alamy. **p. xxxiv:** Comstock Images/Jupiterimages. **p. xxxviii:** Burke/ Triolo/Brand X Pictures/Jupiterimages. **xl:** Dynamic Graphics/Jupiterimages. **Chapter 1 p. 2:** Stuart McClymont/Stone+/Getty Images. **Module 1: p. 7:** liquidlibrary/ PictureQuest. **p. 9:** WireImage/Getty Images. **Module 2: p. 13:** (man) Bettmann/CORBIS. **p. 13:** (coffee cup) ©Pixtal/SuperStock. **p. 14:** (bottom) Hulton Archive/Getty Images. **p. 14:** (picture frame) ©1996 Image Farm, Inc. **p. 17:** (on t-shirt) Bettmann/CORBIS. **p. 18:** RubberBall Productions. **p. 19:** Oakland County Prosecutors Office/Jeff Kowalsky/ Handout/epa/CORBIS. **p. 21:** Brand X Pictures. **Module 3: p. 27:** Robert I.M. Campbell/National Geographic Image Collection. **p. 27:** (gorilla) ©Digital Vision/ Getty Images. **p. 28:** Alex Segre/Alamy. **p. 31:** M. Wexler/Woodfin Camp and Assoc. **Module 4: p. 37:** Jose Luis Banus-March/Getty Images. **p. 38:** Douglas Faulkner/Photo Researchers, Inc. **Chapter 2 pp. 46–47:** Nancy Kaszerman/ ZUMA/CORBIS. **Module 5: p. 50:** Tom Hoenig/Getty Images. **p. 52:** David Muir/Getty Images. **p. 53:** AFP/Getty Images. **p. 54:** RubberBall Productions. **Module 6: p. 56:** PhotoLink/Getty Images. **p. 60:** (top) Gabriela Medina/Getty Images; (bottom) Comstock/ CORBIS. **p. 61:** Getty Images. **Module 7: p. 65, Figure 1:** (A) Hank Morgan/Photo Researchers, Inc., (B) ©Volker Steger/Peter Arnold; (C) Bryan Christie Design, (D) ©Roger Ressmeyer/Corbis Images. **p. 65:** (bottom) Martin M. Rotker/Photo Researchers, Inc. **p. 70, Figure 6:** (top) Natural History Museum, London; (bottom) From Damasio, H., Grabowski, T., Frank, R., Galaburda, A. M., Damasio, A. R.: The Return of Phineas Gage: Clues about the brain from the skull of a

famous patient. *Science*, 264:1102–1105, 1994. Department of Neurology and Image Analysis Facility, University of Iowa. **p. 72:** Time & Life Pictures/Getty Images. **p. 74:** Comstock Select/CORBIS. **Chapter 3 pp. 82–83:** Trinette Reed/Blend Images/CORBIS. **Module 8: p. 85:** Stephen Studd/Getty Images. **p. 86:** Tetra Images/Getty Images. **p. 87:** Getty Images. **Module 9: p. 91:** Biophoto Associates/ Photo Researchers, Inc. **p. 94:** Mango Productions/CORBIS. **p. 95:** Tom Grill/ CORBIS. **Module 10: p. 100:** Professor Pietro M. Motta/Photo Researchers, Inc. **p. 101:** Omikron/Photo Researchers, Inc. **p. 103:** Royalty-free/CORBIS. **p. 104:** Comstock/ CORBIS. **Module 11: p. 111:** Cary Wolinsky/ Stock Boston. **p. 112:** (top) AFP/Getty Images; (bottom) Comstock Select/CORBIS.

Chapter 4 p. 122: Flint/CORBIS. **Module 12: p. 124:** Stockbyte/Getty Images. **p. 127:** Ted Spagna/Photo Researchers, Inc. **p. 131:** Ryan McVay/Getty Images. **p. 132:** Photodisc/ Getty Images. **p. 134:** (top) Glyn Jones/ CORBIS; (center) Stockbyte/Getty Images; (bottom) Sabine Scheckel/Digital Vision/Getty Images. **Module 13: p. 138:** (top) Associated Press; (bottom) Design Pics Inc./Alamy. **p. 139:** liquidlibrary/PictureQuest. **Module 14: p. 143:** David Seed Photography/Getty Images. **p. 144:** Comstock Select/CORBIS. **p. 145:** David Zurick. **p. 148:** Getty Images. **p. 149:** Andrew Brookes/CORBIS. **p. 151:** Royalty-Free/ CORBIS. **p. 152:** Getty Images. **Chapter 5 p. 160:** James A. Sugar/Getty Images. **Module 15: p. 163:** Culver Pictures. **p. 166:** CORBIS Premium RF/Alamy. **p. 167:** Dave Nagel/Taxi/Getty Images. **Module 16: p. 174:** Design Pics Inc./Alamy. **Module 17: p. 186:** (top) Courtesy Albert Bandura; (bottom) Henrik Sorensen/Taxi/Getty Images. **p. 187:** Getty Images. **p. 188:** Tetra Images/Getty Images. **p. 192:** Clarissa Leahy/Stone/Getty Images. **Chapter 6 p. 198:** Will Crocker/ Photodisc/Getty Images. **Module 18: p. 200:** Jaume Felipe/age footstock. **p. 202:** Paul Avis/ Stone/Getty Images. **p. 203:** CORBIS. **p. 204:** Photodisc/Getty Images. **Module 19: p. 209:** (left) Library of Congress; (right) Time & Life Pictures/Getty Images. **p. 211:** Photodisc/ Getty Images. **Module 20: p. 221:** (top) Getty Images; (bottom) Brand X Photography/Veer. **p. 231:** (bottom) Somos/Veer/Getty Images. **p. 233:** (top) Cade Martin/Uppercut Images/ Getty Images; (bottom) David Rosenberg/ Stone/Getty Images. **Module 21: p. 234:** Associated Press. **Chapter 7 pp. 242–243:** PAULO WHITAKER/Reuters/CORBIS. **p. 243:** Getty Images. **p. 245:** Dynamic Graphics/Jupiterimages. **p. 246:** (left) Somos/ Veer/Getty Images; (center) Tanya Constantine/Digital Vision/Getty Images, (right) Somos/Veer/Getty Images. **p. 249:** WireImage/Getty Images. **p. 251:** CORBIS. **Module 23: p. 255:** Lew Robertson/Stockfood Creative/Getty Images. **p. 256:** Ed Quinn/ CORBIS. **p. 257:** Copyright © 2008 ScienceDirect. All rights reserved. ScienceDirect® is a registered trademark of Elsevier B.V. **p. 261:** Queerstock/Getty Images.

NAME INDEX

Eynan, R., 415
Eysenck, H. J., 348–349

Fagan, J. F., 380
Fallon, A., 36
Fallon, B. A., 404
Fanselow, M. S., 52
Farrell, B., 94
Fassler, O., 138
Fast, K., 101
Faust, D., 445
Fearing, V. G., 442
Feeney, B. C., 472
Feinberg, A. W., 325
Feinstein, S., 404
Feldhusen, J. F., 204
Feldman, R. S.., 217
Fergusson, D. M., 315
Fernandez, L. C., 15
Ferraro, R. F., 208
Festinger, L., 15f, 468
Fields-Meyer, T., 309
Fillingim, R. B., 104, 248
Finch, H., 263
Fine, L., 140
Fingelkurts, A., 138
Fink, A., 369
Finkler, K., 141
Finlay, F. O., 310
Finley, C. L., 134
Finn-Stevenson, M., 289
Firestein, B. A., 261
First, M. B., 394
Fischer, A. H., 268, 272
Fischer, K. W., 268f
Fischer, T. M., 87
Fishbach, A., 226
Fisher, C. B., 36
Fisher, J. E., 446
Fisher, L., 203
Fiske, S. T., 470, 484
Fitch, K. L., 230
Fitch, W. T., 232
Flam, F., 100
Flavell, S. W., 52
Fleischman, D. A., 324
Fleminger, S., 416
Flouty, M., 429
Flynn, P. M., 151
Fogel, A., 295
Folkman, S., 499, 505, 506
Forer, B., 358
Forlenza, M. J., 56
Fossey, D., 27
Foster, D. H., 96
Foster, K. M., 192
Fountoulakis, K. N., 452
Fowler, R., 100
Fox, K., 263
Fox, M. J., 53, 54
Fox, S., 371
Frances, A., 394
Francis, J. L., 54, 412
Frank, L. R., 454
Frankenburg, W. K., 294f
Frankham, P., 254
Franzek, E., 411
Freedman, D. S., 256
Freeman, A., 439

Freire, J. C., 442
Frensch, P. A., 185
Freud, A., 14, 15, 341
Freud, S., 14f, 17, 27, 129–130, 262,
    336–342, 391, 492
Fricker, B., 465
Friedberg, R. D., 437
Friederici, A. D., 295
Friedman, J. N. W., 414
Friesen, W. V., 274, 275
Frijda, N., 268
Frijda, N. H., 272
Frincke, J. L., 9
Frings, L., 74
Frost, L. E., 389
Frost, R. O., 402, 403
Fuchs-Lacelle, S., 104
Funder, D. C., 350
Funke, G. J., 306
Furnham, A., 343
Furumoto, L., 15
Fyer, A. J., 434

Gabriel, L. T., 376
Gaertner, S. L., 482, 483, 485
Gage, P., 70
Gailliot, M. T., 495
Galanter, E., 85f
Galanter, M., 444
Galatzer-Levy, R. M., 432
Gall, F. J., 12, 14f
Gallo, P., 232
Galvin, D. M., 153
Gami, A. S., 132
Gangestad, S. W., 259
Garb, H. N., 362
Garber, J., 415
Garcia, S. M., 495
Gardini, S., 221
Gardner, C. O., 145, 406
Gardner, E. P., 103
Gardner, H., 85, 367–368
Gardner, S., 15
Garfield, S. L., 434
Garle, M., 61
Garrido-Nag, K., 230
Garwick, G. B., 376
Garza-Guerrero, C., 489
Gass, C. S., 27
Gatchel, R. J., 104
Gathchel, R. J., 257
Gatz, M., 406
Gautreaux, G., 436, 494
Gazzaniga, M. S., 47, 74
Gegenfurtner, K. R., 96
Gelman, R., 295
Genovese, J. E. C., 305
George, J., 444
George, L. K., 325
George, M. S., 272
George, S., 147
Georgeson, M., 94
Geppert, C. M., 444
Gershkoff-Stowe, L., 232
Gerson, K., 322
Gerstel, N., 322
Giacobbi, P. R., Jr., 499
Gibbons, R. D., 451

Gilbert, D. T., 347
Gilligan, C., 312
Gladwell, M., 343, 363, 364
Glass, G. V., 444, 445f
Gleitman, L. R., 232
Glickler, J., 351
Glicksohn, J., 470
Glisky, E. L., 325
Goffin, R. D., 472
Goin, M. K., 429
Gold, P. E., 217
Goldfried, M. R., 444
Goldsmith, H. H., 414
Goldstein, I., 258
Goldstein, S. N., 312
Goldstone, R. L., 221
Goleman, D., 422
Golosheykin, S., 139
Gong, H., 96
Gontkovsky, S. T., 67, 369
Goode, E., 100, 433
Goodheart, C. D., 446
Goodwin, R., 476
Goodwin, R. D., 414
Gooren, L., 262
Gordijn, M. C. M., 133
Gordon, R., 101
Gothard, K. D., 434
Gotlib, I. H., 408
Gottesman, I. I., 283, 284, 411, 412f
Gottfredson, L. S., 367, 378
Gottlieb, D. A., 174, 175
Gould, R. L., 320
Graf, P., 209
Graham, C. A., 409
Graham, J. R., 360
Graham, L., 75f
Graham, S., 37, 416
Granath, F., 61
Grange, D. K., 289
Granic, I., 315
Grann, J. D., 215
Grant, S., 362
Gray, G. C., 495
Gray, H., 470
Gray, R., 290
Greco, C. M., 76
Green, M. C., 466
Green, P. R., 94
Greenberg, R. M., 454
Greene, J. D., 272
Greene, R. L., 361
Greenspan, S., 376
Greenwald, A. G., 485
Greer, R. D., 436, 494
Gregory, R. L., 114
Gretchen, D., 447
Griffin, D. W., 489
Griffiths, R. R., 145
Grigorenko, E. L., 380
Grigoriadis, S., 442
Grilo, C. M., 256
Grossmann, T., 295
Groves, 27
Grusec, J. E., 186, 436
Guarnaccia, P. J., 393, 421, 422
Guéguen, N., 476
Guez, J., 215
Guilleminault, C., 132, 133

Guthrie, R. V., 37
Gutierrez, P. M., 315
Gwynn, M. I., 137

Haberstick, B. C., 145, 287
Hadjistavropoulos, T., 104
Häfliger, A., 208
Haier, R. J., 367
Halford, S., 298
Halgin, R. P., 361f
Hall, N. W., 289
Hall, R. E., 379
Halle, T., 300
Hallschmid, M., 254
Halpern, D. F., 322
Hamann, S. B., 272
Hambleton, R. K., 358
Hamer, D. H., 262
Hamilton, A. C., 202
Hamilton, S. P., 414
Hampson, R., 465
Hand, V. M., 393
Haney, C., 476
Hanley, C., 187
Hansell, S., 335
Hanson, D. R., 283, 411
Harlaar, N., 60
Harlow, H. F., 297
Harlow, J. M., 70
Harned, M. S., 436
Harper, D. J., 454
Harrington, H., 354
Harris, K. R., 369, 416
Hartmann, E., 126f
Hartung, C. M., 421
Harvey, J. H., 261
Harvey, P. D., 412
Harvey-Berino, J., 255
Hattrill, K., 161
Haugen, R., 473
Hauke, C., 343
Hauser, M. D., 232
Havercamp, S. M., 250
Havermans, R. C., 436
Haviland-Jones, J., 101
Hawley, E., 114
Hayflick, L., 323
Hays, P. A., 446, 447
He, X., 233
Heard, H. L., 437
Heath, R. A., 263
Hedgepeth, E., 312
Hedges, D. W., 450
Hedlund, J., 370
Hegarty, P., 378, 466
Heimann, M., 305
Heinrichs, R. W., 410
Heisel, M. J., 415
Heller, S., 342
Heller, W., 72
Helmuth, L., 52
Henderlong, J., 249
Henderson, J., 290
Henderson, N. D., 379f
Hendrick, C., 489
Hendrick, S. S., 489
Hentschel, U., 341
Herman, C. P., 256
Herrán, A., 401

Herrmann, A., 226
Herrnstein, R. J., 378
Herskovits, M. J., 114
Herz, R. S., 101
Heshka, S., 257
Hess, D. W., 75
Hessels, S., 216
Hewstone, M., 470
Heyman, G. D., 235
Hiby, E. F., 174
Hicks, B. M., 495
Hicks, T. V., 260
Hilgard, E., 138
Hill, J. O., 253, 258
Hill, S. S., 36
Hines, M., 72
Hinshaw, S. P., 416
Hippocrates, 14f
Hirsch, J., 256
Hirschler, B., 60
Hirt, E. R., 211
Hobfoll, S. E., 499
Hobson, J., 126f
Hobson, J. A., 131
Hochschild, A., 322
Hock, H. S., 85
Hoff, E., 230, 233
Hoffmann, M., 320
Hofmann, S. G., 436
Hogan, J., 364
Hogan, R., 364
Hogg, M. A., 483
Hojjat, M., 490
Holden, C., 408, 409, 410
Holland, C. R., 380
Hollenstein, T., 315
Hollingworth, L. S., 15
Hollopeter, C., 3
Holloway, L., 234
Holmes, A., 403
Holmes, J. G., 489
Holowka, S., 72
Holt, M., 52
Home, J. A., 129
Hongchun, W., 138
Honzik, C. H., 184
Hope, K., 456
Horn, J. L., 379
Horney, K., 15, 343–344
Hornsey, M. J., 475
Horowitz, H. A., 414
Horowitz, J. L., 415
Horwood, L. J., 315
Houghtalen, R. P., 404
Howard, A., 457f
Howe, C. J., 232
Howells, J. G., 390
Hsu, H. C., 301
Hu, F. B., 258
Hubbard, B., 472
Hubbard, K., 253
Hubel, D. H., 15f, 94
Huber, F., 226
Hudson, W., 115
Hudspeth, A. J., 70
Hughes, L., 281
Huijie, T., 285
Hull, C. L., 37, 245
Humphrey, N., 370

Humphreys, C., 132
Humphreys, G. W., 109
Hungi, N., 217
Hunt, E., 369
Hunt, M., 260, 261
Hussain, R., 377
Huston, A. C., 188
Hutchinson, S. L., 505
Hyde, J., 262
Hyde, J. S., 260
Hyman, M., 432

Ievers-Landis, C. E., 289
Igo, S. E., 27
Ilies, R., 59
Imamura, M., 111
Inhelder, B., 304
Innocenti, G. M., 288
Ireland, M., 315
Irwin, R. R., 140
Isaacson, J. S., 71
Isay, R. A., 262
Isbell, L. M., 486
Ishikawa, S., 439
Iversen, L. L., 54, 152
Iverson, S. D., 54
Ivry, R. B., 47
Iyengar, S. S., 249
Izard, C. E., 274, 297
Izenwasser, S., 145

Jackendoff, R., 233
Jacobs, J. A., 322
Jacobsen, T., 99
Jacobson, N. S., 362f
Jacoby, L. L., 216
Jacquez, F. M., 416
Jaffé, A., 60
Jaglom, M., 453
Jahn, R., 52
Jain, S., 500
James, R. C., 109f
James, H. S., Jr., 249
James, W., 14f, 269
Jamieson, G. A., 138
Jamison, K. R., 405
Jang, S. J., 71
Janson, G. R., 263
Jarlais, D. C. D., 147
Jarvin, L., 372
Jasso, H., 51
Javitt, D. C., 412
Jelley, R. B., 472
Jenkins, 10
Jenkins, S. R., 265
Jennings, D. J., 221
Jensen, A. R., 369
Jequier, E., 255
Jessell, T. M., 56
Jeter, D., 284
Jetten, J., 475
Jinks, A. L., 101
Jobes, D. A., 429
Joe, G. W., 151
Johnson, G. B., 51f, 66f
Johnson, H. D., 264
Johnson, J. G., 188
Johnson-Greene, D., 36

John-Steiner, V., 306
Johnston, L. D., 142f, 143, 151, 152f
Joiner, T. E., Jr., 395
Jones, A. L., 344
Jones, E. E., 433
Jones, R., 310
Jones, S., 413
Jorgensen, G., 312
Josephs, R. A., 148
Jourdan, A., 442
Joyce, J., 388
Juliano, L. M., 145
Julien, R. M., 152
Jung, C. G., 343
Jung, J., 147
Jung, R. E., 367
Jylha, M., 325

Kaasinen, V., 54
Kahneman, D., 225
Kainz, P. M., 94
Kaller, C. P., 226
Kallio, S., 138
Kamphaus, R. W., 363
Kandel, E. R., 70, 103
Kandell, E. R., 56
Kane, M. J., 367
Kanner, A. D., 501f
Kantrowitz, B., 123
Kaplan, J. R., 32
Kaplan, R. M., 358
Kassin, S. M., 19
Kato, T., 407
Katz, J., 104
Kaufmann, C. A., 403
Kawakami, K., 485
Kay, P., 233
Kaya, M. C., 450
Kazdin, A. E., 446
Keating, D. P., 305
Kehrer, C. A., 415
Keillor, J. M., 275
Keller, H., 368
Kellner, C. H., 454
Kelly, D., 369
Kelson, T., 309
Kemeny, M. E., 500
Kempermann, G., 71
Kendler, K. S., 145, 406
Kenneally, 47
Kennedy, J. F., 209
Kenshalo, D. R., 103f
Kenway, L., 131
Kersten, A., 221
Kerwin, R. W., 54
Kesmodel, U., 290
Kessler, D., 328
Kessler, R. C., 419
Khan, A. S., 27
Khayyer, M., 249
Kidd, K. K., 380
Kiecolt, J. K., 322
Kihlstrom, J. F., 138, 208, 404
Kilner, J. M., 94
Kim, H. S., 234
Kim, J-J., 274
Kim, J-W., 274
Kim, K. H., 235, 236f
Kim, S-E., 274

King, R. A., 451
Kinsey, A., 261
Kirk, K. M., 262
Kirkby, J., 130
Kirsch, I., 137
Kirschenbaum, H., 441, 442
Kisac, I., 499
Kitayama, S., 473
Kit-Fong Au, T., 295
Kleiber, D. A., 326
Kleinman, A., 421
Klerman, G. L., 442
Klötz, F., 61
Kluger, J., 399
Kluth, J., 465
Knoblich, G., 116
Knowles, J. A., 403
Knox, J., 138
Koch, K. L., 100
Koestner, R., 249
Koff, W. J., 263
Kohlberg, L., 311–312, 312
Kohler, C. G., 274
Kolata, G., 61
Konczak, J., 113
Kondo, T., 506
Konijn, E., 19
Koocher, G. P., 36
Kopelman, M. D., 416
Koplewicz, H., 416
Kopp, T. G., 355
Kosslyn, S. M., 221
Kostygina, A., 188
Kotov, R., 395
Kovacs, E. A., 301
Kovas, Y., 377
Kozak, A. T., 434
Kozulin, A., 306
Krieger, A., 123
Krieger, K. M., 443
Krijn, M., 434
Krueger, R. G., 495
Kübler-Ross, E., 328
Kuhlman, D. M., 246
Kumari, V., 262
Kunzmann, U., 321
Kuo, L-J., 235
Kuriyama, K., 131
Kvavilashvili, L., 203
Kwon, P., 407
Kwon, S. M., 401

Laas, I., 250
Labouliere, C. D., 434
Lacerda, F., 305
Ladd, D. R., 232
Laederach-Hofmann, K., 401
LaFuci, G., 60
Lagacé-Séguin, D. G., 301
Lai, Y., 105
Laing, D. G., 101
Laird, J. D., 269
Lamal, P. A., 5
Lamb, H. R., 456
Lamb, M. E., 298
Lana, R. E., 233
Lane, A. M., 352
Lane, K. A., 485

Lane, S. D., 152
Lang, A. J., 104
Lang, G., 105
Langan-Fox, J., 362
Langdon, R., 410
Lange, C., 269
Langer, E. J., 39
Langley, J., 245
Lankov, A., 321
Laqueur, T. W., 260
Larcher, V., 60
Laroi, F., 411
Larsen, R. J., 350
Larsen McClarty, K., 352
Larsson, M., 100
Larzelere, R. E., 174
Latané, B., 494f, 495
Latif, T., 454
Latner, J., 20
Latner, J. D., 179
Laucht, M., 148
Laukli, E., 323
Laurenceau, J. P., 407
Lauterbach, D., 437
Lavelli, M., 295
Lawson, M. J., 217
Lazarus, R. S., 500, 506
LeBow, M. D., 256
Leckman, J. F., 451
Lee, F., 235
Lee, H. J., 401
Lee, S., 473
Lee, S. H., 139
Lee, Y. J., 139
Lee-Chai, A. Y., 264
Lee-Chiong, T. L., 133
Lefaucheur, J. P., 454
Leffard, S. A., 363
Lehar, S., 109
Lehman, D. R., 248
Leibel, R. L., 256
Leitenberg, H., 260
Leitner, L. M., 447
Lemay, E. P., Jr., 472
Lemonick, M. D., 144
Lengua, L. J., 299, 301
Lens, W., 264
Lenzenweger, M. F., 411, 412, 414
Leo, R. J., 454
Lepage, J. F., 50, 186
Lepper, M. R., 249
Lepre, A., 498
Lesch, K. P., 59
Leu, J., 235
Levander, S., 450
Levant, R. F., 445
LeVay, S., 262
Levenson, R. W., 275
Levi, A., 468
Levin, J. R., 217
Levine, B., 324
Levine, J. M., 476
Levine, S. Z., 411
Levinson, D. J., 320
Levy, G., 282
Lewin-Epstein, N., 322
Lewinsohn, P. M., 407
Lewis, C. M., 443
Lewis, R., 92f

Mohapel, P., 54
Monteith, M. J., 485
Montejo, M., 187
Montepare, J. M., 489
Montgomery, C., 153
Moody, H. R., 322
Moore, B. C. J., 85
Moore, M. M., 26
Moorey, S., 439
Mora-Giral, M., 256
Moran, A., 221
Morano, M. I., 500
Moreland, R. L., 476
Moritz, S., 411
Morley, S., 104
Morone, N. E., 76
Morran, D. K., 443
Morris, E., 370
Morris, J. F., 263
Morrissey, S., 199
Morrone, A. S., 263
Morrow, J., 75
Morton, B. E., 73
Moselhy, H., 147
Mosher, C. J., 123, 144
Moskowitz, G. B., 470
Moskowitz, J. T., 499, 505, 506
Mu, X., 473
Muammar, O. M., 370
Mullen, B., 484
Müller, H., 109
Munakata, Y., 305
Muris, P., 401
Murphy, G. J., 101
Murphy, G. L., 221
Murphy, T., 429
Murray, D., 378
Murray, R. M., 413
Murray, S. L., 489
Myers, J., 145
Myers, L. L., 256
Myerson, J., 305

Nagai, Y., 76
Nagda, B. A., 486
Nagin, D. S., 415
Nahari, G., 470
Najman, J. M., 289
Nakamizo, S., 111
Nakamura, Y., 60
Nasir, N. S., 393
Nathan, P. E., 444
National Academy of Sciences, 152
National Association for the Education of
    Young Children, 300
National Center for Health Statistics, 296f
National Depression Screening Day, 406f
National Institute on Drug Abuse, 153
National Mental Health Information Center,
    U.S. Department of Health and Human
    Services, 456f
National Research Council, 299
Natvig, G. K., 506
Naveh-Benjamin, M., 215
Neitz, J., 94
Neitz, M., 94
Neron, S., 105
Nesdale, D., 483

Nesheim, S., 289
Nestler, E. J., 147
Nettlebeck, T., 217
Neubauer, A. C., 369
Newby-Clark, I. R., 211
Newell, A., 226
Newman, C. F., 407
Newman, M., 282
Newport, F., 257
Niccols, A., 290
NICHD Early Child Care Research Network,
    299, 300
Nickeas, R., 404
Nielsen, S. L., 444
Nigg, J. T., 414
Nikles, C. D., II, 130
Nimrod, G., 326
Nisbett, R. E., 379
Nissley, W., 47
Nittrouer, S., 86
Nixon, R. D. V., 246
Nolen-Hoeksema, S., 389, 400f, 408, 415
Norcross, J. C., 36, 445
Norton, P. J., 434
Nosek, B. A., 485
Novak, M. A., 37
Novotny, C. M., 444
Nowicki, S., Jr., 414
Noyes, R., Jr., 404
Ntinas, K. M., 179
Nurmi, J-E., 352
Nurnberger, J. I., Jr., 148
Nuss, C. K., 475
Nyberg, L., 204

Oberman, L. M., 51
O'Brien, K. M., 256
O'Doherty, J., 94
O'Donohue, W. T., 446
Oehman, A., 343
Offer, D., 211
Ogbu, J. U., 192
Oh, S-S., 505
Ohara, K., 412
O'Keefe, T., 263
Olatunji, B. O., 404
O'Leary, O. F., 451
Olijslagers, J. E., 54
Oliver, M. B., 260
Olliver-Gray, Y., 191
Olson, D. H., 321
Oltmanns, T. F., 414
Ommundsen, Y., 473
O'Neill, A., 253
Oordt, M. S., 257
Ornat, S. L., 232
Orozco, C., 151
Orwin, R. G., 444
Osborn, M. L., 390
O'Sullivan, M., 274
Ovarnstrom, U., 506

Pachankis, J. E., 444
Pagnin, A., 324
Pagonis, T. A., 61
Pagoto, S. L., 434
Palmerus, K., 174
Paluck, E. L., 486

Paniagua, F. A., 393, 447
Paquette, D., 298
Paquier, P. F., 67
Park, H., 478
Park, L. E., 352
Parke, R. D., 298
Parker-Pope, T., 257
Parnes, A., 202
Parrott, A. C., 153
Parsons, L. M., 67
Pascual, A., 476
Pascual, M. A., 170
Passer, M. W., 59f
Pate, W. E., II, 9
Patterson, D., 289
Patterson, D. R., 105
Paukert, A., 456
Paul, A. M., 364
Paulozzi, L. J., 147
Pavitt, C., 470
Pavlov, I. P., 14f, 162–163
Pazzaglia, F., 221
Pearson, A. R., 482
Pedersen, D. M., 249
Pedersen, P. B., 447
Pedersen, W. C., 493
Pellegrini, S., 175
Pelli, D. G., 94
Pellis, S. M., 298
Pellis, V. C., 298
Pence, D., 468
Penke, L., 379
Penley, J. A., 505
Penn, D. L., 410
Penney, J. B., Jr., 52
People, 281
Perez, R. M., 263
Perfetti, B., 367
Perlis, T., 147
Perrett, D. I., 489
Persinger, M. A., 67
Pervin, L. A., 355
Pesmen, C., 103, 105
Peters, E., 324
Peterson, R. A., 32
Peterson, S., 414
Petersson, K. M., 74
Pettigrew, T. F., 485
Pettito, L. A., 72, 230
Petty, R. E., 467
Phelps, E. A., 434
Philip, P., 129
Piaget, J., 15f, 303–305
Picchioni, D., 130
Pickard, N., 202
Pickering, G. J., 101
Piechowski, M. M., 250
Piel, E., 129
Pilcher, J. J., 128
Pillay, S. S., 401f
Pincus, H. A., 394
Pincus, T., 104
Pineda, J. A., 51
Pinel, J. P. J., 248
Pinker, S., 233, 283
Pinkerton, S. D., 260
Pinna, B., 94
Pintrich, P. R., 263
Piper, W., 443

Scheele, B., 493
Scheff, T. J., 389
Scheier, M., 328
Scheier, M. F., 326, 360
Schieber, F., 323
Schienle, A., 271
Schimpf, P. H., 67
Schlenger, W. E., 153
Schmajuk, N., 185
Schmidt, J. P., 52
Schmidt, N. B., 395
Schmitt, F. A., 324
Schnake, S. B., 470
Schneider, A., 129f
Schneider, D. J., 483
Schredl, M., 129
Schulte-Ruther, M., 50, 186
Schultz, G., 199
Schutt, R. K., 26
Schutte, N. S., 444
Schwartz, B. L., 207
Schwartz, J. H., 56
Schwarz, N., 485
Seamon, M. J., 152
Sebanz, N., 116
Sebel, P. S., 208
Seeley, R., 66f
Sefcek, J. A., 8
Segall, M. H., 114
Seli, H., 245
Seligman, M. E. P., 407, 444,
    445, 505
Sellbom, M., 359
Sells, R., 261
Selove, R., 289
Selsky, A., 317
Selye, H., 503
Semin, G. R., 230, 470
Semykina, A., 264
Seroczynski, A. D., 416
Serpell, R., 378
Sestir, M. A., 188
Shafer, V. L., 230
Shaikholeslami, R., 249
Shapiro, C. J., 416
Shapiro, L. R., 210
Shapiro, S. L., 139
Shastri, J., 299
Shaver, P. R., 268f
Sheehan, S., 409
Shelton, R. C., 451
Shen, C. K., 71
Shen, L., 268
Shier, D., 92f
Shiffrin, R. M., 210
Shimono, K., 113
Shinn, M., 456
Shurkin, J. N., 378
Shweder, R. A., 269
Sidman, M., 174
Siegel, B., 140
Siegel, J. M., 128
Sierra-Biddle, D., 401
Silbersweig, D. A., 412
Silverman, M. M., 429
Silverstein, M. L., 362
Simon, H., 226
Simon, T., 372
Simonds, V. M., 166

Singer, J. E., 271
Sininger, Y. S., 100
Skinner, B. F., 15f, 17, 170–171, 232, 350
Sloan, E. P., 134
Slomkowski, C., 421, 422
Smetana, J., 315
Smetana, J. B., 343
Smetana, J. G., 315
Smith, B. H., 416
Smith, C., 131
Smith, C. A., 506
Smith, C. D., 74
Smith, D., 134
Smith, D. B., 387
Smith, E. R., 470
Smith, K., 132
Smith, L., 232
Smith, M. L., 444, 445f
Smith, R. A., 488
Smith, R. E., 59f
Smith, S. E., 498
Smith, W. B., 344
Smith-Crowe, K., 489
Smitherman, T. A., 434
Snyder, D. J., 101
Snyder, J., 301
Snyder, M., 355
Snyder, S. H., 411, 450
Society for Personality Assessment, 362
Sohr-Preston, S. L., 288
Sokolove, M., 389
Sommer, B., 27
Sommer, R., 27
Sorbring, E., 174
Sorek, S., 215
Sorrell, J. T., 104
Soussignan, R., 275
Spanos, N. P., 105, 137
Spates, C. R., 434
Spearman, C., 367
Spector, P. E., 371
Speirs Neumeister, K. L., 263
Spencer, D., 209
Spencer, S. J., 472
Sperry, R., 74
Spiegel, D., 404, 445
Spiller, L. D., 478
Spillmann, L., 94
Spitoni, G., 367
Sprecher, S., 261
Springen, K., 124
Sriram, N., 485
Staddon, J. E. R., 174
Stagner, B., 456
Staley, J. K., 406
Stankov, L., 324, 367
Stapel, D. A., 230
Stark, J., 71
Stark, R., 271
Stark, S., 71
Steele, C. M., 148
Stegerwald, F., 263
Steiger, A., 128
Stein, L. A. R., 360
Steiner, B., 71
Steiner, R. D., 289
Steinhardt, M. A., 498
Steketee, G., 402, 403
Stemler, S. E., 370

Stenbacka, L., 70
Stenklev, N. C., 323
Stephens, T., 66f
Stephenson, R., 105
Stephenson, R. H., 253
Stepp, S. D., 415
Stern, E., 412
Stern, R. M., 100
Sternberg, R. J., 25, 284, 367, 369, 370, 371f,
    372, 380, 446, 489–490, 490
Stettler, N., 255
Stevens, G., 15
Stevens, P., 454
Stevenson, H. W., 473
Stevenson, R. J., 100
Stewart, A. J., 321
Stewart, P. J., 212
Stewart, W. F., 103
Stickgold, R., 131
Stickgold, R. A., 129
Stickley, T., 404
Stier, H., 322
Stilling, P., 75f
Stillman, T., 259
Stockton, R., 443
Stompe, T., 410
Stouffer, E. M., 185
Strathern, A., 212
Strauss, E., 74
Strayer, D. L., 19
Striano, T., 295
Striegel-Moore, R., 256
Strong, T., 443
Stronski, S. M., 315
Strupp, H. H., 444
Stuart, S. P., 444
Suchecki, D., 245
Sue, D., 446
Sue, D. W., 446
Sue, S., 446
Sullivan, A., 368
Sun, T., 71
Surette, R., 188
Sutin, A. R., 211
Suzuki, L. A., 378
Svartdal, F., 175
Swales, M. A., 437
Swann, W. B., Jr., 352
Swanson, H. L., 416

Tadmor, C. T., 235
Taggi, F., 19
Tajfel, H., 483
Takizawa, T., 506
Talbot, N., 404
Talukdar, S., 299
Tam, T. W., 147
Tamagnan, G., 406
Tangney, B., 369
Tanner, J. M., 310
Taras, H., 289
Tate, P., 66f
Tausch, R., 441
Taylor, F., 129
Taylor, J. A., 399
Taylor, S. E., 506, 507
Tcheremissine, O. V., 152
Tees, R. C., 288
Tellegen, A., 353f

SUBJECT INDEX

Benzedrine, 146f
Bereavement support groups, 444
Beta amyloid precursor protein, 325
Bias
    attribution, 471–473
    experimental, 38–39
Biculturalism, 235
Big Five personality traits, 349, 349f
Bilingual education, 234–235, 235f, 236f
Bilingualism, brain and, 235, 236f
Binocular disparity, 112
Biofeedback, 75–76
    for pain management, 105
Biological and evolutionary approaches to
        personality, 353–354
Biological influences
    in children, 411–412, 412f, 413f
    in emotion, 269–272, 272f
Biomedical therapies, 449–458
    community psychology and, 455–456, 456f
    drug therapy, 449–452, 450f
    electroconvulsive therapy, 454
    patient rights and, 453
    transcranial magnetic stimulation, 454
Biopsychologists, 47
Bipolar disorder, 407
Bisexuality, 261
Blind spot, 91, 92f, 93
BMI. See Body mass index (BMI)
Bodily kinesthetic intelligence, 368f
Body mass index (BMI), 254
Borderline personality disorder, 414–415
Bottom-up processing, 110
Brain, 57, 58f, 64–77
    anorexia nervosa and, 256, 257f
    auditory messages to, 99
    bilingualism and, 235, 236f
    central core of ("old brain"), 66f, 66–67
    cerebral cortex of ("new brain"), 68–70, 69f
    electroencephalography and, 64–65, 65f
    emotion and, 270, 271–272, 272f
    hemispheric specialization and, 71–76
    hunger and, 254
    limbic system of, 67f, 67–68
    mood disorders and, 408, 408f
    neuroimaging of, 64, 65, 65f
    neuroplasticity and, 71
    sexual orientation and, 262
    visual signals to, 91, 93, 93f
Brain stimulation
    for pain management, 105
    transcranial magnetic stimulation, 65,
        65f, 454
Broca's area, 69f
Bulimia, 256

Caffeine, 144f, 144–145
Canabis, 146f
Cannon-Bard theory of emotion, 270, 270f
Caring, morality of, 312
Case study, 27–28, 33f
Castration anxiety, 339
Cataclysmic events, 499
Catharsis, 492–493
Causation, correlation versus, 28–29
Cell phones, driving ability and, 19
Central core, 66f, 66–67
Central nervous system (CNS), 56–57,
    57f, 58f. See also Brain

Central route processing, 467
Central traits, 470
Cerebellum, 66f, 66–67
Cerebral cortex, 66f, 68–70
    association areas of, 69f, 70
    motor area of, 68–69, 69f
    sensory area of, 69f, 69–70
Child care, consequences of, 299f, 299–300
Childhood. See also Infant and
        child development
    psychological disorders in, 415–416
Chlorpromazine, 450
Chromosomes, 60, 286
Chunks, 202
Circadian rhythms, 133f, 133–134
Classical conditioning, 162–168
    application to human behavior, 165
    aversive, 434
    definition of, 163
    extinction in, 165–166, 166f
    operant conditioning versus, 177–178, 178f
    Pavlov's experiments on, 162–163
    spontaneous recovery in, 166
    stimulus discrimination in, 167
    stimulus generalization in, 167
    treatments based on, 434–436
Client-centered therapy, 441–442
Clinical mental health counselors, 431f
Clinical neuropsychology, 6f, 8
Clinical psychologists, 431f
Clinical psychology, 6f, 7
Clinical social workers, 431f
Close relationships, 488. See also
        Interpersonal attraction
Closure, principle of, 108, 108f
CNS. See Brain; Central nervous
    system (CNS)
Cocaine, 145, 146f, 147
Cochlea, 99, 99f
Cognition, social, 469–473
Cognitive appraisal, 439
Cognitive approaches to motivation, 248–249
Cognitive-behavioral approach, 437
Cognitive changes in late adulthood,
    323–325, 324f
Cognitive development
    in adolescence, 310–312
    culture and, 306
    in infancy and childhood, 302–306
    information-processing approaches to,
        305–306, 306f
    Piaget's theory of, 303f, 303–305
    Vygotsky's theory of, 306
Cognitive dissonance, 468–469, 469f
Cognitive learning theory, 183–193
    cultural influences and, 188, 191, 191f
    latent learning and, 184f, 184–185
    observational learning and, 185–188, 187f
Cognitive maps, 185
Cognitive perspective, 16f, 17–18
    on key issues and controversies, 20t
Cognitive perspective on psychological
        disorders, 390f, 391–392
Cognitive psychology, 6, 199. See also
        Language; Memory; Thinking
Cognitive restructuring for pain
        management, 105
Cognitive therapy, 438–439
Cognitive treatment approaches, 437–439

cognitive therapy, 438–439
    evaluation of, 439
    rational-emotive therapy, 438
Cohorts, 285
Collective unconscious, 343
Collectivistic orientation, 473
College students as research subjects, 37
Color vision, 94–96
    opponent-process theory of, 96
    trichromatic theory of, 95–96
Community psychology, 455–456, 456f
Comorbidity, 419
Companionate love, 489
Compliance, 477–478
Compulsions, 402
Concept(s), 221–222, 222f
Conception, 286
Concrete operational stage, 303f, 304
Conditional positive regard, 355
Conditioned response (CR), 164
Conditioned stimulus (CS), 164
Conditioning. See Classical conditioning;
    Operant conditioning
Cones, 91, 92f
Conformity, 475–477, 476f
    to social roles, 476–477
Conscience, 338
Conscientiousness, 349, 349f
Consciousness
    altered states of. See Altered states of
        consciousness
    definition of, 123
Conscious versus unconscious determinants
    of behavior issue, 20f, 21
Consent, informed, 36
Constructive processes in memory, 210–213
Contingency contracting, 436
Continuous reinforcement schedule, 174–175
Control group, 30
Conversion disorders, 404
Coping with stress, 504–507
    effective strategies for, 506–507
    learned helplessness and, 505
    social support and, 505–506
Cornea, 90, 92f
Corpus callosum, 66f
    cutting of, 74–75
Correlation(s), 28–29
    causation versus, 28–29
Correlational research, 28–29, 29f, 33f
Counseling psychologists, 431f
Counseling psychology, 6f, 7
CR. See Conditioned response (CR)
Critical periods in fetal development, 288
Cross-cultural psychology, 6f, 7
Cross-sectional research, 285
Crystallized intelligence, 324, 367
CS. See Conditioned stimulus (CS)
Cue-dependent forgetting, 215–216
Culture
    altered states of consciousness and, 140–141
    biculturalism and, 235
    cognitive development and, 306
    emotional expression and, 273f, 273–275
    fundament attribution bias and, 472–473
    intellectual ability and, 378
    learning and, 188, 191, 191f
    memory and, 212
    perception and, 115f, 115–116

Forensic psychology, 6f, 7
Forgetting, 213–217, 214f
  cue-dependent, 215–216
  decay and, 215
  encoding failure and, 215
  interference and, 215, 216, 216f
  reasons for, 215f, 215–216
Formal operational stage, 303f, 304–305
Fovea, 91, 92f
Free association, 432
Free will, 18, 21
Free will versus determinism issue, 20f, 21
Freudian slips, 336–337
Freud's theory of personality. *See*
    Psychoanalytic theory
Frontal lobes, 68, 69f
Frustration-aggression theory, 493
Fugue, dissociative, 405
Functional fixedness, 227
Functionalism, 13
Functional magnetic resonance imaging
    (fMRI), 65
Fundamental attribution error, 472–473

GABA. *See* Gamma-aminobutyric acid
    (GABA)
Gag reflex, 294
Gamma-aminobutyric acid (GABA), 53f
Gardner's multiple intelligences, 367–369,
    368f
GAS. *See* General adaptation syndrome (GAS)
Gate-control theory of pain, 104
Gender roles, 321–322
Gene(s), 60, 286
General adaptation syndrome (GAS), 503f,
    503–504
Generalized anxiety disorder, 401, 402f
Generativity-versus-stagnation stage, 313f,
    314
Gene therapy, 60
Genetic influences. *See also* Nature-nurture
    issue
  on fetus, 289
Genetic programming theories of aging, 323
Genetics
  behavioral, 8, 59–61
  principles of, 286–287, 287f
Genital(s), 258–259, 259f
Genital stage, 340
Genome, 60
German measles, fetal development and, 290f
Germinal period, 287
Gerontologists, 322
Gestalt laws of organization, 108f, 108–109
Gestalt psychology, 13–14
g-factor, 366–367
Giftedness, 377–378
Glutamate, 53f
Graded exposure, 436
Group therapy, 442–443
Gustation, 101–102

Habituation, 162
Hair cells, 99
Hallucinations in schizophrenia,
    410f, 410–411
Hallucinogens, 146f, 151–153
  ecstasy, 153
  marijuana, 146f, 151–152, 152f

MDMA, 146f, 153
Halo effect, 471–472
Hammer, 98, 99f
Hashish, 146f
Hash oil, 146f
Health psychology, 6f, 7
Hearing, 99–100
Heart, hormone of, 62f
Helping behavior, 494f, 494–495
Helplessness, learned, 505
Hemimegalencephaly, 47
Hemispheres of brain, 71–76
Hemispheric specialization, 71–76
Heritability of intellectual ability, 379, 379f
Heroin, 146f, 151
Heterosexuality, 260
Heuristics, 223
Hindbrain, 66
Hippocampus, 67, 67f
  emotion and, 272
Homeostasis, 67, 245–246
Homosexuality, 261–263
Hormone(s), 61, 62f
  sex, 258, 262
Hormone replacement therapy (HRT), 61
Hormone therapy (HT), 320
Horney's neo-Freudian perspective, 343–344
Hotlines for drug and alcohol problems, 154
HRT. *See* Hormone replacement therapy
    (HRT)
HT. *See* Hormone therapy (HT)
Humanistic approaches to personality,
    354–355
Humanistic perspective, 16f, 18
  on key issues and controversies, 20f
  on psychological disorders, 390f, 392
Humanistic therapy, 441–442
  evaluation of, 442
  person-centered therapy, 441–442
Hunger and eating, 253–258, 254f
  biological factors in regulation of hunger
    and, 254–255
  dieting and weight loss and, 257–258
  eating disorders and, 256–257, 257f
  obesity and, 253–254, 255–256
  social factors in eating and, 255
Hypnosis, 137–138
  for pain management, 105
Hypochondriasis, 403–404
Hypothalamus, 66f, 67
  hormones of, 62f
  hunger and, 254
Hypotheses, 25

IAT. *See* Implicit Association Test (IAT)
Id, 337, 337f, 338
Identical twins, 284
Identification, 339–340
Identity, 312
Identity-versus-role confusion stage,
    312–313, 313f
Ill-defined problems, 224
Illness, maternal, prenatal development
    and, 289, 290f
Illusions, 113–116, 114f, 115f
Immersion programs for bilingual education,
    234–235
Implicit Association Test (IAT), 484–485
Implicit memory, 209

Impression formation, 470–471
Incentive approaches to motivation, 246, 248
Independent variable, 30–31
Individual differences versus universal
    principles issue, 20f, 21
Individualist orientation, 473
Industrial-organizational (I/O)
    psychology, 6f, 478
Industry-versus-inferiority stage, 302, 313f
Ineffability, 141
Infant(s)
  newborn. *See* Newborns
  preterm, 288–289
Infant and child development, 296–306
  cognitive, 302–306
  physical, 296, 296f
  social, 297–302
Inferiority complex, 344
Information processing, 18
Information-processing approach
  to cognitive development, 305–306, 306f
  to intelligence, 368f
Informed consent, 36
Inhibitory messages, 52
Initiative-versus-guilt stage, 302, 313f
Inner ear, 99, 99f
Insomnia, 132
Instincts, 244
  aggression and, 492–493
Intellectual disabilities, 376–377
Intellectually gifted, 377–378
Intelligence, 366–381
  assessment of. *See* Intelligence tests
  crystallized, 324, 367
  definition of, 366
  emotional, 370–371, 371f
  fluid, 324, 367
  Gardner's multiple intelligences and,
    367–369, 368f
  genetics and environment and,
    378–380, 379f
  g-factor and, 366–367
  giftedness and, 377–378
  information-processing approach to, 368f
  mental retardation and, 376–377
  practical, 370, 371f
Intelligence quotient (IQ), 373f, 373–374
Intelligence tests, 371–376
  contemporary, 374f–375f, 374–376
  culture-fair, 378
  development of, 372–374, 373f
  group, 375–376
  scores on, 373f, 373–374
Interactionist approach to language
    development, 233
Interference, 215, 216, 216f
Intermittent reinforcement schedule, 174–175
Interneurons, 57
Interpersonal attraction, 488–491
  liking and, 488–489
  love and, 489–491, 490f, 491f
Interpersonal intelligence, 368f
Interpersonal therapy (IPT), 442
Intimacy-versus-isolation stage, 313f, 314
Intrapersonal intelligence, 368f
Intrinsic motivation, 248–249
Introspection, 13
I/O psychology. *See* Industrial-organizational
    (I/O) psychology

Nature versus nurture issue, 20f, 21
Needs
    for achievement, 263
    for affiliation, 264
    Maslow's hierarchy of, 249–250, 250f
    for power, 264–265
Negative correlations, 28
Negative punishment, 172
Negative reinforcers, 171–172, 173f
Negative-symptom schizophrenia, 411
Nembutal, 146f
Neo-Freudian psychoanalysts, 342
Neo-Freudian theories of personality,
    342–344
Neonates, 293. See also Newborns
Nerve stimulation for pain management, 105
Nervous system, 56–61
    central, 56–57, 57f, 58f. See also Brain
    peripheral, 56, 57f, 58
Neural impulses, 49
Neurogenesis, 71
Neuroimaging, 64, 65, 65f
Neurons, 48–54
    firing of, 49–51, 50f
    ions, 57
    mirror, 51–52, 186
    motor (efferent), 57
    sensory (afferent), 57
    structure of, 48–49, 49f
    synapses between, 51f, 51–52
Neuroplasticity, brain and, 71
Neuroscience perspective, 16f, 16–17
    on key issues and controversies, 20f
Neuroscientists, 47
Neuroticism, 348f, 348–349, 349, 349f
Neurotic symptoms, 430
Neurotransmitters, 52–54, 53f
Neutral stimulus, 163
Newborns, 293–296
    preterm, 288–289
    reflexes of, 294, 294f
    sensory development of, 295f, 295–296
"New brain," 68–70, 69f
Nicotine use, 145
    maternal, prenatal development and,
        290, 290f
Night terrors, 132
Noise in psychophysics, 85
Nondeclarative memory, 204
Norms
    conformity and, 475
    psychological tests and, 359
    reducing prejudice and discrimination
        and, 485
Note taking, 217
Not-so-free sample, 478
Nutrition, maternal, prenatal development
    and, 289, 290f

Obedience, 478–480, 479f
Obesity, 20
    roots of, 255–256
Object permanence, 303–304
Observable behavior versus internal mental
    processes issue, 20f, 21
Observation, naturalistic, 26–27, 33f
Observational learning, 185–188, 187f
    of aggression, 493–494
    personality and, 351

of prejudice and discrimination, 483–484
    therapeutic use of, 436
    violence in television and, 187–188
Obsessions, 40
Obsessive-compulsive disorder, 401–402
Occipital lobes, 68, 69f
Oedipal conflict, 339
"Old brain," 66f, 66–67
Olfaction, 100–101
Olfactory cells, 100, 101
Openness to experience, 349, 349f
Operant conditioning, 170–181
    behavior analysis and behavior modification
        and, 178–181
    classical conditioning versus, 177–178, 178f
    definition of, 170
    reinforcement and. See Reinforcement
    Skinner's experiments on, 170–171, 171f
    treatments based on, 436
Operational definitions, 25
Opponent-process theory of color vision, 96
Optic chiasm, 93, 93f
Optic nerve, 91, 93, 93f
Oral stage, 338–339, 339f
Organization cues, 217
Otoliths, 100
Ovaries, hormones of, 62f
Overgeneralization, 231–232
Overlearning, 217
Ovulation, 258–259

Pain
    gate-control theory of, 104
    management of, 104–105
Pancreas, hormone of, 62f
Panic attacks, 400–401
Panic disorder, 400–401
Parasympathetic division, 57f, 58, 59
Parenting, father's role in, 298
Parenting styles
    social development and, 300f, 300–301
    and temperament, 301
Parietal lobes, 68, 69f
Parkinson's disease, 53, 54
Partial reinforcement schedule, 174–175
Participants
    expectations of, 38–39
    in research studies, 30
Passionate love, 489
Patient rights, 453
Peer relationships in childhood, 298–299
Perception, 107f, 107–117
    culture and, 115f, 115–116
    definition of, 84
    depth, 111–113
    gestalt laws of organization and, 108f,
        108–109
    illusions and, 113–116, 114f, 115f
    motion, 113
    perceptual constancy and, 110–111
    top-down and bottom-up processing and,
        109–110, 110f
Perceptual constancy, 110–111
Perceptual disorders in schizophrenia, 410f,
    410–411
Peripheral nervous system (PNS), 56, 57f, 58
Peripheral route processing, 467
Peripheral vision, 91
Permissive parents, 300, 300f, 301

Personality
    assessment of. See Personality assessment
    biological and evolutionary approaches to,
        353–354
    comparing approaches to, 255, 256f
    definition of, 335
    humanistic approaches to, 354–355
    learning approaches to, 350–352
    psychodynamic approaches to, 336–342
    social cognitive approaches to, 351–352
    trait theories of, 348–350
Personality assessment, 358–365
    assessment of, 364
    behavioral, 363–364
    projective methods for, 362, 362f
    self-report measures for, 359–361, 361f
Personality disorders, 413–415
Personality psychology, 6f, 7
Personal stressors, 499
Person-centered therapy, 441–442
Perspective, linear, 113
Persuasion, 466–469
    link between attitudes and behavior and,
        468–469, 469f
    routes to, 467, 468f
PET. See Positron emission tomography (PET)
Phallic stage, 339
Ph.D. degree, 10
Phenobarbital, 146f
Phenylketonuria (PKU), 289
Phobias, 300f, 399–400
Phobic disorder, 300f, 399–400
Photosynthesis, real-world applications of,
    18–20
Physical attractiveness, liking and, 489
Physical development
    in adolescence, 309–310, 310f
    in adulthood, 319–320
    in infancy and childhood, 296, 296f
Piaget's theory of cognitive development,
    303f, 303–305
Pineal gland, hormone of, 62f
Pituitary gland, 61, 62, 62f, 66f
    hormones of, 62f
PKU. See Phenylketonuria (PKU)
Placebos, 39
Plasticity, brain and, 71
Pleasure principle, 337
PNI. See Psychoneuroimmunology (PNI)
PNS. See Peripheral nervous system (PNS)
Pons, 66, 66f
Populations, 27
Positive correlations, 28
Positive punishment, 172
Positive reinforcers, 171–172, 173f
Positive-symptom schizophrenia, 411
Positron emission tomography (PET), 65
Posttraumatic stress disorder
    (PTSD), 499–500
Power, need for, 264–265
Practical intelligence, 370, 371f
Practice, 217
Preconscious, 336–337
Predisposition model of schizophrenia, 413
Prejudice, 482–486
    foundations of, 483–484
    measurement of, 484–485
    reducing, 485–486
Premarital sex, 260

Prenatal development, 286–290
  embryonic period of, 287–289
  environmental influences in, 289–290, 290f
  fetal period of, 287–289, 288f
  genetic influences in, 289
  genetic principles and, 286–287, 287f
  germinal period of, 287–289
  sensitive (critical) periods in, 288
Preoperational stage, 303f, 304
Preterm infants, 288–289
Primary drives, 245
Primary reinforcers, 171
Principle of conservation, 304
Proactive interferences, 216, 216f
Problem solving, 223f, 223–227, 224f
  evaluating solutions and, 226
  generating solutions and, 225–226
  impediments to solutions and, 226–227, 227f, 228f
  understanding and diagnosing problems and, 224–225, 225f
Procedural memory, 204
Profound retardation, 376
Progesterone, 258
Program evaluation, 6f
Projection, 341f
Projective personality tests, 362, 362f
Prosocial behavior, 494f, 494–495
Prototypes, 222
Proximity
  liking and, 488
  principle of, 108, 108f
Psychedelic drugs. See Hallucinogens
Psychiatric social workers, 431f
Psychiatrists, 431f
Psychoactive drugs, 142f, 142–154, 143f
  addiction and, 143
  depressants, 146f, 147f, 147–149, 149f
  hallucinogens, 146f, 151–153
  identifying drug and alcohol problems and, 153–154
  identifying problems with, 153–154
  narcotics, 146f, 151
  stimulants, 144f, 144–147, 146f
Psychoanalysis, 342, 432
Psychoanalysts, 431f
Psychoanalytic perspective on psychological disorders, 390f, 391
Psychoanalytic theory, 336–342
  defense mechanisms and, 340–341, 341f
  evaluation of, 341–342
  personality structure and, 337f, 337–338
  psychosexual stages and, 338–340, 339f
Psychodynamic approaches to personality, 336–342
Psychodynamic perspective, 16f, 17
  on key issues and controversies, 20f
Psychodynamic therapy, 430–433
  contemporary approaches to, 433
  evaluation of, 433
  psychoanalysis, 432
Psychological disorders, 386–426
  abnormality defined and, 388–389
  anxiety disorders, 397–403
  behavioral perspective on, 390f, 391
  in childhood, 415–416
  classification of, 393–395, 394f
  cognitive perspective on, 390f, 391–392
  dissociative disorders, 404–405

eclectic approach to, 429, 446
  humanistic perspective on, 390f, 392
  medical perspective on, 390f, 390–391
  mood disorders, 405–409
  personality disorders, 413–415
  prevalence of, 419–420, 420f
  psychoanalytic perspective on, 390f, 391
  schizophrenia, 409f, 409–413, 410f
  seeking help for, 422
  social and cultural context of, 420–422
  sociocultural perspective on, 390f, 392–393
  somatoform disorders, 403–404
  treatment of, 428–458. See also Biomedical therapies; Psychotherapy
Psychological tests, 27, 358–359
Psychologists, 8f, 8–9, 431f
  education of, 10
Psychology
  definition of, 4
  key issues and controversies in, 20–22
  perspectives on, 16f, 16–18
  roots of, 13–15, 15f–16f
  subfields of, 4–8
  testing your knowledge of, 5
Psychology of women, 6f
Psychoneuroimmunology (PNI), 504
Psychophysics, 85
Psychophysiological disorders, 501
Psychosexual stages, 338–340, 339f
Psychosocial development, Erikson's theory of, 301–302, 312–314, 313f
Psychosomatic disorders, 501
Psychotherapy, 430–447
  behavioral approaches to, 433–437
  choosing therapist for, 457f, 457–458
  cognitive approaches to, 437–439
  evaluation of, 444–446, 445f
  family, 443
  group, 442–443
  humanistic, 441–442
  interpersonal, 442
  psychodynamic, 430–433
  racial and ethnic factors in, 446–447
  self-help, 443–444
  therapists providing, 430, 431f
Psychoticism, 348f, 348–349
Psy.D. degree, 10
PTSD. See Posttraumatic stress disorder (PTSD)
Puberty, 310
Punishment, 172–174, 173f
  positive and negative, 172
  reinforcement versus, 173–175
Pupil, 90, 91f

Radiation, prenatal development and, 290f
Random assignment to condition, 31–32
Rapid eye movement (REM) sleep, 125, 126f, 127, 128
Rational-emotive therapy, 438
Rationalization, 341f
Reaction formation, 341f
Reasoning, 222–227
  algorithms and, 223
  heuristic autonomic nervous system, 223
  moral, 311f, 311–312
  problem solving and, 223f, 223–227, 224f
Rebound effect, REM sleep and, 127
Receptive learning style, 189–190, 191f

Reciprocity-of-liking effect, 489
Recognition, 207, 207f, 208f
Reflexes, 56–57, 294
  in newborn, 294, 294f
Refraction, 90
Regenerative powers of brain, 71
Regression, 341f
Rehearsal, 203, 217
Reinforcement, 171–177
  positive and negative reinforcers and, 171–172, 173f
  punishment and, 172–174, 173f
  punishment versus, 173–175
  schedules of, 174–177
Reinforcers, 171–172
  positive and negative, 171–172, 173f
  primary and secondary, 171
Relational learning style, 191–192
Relationships
  close, 488. See also Interpersonal attraction
  style of, 492
Relative size, 113
Relaxation techniques for pain management, 105
REM sleep, 125, 126f, 127, 128
Replication, 32
Repressed memories, 405
Repression, 340–341, 341f
Research, 24–34, 33f
  animals as subjects for, 37–38
  cross-sectional, 285
  descriptive, 26–29, 33f
  ethics of, 36–37
  evaluating, 39–40
  experimental, 29–32, 33f
  experimental bias in, 38–39
  longitudinal, 285–286
  scientific method and, 24–26, 25f
  sequential, 286
Resistance stage of general adaptation syndrome, 503
Response
  conditioned, 164
  unconditioned, 163
Responsibility, diffusion of, 494–495
Resting state, 49
Reticular formation, 66f, 67
Retina, 91, 92f
Retrieval cues, 207, 207f, 208f
Retroactive interferences, 216, 216f
Reuptake, 52
Rites of passage, 317
Rods, 91, 92f
Rogers' humanistic approach to personality, 354–355
Rohypnol, 146f, 149
Roles
  gender, 321–322
  social, conformity to, 476–477
Romantic love, 489
Rooting reflex, 294
Rorschach test, 362, 362f
Rubella, fetal development and, 290f

St. John's wort, 451
Samples, 27
Scaffolding, 306
Schachter-Singer theory of emotion, 270f, 271
Schedules of reinforcement, 174–177

Schemas
  memory and, 211
  social cognition and, 469–470
Schizophrenia, 409f, 409–413, 410f
  biological causes of, 411–412, 412f, 413f
  characteristics of, 410f, 410–411
  definition of, 409
  environmental perspectives on, 412–413
  multiple causes of, 413
  positive and negative symptoms of, 411
  predisposition model of, 413
  types of, 409, 409f, 411
Scientific method, 24–26, 25f
  hypotheses and, 25
  theories and, 24–25
Seconal, 146f
Secondary drives, 245
Secondary reinforcers, 171
Securely attached babies, 297–298
Selective serotonin reuptake inhibitors
    (SSRIs), 450f, 451
Self-actualization, 249–250
  Obesity, 253–254, 354–355
Self-concept, 354–355
Self-efficacy, 351–352
Self-esteem, 352
Self-fulfilling prophecies, 482–483
Self-help therapy, 443–444
Self-report measures of personality,
    359–361, 361f
Self-serving bias, 472
Semantic memory, 204
Semicircular canals, 99f, 100
Sensation, 82–117, 84–87. See also Hearing;
    Vision
  absolute threshold and, 85, 85f
  definition of, 84
  light and, 89f, 89–90
  sound and, 98–100, 99f
Sensation seeking, 247–248
Sensitive periods in fetal development, 288
Sensorimotor stage, 303f, 303–304
Sensory adaptation, 87
Sensory area of cerebral cortex, 69f,
    69–70
Sensory development in infancy, 295f,
    295–296
Sensory memory, 201, 201f, 202
Sensory neurons, 57
Sequential research, 286
Serotonin, 53f
Set point for weight, 254–255
Severe retardation, 376
Sex determination, 286–287
Sex hormones, 258
Sexual behavior, 258–263, 259f
  heterosexuality and, 260
  marital sex and, 260–261
  masturbation and, 260
  premarital sex and, 260
  sexual orientation and, 260, 261–263
Sexuality in adolescence, 310
Sexual orientation, 260, 261–263
Shaping, 177–178
  classical versus operant conditioning and,
    177–178, 178f
Sickle-cell anemia, 289
SIDS. See Sudden infant death syndrome
    (SIDS)

Similarity
  liking and, 489
  principle of, 108f, 109
Simplicity, principle of, 108f, 109
Situational causes, 471
Size, relative, 113
Skinner's behaviorist approach to personality,
    350–351
Skin senses, 102–105, 103f
Sleep, 124–129
  amount needed, 128f, 128–129
  disturbances of, 132–133
  dreaming and, 129f, 129–131, 130f
  functions of, 128
  improving, 134
  REM, 125, 126f, 127, 128
  stages of, 124–127, 126f
Sleep apnea, 132
Sleep spindles, 125
Sleeptalking, 133
Sleepwalking, 133
Small intestine, hormones of, 62f
Smell sense, 100–101
Social bonds in infancy, 297, 297f
Social cognition, 469–473
  attribution and, 471–473
  impression formation and, 470–471
  understanding others and, 469–470
Social cognitive approaches
  to learning, 185
  to personality, 351–352
Social development
  in adolescence, 312–317
  in adulthood, 320–321
  in infancy and childhood, 297–302
Social factors
  in eating, 255
  in psychological disorders, 420–421
Social identity theory of prejudice and
    discrimination, 483–484
Social influence, 475–480
  definition of, 475
Social phobia, 400f
Social psychology, 6f, 7, 464–507
  aggression and, 491–494
  compliance and, 477–478
  conformity and, 469–473
  definition of, 465
  liking and love and, 488–491
  obedience and, 478–480, 479f
  persuasion and, 466–469
  prejudice and discrimination and, 482–486
  prosocial behavior and, 494f, 494–495
  social cognition and, 475–477, 476f
  stress and. See Stress
Social roles, conformity to, 476–477
Social support, coping with stress and,
    505–506
Social workers, 431f
Social world in late adulthood, 325–328
Sociocultural perspective on psychological
    disorders, 390f, 392–393
Somatic division, 57f, 58
Somatoform disorders, 403–404
  conversion disorders, 404
  hypochondriasis, 403–404
Somatosensory area of cerebral cortex, 69f, 70
Sound, sensing, 98–100
Sound localization, 98

Spatial intelligence, 368f
Specific phobias, 400f
Spermarche, 310
Spinal cord, 56–57, 58f, 66f
Split brain patients, 74–75
Spontaneous recovery, 166
Spontaneous remission, 444
Sport psychology, 6t
SSRIs. See Selective serotonin reuptake
    inhibitors (SSRIs)
Stage 1 sleep, 125, 126f, 127
Stage 2 sleep, 125, 126f, 127
Stage 3 sleep, 125, 126f, 127
Stage 4 sleep, 124, 126f, 127
Stanford-Binet Intelligence Scale, 374
Startle reflex, 294
Stereotypes, 482
  reducing prejudice and discrimination and,
    485, 486
Steroids, 61, 62, 62f
Stimulants, 144f, 144–147, 146f
Stimulus, 84
  conditioned, 164
  neutral, 163
  unconditioned, 163
Stimulus discrimination, 167
Stimulus generalization, 167
Stirrup, 99, 99f
Stomach, hormones of, 62f
Stress, 498–507
  assessing level of, 502
  coping with, 504–507
  cost of, 500–502, 502f
  definition of, 498
  general adaptation syndrome and, 503f,
    503–504
  psychoneuroimmunology and, 504
  stressors and, 498–500
Stressors, 498–500
  categorizing, 499–500, 501f
Structuralism, 13
Subjects in research studies, 30
Sublimation, 341f
Substance P, 103
Sucking reflex, 294
Sudden infant death syndrome (SIDS), 132
Suicide in adolescence, 315–316, 316f
Sulci, 68
Superego, 337f, 338
Surgery for pain management, 105
Survey research, 27, 33f
Sympathetic division, 57f, 58, 59
Synapses, 51f, 51–52
Syphilis, fetal development and, 290f
Systematic desensitization, 434–435, 435f

Taste buds, 101, 102
Taste sense, 101–102
TAT. See Thematic Apperception Test (TAT)
Telegraphic speech, 231
Television, violence in, 187–188
Temperament, 353–354
  parenting styles and, 301
Temporal lobes, 68, 69f
Teratogens, 289–290, 290f
Terminal buttons, 49, 49f
Testes, hormones of, 62f
Test standardization, 361
Texture gradient, 113

Thalamus, 66f, 67
That's-not-all technique, 478
Thematic Apperception Test (TAT), 264, 362
Theory of mind, 306
Theory of multiple intelligences, 367–369, 368f
Therapists, 430, 431f
  choosing, 457f, 457–458
Thinking, 220–222
  concepts and, 221–222, 222f
  influence of language on, 233–236
  mental images and, 221
Thought disturbances in schizophrenia, 410
Thresholds
  absolute, 85
  difference, 86
Thyroid, hormones of, 62f
Tip-of-the-tongue phenomenon, 207
TMS. See Transcranial magnetic stimulation (TMS)
Token systems, 436
Top-down processing, 109–110, 110f
Tower of Hanoi problem, 223f, 223–224
Traits, 348
  Big Five, 349, 349f
  central, 470
Trait theories of personality, 348–350
  Big Five traits and, 349, 349f
  evaluation of, 349–350
  of Eysenck, 348f, 348–349
Transcranial magnetic stimulation (TMS), 65, 65f, 454
Transference, 432
Transgenderism, 263
Transsexualism, 263
Treatments
  in experimental research, 30
  for psychological disorders. See Biomedical therapies; Psychotherapy
Trephining, 12
Trichromatic theory of color vision, 95–96
Tricyclic drugs, 450f, 450–451
Trust-versus-mistrust stage, 313f
Trust-versus-mistrust state, 302
Twins, identical, 284

UCR. See Unconditioned response (UCR)
UCS. See Unconditioned stimulus (UCS)
Unconditional positive regard, 355, 442
Unconditioned response (UCR), 163
Unconditioned stimulus (UCS), 163
Unconscious, 336–337
  collective, 343
Unconscious wish fulfillment theory of dreaming, 129–130, 131f
Uninvolved parents, 300f, 301
Uplifts, 500

Variable-interval schedules, 175–176, 176f, 177
Variable-ratio schedules, 175, 176f
Variables, 28
Vernix, 293
Viability, age of, 288
Violence in television, 187–188
Visceral experience, 269
Vision, 89f, 89–97, 90f
  color, 94–96
  eye structure and, 90–94
  peripheral, 91
Visual accommodation, 90
Visual area of cerebral cortex, m 69f, 69, 70
Visual illusions, 113–116, 114f, 115f
Visual message
  processing of, 94
  transmission to brain, 91, 93, 93f
Visual spectrum, 89, 89f
Vygotsky's theory of cognitive development, 306

Wear-and-tear theories of aging, 323
Weber's law, 86
Wechsler Adult Intelligence Scale-IV, 375
Wechsler Intelligence Scale for Children-IV (WISC-IV), 375
Weight loss, 257–258
Well-defined problems, 224
Wernicke's area, 69f
WISC-IV. See Wechsler Intelligence Scale for Children-IV (WISC-IV)

Withdrawal, in schizophrenia, 411
Women
  in field of psychology, 14–15
  moral development in, 312
  psychology of, 6f
  working, 322
Working mothers, 322

X chromosome, 287
X rays, prenatal development and, 290f

Y chromosome, 287

Zone of proximal development (ZPD), 306
Zygote, 287